Windows on Writing

PRACTICE IN CONTEXT

Annotated Instructor's Edition
(student text available with or without additional readings)

Windows on Writing

PRACTICE IN CONTEXT

Annotated Instructor's Edition
(student text available with or without additional readings)

Laurie G. Kirszner
Philadelphia College of Pharmacy and Science

Stephen R. Mandell
Drexel University

St. Martin's Press
New York

Editor: Nancy Lyman
Development editor: Mark Gallaher
Managing editor: Patricia Mansfield Phelan
Senior project editor: Erica Appel
Production supervisor: Patricia Ollague
Art director: Lucy Krikorian
Text design: Patricia McFadden
Cover design: Patricia McFadden
Cover photo: Gary San Pietro

Library of Congress Catalog Card Number: 95-72090

Copyright © 1996 by St. Martin's Press, Inc.

All rights reserved. No part of this book may be reproduced, stored in a retrieval system, or transmitted by any form or by any means, electronic, mechanical, photocopying, recording, or otherwise, except as may be expressly permitted by the applicable copyright statutes or in writing by the Publisher.

Manufactured in the United States of America.

0 9 8 7 6
f e d c b a

For information, write:
St. Martin's Press, Inc.
345 Park Avenue South
New York, NY 10010

ISBN: 0-312-13673-0

Acknowledgments

Maya Angelou, "Graduation" (excerpt) from *I Know Why the Caged Bird Sings.* Copyright © 1969 by Maya Angelou. Reprinted with the permission of Random House, Inc.
Dave Barry, "How Your Body Works" from *Stay Fit and Healthy Until You're Dead.* Copyright © 1985 by Dave Barry. Reprinted with the permission of the author and Rodale Press, Inc., Emmaus, PA 18098. For ordering information, please call 1-800-848-4735.
Suzanne Britt Jordan, "That Lean and Hungry Look" from "My Turn," *Newsweek On Campus* (1978). Reprinted with the permission of the author.
José Antonio Burciaga, "Tortillas" (editor's title, originally titled "I Remember Masa") from *Weedee Peepo* (Edinburg, TX: Pan American University Press, 1988). Reprinted with the permission of the author.
John Egerton, recipe for fried chicken from *Southern Food.* Copyright © 1987 by John Egerton. Reprinted with the permission of Alfred A. Knopf, Inc.
Entry for "Broad Lighting" from *Encyclopedia of Photography.* Copyright © 1984. Reprinted with the permission of Crown Publishers.
Leona Frankel, "History on the Head," *The New York Times* (April 25, 1993). Copyright © 1964 by The New York Times Company. Reprinted with the permission of *The New York Times.*
Martin Gansberg, "38 Who Saw Murder Didn't Call Police" from *The New York Times,* March 27, 1964. Copyright © 1964 by The New York Times Company. Reprinted with the permission of *The New York Times.*

Acknowledgments and copyrights are continued at the back of the book on page 607, which constitutes an extension of the copyright page.

Contents

Preface xiii

Teaching with *Windows on Writing*
Overview AIE-1
Some Advice for the New Teacher of Basic Writing AIE-5
Using *Windows on Writing* to Teach the Skills Required by Writing Assessment Tests AIE-9

WRITING PARAGRAPHS AND ESSAYS 1

▶ Unit 1 The Writing Process 1

1 Planning, Drafting, and Revising 1

  A. Getting Your Bearings 1
  B. Using Invention Strategies 3
  C. Selecting and Arranging Ideas 10
  D. Drafting 13
  E. Revising 14

▶ Unit 2 Focus on Paragraphs 19

2 Writing Effective Paragraphs 19

  A. Unity: Using Topic Sentences 19
  B. Development: Supporting the Topic Sentence 25
  C. Coherence: Connecting Ideas 28

3 Patterns of Paragraph Development 38

  A. Exemplification 38
  B. Narration 42

C. Description   45
D. Process   49
E. Cause and Effect   53
F. Comparison and Contrast   57
G. Classification and Division   63
H. Definition   67
I. Argument   71

Unit 2 Review   81

▶ Unit 3 Paragraphs into Essays   86

4 Thesis and Support   86

A. Building Paragraphs and Essays   86
B. Understanding Thesis and Support   91
C. Moving from Topic to Thesis   97
D. Stating the Thesis   100

5 Introductions and Conclusions   106

A. Introductions   106
B. Conclusions   111

Unit 3 Review   118

REVISING AND EDITING YOUR WRITING   121

▶ Unit 4 Writing Simple Sentences   121

6 The Basic Sentence Pattern: Subjects and Verbs   121

A. Identifying Subjects   122
B. Identifying Prepositional Phrases   125
C. Identifying Verbs   127

7 Avoiding Sentence Fragments   134

A. Including Subjects and Verbs   135
B. Including Complete Verbs   137
C. Expressing Complete Thoughts   139

8 Subject-Verb Agreement   147

A. Understanding Subject-Verb Agreement   148
B. Avoiding Problems with *Be, Have,* and *Do*   152

CONTENTS • vii

    C. Avoiding Problems When Words Come between the Subject and the Verb   155
    D. Avoiding Problems with Indefinite Pronouns As Subjects   157
    E. Avoiding Problems When the Verb Comes before the Subject   158
    F. Avoiding Problems with the Relative Pronouns *Who*, *Which*, and *That*   160

Unit 4 Review   166

▶ Unit 5 Understanding Verbs   169

9 The Past Tense   169

    A. Understanding Regular Verbs in the Past Tense   170
    B. Understanding Irregular Verbs in the Past Tense   173
    C. Using *Be* in the Past Tense   177
    D. Using *Can/Could* and *Will/Would*   180

10 Past Participles and the Perfect Tenses   186

    A. Recognizing Regular Past Participles   187
    B. Recognizing Irregular Past Participles   189
    C. Using the Present Perfect Tense   195
    D. Using the Past Perfect Tense   199
    E. Using Past Participles As Adjectives   202

11 Present Participles and the Progressive Tenses   208

    A. Recognizing Present Participles and Using the Present Progressive Tense   209
    B. Using the Past Progressive Tense   213

Unit 5 Review   219

▶ Unit 6 Building Sentences   222

12 Combining Sentences with Coordination   222

    A. Using Coordinating Conjunctions to Form Compound Sentences   223
    B. Using Semicolons to Form Compound Sentences   228
    C. Using Semicolons and Conjunctive Adverbs to Form Compound Sentences   230

13 Combining Sentences with Subordination 239

A. Using Subordinating Conjunctions to Form Complex Sentences 240
B. Using Relative Pronouns to Combine Sentences 245
C. Using Relative Pronouns to Introduce Restrictive and Nonrestrictive Ideas 250

14 Avoiding Run-Ons and Comma Splices 257

A. Identifying Run-Ons and Comma Splices 258
B. Correcting Run-Ons and Comma Splices 259

Unit 6 Review 269

▶ Unit 7 Revising for Clarity and Effectiveness 272

15 Avoiding Illogical Shifts 272

A. Avoiding Illogical Shifts in Tense 273
B. Avoiding Illogical Shifts in Person 276
C. Avoiding Illogical Shifts in Number 278
D. Avoiding Illogical Shifts in Discourse 281
E. Avoiding Illogical Shifts in Voice 283

16 Using Parallelism 291

A. Recognizing Parallel Structure 292
B. Using Parallel Structure 294

17 Revising for Sentence Variety 303

A. Varying Sentence Types 304
B. Varying Sentence Openings 307
C. Combining Sentences 310
D. Varying Sentence Length 318

18 Revising Words 328

A. Choosing Exact Words 329
B. Using Concise Language 333
C. Avoiding Trite Expressions 337
D. Using Similes and Metaphors 340
E. Avoiding Sexist Language 343

Unit 7 Review 349

Unit 8 Understanding Nouns, Pronouns, and Other Parts of the Sentence 353

19 Using Nouns and Pronouns 353

A. Recognizing Nouns and Forming Plural Nouns 354
B. Recognizing Personal Pronouns 357
C. Understanding Pronoun Case 359
D. Understanding Pronoun-Antecedent Agreement 365
E. Solving Special Problems with Pronoun-Antecedent Agreement 367
F. Understanding Reflexive and Intensive Pronouns 376

20 Using Adjectives and Adverbs 382

A. Understanding Adjectives and Adverbs 383
B. Understanding Comparatives and Superlatives 387
C. Using Demonstrative Adjectives 392

21 Using Prepositions 398

A. Understanding Prepositions 399
B. Using Prepositions in Familiar Expressions 401

Unit 8 Review 408

Unit 9 Special Problems with Punctuation, Mechanics, and Spelling 411

22 Using Commas 411

A. Using Commas in a Series 412
B. Using Commas to Set Off Introductory Phrases and Transitional Words and Expressions 414
C. Using Commas with Appositives 416
D. Using Commas in Dates and Addresses 418

23 Using Apostrophes 423

A. Using Apostrophes to Form Contractions 424
B. Using Apostrophes to Form Possessives 426
C. Revising Incorrect Use of Apostrophes 429

24 Setting Off Proper Nouns, Direct Quotations, and Titles 434

A. Capitalizing Proper Nouns 435
B. Punctuating Direct Quotations 438
C. Setting Off Titles of Books, Stories, and Other Works 442

25 Understanding Spelling 449

A. Understanding Spelling and Pronunciation 450
B. Deciding between *ie* and *ei* 453
C. Understanding Prefixes 455
D. Understanding Suffixes 455
E. Learning Commonly Confused Words 459
F. Becoming a Better Speller 470

Unit 9 Review 476

APPENDIXES 481

Appendix A: Writing Paragraphs and Essays in an Exam Setting 481

A. Before the Exam 481
B. At the Exam 482
C. Writing a Paragraph 484
D. Writing an Essay 485

Appendix B: Tips for ESL Writers 488

A. Including Subjects in Sentences 488
B. Avoiding Special Problems with Subjects 488
C. Indicating Whether Nouns Are Singular or Plural 489
D. Understanding Count and Noncount Nouns 489
E. Using Determiners with Count and Noncount Nouns 491
F. Understanding Articles 492
G. Forming Negatives and Questions 494
H. Indicating Verb Tense 495
I. Recognizing Verbs That Do Not Form the Progressive Tenses 495
J. Placing Adjectives in Order 495
K. Learning Prepositions 496

L. Understanding Prepositions in Two-Word Verbs 497

Appendix C: The Reading Process 498

  A. Approaching a Reading Assignment 498
  B. Highlighting a Reading Assignment 501
  C. Annotating a Reading Assignment 503
  D. Outlining a Reading Assignment 505
  E. Writing a Response Paragraph 506

Appendix D: Patterns of Essay Development: Readings for Writers 508

  A. Exemplification 509

    Timothy E. Miles, *Fighting Fire with Fire Safety Education* (student essay) 511
    Richard Lederer, *English Is a Crazy Language* 513
    Ellen Goodman, *The Suspected Shopper* 516

  B. Narration 519

    Mark Cotharn, *Swing Shift* (student essay) 521
    Jaime O'Neill, *Falling into Place* 523
    Martin Gansberg, *38 Who Saw Murder Didn't Call the Police* 526

  C. Description 530

    Alisha Woolery, *African Violet* (student essay) 532
    Maya Angelou, *Graduation* 534
    Gary Soto, *The Grandfather* 537

  D. Process 540

    Mai Yoshikawa, *Under Water* (student essay) 542
    Merrill Markoe, *Showering with Your Dog* 544
    Joyce Howe, *Indelible Marks* 547

  E. Cause and Effect 549

    Andrea DiMarco, *How My Parents' Separation Changed My Life* (student essay) 551
    Anna Quindlen, *The Old Block* 553
    Carol Sanger, *Just Say "No," Just Hear "No"* 556

  F. Comparison and Contrast 559

    Cheri Rodriguez, *Jason Voorhees, Meet Count Dracula* (student essay) 561

Suzanne Britt Jordan, *That Lean and Hungry Look* 564
Brent Staples, *Role Models, Bogus and Real* 567

G. Classification and Division 569

Deborah Ulrich, *Sports Fans Are in a Class by Themselves* (student essay) 571
Dave Barry, *How Your Body Works* 573
Mary Mebane, *Shades of Black* 578

H. Definition 583

Kristin Whitehead, *Street Smart* (student essay) 585
José Antonio Burciaga, *Tortillas* 587
Leora Frankel, *History on the Head* 589

I. Argument 593

John Fleeger, *Why Isn't Pete Rose in the Hall of Fame?* (student essay) 595
Martin Luther King, Jr., *I Have a Dream* 598
Richard Pothier, *Animal Tests Saved My Life* 602

Teaching with *Windows on Writing:* A Chapter-by-Chapter Guide

Writing Paragraphs and Essays (Units 1–3) Teaching Notes – 1
Revising and Editing Your Writing (Units 4–9) Teaching Notes – 4
Appendixes A–D Teaching Notes – 13

Index

Preface

As we worked on *Windows on Writing: Practice in Context*, our goal was to write a book that would live up to its title. First, we wanted the text to be a "window" that would offer students a view of both the ideas they have to communicate and the writing and thinking skills they need to make such communication possible. Second, we wanted the text to offer "practice in context," presenting as much instruction as possible in the context of students' own writing. We also wanted the text to be a writing-centered workbook, integrating skill-building exercises with actual revision and editing tasks. Finally, we wanted this book to help students gain access to the ongoing exchange of ideas taking place in their schools, their communities, and their world.

We wrote *Windows on Writing* for our students, whom we see as interested, concerned, involved adults. We wanted to write a book whose basic approach and content would show our respect for our students and earn their respect in return. For this reason, we tried to avoid the sort of artificial exercises that teach students nothing more than that writing is a dull, repetitive, and ultimately pointless activity. Instead, most of the exercises we developed focus on revision and editing. We also made a point of seeking out fresh, contemporary content for examples, exercises, and student writing, and of avoiding childish and insulting topics like "Write about your favorite pet" or "Tell about a visit to the circus." The result is a diverse assortment of exercises and writing assignments on issues of real interest and concern to students of various ages and backgrounds.

Another important goal was for the book's style and tone to demonstrate our respect for our subject—the English language—as well as for our audience. To accomplish this, we used a level of diction that talks *to* (not *down to* or *at*) students. And, on every page, we tried to be concise without being abrupt, thorough without being repetitive, direct without being rigid, specific without being prescriptive, and flexible without being structureless.

Organization

The organization of *Windows on Writing* is logical yet flexible. In the first section of the book, titled Writing Paragraphs and Essays, Units 1–3 (Chapters 1–5) provide a focused but thorough treatment of the writing process (including a variety of invention strategies), paying special attention to writing and revising paragraphs and to expanding paragraphs into essays. Unit 1 begins with a general discussion of the writing process, paying special attention to the problems of beginning writers—in particular, gathering, selecting, and arranging ideas. Unit 2 applies these principles to writing effective paragraphs, explaining and illustrating various patterns of paragraph development—exemplification, narration, description, process, cause and effect, comparison and contrast, classification and division, definition, and argumentation. Encouraging students to expand on the skills they have already acquired, Unit 3 shows them how to expand paragraphs into essays. This unit also introduces students to the concept of thesis and support and offers instruction in writing effective introductions and conclusions.

The center of the book, Revising and Editing Your Writing (Units 4–9), provides a thorough review of sentence skills, grammar, punctuation, and mechanics in the context of revising and editing paragraphs and essays. Unit 4 (Chapters 6–8) discusses the simple sentence and highlights potential problem areas, such as sentence fragments and subject-verb agreement, while Unit 5 (Chapters 9–11) is a detailed review of verb tenses. Unit 6 (Chapters 12–14) shows how students can use coordination, subordination, and participles to combine simple sentences into compound and complex sentences, and an entire chapter in this unit is devoted to avoiding run-on sentences and comma splices. This section of the text ends with an overview of options for revising sentences for clarity and effectiveness in Unit 7 (Chapters 15–18); a review of nouns and pronouns, pronoun-antecedent agreement, adjectives and adverbs, and prepositions in Unit 8 (Chapters 19–21); and a discussion of some general problems with punctuation, mechanics, and spelling in Unit 9 (Chapters 22–25). Throughout these units, abundant practice exercises reinforce explanations and offer material for students to edit and evaluate.

Windows on Writing closes with three appendixes that students can refer to as the need arises. Appendix A gives advice for taking written exams, and Appendix B offers advice about some of the more common problems that arise for nonnative speakers. To help students to become more active readers, Appendix C introduces the reading process, focusing on a variety of skills such as highlighting, annotating, outlining, and writing a response paragraph.

Windows on Writing with Additional Readings is available to instructors who also ask their students to read short essays. This alternate edition contains everything found in *Windows on Writing* plus Appendix D: Patterns of Essay Development: Readings for Writers. This appendix builds on the discussion in Unit 3, showing students how the same patterns they use to develop paragraphs can also be used to develop complete essays. Here, along with charts showing options for organizing each pattern of essay and a writing checklist for each pattern, we include eighteen professional and nine student essays, rhetorically arranged. These readings range in style and tone from Gary Soto's lyrical "Grandfather" to Merrill Markoe's humorous "Showering with Your Dog" to Martin Luther King, Jr.'s, "I Have a Dream." Our goal is to achieve a blend of personal and reportorial voices, formal and informal styles. Each of the professional reading selections is accompanied by four sets of questions designed to encourage critical thinking—Reacting to Reading, Reacting to Words, Reacting to Ideas, Reacting to the Pattern—as well as by additional Writing Practice topics.

Features

Central to *Windows on Writing* are a number of features developed to engage students and to make their writing practice more purposeful, more productive, and (not incidentally) more enjoyable.

- **Overview Boxes** Every chapter opens with a boxed Overview that previews the chapter's key terms and concepts.

- **Paragraph Practice** For each chapter in the section Revising and Editing Your Writing, the first activity is a Paragraph Practice exercise that asks students to write an informal paragraph-length response to a specific assignment. Blank space encourages students to use invention strategies before writing their paragraph. This exercise offers students regular opportunities for informal writing practice.

- **Flashback Exercises** Throughout each chapter in Revising and Editing Your Writing, frequent Flashback exercises give students opportunities to learn sentence-level skills in the context of their own writing as they apply each lesson in turn to revising the Paragraph Practice response.

- **Focus Boxes** Throughout the text, Focus boxes visually highlight key points and potentially difficult concepts, while providing concise explanations and clear examples.

- **Practice Exercises** These include a full range of writing, revision, and editing activities that test and reinforce students' understanding of the concepts and practical issues covered in each chapter. We have tried to focus on exercises that treat students with respect as readers and writers, asking them to write about topics of their own choice rather than in response to artificial prompts far from their frame of reference, to analyze actual student writing rather than unrealistic examples, and to edit for errors in passages with content of real interest to young adult and adult learners rather than in essentially contentless individual exercises.

- **Extensive Review Aids** Every chapter closes with a **Review** box that reinforces key terms and concepts. **Chapter Reviews** at the end of most chapters include three kinds of exercises:

  1. revision of a student-written passage
  2. a final review of students' paragraph practices
  3. collaborative activities for group work

  Finally, **Unit Reviews** contain collaborative activities for writing, revising, and editing; writing topics for essay-length writing; and a sample student essay for editing.

- **Appendixes for Specific Needs** Writing Paragraphs and Essays in an Exam Setting—Appendix A—provides advice for writing under pressure, and Tips for ESL Writers are provided in Appendix B.

- **Appendixes on Reading and Writing** Appendix C provides guidance in the reading process and, for those who choose *Windows on Writing with Additional Readings*, Appendix D provides a rhetorically-arranged collection of twenty-seven readings.

Model Paragraphs and Essays

Windows on Writing includes over thirty full-page examples of student writing at the ends of most chapters and units, as well as numerous paragraph-length examples. These enable students to develop and practice revision and editing skills on writing samples that are accessible and inviting to them. They also permit students to read and respond to examples of writing on topics and assignments similar to those they will encounter in their own college courses in various disciplines. In addition to these student models there are many paragraph-length examples by professional writers. *Windows on Writing with Additional Readings* includes twenty-seven additional selections—nine student and eighteen professional essays. We include these professional essays to provide springboards for class discussion as well as topics for student writers. Perhaps more important, we want all these essays to show students that the writing they do is not just an exercise but something that has a place in the real world.

Ancillaries

Windows on Writing is accompanied by a full teaching package, available to adopters of the text. The package includes the following:

- **Annotated Instructor's Edition,** which contains answers to all the exercises
- **Alternate Editions,** one with additional readings and one without readings
- **Transparency Masters** drawn from the text
- **Supplemental Exercises,** in disk or booklet form
- **Computerized Test Item File**
- **Editing/Proofreading Exercises,** on disk only
- **Micrograde,** a computerized grade management system

Some Final Thoughts

All in all, our goal in *Windows on Writing* has been to provide a text that can help basic writers develop college and real-world writing skills by practicing these skills in the context of writing and revising their own paragraphs and short essays. We have tried to design a book that allows true flexibility, so that instructors can use its features to complement their own individual teaching styles and to meet the needs of students at various levels of writing proficiency. Most of all, we have tried to write a text that is respectful of its audience—that treats basic writers as college-level learners, as adults who can take responsibility for their improvement as writers.

Acknowledgments

Windows on Writing was not an easy book to write; it took time, patience, and stamina. Luckily, all the hard work we did was shared. We owe a lot of people a lot of gratitude: Nancy Barlow, Brookhaven College; Robert Bator, Community College of Chicago–Olive Harvey College; Barbara Beauchamp, County College of Morris; Ellen H. Bell, Manatee Community College; Robin Browder, Tidewater Community College; Jo Ann Buck, Guilford Technical Community College; Nancy Corbett, Ashland Community College; Michael Felker, South Plains College; Lillie Fenderson, Seminole Community College; Patricia Gaston, West Virginia University–Parkersburg; Margaret Glazier, Merced College; Judy A. Harris, Rochester Community College; Susan Lagunoff, St. Louis Community College–Florissant Valley; Ted McFerrin, Collin County Community College; James McGowan, Parkland College; Benjamin McKeever, Sinclair Community College; Rebecca Munshaw-Heintz, Polk Community College; Troy Nordman, M.F.A., Butler County Community College; Maureen Hogan O'Brien, Springfield Technical Community College; Frank Pintozzi, Kennesaw State College; Joyce Powell, North Lake College; Charlene Roesner, Kansas Wesleyan University; Carolyn Russell, Rio Hondo Community College; Isara J. Tyson, Manatee Community College; Russ Ward, Aims Community College; Julie Warmke-Robitaille, Santa Fe Community College; Suzanne Weisar, San Jacinto College South; Linda Whisnet, Guilford Technical Community College.

The person to whom we owe the most is Mark Gallaher, baritone *extraordinaire*, who challenged us to write this book and browbeat us until it was finished. His creative exercises helped to define the text's voice, and his constant willingness to rethink, re-see, and revise taught us a thing or two about the recursive (and collaborative) nature of the writing process.

At St. Martin's Press, Senior Editor Karen Allanson kept us on track (and on schedule) and encouraged and supported our efforts to write a book that would meet all our standards. Her assistant, Christine Kline, was a marvel of efficiency who used Post-it notes with grace and style. Our copy editor, Marcia Muth, did an impressively thorough, professional job of sorting through the manuscript, and Senior Project Editor Erica Appel guided it swiftly and skillfully through production. In fact, the entire St. Martin's team—Nancy Lyman, Acquisitions Editor; Barbara Heinssen, Director of Development; Patricia McFadden, Senior Designer; Patricia Ollague, Production Manager; Janice Wiggins, Executive Marketing Manager; and Darby Downey, Manager of Marketing Communications—was consistently enthusiastic and professional. To these people, and to many others, we are grateful.

We are grateful too for the continued support of our families—Mark, Adam, and Rebecca Kirszner and Demi, David, and Sarah Mandell. We thank them here for services rendered: computer expertise supplied, writing samples contributed and evaluated, faxes untangled, phone messages taken, piles of manuscript picked up and delivered, vacations interrupted. Finally, we are grateful for the survival and growth of the writing partnership we entered into in 1975, when we were graduate students. We had no idea then of the wonderful places our collaborative efforts would take us. Now, we know.

Teaching with *Windows on Writing*

▶ OVERVIEW

Devising a Syllabus

Windows on Writing is a comprehensive text for basic writers, including full instruction in drafting and revising paragraphs and essays as well as ample treatment of sentence-level skills. The text is divided into three main sections. The first, Writing Paragraphs and Essays, covers the writing process; paragraph unity, development, and coherence; patterns of paragraph development; and the essay (thesis and support, introductions, and conclusions). The second section, Revising and Editing Your Writing, covers a full range of grammar, punctuation, and mechanics skills: maintaining subject-verb agreement, avoiding sentence fragments, understanding verb tenses, combining sentences, avoiding run-ons and comma splices, revising for clarity and effectiveness, using commas correctly, spelling, and so forth. The final section, Appendixes, offers advice for writing paragraphs and essays on exams, provides help with common problems encountered by nonnative speakers of English, and covers the reading process. The final Appendix D, included in *Windows on Writing with Additional Readings*, offers instruction in writing essays based on each of the nine rhetorical patterns, along with nine student and eighteen professional models.

Windows on Writing has been written and organized with an eye toward classroom flexibility. Units and chapters are essentially self-contained so that instructors can present them in any order that suits their teaching methods and their students' needs. We do recommend, however, that you start with the overview of the writing process in Chapter 1, which offers instruction basic to both paragraphs and essays. After working through Chapter 2, which focuses on the basic paragraph, instructors have several options. One is to continue to have students work on individual paragraphs, concentrating in detail on the patterns of paragraph development in Chapter 3 before moving on to essays. Another is to skip from Chapter 2 to Chapters 4 and 5, which apply the concepts of the basic paragraph to the writing of multi-paragraph essays; such a syllabus might then combine instruction in the patterns of paragraph development in Chapter 3 with instruction in using the same patterns for essay development in Appendix D.

There are also several alternatives for assigning Chapters 6 through 25, which cover sentence-level skills. If your students do not need a basic review of subjects and verbs, for example, you may choose to skip Unit 4 and Unit

5 and assign only Unit 6 (Building Sentences) and Unit 7 (Revising for Clarity and Effectiveness) to the whole class. Chapters that cover common problems—such as sentence fragments (Chapter 7), subject-verb agreement (Chapter 8), run-ons and comma splices (Chapter 14), and use of commas (Chapter 22)—might also be assigned to the class as a whole. You might also choose to assign many of these chapters on an individual basis to students who seem to need some basic review or who consistently have trouble with a particular issue of grammar, punctuation, or mechanics.

The professional and student essays in Appendix D are presented as rhetorical models, but they need not only be taught this way. For example, if you assign your students to write only exemplification, narration, comparison and contrast, and argument essays, then you would probably use the corresponding essays in Appendix D as models; but you could also have your students read some of the other essays simply for their content—as subjects for class discussion or ideas for writing topics or as examples of effective writing at the sentence level. (The discussion of Appendix D on Teaching Notes page 14 at the back of the book includes suggested thematic groupings for these essays.)

Here are two sample syllabi based on a twelve-week term, with two class meetings a week. These are meant only as general guides and can be easily adapted to different term lengths and to different course requirements by dropping, adding, or substituting chapters for those listed.

Sample Syllabus: Paragraph to Essay

Week 1	Chapter 1 The Writing Process
	Chapter 2 Writing Effective Paragraphs
Week 2	Chapter 3A Paragraph Development—Exemplification
	Chapter 6 The Basic Sentence Pattern
	Chapter 7 Avoiding Sentence Fragments
Week 3	Chapter 3B Paragraph Development—Narration
	Chapter 3C Paragraph Development—Description
	Chapter 8 Subject-Verb Agreement
	Unit 4 Review
Week 4	Chapter 3E Paragraph Development—Cause and Effect
	Unit 5 Understanding Verbs
Week 5	Chapter 3F Paragraph Development—Comparison and Contrast
	Chapter 12 Combining Sentences with Coordination
	Chapter 13 Combining Sentences with Subordination
Week 6	Chapter 3G Paragraph Development—Classification and Division
	Chapter 14 Avoiding Run-ons and Comma Splices
	Unit 6 Review

Week 7	Chapter 3I Paragraph Development—Argument Chapter 15 Avoiding Illogical Shifts Chapter 16 Using Parallelism
Week 8	Unit 3 Paragraphs into Essays Chapter 17 Revising for Sentence Variety
Week 9	Appendix D,A Essay Development—Exemplification Chapter 18 Revising Words Unit 7 Review
Week 10	Appendix D,F Essay Development—Comparison and Contrast Chapter 22 Using Commas
Week 11	Appendix D,I Essay Development—Argument Chapter 23 Using Apostrophes Unit 9 Review
Week 12	Review

Note: Individual exercises from Chapter 25 Understanding Spelling are assigned throughout the term with this syllabus.

Sample Syllabus: Focus on the Essay

Week 1	Chapter 1 The Writing Process Chapter 2 Writing Effective Paragraphs
Week 2	Chapter 4 Thesis and Support Chapter 5 Introductions and Conclusions
Week 3	Chapter 3A Paragraph Development—Exemplification Appendix D,A Essay Development—Exemplification Chapter 12 Combining Sentences with Coordination
Week 4	Chapter 13 Combining Sentences with Subordination Chapter 14 Avoiding Run-ons and Comma Splices Unit 6 Review
Week 5	Chapter 3B Paragraph Development—Narration Appendix D,B Essay Development—Narration Chapter 15 Avoiding Illogical Shifts
Week 6	Chapter 16 Using Parallelism Chapter 17 Revising for Sentence Variety Appendix D Martin Luther King, Jr., "I Have a Dream"
Week 7	Chapter 3F Paragraph Development—Comparison and Contrast

	Appendix D,F Essay Development—Comparison and Contrast
	Chapter 18 Revising Words
	Unit 7 Review
Week 8	Chapter 22 Using Commas
	Appendix D Carol Sanger, "Just Say 'No,' Just Hear 'No'"
Week 9	Chapter 3G Paragraph Development—Classification and Division
	Appendix D,G Essay Development—Classification and Division
	Chapter 23 Using Apostrophes
Week 10	Chapter 25 Understanding Spelling
Week 11	Chapter 3I Paragraph Development—Argument
	Appendix D,I Essay Development—Argument
Week 12	Review

Using the Paragraph Practices and Flashbacks

One distinctive feature of *Windows on Writing* is that each chapter in the section Revising and Editing Your Writing begins with a brief writing prompt (Paragraph Practice) that offers an interesting topic for a student paragraph to be drafted right in the book on lines that follow the prompt. Then, throughout the chapter, Flashbacks direct students back to their draft paragraphs to see if any revisions or corrections need to be made based on the specific lessons being taught in that chapter. The purpose is to provide a real writing context within which students can learn sentence-level skills.

While you may not wish to have students complete the Paragraph Practice/Flashback sequence for every chapter you assign, we encourage you to do so whenever time permits. These should not generally be graded, nor should they be considered formal assignments. Research shows that the more writing students do in connection with their writing courses, the more adept writers they become. The Paragraph Practices can allow students to write fairly freely, without fear of judgment or criticism, and to review their work on their own with specific areas of improvement or correction immediately in mind. We believe that the transfer of sentence-level skills to real writing can be better achieved in this way than by the completion of workbook exercises alone.

One good way of using the Paragraph Practices is to have students begin drafting them in class when you assign a chapter. You could, for example, give students ten minutes at the end of a class session to begin drafting a chapter's Paragraph Practice, with the instruction that they complete the rest of the chapter—or the specific sections you wish them to work on—before the next class session. Alternatively, you could have students complete the Paragraph Practice at the beginning of the class session, returning to it as you work through sections of the chapter in class. Of course, you also have the option of having students complete both Paragraph Practices and chapter exercises on their own time.

Supervising Collaborative Activities

Each Chapter Review and Unit Review in *Windows on Writing* includes a section of Collaborative Activities. These are designed to be completed by students working independently in small groups. Most can also be completed by the whole class working together, but many students contribute more freely in small groups, and small groups give every student a chance to participate.

Groups of three to five students are generally the most productive. Group members may be selected randomly, or you may try to put groups together based on ability or congeniality. (You may also allow students to choose their own groups, but if you do so, you run the risk of having certain students feel uncomfortable or excluded; self-selected groups are sometimes more difficult to manage, as well.) You may want to alter groups for each activity; however, if you have students working together in writing groups for a particular paragraph or essay assignment, you may want to maintain the same groups for Collaborative Activities. In altering groups, try to mix students based on your observations of the roles they generally assume—that is, some students will naturally take more initiative in organizing the elements of the activity and seeing that group members stay involved, others will serve as especially good recorders, and so forth. Try to balance groups so that each includes members who will help facilitate the success of the group as a whole.

Most of the Collaborative Activities ask students to produce some final document to which they have all contributed. Give them a set amount of time to do so—say twenty minutes. One member should be designated the secretary or recorder; this student will make any notes required by the activity and will be responsible for writing out the final document. Give each group five minutes' notice of the end of the activity, and after you call time, allow them a few minutes more to review the final document.

During these sessions, sit in on a few minutes of discussion in several or all the groups. Feel free to answer questions and even contribute a suggestion or two if the group seems to have trouble getting started or is stalled at a particular point. If you notice that some students make very few contributions, make irrelevant or disruptive contributions, refuse to cooperate, or treat other group members with a lack of respect, talk to them about your observations privately and in as positive a manner as possible. Students should realize that much of what goes on in the professional world depends on the ability to work productively in small groups.

▶ SOME ADVICE FOR THE NEW TEACHER OF BASIC WRITING

Students in basic writing courses are often the most diverse of those enrolled in any course on a college or community college campus—in terms of cultural background and expectations, basic English language skills, age, and life experience. Some may be surprisingly fluent and imaginative writers who simply haven't mastered the art of the placement test. Some may express ideas competently but produce work that is marred significantly by surface errors or a shaky command of the conventions of standard English. Some, who have been out of an academic environment for a while, may just need a refresher on the conventions of essay writing. Others may be quite inarticulate and have a basic difficulty producing a coherent paragraph.

The challenge for a new instructor is often in recognizing these differences. It does little good, for example, to start out by marking an inarticulate student's papers for errors, when what the student needs is encouragement to feel more comfortable in the written "dialect" of English. Similarly, it is easy to fail to recognize the rhetorical strengths of a paper that is riddled with surface errors. In evaluating and responding to student work, the basic writing instructor should try to begin by looking for matters to praise, to point out any strengths that can be built upon in revision. Once positive rapport has been established, then constructive criticism can have a positive effect.

Learning by Writing

Many basic writers have relatively little experience as writers, at least in a formal sense, so in general the more they are required to write, the better. However, this does not mean that instructors need to comment on all of the writing they assign—and, in fact, they need not even read all the writing they assign. Students may keep journals that instructors look over only several times a semester to confirm that students are keeping up with their entries. Similarly, students may be assigned to write informally in class at every session or once a week. (One of us uses exam "blue books" for these in-class writings because they are easy to collect and redistribute.) As suggested earlier, the Paragraph Practices in *Windows on Writing* provide good possibilities for informal writing that need not be shared with the instructor.

Students may also be asked to write informally about themselves as writers. A particularly good idea during the first week of class is to ask students to write about their "writing history": their earliest memories of writing, their best experiences and worst experiences, their biggest concerns as writers, why they think they have had to enroll in the course, what they hope to accomplish in the course. (You may be surprised at how much you may learn from these histories.) And following completion of the final version of each formal writing assignment for the class, students may be asked to write informally about their own writing process for the assignment—what they found difficult, what they feel they learned, what they think they could improve if they had more time to complete the assignment. Such self-analysis of their roles as writers can help students and their instructors recognize some basic stumbling blocks to improvement.

Revising (and Revising)

Basic writers are often unskilled in effective revision. Many have difficulty reviewing an initial draft and identifying its strengths and weaknesses:

Some may see no strengths at all in their own writing, while others may see no areas in need of improvement. Either way, when called on to revise a paper, basic writers often don't know where to begin and so start all over on what is essentially a new first draft.

One way to help them is to demonstrate the process directly. Chapter 1 of *Windows on Writing* provides an example of a first draft, hand-edited revision, and final draft of a student paragraph, which you can discuss with your students in detail. If possible, share drafts and revisions of other student papers from previous semesters or particularly effective examples of revisions of papers in progress in the current class.

In reviewing and discussing drafts with students, you will generally point out specific possibilities for revision. However, try to communicate to students that they should do more than simply attempt to respond to your comments as they revise. They need to take personal, individual responsibility for their work, evaluting for themselves what works and what doesn't. They should look on their own for places where detail is skimpy, for ideas that do not pertain to the topic, for lack of clarity in the connections among ideas. They should experiment on their own, for example, with ways of making introductions interesting and conclusions satisfying. Students need your guidance, obviously; but they also need to know that real improvement can only be achieved on their own.

Of course, in one of the most common academic writing situations—the essay exam—and in much on-the-job writing, students won't have time for extensive revision. You do something of a disservice, then, if you don't encourage students to become proficient at producing stronger first drafts, at the same time that they are learning to revise more effectively. Doing so requires the ability to plan a piece of writing before beginning to draft. Work through such a planning process with the class several times over the course of a term. Select a topic—try to make it a "real" topic (such as a campus issue or something from the news)—and a format (such as a letter to the editor or an essay exam), and have students brainstorm some ideas that you record on the board. Then, based on some of those ideas, draft a thesis or organizing statement, and map out an organizational strategy. Show that the process of planning a piece of writing need not take a great deal of time yet can result in fuller, more coherent drafts.

Editing and Improving Sentence-Level Proficiency

Instructors have varying levels of tolerance for surface or sentence-level error. Helping students improve their sentence-level skills without inhibiting their development as thoughtful, articulate writers has been an area of much discussion in developmental studies.

Instructors must realize that it is the rare writer at any level whose work is completely error-free. Grading papers by marking many errors is almost always counterproductive. Faced with a page full of circled words and marginal annotations such as "fragment" and "subject-verb agreement," a student is unlikely to assimilate the barrage of information. It is better to focus on one type of error per draft, marking several instances and referring the writer to the appropriate text discussion. If the same error persists in drafts for later assignments, tell the student about it rather than pointing it out directly (for example, in your comments at the end of the paper you might indicate that the writer should check carefully for subject-verb agreement because you found several sentences in which subjects and verbs do not agree). As much as possible, give students responsibility for finding as well as correcting errors.

Also encourage students as they revise and edit to look for ways to improve their work stylistically—for example, by combining sentences (Unit 6) and using parallelism (Chapter 16). Let them know that editing is more than a matter of looking for "mistakes": It also involves clarifying the connections among ideas and refining the way they express those ideas.

Some instructors have students create personal checklists of their most common sentence-level problems. Students are then expected to follow these checklists as part of the process of preparing to hand in every paper. Such checklists can be quite effective because, by breaking it down into steps, they make the initial editing process seem more manageable.

If your students are editing on word processors, you can help them discover strategies to use when looking for problems that often turn up in their writing. For example, students who often mistake *its* and *it's* can run the search function for both these words in order to check for correct usage. Similarly, students who often use *they* and *their* to refer to a singular antecedent or *been* without a form of *have* can search for instances of these words.

Peer Review and Writing Groups

Some instructors of basic writing shy away from having students comment on one another's work because they believe writers at this level are not adept enough to help one another and may actually give poor advice or reinforce bad habits. While there may be some occasional risk of this possibility, most current theory suggests that feedback from other students has a positive effect. Basic writers often have significant difficulty with the concept of audience; writing has never seemed real for them because they have never thought much about the needs of readers. Having students read and comment on one another's work gives such writers an audience they can conceive of clearly as they draft.

As we suggested in our discussion of *Windows on Writing*'s Collaborative Activities, groups of three to five students generally work best. Some instructors maintain the same groups for the entire term, while others create new groups for each new assignment. The choice depends on the size and makeup of the class.

Writing groups are most effective when they are given specific guidelines or goals for each meeting. Sometimes students will come to class prepared to share their ideas for a new paper with other group members. Sometimes they will share drafts, focusing on one or two particular elements, such as organization, use of detail, or paragraph unity. (Whenever possible, let the class know in advance what the next class's peer feedback session will focus on so that students can have that in mind as they draft or revise.) While you need not discourage students from commenting on the content of the draft, pointing out information they found interesting or particularly vivid details, encourage them in every case to comment on some specific rhetorical feature that you have defined in advance.

Depending on the size of the groups, members may share their comments on one another's drafts orally or in writing. Smaller groups will usually have time for members to read one another's drafts and then discuss them together, which often provides more extensive and integrated commentary. With larger groups the reading will take more time, so written comments may be more convenient. Some instructors distribute a peer review form that includes specific questions about the draft and space for comments and suggestions. The benefit of written comments is that each student writer has them to refer to before beginning to revise, so if students discuss drafts orally, you might have each member provide a brief written summary of his or her commens or, alternatively, ask each writer to summarize in writing the discussion of his or her paper. (Some instructors have students read their papers aloud to the rest of the group rather than sharing papers, but we feel that many basic writers need to see words and paragraph breaks on the page in order to comment about clarity and development.)

In setting up writing groups, make sure students realize that they don't have to take the advice of other group members but that they need to consider carefully what that advice suggests about their drafts. They may find a better way to solve what has been pointed out as a problem. Whether or not you have students point out sentence-level problems is a choice you will make based on your students and your own teaching strategies. Some instructors try to include one student in every group whose sentence-level skills are fairly strong and who will presumably help other members with some such matters. Other instructors feel that allowing comment on sentence-level issues is not very productive and can deflect students from the goal of considering audience in organizing and developing their ideas.

▶ USING *WINDOWS ON WRITING* TO TEACH THE SKILLS REQUIRED BY WRITING ASSESSMENT TESTS

In some states and school systems, students must pass standard tests of basic competency in reading, mathematics, and writing skills. Following are lists of the skills tested by two such writing tests, along with the chapters or sections in *Windows on Writing* in which those skills are covered.

The Texas Academic Skills Program (TASP)

The multiple-choice section of the test focuses on the following skills.

1. *Recognizing audience, purpose, and occasion for writing*
   1A (audience and purpose); Appendix D (responding to writing assignments)

2. *Understanding unity, focus, and development*

   2A (topic sentences); 2B (developing topic sentences); 3 (methods of paragraph development); 4 (thesis and support); Appendix D (methods of essay development)

3. *Organizing effectively*

   2C (coherence); 3 (paragraph organization); Appendix D (essay organization)

4. *Writing effective sentences*

   6 (basic sentence pattern); 7 (avoiding sentence fragments); 8 (subject-verb agreement); 12 and 13 (combining sentences); 14 (avoiding run-ons and comma splices); 16 (using parallel structures); 18 (effective word choice); 20 (adjectives and adverbs); Appendix B (sentence problems for ESL writers)

5. *Exhibiting standard usage*

   9, 10, and 11 (standard use of verbs); 19 (standard use of nouns and pronouns); 22, 23, and 24 (standard use of punctuation); Appendix B (usage problems for ESL writers)

The writing sample of the TASP measures the following skills, which overlap with those tested in the multiple-choice portion of the test.

1. *Using language and style appropriate to audience and purpose*

   1A (audience and purpose); 12 and 13 (writing effective sentences); 17 (varying sentences); 18 (using words effectively)

2. *Maintaining unity and focus on a main idea*

   2 and 3 (unified paragraphs); 4 and Appendix D (unified essays)

3. *Developing ideas: amount, depth, and specificity of detail*

   1B (generating ideas); 2B and 3 (developing paragraphs); 4 and Appendix D (developing essays)

4. *Organizing ideas clearly*

   1C (arranging ideas); 3 (organizing paragraphs); Appendix D (organizing essays)

5. *Understanding standard sentence structure and usage*

   7 (avoiding sentence fragments); 8 (subject-verb agreement); 9, 10, and 11 (standard verb forms); 14 (avoiding run-ons and comma splices); 15 (avoiding illogical shifts); 16 (parallel structures); 19 (nouns, pronoun case, and pronoun-antecedent agreement); 20 (adjectives and adverbs); 21 (prepositions); Appendix B (sentence structure and usage problems for ESL writers)

6. *Understanding mechanical conventions*

   22, 23, and 24B–C (punctuation); 24A (capitalization); 25 (spelling)

The Florida College-Level Academic Skills Test (CLAST)

The writing sample should give evidence that the student can do the following.

1. *Select a subject that lends itself to development*
   1B–C (generating and selecting ideas); 3 (developing paragraphs); Appendix D (developing essays)

2. *Determine the purpose and the audience for writing*
   1A (purpose and audience); Appendix D (responding to writing assignments)

3. *Limit the subject to a workable topic given time, audience, and purpose*
   2A (narrowing topics); 4A (focusing essays); 4C (topic to thesis)

4. *Formulate a thesis or statement of main idea that focuses the essay*
   4B–D (thesis and support); Appendix D (sample thesis statements)

5. *Develop the thesis or main idea statement by*
   a. *providing adequate support using generalized and specific evidence*
      1B (generating ideas); 2B (supporting topic sentences); 3 (paragraph development); 4B (thesis and support)
   b. *arranging the ideas and supporting details logically*
      1C (arranging ideas); 3 (logical development of paragraphs); Appendix D (logical development of essays)
   c. *writing unified prose with all supporting material relevant to the thesis*
      2A (paragraph unity); 3 (patterns of paragraph unity); 4 (supporting a thesis); Appendix D (patterns of essay unity)
   d. *writing coherent prose and providing effective transitions*
      2C (paragraph coherence); Appendix D (essay coherence and transitions)

6. *Demonstrate effective word choice by*
   a. *using words that convey appropriate denotative and connotative meanings*
      18A (exact words); 18D (similes and metaphors); 25E (commonly confused words)
   b. *avoiding inappropriate language*
      18C (avoiding trite expressions); 18E (avoiding sexist language)
   c. *avoiding wordiness*
      18 (concise language)

7. *Employ conventional sentence structure by*
   a. *placing modifiers correctly*
      13B–C (relative clause modifiers); Appendix BJ (placing adjectives in order)
   b. *coordinating and subordinating sentence elements according to their relative importance*
      12 (coordination); 13 (subordination)

c. *using parallel expressions*
   16 (parallelism)
d. *avoiding fragments, comma splices, and fused sentences*
   7 (avoiding sentence fragments); 14 (avoiding comma splices and fused sentences); Appendix B,A–B (sentence-structure problems for ESL writers)

8. *Employ effective sentence structure by*
   a. *using a variety of sentence patterns*
      6 (the basic sentence pattern); 12 and 13 (combining basic sentences); 17 (sentence variety)
   b. *avoiding overuse of passive constructions*
      15E (shifts to passive)

9. *Observe the conventions of standard American English grammar and usage by*
   a. *using standard verb forms*
      9, 10, and 11 (standard verb forms); Appendix B,G–I (verb problems for ESL writers)
   b. *maintaining agreement between subjects and verbs, pronouns and antecedents*
      8 (subject-verb agreement); 15C (shifts in number; 19D–E (pronoun-antecedent agreement)
   c. *avoiding inappropriate shifts in tense*
      15A (illogical shifts in tense)
   d. *using proper case forms*
      19C (understanding pronoun case)
   e. *maintaining a consistent point of view*
      15B (illogical shifts in person)
   f. *using adjectives and adverbs correctly*
      20 (adjectives and adverbs)
   g. *making logical comparisons*
      20B (comparatives and superlatives)

10. *Use standard practice for spelling, punctuation, and capitalization*
    25 (spelling); 22, 23, 24B–C (punctuation); 24A (capitalization)

11. *Revise, edit, and proofread work to ensure clarity, consistency, and conformity to the conventions of writing*
    1E (revising and editing checklists)

Windows on Writing

PRACTICE IN CONTEXT

Annotated Instructor's Edition
(student text available with or without additional readings)

1 Planning, Drafting, and Revising

> **Overview**
>
> In this chapter you will learn
> - To understand your assignment, audience, and purpose
> - To use invention strategies to find ideas for writing
> - To select and arrange ideas
> - To write a first draft
> - To revise your draft
> - To edit your work

A GETTING YOUR BEARINGS

Before you begin any writing assignment, you should get a sense of what you are being asked to do. Instead of plunging in headfirst and starting to write, take the time to ask some questions about your assignment, your audience, and your purpose for writing. Finding out the answers to these questions now will save you time in the long run.

QUESTIONS ABOUT ASSIGNMENT, AUDIENCE, AND PURPOSE

Assignment

- What is my assignment?
- When is my assignment due?
- Will I be expected to complete my assignment at home or in class?
- Will I be allowed to revise after I hand in my assignment?

Audience

- Who will read my paper—just my instructor or other students too?
- What will my readers expect?

Purpose

- Why am I writing?
- Am I expected to express personal reactions—for example, to tell how I feel about a piece of music or a shocking news event?
- Am I expected to present information—for example, to answer an exam

question, describe a process in a lab report, or summarize a story or essay I have read?
- Am I expected to take a stand or argue in support of a position on a controversial issue?

PRACTICE 1-1

Think about how you would approach the following writing assignments, given the different audience and purpose for each. What information would you include for each? Would you use formal or informal language? Would you use mostly personal experiences and reactions, or would you include more hard facts and objective information? What do you think your readers would expect? On the lines below each assignment, make some notes about your approach. Then, with your class or in a small group, discuss your responses, and identify any differences in your approaches.

1. For the other students in your writing class, write a paper in which you describe your one best educational experience and your one worst educational experience.

   Answers will vary, but language would probably be informal, and personal experience would be used.

2. For the professor of an introductory psychology course, write a paper discussing how early educational experiences can affect students' performance throughout their schooling.

   Answers will vary, but language would probably be formal, and facts and objective information would be used.

3. Write a letter to the editor of your local newspaper in which you try to convince your community to make two or three specific changes that you believe would improve the schools you attended or those your children might attend.

   Answers will vary, but language would be formal, and both personal experiences and objective information could be used.

4. Write a letter to your favorite teacher—either past or present—expressing what you appreciate about his or her teaching methods and how they have contributed to your development as a student.

   Answers will vary, but language would be informal, and personal experiences would be used.

B USING INVENTION STRATEGIES

Once you know what, why, and for whom you are writing, you can begin to gather ideas. Sometimes called *prewriting* or *discovery*, **invention**—the process of finding material to write about—is not the same for every writer. You may be the kind of person who likes a systematic, structured approach, or you may prefer a more relaxed, less structured, method of finding ideas.

The pages that follow illustrate how four different invention strategies—*freewriting, brainstorming, clustering,* and *journal writing*—can be used to find ideas on the topic of personal heroes. When you write, try each of these four strategies to see which ones work best for you.

Freewriting

When you **freewrite**, you write for a set period of time—perhaps five minutes—without stopping, even if what you are writing doesn't seem to have a point or a direction. Your goal is to relax your mind and let ideas take shape. You can freewrite without a particular topic in mind, or, if you know your topic, you can focus your attention on it as you freewrite. This strategy is called **focused freewriting**.

When you finish freewriting, read what you have written, and underline any ideas you think you might be able to use. If your freewriting introduces an idea you want to explore further, you can freewrite again, this time using the idea as a starting point. An example of focused freewriting on the topic of personal heroes appears below.

Heroes? Didn't I already do this – in fifth grade? My hero (heroine?) was Lucretia Mott, the abolitionist. Maybe write about her now – but can't remember much – not much – she was a Quaker and lived in Philadelphia. Not much to start with. Maybe a sports hero – but not exactly heroes except Dr. J. – he did a lot for the community – spoke at school once. I don't know much about sports – maybe TV stars?

(continued on the following page)

(continued from previous page)

> Cartoon characters? Bugs Bunny always outsmarted Elmer Fudd. My little sister wanted to be She-Ra — the action figure came with a sword, a shield, + a comb. Not my hero — my hero — I used to think Mike Schmidt was pretty impressive (why?) but not really a hero. Now it's athletes again — again - who else? Not Charles Barkley — he said people shouldn't think of him as a role model — but I forget why. I keep thinking of athletes. Who isn't an athlete? Ben Franklin — I named my Cabbage Patch doll after him (why?). This is a lot harder than I thought - + why am I thinking about people who were my heroes when I was a kid? I need some heroes for <u>now</u>. (I guess we all do.)

Freewriting

PRACTICE 1-2

Reread the above example of freewriting on the topic of personal heroes. If you were advising this student writer, what ideas would you suggest she might explore further? Note your thoughts on the lines below. Then, with your class or in a small group, discuss your reasons for choosing these ideas.

Answers will vary.

PRACTICE 1-3

Practice freewriting about any five of the following topics. (You might also choose to freewrite about your personal heroes, and your instructor may suggest other topics or allow you to choose topics of your own.) Use a blank sheet of lined paper for each topic, and freewrite on each for *at least five minutes without stopping*. If you have trouble thinking of anything to write, recopy the last word you have written until something else comes to mind. When you have finished each freewriting, reread what you have written, and underline any ideas that you might be able to use if you were writing a paper about that topic.

Achieving a personal goal	Early educational experiences
Healthy or unhealthy diets	Holidays
Clothing styles or fads	A problem facing your community
Work pressures or pleasures	People who have influenced you
Things that annoy you	Learning a new language
MTV or a type of music	Animal rights
A problem at your school	A recent item in the news
Telling lies	A problem facing young people

PRACTICE 1-4

Reread the freewriting you did for Practice 1-3. For which topic did you come up with your most interesting ideas? Choose one idea, and use it as a starting point for a focused freewriting exercise.

Brainstorming

When you **brainstorm**, you jot down all the ideas about your topic that come to mind. Unlike freewriting, which is linear, brainstorming can be scattered all over the page. You don't have to use complete sentences—single words or phrases are fine—and you can ask questions; list points; draw arrows to connect related ideas; and underline, star, or box important points.

> ▶ **FOCUS** ON BRAINSTORMING ◀
>
> Sometimes your instructor may allow you and another student to brainstorm together; at other times, the class might brainstorm as a group with your instructor writing ideas on the board so the class can later evaluate them. However you brainstorm, your objective is the same: to come up with as much material on your topic as you can.

An example of brainstorming on the topic of personal heroes appears below.

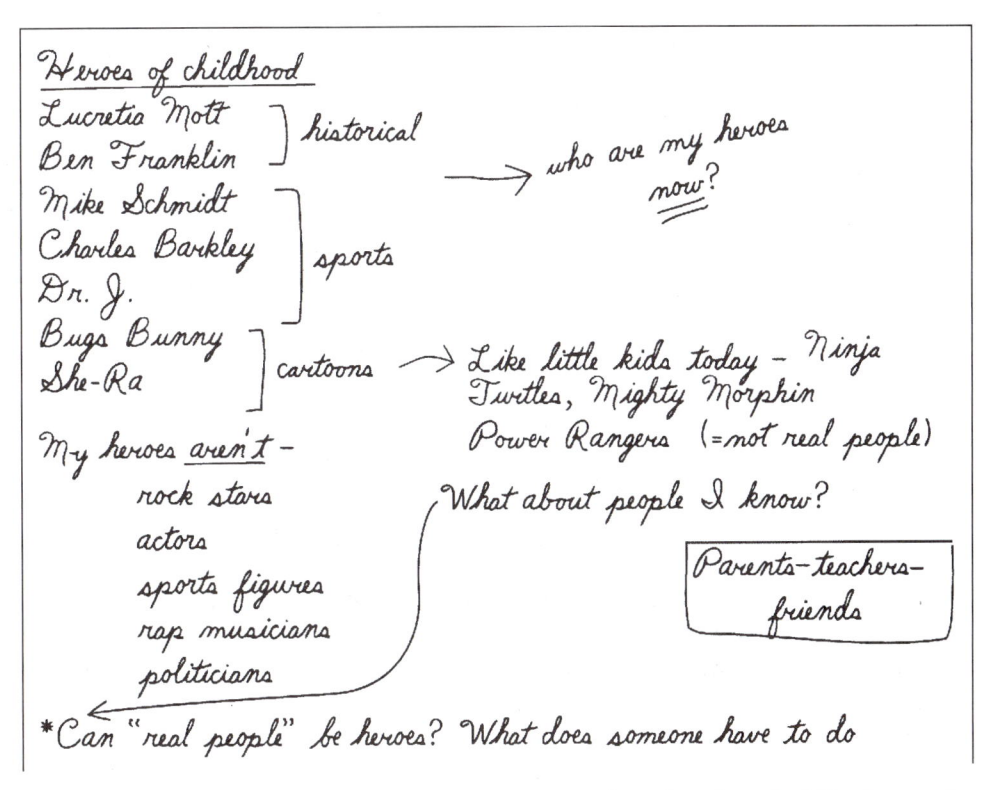

```
Heroes of childhood
Lucretia Mott    ] historical     → who are my heroes
Ben Franklin     ]                   now?
Mike Schmidt     ]
Charles Barkley  ] sports
Dr. J.           ]
Bugs Bunny       ] cartoons  → Like little kids today — Ninja
She-Ra           ]              Turtles, Mighty Morphin
                                Power Rangers (=not real people)
My heroes aren't —
    rock stars          What about people I know?
    actors
    sports figures              [ Parents–teachers–
    rap musicians                   friends ]
    politicians
*Can "real people" be heroes? What does someone have to do
```

(continued on the following page)

6 · UNIT 1 The Writing Process

(continued from previous page)

> to be a hero? Rescue someone? Risk life? Fight in war? Sacrifice for others? Overcome some disability?
> - Work hard
> - Stick to principles
> - Do the right thing
> - Give something back
>
> (Malcolm X, Nelson Mandela, Cesar Chavez, Mother Teresa, ?)
>
> Most people say they have no heroes — or they think musicians and athletes are heroes because they have $ + fame + power.
>
> Parents' heroes = war heroes, heroes of civil rights movement. It's different today.

Brainstorming

PRACTICE 1-5

Reread the above example of brainstorming on the subject of personal heroes. How is it similar to and different from the student's freewriting on the same subject? If you were advising this student writer, what ideas would you suggest that she delete as she continues to explore the subject? Note your thoughts on the lines below. Then, with your class or in a small group, discuss your reasons for deleting these ideas.

Answers will vary.
_____
_____
_____

PRACTICE 1-6

Practice brainstorming on two or three of the topics you used for freewriting in Practice 1-3 or on different topics from that list or other topics that your instructor suggests. Use a separate blank sheet of unlined paper for each topic. Write quickly, without worrying about using complete sentences or making each word follow the next. Write on different parts of the page, make lists, and draw arrows to connect ideas if it seems helpful to do so. When you have finished, look over what you have written. What are the most interesting ideas that appear on each of your brainstorming pages? If you have brainstormed on topics you also freewrote about, what new ideas have

CHAPTER 1 Planning, Drafting, and Revising • 7

you come up with? How might you use any of these ideas in a paper on that topic?

PRACTICE 1-7

With your class or in a small group, practice collaborative brainstorming. First, agree as a group on a topic for brainstorming. (Your instructor may choose a topic for you.) Next, choose one member to write down ideas on a blank sheet of paper or on the board. (If your group is large enough, you might choose two secretaries, who can compare notes at the end of the group brainstorming session.) Then discuss the topic informally, with every member contributing at least one idea. The person who is writing down ideas should slow down the conversation if he or she is having trouble keeping up. After fifteen minutes or so, review the ideas that have been written down. As a group, look for interesting connections among ideas and for ideas that might be explored further in a paper.

Clustering

Some writers like to use a more visual invention strategy. **Clustering**, sometimes called *mapping*, is one such strategy. When you cluster, you begin by writing your topic in the center of a piece of paper. Then you branch out, drawing lines from the center to the corners of the page, becoming more specific as you move out from the center. When you finish your first cluster exercise, you can cluster again on a new sheet of paper, this time beginning with a topic from one of the branches. Sometimes one branch of your exercise will give you all the material you need; at other times you may decide to write about the ideas on several branches.

An example of clustering on the topic of personal heroes appears on page 8.

PRACTICE 1-8

Reread the example of clustering on the subject of personal heroes (p. 8). How is it similar to and different from the student's brainstorming on the same subject? If you were advising this student writer, which branch would you say seems most promising? Why? Can you add any branches? Note your thoughts on the lines below. Then, with your class or in a small group, discuss your ideas about this sample of clustering.

Answers will vary.

_____

_____

_____

PRACTICE 1-9

Practice clustering on two or three of the topics you have used to practice freewriting or brainstorming, or use different topics from the list in

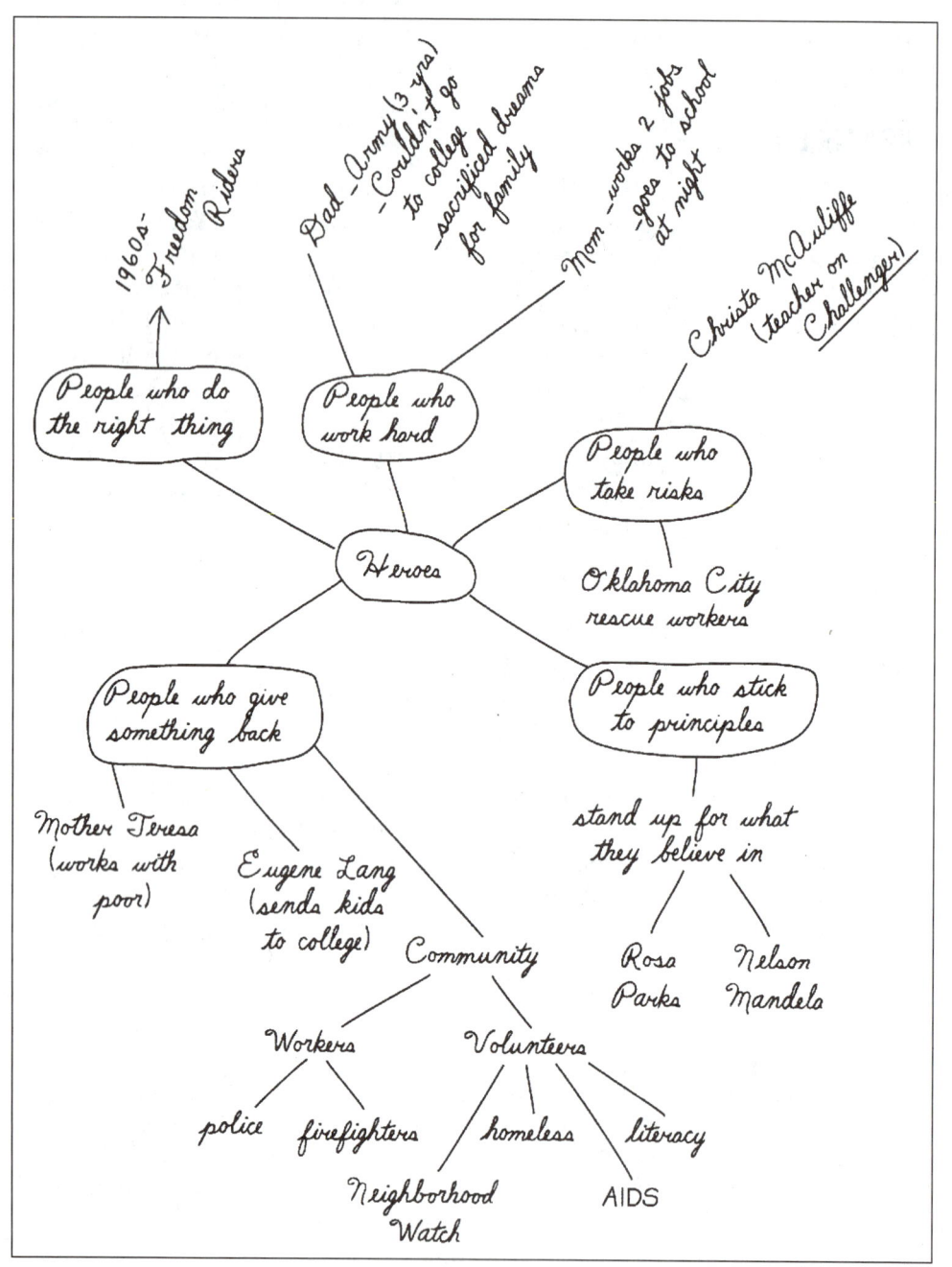

Clustering

A hand-drawn cluster diagram with "Heroes" at the center, branching to:

- **People who do the right thing** → 1960s–Freedom Riders
- **People who work hard** → Dad—Army (3 yrs)—Couldn't go to college—sacrificed dreams for family; Mom—works 2 jobs—goes to school at night
- **People who take risks** → Christa McAuliffe (teacher on Challenger); Oklahoma City rescue workers
- **People who stick to principles** → stand up for what they believe in → Rosa Parks, Nelson Mandela
- **People who give something back** → Mother Teresa (works with poor); Eugene Lang (sends kids to college); Community
  - Community → Workers (police, firefighters, Neighborhood Watch); Volunteers (homeless, AIDS, literacy)

Practice 1-3 or other topics that your instructor suggests. Begin by writing the topic in the center of a blank sheet of unlined paper. Circle the topic, and then branch out with specific ideas and examples, continuing to the edge of the page if you can. When you have finished, look over what you have written. What are the most interesting items that appear in your cluster diagram? Which branches seem most promising as the basis for further writing? If you have clustered on topics you also used for freewriting or brainstorming, what new ideas have you come up with?

Journal Writing

A **journal** is an informal record of your thoughts and ideas. In a journal, you can reflect, question, summarize, or even complain. When you are actively involved in a writing project, your journal is a place where you can jot down ideas to write about, think on paper about your assignment, try to resolve a problem or restart a stalled project, argue with yourself about your topic, critique a draft, try out different versions of sentences, keep track of details or examples, or keep a record of potentially useful things you read or observe. A journal can be whatever you make it.

You might begin by buying a notebook, looking for one that suits your writing habits and personality. A visit to a large stationery store or to your school's bookstore will give you a sense of your options. For example, you may feel most comfortable with a standard 8½-by-11-inch notebook, like the ones you use for class notes, or you may prefer a smaller one that you can easily carry with you. You may select a book with white paper or one with paper in a favorite color, a spiral-bound book or a looseleaf notebook. In addition, you can choose a book with narrow- or wide-ruled lines—or, if you like to doodle or draw pictures, you may want a notebook with no lines at all. Make your selection carefully; the better your journal suits you—the more you feel it belongs to you—the more likely you are to write in it. If you write in your journal regularly and take it seriously, it can be a valuable source of ideas for your writing.

An example of a journal entry on the topic of personal heroes appears below.

> It's been really hard to figure out who my heroes are, or even what a hero is. Heroes are different when you're a kid. Who your heroes are probably has a lot to do with what you like — what music, TV shows, books, sports, etc. Now that I'm older, maybe I need more female heroes because I'm female. Maybe my heroes have to be people I could become, people who are like me. Or maybe they have to be people who <u>aren't</u> like me, but people I wish I could be, male or female. The main thing is, a hero doesn't have to be someone important or famous. He or she can be an ordinary person who does something out of the ordinary. I keep coming back to the idea of a hero being someone who sticks to principles, speaks out, works hard, etc. I've read about plenty of people like this, and I even know some of them. That's what I should write about.

Journal Entry

PRACTICE 1-10

Buy a notebook appropriate for keeping a journal. (Your instructor may require a specific size and format, particularly if journals are going to be collected at some point.) Find a regular time to write for fifteen minutes or so in your journal—during your lunch break, for example, or before you go to bed. Make entries daily or several times a week, depending on your own schedule and your instructor's suggestions. The following topics offer some suggestions for what you might write about in your journal.

- *Your school work.* Of course, you can use your journal to explore your ideas for writing assignments in your composition course or in other courses for which papers are assigned. But keep in mind that your journal can also be a place where you think about what you have learned, where you ask questions about things you're having difficulty understanding, and where you examine new ideas and new ways of seeing the world. Writing regularly in a journal about what you're studying in school can actually help you become a better student.

- *Your ideas about current events.* Expressing your opinions in the privacy of your journal can be quite satisfying. Your entries may even spur you to write letters to your school or local newspaper or to public officials—and even to become involved in community projects or political activities.

- *Your impressions of what you see around you.* Many professional and amateur writers carry their notebooks or journals with them everywhere, so they can record any interesting or unusual or funny things they observe in the course of their daily lives. Rather than relying on memory—which can be faulty—they try to jot down images of memorable people or places as soon as possible after they observe them. One of the pleasures of writing is that you can return to what you've written and recall such moments, perhaps even incorporating them into stories or other pieces of writing.

- *Aspects of your personal life.* Although you may not want to record the intimate details of your life if your instructor is collecting journals, such entries are probably the most common of all in a private journal. Writing about relationships with family and friends, personal problems, hopes and dreams—all the details of your life—can help you reach a better understanding of yourself and of others.

Once you have started making regular entries in a journal, take the time every week or so to go back and reread what you have written. You may find ideas for your writing or even discover new topics for further journal entries.

C   SELECTING AND ARRANGING IDEAS

When you are satisfied that you have enough material to write about, you can move on to the next stage of the writing process: finding a workable idea to develop and selecting and organizing the details that will support that idea most effectively.

Finding an Idea to Develop

Begin by taking stock of what you have gotten down on paper. As you read through your freewriting, brainstorming, clustering, and journal entries, you want to look for one particular point or idea that your material can support. This central idea will give your writing its focus.

The student working on the topic of her heroes thought her invention suggested a number of promising directions for her writing. She decided to develop the idea that her heroes are not just famous people but also ordinary, hardworking citizens who give something back to their communities.

> ### ▶ FOCUS ◀ ON THE WRITING PROCESS
>
> At any time during the writing process, you may find yourself running out of ideas. If this happens, return to the invention strategies you found most helpful, and use them to help you discover additional material about your topic.

Choosing Details

After you select an idea to develop, you should review your accumulated material once again. This time, your objective is to select those points (details, examples, and so on) that you think will support your central idea most effectively. As you review your notes, list those points.

The student writing about her heroes chose these points from her notes.

```
* Work hard (Mom)
* Stick to principles (Mandela)
* Do the right thing
* Give something back
* Take risks
* Not just someone important or famous
* Could be ordinary person
```

Ordering Details

Once you have made a list of points you can use to develop your central idea, you should arrange them in the order in which you plan to present them.

The student writing about her heroes arranged her points in the following order.

```
                My Heroes

People who do the right thing
     * Famous and not famous
          -- Mom (hardworking)
          -- Nelson Mandela (sticks to principles)
```

12 • UNIT 1 The Writing Process

```
* Stand up for what they believe
* Take risks
* Give something back (← most important)
```

PRACTICE 1-11

For Practices 1-3, 1-6, and 1-9, you practiced freewriting, brainstorming, and clustering on several different topics. Now choose one of these topics to write about more formally. Look over all the invention writing you have done on that topic, and decide on a tentative focus—one particular point or idea that your material can support. Write that point or idea on the lines below.

Answers will vary.

_____

_____

Now list the six or seven specific details from your invention writing—or any additional details you think of now—that will support this central idea most effectively.

- _____
- _____
- _____
- _____
- _____
- _____
- _____

Look over these details, and make sure all of them support your central idea. Cross out any that do not. Then, arrange the remaining details on the lines below in the order in which you plan to write about them.

1. _____
2. _____
3. _____
4. _____
5. _____
6. _____
7. _____

D DRAFTING

Once you have found a focus for your writing and arranged the points you will discuss in order, you are ready to write a first draft. When you write a first draft, your main priority is to get your ideas down on paper. Keeping an eye on the list of points you intend to discuss, write without worrying whether the wording of each sentence is perfect and without getting bogged down in concerns about correct spelling or punctuation. If a new idea, one that is not on your list, occurs to you, write it down. Don't worry about where (or if) it fits. Your goal is not to produce a perfectly polished piece of writing but simply to create an unfinished draft. When you revise, you will have a chance to rethink ideas and rework sentences.

Because you know you will revise—add or cross out words and phrases, reorder ideas and details, clarify connections between ideas, and rephrase—it makes sense as you draft to leave plenty of room for rewriting. Leave wide margins, write on every other line (or triple-space if you type your draft or write on a computer), and leave extra space in places where you think you might need to add more material. Feel free to be messy and to cross out; remember, the only person who will work on this draft is you.

When you have finished your draft, try not to start tearing it apart right away. Take a break and think about something—anything—else. Then, return to your draft, and read it with a fresh eye.

A draft of a paragraph on the topic of personal heroes appears below.

My Heroes

My heroes are people who do the right thing. Some of my heroes are famous people, and others are people I know. They work hard, sometimes at more than one job, like my Mom. They stick to their principles. Nelson Mandela is a good example of this. They stand up for what they believe in. They take risks. And they give something back to their communities. I think this last quality is really the most important. Some people work with charities, and others are active in their communities in other ways. They do these things even though they don't have to do them. That makes them heroes to me.

Draft

14 ▪ UNIT 1 The Writing Process

PRACTICE 1-12

Reread the draft paragraph about heroes. If you were advising this student writer, what would you suggest that she change in the draft? What might be added? What might be crossed out? Note your thoughts on the lines below. Then, with your class or in a small group, discuss your ideas about this draft paragraph.

Answers will vary.

PRACTICE 1-13

Using the material you came up with for Practice 1-11, draft a paragraph about your topic, being sure to state your central idea and support it with as many specific details as you can. Be sure to allow plenty of margin space; if you like you may leave every other line blank. When you are finished, give your paragraph a title.

E REVISING

Revision is the act of re-seeing, rethinking, reevaluating, and rewriting your work. The revision process involves much more than substituting one word for another or correcting a comma here and there. Often, revision means moving sentences, adding words and phrases, and even changing the direction or emphasis of your ideas. To get the most out of the revision process, begin by carefully rereading your draft, trying to approach it with a critical eye.

THINKING CRITICALLY ABOUT WRITING

- Do I need to state my central idea more clearly?
- Do I need to look back at my notes or try another invention strategy to find additional supporting material?
- Should I cross out any ideas?
- Do I need to add more examples or details?
- Do I need to explain anything more fully?
- Does every sentence say what I mean?
- Can I state any idea more clearly?
- Can I combine any sentences to make my writing smoother?
- Should I move any sentences?
- Are all my words necessary, or can I cut some?
- Should I change any words?

CHAPTER 1   Planning, Drafting, and Revising   •   15

The student who drafted the paragraph about her heroes (page 13) approached her draft from a critical perspective and made a number of revisions. Her revised paragraph appears below.

> My Heroes
>
> My heroes are people who do the right thing, ^even when it's not the easiest thing. Some of my heroes are famous people, but ^many others are people I know. They work hard, sometimes at more than one job, like my Mom ^(who also goes to school at night). They stick to their principles, ^and ~~Nelson Mandela is a good example of this.~~ ~~They~~ stand up for what they believe in, ^like Nelson Mandela, Rosa Parks, and Cesar Chavez. They take risks, like Christa McAuliffe, who died in the Challenger explosion, ^like the Oklahoma City rescue workers, and like the police officers and firefighters who work in my neighborhood. ~~And they~~ ^Most important, heroes give something back to their communities. ~~I think this last quality is really the most important. Some people work~~ ^A New York City businessman named Eugene Lang did this when he set up the I Have a Dream Foundation to send all the graduates of his elementary school to college. Mother Teresa gives ~~with charities, and others are active in other ways.~~ something back every day. The heroes of my community are volunteers. They work without pay in food banks and soup kitchens. They participate in Neighborhood Watch, and they tutor in literacy programs. They volunteer to be Big Brothers and Big Sisters, work in the schools, deliver meals to the elderly, and care for AIDS babies. They do these things even though they don't have to do them, ^and ~~T~~hat makes them heroes to me.

Revised Draft

When she revised, the student author of this paragraph did not worry about being neat. She crossed out, added material, and made major changes in the words, sentences, and ideas of her paragraph. For instance, she added some more examples of heroic figures, both famous and familiar, and she expanded her paragraph to explain what she meant by "give something back" and why she felt this was so important. The final typed version of her revised paragraph appears below.

16 ▪ UNIT 1 The Writing Process

                My Heroes

   My heroes are people who do the right thing, even when
it's not the easiest thing. Some of my heroes are famous
people, but many others are people I know. They work hard,
sometimes at more than one job, like my Mom (who also goes
to school at night). They stick to their principles, and
they stand up for what they believe in--like Nelson Mandela,
Rosa Parks, and Cesar Chavez. They take risks, like Christa
McAuliffe, who died in the Challenger explosion, like the
Oklahoma City rescue workers, and like the police officers
and firefighters who work in my neighborhood. Most important,
heroes give something back to their communities. A New York
City businessman named Eugene Lang did this when he set up
the I Have a Dream Foundation to send all the graduates of
his elementary school to college. Mother Teresa gives
something back every day. The heroes of my community are the
volunteers. They work without pay in food banks and soup
kitchens. They participate in Neighborhood Watch, and they
tutor in literacy programs. They volunteer to be Big
Brothers and Big Sisters, work in the schools, deliver meals
to the elderly, and care for AIDS babies. They do these
things even though they don't have to do them, and that
makes them heroes to me.

▶ FOCUS ON EDITING ◀

Do not confuse revision with editing. Revision involves serious rewriting and rearranging, and it can be hard work. Editing comes after revision. When you **edit**, you concentrate on the details and surface features of your writing, checking for clarity and for correct grammar, punctuation, mechanics, and spelling. You also need to proofread carefully for typos that a computer spell checker may not identify. Although editing is a lot less comprehensive than revision, it is nevertheless a vital last step in the writing process. Many readers will not take you seriously if you have made grammatical or mechanical errors in your work, and correctness goes a long way toward establishing your competence and authority with your audience.

EDITING CHECKLIST

Editing for Grammar

- Have I avoided sentence fragments? (See Chapter 7.)
- Do my subjects and verbs agree? (See Chapter 8.)
- Are my verb forms and tenses correct? (See Chapters 9, 10, and 11.)
- Have I avoided run-ons and comma splices? (See Chapter 14.)
- Have I used singular and plural nouns correctly? (See Chapter 19.)

- Have I used pronoun case correctly, and are my pronoun references clear? (See Chapter 19.)
- Do my pronouns and antecedents agree? (See Chapter 19.)
- Have I used adjectives and adverbs correctly? (See Chapter 20.)
- Have I used appropriate prepositions? (See Chapter 21.)

Editing for Clarity and Effectiveness

- Have I avoided illogical shifts? (See Chapter 15.)
- Have I used effective parallel structure in my sentences? (See Chapter 16.)
- Have I varied sentence type, structure, and length? (See Chapter 17.)
- Have I used exactly the words I mean? (See Chapter 18.)

Editing for Punctuation, Mechanics, and Spelling

- Have I used commas correctly? (See Chapter 22.)
- Have I used apostrophes correctly? (See Chapter 23.)
- Have I used capital letters where they are required? (See Chapter 24.)
- Have I used quotation marks correctly where they are needed? (See Chapter 24.)
- Have I spelled every word correctly? (See Chapter 25.)

PRACTICE 1-14

Reread the revised version of the paragraph about heroes (page 15). What kinds of changes did the writer make? Which do you think are the most effective changes? Why? Note your thoughts on the lines below. Then, with your class or in a small group, discuss your ideas about the revised paragraph.

Answers will vary.

PRACTICE 1-15

Evaluate the paragraph you drafted for Practice 1-13, based on the Thinking Critically about Writing questions (page 14). What additions can you make to support your central idea more fully? Should anything be crossed out because it doesn't support your central idea? Can any ideas be stated more clearly? (Your instructor may offer comments and suggestions about your draft or may ask you to exchange papers with another student for comments.) On the lines below, describe some of the changes you feel you should make in your draft.

Answers will vary.

Now, revise your draft, crossing out unnecessary material and material you want to rewrite. Add new and rewritten material on the blank lines and in the margins. Before you prepare a final copy to be handed in to your instructor, look over your draft carefully. Using the Editing Checklist (page 16) as a guide, try to correct any sentence errors or errors in punctuation and spelling.

Review

- Before you start to write, consider your assignment, audience, and purpose for writing. (See 1A.)
- Use invention strategies—freewriting, brainstorming, clustering, and journal writing—to find ideas. (See 1B.)
- Select ideas from your notes, and arrange them in a logical order. (See 1C.)
- Write a first draft. (See 1D.)
- Revise your draft. (See 1E.)
- Edit your draft. (See 1E.)

2 Writing Effective Paragraphs

UNIT 2

Overview

In this chapter you will learn
- To state the main idea of a paragraph in a topic sentence
- To understand the characteristics of a good topic sentence
- To write a unified paragraph
- To write a well-developed paragraph
- To write a coherent paragraph

A **paragraph** is a group of related sentences, each of which develops part of a main idea. A paragraph can stand alone, as it does in a one-paragraph classroom exercise or exam answer, or it can be part of a longer piece of writing, as it is in an essay. Because paragraphs play a part in every writing assignment, learning to write a paragraph is the first step toward becoming a competent writer. This chapter gives advice on how to write effective paragraphs—paragraphs that are *unified, well developed*, and *coherent*.

A UNITY: USING TOPIC SENTENCES

A paragraph is **unified** when it focuses on a single **main idea**. Many paragraphs state this main idea in a sentence called a **topic sentence**. Because it states the main idea, the topic sentence is usually the most general sentence in a paragraph. The other sentences are more specific because they discuss or illustrate the main idea.

An effective topic sentence should present an idea that you can discuss in a single paragraph. If your topic sentence is too broad, you will not be able to discuss it in the limited space you have. If it is too narrow, you will not be able to think of much to say about it. Consider the following topic sentences.

> Students with disabilities have special needs.
>
> The science building has an access ramp for wheelchairs.

The first sentence above is much too general to serve as the topic sentence for a single paragraph. The second sentence is so narrow that it is almost impossible to develop. The following sentence, however, is a good topic sentence.

> Establishing a buddy system to pair student volunteers with students with physical disabilities would make our campus more accessible to students with special needs.

Not only does this sentence state a main idea, but it also focuses on an idea that can be developed in a single paragraph.

▶ FOCUS ON TOPIC SENTENCES ◀

Remember that there is a difference between a topic and a topic sentence: The topic is what a paragraph is about; the topic sentence makes a point about the topic. The topic sentence can also suggest the paragraph's purpose.

Topic	Topic Sentence
television violence	Violent television shows have had a negative effect on my younger brothers.
animal testing	Tests used for cosmetics often cause physical harm to animal subjects.
heroes	My heroes are people who do the right thing even when it's not the easiest thing.

Keep in mind that a topic sentence can be placed anywhere in a paragraph—at the beginning, in the middle, or at the end. For the time being, however, it is a good idea to begin each of your paragraphs with the topic sentence. Not only will the topic sentence at the beginning immediately tell your readers what you are writing about, but it also will help keep you on track.

▶ FOCUS ON TOPIC SENTENCES ◀

As a rule, a topic sentence that makes a point about your topic is more interesting and engaging than one that doesn't.

Topic Sentence That Doesn't Make a Point

I was raised in a rural community in Pennsylvania.

Topic Sentence That Makes a Point

The changing economic picture has led many people to move away from the rural Pennsylvania community where I was raised, and this in turn has changed the community.

Revising for Unity

A paragraph lacks **unity** when its sentences do not focus on its main idea. You can correct this problem by carefully rereading your paragraphs and rewriting or deleting sentences that do not support the main idea stated in the topic sentence.

Paragraph Not Unified

<u>The changing economic picture has led many people to move away from the rural Pennsylvania community where I was raised, and this in turn has changed the community.</u> Over the years, farmland has become more and more expensive. Years ago, a family could buy each of its children twenty-five acres on which they could start farming. Today, the price of land is so high that the average farmer cannot afford to buy this amount of land. I am tired of seeing my friends move away. After I graduate, I intend to return to my town and get a job there. Even though many factories have moved out of the area, I think I can get a job. My uncle owns a hardware store, and he told me that after I graduate, he will teach me the business. I think I can contribute something to the business and to the town.

This paragraph is not unified. After presenting one reason why people are moving away (sentences 2 through 4), the writer abandons his topic and starts to complain about his friends and outline his future plans. Sentences 5 through 9 are digressions that do not support the paragraph's topic sentence.

Paragraph Unified

<u>The changing economic picture has led many people to move away from the rural Pennsylvania community where I was raised, and this in turn has changed the community.</u> Over the years, farmland has become more and more expensive. Years ago, a family could buy each of its children twenty-five acres on which they could start farming. Today, the price of land is so high that the average farmer cannot afford to buy this amount of land, and those who choose not to farm have few alternatives. They just can't get good jobs anymore. Factories have moved out of the area and have taken with them the jobs that many young people got after high school. As a result, many eighteen-year-olds have no choice but to move to Pittsburgh to find employment. Clearly, the area has changed. Once my hometown was a quiet little rural community. Now, it is almost a suburb of Pittsburgh. Housing developments have replaced farms, and large shopping malls have driven local business away. Many people who have lived here for years have moved to rural areas in Ohio and Indiana to get away from the crowds and the congestion.

This paragraph is unified. It discusses only what the topic sentence promises: the reasons why people have moved away and the ways in which their departure has affected the community.

22 • UNIT 2 Focus on Paragraphs

PRACTICE 2-1

Decide whether or not the following statements could be effective topic sentences for paragraphs. If the sentence is too broad, write "too broad" in the blank following the sentence. If it is too narrow, write "too narrow" in the blank. If the sentence is an effective topic sentence, write "OK" in the blank following the sentence.

Example: Thanksgiving always falls on the fourth Thursday in November. __too narrow__

1. Computers are changing the world. __too broad__
2. There are five computer terminals in the campus library. __too narrow__
3. The computer I use at work makes my job easier. __OK__
4. Lenny Wilkins coaches the Atlanta Hawks basketball team. __too narrow__
5. Americans enjoy watching many types of sporting events on television. __too broad__
6. There is one quality that distinguishes a good coach from a mediocre one. __OK__
7. Vegetarianism is a healthy way of life. __too broad__
8. Uncooked spinach has fourteen times more iron than steak does. __too narrow__
9. Fast-food restaurants are finally beginning to respond to the growing number of customers who are vegetarians. __OK__
10. There are many different kinds of cars to choose from. __too broad__
11. When you are shopping for a used car, you should check for three things. __OK__
12. A used car is usually cheaper than a new one. __too narrow__
13. This building is a smoke-free facility. __too narrow__
14. Smoking is a very controversial subject. __too broad__
15. Experts offer the following advice for people who want to quit smoking. __OK__

CHAPTER 2 Writing Effective Paragraphs • 23

PRACTICE 2-2

Decide whether or not each of the following potential topic sentences makes a point about its topic. If so, write "OK" in the blank. If not, write "no point."

Example: Davis Community College opened in 1974. *no point*

1. The class schedule at Davis Community College offers great flexibility for students. *OK*

2. Many college students hold down one or more jobs in addition to doing their school work. *no point*

3. Juggling work, school, and family life can be stressful for many college students. *OK*

4. In my psychology class, we have been studying body language. *no point*

5. Anthropologist Desmond Morris has written several books on body language. *no point*

6. You can learn some very specific things about other people by understanding the signals they send through their body language. *OK*

7. I have observed some of the different ways men and women communicate. *no point*

8. Women and men communicate in different ways, which can lead to misunderstandings between wives and husbands. *OK*

9. My younger son loves sports, and my older son loves art and music. *no point*

10. My two sons are as different as night and day. *OK*

PRACTICE 2-3

The following paragraphs are not unified because not every sentence clearly relates to or supports the opening topic sentence. Cross out the sentence or sentences in each paragraph that do not belong.

1. A vegetarian diet benefits one's health, one's well-being, and even the environment. First, a low-fat vegetarian diet can prevent heart disease and help lower blood pressure, as well as fight diabetes. ~~Not many people realize that almost 6 percent of Americans are diabetic and that there is no cure.~~ Muscles, strength, and endurance are also enhanced by a vegetarian diet. In addition to the health benefits, vegetarians say they feel better about themselves spiritually than they did when they were eating meat. It is as if people discover a greater awareness of their connection with the plant and animal world. This awareness is related to the satisfaction of knowing that vegetarianism benefits the environment. Less water is used in the cultivation of vegetables than in the production of livestock, and much more fossil fuel is required to produce the same amount of protein from beef as from grain. ~~More and more young people are turning to vegetarianism.~~ Given the benefits, it is no wonder over twelve million Americans today consider themselves vegetarians.

2. Studies conducted by Dr. Leonard Eron over the last thirty years suggest that the more television violence children are exposed to, the more aggressive they are as teenagers and adults. In 1960 Eron questioned parents about how they treated their children at home, including how much television their children watched. ~~There is more violence on television today than there was then.~~ Ten years later he interviewed these families again and discovered that whether teenage sons were aggressive depended less on how they had been treated by their parents than on how much violent television they had watched as children. Returning in 1990, he found that these same young men, now in their thirties, were still more likely to be aggressive and to commit crimes. ~~Researchers estimate that a child today is likely to watch 100,000 violent acts on television before finishing elementary school.~~

3. The three possessions I could not live without are my car, my portable tape recorder, and my bed. In addition to attending school full time, I hold down two part-time jobs that are many miles from each other, from where I live, and from school. Even though my car is almost twelve years old and has close to 120,000 miles on it, I couldn't manage without it. ~~I'm thinking about buying a new car, and I always check the classified ads, but I haven't found anything I want that I can afford. If my old car breaks down, I guess I'll have to, though.~~ I couldn't live without my portable tape recorder because I use it to record all the class lectures I attend. Then I can play them back while I'm driving or during my breaks at work. ~~Three nights a week and on weekends I work as a counselor at a home for teenagers with problems, and my other job is in the tire department at Sam's.~~ Finally, I couldn't live without my bed, because I spend so much of my time on the go. When I'm home, all I want to do is sleep!

4. Libraries today hold a lot more than just books. Of course, books still outnumber anything else on the shelves, but more and more libraries are expanding to include other specialized services. For example, many libraries now offer extensive collections of tapes and CDs, ranging from classical music to jazz to country to rock. Many have also increased their holdings of videotapes, both instructional programs and popular recent and vintage movies. ~~However,~~

~~most people probably still get more movies from video stores than from libraries.~~ In addition, the children's section often has games and toys young patrons can play with in the library or even check out. Most important, libraries are offering more and more computerized data services, which can provide much more detailed and up-to-date information than printed sources. These expanding non-print sources are the wave of the future for even the smallest libraries and will allow patrons access to much more information than books or magazines ever could. ~~People who don't know how to use a computer are going to be out of luck.~~

PRACTICE 2-4

Trade a draft of a paragraph you are working on for one written by a classmate or by a member of your writing group. First, decide whether the draft paragraph you are reading has a clear topic sentence. If it does not, suggest a sentence that might make a clearer topic sentence. Then, make sure that the topic sentence is not too broad or too narrow and that it makes a point about the topic. Finally, review each other's paragraphs for unity, and point out any sentences that don't support or relate to the topic sentence. Based on the comments you receive, revise your paragraph so that it has a clear, effective topic sentence and is unified.

B DEVELOPMENT: SUPPORTING THE TOPIC SENTENCE

A paragraph is well **developed** when it contains enough specific details and concrete examples to support the main idea in the topic sentence. Every one of your paragraphs needs a certain amount of information to explain or illustrate its main idea. Without this material, readers will not understand or accept what you are saying. As you write, you should imagine your readers asking, "What do you mean?" or "What support do you have?" If the answers to these questions are clear, then you probably have enough support. If they are not, then you should add more specific details and examples.

Keep in mind that although length does offer room for development, length alone does not *guarantee* adequate development. The amount and kind of support you need depend on two things. First, you need to consider how complicated your main idea is. It stands to reason that a complicated main idea will need more explanation than a relatively simple one. Second, you need to consider how much your readers know about your main idea. If, for example, they already know a lot about the food offered by your school's food service facilities, you do not need to give many examples to convince them that the food is bad. If, on the other hand, your readers are not familiar with the food at your school, you have to supply several examples to establish your point. Remember, a paragraph that leaves too many questions unanswered, too many claims unsupported, or too many ideas unillustrated will not be successful. By adding details and examples, you can turn a relatively unconvincing paragraph into a convincing and interesting one.

► FOCUS ON DEVELOPMENT ◄

Specific details help explain ideas to readers. Let's say, for example, that you write a paragraph in which you state that some cities have taken action against pit bulls and their owners. In itself, this statement means very little. You need to clarify it by supplying specific details—in this case identifying the cities and the particular actions they have taken. Such additional information makes your discussion more interesting as well as clearer.

Examples illustrate your statements and thus make them clear to your readers. Let's say that in your paragraph about pit bulls you claim that these dogs are sometimes mistreated. This general statement would be more convincing and easier to understand if you supplied a particular instance of mistreatment. In this case, you could add an example illustrating how some dogs are mistreated by owners to make them more aggressive than they naturally are.

Revising for Development

A paragraph lacks **development** when it does not contain the support readers need to understand or accept its main idea. You can correct this problem by looking for unsupported generalizations and supplying the details and examples you need to support them.

Undeveloped Paragraph

   Although pit bulls have been bred to fight, they can actually make good pets. Today, many people are afraid of pit bulls. These dogs are sometimes mistreated. As a result, they become more aggressive. For this reason, they are misunderstood and persecuted. In fact, some municipalities have taken action against them. But pit bulls do not deserve their bad reputation. Contrary to popular opinion, pit bulls can make good pets.

This paragraph is not well developed. It contains a series of general statements that leave the writer's points unclear and, therefore, do not provide adequate support for the main idea.

Well-Developed Paragraph

   Although pit bulls have been bred to fight, they can actually make good pets. Breeders say the pit bull is descended from the Staffordshire terrier. They were bred mainly for fighting and were used extensively for this purpose in the rural South and Southwest. Their powerful jaws, short muscular legs, and large teeth are ideally suited to this purpose. Some pit bulls—especially males—can be aggressive toward other dogs, but most pit bulls like human beings and are quite friendly. Owners report that pit

(continued on the following page)

> *(continued from the previous page)*
>
> bulls are affectionate, loyal, and good with children. Recently, however, pit bulls have gotten a bad reputation, and they have become the weapon of choice for some drug dealers. Quite often these dogs are horribly mistreated by their owners to make them more aggressive than they naturally are. Because of this aggressiveness, some municipalities have passed ordinances against pit bulls. For example, officials in Chicago tried to pass an ordinance prohibiting pit bulls in public housing. When dog owners and local SPCA officials protested, the city withdrew its objections. Perhaps if people would take the time to look at the breed itself, they would realize that the pit bull does not deserve the bad reputation it has gotten.
>
> This paragraph is well developed. General statements are clarified by specific examples or details. As a result, readers are likely to accept the idea that some pit bulls are mistreated and that the breed's bad reputation is undeserved.

PRACTICE 2-5

The following two paragraphs are not well developed with specific details and examples. On the lines that follow each paragraph, write down three questions or suggestions that might help the writer develop his or her ideas more fully.

1. Other than my parents, the biggest influence on my life was probably my Aunt Sylva. When I was little, she used to baby-sit for me every day, and she always found interesting and educational things for us to do, either at home or on trips downtown. She had lived in Mexico City for many years, and I always admired her exotic looks. As a teenager, I tried to copy the way she walked, talked, and even dressed. Even today I often think of her when I catch myself putting on the sort of outfit she might have worn. Tragically, she died just before my eighteenth birthday.

Answers will vary, but students might suggest supplying more details about the activities done with Aunt Sylva, her appearance and dress, and her death.

2. Computerized special effects have made a big difference in movies over the last ten years. Science fiction films are more spectacular than ever, and filmmakers are able to take moviegoers to places they've never been before. New special effects techniques can also create fierce monsters, more terrifying than anything seen on the screen before. Other effects have been used in comedies to create hilarious visual gags. It's likely that the future will bring even more impressive effects for the enjoyment of movie audiences.

Answers will vary, but students might suggest supplying titles of movies, names of monsters, and specific visual gags.

PRACTICE 2-6

Trade a draft of a paragraph you are working on for one written by a classmate or by a member of your writing group. Read over each other's paragraphs, and decide how well developed they are. If you think certain points are not developed with enough specific examples and details, suggest questions or ideas for the writer to consider when revising. Based on the comments you receive, revise your paragraph to improve its development. Before you begin to revise, you may want to repeat some of the invention strategies discussed and illustrated in Chapter 1 to help you come up with new ideas.

C COHERENCE: CONNECTING IDEAS

A paragraph is **coherent** if all its sentences are arranged in a clear, logical order. You can make a paragraph coherent by arranging details logically and by supplying transitional words that show the connections between sentences.

Arranging Details Logically

In general, you can arrange the ideas in a paragraph according to *time order, spatial order,* or *sequential order.*

Paragraphs that are arranged in **time order** present events chronologically—often in the exact order in which they occurred. Time order is central to narrative and process paragraphs. Stories, historical accounts, and instructions are generally arranged in time order.

The paragraph below presents events in **time order**. Note that words like *before, once, then,* and *finally* indicate the sequence of events in the paragraph.

> In 1856, my great-great-great grandparents, Anne and Charles McGinley, came to the United States to start a new life. Before they left Ireland, their English landlords had raised the taxes on their land so high that they could not afford to pay them. It took them three years to save the money for passage. Once they had saved the money, they had to look for a ship that was willing to take them. Then, my great-great-great grandparents were on their way. They and their ten children spent four long, grueling months on a small sailboat. Storms, strong tides, and damaged sails made the trip longer than it should have been. Finally, in November of 1856, they sighted land, and two days later they sailed into New York Harbor. After they were admitted to the United States, they took a train to Baltimore, Maryland, where some cousins lived.

Paragraphs that are arranged in **spatial order** present details in the order in which they are observed—top to bottom, near to far, or right to left, for example. Spatial order is central to descriptive paragraphs, which tell what a person, place, animal, or object looks like (and perhaps what it sounds, smells, tastes, and feels like).

The following paragraph presents events in **spatial order**. Notice how words like *directly in front, next to, behind*, and *inside* help establish the order—far to near—from which readers will view the details of the scene.

> The day I arrived at the Amish school I knew it was unlike any other school I had seen before. A long, tree-lined dirt road led to the small wooden schoolhouse. <u>Directly in front of</u> the school was a line of bicycles and metal scooters. A small baseball diamond had been carved into the dirt in the yard <u>next to</u> the schoolhouse. <u>Behind</u> the school two little outhouses stood next to each other with a green water pump <u>in between</u>. The schoolhouse itself was a small one-story structure. White paint curled off its clapboard siding, and a short steeple, holding a brass bell, sat firmly <u>on top of</u> the roof. <u>Inside</u> the open door, a long line of black hats hung on pegs. <u>In the center of</u> the small schoolhouse was an iron potbellied stove surrounded by the desks of the children.

Paragraphs that are arranged in **sequential order** present ideas in a logical sequence—from least important to most important, general to specific, or most familiar to least familiar, for example. Writers often build suspense by presenting the least important idea first and then leading up to the most important one.

The paragraph below presents ideas in **sequential order**. Here the phrases *the first rule, an even sillier rule,* and *the most ridiculous rule* establish the order in which the rules are presented and help readers move from one point to another.

> My high school had three rules that were silly at best and ridiculous at worst. <u>The first rule</u> was that only seniors could go outside the school building for lunch. In spite of this rule, many students went outside to eat because the cafeteria was not big enough to accommodate all the students if they decided to stay. Understanding the problem, the teachers and the principal looked the other way as long as we returned to school after lunch period was over. <u>An even sillier rule</u> was that we had to attend ninety-five percent of the classes for every course. This rule meant that a person could only miss about six days of class every semester. Naturally, this rule was never enforced because if it had been, half of the school would have failed. <u>The most ridiculous rule</u>, however, was that students could not throw their hats into the air during graduation. At one point in the past—no one seems to know when—a parent complained that this activity could cause someone to get poked in the eye. As a result, graduating classes were told that under no circumstance could they throw their hats. Naturally, on graduation day we did what every previous graduating class had done—ignored the rule and threw our hats into the air.

PRACTICE 2-7

Read each of the following topic sentences carefully. Would you expect the details for a paragraph introduced by the sentence to be arranged in time

30 • UNIT 2 Focus on Paragraphs

order, spatial order, or sequential order? Write your answer in the blank following each topic sentence.

Example: It is important to keep several things in mind when shopping for a new stereo. _sequential order_

1. My senior year of high school began badly but ended more happily than I ever could have expected. _time order_

2. People would get along better if everyone practiced a few important rules of common courtesy. _sequential order_

3. My son's bedroom reflects his many different interests and hobbies. _spatial order_

4. There are three reasons why the Mustangs are a stronger team than the Bobcats. _sequential order_

5. Babies develop in amazing ways over the first three months of life. _time order_

6. When you interview for a job, keep in mind that most employers look for the same qualities in a prospective employee. _sequential order_

7. Dressing for success means looking your best from the hair on your head to the shoes on your feet. _spatial order_

8. I had always felt safe in my neighborhood until last year when something happened that changed my attitude completely. _time order_

9. To protect yourself on campus after dark, you should always take the following precautions. _sequential order_

10. The new Southern Trust Bank in Gaston is one of the ugliest buildings in town. _spatial order_

PRACTICE 2-8

Using one of the invention strategies described and illustrated in Chapter 1, develop a topic sentence. Then, draft a paragraph for one or more of the following assignments, according to your instructor's directions. Be sure to arrange details logically in the order suggested.

1. Write a paragraph about something you did that you were later ashamed of. Be sure to be clear about when this event took place, how long it lasted, when you began to feel ashamed, and what you did about your feelings. Use time order to arrange the details in your draft paragraph.

2. In a newspaper or magazine, find an interesting illustration or photograph that includes a lot of visual details. Write a paragraph describing what you see in the photograph so that readers will be able to "see" it almost as clearly as you can. Decide on a specific spatial order—top to bottom, left to right, clockwise from the center, or another arrangement that makes sense to you. Use that spatial order to organize the details in your draft paragraph.

3. Write a paragraph explaining your reasons for attending college, focusing on at least three specific reasons. Arrange your reasons in order of their importance to you personally.

Transitional Words and Phrases

In the paragraphs illustrating coherence (pages 28–29), certain **transitional words and phrases** indicate the relationship among sentences. By establishing the time order, spatial order, and sequential order of the ideas in a paragraph, these words and expressions enable readers to see the connections among ideas.

Transitional Words and Phrases

Words and Phrases That Signal Time Order

after	later
afterward	next
at first	now
before	soon
earlier	then
finally	dates—for example, "In June"

Words and Phrases That Signal Spatial Order

in front	over	below
in back	near	beside
on the right	on top	next to
on the left	on the bottom	behind
under	above	

Words and Phrases That Signal Sequential Order

the most important	in addition
the least important	last
equally important	next
first . . . second . . . third	one . . . another
not only . . . but also	furthermore

Revising for Coherence

Because transitional words and phrases establish **coherence**, a paragraph that lacks transitions can be very difficult to understand. You can correct this problem by supplying the words and phrases that make the relationships among the ideas in your paragraph clear.

Paragraph without Transitional Words and Phrases

During his lifetime, Jim Thorpe faced many obstacles. Thorpe was born in 1888 in Indian territory, the son of an Irish father and a Native American mother. He was sent to the Carlisle Indian School in Pennsylvania. "Pop" Warner, the legendary coach at Carlisle, discovered Thorpe when he saw him jump over six feet while he was wearing street clothes. Thorpe became a star on the Carlisle track team and a substitute on the football team. Thorpe left Carlisle to play baseball for two seasons in the newly formed East Carolina minor league. Thorpe returned to Carlisle, played football, and was named to the All-American team. Thorpe went to the 1912 Olympic games in Stockholm, where he won two gold medals. King Gustav V of Sweden said to him, "Sir, you are the greatest athlete in the world." Thorpe's career took a dramatic turn for the worse when a sportswriter who had seen him play baseball in North Carolina exposed him as a professional. The Amateur Athletic Union stripped him of his records and medals. The International Olympic Committee returned Thorpe's Olympic medals to his family.

This paragraph is not coherent. It does not contain the transitional words and phrases necessary to establish how the events relate to one another.

Paragraph with Transitional Words and Phrases

During his lifetime, Jim Thorpe faced many obstacles. Thorpe was born in 1888 in Indian territory, the son of an Irish father and a Native American mother. <u>In 1904</u> he was sent to the Carlisle Indian School in Pennsylvania. <u>The next year</u>, "Pop" Warner, the legendary coach at Carlisle, discovered Thorpe when he saw him jump over six feet while he was wearing street clothes. <u>Almost immediately</u>, Thorpe became a star on the Carlisle track team and a substitute on the football team. Thorpe left Carlisle <u>in 1909</u> to play baseball for two seasons in the newly formed East Carolina minor league. <u>In 1911</u>, Thorpe returned to Carlisle, played football, and was named to the All-American team. Thorpe's most notable achievement came at the 1912 Olympic games in Stockholm, where he won two gold medals. <u>At the games</u>, King Gustav V of Sweden said to him, "Sir, you are the greatest athlete in the world." <u>The next year, however</u>, Thorpe's career took a dramatic turn for the worse when a sportswriter who had seen him play baseball in North Carolina exposed him as a professional. <u>As a result</u>, the Amateur Athletic Union stripped him of his records and medals. <u>After years of appeals</u>, the International Olympic Committee returned Thorpe's Olympic medals to his family in 1982, more than thirty years after his death.

(continued on the following page)

CHAPTER 2 Writing Effective Paragraphs • 33

> *(continued from the previous page)*
>
> This paragraph is coherent. It contains transitional words and phrases—*almost immediately, the next year,* and *after years of appeals,* for example—that establish the time order of key events in Thorpe's life.

PRACTICE 2-9

Underline the transitional words and phrases in the following paragraphs. Then decide what order—time order, spatial order, or sequential order—the writer has chosen for arranging details in the paragraph.

1. Alarmed that teenage girls today get only half as much exercise as boys, researchers are trying to find out why. <u>One reason</u>, they say, is the amount of television girls watch. <u>Another</u> is the amount of fast food they consume. But these are not real explanations since boys generally watch as much television and eat as much fast food as girls do. <u>A more important reason</u> is that girls don't have available to them the sorts of organized high school athletic programs that are available to boys. Furthermore, because both parents often work now, girls are more likely to have responsibilities at home that leave them less free time than boys have to pursue physical activity. <u>Most important</u>, though, may be the lingering attitude that boys aren't attracted to girls who are athletic. Being "feminine," in this view, means avoiding anything that might mess up one's hair or make one perspire. Unless these habits and attitudes change, the current generation of teenage girls may grow into a generation of women plagued with serious health problems.

Order: _sequential order_

2. The high school I attended is unusual because, instead of being a single building, it is actually a campus consisting of six separate buildings located on a small hill. <u>The front building</u>, which faces the street, houses administrative offices, the library, and the cafeteria. <u>Beside the administration building</u> is a large structure that contains the gym, a swimming pool, and rehearsal rooms for band and chorus. <u>In back of the administration building</u> is a parallel building where English and foreign language classes are held. <u>Behind this</u> is a large grassy space flanked by two buildings that run at right angles to the English building. The building <u>on the right</u> is for social studies and business courses, while the building <u>on the left</u> is for math and the sciences. <u>At the far end of the grassy space</u> is a small A-frame building containing the art studio and the shop. <u>Between the buildings</u> are covered cement walkways, and changing classes requires going from building to building. This is usually a nice break—except in the dead of winter, when everyone freezes getting from class to class.

Order: _spatial order_

3. The Caribbean island of Puerto Rico has a complex history. <u>Before the 1400s</u>, its inhabitants for centuries were the native Arawak Indians. <u>In 1493</u>, Christopher Columbus and his crew were the earliest Europeans to reach the island. <u>Fifteen years later</u>, Ponce de Leon conquered the island for Spain,

34 ▪ UNIT 2 Focus on Paragraphs

and the Spanish subjected the Arawaks to virtual slavery to develop a sugar industry. <u>Finally</u>, these native people were annihilated completely, slaughtered by the sword and by European diseases for which they had no immunity. The Arawaks were <u>soon</u> replaced by African slaves, as a European plantation culture flourished. <u>After the Spanish-American War</u>, the island was ceded to the United States in 1898. <u>The next year</u>, the United States designated Puerto Rico a colony under an American governor. <u>Later</u>, in 1917, Puerto Ricans were granted U.S. citizenship, and the country became a U.S. commonwealth in 1952. <u>Since then</u>, Puerto Ricans have debated this status, with some arguing for statehood and others for independence. For now, the island remains a commonwealth, and its citizens share most of the rights and obligations of U.S. citizenship.

Order: _____*time order*_____

PRACTICE 2-10

Look back at the paragraph or paragraphs you drafted for Practice 2-8. Underline the transitional words and phrases that you have used to show the connections among ideas, objects, and events. Then, revise each paragraph, adding transitional words and phrases as necessary.

• • • • • • • • • • • • • • • **REVIEW** • • • • • • • • • • • • • •

CHAPTER REVIEW: STUDENT WRITING

Read the following paragraphs, and evaluate each in terms of its unity, development, and coherence. First, underline each topic sentence. Then, cross out any sentences that do not support the topic sentence, and add transitional words and phrases where needed. Finally, discuss in class whether additional details and examples could be added to each paragraph.

1. <u>In 1979, a series of mechanical and human errors in Unit 2 of the nuclear generating plant at Three Mile Island, near Harrisburg, Pennsylvania, caused an accident that profoundly affected the nuclear power industry</u>. A combination of stuck valves, human error,

and poor decisions caused a partial meltdown of the reactor core. Large amounts of radioactive gases were released into the atmosphere. The governor of Pennsylvania immediately evacuated pregnant women from the area. People soon panicked and left their homes. The nuclear regulatory agency later claimed that the situation was not really dangerous and that the released gases were not a health threat, but activists and local residents disputed this. ~~The reactor itself remained unusable for more than ten years.~~ Massive demonstrations followed the accident, including a rally of over 200,000 people in New York City. ~~Some people came because the day was nice.~~ By the mid 1980s, new construction of nuclear power plants in the United States had stopped.

2. <u>A survey of cigarette commercials shows how tobacco companies have consistently encouraged people to continue smoking</u>. One of the earliest television ads showed two boxes of cigarettes dancing to an advertising jingle. The approach in this ad was simple: Create an entertaining commercial, and people will buy your product. ~~Many people liked these ads. Other~~ Later, other commercials were more subtle. Some were aimed at specific audiences. Marlboro commercials, with the rugged Marlboro man, targeted men. Virginia Slims made an overt pitch to women by saying, "You've come a long way, baby!" Salem, a mentholated cigarette, showed

rural scenes and targeted people who liked the freshness of the outdoors. Kent, with its "micronite filter," appealed to those who were health conscious by claiming that Kent contained less tar and nicotine than any other brand. ~~This claim was not entirely true. Other brands had less tar and nicotine.~~ Cigarette companies *now* are responding to the worldwide decline in smoking by directing advertising at the less well educated. Camels, with the cartoon character Joe Camel, are aimed at teenagers and young adults. Merit and other high-tar and high-nicotine cigarettes use commercials that are specifically directed at minorities.

3. Cities created police forces for a number of reasons. The first reason was status. After the Civil War, it became a status symbol for cities to have a uniformed police force. ~~A~~ *Second, a* police force provided a large number of political jobs. Politicians were able to promise jobs to people who would work to support them. *Third, police* ~~Police~~ made people feel safe. *For example,* ~~P~~olice helped visitors find their way. *In addition,* They took in lost children and sometimes fed the homeless. They *also* directed traffic, enforced health ordinances, and provided a series of other services. *Finally, police* ~~Police~~ kept order. Without a visible, uniformed police force, criminals would have made life in nineteenth-century cities unbearable.

CHAPTER REVIEW: COLLABORATIVE ACTIVITIES

1. List all the reasons why you decided to attend your school. Then, arrange these reasons in order of their increasing importance, and write a paragraph in which you discuss them. As a group, decide on a topic sentence that presents the main idea of each student's paragraph.
2. Write three sentences, each of which could serve as a topic sentence for a paragraph about a different current issue. Choose one of these topic sentences, and write several sentences that support it. Then, exchange paragraphs with another person in your group, and make a list of suggestions about how to make each paragraph unified, well developed, and coherent.
3. Bring to class a paragraph that you have cut out or duplicated from a newspaper or a magazine. As a group, decide whether the paragraph is unified, well developed, and coherent. If it is not, try to rewrite the paragraph to make it more effective.

Review

- A paragraph is unified when it focuses on a single main idea. (See 2A.)
- Many paragraphs state the main idea in a sentence called the topic sentence, which makes a point about the topic. (See 2A.)
- Although a topic sentence can be placed anywhere in a paragraph, often it is the first sentence. (See 2A.)
- A paragraph is well developed when it contains enough specific details and concrete examples to support the main idea in the topic sentence. (See 2B.)
- A paragraph is coherent if all its sentences are arranged in a clear, logical order. (See 2C.)
- You can make a paragraph coherent by arranging details logically and by supplying transitional words that show the connections among ideas. (See 2C.)

3 Patterns of Paragraph Development

> **Overview**
>
> In this chapter you will learn
> - To write exemplification paragraphs
> - To write narrative paragraphs
> - To write descriptive paragraphs
> - To write process paragraphs
> - To write cause-and-effect paragraphs
> - To write comparison-contrast paragraphs
> - To write classification-and-division paragraphs
> - To write definition paragraphs
> - To write argument paragraphs

In Chapter 2, you learned how to write unified, well-developed, and coherent paragraphs. In this chapter, you will become acquainted with the many options you have for organizing ideas within paragraphs. As you write, you will see that your ideas tend to develop in ways that reflect the way your mind works—you give examples, tell what happened, describe appearances, explain how something operates, identify causes or predict effects, find similarities and differences, divide a whole into parts and classify information into categories, define, or persuade. These methods correspond to specific patterns of development: exemplification, narration, description, process, cause and effect, comparison and contrast, classification and division, definition, and argument. Not surprisingly, you can also use these patterns to develop an entire essay. Recognizing these patterns and understanding how they help you organize your ideas will enable you to become a better, more confident writer.

A EXEMPLIFICATION

An **exemplification** paragraph develops a general statement—the topic sentence—with one or more specific examples. Not only do these examples illustrate and explain the topic sentence, but they also make your writing more interesting and more convincing. The following paragraph about the 1969 Woodstock festival uses a number of short examples to illustrate its main idea.

> In most respects, after all, Woodstock was a disaster. To begin with, it rained and rained for weeks before the festival, and then, of course, it rained during the festival. The promoters lost weeks of preparation time when the site had to be switched twice. They rented Yasgur's field less than a month before the concert. The stage wasn't finished, and the sound system was stitched together perilously close to the start of the show. As soon as the festival opened, the water- and food-delivery arrangements broke down, the gates and fences disintegrated, and tens of thousands of new bodies kept pouring in. (One powerful lure was the rumor that the revered Bob Dylan was going to perform; he wasn't.) In response to an emergency appeal for volunteers, fifty doctors were flown in. The Air Force brought in food on Huey helicopters, and the Women's Community Center in Monticello sent thirty thousand sandwiches. One kid was killed as he was run over by a tractor, one died of appendicitis, and another died of a drug overdose.
>
> Hal Espen, "The Woodstock Wars"

Topic sentence

Series of short examples

The writer of this paragraph piles on many examples, one after the other, to support his main idea. Each example gives a specific illustration of how Woodstock was a disaster: it rained, the promoters had to switch sites, water and food were not delivered as planned, and so on.

If a single example is particularly vivid and compelling, it can sometimes be enough to support a topic sentence. The following paragraph uses one extended example to support its main idea—that fear can move one to action.

> Sometimes fear can be a great motivator. Once when I was in high school, I tried out for a part in the school play. I was surprised and thrilled when I was given one of the leads. Never for a moment, however, did I consider how long my part was or how hard I would have to work to memorize it. All I could think of was how much attention I was getting from my friends. I even ignored the warnings of the play's director who told me I would be in trouble if I did not begin to memorize my lines. The reality of my situation finally sank in during our first dress rehearsal when I stumbled all over my lines, and the rest of the cast laughed at me. That night, and for the two weeks leading up to the play, I spent hours going over my lines. Miraculously, I got through the first night of the play without missing (at least obviously missing) many of my lines. As a result of that experience, I learned two things: first, that I could do almost anything if I was frightened enough and second, that I would never try out for another play.
>
> Jerry Doyle (student)

Topic sentence

Single extended example

Notice that, in the paragraph above, the single extended example that illustrates the topic sentence is a narrative. Often a personal experience like this one can be an interesting and powerful way of illustrating your ideas to your readers.

PRACTICE 3-1

Read this exemplification paragraph, and answer the questions that follow.

Youthful Style?

<u>As a teenager in the late 1960s and early 1970s, I was always pretty tolerant about radical clothing styles, but more and more today I find myself asking, "Why do these kids want to look so weird?"</u> For example, I do not understand why a boy would wear a baseball cap backwards on his head. To me, this just looks goofy, like something a person would do and then talk in a really stupid voice to make his friends laugh. Under the backward cap, the boy probably has his hair in a buzz cut, except for one long strand of hair reaching halfway down his back. I can't imagine who thought up this hairstyle, unless it was an ex-monk. Furthermore, every boy I see today seems to be wearing a T-shirt that looks ten sizes too big for him and comes down below his knees, or, if not that, he's got all his clothes on inside out or backwards or both! Then, there are the girls. Since when did it become stylish to wear your underwear on top of your regular clothes? Who decided that it was attractive to combine a white T-shirt and a long, sheer, flowing jumper with a pair of huge black jackboots? I'm so confused. It all just makes me nostalgic for the days of frayed bell-bottoms, tie-dyed tank tops, strands of hippie beads, and headbands circling heads of long, stringy hair.

Willa Kincaid (student)

1. Underline the topic sentence of the paragraph.
2. List the specific examples the writer uses to develop her topic sentence. The first example has been listed for you.

boys wearing baseball caps backwards

buzz-cut hair with one long strand

oversize T-shirt

clothes inside out

girls wearing underwear on top of clothing

sheer flowing jumper with black jackboots

CHAPTER 3 Patterns of Paragraph Development · 41

3. Do you find this exemplification paragraph effective? _____

   Why, or why not? _Answers will vary._

   _____

   _____

   _____

PRACTICE 3-2

Choose one of the topics below as the basis for an exemplification paragraph.

Effective (or ineffective) politicians	Exercise training
Qualities that make a song popular	Terrible dates
Successful comedies (or another type of movie)	Racial conflicts
Challenges facing students	Role models
The appeal (or silliness) of a soap opera	Rude behavior
Unattractive clothing styles	Great athletes
Peer pressure	Acts of bravery
The benefits of cooperation	Difficult jobs

Now, carry out the following process for writing an exemplification paragraph.

- ▶ First, use one or more of the invention strategies described in Chapter 1 to help you come up with as many examples as you can that relate to your topic.
- ▶ Then, focus on examples that are related in some way and that you think you can develop an interesting point about. For example, if your invention topic is rude behavior, you might find that you have a number of examples of rude driving habits or rude sales techniques. (As an alternative, you may decide to write about one especially pertinent example that you can develop in detail.)
- ▶ With your audience and examples (or single example) in mind, draft a topic sentence that introduces your topic and communicates your point.
- ▶ If you are having trouble at this point, you may want to repeat the previous steps, using a different topic from the list.
- ▶ Evaluate your topic sentence, making sure that it is not too broad and that it makes an interesting point about your examples.
- ▶ Briefly list your examples or the facts related to your single example, arranging them in a logical order, such as order of importance.
- ▶ Draft your exemplification paragraph.
- ▶ Review your draft paragraph for development. If you think you should expand the number of examples or further develop your discussion of your examples (or your single example), return to the invention strategies to come up with more ideas. Also consider whether you need to find examples that are more clearly related and narrowly focused.

- Review your draft paragraph for unity. Cross out any examples or facts that don't relate directly to your topic sentence, or revise your topic sentence so that it relates better to the rest of the paragraph.
- Review your draft paragraph for coherence. Rearrange examples and facts if needed, and add any helpful transitional words or phrases.
- Prepare a final, edited draft of your paragraph.

B NARRATION

A **narrative** paragraph relates a sequence of events to tell a story, but it is more than just a story. A narrative paragraph generally makes a point that is stated in a topic sentence, and the rest of the paragraph develops this point, with ideas arranged in time order.

In the following paragraph, Vietnam War veteran Ron Kovic tells how he celebrated his birthday when he was a child.

Topic sentence

Events presented in time order

When the Fourth of July came, there were fireworks going off all over the neighborhood. <u>It was the most exciting time of year for me next to Christmas</u>. Being born on the same exact day as my country I thought was really great. I was so proud. And every Fourth of July, I had a birthday party and all my friends would come over with birthday presents and we'd put on silly hats and blow these horns my dad brought home from the A&P. We'd eat lots of ice cream and watermelon and I'd open up all the presents and blow out the candles on the big red, white, and blue birthday cake and then we'd all sing "Happy Birthday" and "I'm a Yankee Doodle Dandy." At night everyone would pile into Bobby's mother's old car and we'd go down to the drive-in, where we'd watch the fireworks display. Before the movie started, we'd all get out and sit up on the roof of the car with our blankets wrapped around us watching the rockets and Roman candles going up and exploding into fountains of rainbow colors, and later after Mrs. Zimmer dropped me off, I'd lie on my bed feeling a little sad that it all had to end so soon. As I closed my eyes I could still hear strings of firecrackers and cherry bombs going off all over the neighborhood.

Ron Kovic, *Born on the Fourth of July*

Notice that in this paragraph all the incidents relate back to the topic sentence. In addition, transitional words and phrases—*at night, later,* and *as I closed my eyes*—signal the order in which the events occurred.

In the next paragraph, Puerto Rico–born writer Judith Ortiz Cofer uses vivid details to make the individual events of her story come alive for her readers.

CHAPTER 3   Patterns of Paragraph Development   ▪   43

> My first public poetry reading took place in Miami, at a restaurant where a luncheon was being held before the event. I was nervous and excited as I walked in with a notebook in hand. An older woman motioned me to her table, and thinking (foolish me) that she wanted me to autograph a copy of my newly published slender volume of verse, I went over. She ordered a cup of coffee from me, assuming that I was the waitress. (Easy enough to mistake my poems for menus, I suppose.) I know it wasn't an intentional act of cruelty. <u>Yet of all the good things that happened later, I remember that scene most clearly, because it reminded me of what I had to overcome before anyone would take me seriously.</u> In retrospect I understand that my anger gave my reading fire. In fact, I have almost always taken any doubt in my abilities as a challenge, the result most often being the satisfaction of winning a convert, of seeing the cold, appraising eyes warm to my words, the body language change, the smile that indicates I have opened some avenue for communication. So that day as I read, I looked directly at that woman. Her lowered eyes told me she was embarrassed at her faux pas, and when I willed her to look up at me, she graciously allowed me to punish her with my full attention. We shook hands at the end of the reading and I never saw her again. She has probably forgotten the entire incident, but maybe not.
>
> Judith Ortiz Cofer, "The Latina Stereotype"

Events presented in time order

Topic sentence

In this paragraph, all the events develop the point stated in the topic sentence, and transitional words and phrases—*first, later,* and *as I read*—connect the events in time.

▶ FOCUS ON NARRATIVE ◀

Not all narrative paragraphs have topic sentences. Sometimes a writer uses a narrative just to tell an interesting story, not to make a point. Even so, the events in the paragraph all contribute to a single idea—that an experience was exciting or unusual, for example.

PRACTICE 3-3

Read this narrative paragraph, and answer the questions that follow.

```
         The Trip to a Brand-New Life
```

<u>When I was seven, my family took a trip that changed our entire lives--the trip to America.</u> Leaving our native Vietnam illegally, we (first) traveled three days in a small

44 ▪ UNIT 2 Focus on Paragraphs

boat with about fifty other people. We soon ran out of food and supplies, and I thought we would never make it, but at last we reached Malaysia. The people who met us on shore led us to a campsite where there were hundreds of other Vietnamese refugees. For nine months my family stayed there, living in a shelter consisting of logs covered with thick plastic. During this time, we were called in to present our situation to representatives from a variety of countries so they could process our documents and decide whether to accept us as immigrants. We were among the fortunate ones accepted by the United States. Next, we were transferred to a camp in the Philippines where the houses were more stable and the floors were cement instead of dirt. For three months we continued to study English and waited for the happy moment when we learned that we would be leaving for America. A few days later, we were headed for New York, changing planes in several countries before reaching our destination. As the last plane landed, I was overwhelmed by the realization that my family and I had finally reached the end of our dreams. I knew that my first step on the ground would lead me to a new future and a completely new life. I was scared, but I did not hesitate.

Anne Duong (student)

1. Underline the topic sentence of the paragraph.
2. List below the major events of the narrative. The first event has been listed for you.

   The family left Vietnam and spent three days on the water.

   When they reached Malaysia, they entered a refugee camp.

   For nine months they waited to be accepted by another country.

   After being accepted by the U.S., they moved to the Philippines for three months.

   Finally, they were flown to New York to begin their new life.

3. Reread the narrative, circling the transitional words and expressions the writer uses to create a clear time order.
4. Do you find this narrative paragraph effective? _____ Why, or why not? *Answers will vary.*

CHAPTER 3 Patterns of Paragraph Development • 45

PRACTICE 3-4

Choose one of the topics below as the basis for a narrative paragraph.

A difficult choice	An embarrassing situation
A frightening experience	A memorable holiday
A time of rejection	A sudden understanding
A triumph	Something funny a friend did
An act of violence	An unexpected failure
A lesson learned	A conflict with authority
Your happiest moment	An event that changed your life
An instance of injustice	An important decision

Now, carry out the following process for writing a narrative paragraph.

- First, use one or more of the invention strategies described in Chapter 1 to help you come up with several personal experiences that relate to your topic.
- Then, choose the experience that you think would make the best subject for a narrative paragraph—one that would interest others and be meaningful to write about. Use one or more of the invention strategies to help you remember details about this experience.
- Draft a topic sentence that summarizes the point of the experience.
- If you are having trouble at this point, you may want to repeat the previous steps using a different topic from the list.
- Briefly list the events of your experience, arranging them in time order.
- Draft your narrative paragraph.
- Review your draft paragraph for development. If you think you should add more details to make your narrative clearer or livelier, return to the invention strategies to come up with more ideas.
- Review your draft paragraph for unity. Cross out any details that aren't directly related to the point you make in your topic sentence, or revise your topic sentence so that it takes into account these additional details.
- Review your draft paragraph for coherence. Make sure your narrative proceeds in clear time order, and add any helpful transitional words or phrases.
- Prepare a final, edited draft of your paragraph.

C DESCRIPTION

A **descriptive** paragraph paints a word picture that conveys your sensory impressions of a person, place, or thing. You use description when you want readers to see what you see, hear what you hear, smell what you smell, taste what you taste, and feel what you feel. In a descriptive paragraph, information usually is arranged in spatial order.

46 ▪ **UNIT 2** Focus on Paragraphs

In general, there are two kinds of description. If a writer's purpose is primarily to describe something precisely, without emotion, he or she will use **objective** description. This kind of description is often used in technical or scientific writing, but it can also be used in other kinds of writing. In the following paragraph, the writer uses precise language and concrete details to describe an object to readers.

Topic sentence

Specific, concrete details

<u>Once in a long while, four times so far for me, my mother brings out the metal tube that holds her medical diploma.</u> On the tube are gold circles crossed with seven red lines each—"joy" ideographs in abstract. There are also little flowers that look like gears for a gold machine. According to the scraps of labels with Chinese and American addresses, stamps, and postmarks, the family airmailed the can from Hong Kong in 1950. It got crushed in the middle, and whoever tried to peel the labels off stopped because the red and gold paint came off too, leaving silver scratches that rust. Somebody tried to pry the end off before discovering that the tube pulls apart. When I open it, the smell of China flies out, a thousand-year-old bat flying heavy-headed out of the Chinese caverns where bats are as white as dust, a smell that comes from long ago, far back in the brain. Crates from Canton, Hong Kong, Singapore, and Taiwan have that smell too, only stronger because they are more recently come from the Chinese.

Maxine Hong Kingston, *The Woman Warrior*

Because the writer's purpose is to enable readers to picture the object she describes—the tube that contains her mother's diploma—her description is primarily objective. Transitional words and phrases that convey the spatial relationships—*on the tube* and *in the middle*—connect various details within the description. Specific, concrete details—*gold circles, seven red lines, silver scratches that rust*—give readers a clear picture of the tube. Still, the paragraph is not entirely without emotion—for example, Kingston describes the "smell of China" in very subjective terms.

If a writer's purpose is primarily to convey personal reactions to a subject, he or she will use **subjective** description. Instead of limiting the description to just the facts, the writer includes feelings and emotions. The following paragraph presents the writer's impressions of the all-female household in which she grew up.

Topic sentence

Details convey writer's feelings

Growing up, I could have died from overexposure to femininity. <u>Women ruled at 2239</u>. A grandmother, a mother, occasionally an aunt, grown-up girlfriends from at least two generations, all the time rubbing up against me, fixing my food, running my bathwater, telling me to sit still and be good in those grown-up girly-girl voices. Chanel and Prince Matchabelli wafting through the bedrooms. Bubble bath and Jergens came from the bathroom, scents unbroken by aftershave, macho beer breath, a good he-man funk. I remember a house full of 'do rags and rollers, the soft, sweet allure of Dixie peach and bergamot; brown-skin queens wearing pastel housecoats and worn-out size six-and-a-half flip flops that slapped softly against the wood as the royal women climbed the stairs at night carrying their paperbacks to bed.

Bebe Moore Campbell, *Sweet Summer*

Because the writer's purpose is to communicate her feelings about her household and its effect on her, her description is primarily subjective. All the details in the description support the main idea of the paragraph—that the household was dominated by females. In addition, the paragraph contains subjective phrases—*a good he-man funk; the soft, sweet allure of Dixie peach;* and *royal women*—that convey the writer's emotional response to the world she describes.

> ► **FOCUS** ON DESCRIPTION ◄
>
> Most descriptive paragraphs mix objective and subjective description. Although one kind will dominate, the other will most likely be present as well. Whether subjective or objective description is dominant depends on the writer's purpose and on the audience for which he or she is writing.

PRACTICE 3-5

Read through this descriptive paragraph, and answer the questions that follow.

```
                    Camaro Joe

    When I was growing up, my older sister Roxanne in-
variably managed to come up with the greasiest lowlifes
for boyfriends, generally characterized by their lip-
snarling, cigarette-smoke-trailing, "I-just-might-die-
tomorrow-and-I-might-as-well-take-someone-with-me" atti-
tudes. Usually named Mitch or Jake, these guys would hoist
my delicate sister on the back of their black, chrome-
laden motorcycles and tear off in a cloud of dirt and ex-
haust fumes. I particularly remember the one we called
Camaro Joe, Roxanne's suitor the summer I was twelve. When
he first squealed into our driveway in a sputtering, dirty-
gold Camaro with a thumping stereo that shook the trees,
we knew my sister had picked another winner. Joe's cowboy
boots swung from his car onto the gravel of our driveway,
and we watched as he launched his massive beer belly from
```

the low seat. His waddle up to the house reminded me of a
penguin. Joe was short and stocky with beady, black eyes
and a thin, fuzzy mustache. He wore his black hair slicked
back with grease, and a Camel cigarette hung from his
lower lip as if it were glued there. Like any good Nean-
derthal, he communicated mostly in grunts. My father eventually laid down the law and insisted that Roxanne stop
seeing Joe, and much to his satisfaction she did. Of
course, it wasn't long before Joe was replaced by another
Mitch--or was it Jake?

Susan Burkhart (student)

1. Underline the topic sentence of the paragraph.
2. In a few words, summarize the main impression the writer wants to give of her subject, Camaro Joe. *Joe is a greasy, unattractive lowlife.*

3. What are some of the details the writer uses to create this main impression? The first detail has been listed for you.

   drives a dirty Camaro

   big beer belly

   waddles

   thin, fuzzy mustache

   slicked-back hair

   grunts

4. Do you find this descriptive paragraph effective? _____ Why, or why not? *Answers will vary.*

PRACTICE 3-6

Choose one of the topics below as the basis for a descriptive paragraph.

A favorite place from childhood   A treasured possession
A place you felt trapped in   Your workplace
An interesting spot on campus   An ugly outfit

An unusual-looking person	An interesting object in nature
A place you find depressing	A pet
A family member or friend	A place you find soothing
A neighborhood character	Your car or truck
A work of art	A scenic spot

Now, carry out the following process for writing a descriptive paragraph.

▶ First, use one or more of the invention strategies described in Chapter 1 to help you come up with a specific person, place, animal, or object you think would make a good subject for a descriptive paragraph—one that would interest others and be meaningful to write about.
▶ Then, use one or more of the invention strategies to help you remember details about this person, place, animal, or object. Even better, if your subject is available to you, spend some time observing it directly, making detailed notes about your observations.
▶ Draft a topic sentence that summarizes the main impression you want your readers to have of your subject.
▶ If you are having trouble at this point, you may want to repeat the previous steps using a different topic from the list.
▶ Briefly outline your description, arranging the details in some logical spatial order—top to bottom, left to right, far to near, or whatever seems to suit the subject.
▶ Draft your descriptive paragraph.
▶ Review your draft paragraph for development. If you think you should add more details to make your description clearer or more interesting, return to one of the invention strategies to come up with ideas. Consider whether you need to include more objective description to make your subject clear or more subjective description to express your feelings about your subject.
▶ Review your draft paragraph for unity. Cross out any details that don't relate to your topic sentence or that aren't consistent with the main impression you want to give of your subject.
▶ Review your draft paragraph for coherence. Make sure your description proceeds in a logical spatial order, and add any helpful transitional words or phrases.
▶ Prepare a final, edited draft of your paragraph.

D PROCESS

A **process** paragraph explains how something works or how to do something. In general, there are two types of process paragraphs: *process explanations* and *instructions*. In a **process explanation** the writer's purpose is simply to help readers understand a process, not perform it. The following paragraph is a process explanation.

50 • UNIT 2 Focus on Paragraphs

Topic sentence
Stage one

Stage two

Stages three and four

End of process

<u>Once asleep, we go through four distinct stages</u>. The first stage of sleep is marked by an easing of muscle tension and a change in brain-wave activity. This transitional stage is especially light and typically lasts about 20 minutes, during which time you may be easily awakened. In stage two, brain waves slow and slumber grows deeper. Even with the eyes taped open, we are quite literally blind during this phase and would be incapable of seeing anything—even a hand passing over the face—since the eye-brain connection has been shut off. More than half of the time devoted solely to sleep is spent in stage two, and no dreaming occurs. Stages three and four are marked by even slower brain waves, but the deepest sleep occurs in stage four. Mysteriously, the highest levels of the body's growth hormone are released during this sleep stage. After cycling back for a few minutes of stage-two sleep, dreaming begins. The first dream phase, lasting only a few minutes, is the shortest of the night. When dreaming is over, the sleeper retraces all the stages back to lighter sleep and then repeats the deep-sleep stages back to dreaming.

Mark McCuchen, *The Compass in Your Nose and Other Astonishing Facts about Humans*

The topic sentence identifies the process, and the rest of this paragraph presents the steps. As is common in process explanations, the writer presents the steps in strict chronological order. Throughout the paragraph, transitional words and phrases—*the first stage, in stage two,* and *stages three and four*—identify individual steps in the process.

Other process paragraphs present **instructions**. Here the writer's purpose is to give readers the information they actually need to perform a task or activity. The following paragraph presents a set of instructions telling skaters how to check a pair of in-line skates before beginning to skate.

Topic sentence

Step one

Step two

Step three

Step four

<u>Now that you are the proud owner of in-lines, you must be sure your skates are fine-tuned and road-worthy, so before you roll, be sure to do the following.</u> First, sit down and place your blades between your legs, wheels facing up. Make certain they are clean so you won't get dirty. Next, wiggle each wheel, making certain there is no lateral play (side-to-side). If bolts are loose, tighten them with the Allen, socket, or crescent wrenches supplied by the manufacturer. Then, spin each wheel so they all spin smoothly and evenly. Feel and listen for any grinding. If this occurs, the bearings may need to be cleaned or replaced. After checking the wheels, look at your brake. Some stoppers screw on, while others have bolts on the side or through the center. Jiggle the stopper, and if it's loose, tighten it. If it is worn, replace it. It is best to replace your brake before you start to wear it down to the metal, or you might strip the threads of the bolt and have to saw off the brake, a time-

CHAPTER 3 Patterns of Paragraph Development · 51

consuming and difficult process. Finally, check your laces or buckles for any wear and tear. Properly serviced, a pair of skates will have a long life span and allow you to roll more easily and smoothly.

Step five

Joel Rappelfeld, *The Complete Blader*

Because the writer of this process paragraph expects readers to follow his instructions, he addresses them directly, using commands to tell them what to do (for instance, "Sit down and place your blades between your legs . . ."). He uses clear transitional words and expressions—*next, then,* and *after checking the wheels,* for example—to make sure readers know the exact sequence in which the steps are to be performed. He even includes cautions and reminders ("Make certain they are clean so you won't get dirty," for example) and explains the purpose for some steps, such as replacing a worn brake.

> ▶ **FOCUS** ON PROCESS ◀
>
> Like narrative paragraphs, process paragraphs present a sequence of events. Unlike narrative paragraphs, however, process paragraphs describe a sequence that occurs—or should occur—in exactly the same way every time.

PRACTICE 3-7

Read this process paragraph, and answer the questions that follow.

An Order of Fries

   I had always enjoyed the french fries at McDonald's and other fast food restaurants, but I never realized just how much work goes into making them until I worked at a potato processing plant in Hermiston, Oregon. The process begins with freshly dug potatoes being shoveled from trucks onto conveyor belts leading into the plant. During this stage, workers must sort out any rocks that may have been dug up with the potatoes because these could cause severe damage to the automated peelers. After the potatoes have gone through the peelers, they travel on a conveyor belt through the "trim line." Here, workers cut out any bad spots, being careful not to waste potatoes by trimming too much. The potatoes next are sliced in automated cutters and then fried for about a minute. Following this, they continue along a conveyor

52 ▪ UNIT 2 Focus on Paragraphs

```
belt to the "wet line." Here, workers again look for bad
spots, discarding any rotten pieces. At this point, the
potatoes go to a second set of fryers for three minutes
before being moved to subzero freezers for ten minutes.
Then it's on to the "frozen line" for a final inspec-
tion. The inspected fries are weighed by machines and
then sealed into five-pound plastic packages, which are
weighed again by workers who also check that they are
properly sealed. The bags are then packed in boxes and
made ready for shipment to various McDonald's and other
restaurants across the western United States. This
process goes on continuously, twenty-four hours a day,
to bring us consumers the tasty french fries we all en-
joy so much.
```

Cheri Rodriguez (student)

1. Underline the topic sentence of the paragraph.
2. Is this a process explanation or instructions? _____*process*_____
   _____*explanation*_____ How do you know? _____*Verbs are not commands.*_____

3. List the steps of the process. The first step has been listed for you.

   The potatoes are unloaded, and the rocks are sorted out.

   They are peeled and carried to the "trim line."

   They are sliced and fried for a minute.

   They are carried to the "wet line."

   They are fried again, then frozen.

   They get a final inspection on the "frozen line."

   They are weighed, packaged, and boxed for shipment.

4. Do you find this process paragraph effective? _____ Why, or why not? *Answers will vary.*

PRACTICE 3-8

Choose one of the topics below as the basis for a process paragraph.

A popular dancing style
A daily workplace task
Strategies for winning a particular game
A hairstyling technique
Planning an event
Your average work/school day
A scientific process
An exercise/workout routine
A specific car or household repair
The stages of a plant's development
A baby animal's first six weeks
Running a computer program
A process involved in a hobby
The stages of a love affair
A simple medical procedure
A process you've observed in nature

Now, write a process paragraph using the instructions that follow.

▶ If you don't already have a process in mind, use one or more of the invention strategies described in Chapter 1 to help you decide on the specific process you want to write about.
▶ Then, freewrite or brainstorm about the process, listing all its steps or stages and details about each.
▶ Read over what you have written, and decide whether you will develop your process paragraph as a set of instructions that a reader could follow or as an explanation meant just to help your reader understand the process.
▶ If you are having trouble at this point, you may want to repeat the previous steps using a different topic from the list.
▶ Draft a topic sentence that reflects the purpose of your process paragraph.
▶ List the steps or stages of the process, arranging them in exact chronological order.
▶ Draft your process paragraph.
▶ Review your draft paragraph for development. If you have missed any steps or stages or think that readers would understand the process better if you described one or more steps in greater detail, use the invention strategies to find more ideas about what you still need to include.
▶ Review your draft paragraph for unity. Cross out any information that doesn't relate directly to the process or that might confuse readers.
▶ Review your draft paragraph for coherence. Rearrange steps or stages if necessary, and add any helpful transitional words or phrases.
▶ Prepare a final, edited draft of your paragraph.

E CAUSE AND EFFECT

A **cause-and-effect** paragraph can analyze causes (what made a particular event or outcome occur) or consider effects (the probable outcomes of a particular activity or behavior). Like other kinds of paragraphs, a cause-and-effect paragraph makes a point about its topic in its topic sentence. You write cause-and-effect paragraphs when your purpose is to help readers understand why something happened or is happening or when you want to show readers how something affects people or some part of the world. You can even use cause-and-effect to predict future events.

The main difficulty you may have when planning a cause-and-effect paragraph is making sure one event actually caused another event, not just preceded it in time. Another problem is making sure you consider all possible causes and effects, not just the most obvious or most important ones. As you write, be sure you accurately assess the importance of the causes or effects you discuss. Don't mistakenly make a particular cause or effect stronger than it actually is just to strengthen your case.

The following paragraph identifies causes.

Topic sentence: effect

First (minor) cause: paper costs

Second (major) cause: illiteracy

<u>Newspapers are folding.</u> Paper costs are high, but loss of literate readers is much higher. Forty-five percent of adult citizens do not read newspapers. Only 10 percent abstain by choice. The rest have been excluded by their inability to read. Even the most distinguished daily papers are now written at an estimated tenth-grade level. Magazines such as *The Nation, The New Republic, Time, Newsweek,* and *The National Review* are written at a minimum of twelfth-grade level. Circulation battles represent a competition for the largest piece of a diminished pie. Enlargement of that pie does not yet seem to have occurred to those who enter these increasingly unhappy competitions. The only successful major paper to be launched in the last decade, *USA Today,* relies on a simplistic lexicon, large headlines, color photographs, and fanciful weather maps that seek to duplicate the instant entertainment on TV.

Jonathan Kozol, *Illiterate America*

The topic sentence identifies the effect the paragraph will discuss. After mentioning one relatively minor cause of the problem (the cost of paper), the paragraph goes on to analyze the primary cause of the problem—illiteracy.

The next paragraph discusses effects.

Topic sentence: cause

First effect: pain disappears

<u>Professional athletes are sometimes severely disadvantaged by trainers whose job it is to keep them in action.</u> The more famous the athlete, the greater the risk that he or she may be subjected to extreme medical measures when injury strikes. The star baseball player whose arm is sore because of a torn muscle or tissue damage may need sustained rest more than anything else. But his team is battling for a place in the World Series; so the trainer or team doctor, called upon to work his magic, reaches for a strong dose of butazolidine or other powerful pain suppressants. Presto, the pain disappears! The pitcher takes his place on the mound and does superbly. That could be the last game, however, in which he is able to throw a ball with full strength. The drugs didn't repair torn

muscle or cause the damaged tissue to heal. What they did was to mask the pain, enabling the pitcher to throw hard, further damaging the torn muscle. Little wonder that so many star athletes are cut down in their prime, more the victims of overzealous treatment of their injuries than of the injuries themselves.

Second effect: muscle damaged further

Norman Cousins, "Pain Is Not the Ultimate Enemy"

The topic sentence identifies the cause of the problem the paragraph will consider. The paragraph then goes on to discuss two effects—the second more important than the first—of the trainer's actions.

> ▶ **FOCUS** ON CAUSE AND EFFECT ◀
>
> Because of its limited length, a single paragraph is not usually able to discuss *both* causes and effects.

PRACTICE 3-9

Read this cause-and-effect paragraph, and answer the questions that follow.

The Ultimate High

<u>Some people associate running only with panting, sweating, and plain and simple torture, but for me and other experienced runners the effect of running is pure and utter pleasure.</u> When I run, it might look as though I'm in agony, with my gaping mouth, soaked brow, and constantly contracting leg muscles. In fact, however, my daily half-hour run represents a time of complete physical and mental relaxation. As I begin my run, my lungs escape the stuffy atmosphere of my job and school and are immediately refreshed by the clean, open air. The daily tensions built up in my body ease as my muscles stretch and pump, releasing all feelings of anger or frustration. I mentally dive into my run and feel as though I am lifting my feet from the pavement and ascending into the air. My mind wanders toward the outer limits of my imagination, and I seem to float, daydreaming about wherever my thoughts take me. I take pride in the salty perspiration that trickles down my face and body, signifying my effort and ambition. After I complete my run and cool down with long, deep breaths, my body tingles slightly and feels ener-

gized, as if I had just come off a roller coaster. I am more alert, my concentration is sharper, and my state of mind is relaxed and peaceful. I feel alive. Beginning runners who initially experience soreness and fatigue rather than this kind of "high" should be patient. As the body builds up strength and tolerance, they will no longer equate running with pain but rather with relief from tension and with greater emotional well-being.

Scott Weckerly (student)

1. Underline the topic sentence of the paragraph.
2. Does this paragraph deal mainly with the causes or the effects of running?

   effects How do you know? _The topic sentence says the paragraph will focus on the "effect of running."_

3. List some of the effects the writer describes. The first effect has been listed for you.

   His lungs are refreshed with clean air.

   Tension and frustrations are released.

   He escapes into an imaginative other world.

   He feels proud of his effort.

   He feels energized afterwards, alert and at the same time relaxed.

4. Do you find this cause-and-effect paragraph effective? _____ Why, or why not? _Answers will vary._

PRACTICE 3-10

Choose one of the topics below as the basis for a paragraph examining causes or effects.

Why a current television show or movie is popular
Some personal causes (or effects) of stress
Why many Americans don't vote
The effects of treating others with respect

CHAPTER 3   Patterns of Paragraph Development   •   57

Why teenagers smoke, drink and drive, or do another dangerous thing
Some reasons why relationships break up
Effects of a particular medication or medical treatment
Why you would consider becoming (or could never become) a vegetarian
The beneficial effects of running or another physical exercise
Why a particular video game is popular
The effects an influential person in your life had on you
Why some people find writing difficult
Effects of a new baby on a household
Major reasons high school or college students drop out of school
How managers can get the best (or the worst) from their employees

Now, carry out the following process for writing a cause-and-effect paragraph.

- ▶ First, freewrite or brainstorm about your topic, trying to think of as many causes or effects as you can.
- ▶ Next, review your notes and create a cluster diagram (see page 8). Write your topic in the center of the page, and then draw arrows branching out to the various specific causes or effects.
- ▶ Choose the two to four causes or effects from your cluster diagram that you think are most important and that your audience would find most interesting.
- ▶ If you are having trouble at this point, you may want to repeat the previous steps using a different topic from the list.
- ▶ Draft a topic sentence introducing your topic and suggesting your purpose or main point.
- ▶ Briefly outline the causes or effects you will discuss, arranging them in an effective order, perhaps in order of importance.
- ▶ Draft your cause-and-effect paragraph.
- ▶ Review your draft paragraph for development. Might there be other important causes or effects you haven't yet thought of? Might your audience want more information about any of the causes or effects you do include? Do some more invention to clarify what you still need to include.
- ▶ Review your draft paragraph for unity. Cross out any information that doesn't relate directly to your topic sentence or to the causes or effects you are discussing. You may also decide to revise your topic sentence to accommodate any new ideas.
- ▶ Review your draft paragraph for coherence. Rearrange causes or effects if you think they should be arranged more clearly, and add any helpful transitional words or phrases.
- ▶ Prepare a final, edited draft of your paragraph.

(F)   COMPARISON AND CONTRAST

When you **compare** two things, you tell how they are similar. When you **contrast** two things, you tell how they are different. Sometimes your purpose in a comparison or contrast is to analyze two subjects in order to clarify what makes each unique. At other times, your purpose may be to evaluate two subjects in order to determine which has greater merit or worth.

In general, you can organize information in a comparison-contrast paragraph in two ways. One way is a **subject-by-subject** arrangement in which you discuss all of your points for one subject and then all of your points for the other subject. The following paragraph is an example of a subject-by-subject comparison.

Topic sentence
Subject one:
women's
conversations

Subject two:
men's
conversations

First, it is important to note that men and women regard conversation quite differently. For women it is a passion, a sport, an activity even more important to life than eating because it doesn't involve weight gain. The first sign of closeness among women is when they find themselves engaging in endless, secretless rounds of conversation with one another. And as soon as a woman begins to relax and feel comfortable in a relationship with a man, she tries to have that type of conversation with him as well. However, the first sign that a man is feeling close to a woman is when he admits that he'd rather she please quiet down so he can hear the TV. A man who feels truly intimate with a woman often reserves for her and her alone the precious gift of one-word answers. Everyone knows that the surest way to spot a successful long-term relationship is to look around a restaurant for the table where no one is talking. Ah . . . now *that's* real love.

Merrill Markoe, "Men, Women, and Conversation"

This subject-by-subject comparison begins with a topic sentence that states the main idea of the paragraph and indicates that the paragraph will focus on differences. The writer then discusses each subject separately, enabling readers to understand how women and men communicate differently. Notice how the transition *however* signals the writer's shift from one subject to the other.

The other way to organize information in a comparison-and-contrast paragraph is a **point-by-point** arrangement, in which you discuss each point for both subjects before going on to the next point. The following paragraph is an example of a point-by-point comparison.

Topic sentence
Point one

Point two

Point three
Point four

After a short time in England, I began to see why the English see Americans as loud and ill-mannered. Americans are open and confident. The English are reserved and modest. Americans frequently spend money blatantly; the English spend money quietly. For example, when Americans tip a doorman at a hotel, they hand him the money in full view. When the English perform the same act, they fold the bill and slip it into the person's hand. Americans seem to swagger when they walk; the English walk deliberately—to get from one place to another. Finally, and perhaps most irritating to the English, Americans frequently call people they have met by their first names. Most English people will call someone by his or her first name only after they have been asked to.

Beth Haurin (student)

Like a subject-by-subject comparison, this point-by-point comparison begins with a topic sentence that states the main idea of the paragraph and indicates that the paragraph will concentrate on differences. The rest of the paragraph develops four points of contrast, one at a time, for both Americans and English people. In addition, it gives an example for one of the points—spending money. The shift from one subject to another is signaled by the use of the words *Americans* and *English*.

> ▶ **FOCUS** ON COMPARISON AND CONTRAST ◀
>
> Because of its limited length, a comparison-and-contrast paragraph will usually focus on similarities *or* on differences, not on both.

PRACTICE 3-11

Read this comparison-and-contrast paragraph, and answer the questions that follow.

Comparing the British and
American Education Systems

The British system of education is common not only in England but in countries all over the world that were once British colonies. It differs from the American system in a number of ways. First, most American children have only one year of kindergarten, beginning at age five. Under the British system, children begin kindergarten at age four and then go on to another year of more advanced kindergarten called "preparatory" or "prep," which is comparable to American first grade. Starting in seventh grade, most American students study basic subjects separately, devoting a semester to algebra, for example, and another semester to geometry. However, under the British system, algebra, geometry, and trigonometry are taught together in a single course which is then repeated at a higher level every term. Also, in American high schools some classes, particularly electives, may include sophomores, juniors, and seniors. In schools run according to the British system, students at different levels, or "forms," are not mixed in classes; each form attends all its classes together. Finally, American students gener-ally graduate after their twelfth year of school, and senior year is just another year of course work. British students, on the other hand, finish everything they need to learn in secondary school during the first term of their eleventh year of school. Then, during the second term, they study for comprehensive final exams that cover everything they have been learning for the last four years. These exams, which include three separate tests for every subject, are taken during the final term.

Lisa Van Hoboken (student)

1. Underline the topic sentence of the paragraph.

2. Does this paragraph deal mainly with similarities or differences?

   differences How do you know? _The topic sentence points to differences._

3. Is this paragraph organized subject by subject or point by point?

   point by point How do you know? _Discussion of points alternates between American and British systems._

4. List some of the contrasts the writer describes. The first contrast has been listed for you.

   American students start kindergarten at five, while British-school students start kindergarten at four.

   American students study subjects separately, while British-system students study all branches of a subject in one course.

   American classes may include students in different grades, but British-system classes do not mix levels.

   American students don't prepare for comprehensive tests in their final year as British-school students do.

5. Do you find this comparison-and-contrast paragraph effective? _____
   Why, or why not? _Answers will vary._

CHAPTER 3 Patterns of Paragraph Development • 61

6. How is the following revised version of the previous paragraph different from the original? _subject-by-subject arrangement_

   Which version do you find more effective? Why?

   Answers will vary.

   The British system of education is common not only in England but in countries all over the world that were once British colonies. It differs from the American system in a number of ways. Most American children have only one year of kindergarten, beginning at age five. Starting in seventh grade, most American students study basic subjects separately, devoting a semester to algebra, for example, and another semester to geometry. In American high schools, some classes, particularly electives, may include sophomores, juniors, and seniors. In addition, American students generally graduate after their twelfth year of school, with senior year being just another year of course work. Under the British system, however, children begin kindergarten at age four and then go on to another year of more advanced kindergarten called "preparatory" or "prep," which is comparable to American first grade. For older students, advanced subjects like algebra, geometry, and trigonometry are taught together in a single course which is then repeated at a higher level every term. Also, students at different levels, or "forms," are not mixed in classes; each form attends all its classes together. Finally, British-school students finish everything they need to learn in secondary school during the first term of their eleventh year of school. Then, over the second term, they study for comprehensive final exams that cover everything they have been learning for the last four years. These exams, which include three separate tests for every subject, are taken during the final term.

PRACTICE 3-12

Choose one of the topics below as the basis for a paragraph exploring similarities or differences.

Two popular entertainers, TV or radio talk-show hosts, politicians, or athletes
Two related styles of music, such as reggae and dancehall
High school seniors and first-year college students
A common stereotyped image of something versus its reality
How you act in two different situations (home and work, for example) or with two different sets of people (such as your family and your friends)
Two modes of transportation
Two ads for similar products directed at different audiences

Two different management or teaching styles
Two different bosses or teachers
Men's and women's attitudes toward dating
Your goals or values as a child versus your goals or values today
Smokers versus nonsmokers
Two competing consumer goods, such as two models of automobile, two video-game systems, or two pizza chains
Two relatives who have very different personalities
Two animal species of the same genus
Two generations' attitudes toward a particular issue or subject (for example, how people in their forties and people in their teens view MTV)

Now, carry out the following process for writing a comparison-and-contrast paragraph.

▶ First, use one or more of the invention strategies described in Chapter 1 to help you decide on the two specific subjects you will compare or contrast.
▶ Then, freewrite or brainstorm about your two subjects, trying to think of as many similarities and differences as you can. (You might create two columns with each subject at the top of one, and then list corresponding features for each.) Another possibility is to create a separate cluster diagram for each subject.
▶ Review your notes and decide whether to focus on similarities or on differences. Also consider your purpose for writing about these two subjects together. Will your paragraph clarify what makes each subject unique? Will it describe the relative merits of one over the other? Will it explain why differences exist? Will it look at some surprising similarities or differences?
▶ Based on your purpose, choose three to five similarities or differences that help make your point about your two subjects.
▶ If you are having trouble at this point, you may want to repeat the previous steps using a different topic from the list.
▶ Draft a topic sentence introducing your two subjects and suggesting your purpose for comparing or contrasting them.
▶ Briefly outline a plan for your paragraph. Decide whether you will organize your paragraph as a subject-by-subject comparison or as a point-by-point comparison. If you plan to use a subject-by-subject arrangement, then decide which subject you should discuss first and which second. If you plan to use a point-by-point arrangement, then decide on the order in which you will present your points—perhaps from least to most important.
▶ Draft your comparison-and-contrast paragraph.
▶ Review your draft paragraph for development. If you think you need to include more similarities or differences or more information about any similarities or differences, do some more invention to develop more ideas.
▶ Review your draft paragraph for unity. Cross out any information

that doesn't relate directly to your topic sentence and to the similarities or differences between your two subjects. You may also need to revise your topic sentence to accommodate any new information.
- Review your draft paragraph for coherence. Rearrange your similarities or differences if you think a different order would be more effective. If your paragraph is a subject-by-subject comparison, be sure that the features of the second subject are treated in the same order as the features of the first subject. Add any helpful transitional words or phrases.
- Prepare a final, edited draft of your paragraph.

G CLASSIFICATION AND DIVISION

When you use classification and division, your purpose is to help readers understand how items are related to one another and to the whole. A **classification** paragraph sorts information into groups. For example, animals can be classified as birds, mammals, insects, and so on, and cars can be classified as vehicles with front-wheel, rear-wheel, and four-wheel drive. The topic sentence of a classification paragraph identifies the subject being discussed and the categories into which individual items will be classified.

> I can classify my friends into three categories: those who know what they want out of life; those who don't have a clue; and those who are searching for goals. The first category, those who know what they want, are the most mature. They know exactly what they want to do for the rest of their lives. Although these friends will most likely be successful, they are the most boring. The second category, those who don't have a clue, are the most immature. They seem to live for the minute and don't think much about the future. If there is a party the night before a big test, they will go to the party and try to study when they get back. Although these friends can be a bad influence, they are the most fun. The third category, those who are searching for goals, are somewhere between the other two when it comes to maturity. They do not know exactly what they want to do with their lives, but they realize that they should be trying to find a goal. Although these friends can sometimes be unpredictable, they are by far the most interesting.
>
> Daniel Corey (student)

Topic sentence

Category one

Category two

Category three

The topic sentence clearly identifies the paragraph's subject—friends—and the three categories into which individual friends will be sorted. The rest of the paragraph discusses each category, one at a time. The shift from one category to another is signaled by the transitional phrases *the first category, the second category,* and *the third category.*

64 ▪ UNIT 2 Focus on Paragraphs

> ► **FOCUS** ON CLASSIFICATION AND DIVISION ◄
>
> Keep in mind that the same kind of information can be classified in more than one way. Animals, for example, can be classified by their behavioral traits—aggressiveness, docility, friendliness, and so on—as well as by species, and cars can also be classified by type—sedan, convertible, and so on. The topic of the paragraph above, friends, could be classified by age or gender, for example, instead of goals.

A **division** paragraph separates a whole into its parts. For example, blood may be separated into white cells, red cells, platelets, and so on. A division paragraph may also examine the relationship of the parts to one another and comment on the significance or value of the whole. The topic sentence in a division paragraph frequently identifies the topic of the paragraph and sometimes the reason for dividing it.

Topic sentence

Parts into which whole is divided

About 90 percent of plasma is water, in which a great variety of substances are held in suspension or in solution. These include proteins, such as fibrinogen, albumin and the globulins, and also sugar, fat and inorganic salts derived from food or from the storage depots of the body. Plasma contains urea, uric acid, creatine and other products of the breakdown of proteins. There are enzymes, such as adrenal hormones, thyroxine and insulin, derived from the glands of internal secretion. There are also various gases: oxygen and nitrogen, diffused into the blood from the lungs; and carbon dioxide, diffused into the blood from the tissues.

Louis Faugeres Bishop, *The Book of Popular Science*

The topic sentence identifies plasma as the subject that will be divided into parts. It then goes on to list the components of plasma—proteins, sugar, and so on.

> ► **FOCUS** ON CLASSIFICATION AND DIVISION ◄
>
> Classification and division are related processes. In many cases, when you classify, you divide, and when you divide, you classify. For example, the paragraph above uses division when it says that plasma is composed of proteins and other components; it uses classification when it groups fibrinogen, albumin, and the globulins together under the category of proteins.

CHAPTER 3   Patterns of Paragraph Development • 65

PRACTICE 3-13

Read this classification-and-division paragraph, and answer the questions that follow.

```
                        Baldness

     There are three basic categories of balding men.
Most common are those who lose hair beginning at the
crowns of their heads. Some men's hair remains very thin
in this area without falling out completely, so just a
bit of the scalp shows through. Other men, however, do
lose the hair completely to reveal a circle of bare
scalp, often so shiny that it appears polished. The cir-
cle usually increases in circumference as time goes by.
Second most common are men with receding hairlines. In
most such cases, the hairline only recedes from the
sides of the forehead, often leaving enough hair at the
front to disguise the loss at the sides fairly easily.
Depending on the shape of his head, his facial features,
and the texture of his hair, a man's appearance can ac-
tually be improved by a slightly receding hairline.
Least common are the unlucky men who suffer from both
these patterns of baldness at once. The balding crown
expands as the hairline recedes, often leaving just a
tuft of hair at the front and a fringe around the sides
and back. In an attempt to hide their condition, some of
these men go so far as to allow the hair on one side of
their heads to grow long enough so that they can care-
fully plaster it over the scalp to resemble normal hair
parted on the side. Others choose to celebrate their
condition by shaving their heads, which is generally
necessary if a man is to be completely bald; oddly
enough, it is very uncommon for any man to lose the hair
at the sides and around the back of his head.

                                 Peter Likus (student)
```

1. Underline the topic sentence of the paragraph.

2. Is this a paragraph of classification or division? ___*classification*___ How do you know? ___*It classifies bald men according to the way they go bald.*___

3. What is the subject of the paragraph? ___*categories of bald men*___ What three categories of the subject does the writer describe?

   men who lose hair at the crown

   men with receding hairlines

   men who lose hair both ways

66 ▪ UNIT 2 Focus on Paragraphs

4. Do you find this classification-and-division paragraph effective? _____
   Why, or why not? *Answers will vary.* _____
   _____
   _____
   _____

PRACTICE 3-14

Choose one of the topics below as the basis for a paragraph of classification or division.

Classify:
> Your friends according to their interests or hobbies
> Kinds of automobile drivers
> Kinds of commuters on public transportation
> Types of television game shows or situation comedies
> Types of employees or bosses
> Kinds of parents
> Types of shoppers, laundromat users, or fast-food customers
> Kinds of sports fans
> Types of radio stations
> Types of diets or fitness routines

Divide:
> An appliance or machine into its principal parts
> Your community into its distinctive neighborhoods or geographic areas
> A governmental or business organization—or perhaps the place where you work—by departments or employee functions
> A typical "slasher," kung fu, or other type of movie into its standard plot parts
> A scientific family of animals into individual species
> A magazine you read into its regular components

Now, carry out the following process for writing a classification or division paragraph.

▶ First, determine the specific subject you will classify or divide.
▶ Then, use one or more of the invention strategies described in Chapter 1 to help you explore your subject in detail. If you're writing a classification paragraph, begin by jotting down as many specific examples as you can. If you're writing a division paragraph, try to recall as much as you can about your subject and its parts.
▶ Review your notes. If you're writing a classification paragraph, focus on grouping similar examples into three or four specific categories and naming those categories. If you're writing a division paragraph, focus separately on three or four major parts of your subject and the important details about each part.

CHAPTER 3 Patterns of Paragraph Development • 67

- If you are having trouble at this point, you may want to repeat the previous steps using a different topic from the lists.
- Draft a topic sentence introducing your subject and its categories or major divisions.
- Briefly outline a plan for your paragraph, indicating the order in which you will discuss each category or division. Categories might be arranged in order of importance. Divisions might be arranged in time order, space order, or order of importance, depending on the subject.
- Draft your classification or division paragraph.
- Review your draft paragraph for development. If you think you need to include more categories or divisions or more examples or specific information for any category or division, do some more invention to come up with the ideas you need.
- Review your draft paragraph for unity. Cross out any information that doesn't relate directly to your topic sentence and to your subject and its categories or divisions. You may also need to revise your topic sentence to include added information.
- Review your draft paragraph for coherence. Rearrange categories or divisions if you think they could be more effectively ordered. Add any helpful transitional words or phrases.
- Prepare a final, edited draft of your paragraph.

H DEFINITION

A **definition** explains what a term means and sometimes how it is different from other similar terms. Anytime you want to make certain your readers know exactly how you are using a particular term or what an unfamiliar concept means, you use definition.

A formal dictionary definition defines a word in a sentence or two. A single sentence, however, is often not enough to define an abstract concept—*envy* or *democracy*, for example—a technical term, or a complex subject. In such cases, you may have to write a definition paragraph. In a definition paragraph, the topic sentence identifies the term to be defined (and, in fact, may briefly define it as well). The rest of the paragraph develops the definition by means of exemplification, comparison and contrast, classification, or another pattern or combination of patterns.

The following paragraph defines what it means to be a traveler.

<u>How do you know if you are a traveler?</u> What are the telltale signs? As with most compulsions, such as being a gambler, a kleptomaniac, or a writer, the obvious proof is that you can't stop. If you are hooked, you are hooked. One sure sign of travelers is their relationship to maps. I cannot say how much of my life I have spent looking at maps, but there is no map I won't stare at and study. I love to measure each detail with my thumb, to see how far I have come, how far I've yet to go. I love maps the way stamp collectors love stamps. Not for their usefulness,

Topic sentence: identifies term to be defined

Series of examples

but rather for the sheer beauty of the object itself. I love to look at a map, even if it is a map of Mars, and figure out where I am going and how I am going to get there, what route I will take. I imagine what adventures might await me even though I know the journey is never what we plan for; it's what happens between the lines.

Mary Morris, *Nothing to Declare*

The topic sentence, in the form of a question, presents the term the rest of the paragraph will define. The rest of the paragraph defines the term and uses several short, personal examples to establish that the writer is indeed a traveler.

The next definition paragraph defines a technical term from the field of gymnastics, the pommel horse.

Topic sentence

History and background: contrast

Explanation of current function: process

The pommel horse is of ancient origin. The Romans used it for the very practical purpose of training soldiers to mount horses. Some suggest it was used even earlier, by the bull dancers of Minoan Crete. Jumping over the bulls by doing springs off the animals' horns, these dancers surely must have practiced on something a little tamer than a live bull. Today, the pommel horse events are less exciting. The gymnast performs intricate leg-swinging movements while supporting his weight on his hands, which are either grasping the pommels or lying flat on the leather of the horse. As he swings his legs so that one follows, or "shadows," the other, the gymnast demonstrates strength, balance, and timing. Exercises such as single or double leg circles and scissors must be done continuously and in both directions. The pommel horse is difficult to master and not a favorite among gymnasts; they call it "the beast."

Ford Hovis, *The Sports Encyclopedia*

Here, the writer defines a specialized object in terms of its background and its current functions, using the patterns of contrast and process.

▶ **FOCUS** ON DEFINITION ◀

In general, you should not include a dictionary or encyclopedia definition in your definition paragraph. Readers can look up a term themselves. Your definition paragraph should show your ideas, not those of a reference book.

CHAPTER 3 Patterns of Paragraph Development • 69

PRACTICE 3-15

Read this definition paragraph, and answer the questions that follow.

```
         The Agony Called Writer's Block

     Have you ever sat staring at a blank notebook page or
piece of typing paper or computer screen, searching your
brain for words and ideas, fidgeting with frustration, and
longing to be anywhere else? If so, you probably want to
know more about writer's block. Writer's block is a
condition that afflicts ten out of ten writers at least
sometime during their lives. It is, simply stated, the
inability to get started on a piece of writing. For
novelists and other creative writers, writer's block can
be a disaster. Remember Jack Nicholson as a novelist in
Stephen King's The Shining typing over and over again "All
work and no play makes Jack a dull boy"--just before he
goes after his family with a butcher knife? For nonpro-
fessionals, writer's block almost always involves a
writing assignment of some kind, such as a paper for
school or a report for work; after all, people rarely feel
blocked when they are writing simply for pleasure.
Sometimes writer's block is caused by poor preparation.
The writer has not allowed enough time to think and make
notes that will pave the way for the actual writing of a
draft. However, even prepared writers with many ideas
already on paper can experience the freeze of writer's
block. It's comparable to being tongue-tied, only this
kind of writer's block is more like being brain-tied; all
the ideas keep bouncing around but won't settle into any
order, and the writer can't think of what to say first.
When the agony of writer's block strikes, often the only
cure is to give up and wait for another time to get
started.

                              Thaddeus Eddy (student)
```

1. Underline the topic sentence of the paragraph.

2. What is the subject of this definition? _writer's block_

3. What is the writer's one-sentence definition of the subject?

   the inability to get started on a piece of writing

4. List some of the specific information the writer uses to define his subject. The first example has been listed for you.

   It is a disaster for creative writers like the Jack Nicholson character in The Shining.

It usually involves a writing assignment.

It can be caused by poor preparation.

It's like being "brain-tied."

5. Do you find this definition paragraph effective? _____ Why, or why not? *Answers will vary.*

PRACTICE 3-16

Choose one of the topics below as the basis for a definition paragraph.

A positive quality, such as loyalty or bravery
A negative quality, such as envy or dishonesty
An ideal, such as the ideal friend or the ideal politician
A type of person, such as a worrier or an egomaniac
A social concept, such as equality, opportunity, or discrimination
A common strategic play in a particular sport or game
A hobby you pursue or some technique associated with that hobby
A term or device used in your job
An object or article of clothing that is symbolic of your religious or ethnic culture
A basic concept in a course you are taking
A particular style of music or dancing
A controversial subject whose definition not all people agree on, such as affirmative action or date rape

Now, carry out the following process for writing a definition paragraph.

▶ First, decide on the specific subject your paragraph will define.
▶ Then, freewrite or brainstorm about that subject, trying to get down on paper as many facts and ideas about it as you can. Name it, describe it, give examples of it, tell how it works, explain its purpose, consider its history or future, compare it to other similar things—do whatever makes sense in terms of your specific subject. You might also create a cluster diagram, as described in Chapter 1.
▶ Next, review your notes, and focus on the most important or interesting facts and ideas.
▶ If you are having trouble at this point, you may want to repeat the previous steps using a different topic from the list.

CHAPTER 3 Patterns of Paragraph Development ▪ 71

- ▶ Draft a topic sentence summarizing your main idea about the term you are going to define.
- ▶ List your facts or ideas, arranging them in an appropriate order.
- ▶ Draft your definition paragraph.
- ▶ Review your draft paragraph for development. If you think you need more information about your subject to define it clearly for your audience or to make your point about it effectively, do some more invention to develop other ideas.
- ▶ Review your draft paragraph for unity. Cross out any information that doesn't relate directly to your subject and your topic sentence. You may also need to revise your topic sentence to accommodate added information.
- ▶ Review your draft paragraph for coherence. Rearrange information if you think a different order might be clearer or more interesting to readers, and add any helpful transitional words or phrases.
- ▶ Prepare a final, edited draft of your paragraph.

I ARGUMENT

An **argument** paragraph takes one side of a debatable subject. When you write an argument, your purpose is to persuade readers that your position has merit. The topic sentence is an assertion that the rest of the paragraph supports with facts and examples, or evidence. If the evidence is effective and the reasoning is sound, the paragraph is likely to lead to a conclusion that readers will accept as reasonable.

The following paragraph argues against the use of Astroturf surfaces in sports stadiums.

Sports stadiums built during the 1960s and 1970s use Astroturf because it requires little maintenance and it creates a uniform playing surface. <u>But recently it has become clear that Astroturf has caused so many injuries that it should be eliminated from all pro sports stadiums.</u> Anyone who follows baseball or football knows that Astroturf causes many knee and ankle injuries. The main reason for this situation is that it does not absorb impact the way a natural grass surface does. Astroturf is a layer of rough artificial grass on top of a layer of padding. Beneath these layers is a cement pad. Players who fall on Astroturf or, in the case of football, are thrown down on it, risk serious injury. The New York Giants, for example, lost tight end Mark Bavaro to knee injuries caused by his falling onto his knees on the artificial surface of the Meadowlands Stadium. And the Astroturf surface in Philadelphia's Veterans Stadium, long known by players to be the worst in the country, has caused the Eagles to lose a number of key players. Sitting in the stands of Veterans

Topic sentence: asserts that Astroturf should be eliminated

Examples: provide evidence that supports the topic sentence

72 ▪ UNIT 2 Focus on Paragraphs

Conclusion

Stadium, you can see the gaps where sections of the Astroturf do not meet properly. When a player catches a foot in these gaps, the result can be a painful sprain or worse. The situations in Philadelphia and New Jersey are not unique. You can see the same problems in every stadium that has an Astroturf playing surface. For this reason, players, owners, and fans should insist that stadiums remove Astroturf and return to natural grass surfaces.

Toni-Ann Marro (student)

The paragraph begins with a sentence that briefly provides some background. Then, the topic sentence states the main idea—the writer's position. After explaining what Astroturf is, the paragraph presents examples that support the assertion in the topic sentence. The paragraph ends with a conclusion based on the evidence presented. Throughout the paragraph, transitional words and phrases—*the main reason, for example*, and *for this reason*—lead readers through the argument.

The next paragraph uses a different technique to argue in favor of capital punishment.

Topic sentence: compares the death penalty with cancer

Comparison continues

Conclusion

Admittedly, capital punishment is not a pleasant topic. However, one does not have to like the death penalty in order to support it any more than one must like radical surgery, radiation, or chemotherapy in order to find necessary these attempts at curing cancer. Ultimately we may learn how to cure cancer with a simple pill. Unfortunately that day has not yet arrived. Today we are faced with the choice of letting the cancer spread or trying to cure it with the methods available, methods that one day will almost certainly be considered barbaric. But to give up and do nothing would be far more barbaric and would certainly delay the discovery of an eventual cure. The analogy between cancer and murder is imperfect, because murder is not the "disease" we are trying to cure. The disease is injustice. We may not like the death penalty, but it must be available to punish crimes of cold-blooded murder, cases in which any other form of punishment would be inadequate and, therefore, unjust. If we create a society in which injustice is not tolerated, incidents of murder—the most flagrant form of injustice—will diminish.

Edward I. Koch, "Death and Justice: How Capital Punishment Affirms Life"

Rather than being supported by facts, as the first sample argument is, this second argument is supported by an imaginative comparison between cancer and murder. Even though such an argument can be quite persuasive, it is most convincing if it is also supported by factual evidence. In college writing you will usually be required to write an argument based on facts.

CHAPTER 3 Patterns of Paragraph Development 73

> ### ▶ FOCUS ON ARGUMENT ◀
>
> Not only must you present evidence to support your argument, but you must also consider the effect of your argument on your audience. Before you write, try to determine whether your readers are hostile, friendly, or neutral to your position, and let your analysis of your audience determine the approach you use.
>
> For example, if you suspect your audience may not be receptive to your position, you might mention (and refute) their possible objections in your topic sentence.
>
> > While some people may argue that students won't get a well-rounded education [possible objection], limiting course requirements will actually benefit most community college students [position].
>
> In addition, you might consider saving your topic sentence for the end of your paragraph, so you can lead up to it gradually.

PRACTICE 3-17

Read this argument paragraph, and answer the questions that follow.

```
     Did Popeye Watch Too Many Violent Cartoons?

     My four-year-old son recently talked about a televi-
sion character being "killed." Since our children are not
allowed to watch violent television programs, I wondered
what he had seen and decided that monitoring the cartoons
he watches might be a good idea. Surprisingly, nearly all
of them, from Daffy Duck to Power Rangers, contain some
sort of violence. Popeye cartoons, which were childhood
favorites of mine, are among the worst. In one episode,
Bluto is smashed over the head with a telephone pole, and
Popeye is thrown into wet cement and then freed when his
head is drilled with a pile driver. In another, Olive is
beaten up for spurning Bluto's amorous attentions. At a
time when children and teenagers are assaulting and even
killing others for clothes, bicycles, and money, I believe
it is time to consider limiting the amount of violence in
children's programs. Just as superior programs such as
Sesame Street have favorable effects because they teach
children useful skills and positive values, violent pro-
grams must also have some effect on impressionable minds.
When violence is depicted as a legitimate means of set-
tling disputes, for example, children learn to turn to vi-
olence as an answer. Of course, cartoons are not entirely
to blame, and other factors, such as home life and even
```

74 • UNIT 2 Focus on Paragraphs

biological conditions, can lead to violence among children. <u>Nonetheless, concerned parents should pay more attention to the "harmless" programming aimed at children, limit their children's access to such programming, and lobby networks and local stations to provide more positive, less violent programs for children.</u>

Tom Woller (student)

1. Underline the topic sentence of the paragraph. Why do you think the writer places the topic sentence where he does? <u>Because he isn't certain his audience will be receptive to his position, he wants to lead up to it gradually with convincing examples.</u>

2. What is the controversial subject that the writer is dealing with? <u>violence in children's television programs</u>   What is the writer's position on the subject? <u>It should be limited.</u>

3. List some of the evidence the writer uses to support his position. The first piece of evidence has been listed for you.

   Most cartoons contain violence (examples from Popeye).

   <u>Violent programs may make violence seem like a legitimate way of settling disputes. They may be contributing to the violence being inflicted by children and teenagers on their peers.</u>

4. Do you find this argument paragraph effective? _____ Why, or why not? <u>Answers will vary.</u>

PRACTICE 3-18

Choose one of the topics below as the basis for an argument paragraph.

An issue related to your school, such as grading procedures, required courses, entrance requirements, attendance policies, course offerings, student activity fees, the condition of classrooms or other facilities, accessibility to students with disabilities, or child-care facilities

A community issue, such as the need for a traffic signal, youth center, or something else you think would benefit the community; an action you think local officials should take, such as changing school hours, cleaning up a public eyesore, or improving a specific service; a new law you would like to see enacted or a current law you would like to see changed or revoked

A current controversy that you've been following in the news

Now carry out the following process for writing an argument paragraph.

- ▶ First, use one of the invention strategies described in Chapter 1 to help you identify an issue for your argument. (You might spend some time freewriting or brainstorming about each of the three topics suggested above.)
- ▶ Once you have decided on an issue, freewrite or brainstorm about your position on the issue. Ask yourself questions like the following: Why do you feel the way you do? Do many other people share your views, or are you likely to be in the minority? What specific actions do you think should be taken, and how would they make a difference? What objections are likely to be raised against your position or recommendation? How could you answer those objections?
- ▶ Now, review your notes, and pick out the facts and ideas that best support your position. Also, identify the strongest objections to your position and your best arguments against those objections. Ask yourself honestly whether you know enough about opposing positions on the issue to make a convincing case to an audience of well-informed readers.
- ▶ If you are having trouble at this point, you may want to repeat the previous steps using a different topic.
- ▶ Draft a one-sentence statement that clearly expresses your position, perhaps even mentioning possible objections.
- ▶ Spend a few minutes defining your audience. Are you writing for fellow students, for an administrator or governing body, or for the people who read your local newspaper's letters to the editor? How are they likely to feel about the issue and your position? Hostile? Friendly? Neutral?
- ▶ Briefly list your facts and ideas in an effective order that you think will be convincing to the audience you have defined.
- ▶ Draft your argument paragraph. Keep in mind that you may save your topic sentence to the end so that your paragraph gradually leads your readers to accept your position.
- ▶ Review your draft paragraph for development. If you think you need more facts or other evidence about the issue to convince your audience to accept your position, do some more invention to develop additional ideas.
- ▶ Review your draft paragraph for unity. Cross out any information that doesn't relate directly to your topic sentence, your position on the issue, or pertinent opposing positions. You may also revise your topic sentence to accommodate any new ideas.
- ▶ Review your draft paragraph for coherence. Rearrange information if you think a different order might be more convincing to readers, and add any helpful transitional words or phrases.
- ▶ Prepare a final, edited draft of your paragraph.

REVIEW

CHAPTER REVIEW: STUDENT WRITING

Read the following paragraphs. First, underline each topic sentence, and then determine which pattern of development each paragraph uses to support the topic sentence—for example, "process." Finally, underline any transitional words or phrases the writer uses to connect the ideas in the paragraph.

1. <u>My family loves to celebrate, and for us there is no better time to celebrate than on holidays.</u> They are very special times. <u>Because</u> we are Irish Catholic, Christmas not only has religious significance, but it is also an excuse for a party. All my cousins, aunts, and uncles gather at my grandmother's house. <u>First</u>, we dance, decorate the tree, and kiss under the mistletoe. <u>Then</u>, my mother plays the piano while we sing carols, and my grandmother gives out the gifts. Easter is <u>also</u> a time for celebrating. <u>On Easter morning</u> we all wake up early and go to services and <u>then</u> come home to a big breakfast of eggs, pancakes, sausages, and coffee. <u>After</u> we have eaten, my grandmother and my uncles clear the table, and the children dye eggs. <u>In the afternoon</u> we go on an egg hunt, and whoever finds the most eggs gets a special prize--a two-pound chocolate egg. It is a great time, and everyone joins in.

   Pattern of development: *exemplification*

2. <u>I'll never forget my high school biology classroom.</u> There was something in the air, in the flavor of the room. There were the fossils lying on the wooden tables

CHAPTER 3 Patterns of Paragraph Development ▪ 77

<u>in the back</u> of the room and human anatomy charts <u>on the side walls</u>. <u>In the front</u> of the room was a long table that held the objects that the teacher, Mr. Stuppy, was going to tell us about. There was even something that touched me deeply in Mr. Stuppy's attitude as he sat <u>at his old oak desk</u> drinking coffee from a white china mug bearing the words "Over 50 and proud of it!" Two years before this class I had hated science; now I loved it. That year, the year I took biology, I decided to devote my life to science and to teaching.

Pattern of development: ___*description*___

3. During the past twenty years, the Federal Communications Commission has challenged the freedom of speech of many college radio stations. <u>For example</u>, in 1973 the Yale Broadcasting Company was told not to play songs that had objectionable lyrics, and in 1975 the University of Pennsylvania's radio station almost lost its license because of objectionable language used during a call-in program. The same situation <u>also</u> exists today at our college station, WKDU. The FCC is telling the station that it can no longer play certain songs on the air. The students who work at the station are angry, and so are the listeners who will not be able to hear their favorite music. <u>In fact</u>, the FCC's policy challenges our right of free speech. The Communications Act of 1934 states that the FCC cannot pass any regulation that interferes with the right of free speech

on the radio. By limiting the kind of music WKDU is allowed to play, the FCC is clearly interfering with the station's right to determine its own programming. Government censorship is not something that any of us should take lightly. <u>For this reason, the infringement on WKDU's right of free speech is wrong and should be opposed by all of us.</u>

Pattern of development: _____*argument*_____

4.   For me, a utopia would be Dr. Martin Luther King's world where people are not judged by race, color, or creed, but by character. <u>However</u>, I don't think this will ever occur. Our world is too racially divided to become this type of utopia. <u>Therefore</u>, I would settle for a "second-degree" utopia. This world would be Malcolm X's world, in which people would work to educate themselves and their children. This world is more possible than Dr. King's, but it <u>too</u> is a long way off. <u>So</u>, I think that I will have to settle for a "third-degree" utopia, in which blacks and whites may not love one another but do respect one another's rights. <u>Although this utopia is not the one I would hope for, it is the one that I think can be achieved</u>.

Pattern of development: *definition (using classification)*

5.   <u>According to Richard Rodriguez in his essay "The Fear of Losing a Culture," Hispanic Americans are torn between two extremes.</u> <u>On the one hand,</u> they want to come

to the United States and achieve the American Dream. Like other immigrants, they want to realize the promise of freedom and opportunity that this country offers. <u>In the process</u>, they want their children to get an education--something they often can't get in their native country--and a chance to move up in the world. <u>On the other hand</u>, Hispanic Americans have a strong desire to hold on to their native culture. <u>According to Rodriguez</u>, the immigrants come to this country to achieve their dreams, but they continue to speak Spanish. Some are so afraid of losing their ethnic identity that they resist assimilation. The trick, <u>however</u>, is to do both--to be Latino and also to be part of the American mainstream.

Pattern of development: *comparison and contrast*

CHAPTER REVIEW: COLLABORATIVE ACTIVITIES

1. As a group, decide on an activity that all of you do regularly—commute or study, for example. Then, write a process paragraph in which you describe the specific steps you follow when you perform this activity. Make sure you include a topic sentence that identifies the subject of your paragraph.

2. Decide on an issue about which the members of your group agree. Then, brainstorm to find ideas about your subject. Finally, write an argument paragraph in which you present your ideas. Make sure you include a topic sentence that states your position and specific examples to support your assertions.

3. What services or facilities on your campus—for example, the gym or the career counseling center—operate most efficiently? As a group, write a topic sentence that presents your favorable opinion of the subject you choose, and then list several examples that support your topic sentence. Finally, write an exemplification paragraph in which you present your assessment.

Review

- An exemplification paragraph supports a general statement with one or more specific examples. (See 3A.)
- A narrative paragraph relates a sequence of events—in time order—to tell a story. (See 3B.)
- A descriptive paragraph tells how something looks, sounds, smells, tastes, and feels. An objective description describes a subject in precise and concrete terms, without emotion. A subjective description includes a writer's feelings about a subject. (See 3C.)
- A process paragraph explains how something works or how to do something. In a *process explanation,* the writer wants readers to understand a process, not to perform it. *Instructions* give readers the information they need to perform a task or activity. (See 3D.)
- A cause-and-effect paragraph analyzes causes (what made a particular event or outcome occur) or discusses effects (the probable outcomes of a particular activity or behavior). (See 3E.)
- A comparison-and-contrast paragraph tells how two things are similar or how two things are different. In a *subject-by-subject* comparison, you discuss all your points for one subject and then all of your points for the other subject. In a *point-by-point* comparison, you discuss each point for both subjects before going on to the next point. (See 3F.)
- A classification paragraph sorts information into groups. A division paragraph separates a whole into its parts. (See 3G.)
- A definition paragraph explains the meaning of a term or concept by means of exemplification, comparison and contrast, classification, or another pattern (or combination of patterns). (See 3H.)
- An argument paragraph takes one side of a debatable subject. (See 3I.)

Unit 2 Review

The collaborative activities, writing practice topics, and student writing samples that follow provide opportunities for you to review what you have learned in Chapters 2 and 3.

COLLABORATIVE ACTIVITIES

1. Working in groups, design a questionnaire whose objective is to determine how the people in your class learn about local and national news events. You may, for example, ask people if they get most of their news from the newspaper, television, or radio. Respondents should indicate how old they are and whether they are male or female. Your questionnaire should contain no more than ten questions.
2. Distribute your questionnaire to the class. After you have collected the questionnaires, tabulate the responses. Have one person keep a record while the others read the responses. After recording the responses, try to draw some conclusions about your class. Do most people get the news from television or from newspapers? Do more people of one gender or age group get their news from television?
3. Write three paragraphs about your findings. In the first paragraph, describe the procedure you used to design the questionnaire. In the second paragraph, go through the questions one at a time, and report on your findings. In the last paragraph, draw a general conclusion about how people in your class get their news. Support your conclusion with specific examples from responses to your questionnaire. Make sure each of your paragraphs has a clear topic sentence that states its main idea.

WRITING PRACTICE

1. Assume a television producer has asked you to think of an incident in your life that would make a good half-hour television show. Write a narrative paragraph about the incident. Give your paragraph a title that indicates whether the show you envision would be a comedy or a drama.
2. Think of a word that you or members of your peer group or ethnic group use regularly—for example, a slang term or a word in a language other than English. Then, write a paragraph in which you define the word for

someone who does not know what it means. Include one or two examples to make your definition clear to your readers. Don't forget to begin your paragraph with a topic sentence that identifies the term you are going to discuss.

3. Write a paragraph for three of the following topic sentences. Then, check to make sure that each of the paragraphs is unified, well developed, and coherent. Finally, determine what pattern of development you have used, and label each of the paragraphs.

- I'll never forget the worst day I ever had.
- Males and females definitely have different ways of looking at the world.
- If I could change one thing about myself, I know what it would be.
- One person has made it possible for me to be where I am today.
- My teachers fall into four categories.
- The word *patriotism* has a definite meaning to me.
- When I look around my bedroom, I realize that it reveals a lot about me.
- Whenever I get ready to go to a party, I go through the same routine.
- If someone asked me my opinion about banning smoking, I would have no trouble telling him or her what I thought.
- Although most people would agree that lying is wrong, sometimes it seems justified.

STUDENT WRITING

Read the following student paragraphs. Underline the topic sentence in each one, and decide what pattern of development is used. Then, with your class identify the elements that make each paragraph unified, coherent, and well developed.

1. My father began studying martial arts while he was in the Air Force in the 1960s. During this period, martial-arts techniques in Japan were the closely guarded secrets of individual families. Although some masters took other Japanese as students, few would take a foreigner as a serious lifelong student. My father, however, believed he had a serious calling to the martial arts. He was also persistent--so persistent that he overcame the distrust many Japanese have for foreigners. As a result of his persistence he became the

first African American to receive personal training in hand-to-hand fighting and swordsmanship from a true Japanese master.

Pattern of development: __cause and effect__

2. Sundays were always the same. Bright and early my mom and I would take our trash bags of clothes to the Magee Avenue Laundromat. It was always an educational experience. All it took was a woman yelling at her two little children or an old man washing a few belongings for me to realize how lucky we were to have my mom. First, we would sort the clothes, and my sister and I would carry loads to separate washing machines. Then, we would put the soap and the coins into the machines. During the time the clothes were being washed, the three of us would sit and talk. The times we spent together showed us that we all had the same fears and hopes for the future. After the clothes were washed, we would put them in the dryer and talk some more. Later, we would sit around the kitchen table eating Sunday dinner and continue our discussion.

Pattern of development: __process__

3. Hip hop is not just a language. It's rap, a style of clothing, and even a way of life. Hip hop is Puma sneakers, hooded sweatshirts, baggy jeans, hiking boots, a large assortment of hats and vests, and, most of all, an attitude. Hip hop is about hearing new songs and wearing the newest clothes. Hip hop is how you say "I

love you" to a hip-hop junkie. It's your password into the cult of hip-hop infomaniacs. You know hip hop when you see it and hear it.

Pattern of development: _definition (using exemplification and description)_

4. <u>Every time I receive a letter from my uncle in Poland I am glad I came to live in the United States</u>. In his letters my uncle tells me how the lack of consumer goods in Eastern Europe makes his life difficult. Essential items such as toothpaste, clothing, bread, and poultry are among the most difficult for him to obtain. To acquire such goods, he must wait in long lines or pay extremely high prices. Here in the United States, however, supermarket shelves are so well stocked that it takes time to decide what brand, flavor, or size of a product to buy. Stores have racks full of reasonably priced clothes of different colors, materials, and styles. Delicatessens have so much variety that the average consumer is baffled by the selection of meats, cheeses, and breads available.

Pattern of development: _comparison and contrast_

5. <u>Because the death penalty is disproportionately applied to people in certain segments of society, it is not a proper response to violent crime</u>. Recently, Amnesty International reported that most of those sentenced to death in the United States are poor and unemployed. The nation's death rows are populated by the illiterate, members of oppressed minorities, drug

addicts, alcoholics, and other outcasts. Subject to the worst conditions of society, these individuals are the ones most likely to commit crimes punishable by death. In addition, because they are poor, these defendants cannot afford the high legal fees that enable the rich literally to get away with murder. As a result, the poor are forced to rely on court-appointed public defenders who frequently lack resources, expertise, and experience.

Pattern of development: _____*argument*_____

UNIT 3

4 Thesis and Support

> **Overview**
>
> In this chapter you will learn
> - To expand a paragraph into an essay
> - To use a thesis-and-support structure for an essay
> - To move from a topic to a thesis
> - To develop a clear, specific thesis statement that explains a point or takes a stand

Although being able to write a well-constructed paragraph is important, most of the writing you do in college will be longer than a paragraph. Frequently, you will be asked to write an **essay**—a group of paragraphs on a single subject. This unit will show you how to apply the paragraph skills you have learned to writing essays.

> ▶ **FOCUS** ON PARAGRAPHS AND ESSAYS ◀
>
> When you write a paragraph, you follow the same process you use when you write an essay: You move from invention to selecting and arranging ideas to drafting, revising, and editing. (See Chapter 1.)

A BUILDING PARAGRAPHS AND ESSAYS

Both essays and paragraphs are unified by a single main idea. In a paragraph, the **topic sentence** presents the main idea, and the rest of the paragraph develops the main idea.

Paragraph

```
Topic sentence   states the main idea of the
paragraph

Support   develops the main idea with reasons,
details, and examples
_____
_____
_____
```

In an essay, the first paragraph begins with opening remarks and closes with a **thesis statement,** which—like a paragraph's topic sentence—presents the main idea. The **body** of the essay is made up of several paragraphs that support the thesis with reasons, details, and examples. Each of these paragraphs begins with a topic sentence that states its main point. The last paragraph, which may restate the thesis, offers the writer's concluding thoughts on the subject.

Essay

```
Opening remarks   introduce the subject to
be discussed
_____
_____
_____

Thesis statement   presents the main idea of the
essay
```

Introductory Paragraph

Topic sentence (first main point)

Support (reasons, details, examples)

Topic sentence (second main point)

Support (reasons, details, examples)

Topic sentence (third main point)

Support (reasons, details, examples)

} *Body Paragraphs*

Restatement of thesis summarizes essay's main idea

Closing remarks present writer's last words on the subject

Concluding Paragraph

PRACTICE 4-1

The following paragraph can be expanded into a full essay. To see how, first underline the topic sentence. Then underline the four sentences that state the writer's main points. Finally, underline the sentence that restates the topic sentence.

<u>Several strategies can help smokers stop smoking.</u> <u>The first and easiest strategy is finding something to substitute for the physical cigarette that they've gotten used to handling.</u> Some people use a pencil or a straw, while others find a coin helpful, but almost any small object will work. <u>Next, people who quit smoking generally find a substitute for the stimulation they get from cigarettes.</u> They might chew a strongly flavored sugarless gum, for example, or take fast, short breaths or do anything that gives a physical jolt to the system. <u>A third strategy is to alter habits associated with smoking.</u> For example, people who associate cigarettes with drinking coffee might temporarily switch to tea or another beverage with caffeine. <u>Finally, most people who successfully quit smoking prepare themselves to resist temptation in a moment of stress or discomfort.</u> Rather than reaching for a cigarette, they have another sort of treat ready for themselves. <u>These four antismoking strategies have worked for many ex-smokers, who recommend them highly.</u>

Now, assume the writer is going to expand this paragraph into a six-paragraph essay, adding further details and developing each of the four main points in a separate body paragraph. Fill in the following essay diagram with the appropriate sentences from the original paragraph to create an outline for this planned essay about smoking.

Thesis statement: *Several strategies can help smokers stop smoking.*

Topic sentence: The first and easiest strategy is finding something to substitute for the physical cigarette that they've gotten used to handling.

Topic sentence: Next, people who quit smoking generally find a substitute for the stimulation they get from cigarettes.

Topic sentence: A third strategy is to alter habits associated with smoking.

Topic sentence: Finally, most people who successfully quit smoking prepare themselves to resist temptation in a moment of stress or discomfort.

CHAPTER 4   Thesis and Support ▪ 91

> **Restatement of thesis:** *These four antismoking strategies have worked for many ex-smokers, who recommend them highly.*

PRACTICE 4-2

Suppose you were asked to expand a paragraph you wrote earlier into a five- or six-paragraph essay. First, look for a paragraph in which you included three or four main points to support your topic sentence. These should be points about which you could give more details or explanation. As an alternative, brainstorm about one of your topic sentences, and come up with three or four main supporting points, each of which could be developed in its own paragraph. Write your topic sentence and three or four main points on the lines below.

Answers will vary.

Topic sentence: _____

First main point: _____

Second main point: _____

Third main point: _____

Fourth main point: _____

B   UNDERSTANDING THESIS AND SUPPORT

The concept of **thesis and support**—stating a thesis and supporting it with facts, examples, or reasons—is an important one. Because it enables you to present your ideas clearly and persuasively, it is central to much of the writing you will do. Regardless of the specific pattern of development you may use for a particular essay, each of your essays should have this essential thesis-and-support structure.

The student writer of the following essay uses a thesis-and-support structure to present her ideas.

```
                         Working

     Ever since I began college, I have been working.
While some of my friends sat around wasting time, I
have managed to get several part-time jobs. Even
though there have been times when I wished I didn't
have to work, I have gained a lot by working. A part-
time job is a valuable part of any college student's
education.
     The first reason to work is that a job provides a
steady income. The jobs I hold during the year pay for
most of my weekly expenses. When I want to buy books or
an item of clothing, I usually can. If an unexpected
expense comes up, I can usually increase my hours so I
can earn more. Last year, for example, I unexpectedly
had to buy supplies for a photography course I was
taking. At first I thought I would have to drop the
course because I couldn't afford the supplies. After
talking to my boss, however, I was able to arrange to
work a few extra hours and earn enough to buy the
supplies I needed.
     Another reason for working is that a job can help
pay tuition. Even though my parents have never said
anything to me, I know that paying my tuition is a
hardship. Both my parents work, and they are able to
make ends meet. Even so, they don't have the money to
pay all my tuition. In addition, my brother will be
going to college next year, and they have to save for
him. Every summer I try to earn enough money to pay
part of my tuition. This past year, I was able to pay
half my tuition and almost all of my living expenses.
     The most important reason for working is that a job
gives satisfaction. By working, I feel that I am earning
the respect of my parents. I am not a drain on the
family, and I set a good example for my brother. I would
feel horrible if I had to run to my parents every time I
needed money. I would also feel like a kid, not an
adult. By working, I am developing the confidence I will
need when I graduate and enter the work force. Because I
have been able to earn my own way, I know I can support
myself no matter what happens.
     I would advise any student to consider getting a
part-time job. Working supplements income and helps pay
tuition, and it also provides a great deal of
satisfaction.
```

CHAPTER 4 Thesis and Support • 93

An outline of this essay shows that it follows a thesis-and-support pattern.

Opening remarks

Thesis: A part-time job is a valuable part of any college student's education.

Introductory Paragraph

Topic Sentence: The first reason to work is that a job provides a steady income.

Support

Topic Sentence: Another reason for working is that a job can help pay tuition.

Support

Body Paragraphs

(continued on the following page)

94 • UNIT 3 Paragraphs into Essays

(continued from the previous page)

> **Topic sentence:** The most important reason for working is that a job gives satisfaction.
>
> **Support**

> **Restatement of thesis:** I would advise any student to consider getting a part-time job.
>
> **Closing remarks**

Concluding Paragraph

> ▶ **FOCUS** ON THESIS AND SUPPORT ◀
>
> Notice that every topic sentence in a thesis-and-support essay focuses on one aspect of the thesis—in the example above, one reason for working.
> - The first reason to work is that a job provides a steady income.
> - Another reason for working is that a job can help pay tuition.
> - The most important reason for working is that a job gives satisfaction.
>
> These topic sentences not only reinforce the thesis, but they also keep readers on track by reminding them what the main idea of the essay is.

PRACTICE 4-3

Following is an essay expanded from the paragraph on smoking in Practice 4-1. As you read, underline the thesis, the topic sentence of each body

CHAPTER 4   Thesis and Support · 95

paragraph, and the restatement of the thesis in the conclusion. Then, answer the questions at the end, comparing the original paragraph on page 89 to the expanded essay. Discuss your answers with your class or writing group.

> More and more smokers today are aware of the serious risks smoking poses both for themselves and for the nonsmokers around them. Many of them would like to quit but just don't think they can. <u>However, several strategies can help smokers achieve this goal.</u>
> <u>The first and easiest strategy is finding something to substitute for the physical cigarette that they've gotten used to handling.</u> Some people use a pencil or a straw, while others find a coin helpful. I have a friend who started using a Japanese fan. There are even special products available to keep people's hands busy, such as worry beads and small rubber balls. Almost any small object will work as long as it is satisfactory for the individual.
> <u>Next, people who quit smoking generally find a substitute for the stimulation they get from cigarettes.</u> They might chew a strongly flavored sugarless gum, for example, or take fast, short breaths. Other people splash their faces with ice cold water or do some light exercise. Some even claim that standing on their heads has helped. The point is to find something that gives a physical jolt to the system.
> <u>A third strategy is to alter habits associated with smoking.</u> For example, people who associate cigarettes with drinking coffee might temporarily switch to tea or another beverage with caffeine, while people who generally smoke on the telephone might try writing letters rather than making long-distance calls. Unfortunately, some smoking-associated activities are difficult to eliminate. People who associate smoking with being in their cars obviously can't give up driving. The point, though, is to alter as many habits as possible to eliminate times when one would normally reach for a cigarette.
> <u>Finally, most people who successfully quit smoking prepare themselves to resist temptation in a moment of stress or discomfort.</u> Rather than reaching for a cigarette, they have another sort of treat ready for themselves. Some people, understandably, choose candy or sweets of some kind, but these are not the best alternatives for obvious reasons. A better idea is to use the money saved by not buying cigarettes to purchase something to pamper oneself with, such as expensive cologne or a personal CD player.
> No one would say that it's easy to quit smoking, but this fact shouldn't keep people from recognizing that they can kick the habit. <u>These four antismoking strategies have worked for many ex-smokers, who recommend them highly.</u>

1. What did the writer add to expand the opening sentence of the original paragraph into a separate introductory paragraph? *more background about smokers and smoking*

2. What did the writer add to expand the first main point? *more examples of substitutes for handling cigarettes*

96 • UNIT 3 Paragraphs into Essays

3. What did the writer add to expand the second main point? _more examples of substitutes for the stimulation of cigarettes_

4. What did the writer add to expand the third main point? _more examples of ways to break habits and advice for doing so_

5. What did the writer add to expand the fourth main point? _more examples of treats_

6. What remarks did the writer add to expand the closing sentence into a separate concluding paragraph? _sentence about the difficulties of quitting smoking_

PRACTICE 4-4

Look at each of the main points you listed for Practice 4-2. On the lines that follow, brainstorm to develop additional details or examples that you might add to expand each point into a paragraph.

Answers will vary.

First main point: _____

Additional details: _____

Second main point: _____

Additional details: _____

Third main point: _____

   Additional details: _____

   _____

   _____

   _____

Fourth main point: _____

   Additional details: _____

   _____

   _____

   _____

C MOVING FROM TOPIC TO THESIS

Most of the writing you will do in college will begin with a **topic** suggested by an **assignment** your instructor gives you.

- Describe the worst job you ever had.
- Discuss some things you would change about this college.
- What can college students do to improve the environment?

Because they are so general, responding to any of these assignments in their present form would be difficult, if not impossible. What job would you write about? What things about your school would you change? Exactly what can college students do to improve the environment? Answering these questions will help you find a topic.

Assignment	Topic
Describe the worst job you ever had.	My summer job at the Concord Hotel
Discuss some things you would change about this college.	Three things I would change about Jackson Community College
What can college students do to improve the environment?	The campus recycling project

Before you can write about a topic, you have to narrow it and decide on a workable thesis. In some cases, ideas might come to you easily, but most often you will have to use the systematic approach described in Chapter 1 to discover what you want to say. Begin by using the **invention strategies** (see 1B) to help you to discover ideas about your topic and to narrow your focus. Once you have gathered information about your topic, you can decide exactly what you want to say about it. By selecting and rejecting ideas and discovering connections among them, you can determine the point you

98 • UNIT 3 Paragraphs into Essays

want your essay to make. You can then express this point in a **thesis statement:** a single sentence that clearly expresses your essay's main idea.

Topic	Thesis
My summer job at the Concord Hotel	Working as a waitress at a large resort was the worst job I ever had.
Three things I would change about Jackson Community College	If I could change three things about Jackson Community College, I would improve the food choices, decrease class size in first-year courses, and ship some of my classmates to the North Pole.
The campus recycling project	The recycling project recently begun on our campus has already done a lot to improve the environment.

PRACTICE 4-5

Decide whether the following topics are narrow enough for an essay of four to six paragraphs. If a topic is suitable, write "OK" in the blank. If it is not, write in the blank a narrower version of the same topic for a brief essay.

Examples: successful strategies for quitting smoking _____*OK*_____

horror movies _____*1950s Japanese monster movies*_____

1. violence in American public schools *Answers will vary.*

   Example: banning weapons in a local high school.

2. ways to improve your study skills *OK*

3. using pets as therapy for nursing home patients *OK*

4. teachers *Answers will vary. Example: qualities of an effective teacher*

5. safe ways to lose weight *OK*

6. clothing styles *Answers will vary. Example: the influence of MTV on*

   teenagers' clothing styles

CHAPTER 4 Thesis and Support • 99

7. parent-child relationships *Answers will vary. Example: strategies for communicating with your child*

8. reasons children lie to their parents *OK*

9. college education *Answers will vary. Example: the cost of going to college versus the benefits*

10. television's impact on children *Answers will vary. Example: the influence of violent cartoons on children's aggressive behavior*

PRACTICE 4-6

Choose five topics that interest you from the previous exercise. If the original topic was too broad, be sure you have narrowed it to a more manageable topic. Then, draft a thesis statement for a possible essay on each of these five topics.

1. Topic: *Answers will vary.*

    Thesis statement: _____

2. Topic: *Answers will vary.*

    Thesis statement: _____

3. Topic: *Answers will vary.*

    Thesis statement: _____

4. Topic: *Answers will vary.*

    Thesis statement: _____

5. Topic: *Answers will vary.*

    Thesis statement: _____

D STATING THE THESIS

Like a topic sentence, a thesis statement tells readers what to expect. An effective thesis has two important characteristics.

1. An effective thesis statement makes a point about a topic or takes a stand on an issue; for this reason, it must do more than state a fact or announce your intention.

Statement of fact
Football fans cause problems.

Announcement
In this essay I will discuss the problems caused by football fans.

Effective thesis statement
Officials at Pittsburgh's Three Rivers Stadium should take specific action to control the behavior of football fans.

Statement of fact
Many college students work.

Announcement
I would like to present my opinion about whether college students have to work.

Effective thesis statement
A part-time job is a valuable part of any college student's education.

To be effective, a **thesis statement** should make a point about your topic or take a definite stand. A statement of fact is not an effective thesis statement because it gives you nothing to develop in your essay. For example, how much can you say about the *fact* that many college students work? An announcement of your intention also gives readers no indication of the point your essay will make. It is not enough for a thesis statement to say that you plan to discuss the problems football fans cause. A thesis can, however, say that officials should take specific steps to control the behavior of football fans or that a part-time job is a valuable part of a college student's education.

2. An effective thesis statement is clearly worded and specific.

Vague statement
I think my school has some problems.

Effective thesis statement
Administrators at my school should make four changes to improve the quality of student life.

Vague statement
Television commercials aren't like real life.

Effective thesis statement
Television commercials do not present accurate pictures of minority groups.

One way to make sure that your thesis statement clearly communicates your main idea is to be specific. Often an effective thesis statement not only tells readers what an essay will be about, but also suggests the direction the essay will take. The vague statements above convey little information to readers about what the essays will discuss or how they will present or organize their ideas. The effective thesis statements are more focused. They tell readers that the first essay will discuss four changes administrators should make and the second will give examples of television commercials that do not present accurate pictures of minority groups.

> ▶ **FOCUS** ON STATING THE THESIS ◀
>
> Keep in mind that not all essays have a stated thesis. For example, if a writer wants to build suspense or to avoid opening with a controversial statement, he or she might decide to *imply*—that is, just suggest—the essay's thesis. Even when the thesis is not directly stated, it should still be obvious to readers. If readers can tell what your thesis is, they can follow your essay's ideas.

PRACTICE 4-7

On the lines below, indicate whether each of the following is a fact, an announcement, a vague statement, or an effective thesis.

Examples: My commute between home and school takes over an hour each way. ___*fact*___

I don't like my commute between home and school. ___*vague*___

1. Students who must commute a long distance to school are at a disadvantage compared to students who live close by. ___*effective*___

2. In this paper I will discuss cheating and why students shouldn't cheat. ___*announcement*___

102 • UNIT 3 Paragraphs into Essays

3. Any school can establish specific policies that will discourage students from cheating. ___effective___

4. Cheating is a problem for both students and teachers. ___vague___

5. Television commercials are designed to sell products. ___fact___

6. I would like to explain why some television commercials are funny. ___announcement___

7. Single parents have a rough time. ___vague___

8. The news reports that young people are starting to abuse alcohol and drugs at earlier ages than in the past. ___fact___

9. Alcohol and drug abuse are major problems in our society. ___vague___

10. Families can use several strategies to help children avoid alcohol and drugs. ___effective___

11. This essay will look at alcohol, drugs, and the average teenager. ___announcement___

12. There is a lot of controversy about the number of young, unmarried mothers in the United States. ___fact/vague___

13. Teenage mothers trying to raise a child alone face some difficult problems that every young person should think about. ___effective___

14. In today's competitive society, it can be hard to succeed. ___vague___

15. Success in the business world involves working hard, feeling secure about yourself, and looking out for opportunities. ___effective___

PRACTICE 4-8

Look back at your work for Practices 4-2 and 4-4. Revise your topic sentence in Practice 4-2 so that it is an effective thesis statement for an essay of five or six paragraphs. Make sure that it is not an announcement, a statement of fact, or a vague statement. Then, use your outline from Practice 4-4 as the basis for a draft of a thesis-and-support essay. Make sure that you state your thesis in your introductory paragraph, that each body paragraph contains a clear topic sentence, and that you end with a separate concluding paragraph. Before handing in a final copy of your essay, consult the Editing Checklist (page 16).

CHAPTER 4 Thesis and Support 103

• • • • • • • • • • • • • • REVIEW • • • • • • • • • • • • •

CHAPTER REVIEW: STUDENT WRITING

After reading the following essay, write an appropriate thesis statement on the lines provided. (Make sure your thesis statement clearly communicates the essay's main idea and suggests the direction the essay will take.) Then, fill in the topic sentences. Finally, restate the thesis in different words in your conclusion.

```
          Preparing for a Job Interview
    I have read a lot of books that give advice on how to do
well on a job interview. Some recommend practicing your hand-
shake, and others suggest rehearsing answers to typical ques-
tions. This advice is useful, but not many books tell how to
get mentally prepared for an interview.
```
Planning to make a good appearance, working on a positive attitude, and doing some research about the job are my most effective mental preparations for a job interview.

Before my interview, I think about how I should look in order to make a good impression.

```
Feeling good about how I look is important, so I usually wear
a jacket and tie to an interview. Even if you will not be
dressing this formally on the job, you should try to make a
good first impression. For this reason, you should never come
to an interview dressed in jeans or shorts. Still, you should
be careful not to overdress. For example, wearing a suit or a
dressy dress to an interview at a fast-food restaurant might
make you feel good, but it could also make you look as if you
don't really want to work in a casual setting.
```

Another way I prepare for an interview is by concentrating on positive thinking.

Going on an interview is a little like getting ready to participate in an important sporting event. You have to go in with the right attitude. If you think you are not going to be successful, chances are that you won't be. So before I go on any interview, I spend some time building my confidence. I tell myself that I can do the job and that I will do well in the interview. By the time I get to the interview, I am convinced that I am the right person for the job.

Finally, I make sure I do some research about the job.

Most people go to an interview knowing little or nothing about the job. They expect the interviewer to tell them what they will have to do. Once an interviewer told me that he likes a person who has taken the time to do his or her homework. Since that time I have always done some research before I go on an interview--even for a part-time job. (Most of the time my research is nothing more than a call to a person who has a job where I want to work.) This kind of research really pays off. At my last interview, for example, I was able to talk in specific terms about the job's duties and indicate which shift I would prefer. The interviewer must have been impressed because she offered me the job on the spot.

Mentally preparing for an interview can help sharpen your appearance, your attitude, and your knowledge about the job.

Of course, following my suggestions will not guarantee that

CHAPTER 4 Thesis and Support · 105

you get a job. You still have to do well at the interview itself. Even so, getting mentally prepared for the interview will give you an advantage over others who do almost nothing before they walk in the door.

CHAPTER REVIEW: COLLABORATIVE ACTIVITIES

1. Find a paragraph in a magazine or a newspaper about a controversial issue that interests you. Working in groups, compare the paragraphs and select the best one. On a clean sheet of paper, brainstorm about the information in the paragraph. Then, select three points you could discuss in a short essay. Finally, write a sentence that could serve as the thesis statement for the essay.
2. Working in a group, come up with thesis statements suitable for essays on three of the following topics.
   - College sports
   - Talk radio
   - Vegetarians
   - Rock lyrics
   - Cheating
   - Welfare
   - Class size
   - College entrance exams
   - Handguns
   - Commuting
3. Exchange your group's three thesis statements with those of another group. Then, choose the best one of the other group's thesis statements. A member of each group can then read the thesis statement to the class and explain the group's choice.

Review

- In a paragraph, the topic sentence presents the main idea, and the rest of the paragraph develops the main idea. In an essay, the thesis statement presents the main idea, and the body paragraphs support the thesis. (See 4A.)
- A thesis-and-support essay has an introductory paragraph that states the thesis and a concluding paragraph that restates the thesis and brings the essay to a close. It also has several body paragraphs that support the thesis. (See 4B.)
- After you are given a writing assignment, you need to narrow your topic and express your main idea in a single sentence. (See 4C.)
- An effective thesis statement should explain a point or take a stand, not just state a fact or announce your intention. (See 4D.)
- An effective thesis statement should be clearly worded and specific. (See 4D.)

5 Introductions and Conclusions

> **Overview**
>
> In this chapter you will learn
> - To write effective introductions for essays
> - To choose appropriate titles for essays
> - To write effective conclusions for essays

A INTRODUCTIONS

An **introduction** is the first thing people see when they read your essay. If the introduction is interesting and effective, readers are likely to be drawn into your essay. If it isn't, they may be bored or even form a negative impression.

Your introduction should prepare readers for the essay to follow by giving them the information they need to understand your discussion. For this reason, the introduction should include a **thesis statement** that presents the main idea of your essay. The thesis statement usually appears at the end of the introduction, but it can also appear earlier.

In addition to containing the thesis statement, the introduction should make people want to read further. To heighten reader interest, it can begin with a question or a narrative or even an unusual comparison. Because the introduction has so many functions to perform, it should be a full paragraph. (In long essays, in fact, the introduction may be several paragraphs. In such cases, the thesis statement may not appear until the second or third paragraph.)

> ▶ **FOCUS** ON INTRODUCTIONS ◀
>
> Don't begin your essays by announcing what you plan to write about. Instead, begin with an introduction that is a part of your essay and flows naturally into the rest of it, and avoid unnecessary statements like *This essay is about*, *Today I will talk about*, or *In my essay I will discuss*.

The following options can help you write varied and interesting introductions.

1. Begin with a Direct Approach

Quite often the best way to open an essay is by presenting a few opening remarks and then listing the points you will discuss in your essay. This straightforward approach moves readers directly to the central concerns of your essay. Once you feel comfortable with this strategy, you can experiment with the other approaches discussed in the rest of this section.

> In 1994 the Republicans won a majority in both the House and the Senate for the first time in forty years. After their victory, there was quite a bit of finger pointing and discussion in the Democratic Party. Some thought the defeat of President Clinton's health care bill was to blame. Others said so many Democrats lost because the party was out of touch with the voters. Certainly both these issues were important, but even more important were taxes, welfare, and anxiety about the national debt.
>
> Serge Komanawski (student)

2. Begin with a Narrative

You can begin an essay with a narrative drawn from your personal experience or from a current news event. If your story is interesting, it can involve readers almost immediately. Notice how the narrative in the following introduction sets the stage for an argument in favor of animal testing. Also note that this introductory paragraph does not include a thesis statement. Because the writer considers his thesis to be extremely controversial, he does not state it until his conclusion.

> In a desperate—and successful—attempt to save the life of a dying man, woman, child or infant sometime in the next few months, surgeons will implant another heart or liver from a baboon or perhaps even a pig into a human body. Then, two things will happen. Doctors will decide whether the recipient will use the animal organ as a "bridge," until a human organ can be located for transplant, or if the patient will keep the animal organ as a permanent transplant. Second, animal-rights activists will picket the hospital where the medical miracle took place.
>
> Richard Pothier, "Animal Tests Saved My Life"

3. Begin with a Question

Using a question at the beginning of your essay is an effective introductory strategy. Because readers know you will answer the question in your essay—perhaps even in your thesis statement—they will want to read further. Notice how two questions in the following introduction catch the reader's eye.

> Imagine this scene: A child is sitting under a Christmas tree opening her presents. She laughs and claps her hands as she gets a doll, a pair of shoes, and a sweater. What could spoil this picture? What information could cause the child's parents to feel guilt? The answer is this: that children from developing countries most likely worked long hours in substandard conditions so this American child could receive her gifts.
>
> Megan Davia (student)

4. Begin by Establishing Common Ground

Beginning with a general, easily accepted statement can establish a connection between you and your readers by showing them that your ideas are similar to theirs. And, as the following introduction illustrates, establishing common ground can also smoothly pave the way for an unusual, even offbeat, thesis statement.

> Let's face it. Even the most beloved dog can be very stinky at times. And where pet hygiene is concerned, the enlightened pet guardian (and, of course, by that I mean me) has no choice but to share the indoor facilities with the animal.
>
> Merrill Markoe, "Showering with Your Dog"

5. Begin with a Definition

A definition at the beginning of your essay can give valuable information to readers. Such information can explain a confusing concept or clarify a complicated idea. As the following paragraph about the kaffiyeh demonstrates, a definition can also arouse interest by introducing an unfamiliar concept.

CHAPTER 5 Introductions and Conclusions • 109

> It is the ultimate cultural survivor in the Middle East: the plain or stitched cotton cloth that Arabs wear on their heads and draped down the back or shoulders. Designed more than 1,000 years ago, it originally protected against the harsh desert climate. Today, it's also an emblem of masculinity, maturity and nationalism. A substitute flag, a mask, a shield. A political or a fashion statement.
>
> Leora Frankel, "History on the Head"

▶ FOCUS ON INTRODUCTIONS ◀

Don't introduce a definition with a tired opening phrase such as *According to Webster's* or *The American Heritage Dictionary defines*. . . .

6. Begin with a Background Statement

A background statement can provide an overview of a subject and set the stage for the discussion to follow. It can also—as the following introduction illustrates—help prepare readers for a surprising or controversial thesis statement.

> English is the most widely spoken language in the history of our planet, used in some way by at least one out of every seven human beings around the globe. Half of the world's books are written in English, and the majority of international telephone calls are made in English. English is the language of over sixty percent of the world's radio programs, many of them beamed, ironically, by the Russians, who know that to win friends and influence nations, they're best off using English. More than seventy percent of international mail is written and addressed in English, and eighty percent of all computer text is stored in English. English has acquired the largest vocabulary of all the world's languages, perhaps as many as two million words, and has generated one of the noblest bodies of literature in the annals of the human race.
>
> Nonetheless, it is now time to face the fact that English is a crazy language.
>
> Richard Lederer, "English Is a Crazy Language"

7. Begin with an Unusual Comparison

Using an unexpected comparison is a good way to draw readers into an essay. As the following example shows, introducing an essay with an unusual comparison can provide a humorous context for a discussion.

> Your body is like a superbly engineered luxury automobile: if you use it wisely and maintain it properly, it will eventually break down, most likely in a bad neighborhood. To understand why this is, let's take a look inside this fascinating "machine" we call the human body.
>
> Dave Barry, "How Your Body Works"

8. Begin with a Quotation

An appropriate saying or an interesting piece of dialogue can immediately draw readers into your essay. Notice how the quotation below not only creates interest but also leads smoothly and logically into the thesis statement at the end of the introduction.

> According to the comedian Jerry Seinfeld, "When you're single, you are the dictator of your own life. . . . When you're married, you are part of a vast decision-making body." In other words, before you can do anything, you have to discuss it with someone else. These words kept going through my mind as I thought about asking my girlfriend to marry me. The more I thought about Seinfeld's words, the more I hesitated. Unfortunately, I never suspected I would pay a price for my indecision.
>
> Dan Brody (student)

▶ **FOCUS** ON TITLES ◀

Every essay you write should have a **title**. Like an introduction, a title should suggest the subject of your essay and make people want to read further.

(continued on the following page)

(continued from the previous page)

- A title can be a straightforward announcement.
    How Your Body Works
- A title can be a question.
    Is a Tree Worth a Life?
- A title can be an announcement of a controversial position.
    The Case against Animal Testing
- A title can establish a personal connection with readers.
    Animal Tests Saved My Life
- A title can establish an unusual slant or perspective.
    Showering with Your Dog

PRACTICE 5-1

Look back at the essay you wrote for Practice 4-8 or any other essay you are currently working on. Evaluate your opening paragraph. Is it suitable for your topic and thesis? Is it likely to interest readers? Try drafting a different opening paragraph, using one of the options presented in this chapter. Be sure to include a clear statement of your thesis. In what ways, if any, is this new opening paragraph an improvement?

Now, think about your title. Brainstorm to come up with one that will get your readers' attention.

B CONCLUSIONS

Because your **conclusion** is the last thing readers see, they may judge your entire essay by the effectiveness of the conclusion. For this reason, conclusions should be planned, drafted, and revised with care. Like an introduc-

> ▶ FOCUS ON CONCLUSIONS ◀
>
> In essay exams—when time is limited—a one-sentence restatement of your thesis is often enough for a conclusion. Likewise, an in-class essay exam may have just a one- or two-sentence introduction. (See Appendix A, "Writing Essays and Paragraphs in an Exam Setting.")

tion, a conclusion is usually a full paragraph. (Long essays may have a conclusion that is several paragraphs long.)

Your conclusion should give readers a sense of completion. One way you can accomplish this is by restating the essay's thesis. Keep in mind, however, that a conclusion is more than a word-for-word restatement of the thesis. If you return to your thesis here, you should rephrase it, expand upon it, go on to make some general concluding remarks, and end with a sentence that readers will remember.

> ### ▶ FOCUS ON CONCLUSIONS ◀
>
> Familiar phrases that announce your essay is coming to a close—for example, *in summary* or *in conclusion*—are unnecessary and can be annoying. Try to avoid them. Also, avoid words and phrases that weaken your readers' confidence in you, such as *I may not be an expert*, *at least that's my opinion*, and *I could be wrong, but*.

Here are some options you can try when you write your conclusions.

1. Conclude with a Restatement of Your Thesis

This no-nonsense conclusion allows you to reinforce your points by restating your thesis in different words. Notice how the following essay ends by simply reviewing the main points of the argument.

> In 1994, voters' concerns about high taxes, increased welfare costs, and the huge national debt helped propel the Republicans into the House and the Senate. Republican candidates used these issues to exploit the public's distrust of government. For their part, voters did not seem to care that taxes were not as high as they were in the 1960s and 1970s, that welfare costs were a small part of federal spending, and that the national debt was lower than it had been just two years before.
>
> Serge Komanawski (student)

2. Conclude with a Narrative

A narrative conclusion can bring a situation or event discussed in the essay to a logical, satisfying close. The conclusion below uses a narrative to tie up the essay's loose ends.

> After twenty years, the tree began to bear. Although Grandfather complained about how much he lost because pollen never reached the poor part of town, because at the market he had to haggle over the price of avocados, he loved that tree. It grew, as did his family, and when he died, all his sons standing on each other's shoulders, oldest to youngest, could not reach the highest branches. The wind could move the branches, but the trunk, thicker than any waist, hugged the ground.
>
> Gary Soto, "The Grandfather"

3. Conclude with a Question

By ending with a question, you leave readers with something to think about. The question you ask should build on the thesis statement and not introduce any new issues. Notice how the conclusion below asks a series of questions before restating the essay's thesis.

> Why is it that when the sun or the moon or the stars are out, they are visible, but when the lights are out, they are invisible, and that when I wind up my watch, I start it, but when I wind up this essay, I shall end it?
> English is a crazy language.
>
> Richard Lederer, "English Is a Crazy Language"

4. Conclude with a Prediction

This type of conclusion not only sums up the main point of the essay but also goes a step farther and makes a statement about the future. The following conclusion uses this technique to paint a troubling picture of the future of American cities.

> On that little street were the ghosts of the people who brought me into being and the flesh-and-blood kids who will be my children's companions in the twenty-first century. You could tell by their eyes that they couldn't figure out why I was there. They were accustomed to being ignored, even by the people who had once populated their rooms. And as long as that continues, our cities will burst and burn, burst and burn, over and over again.
>
> Anna Quindlen, "The Old Block"

5. Conclude with a Recommendation

Once you think you have convinced readers that a problem exists, you can make recommendations about how the problem should be solved. Notice how the following paragraph makes a series of recommendations about a cancer drug made from the Pacific yew tree.

> Every effort should be made to ensure that the yew tree is made available for the continued research and development of taxol. Environmental groups, the timber industry, and the Forest Service must recognize that the most important value of the Pacific yew is as a treatment for cancer. At the same time, its harvest can be managed in a way that allows for the production of taxol without endangering the continual survival of the yew tree.
>
> Sally Thane Christensen, "Is a Tree Worth a Life?"

6. Conclude with a Quotation

Frequently a well-chosen quotation—even a brief one—can add a lot to your essay. In some cases, a quotation can add authority to your ideas. In others, as in the paragraph below, the quotation can sum up the main point of the essay.

> It was 4:25 A.M. when the ambulance arrived to take the body of Miss Genovese. It drove off. "Then," a solemn police detective said, "the people came out."
>
> Martin Gansberg, "38 Who Saw Murder Didn't Call the Police"

> ▶ **FOCUS** ON INTRODUCTIONS AND CONCLUSIONS ◀
>
> The content of your introductions and conclusions depends on the points you make in the body of your essay. For this reason, it makes little sense to spend much time writing introductions or conclusions until you have drafted the body paragraphs. Once you see the direction in which your essay has developed, you can concentrate on revising your introductions and conclusions so they are consistent with what you say in the body of your essay.

CHAPTER 5 Introductions and Conclusions ▪ 115

PRACTICE 5-2

Look back at the essay you wrote for Practice 4-8 or any other essay you are currently working on. Evaluate your conclusion. Is it suitable for your topic and thesis? Does it bring your essay to a clear and satisfying close that will leave a strong impression on readers? Try drafting a different conclusion, using one of the options presented in this chapter. In what ways, if any, is this new concluding paragraph an improvement?

• • • • • • • • • • • • • • REVIEW • • • • • • • • • • • • • •

CHAPTER REVIEW: STUDENT WRITING

The following essay has a weak introduction and conclusion. Choose an appropriate introductory and concluding strategy, and, on a separate sheet of paper, rewrite both the introduction and the conclusion to make them more effective. Then, choose a suitable title for the essay.

Answers will vary.

    Geraldine Ferraro's life shows how someone who comes from a poor background can make a difference.
    Geraldine Ferraro came from humble beginnings. Her father was an Italian immigrant who died when she was eight years old. Her mother supported the family by sewing beads on women's clothes. After graduating from college, Ferraro taught elementary school, worked as a legal secretary, and eventually graduated from law school.
    Throughout the 1960s, Ferraro raised a family and practiced law on a part-time basis. Her cousin, who was a district attorney in Queens, New York, helped her get a job as an assistant district attorney. In 1978, when the congressional representative in her district retired, Ferraro ran for his seat and won. While in the House of Representatives, she worked tirelessly for the people in her district, and, as a result, she was reelected in 1980 and 1982. Because of her hard work and her involvement in party affairs, she was named chair of the Democratic National Committee in 1984.
    At the 1984 Democratic National Convention, Ferraro was asked to be Walter Mondale's running mate. By accepting the nomination, Ferraro became the first woman to become a vice-presidential candidate from a major party. Ferraro was chosen for at least two reasons.

First, she was a smart, aggressive campaigner. In addition, she could help the Democratic Party appeal to women, Catholics, and blue-collar workers. Throughout the campaign, she handled herself with dignity, responding well to attacks questioning her ability to lead. Although the Democrats were defeated, Ferraro's nomination established once and for all that women were a major force in American politics.

As Geraldine Ferraro's life shows, someone who comes from a poor family can work hard and make a difference.

CHAPTER REVIEW: COLLABORATIVE ACTIVITIES

1. Bring in several copies of an essay you have written for another class. Have each person in your group comment on its introduction and conclusion. Then, revise your essay's introduction and conclusion in response to their suggestions.

2. Find a magazine or newspaper article that interests you. Delete the introduction and conclusion, and bring the body of the article to class. Ask your group to decide on the best strategy for introducing and concluding the article. Then, collaborate on writing new opening and closing paragraphs and an appropriate title.

3. Working in a group, devise interesting and appropriate titles for essays on each of the following topics.
   - The high salaries of sports figures
   - The evils of eating junk food
   - The need for regular exercise
   - The joys of living in the city (or in the country)
   - The rights of smokers
   - Television violence
   - Applying to college
   - Contemporary rock music
   - Holiday shopping
   - Parents (or being a parent)

Review

- The introduction of an essay should contain a thesis statement and should create interest. (See 5A.)
    - An essay can begin with a direct approach.
    - An essay can begin with a narrative.
    - An essay can begin with a question.
    - An essay can begin by establishing common ground.
    - An essay can begin with a definition.
    - An essay can begin with a background statement.
    - An essay can begin with an unusual comparison.
    - An essay can begin with a quotation.

- A title should suggest the subject of your essay and make people want to read further. (See 5A.)

- The conclusion of an essay should restate the thesis and make some general concluding remarks. (See 5B.)
    - An essay can conclude with a restatement of your thesis.
    - An essay can conclude with a narrative.
    - An essay can conclude with a question.
    - An essay can conclude with a prediction.
    - An essay can conclude with a recommendation.
    - An essay can conclude with a quotation.

Unit 3 Review

The collaborative activities, writing practice topics, and student writing sample that follow provide opportunities for you to review what you have learned in Chapters 4 and 5.

COLLABORATIVE ACTIVITIES

1. Bring in copies of a magazine article, and distribute it to your group. Identify the introduction, body, and conclusion. Underline the thesis statement and the topic sentences. Put a check mark next to any paragraphs that do not seem to have a topic sentence. Discuss your findings as a group, and try to resolve any differences of opinion.

2. Think of a term that you could define in an essay—*couch potato* or *jock*, for example. As a group, brainstorm to identify as many characteristics as possible of the term you are going to define. Then, choose your subject's three or four most distinctive characteristics—those you could best illustrate in an essay. Finally, decide on a thesis you could support with the material your group has generated.

3. Working on your own, write a short essay using the material your group generated in the preceding activity. When you have finished, exchange your essay with another person in the group. Check your partner's essay to make sure it has a thesis-and-support structure as well as an effective introduction, conclusion, and title.

WRITING PRACTICE

1. Write an essay in which you discuss three roles you assume daily. For example, you could be a student, a worker, and a parent or child. Make sure your essay has a thesis statement as well as clear topic sentences.

2. Imagine that, while walking on the beach, you find a bottle with a genie in it. The genie offers to grant you three wishes. Unfortunately for you, the genie wants all requests for wishes in writing. Write a thesis-and-support essay in which you state your wishes and explain your reasons for wanting them. Make sure each of your body paragraphs focuses on a single wish.

3. Write a letter to one of your instructors explaining what you like about his or her class. For example, you could discuss how well the instructor responds to student questions or how interesting the classes are. Make

sure your letter has an effective introduction and conclusion and a thesis statement that conveys its main idea.

STUDENT WRITING

Read the following student essay. Underline the thesis statement and the topic sentences. Then, examine the introduction and the conclusion. What strategies does the writer use? What other strategy would work? On a separate sheet of paper, rewrite the introduction and conclusion, using an alternative strategy for each. Finally, choose an appropriate title for the essay.

Answers will vary.

    Why would anyone want to spend one or two afternoons a week doing something for no pay? That is the question some of my friends ask me. <u>They don't know, however, that the satisfaction I get from my volunteer job at an after-school program more than makes up for the time I spend or the money I could earn somewhere else.</u>

    <u>The first reason volunteer work gives me satisfaction is that I like children.</u> I come from a large family, and I love to be around little children. My brothers and sisters are all grown up, and being with the children at the after-school program reminds me of how my own family used to be. In addition, the after-school program gives me the opportunity to work with the children I like the best--those between five and six years old. I find children in this age group to be the most responsive. They will usually try hard to please and will respond to kindness and attention; I can usually get them to open up with just a joke or a kind word.

Another reason volunteer work gives me satisfaction is that it makes me feel as if I am appreciated. The children show me they appreciate me in a lot of little ways. When I arrive in the afternoon, they run to greet me. Some of them are so excited they pull me into the room. Last month, on my birthday, the children and the teacher even had a surprise party for me. They sang songs, gave me cookies they had baked, and even drew a picture for me. Where else could I get this kind of treatment?

The last reason doing volunteer work gives me satisfaction is that it enables me to get firsthand experience in my major--early childhood development. My job at the after-school program is to help the full-time teachers. Usually I read stories to the children and help them with letter and number recognition skills. Occasionally, the teacher lets me plan a lesson that I can teach. Last week, for example, I had the children color in pictures made up of the numbers one to ten. Even though I am two years away from student teaching, I have gotten a good deal of practical experience from volunteering in my field.

As you can see, volunteer work gives me a lot of satisfaction. I can't imagine doing anything more enjoyable or useful. And who knows? In three years I might be working in an after-school program and being paid, too.

6 The Basic Sentence Pattern: Subjects and Verbs

Overview

In this chapter you will learn
- To identify sentence subjects, both singular and plural
- To distinguish prepositional phrases from subjects
- To identify action verbs, linking verbs, and complete verbs (a main verb plus any helping verbs)

PARAGRAPH PRACTICE

Write a descriptive paragraph about a person you admire or with whom you would like to trade places. Be very specific about what this person is like, what he or she does, and what kind of life he or she lives. What exactly do you admire or envy about the person? Use the blank space below for invention. Then, write your paragraph on the lines that follow.

UNIT 4

A **sentence** is a group of words that expresses a complete thought. In a sentence a writer tells readers a complete idea about someone or something. Every sentence includes a subject and a verb.

A IDENTIFYING SUBJECTS

The **subject** of a sentence tells who or what the sentence is about.

<u>Derek Walcott</u> won the 1992 Nobel Prize in literature.

<u>St. Lucia</u> is an island in the Caribbean.

In the first sentence above, the subject is *Derek Walcott*. In the second sentence above, the subject is *St. Lucia*.

Every complete sentence must include a subject. This subject can be a noun or a pronoun. A **noun** names a person, place, or thing—*Derek Walcott, St. Lucia, Nobel Prize, literature, island,* or *Caribbean*. A **pronoun** takes the place of a noun. The pronouns *I, you, he, she, it, we,* and *they* can all be used as subjects.

CHAPTER 6 The Basic Sentence Pattern: Subjects and Verbs

> ▶ **FOCUS** ON SIMPLE AND COMPLETE SUBJECTS ◀
>
> A sentence's **simple subject** is a noun or pronoun alone.
>
>   house   witch   she   it   they
>
> A sentence's **complete subject** is a noun along with any words that describe it.
>
> the haunted house
> our house on the hill
> the wicked witch who frightened Dorothy
>
> A two-word name, such as *Victor Frankenstein*, is a simple subject.

PRACTICE 6-1

Underline the complete subject of each sentence in the paragraph below. Be sure you underline not only the noun or pronoun that tells who or what the sentence is about but also all the words that describe the subject. Put a check over the simple subject.

    Example: The poet's ✓parents were both teachers.

(1) Derek ✓Walcott was born in 1930. (2) His ✓ancestors came from Africa, the Netherlands, and England. (3) His early ✓years were spent on the island of St. Lucia. (4) His early ✓poems were published in Trinidad. (5) ✓He later studied in Jamaica and in New York and founded the Trinidad Theatre Workshop. (6) ✓Walcott eventually gained wide recognition as a poet. (7) ✓He was a visiting lecturer at Harvard in 1981. (8) This renowned ✓poet published *Omeros* in 1990. (9) This book-length ✓poem sets classic Greek heroes in the West Indies. (10) The sixty-two-year-old Caribbean ✓poet was honored in 1992 with a Nobel Prize.

▶ FLASHBACK ◀

Look back at your response to the Paragraph Practice at the beginning of the chapter. *Who* or *what* are most of your sentences about? Write the answer here: _____.
Underline the subject of each of your sentences. Then, list all of those subjects on the lines below.

_____   _____

_____   _____

_____   _____

_____   _____

Do you see any sentence whose subject consists of more than just a noun or pronoun? Write one such complete subject on the line below, and put a check over the simple subject.

_____

▶ FOCUS ON SINGULAR AND PLURAL SUBJECTS ◀

A **singular subject** is one person, place, or thing.

    I   Lewis   he   woman   she   dictionary   it

In the following sentence, *Simón Bolívar* is a singular subject:

    <u>Simón Bolívar</u>, a South American revolutionary leader, was known as "the Liberator."

A **plural subject** is more than one person, place, or thing.

    we   Lewis and Clark   they   women   dictionaries

In the following sentence, *South Americans* is a plural subject:

    <u>South Americans</u> still admire Bolívar, who died in 1830.

Note that two singular subjects can be connected by *and* to form a plural subject.

    <u>Peru and Bolivia</u> are two countries Bolívar helped to liberate.

CHAPTER 6 The Basic Sentence Pattern: Subjects and Verbs • 125

PRACTICE 6-2

All of the words listed below could be subjects of sentences. Some are singular, and some are plural. Write *S* after each word that could be a singular subject, and write *P* after each word that could be a plural subject.

Examples: New York _S_
New Yorkers _P_
New York and New Jersey _P_

1. an albino rat _S_
2. World War I _S_
3. the Osage Indians _P_
4. The Declaration of Independence _S_
5. a jack and a queen _P_
6. our mother _S_
7. James Weldon Johnson _S_
8. chili dogs _P_
9. his two favorite courses _P_
10. Jack and Jill _P_

••••••••▶ **FLASHBACK** ◀••••••••

Look back at your response to the Paragraph Practice at the beginning of the chapter. Can you find any plural subjects? Write them on the lines below.

_____   _____

_____   _____

_____   _____

B IDENTIFYING PREPOSITIONAL PHRASES

A **phrase** is a group of words that has no subject or verb and therefore cannot stand alone as a sentence. A **prepositional phrase** consists of a preposition (such as *on*, *to*, *in*, or *with*) and its object (a noun or pronoun).

Preposition	+	**Object**	=	**Prepositional phrase**
on		the stage		on the stage
to		Nia's house		to Nia's house
in		my new car		in my new car
with		them		with them

Because the object of a preposition is a noun or a pronoun, you may sometimes think it is the subject of a sentence. However, the object of a preposition can never be the subject of a sentence. Look at this sentence:

The cost of the repairs was astronomical.

Here, the noun *cost* is the subject. Because the word *repairs* is also a noun, you might think at first that it is the sentence's subject. *Repairs*, however, is the object of the preposition *of*. Therefore, it cannot be the subject of the sentence.

Now consider this next sentence:

At the end of the novel, after an exciting chase, the lovers flee to Mexico.

The subject of this sentence is the noun *lovers*. Each of the other nouns in the sentence—*end*, *novel*, *chase*, and *Mexico*—is the object of a preposition. Therefore, none of them can be the subject of the sentence.

To avoid confusion as you try to identify a sentence's subject, enclose each prepositional phrase in parentheses.

The <u>cost</u> (of the repairs) was astronomical.
(At the end) (of the novel) (after an exciting chase,) the <u>lovers</u> flee (to Mexico.)

Now the subject of each sentence is clear.

In order to identify prepositional phrases easily, you should become familiar with the most commonly used prepositions. (See the list in 21A.)

PRACTICE 6-3

Each sentence below includes at least one prepositional phrase. To help you identify each sentence's subject, enclose each prepositional phrase in parentheses. Then, underline the subject of the sentence.

Example: (In twentieth-century presidential elections), <u>third-party candidates</u> have attracted many voters.

1. (With over 27 percent of the vote,) Theodore Roosevelt was the strongest third-party presidential candidate (in history.)
2. (In the 1912 race) (with Democrat Woodrow Wilson and Republican William H. Taft,) Roosevelt ran second (to Wilson.)
3. Other candidates (on the ballot) were Socialist Eugene V. Debs and Eugene W. Chafin (of the Prohibition Party.)
4. (Until Roosevelt,) <u>no third-party candidate</u> had won more than 2 or 3 percent (of the vote.)
5. However, some candidates (of other parties) were able to make strong showings (after 1912.)
6. (For example,) Robert M. LaFollette (of the Progressive Party) won about 16 percent (of the vote) (in the 1924 race.)

CHAPTER 6 The Basic Sentence Pattern: Subjects and Verbs • 127

7. (In 1968,)(with more than 13 percent)(of the popular vote,) American Independent Party candidate George C. Wallace placed third (behind Republican Richard M. Nixon and Democrat Hubert H. Humphrey.)
8. (In 1980,) John B. Anderson, an Independent, challenged Republican Ronald Reagan and Democrat Jimmy Carter and got 6.6 percent (of the vote.)
9. (With nearly 19 percent)(of the popular vote,) Independent Ross Perot ran a strong race (against Democrat Bill Clinton and Republican George Bush)(in 1992.)
10. (During the twentieth century,) the two-party system (of the United States) has remained intact (despite the many challenges)(by third-party candidates.)

•••••••••▶ **FLASHBACK** ◀•••••••••

Reread your response to the Paragraph Practice at the beginning of the chapter. Can you identify any prepositional phrases in your paragraph? List as many as you can on the lines below.

_____   _____   _____

_____   _____   _____

_____   _____   _____

_____   _____   _____

C IDENTIFYING VERBS

Every sentence includes both a subject and a verb. The subject tells who or what the sentence is about, and the **verb** tells what the subject does or connects the subject to words that describe or rename it. Without a verb, a sentence is not complete.

Action Verbs

An **action verb** tells what the subject is, was, or will be doing.

Roy Campanella played baseball.

Amelia Earhart flew across the Atlantic.

Action verbs also include those verbs that show mental and emotional actions.

Renee understood the problem.

Travis worried about his job.

128 ■ UNIT 4 Writing Simple Sentences

A sentence may have one action verb, or it may have two or more.

He <u>hit</u> the ball, <u>threw</u> down his bat, and <u>ran</u> toward first base.

Linking Verbs

Not all verbs tell what action the subject is performing. A **linking verb** does not show action; instead, it connects the subject to a word or words that describe or rename it.

Subject ⟷ Linking verb ⟷ Word or words that describe or rename the subject

The following sentence contains a linking verb:

A googolplex is an extremely large number.

The subject of this sentence, *googolplex*, is connected to the words that describe it, *an extremely large number*, by the verb *is*.

A googolplex ⟷ is ⟷ an extremely large number.

Because *is* links the subject and the words that describe it, *is* is a linking verb.

Many linking verbs, like *is*, are forms of the verb *be*. Other commonly used linking verbs refer to the senses (*look*, *feel*, and so on).

The photocopy ⟷ looks ⟷ blurry.
Some students ⟷ feel ⟷ anxious about the future.

Commonly Used Linking Verbs		
act	feel	seem
appear	get	smell
be (am, is, are, was, were)	grow	sound
	look	taste
become	remain	turn

PRACTICE 6-4

Underline the verbs in each sentence. Then, in the blank, indicate whether the verb is an action verb (AV) or a linking verb (LV).

Example: Emily <u>looked</u> pale. **LV**

1. Ann Radcliffe wrote *The Mysteries of Udolpho*, an eighteenth-century Gothic novel. **AV**
2. The novel tells the story of Emily St. Aubert. **AV**
3. Emily is intelligent and talented. **LV**
4. However, she seems remarkably naive. **LV**
5. She often feels weak and faint. **LV**
6. Emily loves a noble but dull young man named Valancourt. **AV**
7. She lives with her foster uncle Montoni, the novel's villain. **AV**

CHAPTER 6 The Basic Sentence Pattern: Subjects and Verbs ▪ 129

8. Montoni <u>appears</u> alarmingly evil. <u>LV</u>
9. As the story progresses, Montoni <u>frightens</u> Emily. <u>AV</u>
10. After Montoni's death, however, Emily and Valancourt <u>are</u> happy. <u>LV</u>

> **▶ FLASHBACK ◀**
>
> Reread your response to the Paragraph Practice at the beginning of the chapter. Underline any verbs you find. Then, write them on the lines below, and identify them as action verbs (AV) or linking verbs (LV).
>
> _____   _____   _____   _____
>
> _____   _____   _____   _____

Complete Verbs

Many verbs are made up of more than one word. The verb in the following sentence consists of two words:

Minh <u>was thinking</u> about his future.

In this sentence, *thinking* is the **main verb,** and *was* is the **helping verb.** A sentence's **complete verb** is made up of a main verb plus any helping verbs that accompany it. In the following sentences, the complete verb is underlined, and the main verb is checkmarked. (Note that sometimes a word can come between the parts of a complete verb.)

Minh <u>should have ✓gone</u> earlier.

<u>Did Minh ✓ask</u> the right questions?

Minh <u>will ✓work</u> hard.

Minh <u>can really ✓succeed</u>.

> **▶ FOCUS ON USING COMPLETE VERBS ◀**
>
> Some words, such as *thinking* and *gone,* cannot stand alone as main verbs in a sentence. They need a helping verb—such as *will, would, may, might, must, should, can,* or *could* or a form of *be* or *have*—to make them complete. See 7B.

PRACTICE 6-5

Some of the verbs in the sentences below consist of only one word. Others consist of a main verb and one or more helping verbs. In each sentence, underline the complete verb, and put a check mark above the main verb.

Example: The Salk polio vaccine <u>was ✓given</u> to more than a million schoolchildren in 1954.

1. During the 1950s, polio <u>✓was</u> a terrifying disease.
2. For years it <u>had ✓puzzled</u> doctors and researchers.
3. Thousands <u>were ✓becoming</u> ill each year in the United States alone.
4. Children <u>should have been ✓playing</u> happily.
5. Instead, they <u>were ✓getting</u> very sick.
6. Polio was sometimes <u>✓called</u> infantile paralysis.
7. In fact, it <u>did ✓cause</u> paralysis in children and in adults as well.
8. Some patients <u>could ✓breathe</u> only with the help of machines called iron lungs.
9. Others <u>would ✓remain</u> in wheelchairs for life.
10. By 1960, Jonas Salk's vaccine <u>had ✓reduced</u> the incidence of polio in the United States by over 90 percent.

▶ **FLASHBACK** ◀

Look back at your Paragraph Practice response at the beginning of the chapter. In every sentence, underline the complete verb, and put a check mark above the main verb.

CHAPTER 6 The Basic Sentence Pattern: Subjects and Verbs — 131

REVIEW

CHAPTER REVIEW: STUDENT WRITING

Read the student passage below. Then, underline the complete subject of each sentence once, and underline the complete verb of each sentence twice. Label the simple subject (S) and the verb (AV for action verb or LV for linking verb). If you think you will have trouble locating the subject, try enclosing any prepositional phrases within parentheses before you begin. The first sentence has been done for you.

Escape to Freedom

(On April 14, 1979,)(at 10 p.m.,) <u>my family and I</u> <u><u>left</u></u> Vietnam. <u>My mother</u> <u><u>had hidden</u></u> gold and jewelry (in water pipes.) Now <u>we</u> <u><u>could use</u></u> these unconfiscated items. <u>We</u> <u><u>could buy</u></u> seats (on a fishing boat.) Then, <u>we</u> <u><u>could escape</u></u> (to freedom.) <u>The trip</u> <u><u>was</u></u> extremely dangerous. <u>Forty-two people</u> <u><u>drifted</u></u> aimlessly (on the water.) <u>We</u> <u><u>drifted</u></u> (for four days and five nights)(on the Pacific Ocean.)(At last,)(on the 18th of April,) <u>we</u> <u><u>saw</u></u> land. <u>We</u> <u><u>stopped</u></u> (at Natuna Besar, Indonesia,) (for three days.) Then, (on the 21st,) <u>we</u> <u><u>came</u></u> (to Sedanau,) another island (of Indonesia.)(After a stay)(of one month,) <u>we</u> <u><u>traveled</u></u> (to Tanjungpinang, Indonesia.) <u>We</u> <u><u>stayed</u></u> there (for three and a half months.) <u>Life</u> (in the refugee camp) <u><u>was</u></u> no luxury. <u>Living space</u> <u><u>was</u></u> very limited. <u>Food</u> <u><u>was</u></u> scarce. Luckily, <u>my father</u> <u><u>had once been</u></u> a captain (in the army.)(As a result,) <u>our family</u> <u><u>was quickly resettled</u></u> (to the United States.)

CHAPTER REVIEW: EDITING PRACTICE

Look back at your response to the Paragraph Practice at the beginning of this chapter. If you haven't already done so, label every action verb *AV*. Then, try to change some of the action verbs you have identified to different action verbs that express more precisely what the subject of each sentence is, was, or will be doing. When you have finished, see if you can improve your use of action verbs in a piece of writing you have done for another assignment.

CHAPTER REVIEW: COLLABORATIVE ACTIVITIES

1. Fold a sheet of paper in half vertically. In a group of three or four students, work together to list as many nouns as you can in the column to the left of the fold. Limit yourselves to two minutes. When your time is up, exchange papers with another group of students. Now, limiting yourselves to five minutes, write an appropriate action verb beside each noun. Each noun will now be the simple subject of a short sentence.

2. Choose five short sentences from the list you worked on in Collaborative Activity 1. Again working in a group, build on the short sentences on the list to create more fully developed sentences. First, expand each simple subject by adding words that describe or rename it. (For example, you could expand *boat* to *the small, leaky boat with the red sail.*) Then expand each sentence further, adding ideas after the verb. (For example, you might continue expanding until you have this sentence: *The small, leaky boat with the red sail bounced helplessly on the water.*)

3. Collaborate in a group of three or four students to write one original sentence for each of the linking verbs listed in 6C. When you have finished, exchange papers with another group. Now, try to add ideas to their sentences to make them more interesting.

Review

- A sentence expresses a complete thought. The subject tells who or what the sentence is about. (See 6A.)

    <u>Derek Walcott</u> won the 1992 Nobel Prize in literature.

- Subjects can be singular or plural. (See 6A.)

    Singular: Simón Bolívar
    Plural: South Americans
    Plural: Peru and Bolivia

(continued on the following page)

(*continued from previous page*)

- The object of a preposition cannot be the subject of a sentence. (See 6B.)

    The <u>cost</u> (of the repairs) was astronomical.

- An action verb tells what the subject is, was, or will be doing. (See 6C.)

    Amelia Earhart <u>flew</u> across the Atlantic.

- A linking verb connects the subject to a word or words that describe or rename it. (See 6C.)

    A googolplex <u>is</u> an extremely large number.

- Many verbs are made up of more than one word. The complete verb in a sentence includes the main verb plus any helping verbs. (See 6C.)

    Minh <u>was thinking</u> about his future.

7 Avoiding Sentence Fragments

> **Overview**
>
> In this chapter you will learn
> - To identify sentence fragments
> - To write sentences that include both subjects and verbs
> - To write sentences that include complete verbs
> - To write sentences that express complete thoughts

PARAGRAPH PRACTICE

Write a paragraph in which you explain how you and your family celebrate a particular holiday. Describe some typical activities and foods, supplying enough specific details to give your readers a sense of why this holiday is important to you. Use the blank space below for invention. Then, write your paragraph on the lines that follow.

CHAPTER 7 Avoiding Sentence Fragments ▪ **135**

A **sentence fragment** is an incomplete sentence. Every sentence must include at least one subject and one verb, and every sentence must also express a complete thought. If a word group does not do all these things, it is not a sentence—even if it begins with a capital letter and ends with a period.

A INCLUDING SUBJECTS AND VERBS

A sentence must include both a subject and a verb. Each of the following is a complete sentence:

The casting of the play *Into the Woods* was color blind.

The actors were ethnically diverse.

The following, however, are *not* complete sentences:

The casting of the play *Into the Woods*.

Were ethnically diverse.

The first group of words, "The casting of the play *Into the Woods*," has no verb: What *point* is being made about the play's casting? The second group of words, "Were ethnically diverse," has no subject: *What* was ethnically diverse? Because a sentence must have both a subject and a verb, neither of these is a sentence. Both are fragments. To correct this kind of fragment, supply the missing subject or verb.

136 · UNIT 4 Writing Simple Sentences

▶ FOCUS ON SENTENCE FRAGMENTS AND SENTENCES ◀

Sentence fragments do not occur in isolation. They appear in paragraphs and longer passages, right beside complete sentences.

┌── complete sentence ──┐ ┌────────── fragment ──────────
Celia took two electives. Computer Science 320 and Spanish 101.

The fragment here does not have a verb. The complete sentence, however, has both a subject (*Celia*) and a verb (*took*).

Often, you can correct a sentence fragment by attaching the fragment to a nearby sentence that supplies the missing element.

Celia took two electives, Computer Science 320 and Spanish 101.

The fragment is now attached to a complete sentence that supplies the missing verb.

PRACTICE 7-1

In the following passage, some of the numbered groups of words are missing a subject, a verb, or both. Identify each fragment by labeling it *F*. Then, attach each fragment to a nearby word group to create a complete new sentence. Finally, rewrite the entire passage, using all complete sentences, on the lines below it.

(1) Sara Paretsky writes mystery novels. __ (2) Such as *Burn Marks* and *Guardian Angel*. _F_ (3) These novels are about V. I. Warshawski. __ (4) A private detective. _F_ (5) V. I. lives and works in Chicago. __ (6) The Windy City. _F_ (7) V. I. takes risks. __ (8) Every day as a detective. _F_ (9) V. I. is tough. __ (10) She is also a woman. __

Rewrite: *Sara Paretsky writes mystery novels, such as Burn Marks and Guardian Angel. These novels are about V. I. Warshawski, a private detective. V. I. lives and works in Chicago, the Windy City. V. I. takes risks every day as a detective. V. I. is tough. She is also a woman.*

CHAPTER 7 Avoiding Sentence Fragments • **137**

> ••••••••▶ **FLASHBACK** ◀••••••••
>
> Reread your response to the Paragraph Practice at the beginning of the chapter. Do all your sentences seem to be complete? If you think any are not complete, copy them on the lines below.
>
> _____
>
> _____
>
> _____

B INCLUDING COMPLETE VERBS

A **complete verb** is made up of a main verb plus any helping verbs. Each of the following sentences includes a complete verb:

The sun is setting.
The sun was hidden behind the clouds.

Now compare the sentences above with the following:

The sun setting.
The sun hidden behind the clouds.

Present participles, like *setting*, and past participles, like *hidden*, are not complete verbs and cannot stand alone without a helping verb. Because neither example above includes a complete verb, both are fragments.

To serve as the main verb of a sentence, a present participle must be completed by a form of the verb *be*.

Helping verb(s)	+ Present participle	= Complete verb
am	setting	am setting
was	setting	was setting
has been	setting	has been setting

Adding a form of *be* to complete the verb changes the first fragment above into a sentence.

Fragment: The sun setting.
Sentence: The sun is setting.

To serve as main verbs of sentences, many past participles must be completed by forms of the verbs *be* or *have*.

Helping verb(s)	+ Past participle =	Complete verb
am	hidden	am hidden
was	hidden	was hidden
has	hidden	has hidden
has been	hidden	has been hidden

Adding a form of *be* to complete the verb changes the second fragment above into a sentence.

Fragment: The sun hidden behind the clouds.
Sentence: The sun <u>was</u> hidden behind the clouds.

For more information about forming complete verbs using present participles, see Chapter 11. For more on past participles, see Chapter 10.

PRACTICE 7-2

Each of the following is a fragment because the verb is not complete. Turn each fragment into a sentence by adding a helping verb to complete the verb.

Example: Justice Marshall ^*had*^ given a lot of thought to his decision.

1. David Henry Hwang ^*has*^ written plays about the Chinese-American experience.
2. Tom Joad ^*had*^ been on a long trip.
3. You ^*are*^ never going to get ahead if you do not study.
4. Dawn ^*was*^ chosen to play Mama in *A Raisin in the Sun*.
5. The students in my chemistry lab ^*are*^ always complaining about the lab manual.
6. Asbestos ^*had*^ fallen from the heating ducts.
7. Before last Wednesday, we ^*had*^ never known about the policy.
8. Some criminals ^*have*^ gotten away with murder.
9. Romeo and Juliet ^*were*^ forbidden to see each other.
10. Karen ^*is*^ minding her own business.

CHAPTER 7 Avoiding Sentence Fragments • **139**

•••••••••▶ **FLASHBACK** ◀•••••••••

Reread your response to the Paragraph Practice at the beginning of the chapter. Do you see any present participles or past participles? List any such participles in the right-hand column below. In the left-hand column, list the helping verb that completes each participle. If no helping verb is present, supply one.

Helping Verb	Participle
_____	_____
_____	_____
_____	_____

C EXPRESSING COMPLETE THOUGHTS

Reading carefully is the first step in testing whether a group of words expresses a complete thought. As you read, ask yourself what the word group says and whether you are left expecting more information. Also, check to see if the word group is introduced by a word that creates an incomplete thought.

Sometimes a group of words includes a subject and a complete verb, but it is still a fragment. The following, for example, is not a complete sentence:

> Although the family had dreamed for years of coming to America.

The group of words above includes a subject (*the family*) and a complete verb (*had dreamed*). However, it does not express a complete thought. Readers expect the idea to continue, but it stops short. What happened to the family's dreams? Did the family ever come to America? If not, what stopped them?

Subordinating conjunctions, such as the word *although*, which introduces the example above, can create incomplete thoughts. (Other commonly used subordinating conjunctions include *because*, *if*, *when*, and *unless*.) When an incomplete thought is created, you need to add another group of words to complete the idea and finish the sentence.

> Although the family had dreamed for years of coming to America, they did not save enough money for the trip until 1985.

The above sentence completes the idea the fragment began. Now it expresses a complete thought. (See 13A for more information on using subordinating conjunctions.)

Relative pronouns, such as *who, which,* and *that,* can also create incomplete thoughts. The following are not complete sentences:

> Novelist Richard Wright, who came to Paris in 1947.
>
> A quinceañera, which is celebrated on a Latina's fifteenth birthday.
>
> A key World War II battle that was fought on an island in the Pacific.

Although each of the word groups above includes a subject (*Richard Wright, quinceañera, battle*) and a complete verb (*came, is celebrated, was fought*), none of the word groups expresses a complete thought. Readers are left up in the air, wondering what Richard Wright did, what a quinceañera commemorates, and what the key battle was called. In each case, readers need more information to complete the thought and finish the sentence.

> Novelist Richard Wright, who came to Paris in 1947, spent the rest of his life there.
>
> A quinceañera, which is celebrated on a Latina's fifteenth birthday, signifies her entrance into womanhood.
>
> A key World War II battle that was fought on an island in the Pacific is Guadalcanal.

(For more information on using relative pronouns, see 13B.)

PRACTICE 7-3

Turn each of these fragments into a complete sentence by adding a group of words that completes the idea.

Example: Before it became a state.
Before it became a state, *West Virginia was part of Virginia.*

Answers will vary.

1. Because so many homeless people are mentally ill, _____

_____

2. The film that frightened me most _____

_____

3. Although people disagree about the effects of violence in children's television shows, _____

_____

4. People who drink and drive _____

_____

CHAPTER 7 Avoiding Sentence Fragments ▪ **141**

5. As competition among college students for athletic scholarships increases, _____
   _____

6. Whenever a new semester begins, _____
   _____

7. Pizza, which is high in fat, _____
   _____

8. Animals that are used in medical research _____
   _____

9. Unless something happens soon, _____
   _____

10. Although it is a very controversial issue, _____
    _____

●●●●●●●▶ FLASHBACK ◀●●●●●●●

Reread your response to the Paragraph Practice at the beginning of the chapter. Consulting the list on page 241, underline every subordinating conjunction in your paragraph. Then underline *which*, *that*, and *who* wherever you find them. Do any of these words create an incomplete thought that is punctuated as if it were a sentence? If so, add a word group to complete each fragment. Write your edited versions below.

_____
_____
_____
_____
_____

PRACTICE 7-4

All of the following are fragments. Turn each fragment into a complete sentence, and write the revised sentence on the line below each fragment. Whenever possible, try creating two different revisions.

Example: The players waiting in the dugout.

Revised: *The players were waiting in the dugout.*

Revised: *The players waiting in the dugout chewed tobacco.*

Answers will vary.

1. Because three-year-olds are still very attached to their parents.

Revised: _____

_____

Revised: _____

_____

2. Going around in circles.

Revised: _____

_____

Revised: _____

_____

3. The prize given for the most unusual costume.

Revised: _____

_____

Revised: _____

_____

4. Students who thought they couldn't afford to go to college.

Revised: _____

_____

Revised: _____

_____

CHAPTER 7   Avoiding Sentence Fragments   •   143

5. On an important secret mission.

Revised: _____

_____

Revised: _____

_____

6. Although many instructors see cheating as a serious problem.

Revised: _____

_____

Revised: _____

_____

7. They never going to get enough chocolate fudge cake.

Revised: _____

_____

Revised: _____

_____

8. The rule that I always felt was the most unfair.

Revised: _____

_____

Revised: _____

_____

9. He always been able to find construction work before.

Revised: _____

_____

Revised: _____

_____

10. The book, which I thought I'd never finish.

Revised: _____

_____

144 ▪ UNIT 4 Writing Simple Sentences

Revised: _____

_____

• • • • • • • • • • • • • • REVIEW • • • • • • • • • • • • • •

CHAPTER REVIEW: STUDENT WRITING

Read the following student passage, in which some incomplete sentences have been introduced. Underline each fragment. Then, correct it by adding the words necessary to complete it or attaching it to a nearby sentence that completes the idea. The first fragment has been underlined and corrected for you.

My First Job

Like many other teenage females, I got my first job when I was in high school. I worked as a salesperson, *i*n a retail clothing chain. At first I was really excited, *l*earning about pricing procedures and arranging displays. I got to see all the new styles, *a*s they were introduced. I also got to use my employee discount, *a* benefit that saved me a lot of money.

People *were* always coming in the store, asking for help in finding things. They would have requests like "Could you tell me where to find a blue and purple lambswool sweater?" and "You're about the same size as my niece. Could you try this on for me?" I felt useful and important, *w*hen I was able to help them.

The job had its bad side, too. I always seemed to be running. *I was c*onstantly straightening the same racks over and over. ~~Also~~ *I was also r*earranging displays several times every night. When the store was busy, it was very hectic. Not all the customers were patient or polite. Some lost their

CHAPTER 7 Avoiding Sentence Fragments · 145

tempers_x Because they couldn't find a particular size or color. Then they took out their anger on me. On slow nights, when the store was almost empty_^ I was restless and bored. Eventually I found a more stimulating position_x At a preschool for developmentally delayed children.

(editorial marks: b over Because; comma insertion after empty; a over At)

CHAPTER REVIEW: EDITING PRACTICE

Reread your response to the Paragraph Practice at the beginning of this chapter. Is every sentence complete? Check every one to be sure that it has a subject and a verb, that the verb is complete, and that the sentence expresses a complete thought. If you identify a fragment, revise it by adding whatever is necessary to complete it or by attaching it to a nearby sentence. Then, choose a piece of writing you have done in response to another assignment, and edit it to correct sentence fragments.

CHAPTER REVIEW: COLLABORATIVE ACTIVITIES

1. Exchange workbooks with another student, and read each other's responses to the Paragraph Practice at the beginning of the chapter. On a separate piece of paper, make a list of five questions for the other student, asking about additional details you would like to know about his or her family's holiday celebration and why it is so meaningful. When your own workbook is returned, answer your partner's questions about your holiday celebration, and add this information to your Paragraph Practice response. Be sure all the sentences you have added are complete.

2. Working in a group of three or four students, add different subordinating conjunctions to each of the sentences listed in the left-hand column below to create several fragments. (See 13A for a list of subordinating conjunctions.) Then, turn each of the resulting fragments into a complete sentence by adding a word group that completes the idea.

   Example:

Sentence	Fragment	New Sentence
I left the party.	As I left the party	As I left the party, I fell.
	After I left the party	After I left the party, the music stopped.
	Until I left the party	Until I left the party, I had no idea it was so late.

   a. My mind wanders.   c. He made a wish.
   b. She caught the ball.   d. Disaster struck.

3. Working in a group of three or four students, build as many sentences as you can around each of the fragments listed below, each of which is introduced by a past or present participle. Use your collective imaginations to create as many interesting, humorous sentences as you can.

Example:

Fragment: Known for his incredible memory

Sentences: Zack, known for his incredible memory, has somehow managed to forget everything he learned about chemistry.

Known for his incredible memory, Monty the Magnificent mesmerized audiences.

a. wandering in the desert
b. stranded in the jungle
c. looking for his ideal mate
d. always using as much ketchup as possible
e. folded, stapled, and mutilated

Review

- An incomplete sentence is called a sentence fragment.

- Some fragments are missing a subject or a verb (or both).

    Were ethnically diverse. (no subject)
    The casting of the play *Into the Woods*. (no verb)

  To correct this kind of fragment, supply the missing subject or verb. (See 7A.)

- Some fragments have a subject and a verb, but the verb is not complete.

    The sun setting.
    The sun hidden behind the clouds.

  To correct this kind of fragment, add a helping verb. (See 7B.)

- Some fragments have a subject and a complete verb but include a subordinating conjunction or relative pronoun, which creates an incomplete thought.

    Although the family had dreamed for years of coming to America.
    A quinceañera, which is celebrated on a Latina's fifteenth birthday.

  To correct this kind of fragment, complete the thought and finish the sentence. (See 7C.)

8 Subject-Verb Agreement

Overview

In this chapter you will learn
- To understand subject-verb agreement with nouns and pronouns
- To make sure subjects agree with the irregular verbs *be*, *have*, and *do*
- To make sure subjects and verbs agree when words come between them
- To make sure verbs agree with indefinite pronouns acting as subjects
- To make sure verbs agree with subjects that follow them
- To make sure verbs agree with the relative pronouns *who*, *which*, and *that*

PARAGRAPH PRACTICE

Describe a place that has special significance to you—a room, a building, or an outdoor location. What does the place look like? Why does it appeal to you? Make sure your description is in the present tense (for example, "A picture *hangs* on the wall"). Use the blank space below for invention. Then, write your paragraph on the lines that follow.

A UNDERSTANDING SUBJECT-VERB AGREEMENT

A sentence's subject (a noun or a pronoun) must **agree** with its verb in number (singular or plural). Agreement can present special problems with present tense verbs because they take different forms with some singular subjects.

Subject-Verb Agreement with Regular Verbs	
Singular	Plural
I p<u>lay</u>	Molly and I/we p<u>lay</u>
you p<u>lay</u>	you p<u>lay</u>
the man/Molly/he/she/it plays	the men/Molly and Sam/they play

> ### ▶ FOCUS ◀ ON THE PRESENT TENSE
>
> **Tense** is the form a verb takes to show when an action or situation took place. The **present tense**, which generally indicates present time, is used in a number of familiar situations.
>
> - Use the present tense to indicate an action or situation that is taking place at the time you are speaking or writing or that takes place regularly.
>
>   Frank <u>works</u> at Rio Brothers Auto Body Shop.
>   Yogini and MaryAnn <u>arrive</u> at school early every morning.
>
> - Use the present tense when you are discussing a literary work (an essay, novel, or short story, for example).
>
>   Louise Erdrich's novel *Love Medicine* <u>focuses</u> on family relationships.
>
> - Use the present tense to indicate a generally accepted belief or a scientific fact.
>
>   The earth <u>revolves</u> around the sun.
>
> The present tense is also sometimes used to indicate an action or situation that will occur in the future.
>
>   Our vacation <u>starts</u> next Monday.

Whether the subject of a sentence is a noun or a pronoun, use a singular form of the verb with a singular subject and a plural form of the verb with a plural subject.

The <u>museum</u> <u>opens</u> at ten o'clock. (Singular noun subject *museum* takes singular verb *opens*.)

The <u>museums</u> <u>open</u> at ten o'clock. (Plural noun subject *museums* takes plural verb *open*.)

<u>She</u> always <u>watches</u> the eleven o'clock news. (Singular pronoun subject *she* takes singular verb *watches*.)

<u>They</u> always <u>watch</u> the eleven o'clock news. (Plural pronoun subject *they* takes plural verb *watch*.)

For more on nouns and pronouns, see Chapter 19.

> ### ▶ FOCUS ON SUBJECT-VERB AGREEMENT ◀
> ### WITH COMPOUND SUBJECTS
>
> The subject of a sentence is not always a single word. It can also be a **compound,** consisting of two or more words.
>
> - When the parts of a compound subject are connected by *and*, the compound subject takes a plural verb.
>
>   John and Marsha share an office.
>
> - If both parts of a compound subject connected by *or* are singular, the compound subject takes a singular verb.
>
>   John or Marsha locks up at the end of the day.
>
> - If both parts of a compound subject connected by *or* are plural, the compound subject takes a plural verb.
>
>   Buses or trains take you to the center of the city.
>
> - If one part of a compound subject connected by *or* is singular and the other is plural, the verb agrees with the word that is closer to it.
>
>   The mayor or the council members meet with community groups.
>   The council members or the mayor meets with community groups.

PRACTICE 8-1

Underline the correct form of the verb in each sentence in the passage below. Be sure the verb agrees with its subject. The first sentence has been done for you.

(1) Jean Toomey (care, <u>cares</u>) for 446 cats. (2) She (run, <u>runs</u>) an endowed home for cats. (3) Over two hundred cats (<u>come</u>, comes) from owners who have left money to Ms. Toomey's home so she will take care of their cats for the rest of their lives. (4) The other cats (<u>come</u>, comes) from the streets.

(5) The cat home (stand, <u>stands</u>) on thirty-five acres of rural land in northwest Connecticut. (6) When you (<u>walk</u>, walks) into the home, you (see, sees) cats everywhere. (7) Some cats (<u>watch</u>, watches) television. (8) Other cats (<u>take</u>, takes) naps on the large wooden deck on the side of the house. (9) Resident cats (<u>come</u>, comes) and (<u>go</u>, goes) through the windows. (10) Cats (<u>run</u>, runs) through five acres of woods, having every adventure a cat could want. (11) Newcomers (<u>stay</u>, stays) in a special room until they get used to their new surroundings. (12) Older cats (<u>live</u>, lives) in the north wing, where the music and food are softer.

(13) Every morning workers (<u>serve</u>, serves) 125 cans of cat food. (14) Dry food (disappear, <u>disappears</u>) during afternoon snacks. (15) A local lum-

beryard (donate, donates) a monthly truckload of sawdust for cat boxes. (16) A veterinarian (provide, <u>provides</u>) discount health care. (17) Some cats (<u>spend</u>, spends) their entire lives at Ms. Toomey's home, while others are adopted.

PRACTICE 8-2

Write in the correct present-tense form of the verb.

Example: Every day she ___*visits*___ the computer lab in the basement of Reinhold Hall. (visit)

1. Lynn ___*writes*___ with a computer. (write)
2. It ___*makes*___ her work easier. (make)
3. I ___*use*___ one too. (use)
4. Our instructors ___*supervise*___ our work. (supervise) They ___*collect*___ our computer disks. (collect)
5. Each week Ms. Keane and Mr. Marlowe ___*give*___ back the disks. (give)
6. The disks ___*contain*___ our instructors' comments. (contain)
7. I ___*put*___ my disk into the computer (put) and ___*read*___ Mr. Marlowe's comments as I revise. (read)
8. We ___*like*___ this technique for marking papers. (like)
9. One student says he ___*hates*___ the computer, however. (hate)
10. The screen ___*gives*___ him headaches. (give)

▶ **FLASHBACK** ◀

Look back at your response to the Paragraph Practice at the beginning of the chapter. Underline the subject of each sentence once and the verb twice. Correct any verbs that do not agree with their subjects.

B AVOIDING PROBLEMS WITH BE, HAVE, AND DO

Most verbs, such as *play, laugh,* and *dance,* are called **regular verbs** because they behave in predictable ways. (For information on singular and plural verb endings for regular verbs, see 8A.) Other verbs, which do not behave in predictable ways, are called **irregular verbs.** Three of the most commonly used irregular verbs are *be, have,* and *do.* These three verbs often present problems with subject-verb agreement in the present tense.

Be

The verb *be* is highly irregular and has more forms in the present tense than other verbs do. Make sure you use the correct form of *be* with singular and plural subjects.

Subject-Verb Agreement with Be

Singular	Plural
I am	we are
you are	you are
he/she/it is	they are
Tran is	Tran and Ryan are
the boy is	the boys are

▶ **FOCUS** ON SUBJECT-VERB AGREEMENT WITH BE ◀

In your college writing, it is not correct to use the verb form *be* as the main verb of a sentence. Always use *is* (singular) or *are* (plural).

Incorrect: He <u>be</u> going to class this morning.
Incorrect: They <u>be</u> going to class this morning.
Correct: He <u>is</u> going to class this morning.
Correct: They <u>are</u> going to class this morning.

Have

Have is another irregular verb that can be troublesome. Be sure to use the proper forms of this verb when you speak or write in college.

Subject-Verb Agreement with *Have*

Singular	Plural
I have	we have
you have	you have
he/she/it has	they have
Shana has	Shana and Robert have
the student has	the students have

Do

Like *be* and *have*, *do* is often misused in everyday speech. Familiarize yourself with the proper forms of this verb.

Subject-Verb Agreement with *Do*

Singular	Plural
I do	we do
you do	you do
he/she/it does	they do
Ken does	Ken and Mia do
the book does	the books do

PRACTICE 8-3

Fill in the correct present tense form of the verbs *be*, *have*, or *do*.

Example: Sometimes, people ____*do*____ damage without really meaning to. (do)

1. Biologists ____have____ serious worries about the damage exotic animals can cause when they move into places where native species have developed few defenses against them. (have)

2. The English sparrow ____is____ one example. (be)

3. It __has__ a role in the decline in the number of bluebirds. (have)

4. On the Galapagos Islands, cats __are__ another example. (be)

5. Introduced by early explorers, they currently __do__ much damage to the eggs of the giant tortoises that live on the islands. (do)

6. Scientists today __are__ worried about a new problem. (be)

7. This __is__ a situation caused by fish and wildlife agencies that deliberately introduce exotic fish into lakes and streams. (be)

8. They __do__ this to please those who enjoy fishing. (do)

9. Although popular with people who fish, this policy __has__ major drawbacks. (have)

10. It __has__ one drawback in particular: Many species of fish have been pushed close to extinction. (have)

11. In California, the brown trout has pushed out the golden trout. It __is__ bigger and more aggressive than the golden trout. (be)

12. Throughout the Great Lakes, Pacific salmon have displaced native lake trout. They too __are__ bigger and more aggressive. (be)

13. An odd case __is__ apparent in Nevada. (be)

14. Guppies, dumped by aquarium hobbyists, have overwhelmed native river fish. As a result, they __are__ near extinction. (be)

15. "It __is__ a pity that fish and wildlife agencies carry out this policy," said one scientist. (be)

16. "They __do__ not seem to understand the consequences of their actions," she continued. (do)

17. "We __have__ to convince them that in the long run they are doing great harm to America's rivers and streams," she concluded. (have)

18. One problem ___is___ that fishing license fees pay for these lake and river stocking programs. (be)

19. According to the head of one state fish and wildlife agency, he and other administrators ___are___ aware of this fact every time they make a decision. (be)

20. "Fishing enthusiasts ___are___ a tough group," he said. (be)

> ••••••••▶ **FLASHBACK** ◀••••••••
>
> Look back at your response to this chapter's Paragraph Practice. Are any of the verbs you underlined forms of *be*, *have*, or *do*? Does each of these verbs agree with its subject? If not, edit those verbs to correct any errors in subject-verb agreement.

C AVOIDING PROBLEMS WHEN WORDS COME BETWEEN THE SUBJECT AND THE VERB

Sometimes a word that comes between the subject and the verb may appear to be the subject when it really is not. Consider the following sentence:

High levels of mercury are found in some fish.

The subject of this sentence (*levels*) is plural, so it requires a plural verb (*are*). Because the prepositional phrase *of mercury* comes between the subject and the verb, it might appear that the subject is singular (*mercury*), but it is not. Here *mercury* is the object of the preposition *of*, and the object of a preposition can never be the subject of the sentence. By adding parentheses around the words that separate the subject and the verb, you can identify the real subject and see whether it agrees with the verb.

High <u>levels</u> (of mercury) <u>are</u> found in some fish.

Words and phrases such as *in addition to*, *along with*, *together with*, *as well as*, *except*, and *including* also introduce prepositional phrases. The nouns and pronouns that follow these phrases are objects of prepositions; therefore, they cannot be subjects.

<u>St. Thomas</u>, (along with St. Croix and St. John,) <u>is</u> part of the United States Virgin Islands.

For more information on prepositional phrases, see 6B. For a list of prepositions, see 21A.

> ▶ FOCUS ON WORDS BETWEEN ◀
> THE SUBJECT AND THE VERB
>
> Other groups of words besides prepositional phrases can come between the subject and verb in a sentence. As with prepositional phrases, enclosing these words in parentheses can also help identify the subject.
>
> The new <u>mall</u>,(which has a food court and many stores,) <u><u>makes</u></u> shoppers happy.

PRACTICE 8-4

Enclose in parentheses the words that separate the subject and the verb in each sentence below. Then, draw a single line under the subject of the sentence. Finally, draw a double line under the verb that agrees with the subject.

Example: The <u>stains</u>(on the carpet)(<u><u>suggest</u></u>, suggests) that they had a party.

1. The <u>Cupids</u> (in the painting) (<u><u>symbolize</u></u>, symbolizes) lost innocence.
2. <u>Fans</u>(at a concert)(<u><u>get</u></u>, gets) angry if a group is late.
3. The <u>appliances</u>(in my kitchen)(<u><u>make</u></u>, makes) strange noises.
4. <u>The United States</u>,(along with Germany and Japan,)(produce, <u><u>produces</u></u>) most of the world's cars.
5. A good <u>set</u>(of skis and poles)(cost, <u><u>costs</u></u>) a lot.
6. Unfortunately, <u>one</u>(out of ten men)(get, <u><u>gets</u></u>) prostate cancer.
7. <u>Workers</u>(in the city)(<u><u>pay</u></u>, pays) a high wage tax.
8. Each summer <u>fires</u>(from lightning)(<u><u>cause</u></u>, causes) hundreds of millions of dollars in property damage.
9. <u>Volunteers</u>,(like my father,)(<u><u>help</u></u>, helps) paramedics in my community.
10. The <u>instructions</u>(for using the computer program)(<u><u>confuse</u></u>, confuses) me.
11. The <u>reaction</u>(in the test tubes)(generate, <u><u>generates</u></u>) a great deal of heat.
12. <u>Calamity Jane</u>,(who has been featured in a number of popular westerns,)(<u><u>is</u></u>, are) the nickname of frontierswoman Martha Jane Burk.
13. The <u>children</u>(in Somalia)(<u><u>need</u></u>, needs) food quickly.
14. <u>The National Cancer Institute</u>,(as well as many smaller groups,)(want, <u><u>wants</u></u>) to ban smoking in all public places.
15. The <u>exhibition</u>,(which will tour eleven U.S. cities,)(include, <u><u>includes</u></u>) the crown of Peter the Great.

CHAPTER 8 Subject-Verb Agreement

▶ FLASHBACK ◀

Look back at your response to this chapter's Paragraph Practice. Can you find any sentences that contain words that come between the subject and the verb? Make sure the subjects and verbs in these sentences agree.

D AVOIDING PROBLEMS WITH INDEFINITE PRONOUNS AS SUBJECTS

An **indefinite pronoun** does not refer to a particular person, place, or idea. Most indefinite pronouns, such as *no one* and *everyone*, are singular and take a singular verb when acting as the subject of a sentence.

No one likes getting up early.
Everyone likes to sleep late.

Singular Indefinite Pronouns

anybody	either	neither	one
anyone	everybody	nobody	somebody
anything	everyone	no one	someone
each	everything	nothing	something

A few indefinite pronouns, however, are plural (*many, several, a few, some*) and take a plural verb.

Many were left homeless by the storm.

▶ FOCUS ON INDEFINITE PRONOUNS AS SUBJECTS ◀

When an indefinite pronoun is followed by a prepositional phrase, the true subject is the indefinite pronoun. (See 8C.)

Each of the boys has a bike. (singular subject takes singular verb)
Many of the boys have bikes. (plural subject takes plural verb)

PRACTICE 8-5

Underline the correct verb in each sentence.

Example: Each of the three streams in our area (<u>is</u>, are) polluted.

1. Some of the streams no longer (<u>have</u>, has) any fish.
2. Another (contain, <u>contains</u>) a lot of algae.
3. Everybody (want, <u>wants</u>) to improve the situation.
4. No one (are, <u>is</u>) willing to do anything.
5. Somebody always (take, <u>takes</u>) control.
6. Everyone (know, <u>knows</u>) that pollution is difficult to control.
7. Neither of the candidates (seem, <u>seems</u>) willing to act.
8. Whenever anyone (ask, <u>asks</u>) them for suggestions, neither (have, <u>has</u>) any.
9. According to the candidates, everything (<u>is</u>, are) being done that can be done.
10. One of my friends (say, <u>says</u>) that she will not vote for either candidate.

FLASHBACK

Look back at your response to the Paragraph Practice at the beginning of this chapter. Do any of your sentences contain indefinite pronouns that act as subjects? Do the verbs in these sentences agree with their indefinite pronoun subjects? If you find any that do not, correct them.

E AVOIDING PROBLEMS WHEN THE VERB COMES BEFORE THE SUBJECT

A verb always agrees with its subject, even if the subject comes after the verb. In questions, for example, word order is frequently reversed, with the verb coming before the subject.

Where <u>is</u> the <u>telephone booth</u>?

What day <u>is</u> <u>it</u>?

Where <u>are</u> <u>we</u> now?

If you have difficulty identifying the subject of a question, turn the question into a statement.

The <u>telephone booth</u> <u>is</u> outside.

It is Tuesday.
We are in Belgium.

> ▶ **FOCUS** ON *THERE IS* AND *THERE ARE* ◀
>
> In a sentence that begins with the phrase *there is* or *there are*, *there* can never be the subject of the sentence. In such sentences, the subject comes after the form of the verb *be*.
>
> There are nine justices on the Supreme Court.
> There is one Chief Justice presiding over the court.

PRACTICE 8-6

Underline the subject of each sentence, and circle the correct form of the verb.

Example: Who ((is), are) the writer who won the 1992 Nobel Prize in literature?

1. Where (is, (are)) the Bering Straits?
2. Why (do, (does)) the compound change color after being exposed to light?
3. Who ((is), are) the artist who painted *Water Lilies*?
4. Why (do, (does)) unemployment go up during a recession?
5. (Is, (Are)) the twins identical or fraternal?
6. ((Has), Have) the government increased funding for job training programs?
7. Who (is, (are)) the women who signed the Declaration of the Rights of Women at Seneca Falls?
8. How (do, (does)) Congress override a presidential veto?
9. What (is, (are)) the three laws of thermodynamics?
10. What ((has), have) this to do with me?

PRACTICE 8-7

Underline the subject of each sentence. Then, circle the correct verb form.

Example: There ((is), are) a copy machine down the hall.

1. There (is, (are)) the silver earrings we bought in New Mexico.
2. There (is, (are)) ten computers in the Writing Center.

160 ■ UNIT 4   Writing Simple Sentences

3. There (is, **are**) over nine million <u>citizens</u> living in Mexico City.
4. There (is, **are**) several reference <u>books</u> in this library that can help you with your research.
5. There (**is**, are) an interesting science <u>museum</u> in Toronto.
6. There (**is**, are) a <u>theory</u> that explains why many comets pass near the earth.
7. There (**is**, are) Charlyce's <u>notebook</u> on the table.
8. There (is, **are**) four <u>reasons</u> why we should save the spotted owl from extinction.
9. There (is, **are**) <u>thousands</u> of teenagers killed each year in automobile accidents.
10. There (**is**, are) a <u>hurricane</u> heading for Florida.

▶ **FLASHBACK** ◀

Choose three sentences from your response to the Paragraph Practice at the beginning of the chapter, and rephrase them as questions on the lines below. Then, try to rewrite one of your original sentences using the phrase *there is* or *there are*.

Questions

1. _____

2. _____

3. _____

There is or *There are* sentence _____

F   AVOIDING PROBLEMS WITH THE RELATIVE PRONOUNS *WHO*, *WHICH*, AND *THAT*

Who, *which*, and *that* are singular when they refer to a singular word and plural when they refer to a plural word. Deciding whether to use a singular or plural verb with *who*, *which*, and *that* can be confusing because the singular and plural forms of these pronouns are the same. Consider the following sentences:

> An author who writes about Chinese immigrants spoke at our college.

In this sentence, the verb *writes* is singular because the pronoun *who* refers to *author*, which is also singular. In the next sentence, however, the verb *have* is plural because the pronoun *that* refers to *computers*, a plural word.

> Computers that have color monitors are expensive.

For more information about *who*, *which*, *that*, and other relative pronouns, see 13B and 13C.

PRACTICE 8-8

Draw an arrow from *who*, *which*, or *that* to the word to which it refers. Then circle the correct form of the verb.

> **Example:** Edgar Allan Poe, who (tell, **tells**) tales of horror, was born in 1809.

1. Poe's "The Fall of the House of Usher" is a story that (have, **has**) entertained many readers.

2. The story, which (contain, **contains**) the poem "The Haunted Palace," was published in 1839.

3. The narrator, who (have, **has**) not seen Roderick Usher for many years, is summoned to the House of Usher.

4. The decaying mansion, which (**is**, are) dark and dreary, stands at the edge of a swamp.

5. Roderick's twin sister Madeline, who (live, **lives**) in the house, has mental and physical problems.

6. At one point in the story, Roderick's sister, who (**is**, are) in a trance, is thought to be dead.

7. Roderick buries her in the family vault that (**is**, are) beneath the house.

8. Later, Madeline, who (**is**, are) dressed in her shroud, walks into the room.

9. Roderick, who (**is**, are) terrified, falls down dead.

10. Running outside, the narrator sees the house, which (have, **has**) split apart, sink into the swamp.

▶ **FLASHBACK** ◀

Look back at your response to the Paragraph Practice at the beginning of the chapter. Can you find any sentences that contain the relative pronouns *who*, *which*, or *that*? Make sure that you have used a singular word when *who*, *which*, or *that* refers to a singular word and a plural word when the reference is to a plural word.

REVIEW

CHAPTER REVIEW: STUDENT WRITING

Read the following student essay, in which errors of subject-verb agreement have been introduced. Decide whether each of the underlined verbs agrees with its subject. If it does not, cross it out and write in the correct form. If it does, write *C* above the verb. The first sentence has been done for you.

Cartoon Violence

Everyone ~~know~~ *knows* cartoons <u>are</u> *C* violent. For some reason, violence, as well as cute animal characters, ~~are~~ *is* entertaining. There <u>are</u> *C* many great old cartoons that ~~illustrates~~ *illustrate* this point. The Roadrunner cartoons, which <u>are</u> *C* staples of children's television, ~~is~~ *are* very violent. The coyote with all his tricks ~~suffer~~ *suffers* many setbacks as he

    attempts
~~attempt~~ to catch the elusive bird. No matter how hard he
    C   C   *seems*
<u>tries</u>, he never <u>succeeds</u>. Everything ~~seem~~ to backfire. The
                                          C
result is that the coyote, who <u>looks</u> pathetically at
          experiences
viewers, ~~experience~~ at least fifteen different episodes of

violence per cartoon.
                                        C
    Another violent cartoon character <u>is</u> Bugs Bunny. Bugs

Bunny, along with Elmer Fudd, Daffy Duck, and Yosemite Sam,
is   C
~~are~~ constantly fighting. A typical cartoon, which <u>stars</u> Bugs
          C   *does*
and Elmer Fudd, <u>has</u> Elmer trying to shoot Bugs. "Why ~~do~~
                                            are
Elmer want to shoot Bugs?" you may ask. There ~~is~~ many

reasons, but the main reason is that it is hunting season.
                             seems
Neither of the two characters ~~seem~~ to be able to resist a
                          C   *walks*
test of wits. Elmer, who <u>is</u> constantly outsmarted, ~~walk~~ away

saying, "Gosh darn wabbit!"
                                  is
    Nothing in these cartoons ~~are~~ good for children.
                                              is
Perhaps the most dangerous idea for children ~~are~~ that they

can shoot someone, set someone on fire, or hit someone with

a hammer and that person will not get hurt.

CHAPTER REVIEW: EDITING PRACTICE

    Rewrite your response to this chapter's Paragraph Practice, changing all the singular subjects to plural subjects and the plural subjects to singular subjects. (For example, *picture* will become *pictures* and *I* will become *we*.) Be sure to change the verbs so they agree with your new subjects.

CHAPTER REVIEW: COLLABORATIVE ACTIVITIES

1. Working in a group of four students, list ten nouns—people, places, or things—on the left-hand side of a sheet of paper. Then, beside each noun, write down the present tense form of a verb to go with each noun. Exchange papers with another group, and check to see that the nouns and verbs agree.

2. Working with your group, expand each noun-and-verb combination you listed in Collaborative Activity 1 into a complete sentence. Then, write a sentence that could logically follow each of these sentences, using a pronoun as the subject of the new sentence. Make sure the pronoun you choose refers to the noun in the previous sentence. *(Alan watches three movies a week. He is a film buff.)* Then, check to be certain the nouns and pronouns in the new sentences agree with the verbs.

3. Exchange responses to the Chapter Review: Editing Practice on page 163 with another student in your group. Answer the following questions about each sentence in his or her Editing Practice.

    - Do any words come between the subject and the verb?
    - Does the sentence contain an indefinite pronoun used as a subject?
    - Does the subject come after the verb?
    - Does the sentence contain *who*, *which*, or *that*?

    As you answer these questions, check to make sure all the subjects agree with their verbs. When your Editing Practice exercise is returned to you, make any necessary corrections.

Review

- Singular subjects (nouns and pronouns) take singular verbs, and plural subjects take plural verbs. (See 8A.)

    The <u>museum</u> <u>opens</u> at ten o'clock.

    The <u>museums</u> <u>open</u> at ten o'clock.

    <u>She</u> always <u>watches</u> the eleven o'clock news.

    <u>They</u> always <u>watch</u> the eleven o'clock news.

- The irregular verbs *be*, *have*, and *do* often present problems with subject-verb agreement in the present tense. (See 8B.)

- Words that come between the subject and the verb do not affect subject-verb agreement. (See 8C.)

    High <u>levels</u> (of mercury) <u>are</u> found in some fish.

- Most indefinite pronouns, such as *no one* and *everyone*, are singular and take a singular verb when they serve as the subject of a sentence. (See 8D.)

    <u>No one</u> <u>likes</u> getting up early.

(continued on the following page)

(*continued from previous page*)

- A verb agrees with its subject even if the subject comes after the verb. (See 8E.)

    Where <u>is</u> the <u>telephone booth</u>?

    There <u>are</u> nine <u>justices</u> on the Supreme Court.

- *Who*, *which*, and *that* are singular when they refer to a singular word and plural when they refer to a plural word. (See 8F.)

    An author <u>who</u> <u>writes</u> about Chinese immigrants spoke at our college.

    Computers <u>that</u> <u>have</u> color monitors are expensive.

Unit 4 Review

The following collaborative activities, writing practice topics, and student writing sample provide opportunities for you to review what you have learned in Chapters 6 through 8.

COLLABORATIVE ACTIVITIES

1. Working in a group of three or four students, compare your responses to the Chapter Review: Student Writing at the end of one of this unit's three chapters. Consider each sentence of the exercise carefully, noting the different editing choices available to you. Then, try to agree on one version of the passage.

2. Working in a group of three or four students, make a list of services, facilities, activities, and organizations on your campus or in your community that need improvement. Try to identify at least two or three specific weaknesses in each. As a group, select one subject from your list. Each member of the group should then write a paragraph discussing one of the weaknesses you have identified.

WRITING PRACTICE

1. Interview a student in your class about a difficulty he or she has overcome. When your questions have been answered, write a short speech in which you nominate the student for an award you have invented. Begin your speech by naming the award and identifying its requirements. Then go on to tell why the student you are nominating deserves to win the award.

2. Write about the worst job you ever had. Begin by listing all the negative aspects of the job that you can remember—hours, pay, boss, coworkers, duties, and so on. Your goal is to help readers understand why you hated the job so much; the more specific detail you include, the more convincing your writing will be. Be sure to check your work for sentence completeness and correct subject-verb agreement.

3. Choose one service, facility, activity, or organization on your campus with which you are dissatisfied, and write a letter of complaint to the person or office responsible for its operation. In your letter, identify all the problems you can, and explain why each presents an inconvenience or hardship for you and your fellow students. In your closing paragraphs, suggest possible solutions to the problems you identify. Keep your letter polite and respectful, but do not be afraid to offer very specific criticisms based on your personal experiences and observations. If you like, you can use

information generated in group work related to Collaborative Activity 2 above.

4. Write two descriptions of a place with which you are familiar. For the first description, assume you are a representative of the local chamber of commerce. Describe the place in positive terms so someone from out of town would want to spend a week there. Talk about the wonderful people, the brilliant sunsets, and the appealing climate. For the second description, assume you are a dissatisfied vacationer. Describe the same place in negative terms so that someone would not be tricked into spending a week there as you were. Describe the unfriendly residents, the smog-laden atmosphere, and the unbearably humid weather. Before writing, review your response to the Paragraph Practice at the beginning of this chapter to see if any information there can be of use to you.

STUDENT WRITING

Read the following student essay in which sentence fragments and errors in agreement have been introduced. Cross out any errors, and write your corrections in the space above the line. The first error has been corrected for you.

```
          Students from the Caribbean

    In many states, immigrant children are entitled to be
taught in their native language. This instruction, which
   gives
~~give~~ them time to adjust to their new environment, is re-
quired by law. But students from English-speaking Caribbean
            are
nations ~~is~~ neither tested nor offered special services. One
high school principal, whose students are largely West In-
       says          are
dian, ~~say~~, "These kids ~~is~~ definitely getting a bad deal."
     are
They ignored because they have problems speaking standard
English.

    In New York City, for example, students from the En-
                              make
glish-speaking Caribbean ~~makes~~ up 21 percent of the new im-
migrants enrolled in schools. Educators don't always recog-
                                             b
nize that they have a language problem. ~~B~~ecause students
```

come from countries where English is spoken. Instead of speaking standard English, however, they speak Creole--a mix of grammar and vocabulary from West African dialects, English, French, Spanish, and Dutch. Linguists are quick to point out, however, that Creole dialects have evolved into languages.

Teachers of these children often have a difficult time understanding them. When they speak. Instead of realizing that a student needs help mastering standard English, teachers automatically assume they are not intelligent. As a result, students from the English-speaking Caribbean often do not succeed in school. There are signs that the situation is changing. Recently, some states have agreed to finance programs for immigrant children from English-speaking Caribbean countries. The teachers in these programs are fluent in Creole-based languages. They not only encourage students to cherish their own language but also to learn the kind of English they will need in school. Many teachers who have taught in these programs gladly volunteer their time to tutor students.

9 The Past Tense

> **Overview**
>
> In this chapter you will learn
> - To use regular verbs in the past tense
> - To use irregular verbs in the past tense
> - To use the past tense of *be* correctly
> - To use *can/could* and *will/would* correctly

PARAGRAPH PRACTICE

Write your own one-paragraph obituary. (Refer to yourself by name or as *he* or *she*.) Assume that you have led a long life and that you have achieved almost everything you hoped you would. Make sure your paragraph has a topic sentence that presents the quality or qualities for which you would most like to be remembered. In addition, include transitional words and phrases that clearly show the relationship of one event in your life to another. Use the blank space below for invention. Then, write your paragraph on the lines that follow.

A UNDERSTANDING REGULAR VERBS IN THE PAST TENSE

The **past tense** is the form a verb takes to show that an action has occurred in the past. **Regular verbs** form the past tense by adding either *-ed* or *-d* to the present tense form of the verb that is used with *I*. This form is called the **base form** of the verb.

> ### ▶ FOCUS ON REGULAR VERBS IN THE PAST TENSE ◀
>
> - Most regular verbs form the past tense by adding *-ed*.
>   > I registered for classes yesterday.
>   > Juan walked to the concert.
>
> - Regular verbs that end in *e* form the past tense by adding *-d*.
>   > Walt Disney produced short cartoons in 1928.
>   > Tisha liked to read romance novels.
>
> *(continued on the following page)*

CHAPTER 9 The Past Tense · 171

(continued from the previous page)

- Regular verbs that end in *y* form the past tense by changing the *y* to *i* and adding *-ed*.

   tr<u>y</u>   tr<u>ied</u>
   appl<u>y</u>   appl<u>ied</u>

- All regular verbs use the same form for both singular and plural in the past tense.

   Singular: I <u>cheered</u> when the San Francisco 49ers won.
   Plural: They <u>cheered</u> when the San Francisco 49ers won.

PRACTICE 9-1

Change the verbs in the following sentences to the past tense. Cross out the present tense form of each underlined verb, and write in the past tense form above it.

Example: My grandparents ~~live~~ *lived* in a small town.

1. My grandparents ~~own~~ *owned* a combination magazine stand and candy store in downtown Madison.

2. They ~~stock~~ *stocked* about three hundred different magazines that ~~range~~ *ranged* in subject matter from health and fitness to guns and ammo to angels and flying saucers.

3. Customers sometimes ~~browse~~ *browsed* for an hour or more.

4. As they ~~look~~ *looked* through the magazines, they often ~~munch~~ *munched* on candy bars or ~~try~~ *tried* a soda.

5. When the candy bar or soda ~~turns~~ *turned* out to be a customer's only purchase, my grandfather ~~wants~~ *wanted* to throw the "library patron" out.

6. My grandmother, however, ~~recognizes~~ *recognized* the importance of customer satisfaction.

172 • UNIT 5 Understanding Verbs

7. She always ~~insists~~ *insisted* that my grandfather be more patient.

8. Still, my grandfather sometimes ~~refuses~~ *refused* to listen to her.

9. He never actually ~~kicks~~ *kicked* a customer out.

10. Sometimes, though, he noisily ~~storms~~ *stormed* out of the store, leaving my grandmother to deal with the startled customer.

PRACTICE 9-2

For each blank in the paragraph below, fill in the past tense form of the appropriate verb from the following list. Use the verb that makes the best sense in context. The first answer has been filled in for you.

agree	apply	discover	score
start	collect	accept	accuse
receive	cause	believe	
earn	answer	apologize	

(1) Cindy Crawford prides herself on having brains as well as beauty. (2) Before she __started__ high school, her father __agreed__ to pay her $200 if she __earned__ straight A's all four years. (3) When she __received__ her final report card, she __collected__ her money. (4) While in high school, Crawford __applied__ to Northwestern University and was __accepted__ into the chemical engineering program. (5) At Northwestern she __discovered__ that her good looks sometimes __caused__ problems. (6) Professors __believed__ that because she was pretty, she must also be dumb. (7) For example, a calculus professor __accused__ her of cheating when she __scored__ 100 percent on a midterm exam. (8) He eventually __apologized__ for his accusation when she __answered__ every question correctly on the final, too.

CHAPTER 9 The Past Tense • 173

> ▶ **FLASHBACK** ◀
>
> Look back at the paragraph you wrote for the Paragraph Practice at the beginning of the chapter. Underline the past tense verbs that end in *-ed* and *-d*. Then, write them in the spaces below.
>
> | | | | |
> |---|---|---|---|
> | | | | |
> | | | | |
> | | | | |
> | | | | |

B UNDERSTANDING IRREGULAR VERBS IN THE PAST TENSE

Unlike regular verbs, whose past-tense forms end in *-d* and *-ed*, **irregular verbs** have irregular forms in the past tense. For example, some irregular verbs use different forms for present and past tense.

Present	Past
c<u>o</u>me	c<u>a</u>me
dr<u>i</u>nk	dr<u>a</u>nk
kn<u>o</u>w	kn<u>e</u>w

Other irregular verbs have the same form in both present and past tense.

Present	Past
Barbers <u>cut</u> hair.	I <u>cut</u> class and finished my homework.
Some gamblers <u>bet</u> compulsively.	I <u>bet</u> ten dollars on the Super Bowl last year.

The following chart lists the base form and past tense form of some of the most commonly used irregular verbs.

Irregular Verbs in the Past Tense

Base Form	Past	Base Form	Past
awake	awoke	get	got
be	was, were	give	gave
beat	beat	go (goes)	went
become	became	grow	grew
begin	began	hang	hanged, hung
bend	bent	have	had
bet	bet	hear	heard
bite	bit	hide	hid
blow	blew	hold	held
break	broke	hurt	hurt
bring	brought	keep	kept
build	built	know	knew
burst	burst	lay (to place)	laid
buy	bought	lead	led
catch	caught	leave	left
choose	chose	lend	lent
come	came	let	let
cost	cost	lie (to recline)	lay
cut	cut	light	lit
do	did	lose	lost
draw	drew	make	made
drink	drank	meet	met
drive	drove	pay	paid
eat	ate	read	read
fall	fell	ride	rode
feed	fed	ring	rang
feel	felt	rise	rose
fight	fought	run	ran
find	found	say	said
fly	flew	see	saw
freeze	froze	sell	sold

(continued on the following page)

(continued from the previous page)

Base Form	Past	Base Form	Past
send	sent	sting	stung
set	set	swear	swore
shake	shook	swim	swam
shrink	shrank	take	took
shut	shut	teach	taught
sing	sang	tear	tore
sit	sat	tell	told
sleep	slept	think	thought
speak	spoke	wake	woke
spend	spent	wear	wore
stand	stood	win	won
steal	stole	wind	wound
stick	stuck	write	wrote

PRACTICE 9-3

In the sentences below, fill in the correct past tense form of the irregular verb in parentheses.

Example: They __*said*__ (say) it couldn't be done.

1. In August 1991, long-jumper Mike Powell __*broke*__ (break) the longest-standing record in track and field.

2. His leap of twenty-nine feet four and one-half inches __*made*__ (make) headlines around the world.

3. Mike Beaman had set the previous record of twenty-nine feet and two and one-half inches when he __*won*__ (win) the Olympics in Mexico City in 1968.

4. Competing against his great rival Carl Lewis, Powell __*swore*__ (swear) to himself that this time he would prevail.

5. He __*felt*__ (feel) that if he __*lost*__ (lose) to Lewis again, his career might suffer.

176 ▪ UNIT 5 Understanding Verbs

6. He ___beat___ (beat) Lewis in that contest, but the world ___saw___ (see) a different story at the Olympics the following year.

7. Lewis ___let___ (let) it be known that he was out to break Powell's record.

8. Before his first jump, Powell ___drew___ (draw) a mark in the sand at twenty-nine feet and six and one-half inches, or nine meters.

9. His jump ___fell___ (fall) far short of that goal.

10. Lewis then ___took___ (take) the Gold Medal by jumping twenty-eight feet and five and one-half inches on his first jump.

11. Powell's best jump of twenty-eight feet and four and one-half inches ___left___ (leave) him with the Silver Medal.

12. However, his August 1991 record still ___stood___ (stand).

PRACTICE 9-4

Edit the following passage for errors in irregular past tense verbs. Cross out any underlined verbs that are incorrect, and write in the correct forms above them. If the verb form is correct, label it *C*. The first error has been corrected for you.

(1) Actor-director Sidney Poitier ~~growed~~ *grew* up in Miami, but he ~~leaved~~ *left* his hometown in the mid-1940s and went *C* to New York City. (2) Once there, he ~~finded~~ *found* that he ~~has~~ *had* to work hard to survive. (3) He ~~become~~ *became* everything from a dock hand to a chicken plucker but eventually ~~beginned~~ *began* to imagine himself as an actor. (4) He applied to the American Negro Theatre but ~~loosed~~ *lost* the job to a more experienced actor. (5) By listening to radio announcers, he ~~teached~~ *taught* himself to improve his speaking skills and reapplied. (6) He fought *C* hard, and this time he was accepted.

(7) After appearing in several plays, Poitier ~~knowed~~ *knew* he wanted to make movies, so he ~~maked~~ *made* the move from New York to Hollywood. (8) His im-

portant films include *Blackboard Jungle*, *The Defiant Ones*, *A Raisin in the Sun*, *Guess Who's Coming to Dinner*, and *Lilies of the Field*, for which he <u>winned</u> ^won an Oscar in 1963. (9) He <u>come</u> ^came a long way from plucking chickens to becoming one of the most powerful African Americans in the entertainment industry.

▶ **FLASHBACK** ◀

Look back at your response to the Paragraph Practice at the beginning of the chapter. Circle the irregular past tense verbs you find, and copy each one in the column on the left. Then, in the column on the right, write down its base form.

Past Tense	Base Form

C USING *BE* IN THE PAST TENSE

The irregular verb *be* can be especially troublesome because it has two different past tense forms. In fact, it is the only verb in English to have more than one form in the past tense.

<u>Carlo</u> <u>was</u> interested in becoming a city planner.
<u>They</u> <u>were</u> happy to help out at the school.

Past Tense Forms of the Verb *Be*

Singular	Plural
I <u>was</u> tired.	We <u>were</u> tired.
You <u>were</u> tired.	You <u>were</u> tired.
He <u>was</u> tired.	
She <u>was</u> tired.	They <u>were</u> tired.
It <u>was</u> tired.	

For detailed information about subject-verb agreement, see Chapter 8.

▶ FOCUS ON THE PAST TENSE OF *BE* ◀

Two familiar contractions use past tense forms of *be*. Keep in mind that the contraction *wasn't* (was + not) contains a singular verb form and is used with a singular subject. *Weren't* (were + not) contains a plural verb form and is used with a plural subject.

Lynette <u>wasn't</u> happy about the school board's decision.
Her <u>parents weren't</u> happy either.

PRACTICE 9-5

Edit the following passage for errors in the use of the verb *be*. Cross out any underlined verbs that are incorrect, and write in the correct forms above them. If the verb form is correct, label it *C*. The first answer has been supplied for you.

(1) Korean-American comic Margaret Cho <u>was</u> *[C]* born in 1969. (2) Her mother and father <u>was</u> *[were]* from prominent families in Korea, but in the United States they <u>wasn't</u> *[weren't]* able to maintain their former standard of living. (3) Eventually, they <u>was</u> *[were]* able to open a bookstore. (4) Cho <u>was</u> *[C]* one of the first successful Asian-American comics in the country, beginning her career at the age of eighteen. (5) Her parents, however, <u>was</u> *[were]* opposed to her career choice.

(6) For years they ~~wasn't~~ *weren't* able to admit to friends that their daughter had a performing career. (7) Cho ~~weren't~~ *wasn't* to be stopped, though. (8) Even when an agent refused to sign her as a client because he said Asians ~~wasn't~~ *weren't* going to go anywhere in the comedy business, Cho didn't back down. (9) Ultimately, her determination was *C* rewarded when she was signed to star in her own television series, *All-American Girl,* which ran during the 1994–95 season. (10) Interestingly, Cho's given name ~~weren't~~ *wasn't* Margaret, which she chose for herself at the age of ten. (11) Her real name ~~were~~ *was* Moran, which in the Korean language denotes a delicate flower that will survive under any circumstances. (12) Cho may not be a delicate flower, but she is certainly a survivor.

▶ FLASHBACK ◀

Look back at your response to the Paragraph Practice at the beginning of the chapter. Find all the sentences in which you use the past tense of *be*. Copy two or three of these sentences in the space below. Make sure you have used the correct form of the verb in each case.

1. _____
   _____

2. _____
   _____

3. _____
   _____

D USING CAN/COULD AND WILL/WOULD

The helping verbs *can* and *could* express the ability to do something, and the helping verbs *will* and *would* refer to action in the future. Their past tense forms are often confused with their present tense forms.

Can/Could

Can, a present tense verb, means "is able to" or "are able to."
First-year students can apply for financial aid.

Could, the past tense of *can*, means "was able to" or "were able to."
Harry Houdini could escape from any prison.

> ▶ **FOCUS** ON COULD ◀
>
> In addition to indicating the past tense of *can*, *could* is used to express possibility or a wish in the future.
> If I started training, I could run the marathon. (possibility)
> I wish I could get an A on my next exam. (wish)

Will/Would

Will, a present tense verb, indicates that an action will take place in the future. *Will* is used to talk about the future from a point in the present—for example, to indicate an intention.

A solar eclipse will occur in ten months.

Would is the past tense of *will*. It generally talks about the future from a point in the past.

I told him yesterday that I would think about it.

Would can also express an intention or wish that cannot be fulfilled.

I would lend you my car, but it's in the shop.

> ▶ **FOCUS** ON WILL AND WOULD ◀
>
> Note that *will* is used with *can*, and *would* is used with *could*.
> I will feed the cats if I can find their food.
> I would feed the cats if I could find their food.

PRACTICE 9-6

Fill in the appropriate helping verb from the choices in parentheses.

Example: Travel took so long years ago that my grandfather ___would___ rarely drive more than ten miles from home. (will/would)

1. In years past, it ___could___ take hours to travel across the state. (can/could)

2. Now, with the new highway, the trip ___can___ take as little as an hour. (can/could)

3. As you make the drive, you ___will___ be surprised. (will/would)

4. Until I made the trip, I ___would___ not have believed the difference. (will/would)

5. Before the new highway opened, you ___could___ get stuck behind a truck on those winding, two-lane roads. (can/could)

6. Now, you ___can___ zip along on four lanes each way. (can/could)

7. Because they were so low, those old roads ___would___ often be flooded. (will/would)

8. The new highway ___will___ never flood because it is elevated. (will/would)

9. If they ___could___ go back to the old ways, some people would do so. (can/could)

10. I ___will___ always try to adapt to progress and change if I can. (will/would)

182 ▪ UNIT 5 Understanding Verbs

FLASHBACK

Look back at your response to the Paragraph Practice at the beginning of the chapter. Add a few sentences that express what you would have accomplished if you had had the chance. Be sure to use *could* and *would* correctly.

_____

_____

_____

_____

_____

_____

_____

REVIEW

CHAPTER REVIEW: STUDENT WRITING

Read the following student passage, in which errors in past tense verb forms have been introduced. Decide whether or not each of the underlined past tense verbs is correct. If it is correct, write *C* above it. If it is not, cross out the verb and write in the correct past tense form. The first sentence has been corrected for you.

Healing

The window seat ~~were~~ *was* our favorite place to sit. I piled comfortable pillows on the ledge and ~~spended~~ *spent* several minutes

CHAPTER 9   The Past Tense   •   183

rearranging them. My friend and I ~~lied~~ [lay] on our backs and propped our feet up on the wall. We sat [C] with our arms around our legs and ~~thinked~~ [thought] about the mysteries of life. We also stared at the people on the street below and ~~wonder~~ [wondered] who they ~~was~~ [were] and where they ~~was~~ [were] going. We imagined that they ~~can~~ [could] be millionaires, foreign spies, or ruthless drug smugglers. We believed that everyone except us ~~leaded~~ [led] wonderful and exciting lives.

I heard [C] a voice call my name. Reluctantly, I ~~rised~~ [rose], tearing myself away from my imaginary world. My dearest and oldest friend--my teddy bear--and I reentered the real world. I grabbed Teddy and ~~brung~~ [brought] him close to my chest. Together we ~~go~~ [went] into the cold sitting room, where twelve other girls ~~sit~~ [sat] around a table eating breakfast. None of them looked happy. In the unit for eating disorders, meals ~~was~~ [were] always tense. Nobody wanted to eat, but the nurses watched us until we ~~eated~~ [ate] every crumb. I set [C] Teddy in the chair beside me and stared gloomily at the food on our plate. I closed my eyes and ~~taked~~ [took] the first bite. I ~~feeled~~ [felt] the calories adding inches of ugly fat. Each swallow ~~were~~ [was] like another nail being ripped from my finger. At last it was [C] over. I had survived breakfast.

Days passed slowly; each passing minute was [C] a triumph. I learned how to eat properly. I learned about other people's problems. I also learned that people loved me. Eventually, even Teddy stopped feeling sorry for me. I ~~begun~~ [began]

to smile--and laugh. Sometimes, I even considered myself happy. My doctors challenged me--and, surprisingly, I ~~rised~~ *rose* to the occasion.

At last, after many weeks, there I stood *C* with Teddy in one hand and my suitcase in the other. Finally, we ~~was~~ *were* on the outside of the building that had held us captive for so long. I strained my eyes and ~~seen~~ *saw* the pane of glass that marked our favorite window seat. I was *C* now one of those people on the sidewalk, ready to face the world.

CHAPTER REVIEW: EDITING PRACTICE

Reread your response to the Paragraph Practice at the beginning of the chapter. Make sure you have used the correct past tense form for each of your verbs. If you have not, cross out the incorrect form, and write the proper past tense form of the verb above the line. When you are finished, do the same for a writing assignment you are currently working on.

CHAPTER REVIEW: COLLABORATIVE ACTIVITIES

1. Working in a group of three or four students, decide on a famous living figure—an actor, a sports star, or a musician, for example—and brainstorm together to identify specific details about this person's life. Then, write a profile of him or her.

2. Working in a group, list several contemporary problems that you think will be solved in ten or fifteen years. Each member of the group should select a problem and write a paragraph or two describing how it could be solved. Use the paragraphs for the body of an essay; as a group, develop a thesis statement and write an introduction and a conclusion. Then, revise the body paragraphs of your essay.

3. Form a group with other students of similar age. What news events do you remember most vividly? Take ten minutes to list news events in the areas of sports, science, entertainment, or politics that you think have defined your generation. Then, on your own, write a short essay in which you discuss the significance of the three events that the members of your group agree were the most important.

Review

- The past tense is the form a verb takes to show that an action has occurred in the past. (See 9A.)
- Regular verbs form the past tense by adding either *-ed* or *-d* to the present tense form of the verb. (See 9A.)

    I registered for classes yesterday.
    Tisha liked to read romance novels.

- Irregular verbs have irregular forms in the past tense. (See 9B.)

    | *present* | *past* |
    | come | came |
    | cut | cut |

- The only verb in English to have more than one form in the past tense is *be*. (See 9C.)
- *Could* is the past tense of *can*. *Would* is the past tense of *will*. (See 9D.)

10 Past Participles and the Perfect Tenses

Overview

In this chapter you will learn
- To recognize past participles
- To form past participles of regular verbs
- To form past participles of irregular verbs
- To use the present perfect tense
- To use the past perfect tense
- To recognize past participles used as adjectives

PARAGRAPH PRACTICE

Write a paragraph about an activity—a hobby or sport, for example—in which you have been engaged for a relatively long period of time. In your topic sentence, identify the activity and state why it has been so important to you. Then, describe the activity, paying particular attention to what you have gained over the years from your participation. Use the blank space below for invention. Then, write your paragraph on the lines that follow.

CHAPTER 10 Past Participles and the Perfect Tenses • 187

_____
_____
_____
_____
_____
_____
_____
_____
_____
_____
_____
_____
_____
_____

A) RECOGNIZING REGULAR PAST PARTICIPLES

Verbs are sometimes combined with other verbs. Consider the following sentences.

> The band has changed its name from The Broken Melons to The Dead Cats.
> The major television networks have introduced their new programs.
> I had finished studying for the test by Tuesday.

Each of the above verbs has two parts: a **helping verb** (a form of the verb *have*) and a **past participle**.

Helping Verb	Past Participle
has	changed
have	introduced
had	finished

The past participle of a regular verb is identical to its past tense form. Both add *-d* or *-ed* to the base form of the verb. (See 9A.) Different helping verbs may be combined with past participles to form the present perfect tense and past perfect tense, which are discussed later in this chapter. (Past participles are also used in forming passive voice verbs. (See 15E.)

> ▶ **FOCUS** ON PAST PARTICIPLES ◀
>
> The helping verb always agrees with its subject, but the past participle of a verb always has the same form.
> I <u>have</u> <u>earned</u> over two thousand dollars this summer.
> Brad <u>has</u> also <u>earned</u> over two thousand dollars this summer.

PRACTICE 10-1

Fill in the correct past participle of the verb in parentheses.

Example: Coffee prices have ___*dropped*___ recently. (drop)

1. Americans have ___*started*___ a coffee craze in the last ten years. (start)

2. Since the early 1980s, over five thousand coffee bars have ___*opened*___ in the U.S. (open)

3. Many of these bars have ___*appeared*___ in metropolitan areas. (appear)

4. However, they have ___*sprouted*___ in suburban malls and small college towns, too. (sprout)

5. One chain alone has ___*increased*___ to over four hundred outlets. (increase)

6. Americans have always ___*enjoyed*___ coffee. (enjoy)

7. In fact, Americans traditionally have ___*consumed*___ one-third of the world's yearly coffee production. (consume)

CHAPTER 10 Past Participles and the Perfect Tenses • 189

8. One survey has __estimated__ that Americans drink 130 million cups a day. (estimate)

9. Tastes have __changed__, though. (change)

10. Today the market has __expanded__ to include espresso and cappuccino. (expand)

▶ FLASHBACK ◀

Look back at your Paragraph Practice at the beginning of the chapter, and find any helping verbs followed by regular past participles. Then, write both the helping verb and the past participle on the lines below.

Helping Verb	Regular Past Participle
_____	_____
_____	_____
_____	_____
_____	_____
_____	_____

B RECOGNIZING IRREGULAR PAST PARTICIPLES

Irregular verbs usually have irregular past participles. In other words, they do not form the past participle by adding *-d* or *-ed* to the base form of the verb.

Base Form	Past	Past Participle
choose	chose	chosen
buy	bought	bought
ride	rode	ridden

The following chart lists the base form, past tense, and past participle forms of some of the most commonly used irregular verbs.

Irregular Past Participles

Base Form	Past Tense	Past Participle
awake	awoke	awoke
be (am, are)	was (were)	been
beat	beat	beaten
become	became	become
begin	began	begun
bend	bent	bent
bet	bet	bet
bite	bit	bitten
blow	blew	blown
break	broke	broken
bring	brought	brought
build	built	built
burst	burst	burst
buy	bought	bought
catch	caught	caught
choose	chose	chosen
come	came	come
cost	cost	cost
cut	cut	cut
do	did	done
draw	drew	drawn
drink	drank	drunk
drive	drove	driven
eat	ate	eaten
fall	fell	fallen
feed	fed	fed
feel	felt	felt

(continued on the following page)

CHAPTER 10 Past Participles and the Perfect Tenses — 191

Base Form	Past Tense	Past Participle
fight	fought	fought
find	found	found
fly	flew	flown
freeze	froze	frozen
get	got	got *or* gotten
give	gave	given
go	went	gone
grow	grew	grown
hang	hung	hung, hanged
have	had	had
hear	heard	heard
hide	hid	hidden
hold	held	held
hurt	hurt	hurt
keep	kept	kept
know	knew	known
lay (to place)	laid	laid
lead	led	led
leave	left	left
lend	lent	lent
let	let	let
lie (to recline)	lay	lain
light	lit	lit
lose	lost	lost
make	made	made
meet	met	met
pay	paid	paid
read	read	read

(continued on the following page)

(continued from the previous page)

Base Form	Past Tense	Past Participle
ride	rode	ridden
ring	rang	rung
rise	rose	risen
run	ran	run
say	said	said
see	saw	seen
sell	sold	sold
send	sent	sent
set	set	set
shake	shook	shaken
shrink	shrank	shrunk
shut	shut	shut
sing	sang	sung
sit	sat	sat
sleep	slept	slept
speak	spoke	spoken
spend	spent	spent
stand	stood	stood
steal	stole	stolen
stick	stuck	stuck
sting	stung	stung
swear	swore	sworn
swim	swam	swum
take	took	taken
teach	taught	taught
tear	tore	torn
tell	told	told

(continued on the following page)

CHAPTER 10 Past Participles and the Perfect Tenses · 193

Base Form	Past Tense	Past Participle
think	thought	thought
wake	woke *or* waked	woken *or* waked
wear	wore	worn
win	won	won
wind	wound	wound
write	wrote	written

PRACTICE 10-2

Fill in the correct past participle of the verb in parentheses.

Example: The program has _____*won*_____ a loyal audience. (win)

1. Nick at Night has _____*found*_____ a receptive audience for old television programs. (find)

2. The cable network Nickelodeon, which broadcasts children's programs during the day, has _____*caught*_____ on with adults at night. (catch)

3. It has _____*drawn*_____ viewers away from current network sitcoms to ones from the 1970s and earlier. (draw)

4. Many viewers have _____*known*_____ and loved these shows since they were children themselves. (know)

5. This is true even if they haven't _____*seen*_____ them for years. (see)

6. They have _____*run*_____ the candy-making machine with Lucy, _____*fallen*_____ in love with Mary, and _____*kept*_____ up with the jokes of Rob and his pals. (run, fall, keep)

7. As they have _____*gotten*_____ older, they have _____*grown*_____ nostalgic for these familiar characters. (got, grow)

194 ▪ UNIT 5 Understanding Verbs

8. Young viewers have ____had____ a chance to discover them for the first time. (have)

9. Both older and younger viewers have ____begun____ to appreciate the shows for their corniness as well as their real humor. (begin)

10. Nick has also ____made____ a name for itself with its clever commercials and station breaks, which parody 1950s style. (make)

PRACTICE 10-3

Edit the following passage for errors in irregular past participles. Cross out any underlined past participles that are incorrect, and write in the correct form above them. If the verb form is correct, label it *C*. The first one has been corrected for you.

(1) The war against wearing fur has ~~became~~ *become* a major campaign in recent years. (2) Some people have always ~~feeled~~ *felt* that killing animals for fur is immoral. (3) Recently, however, activists have ~~took~~ *taken* a more visible role in the struggle against fur. (4) Organizations have ~~fighted~~ *fought* to convince clothing designers not to work with fur, and their efforts have been *C* surprisingly successful. (5) Designers like Calvin Klein and Giorgio Armani have ~~sayed~~ *said* they will no longer include fur in their collections. (6) Many celebrities have ~~choosed~~ *chosen* to take a public stand against furs, and several well-known models have ~~gave~~ *given* their time to pose for antifur ads. (7) They have ~~send~~ *sent* the message that wearing furs is no longer the thing to do. (8) Some critics complain that many of the more radical activists have ~~went~~ *gone* too far. (9) It is true that some have sat *C* chained to racks in department stores and have even ~~tore~~ *torn* fur collars from women's coats. (10) Others have ~~stole~~ *stolen* furs as they were being shipped from warehouses. (11) Such efforts have ~~costed~~ *cost* the fur industry a great deal, so the fur manufacturers and retailers are fighting back with publicity campaigns of their own.

CHAPTER 10 Past Participles and the Perfect Tenses · 195

> ●●●●●●●●▶ **FLASHBACK** ◀●●●●●●●●
>
> Look back at your response to the Paragraph Practice at the beginning of the chapter, and find any helping verbs followed by irregular past participles. Then, write both the helping verb and the irregular past participle below.
>
> **Helping Verb**   **Irregular Past Participle**
>
> _____   _____
>
> _____   _____
>
> _____   _____
>
> _____   _____
>
> _____   _____

C USING THE PRESENT PERFECT TENSE

The **present perfect tense** consists of the present tense of *have* plus the past participle.

The Present Perfect Tense
(*have* or *has* + past participle)

Singular	Plural
I have gained.	We have gained.
You have gained.	You have gained.
He has gained.	
She has gained.	They have gained.
It has gained.	

The past tense (I gained) indicates an action that began and ended in the past. The present perfect tense (I have gained) shows a continuing action—generally one that began in the past and continues into the present. Compare the following two sentences:

> The nurse worked at the Welsh Mountain clinic for two years.
> The nurse has worked at the Welsh Mountain clinic for two years.

In the first sentence, the past tense verb *worked* suggests that the nurse worked at the clinic for two years but now no longer does. In the second sentence, the present perfect verb *has worked* indicates that the nurse worked at the clinic for two years and still works there today. In other words, the action continues into the present.

▶ FOCUS ON THE PRESENT PERFECT TENSE ◀

Use the present perfect tense in these three situations.

- **To indicate an action that began in the past and extends into the present.** When you use the present perfect tense in this way, you frequently use words like *for* or *since* to indicate the duration of the action.

    I have waited in line for two hours. (I am still waiting.)
    Dr. Edenbaum has taught at this school since 1961. (He still teaches here.)

- **To indicate an action that has just ended.** When you use the present perfect tense in this way, you frequently use the words *just, recently, already,* or *yet.*

    They have just arrived at the train station.
    Matt has already quit smoking.

- **To indicate that an action began at an unspecified past time and has now ended.**

    I have read all the books on the syllabus. (I have now finished reading.)

Note that the past tense (not the past perfect) is used to indicate that an action occurred at a specified time in the past.

   I read that book last year.

PRACTICE 10-4

Fill in the appropriate verb tense (past or present perfect) from the choices in parentheses.

CHAPTER 10 Past Participles and the Perfect Tenses · 197

Example: My new kitten *has begun* to dominate the household. (began/has begun)

1. I _have been_ a cat addict all my life. (was/have been)

2. I ___got___ my first cat when I was seven years old. (got/have gotten)

3. I ___named___ him Tweetie after the little bird in the cartoons. (named/have named)

4. Since then I _have owned_ many more felines. (owned/have owned)

5. At one point I ___had___ five cats at once. (had/have had)

6. Last year one ___died___. (died/has died)

7. My sister ___adopted___ another when she got married. (adopted/has adopted)

8. Since then I _have taken_ care of just the other three cats. (took/have taken)

9. Through the years, my cats _have given_ me much pleasure but also a lot of aggravation. (gave/have given)

10. Anyone who _has raised_ cats will understand what I mean. (raised/has raised)

PRACTICE 10-5

Fill in the appropriate verb tense (past or present perfect) of the verb in parentheses. The first answer has been supplied for you.

(1) Newspapers and magazines in America _have presented_ (present) the results of public opinion polls since the mid-1900s. (2) Until the early twentieth century, however, these polls ___were___ (be) unscientific and their results far from accurate. (3) Then, in the 1930s, George Horace Gallup ___devised___ (devise) original techniques for polling. (4) Over the years, these methods _have achieved_ (achieve) considerable success in predicting elec-

tions. (5) Since its development, the Gallup poll _has become_ (become) the most well known of all public opinion polls. (6) Up until now, such polls _have come_ (come) to occupy a larger and larger place in our public lives. (7) In recent years, however, some critics _have begun_ (begin) to argue against the extensive use of polls to chart public opinion. (8) In 1994, for example, many polls _predicted_ (predict) election results fairly inaccurately.

PRACTICE 10-6

Edit the following passage for errors in the use of the past and present perfect tenses. Cross out any underlined verbs that are incorrect, and write in the correct forms above them. If the verb form is correct, label it C. The first error has been corrected for you.

(1) My family ~~has lived~~ *lived* in Miami before we ~~have moved~~ *moved* to the city of Hoboken in New Jersey, where we live now. (2) Since the move ten years ago, we ~~went~~ *have gone* back to Miami many times. (3) I ~~loved~~ *have loved* Miami all my life. (4) It was *C* the place of my birth and the place where I ~~have spent~~ *spent* my happiest years when I ~~have been~~ *was* a child. (5) I ~~missed~~ *have missed* Miami ever since we moved away. (6) I ~~lived~~ *have lived* in Hoboken for many years now, but during all that time, I never have considered *C* it home.

> ••••••••▶ **FLASHBACK** ◀••••••••
>
> Look back at the Paragraph Practice at the beginning of the chapter. Choose three sentences with past tense verbs. Then, rewrite them below, changing past tense to present perfect tense. How does your rewrite change the meaning? Do you have to make other changes when you change the verb tense?
>
> 1. _____
> _____
> _____
>
> *(continued on the following page)*

(continued from the previous page)

2. _____

_____

_____

3. _____

_____

_____

D USING THE PAST PERFECT TENSE

The **past perfect tense** is formed with the past tense of *have* plus the past participle.

The Past Perfect Tense
(had + past participle)

Singular	Plural
I had returned.	We had returned.
You had returned.	You had returned.
He had returned.	
She had returned.	They had returned.
It had returned.	

The past perfect tense describes an action that occurred before another past tense action. Consider the following sentence:

Chief Sitting Bull <u>had fought</u> many battles before <u>he defeated</u> General Custer.

This sentence identifies two actions that happened in the past—the fighting done by Sitting Bull and his defeat of Custer. Notice that the action in the first part of the sentence is in the past perfect tense. This tense indicates that Sitting Bull's battles took place *before* the action in the second part of the sentence, which is expressed in the past tense.

In the sample sentence above, the word *before* clarifies the relationship between the two actions and shows that they took place at different times. Even without words like *before* and *after*, however, the past perfect tense can show the relationship between two past actions. Consider the following sentence:

The witness testified that she had lived in Los Angeles.

Here the past tense verb *testified* indicates that the witness gave testimony at some time in the past. The past perfect tense verb *had lived* expresses the idea that the witness was no longer living in Los Angeles at the time she testified.

> ▶ **FOCUS** ON THE PAST PERFECT TENSE ◀
>
> The past perfect tense and present perfect tense are often confused. Keep the following differences in mind:
>
> - The past perfect tense relates one action that occurred in the past to another that occurred at an earlier time in the past. The past perfect tense is used along with a past tense verb.
>
>   The witness <u>testified</u> (past tense) that she <u>had lived</u> (past perfect) in Los Angeles.
>
> - The present perfect tense relates a continuing action. It is used along with a present tense verb.
>
>   Dr. Edenbaum <u>says</u> (present tense) that he <u>has taught</u> (present perfect) at this school since 1961.

PRACTICE 10-7

Fill in the appropriate verb tense (present perfect or past perfect) from the choices in parentheses.

Example: Although the children __had eaten__ dinner, they still had room for ice cream. (has eaten/had eaten)

1. Ren wondered where he __had left__ his keys. (has left/had left)

2. He believes he __has lost__ them. (has lost/had lost)

3. The receptionist told the interviewer that the applicant __had arrived__. (has arrived/had arrived)

4. The interviewer says that she __has waited__ for an hour. (has waited/had waited)

5. The jury decided that the defendant __had lied__ on the witness stand. (has lied/had lied)

6. The jury members are still deliberating; they _have been_ in the jury room for three days now. (have been/had been)

7. By the time I reached the pizza parlor, I _had decided_ to order a pepperoni pie. (have decided/had decided)

8. By the time my pizza is ready, I usually _have finished_ my pinball game. (have finished/had finished)

9. The movie _had been_ on only ten minutes when I turned it off. (has been/had been)

10. This movie is excellent; I _have seen_ it at least five times. (have seen/had seen)

▶ **FLASHBACK** ◀

Look back at the previous Flashback. Rewrite the three present perfect tense sentences, this time changing them to the past perfect tense. How does your rewrite change the meaning? Do you have to make other changes when you change the verb tense?

1. _____

2. _____

3. _____

E. USING PAST PARTICIPLES AS ADJECTIVES

So far, we have been discussing the past participle as part of a verb form. However, a past participle can also function as an **adjective**, a word that modifies a noun or pronoun. (For more about adjectives, see Chapter 20.) Look at the following sentences:

I cleaned up the broken glass.

The exhausted runner crossed the finish line.

In each of these sentences, the past participle comes before the noun and functions as an adjective. Past participles that function as adjectives can also come after a noun or pronoun, as they do in the following sentences:

Jason seemed surprised.

He looked shocked.

The verbs in these sentences—*seemed* and *looked*—are **linking verbs**, which connect the subject to the word that describes it. (See 6C.)

PRACTICE 10-8

Insert a modifier in the blanks below by filling in the past participle form of the verb in parentheses.

Example: The ___spoiled___ milk turned my stomach. (spoil)

1. I felt ___satisfied___ after the meal. (satisfy)

2. The defendant's mother seemed ___relieved___ by the outcome of the trial. (relieve)

3. A ___sprained___ ankle kept the quarterback out of the game. (sprain)

4. The defense claimed the prosecution's star witness was ___prejudiced___ against their client. (prejudice)

5. On the bar were a ___chipped___ bowl of ___mixed___ nuts, a platter of ___sliced___ bread and meat, some ___bottled___ water, and a pitcher of ___iced___ tea. (chip, mix, slice, bottle, ice)

CHAPTER 10 Past Participles and the Perfect Tenses ▪ 203

PRACTICE 10-9

Edit the following passage for errors in the use of past participle forms as adjectives. Cross out any underlined participles that are incorrect, and write in the correct form above them. If the participle form is correct, label it *C*. The first error has been corrected for you.

(1) College students in their teens and twenties may be ~~surprise~~ *surprised* when they find ~~preapprove~~ *preapproved* applications for credit cards turning up in their mail. (2) Credit card companies also recruit *targeted* [C] students through booths ~~locate~~ *located* near student unions and libraries. (3) The booths are ~~design~~ *designed* to attract new customers with offers of ~~inscribe~~ *inscribed* coffee mugs and tote bags. (4) Why do companies go to all this effort to attract young people? (5) Most older Americans already have at least five credit cards ~~stuff~~ *stuffed* in their billfolds. (6) Banks and credit card companies see younger college students as their major *untapped* [C] market. (7) According to experts, students are also a good credit risk because parents often bail them out when they can't pay a bill. (8) Finally, people tend to feel ~~tie~~ *tied* to their first credit card. (9) Companies want to be the first card ~~acquire~~ *acquired* by a customer.

▶ FLASHBACK ◀

Look back at your response to the Paragraph Practice at the beginning of the chapter. Choose three nouns you used in your paragraph, and list them in the right-hand column below. Then, think of a past participle that can modify each noun, and write the modifier in the left-hand column.

Past Participle	Noun
1. _____	_____

(continued on the following page)

(continued from the previous page)

Past Participle	Noun
2. _____	_____
3. _____	_____

Now, use each of these nouns as the subject of an original sentence followed by a linking verb and a modifier.

1. _____

_____

_____

2. _____

_____

_____

3. _____

_____

_____

• • • • • • • • • • • • • **REVIEW** • • • • • • • • • • • • •

CHAPTER REVIEW: STUDENT WRITING

Read the following student passage, in which errors in past participles and the use of the perfect tenses have been introduced. Decide whether or not each of the underlined verbs or participles is correct. If it is correct, write *C* above it. If it is not, write in the correct past tense form. The first error has been corrected for you.

The U.S. War on Drugs

In our effort to halt the spread of a drug epidemic, the United States has ~~took~~ *taken* extreme measures, some of which

CHAPTER 10 Past Participles and the Perfect Tenses • 205

have ~~had~~ not been in our best interest. Using both internal and external controls, the government has ~~fighted~~ fought the problem on a number of fronts. It has ~~rely~~ relied on internal actions, such as punishing drug traffickers and people found to possess drugs and providing rehabilitation for substance abusers. In addition, it has ~~spended~~ spent funds on external solutions, such as limiting the flow of drugs from other countries. Unfortunately, these efforts have not ~~work~~ worked.

Most internal strategies for dealing with the drug problem have made (C) hardly a dent. In fact, the United States ~~had~~ has discovered that some methods actually create new problems. Stricter laws prohibiting the sale and use of drugs have ~~lead~~ led to longer jail sentences, and longer jail sentences have ~~force~~ forced overcrowded prisons to release dangerous prisoners before their sentences have ~~expire~~ expired. In addition, lack of funding has ~~keeped~~ kept many approved (C) applicants from receiving adequate rehabilitation services.

More frustrating is the failure of the external strategies we ~~had~~ have employed to protect our borders. By the end of 1993, we ~~have~~ had poured millions of dollars of military aid into Latin American countries to encourage them to control traffickers who shipped drugs into the U.S. Much of this money, however, was ~~use~~ used to line the pockets of corrupt government officials. Not only have the officials ~~receive~~ received money from the United States to control drugs, they have also ~~took~~ taken bribes from drug lords. By the time U.S. agents discovered that many corrupt officials ~~have~~ had funneled millions of dollars into foreign bank accounts, the war was basically lost. It is unlikely that our policies did much at all to control the flow of drugs from Latin America.

As good as our intentions may be, our resources ~~had~~ *have* been and continue to be too limited to fight the war on drugs outside our borders. We should concentrate instead on using our resources to protect our borders and to stabilize our domestic situation.

CHAPTER REVIEW: EDITING PRACTICE

Reread the paragraph you wrote for the Paragraph Practice at the beginning of the chapter. Make sure you have used the present perfect and past perfect tenses correctly in your sentences. Also determine whether or not you need to add any of these verb forms to your sentences. If necessary, cross out any incorrect verb forms, and write your corrections above the line. When you have finished, do the same with a writing assignment you are currently working on.

CHAPTER REVIEW: COLLABORATIVE ACTIVITIES

1. Exchange Paragraph Practices with another student. Then, read each other's paragraphs, making sure present perfect and past perfect tenses are used correctly.
2. Working in a group of four students, choose an activity one of you wrote about in the Paragraph Practice for this chapter. Each member of the group should write a paragraph discussing his or her involvement with the activity. (The paragraphs may be serious or humorous.) Then, as a group, edit the paragraphs. After you have finished editing, choose the best paragraph, and read it to the class.

Review

- To form the past participle of regular verbs, add *-d* or *-ed* to the base form. (See 10A.)
- Irregular verbs usually have irregular past participles. (See 10B.)

　　　base form　　　*past*　　　*past participle*
　　　choose　　　　　chose　　　chosen

(continued on the following page)

(continued from previous page)

- The present perfect tense consists of the present tense of *have* plus the past participle. (See 10C.)

    I <u>have waited</u> in line for two hours.
    They <u>have</u> just <u>arrived</u> at the train station.

- The past perfect tense consists of the past tense of *have* plus the past participle. (See 10D.)

    The witness testified that she <u>had lived</u> in Los Angeles.

- The past participle can function as an **adjective**, a word that modifies a noun or pronoun. (See 10E.)

    I cleaned up the <u>broken</u> glass.
    Jason seemed <u>surprised</u>.

11 Present Participles and the Progressive Tenses

> **Overview**
>
> In this chapter you will learn
> - To understand the progressive tenses
> - To recognize present participles
> - To use the present progressive tense
> - To use the past progressive tense

PARAGRAPH PRACTICE

Write a paragraph in which you describe a typical scene in your house or dorm—eating a meal or watching a favorite television show, for example. Make sure you present events as if they are occurring as you write. ("My father is telling my brother to stop eating with his hands"; "We all are sitting in the living room waiting for *Days of Our Lives* to come on.") In addition, include transitional words and phrases, such as *then* and *after that*, that clearly relate one event to another. Use the blank space below for invention. Then, write your paragraph on the lines that follow.

CHAPTER 11 Present Participles and the Progressive Tenses — 209

A) RECOGNIZING PRESENT PARTICIPLES AND USING THE PRESENT PROGRESSIVE TENSE

A **present participle** is formed by adding *-ing* to the base form of the verb. When the base form ends in *e*, drop the *e* before adding *-ing*.

Base Form	Present Participle
grow	growing
merge	merging

The present participle is combined with a helping verb—a form of the verb *be*, in the appropriate tense—to form the *present progressive tense* or the *past progressive tense*.

The **present progressive tense** consists of the present tense of *be* plus the present participle.

> **The Present Progressive Tense**
> (*am*, *is*, or *are* + present participle)
>
> | Singular | Plural |
> |---|---|
> | I <u>am drawing</u>. | We <u>are drawing</u>. |
> | You <u>are drawing</u>. | You <u>are drawing</u>. |
> | He <u>is drawing</u>. | |
> | She <u>is drawing</u>. | They <u>are drawing</u>. |
> | It <u>is drawing</u>. | |

The present progressive tense shows that an action is in progress or that something will happen in the future.

> The rain forests <u>are being</u> destroyed. (They are still being destroyed.)
>
> We <u>are getting</u> our grades next Wednesday. (We will get our grades next Wednesday.)

▶ FOCUS ON THE PRESENT PROGRESSIVE TENSE ◀

Even though they may seem similar, the present tense and the present progressive tense express different meanings. Compare these uses:

present tense

> I <u>go</u> to the movies every Saturday night. (an action that occurs regularly)
>
> Mercury <u>is</u> the closest planet to the sun. (a scientific fact)

present progressive tense

> We <u>are waiting</u> for the bus. (an action in progress now)

Note: Both the present and present progressive tenses can describe an action that takes place in the future.

> The movie <u>opens</u> next week.
>
> The new mall <u>is opening</u> in a month.

See 8A for additional uses of the present tense.

CHAPTER 11 Present Participles and the Progressive Tenses • 211

> ▶ **FOCUS** ON SENTENCE FRAGMENTS ◀
>
> The present progressive tense must include a helping verb. If you accidentally leave out the helping verb, you create a sentence fragment.
>
> **fragment:** Fred <u>watching</u> a boat in the river.
> **correct:** Fred <u>is</u> <u>watching</u> a boat in the river.
>
> See 7B for more information on this type of fragment.

PRACTICE 11-1

Fill in the appropriate tense of the verb (present or present progressive) from the choices in parentheses.

Example: My neighbor ____runs____ early every morning unless it rains. (runs/is running)

1. At the moment I __am watching__ the Knicks game. (watch/am watching)

2. The doctor __is seeing__ a patient at the hospital now. (sees/is seeing)

3. He usually __sees__ patients at his office. (sees/is seeing)

4. Senator Williams __criticizes__ the administration every chance he gets. (criticizes/is criticizing)

5. She __is speaking__ on television right now. (speaks/is speaking)

6. She __is going__ to run for president one day. (goes/is going)

7. I always __believe__ anything I am told. (believe/am believing)

8. Unfortunately, now I __am suffering__ because of my trusting nature. (suffer/am suffering)

9. If you're looking for Bob, he __is working__ at home today. (works/is working)

10. Short hair __is becoming__ fashionable again. (becomes/is becoming)

PRACTICE 11-2

Edit the following passage for errors in the use of the present progressive tense. Cross out any underlined verbs that are incorrect, and write in the correct forms above them. If the verb form is correct, label it *C*. The first answer has been supplied for you.

(1) While Sonic the Hedgehog <u>is spinning</u> [*C*] his way across television screens, real hedgehogs <u>becoming</u> [*are becoming*] more and more popular as household pets. (2) Even though these odd creatures are covered with little spines, they still <u>finding</u> [*are finding*] a place in many people's homes. (3) Owners say they make excellent pets. (4) They are clean, they are quiet, and they <u>are requiring</u> [*require*] little care. (5) Because pet stores today <u>selling</u> [*are selling*] hedgehogs for $150 to $200, many owners <u>looking</u> [*are looking*] at their hedgehogs as an investment, and they <u>are gambling</u> [*C*] that hedgehogs are not just another fad, like potbellied pigs and ferrets. (6) Some experts <u>begin</u> [*are beginning*] to worry that once their novelty wears off, hedgehogs will be neglected. (7) They <u>advising</u> [*are advising*] potential buyers to think carefully before taking home a hedgehog.

•••••••••▶ **FLASHBACK** ◀•••••••••

Look back at your response to the Paragraph Practice at the beginning of the chapter. Underline the present progressive verbs. Then, list the helping verb (a form of *be*) and the present participle that make up each present progressive verb form on the lines below.

Helping Verb   **Present Participle**

_____   _____

_____   _____

(continued on the following page)

CHAPTER 11 Present Participles and the Progressive Tenses • 213

(continued from the previous page)

Helping Verb	Present Participle
_____	_____
_____	_____
_____	_____
_____	_____
_____	_____
_____	_____

B USING THE PAST PROGRESSIVE TENSE

The **past progressive tense** consists of the past tense of *be* plus the present participle.

The Past Progressive Tense
(*was* or *were* + present participle)

Singular	Plural
I was drawing.	We were drawing.
You were drawing.	You were drawing.
He was drawing.	
She was drawing.	They were drawing.
It was drawing.	

The past progressive tense describes an action that took place over a specific period of time in the past. It is often used along with the words *when*, *as*, or *while* to describe two actions that occurred at the same time.

I was reading when the burglar alarm went off.
They were watching as the police pulled into the yard.
While Alicia was sleeping, the police broke down her door.

> ### ▶ FOCUS ON THE PAST PROGRESSIVE TENSE ◀
>
> Even though they may appear to be similar, the past and the past progressive tenses express different meanings.
>
> **past tense**
> The defense <u>used</u> DNA evidence. (an action completed in the past)
>
> **past progressive tense**
> As the defendant testified, the jury <u>was looking</u> at him intently. (an action that took place over a specific period of time in the past)

PRACTICE 11-3

Fill in the appropriate tense of the verb (past or past progressive) from the choices in parentheses.

Example: Last spring, as the neighbors grew more fearful, robberies *were occurring* nearly every day. (occurred/were occurring)

1. The clerk at the shoe store *was emptying* the cash register when a suspicious customer entered. (emptied/was emptying)

2. After he pulled out a gun, she *emptied* the cash into his bag. (emptied/was emptying)

3. Two police officers *were patrolling* the block when the report came in. (patrolled/were patrolling)

4. As they entered the store, the clerk *was telling* a coworker what had happened. (told/was telling)

5. She *repeated* her story to the officers. (repeated/was repeating)

6. She *was getting* ready to close as the robbery occurred. (got/was getting)

CHAPTER 11 Present Participles and the Progressive Tenses • 215

7. The robber ___pulled___ a gun, but no one was hurt. (pulled/was pulling)

8. When he escaped with the money, he _was wearing_ a green jacket, a blue baseball cap, and dark pants. (wore/was wearing)

9. Now that it was over, the clerk just ___wanted___ to go home. (wanted/was wanting)

10. She said she _was beginning_ to think she should find another job. (began/was beginning)

▶ FLASHBACK ◀

Look back at the previous Flashback where you listed present progressive verbs from your Paragraph Practice. Copy the present progressive verb forms in the left-hand column below. Then rewrite them as past progressive verb forms in the right-hand column.

Present Progressive	Past Progressive
_____	_____
_____	_____
_____	_____
_____	_____
_____	_____
_____	_____
_____	_____

216 • UNIT 5 Understanding Verbs

REVIEW

CHAPTER REVIEW: STUDENT WRITING

Read the following student passage, in which errors in the use of the present and past progressive tenses have been introduced. Decide whether or not each of the underlined verbs or participles is correct. If it is, write *C* above it. If it is not, cross it out and write in the correct verb. The first error has been corrected for you.

Making the Team

"Five feet two inches and one hundred three pounds?" asked my coach.

I ~~was stammering~~ *stammered* "Yes, sir."

"You've got to put some meat on those bones," he barked. "If you ~~going~~ *are going* to try out for the college hockey team, you'll have to put on at least fifteen pounds."

That did it. I knew what I ~~was having~~ *had* to do. My mother was the first person to notice that something was changing. *C*

"You hardly ever used to finish your dinner," she said one evening at the dinner table. "Now, you eat all the time. *C* You ~~eat~~ *are eating* us out of house and home."

"That's fine," I said, "but am I gaining weight?"

"I hope you ~~feeling~~ *are feeling* all right," was her only response.

I ~~was realizing~~ *realized* that she was right. I was downing *C* gallons of chocolate shakes, piles of Italian hoagies, and mounds of fries. In fact, I ~~consuming~~ *was consuming* more food in one day than I used to in a week. Many times while I was sitting at the dinner table, shoveling food into my mouth, my brothers

CHAPTER 11 Present Participles and the Progressive Tenses • 217

~~were making~~ *made* sarcastic comments like "Do you think you ~~get~~ *are getting* enough to eat?"

　　Finally, the day came for the hockey team weigh-in. At 9 A.M. I was waiting *C* in line for my turn to step on the scale. After almost four months of gorging myself, I ~~going~~ *was going* to see the payoff. As I ~~was stepping~~ *stepped* on the scale, I was smiling confidently. Then, to my surprise and shock, I heard the coach say, "Brian, I ~~was telling~~ *told* you to gain some weight, not to put on thirty pounds. To make the team, you are going *C* to have to lose at least ten pounds!"

CHAPTER REVIEW: EDITING PRACTICE

　　Reread your response to the Paragraph Practice at the beginning of the chapter. Make sure you have used the correct verb tenses in your sentences. If necessary, cross out the incorrect verb forms, and rewrite your corrections above the line. Check to make sure every progressive verb form includes a helping verb and add helping verbs as necessary to correct sentence fragments. When you have finished, do the same for another of your Paragraph Practice responses or for an assignment you are currently working on.

CHAPTER REVIEW: COLLABORATIVE ACTIVITIES

1. Working in a group of four students, list ten nouns. Then, write five sentences, using two different nouns from the list in each. Make sure that each sentence contains at least one verb in a progressive tense.
2. Working with members of the same group, choose one of the sentences you wrote for Collaborative Activity 1. Develop the ideas in this sentence into a paragraph. Make sure you use both the present progressive and the past progressive tenses in the paragraph.
3. Exchange paragraphs with another group. Read the other group's paragraph to make sure that the progressive tenses are used correctly. Edit the paragraph to correct any errors you find. Then, try to add a sentence or two to the paragraph to make it more interesting. Finally, add any necessary transitions.

Review

- A present participle is formed by adding *-ing* to the base form of the verb. (See 11A.)
- The present progressive tense consists of the present tense of *be* plus the present participle. (See 11A.)

    I am drawing.
    They are drawing.

- The past progressive tense consists of the past tense of *be* plus the present participle. (See 11B.)

    I was drawing.
    They were drawing.

Unit 5 Review

The collaborative activities, writing practice topics, and student writing sample that follow provide opportunities for you to review what you have learned in Chapters 9 through 11.

COLLABORATIVE ACTIVITIES

1. Form groups of five students. Assume that the president of your school has asked your group to design a logo. He or she especially wants a symbol that will convey the history and current strengths of your school. Draw the logo, and write a paragraph that explains its significance. In particular, discuss how the new logo reflects your school's past and how your school is changing today.
2. Exchange logos and paragraphs with another group. This time, assume your group works in the admissions office. Read the other group's paragraph, and then write an evaluation of the group's logo. Make sure your group's evaluation discusses the logo's strengths and weaknesses and why you believe it will (or will not) effectively convey the image of the school to prospective students.
3. Make a list of four or five books that all members of your group have read. Then, imagine that an organization is pressuring the public library to remove these books because they think they are subversive. Write a letter to a local newspaper defending these books. Be sure to discuss how the ideas in these books have affected your views of the world in a positive way.

WRITING PRACTICE

1. Imagine your ideal job: social director of a cruise ship, guide at a national park, or assistant to the president of MTV, for example. Then, write a letter applying for this job. Begin by identifying the position for which you are applying. Then, describe your unique qualifications for this job. Remember that your prospective employer is particularly interested in you as an individual. For this reason, you should describe any experiences you think will identify you as the kind of person he or she is looking for.
2. Write an essay in which you discuss how television portrays people in your age group. Do you think the portrayals are accurate, or do you think they distort reality? Be sure to refer to specific shows and to compare situations they portray with some of your own experiences.

220 · UNIT 5 Review

3. What do you think your school could do to improve student life on your campus? Write an editorial for your school paper in which you identify some areas that you believe need improvement. Then, present your specific recommendations for improvements.

STUDENT WRITING

Read the following student passage, in which errors in the use of verb forms have been introduced. Decide whether or not each of the underlined verb forms is correct. If the form is correct, write *C* above it. If it is not, cross it out, and correct it in the space above the line. The first error has been corrected for you.

My Brother's Wedding

"Do you think now is a good time to call it off?" my brother ~~sayed~~ [*said*] jokingly as we adjusted [*C*] our bow ties and ~~taken~~ [*took*] our cummerbunds off their hangers. In only a few hours, a single event would change [*C*] our lives dramatically. As I watched us fumble with our cuff links and comb our hair, I ~~was realizing~~ [*realized*] that time had cheated [*C*] us. "Everything ~~happening~~ [*is happening*] too fast," I thought to myself. In the months before the wedding day, I ~~passed~~ [*had passed*] some real milestones, including camping alone in the mountains for the first time and catching a home-run ball at a professional game. These events, however, ~~can~~ [*could*] hardly compare with seeing my brother get married.

My brother is ten years older than I am. Like most people of his generation, he ~~grown~~ [*grew*] up listening to Led Zeppelin, following the events of the war in Vietnam, and watching the Flyers win back-to-back Stanley Cups. In high school he met [*C*] Molly, and he ~~realize~~ [*realized*] then that someday they

~~will~~ *would* be married. Now, eight years later, the moment ~~had arrive~~ *had arrived*.

For years, our parents have seen [C] my brother and me as opposites, and in many ways we are. What ~~brung~~ *brought* us together and kept [C] us close, though, were the countless Sundays we spent cheering for our favorite football teams, the many concerts and parties we attended, and the memories of seventeen years ~~spended~~ *spent* growing up in the same household.

In the weeks before the wedding, I often thought [C] about the changes that ~~will~~ *would* take place. First, I realized that my brother would move [C] out of the house, and since he would be living far away, I ~~will~~ *would* only be able to see him once a week. His best friend would now be his girlfriend of eight years, not his brother.

After the wedding I ~~was thinking~~ *thought* often about how quickly life moves. After that day's events I ~~begun~~ *began* to see that life is constantly changing. Soon, I knew, I would start [C] college and set out on my own voyage of maturity. My brother's wedding became a greater milestone in my life than any I ~~have~~ *had* reached before. It ~~allow~~ *allowed* me to remember the good times my family ~~had~~ *had had* throughout our lives and how quickly the years had passed. I also realized that just as time ~~has~~ *had* cheated us, we had cheated time. My brother and I had ~~did~~ *done* a lot in our seventeen years together, and I knew that in the future we ~~can~~ *could* create many more new memories together.

12 Combining Sentences with Coordination

> **Overview**
>
> In this chapter you will learn
> - To form compound sentences with coordinating conjunctions
> - To form compound sentences with semicolons
> - To form compound sentences with semicolons and conjunctive adverbs

PARAGRAPH PRACTICE

Imagine you have invented a new product, such as Velcro, the zipper, aluminum foil, Scotch tape, the safety pin, the paper clip, the rubber band, or Styrofoam. Write a paragraph in which you define the product, describe what it looks like, and give examples of its possible uses to an audience who has never heard of it before. Use the blank space below for invention. Then, write your paragraph on the lines that follow.

CHAPTER 12   Combining Sentences with Coordination   ▪   223

_____
_____
_____
_____
_____
_____
_____
_____
_____
_____
_____

A USING COORDINATING CONJUNCTIONS TO FORM COMPOUND SENTENCES

A simple sentence includes a subject and a verb.

European <u>immigrants arrived</u> at Ellis Island.
Asian <u>immigrants arrived</u> at Angel Island.

Two simple sentences can be joined into one **compound sentence** with a **coordinating conjunction**.

Coordinating Conjunctions			
and	or	for	yet
but	nor	so	

In the following example, the two simple sentences are joined with the coordinating conjunction *but*:

European immigrants arrived at Ellis Island, <u>but</u> Asian immigrants arrived at Angel Island.

You can often make your writing more interesting and more precise than it might otherwise be by combining two short sentences with a coordinating conjunction and creating a compound sentence. To do so, you must first understand how each of the seven coordinating conjunctions works to connect ideas.

- If you want to indicate addition, use *and*.
    He acts like a child, <u>and</u> people think he is cute.

- If you want to indicate contrast or contradiction, use *but* or *yet*.
    He acts like a child, <u>but</u> he is an adult.
    He acts like a child, <u>yet</u> he longs to be taken seriously.

- If you want to indicate a cause-effect relationship, use *so* or *for*.
    He acts like a child, <u>so</u> we treat him like one.
    He acts like a child, <u>for</u> he craves attention.

- If you want to present choices, use *or*.
    He acts like a child, <u>or</u> he is ignored.

- If you want to eliminate choices, use *nor*.
    He does not act like a child, <u>nor</u> does he look like one.

> ▶ **FOCUS** ON PUNCTUATING WITH ◀
> **COORDINATING CONJUNCTIONS**
>
> When you use a coordinating conjunction to link two short sentences into a single compound sentence, always put a comma before the coordinating conjunction.
> Either we will stand in line all night, or we will go home now.

PRACTICE 12-1

Fill in the coordinating conjunction—*and*, *but*, *or*, *nor*, *for*, *so*, or *yet*—that most logically links the two parts of each compound sentence. Remember to insert a comma before each coordinating conjunction.

Example: Fairy tales have been told by many people around the world, <u>but</u> the stories by two German brothers may be the most famous.

(1) Jakob and Wilhelm Grimm lived in the nineteenth century, <u>and</u> they wrote many well-known fairy tales. (2) Most people think fondly of fairy tales, <u>but/yet</u> the Brothers Grimm wrote many unpleasant and violent

CHAPTER 12 Combining Sentences with Coordination • 225

stories. (3) In their best-known works, children are abused, _and_ endings are not always happy. (4) Either innocent children are brutally punished for no reason, _or_ they are neglected. (5) For example, in "Hansel and Gretel" the stepmother mistreats the children, _and_ their father abandons them in the woods. (6) In this story, the events are horrifying, _but/yet_ the ending is still happy. (7) The children outwit the evil adults, _so_ they escape unharmed. (8) Apparently, they are not injured physically, _nor_ are they harmed emotionally. (9) Nevertheless, their story can hardly be called pleasant, _for_ it remains a story of child abuse and neglect.

PRACTICE 12-2

Pair each of the short sentences in the left-hand column with a sentence in the right-hand column to create ten compound sentences. Write these sentences on the lines below, using as many different coordinating conjunctions as you can to connect ideas. Be sure each coordinating conjunction you choose conveys the appropriate relationship between ideas, and remember to put a comma before each one. You may use some of the listed sentences more than once. Note: Many different combinations—some serious and factually accurate, some humorous—are possible.

Answers will vary.

Some dogs wear little sweaters.	Many are named Hamlet.
Pit bulls are raised to fight.	They have strange sexual habits.
Bonobos are pygmy chimpanzees.	One even sings Christmas carols.
Many people fear Dobermans.	They can wear bandanas.
Leopards have spots.	They can play frisbee.
Dalmations can live in firehouses.	Many live in equatorial Zaire.
Horses can wear blankets.	Some people think they are gentle.
All mules are sterile.	They don't get cold in winter.
Great Danes are huge dogs.	They are half horse and half donkey.
Parrots can often speak.	They can be unpredictable.

1. _____

_____

2. _____

_____

3. _____

_____

4. _____
_____

5. _____
_____

6. _____
_____

7. _____
_____

8. _____
_____

9. _____
_____

10. _____
_____

PRACTICE 12-3

Some of the sentences in the passage that follows would be clearer and more effective if they were connected to other sentences. Wherever you think it is necessary, combine sentences with coordinating conjunctions to make the relationship of one idea to another clear. Do not forget to put a comma before each coordinating conjunction you add. The first sentence has been corrected for you.

Other answers may be acceptable.

(1) A centenarian is a man or woman who is at least one hundred years old, and today (2) ~~Today,~~ over thirty-two thousand centenarians are alive in the United States. (3) Most people assume that diet, exercise, and family history account for their long lives, but this (4) ~~This~~ is not necessarily true. (5) Recently, a study was conducted in Georgia that showed surprising common threads among centenarians. (6) They did not necessarily avoid tobacco and alcohol, and they (7) ~~They~~ did not eat low-fat diets. (8) In fact, they ate relatively large

CHAPTER 12 Combining Sentences with Coordination • 227

amounts of fat, cholesterol, and sugar, (9) ~~Diet~~ *so diet* could not explain their long lives. (10) They did, however, share four key survival characteristics. (11) First, all of the centenarians were optimistic about life, (12) ~~All~~ *and all* of them were positive thinkers. (13) They were also involved in religious life and had deep religious faith. (14) In addition, all the centenarians had continued to lead physically active lives, (15) ~~They~~ *and they* remained mobile even as elderly people. (16) Finally, all were able to adapt to loss. (17) They had all experienced the deaths of friends, spouses, and children, (18) ~~They~~ *yet they* were able to get on with their lives. (19) Deaths of loved ones could have depressed them, (20) ~~These~~ *or these* losses could have left them physically weakened. (21) However, they coped unusually well with their losses. (22) Researchers concluded that all the centenarians remained satisfied with their lives, (23) ~~They~~ *for they* saw absolutely no signs of depression in these elderly people.

▶ **FLASHBACK** ◀

Reread your response to the Paragraph Practice at the beginning of the chapter. If you see any compound sentences, bracket them. If you see any pairs of simple sentences that could be combined, rewrite them on the lines below, joining them with appropriate coordinating conjunctions to create compound sentences.

1. _____

2. _____

3. _____

Be sure that each of your compound sentences includes a comma before the coordinating conjunction.

B   USING SEMICOLONS TO FORM COMPOUND SENTENCES

You can also use a **semicolon** to join two simple sentences into one compound sentence.

> The AIDS quilt contains thousands of panels; each panel is shaped like a coffin.

Between two sentences, a semicolon serves the same function as a comma followed by a coordinating conjunction.

> The AIDS quilt contains thousands of panels, and each panel is shaped like a coffin. (comma plus coordinating conjunction)
> The AIDS quilt contains thousands of panels; each panel is shaped like a coffin. (semicolon)

However, a semicolon is not always interchangeable with a coordinating conjunction plus a comma. A semicolon generally indicates a stronger, more forceful link between ideas than a comma followed by a coordinating conjunction does.

▶ **FOCUS** ON USING SEMICOLONS TO JOIN SENTENCES ◀

Remember that a semicolon can only join two *complete* sentences. A semicolon cannot join a sentence and a fragment.

                           ─── Fragment ───
Incorrect: Because thousands are dying of AIDS; more research is clearly needed.
Correct: Because thousands are dying of AIDS, more research is clearly needed.

For more information on sentence fragments, see Chapter 7.

PRACTICE 12-4

Each of the short sentences below can be linked by a semicolon to another short sentence to form a compound sentence. In each case, add a semicolon, and complete the compound sentence with another short sentence.

Example: My brother is addicted to fast food; _he eats it every day._
Answers will vary.

1. Fast-food restaurants have become an American institution _____

   _____

2. Families eat at these restaurants _____

   _____

CHAPTER 12   Combining Sentences with Coordination   •   229

3. Many teenagers work there _____
   _____

4. McDonald's is known for its hamburgers _____
   _____

5. KFC is famous for its fried chicken _____
   _____

6. Taco Bell serves Mexican-style food _____
   _____

7. Pizza Hut specializes in pizza _____
   _____

8. Many fast-food restaurants offer some low-fat menu items _____
   _____

9. Some offer recyclable packaging _____
   _____

10. Some even have playgrounds _____
    _____

▶ FLASHBACK ◀

Review your response to the Paragraph Practice at the beginning of the chapter. Do you see any simple sentences that you could connect with semicolons? If so, rewrite these sentences on the lines below, linking them with semicolons. Be sure your semicolons connect two complete sentences.

_____
_____
_____
_____

C USING SEMICOLONS AND CONJUNCTIVE ADVERBS TO FORM COMPOUND SENTENCES

Another way to combine short sentences is with a semicolon and a **conjunctive adverb**, a transitional word such as *however*, *then*, or *therefore*.

Some college students receive grants; however, others must take out loans.

Notice that the semicolon comes before the conjunctive adverb *however* and that a comma follows it.

Commonly Used Conjunctive Adverbs

also,	instead,	still,
besides,	meanwhile,	then,
consequently,	moreover,	therefore,
furthermore,	nevertheless,	thus,
however,	otherwise,	

The addition of a conjunctive adverb makes a sentence more precise than it would be with a semicolon alone. Because different conjunctive adverbs convey different meanings, you should use the one that best conveys the relationship between the sentences it joins.

- Some conjunctive adverbs signal addition (*also, besides, furthermore, moreover*).

    I have a lot on my mind; also, I have a lot of things to do.

- Some conjunctive adverbs make causal connections (*therefore, consequently, thus*).

    I have a lot on my mind; therefore, I need to concentrate.

- Some conjunctive adverbs indicate contradiction or contrast (*nevertheless, however, still*).

    I have a lot on my mind; nevertheless, I must try to relax.

- Some conjunctive adverbs present alternatives.

    I have a lot on my mind; otherwise, I could relax.
    I will try not to think; instead, I will relax.

- Some conjunctive adverbs convey time sequence.

    I have a lot on my mind; meanwhile, I still have work to do.
    I will relax for an hour; then, I will go to work.

> ### ▶ FOCUS ON TRANSITIONAL EXPRESSIONS ◀
>
> Like conjunctive adverbs, **transitional expressions** can also link two simple sentences into one compound sentence.
>
> He had a miserable time at the party; in addition, he drank too much.
>
> Notice that the transitional expression is preceded by a semicolon and followed by a comma.
>
> **Commonly Used Transitional Expressions**
>
> as a result,   in comparison,
> at the same time,   in fact,
> for example,   on the contrary,
> for instance,   on the other hand,
> in addition,   that is,

PRACTICE 12-5

Add semicolons and commas where required with conjunctive adverbs and transitional expressions. The first sentence has been corrected for you.

(1) The United States has a long history of disastrous fires; in addition, it has a long history of innovations in fire safety. (2) A major fire destroyed much of Boston in 1653; as a result, each house was required to have a ladder and a fire bucket. (3) City governments became more concerned about fires; therefore, volunteer fire companies were started in the mid–eighteenth century. (4) Fire hydrants were installed in Boston, Philadelphia, and New York in the early nineteenth century; however, hydrants sometimes froze. (5) Other innovations were clearly needed; consequently, fire alarm boxes and steam-powered fire engines were developed. (6) These developments helped; nevertheless, fires of disastrous proportions still plagued American cities.

PRACTICE 12-6

Consulting the lists on page 230 and above, choose a conjunctive adverb or transitional expression that can logically connect each pair of sentences below into one compound sentence. Be sure to use punctuation and capital letters appropriately.

Example: Every year since 1927, *Time* has designated a Man of the Year, ~~;The~~ *however, the* Man of the Year has not always been a man.

Other answers may be acceptable.

1. *Time* selects the Man of the Year to honor the person who has most influenced the previous year's events, ~~;The~~ *consequently, the* choice is often a prominent politician.

2. In the 1920s and 1930s, world leaders were often chosen; *for example,* Franklin Delano Roosevelt was chosen twice and Ethiopia's Haile Selassie once.

3. In 1936, the Man of the Year was not a head of state; ~~It~~ *instead, it* was Wallis Warfield Simpson, the woman for whom King Edward VIII of England abdicated the throne.

4. During the war years, Hitler, Stalin, Churchill, and Roosevelt were all chosen; *moreover,* Stalin was featured twice.

5. Occasionally the Man of the Year was not an individual; ~~In~~ *for instance, in* 1950 it was The American Fighting Man.

6. In 1956, The Hungarian Freedom Fighter was Man of the Year; ~~In~~ *in addition, in* 1966, *Time* editors chose The Young Generation.

7. Only a few individual women have been selected; *however,* Queen Elizabeth II was featured in 1952 and Corazon Aquino in 1986.

8. In 1975, American Women were honored as a group; ~~The~~ *still, the* Man of the Year has nearly always been male.

9. Very few people of color have been designated Man of the Year; *nevertheless,* Martin Luther King, Jr., was honored in 1963.

10. The Man of the Year has almost always been one or more human beings; ~~The~~ *however, the* Computer was selected in 1982 and Endangered Earth in 1988.

PRACTICE 12-7

Using the specified topics and conjunctive adverbs or transitional expressions, create five compound sentences. Be sure to punctuate appropriately.

Example:
Topic: fad diets
Transitional expression: for example

People are always falling for fad diets; for example, some people eat only pineapple to lose weight.

1. Topic: laws to protect people with disabilities
   Transitional expression: in addition

   _____
   _____

2. Topic: gay men and lesbians as adoptive parents
   Conjunctive adverb: however

   _____
   _____

3. Topic: prayer in public schools
   Conjunctive adverb: therefore

   _____
   _____

4. Topic: high school proms
   Conjunctive adverb: also

   _____
   _____

5. Topic: course requirements at your school
   Conjunctive adverb: instead

   _____
   _____

> **FLASHBACK**
>
> Reread your response to the Paragraph Practice at the beginning of the chapter. Have you used any conjunctive adverbs or transitional expressions to link sentences? If so, check to make sure that you have punctuated them correctly and that you haven't incorrectly joined any fragments to sentences. Next, check to see that you have used the conjunctive adverb or transitional expression that best expresses the relationship between the ideas in the two sentences. Finally, on the lines below, try rewriting one or two of these compound sentences, experimenting with different conjunctive adverbs or transitional expressions.
>
> _____
>
> _____
>
> _____
>
> _____

• • • • • • • • • • • • • • **REVIEW** • • • • • • • • • • • • • •

CHAPTER REVIEW: STUDENT WRITING

Read the student passage below. Then, revise it by linking pairs of sentences together with a coordinating conjunction, a semicolon, or a conjunctive adverb or transitional expression. Do not forget to put commas before coordinating conjunctions and to use semicolons and commas correctly with conjunctive adverbs. The revision should be a smoothly written passage that connects ideas clearly and logically. The first two sentences have been combined for you.

Other answers may be acceptable.

My Father's Life

My grandparents were born in the Ukraine/ ~~They~~ , but they raised my father in western Pennsylvania. The ninth of their ten children, he had a life I cannot begin to imagine. To me, he is my big, strong, powerful Daddy/ ;~~In~~ *in* reality, he is a child of poverty.

My grandfather worked for the American Car Foundry. The family lived in a company house/, ~~They~~ *and they* shopped at the company store. In 1934, he was laid off/ ; ~~He~~ *then, he* went to work for the government digging sewer lines. At that time, the family was on relief. Every week they were entitled to get food rations/, ~~My~~ *so my* father would go to pick up the food. They desperately needed the prunes, beans, flour, margarine, and other things.

For years my father wore his brothers' hand-me-down clothes/ ; ~~He~~ *in addition, he* wore thrift-shop shoes with cardboard over the holes in the soles. He was often hungry/, ~~He~~ *so he* would sometimes sit by the side of the railroad tracks, waiting for the engineer to throw him an orange. My father would do any job to earn a quarter. Once, for example, he weeded a mile-long row of tomato plants/ ~~He~~ *, and he* was paid twenty-five cents and a pack of Necco wafers. (Twenty-five cents was a lot of money during the Depression.)

My father saved his pennies/ ~~E~~*, and* eventually he was able to buy a used bicycle for two dollars. He dropped out of school at fourteen and got a job/ ~~The~~ *, for the* family badly needed his income. He woke up every day at 4 a.m. and rode his bike to his job at a meatpacking plant/ ; ~~He~~ *then, he* peeled hot dogs for fifty cents a day.

In 1943, at the age of seventeen, my father joined the

Navy/ ~~He~~ *, and he* discovered a new world. For the first time in his life, he had enough to eat. He was always first in line at the mess hall/ ~~He~~ *; moreover, he* went back for seconds and thirds before anyone else. After the war ended in 1945, he was discharged from the Navy. He went to work in a meat market in New York City/ ~~The~~ *; the* only trade he knew was the meat business. Three years later, he had saved enough to open his own store, Pete's Quality Meats.

CHAPTER REVIEW: EDITING PRACTICE

Reread your response to the Paragraph Practice at the beginning of this chapter. Underline each compound sentence you find. Have you used the coordinating conjunction, conjunctive adverb, or transitional expression that best conveys your meaning? Have you punctuated these sentences correctly? Also, look for other sentences that you could combine using one of the methods of coordination discussed in this chapter. Edit your paragraph for clarity and correctness. When you have finished, look over a piece of writing you have done in response to another assignment, and try connecting some simple sentences with coordination.

CHAPTER REVIEW: COLLABORATIVE ACTIVITIES

1. Work in a group of three or four students to create a cast of characters for a movie, a television pilot, or a music video. First, working individually, write five brief descriptive sentences—one about each of five different characters. Then, exchange papers with another student, and use coordinating conjunctions to build new sentences from the sentences on his or her list.

    Example:
    Original sentence: Mark is a handsome heartthrob.
    New sentence: Mark is a handsome heartthrob, but he has green dreadlocks.

    Next, narrow down the list of characters your group has created to those who sound most interesting. Write additional descriptive sentences about those, using coordination to link sentences whenever possible. Your new sentences can provide information about the characters' relationships with one another as well as about their personalities and physical appearances.

2. Decide as a class on a controversial issue to serve as the focus of this exercise. Then, form groups of four students, with two on each side of the issue. Each pair of students should prepare a list of points to support their position (pro or con) on the issue. Then, the two pairs of students in each group should work together to join their opposing points with semicolons and appropriate conjunctive adverbs or transitional expressions to create as many compound sentences as possible.

   Example:
   Controversial issue: Gun control
   Pro: Gun control can reduce the number of accidents involving children.
   Con: Gun control can limit citizens' ability to defend themselves in their homes.
   Compound sentence: Gun control can reduce the number of accidents involving children; however, it can also limit citizens' ability to defend themselves in their homes.
   Compound sentence: Gun control can limit citizens' ability to defend themselves in their homes; however, it can also reduce the number of accidents involving children.

   Working in your original groups of four, select your group's five best compound sentences. Designate a secretary, and have that person write these sentences on the board. Work collaboratively as a class to select those compound sentences that present the most provocative pairs of opposing points, eliminating any overlaps or repetition among the sentences. When you have narrowed the sentences down to the most interesting, edit the remaining sentences carefully, paying particular attention to the suitability of the conjunctive adverbs and transitional expressions that have been selected.

   In class discussion, use the sentences that remain on the board to help you reach a consensus about the controversial issue. Can the class agree on a single position?

Review

- A compound sentence is made up of two parts, each with a subject and a verb. (See 12A.)

    European immigrants arrived at Ellis Island, <u>but</u> Asian immigrants arrived at Angel Island.

- A coordinating conjunction—*and, but, or, nor, for, so,* or *yet*—can join the two parts of a compound sentence. A comma always comes before the coordinating conjunction used to join the two parts of a compound sentence. (See 12A.)

    He acts like a child, <u>so</u> we treat him like one.

    (continued on the following page)

(continued from previous page)

- A semicolon can join two complete sentences into one compound sentence. (See 12B.)

    The AIDS quilt contains thousands of panels; each panel is shaped like a coffin.

- A conjunctive adverb or transitional expression can also join two complete sentences into one compound sentence. When it joins two sentences, a conjunctive adverb or transitional expression is always preceded by a semicolon and followed by a comma. (See 12C.)

    Some college students receive grants; <u>however</u>, others must take out loans.

13 Combining Sentences with Subordination

Overview

In this chapter you will learn
- To understand how subordinating conjunctions are used to create complex sentences
- To punctuate sentences with subordinating conjunctions
- To correct fragments created by subordinating conjunctions
- To understand how relative pronouns are used to create complex sentences
- To correct fragments created by relative pronouns
- To recognize and correctly punctuate restrictive and nonrestrictive clauses introduced by relative pronouns

PARAGRAPH PRACTICE

Write a paragraph in which you describe something that you believe needs to be changed. You could, for example, discuss a rule, a law, a policy, a situation, or a custom. In your topic sentence, identify what you think needs to be changed, and explain why you think a change is necessary. Then, support your position with specific examples. Use the blank space below for invention. Then, write your paragraph on the lines that follow.

A USING SUBORDINATING CONJUNCTIONS TO FORM COMPLEX SENTENCES

A **clause** is a group of words that contains a subject and a verb. An **independent clause** can stand alone as a sentence:

> The French sculptor Auguste Rodin caused a great deal of controversy.

A **dependent clause** is a fragment that cannot stand alone:

> Because his nude figures shocked the sensibilities of many viewers.

When an independent clause is joined with a dependent clause, the result is a **complex sentence:**

> The French sculptor Auguste Rodin caused a great deal of controversy because his nude figures shocked the sensibilities of many viewers.

As you combine sentences, you should keep in mind that the idea expressed in one sentence may be more important than the idea in another, and that one idea may be dependent on another for its meaning. In such cases, **subordinating conjunctions**—words like *although* and *because*—may be used to join the two sentences into one complex sentence and to clarify the relationship between them.

Two sentences

The French sculptor Auguste Rodin caused a great deal of contro-

CHAPTER 13 Combining Sentences with Subordination · 241

versy. His nude figures shocked the sensibilities of many viewers.

Combined (complex sentence)

The French sculptor Auguste Rodin caused a great deal of controversy <u>because</u> his nude figures shocked the sensibilities of many viewers.

Different subordinating conjunctions express different relationships.

Relationship between clauses	Subordinating conjunction	Example
Time	after, before, since, until, when, whenever, while	<u>When the whale surfaced,</u> Ahab threw his harpoon.
Reason or Cause	as, because	Scientists have to scale back the project <u>because of cutbacks in government spending.</u>
Result or Effect	in order to, so, so that	<u>In order to improve students' math scores,</u> many schools have instituted special programs.
Condition	if, even if, unless	The rain forest could disappear by the end of the century <u>unless steps are taken immediately.</u>
Contrast	although, even though, though	<u>Although Edison had almost no formal education,</u> he was one of the most productive inventors of his time.
Location	where, wherever	Pittsburgh was built <u>where the Allegheny and Monongahela Rivers meet.</u>

> ▶ **FOCUS** ON PUNCTUATING WITH ◀
> **SUBORDINATING CONJUNCTIONS**
>
> Always place a comma after the dependent clause when it comes *before* the independent clause in the sentence. Do not use a comma when the dependent clause comes *after* the independent idea in the sentence.
>
> *(continued on the following page)*

> ─── Dependent clause ─── ─ Independent clause ─
> <u>Although</u> she wore the scarlet letter, Hester carried herself proudly.
>
> ─ Independent clause ─ ─── Dependent clause ───
> Hester carried herself proudly <u>although</u> she wore the scarlet letter.

▶ FOCUS ON CORRECTING FRAGMENTS CREATED ◀ BY SUBORDINATING CONJUNCTIONS

A clause that begins with a subordinating conjunction is a dependent clause and does not express a complete thought. It is, therefore, a fragment (see 7C). You can generally correct fragments created by subordinating conjunctions by connecting the fragment to a sentence (an independent clause) that comes before it.

Fragment: Diplomat Alger Hiss always insisted on his innocence. <u>Even though he was convicted of perjury.</u>

Correct: Diplomat Alger Hiss always insisted on his innocence even though he was convicted of perjury.

You can also eliminate the subordinating conjunction and create a complete sentence, but if you choose this option, be sure that deleting the subordinating conjunction does not obscure the connection between two ideas or create a pair of short, choppy sentences.

PRACTICE 13-1

Fill in an appropriate subordinating conjunction in each blank in the sentences below. Look at the list of subordinating conjunctions on page 241 to make sure you choose one that establishes the proper relationship between ideas. (Note that the required punctuation has been provided.) The first answer has been supplied for you.

Other answers may be acceptable.

(1) Eugene V. Debs, the son of Alsatian immigrants, grew up in Terre Haute, Indiana, __*where*__ he was born in 1855. (2) __*After*__ he left

CHAPTER 13 Combining Sentences with Subordination • 243

school at age fourteen, he held various jobs for the railroad. (3) _Because_ he was intelligent and hardworking, he became the grand secretary of the Brotherhood of Locomotive Firemen. (4) By 1877, Debs had become interested in the social conditions of railroad workers. (5) _While_ he had once defended the union, Debs now criticized its policies. (6) He believed the union only served the interests of some workers. (7) _Although_ he did not have much money, he resigned his position with the union and formed the American Railway Union (ARU). (8) The ARU grew rapidly _before_ it went on strike against the Pullman Company. (9) _Because_ violence occurred during the strike, Debs went to jail for six months. (10) Debs had always supported the Democratic Party _until_ he organized the Social Democratic Party of America in 1897. (11) In 1898 it merged with the Socialist Labor Party of America. (12) Debs was nominated as the Socialist Labor Party's presidential candidate five times. (13) _When_ he completed a difficult campaign in 1912, he received 900,000 votes (6 percent of the total), the largest vote ever for a socialist presidential candidate. (14) Debs remained a popular labor leader his entire life _even though_ he was jailed for giving a speech denouncing America's entry into World War I.

PRACTICE 13-2

Combine each of the following pairs of sentences, using a subordinating conjunction to clarify the relationship between the dependent and independent clauses in each sentence. Make sure you include a comma where one is required.

Example: Orville and Wilbur Wright built the first powered plane, ~~They~~ _although they_ had no formal training as engineers.

Other answers may be acceptable.

1. ~~Professional~~ _Although professional_ midwives are used widely in Europe, ~~In~~ _in_ the United States they usually practice in areas where there are few doctors.

244 ■ UNIT 6 Building Sentences

2. ~~John~~ *When* John Deere constructed his first steel plow in 1837~~,~~ *a* ~~A~~ new era began in prairie agriculture.

3. Stephen Crane powerfully describes battles in *The Red Badge of Courage,* ~~He~~ *even though he* never experienced a war.

4. Mary Baker Eddy was sick for many years, *before she* ~~She~~ founded the Christian Science movement.

5. *After* Jonas Salk developed the first polio vaccine in the 1950s, ~~The~~ *the* incidence of polio began to decline rapidly in the United States.

6. ~~The~~ *When the* salaries of baseball players rose dramatically in the 1980s, ~~Some~~ *some* sportswriters predicted that fans would stop attending games.

7. ~~The~~ *Before the* gunpowder manufacturers, the Du Ponts, arrived in Rhode Island from France in 1800, American gunpowder was expensive and inferior to the kind manufactured by the French.

8. *After* Margaret Sanger opened her first birth control clinic in America in 1916, ~~She~~ *she* was arrested and sentenced to thirty days in jail.

9. *Because* Thaddeus Stevens thought plantation land should be distributed to freed slaves, ~~He~~ *he* disagreed with Lincoln's peace terms for the South.

10. *Even though* Steven Spielberg directed some of the most popular movies of all time, ~~He~~ *he* never won an Academy Award until *Schindler's List*.

PRACTICE 13-3

The passage below contains fragments created by subordinating conjunctions. Revise each fragment by connecting it to the independent clause to which it is related. Remember to put a comma after the dependent clause if it comes before the independent clause in the sentence. The first fragment has been corrected for you.

(1) Sharks have been predators of the sea for more than 400 million years, (2) ~~Although~~ *although* they are now being wiped out by the human appetite for shark flesh. (3) Their disappearance could disrupt the ecology of the world's oceans, (4) ~~Because~~ *because* it could throw marine food chains off balance. (5) The

Asian market for shark fins has driven the price of shark fins and tails up to $100 a pound. (6) This demand has led to the deplorable practice of "finning," (7) ~~Where~~ *where* hunters cut off the fins of sharks and dump the live but helpless sharks back into the sea. (8) A strong market for shark meat has also developed in the United States, (9) ~~Even~~ *even* though the National Marine Fisheries Service has published warnings about depleting the shark population. (10) Regulations to control the killing of sharks must be put in place at once, ~~Before~~ *before* it is too late.

▶ FLASHBACK ◀

Reread your response to the Paragraph Practice at the beginning of this chapter. First, underline any subordinating conjunctions. Next, make sure these words do not create any sentence fragments. On the lines below, revise any fragments by attaching each one to a complete sentence. Check to make sure you have punctuated your new sentences correctly.

_____

_____

_____

_____

B USING RELATIVE PRONOUNS TO COMBINE SENTENCES

A **relative pronoun** refers to a particular noun or pronoun in the sentence.

Nadine Gordimer, <u>who won the Nobel Prize in literature in 1991</u>, comes from South Africa.

Many words <u>that are slang</u> eventually become part of the language.

Transistors, <u>which were invented in 1948</u>, have replaced vacuum tubes in radios and television.

Relative Pronouns			
who	which	what	whomever
whom	that	whoever	whose

Like subordinating conjunctions, relative pronouns can be used to combine sentences and to indicate the relationship between the two sentences they link.

Two sentences: The African Company was an all-black acting troop. It performed Shakespeare's plays in the early 1820s.

Combined (complex sentence): The African Company was an all-black acting troop that performed Shakespeare's plays in the early 1820s.

Here the second sentence has been changed to a dependent clause and attached to an independent clause to form a complex sentence.

▶ FOCUS ON USING WHO, WHICH, AND THAT ◀

- *Who* refers to people.

    He is the man who bought the car.

- *Which* refers to things.

    Years of effort produced the Hubble telescope, which is very powerful.

- *That* refers to things or to groups of people.

    The subject that we discussed was how to increase sales.
    The Rockies were the team that won.

▶ FOCUS ON CORRECTING FRAGMENTS ◀
CREATED BY RELATIVE PRONOUNS

A clause that contains a relative pronoun does not by itself express a complete thought; it is therefore a fragment. You can correct this kind of fragment by connecting it to a nearby sentence or by adding the words needed to complete the idea. (See 7C.)

(continued on the following page)

CHAPTER 13 Combining Sentences with Subordination • 247

(continued from the previous page)

Fragment: Dizzy Gillespie was a jazz musician. <u>Who got standing ovations all around the world</u>.

Sentence: Dizzy Gillespie was a jazz musician <u>who</u> got standing ovations all around the world.

Fragment: Susan B. Anthony, <u>who crusaded for women's rights</u>.

Sentence: Susan B. Anthony, <u>who</u> crusaded for women's rights, died in 1922.

PRACTICE 13-4

Combine the following pairs of sentences, using the relative pronoun that follows each pair.

Example: The United States is frightening to many Japanese. It is seen as a place where everyone owns or carries a gun. (which)

The United States, which is seen as a place where everyone owns or carries a gun, is frightening to many Japanese.

1. This image is reinforced by a television show.
   It started several years ago. (which)

   This image, which started several years ago, is reinforced by a television show.

2. On Sunday nights, television viewers tune in to see the latest disaster to happen to Hyota.
   He is a Japanese traveler trying to survive in America. (who)

   On Sunday nights, viewers tune in to see the latest disaster to happen to Hyota, who is a Japanese traveler trying to survive in America.

3. One Sunday Hyota was wandering through the streets, looking for someone to help him.
   They were full of people. (that)

   One Sunday Hyota was wandering through streets that were full of people, looking for someone to help him.

4. His questions were misunderstood.
   They were halfway between English and Japanese. (which)

   His questions, which were halfway between English and Japanese, were misunderstood.

5. This television program is very popular.
   It teaches American street expressions to Japanese viewers. (which)

   This television program, which is very popular, teaches American street expressions to Japanese viewers.

6. Most Japanese learn English in high school by reading formal passages from textbooks.
   They are designed to get them into the university. (that)

   Most Japanese learn English in high school by reading formal passages in textbooks that are designed to get them into the university.

7. The English they learn is of little use in the real world.
   It is not enough to protect them from street hustlers. (which)

   The English they learn, which is not enough to protect them from street hustlers, is of little use in the real world.

8. Some Japanese have been killed or injured in the United States.
   They could not understand spoken English. (who)

   Some Japanese who could not understand spoken English have been killed or injured in the United States.

9. For example, a sixteen-year-old Japanese exchange student was shot.
   He did not understand the command *freeze*. (who)

   For example, a sixteen-year-old Japanese exchange student who did not understand the command freeze was shot.

10. This case has led many Japanese to learn "usable English."
    It will help them when they travel to the United States. (that)

    This case has led many Japanese to learn "usable English" that will help them when they travel to the United States.

CHAPTER 13 Combining Sentences with Subordination · 249

PRACTICE 13-5

The following paragraphs contain fragments introduced by relative pronouns. After locating the fragments, correct them by connecting them to the words they relate to. The first error has been corrected for you.

(1) One thing that constantly mystifies people who study the behavior of violent criminals is how they are tripped up by foolish mistakes. (2) One foolish mistake involved basketball star Michael Jordan's father's murderers, *who* (3) ~~Who~~ made repeated calls on their victim's cellular phone. (4) The phone bill turned into a trail, *that* (5) ~~That~~ led straight to the criminals. (6) Many suspects have also been lured from hiding by gimmicks that are laughable. (7) In 1984 in New York, federal marshals rounded up sixty-five criminals, *who* (8) ~~Who~~ apparently let greed get the best of them. (9) The marshals sent letters saying that the criminals had won big-screen televisions. (10) The criminals were told to wait for a truck, *that* (11) ~~That~~ would deliver their prizes. (12) The truck arrived with the marshals inside. (13) In Washington, D.C., marshals had even better success rounding up fugitives, *who* (14) ~~Who~~ were offered hard-to-get professional football tickets. (15) When the fugitives showed up to collect their tickets, they were handcuffed and led off to jail.

••••••••▶ **FLASHBACK** ◀••••••••

Reread your response to the Paragraph Practice at the beginning of the chapter. First, underline any relative pronouns. Then, draw an arrow that connects each relative pronoun to the noun or pronoun it is related to. Next, check to make sure the relative pronouns do not create any fragments. On the lines below, revise any fragments by attaching each to a complete sentence.

_____

_____

_____

_____

C USING RELATIVE PRONOUNS TO INTRODUCE RESTRICTIVE AND NONRESTRICTIVE IDEAS

Clauses introduced by relative pronouns can be either restrictive or nonrestrictive. A **restrictive** clause is one that is necessary to the meaning of the sentence. Consider the following sentences:

> Many successful rock stars who recorded hits in the 1950s made little money from their songs.
> The "sand" that builds up in the corner of the eye is actually dried mucus.

In the first sentence the clause *who recorded hits in the 1950s* supplies information about successful rock stars that is essential to the meaning of the sentence, as does the phrase *that builds up in the corner of the eye* in the second sentence. Both these clauses are therefore restrictive.

A **nonrestrictive** clause is one that is *not* necessary to the meaning of the sentence. Frequently a nonrestrictive clause interrupts the flow of the sentence by supplying "extra" information. One way to determine whether a clause is restrictive or nonrestrictive is to remove it from the sentence. If the sentence has essentially the same meaning without the dependent clause, then that clause is nonrestrictive. If the sentence has a different meaning, the clause is restrictive. Consider the following sentences:

> Telephone calling-card fraud, which cost consumers and phone companies $4 billion last year, is increasing.
> Robert Frost, who was eighty-six years old at the time, read his poetry at John F. Kennedy's inauguration.

In the sentences above, the underlined clauses provide extra information. The sentences still make sense even without this information.

> Telephone calling-card fraud is increasing.
> Robert Frost read his poetry at John F. Kennedy's inauguration.

Notice though, how eliminating a restrictive clause changes the meaning of this sentence.

> The "sand" is actually dried mucus.

Clearly, the restrictive clause *that builds up in the corner of the eye* is essential to the meaning of the sentence.

▶ FOCUS ON PUNCTUATING RESTRICTIVE ◀ AND NONRESTRICTIVE IDEAS

Because a restrictive idea is necessary for the meaning of a sentence, it is *not* set off by commas. A nonrestrictive idea, which is not essential to meaning, *is* set off by commas.

(continued on the following page)

CHAPTER 13 Combining Sentences with Subordination • 251

> *(continued from the previous page)*
>
> **Restrictive** (not set off by commas):
> People <u>who have lived in our century</u> have experienced more change than any other people in the history of the world.
>
> **Nonrestrictive** (set off by commas):
> Fiber-optic cable, <u>which will be laid during the next twenty years</u>, will bring hundreds of television channels into the home.

PRACTICE 13-6

In the following sentences, the dependent clauses introduced by relative pronouns have been underlined. Put an *R* above each underlined clause that is restrictive. Put an *N* above each underlined clause that is nonrestrictive. Note that commas have been deliberately omitted. Add them for nonrestrictive elements.

    Example: An Alaska museum exhibition <u>that celebrates the Alaska highway</u> [R] has rescued the story of its construction.

(1) During the 1940s, a group of African-American soldiers <u>who defied the forces of nature and human prejudice</u> [R] were shipped to Alaska. (2) They built the Alaska highway <u>which stretches twelve hundred miles across Alaska</u> [N]. (3) The African-American troops <u>who worked on the highway</u> [R] have received little attention in most historical accounts. (4) Fifty years later the men <u>who worked on the road</u> [R] have been remembered. (5) The highway, <u>which cut through some of the roughest terrain in the world</u> [N], was begun in 1942. (6) The Japanese had just landed in the Aleutian Islands, <u>which lay west of the tip of the Alaska Peninsula</u> [N]. (7) Military officials <u>who oversaw the project</u> [R] doubted the ability of African-American troops. (8) As a result, they made the African-American troops work under conditions <u>that made construction difficult</u> [R]. (9) The African-American troops <u>who worked on the road</u> [R] proved their commanders wrong by finishing the highway months ahead of schedule. (10) In one case, white engineers <u>who surveyed a river</u> [R]

252 • UNIT 6 Building Sentences

said it would take two weeks to bridge. (11) To the engineers' surprise, the African-American soldiers, <u>whose honor was at stake</u>, beat the estimate by half a day. (12) A military report <u>that was issued in 1945</u> praised them. (13) It said the goals <u>that the black regiments achieved</u> would be remembered through the ages.

PRACTICE 13-7

Go back to Practices 13-4 and 13-5. Check to make sure that your revised sentences include commas as necessary to set off nonrestrictive elements and that you have *not* set off restrictive elements with commas. Make corrections as necessary.

> ••••••▶ **FLASHBACK** ◀••••••
>
> Reread your response to the Paragraph Practice at the beginning of the chapter, and look back at the sentences you revised for the previous flashback. Then, decide whether the ideas introduced by relative pronouns are restrictive or nonrestrictive, and check to see that you have punctuated each of these elements correctly. Add commas to set off nonrestrictive ideas, and delete any commas that you've used to set off restrictive ideas.

•••••••••••••• **REVIEW** ••••••••••••••

CHAPTER REVIEW: STUDENT WRITING

Read the following student essay, in which errors in the use of subordinating conjunctions and relative pronouns have been introduced. Revise any fragments. Then, add commas to set off dependent ideas at the beginning of sentences or to set off nonrestrictive ideas, and delete any commas that are used incorrectly. Finally, try combining several pairs of short sentences with subordinating conjunctions or relative pronouns. The first error has been corrected for you.

CHAPTER 13 Combining Sentences with Subordination · 253

Other answers may be acceptable.

My Life in Haiti

My father was born in Haiti, ~~Although~~ *although* I was born in the United States. My father and his brother opened a small business in Haiti, ~~When~~ *when* I was a baby. *As* I grew up in Haiti, I experienced the culture as a native, not a foreigner. My friends, who were all Haitian, only wanted to play soccer, *a*~~A~~lthough I tried to teach them baseball and football. Before I learned to speak English, I only spoke the Haitian Creole dialect. *When* I was a toddler, I went to New York to visit my grandmother. One day I was thirsty. I asked her in Creole for a glass of water, *while* I pointed to the refrigerator. My grandmother*, who only spoke English,* had no idea what I meant. ~~She only spoke English.~~ I finally had to point to a glass so she would know what I wanted.

In Haiti I developed close relationships with the neighbors, *who* ~~They~~ lived on our street. They never shut their doors, so I was constantly walking in and out of their houses. Whenever I opened my mouth, one of them fed me some candy or a bowl of curried goat stew. Dina, who was an elderly Cuban woman, was like a grandmother to me. She encouraged me to eat, ~~Because~~ *because* she thought I was too skinny. Lita, another neighbor, was an excellent storyteller. She would tell my friends and me tales of voodoo, until we were afraid to walk home. *Although her* ~~Her~~ stories terrified us*, we* ~~We~~ couldn't wait to hear more.

When I was twelve, my life in Haiti ended. My father, *who had been sick for a year,* died of cancer. ~~He had been sick for a year.~~ *Although* ~~My~~ *my* mother and I could have stayed in Haiti~~,~~ *she* ~~She~~ decided to return to her parents in New York. She sold her share of the business to my uncle~~.~~ *because* ~~Because~~ we needed the money. Sometimes, my mind wanders back to those days. Although my life in Haiti is over**,** I will never forget the people I knew and loved there.

CHAPTER REVIEW: EDITING PRACTICE

Reread your response to the Paragraph Practice at the beginning of the chapter. Correct any errors in your use of subordinating conjunctions and relative pronouns. Then, use subordinating conjunctions or relative pronouns to combine any short sentences. Finally, revise your paragraph, incorporating all these changes.

When you are finished, look back at a Paragraph Practice from another chapter or review a paper you are working on, thinking about your use of complex sentences. Do you find any errors? Are there sentences that could be combined?

CHAPTER REVIEW: COLLABORATIVE ACTIVITIES

1. Working in a group of four students, make a list of four or five of your favorite recording artists. Divide into pairs, and with your partner write two sentences describing each artist. Then, combine the sentences with subordinating conjunctions or relative pronouns. As a group, discuss how the ideas in each sentence are related, and make sure you have used the subordinating conjunction or relative pronoun that best conveys this relationship.

   Example:
   Many of Bob Marley's songs celebrate the lives of poor Jamaicans. He has achieved worldwide recognition.
   Although many of Bob Marley's songs celebrate the lives of poor Jamaicans, he has achieved worldwide recognition.

2. Working in a group of five or six students, write a fairy tale in which all the individuals in your group are characters. You may, if you wish, follow the plot of a well-known fairy tale such as Cinderella or Snow White, or you may make up your own plot. Write the first draft of your fairy tale all in simple sentences. After you have written this draft, work as a group to combine as many sentences as you can with subordinating conjunctions and relative pronouns.

3. Assume that you are in a competition to determine which collaborative group in your class is the best. Prepare a letter to your instructor in which you present the strengths of each individual in your group. Be sure you use a subordinating conjunction or relative pronoun in each of the sentences in your letter.

   Next, exchange letters with one of the other groups in the class. Read the letter from the other group, and make sure that the relative pronouns come directly after the nouns to which they refer, that all sentences are punctuated correctly, and that there are no fragments. When you have finished, return the letter to the group that drafted it.

   Finally, as a class, evaluate the letters from each group. Choose the letter that most successfully convinces you that its group is best.

Review

- When an independent clause is joined with a dependent clause, the result is a complex sentence. (See 13A.)

    The French sculptor Auguste Rodin caused a great deal of controversy because his nude figures insulted the sensibilities of many viewers.

- Subordinating conjunctions—such as *although, after, when, while,* and *because*—can be used to combine two sentences and clarify the relationship between dependent and independent clauses in a sentence. (See 13A.)
- Always use a comma *after* the dependent clause if it comes before the independent clause in the sentence. Do not use a comma if the dependent clause follows the independent clause. (See 13A.)
- When a subordinating conjunction begins a simple sentence, it is a fragment and cannot stand alone. You can correct the fragment by connecting it to an independent clause or by eliminating the subordinating conjunction. (See 13A.)
- Relative pronouns refer to particular nouns or pronouns in a sentence. You can use relative pronouns to join short, choppy sentences. (See 13B.)

    Nadine Gordimer, <u>who won the Nobel Prize in literature in 1991</u>, comes from South Africa.

- A clause that contains a relative pronoun does not express a complete thought and is, therefore, a fragment. (See 13B.)
- Relative pronouns can introduce restrictive or nonrestrictive clauses.

(continued on the following page)

(continued from the previous page)

A restrictive clause, which is necessary for meaning, is *not* set off by commas. A nonrestrictive clause, which is not essential to meaning, *is* set off by commas. (See 13C.)

Restrictive: People <u>who have lived in our century</u> have experienced more change than any other people in the history of the world.

Nonrestrictive: Fiber-optic cable, <u>which will be laid during the next twenty years</u>, will bring hundreds of television channels into the home.

14 Avoiding Run-Ons and Comma Splices

Overview

In this chapter you will learn
- To identify run-on sentences and comma splices
- To correct run-ons and comma splices in three ways

PARAGRAPH PRACTICE

Write a paragraph in which you describe the student population of one of the schools you have attended in terms of its social or economic status, ethnicity, race, and gender. What problems, if any, occurred as a result of the diversity—or lack of diversity—in that school? In what way did the nature of the student population affect you? Use the blank space below for invention. Then, write your paragraph on the lines that follow.

A IDENTIFYING RUN-ONS AND COMMA SPLICES

A **run-on sentence**—also called a **fused sentence**—is an error that occurs when two sentences (independent clauses) are joined without punctuation.

> **Incorrect:** More and more students are earning high school equivalency diplomas the value of these diplomas is currently under debate.

More and more students are earning high school equivalency diplomas and *The value of these diplomas is currently under debate* are each complete sentences. They cannot be joined without punctuation.

A **comma splice** is an error that occurs when two sentences are joined with just a comma.

> **Incorrect:** More and more students are earning high school equivalency diplomas, the value of these diplomas is currently under debate.

A comma alone cannot be used to join the two sentences into one complete sentence.

PRACTICE 14-1

Some of the sentences in this passage are correct, but others are run-on sentences or comma splices. In the answer space after each sentence, identify each as correct (C), run-on (RO), or comma splice (CS). The first answer has been supplied for you.

CHAPTER 14   Avoiding Run-Ons and Comma Splices   ▪   259

(1) In 1919 African-American director Oscar Micheaux filmed *Within Our Gates* this movie examined black life in Chicago. _RO_ (2) The film included scenes of violence, it even depicted two lynchings. _CS_ (3) It also treated interracial relationships white censors banned it. _RO_ (4) Race riots had occurred in Chicago that year, the censors feared violence. _CS_ (5) Micheaux appealed to the board they agreed to the film's release in Chicago. _RO_ (6) The movie was shown, twelve hundred feet of film were omitted. _CS_ (7) Micheaux later made many low-budget movies, but few survive today. _C_ (8) Some are musicals others are melodramas. _RO_ (9) Few are socially conscious films like *Within Our Gates*. _C_ (10) One, *Body and Soul*, was Paul Robeson's first film. _C_ (11) Micheaux died in 1951. _C_ (12) In 1990, an uncut version of *Within Our Gates* was discovered in Madrid, it was shown in Chicago for the first time in 1992. _CS_

▶ **FLASHBACK** ◀

Reread your response to the Paragraph Practice at the beginning of the chapter. Do you see any run-ons or comma splices? If so, put brackets around them.

B   CORRECTING RUN-ONS AND COMMA SPLICES

You can correct a run-on sentence or comma splice in four different ways.

1. Create two separate sentences. If you do not need to indicate the relationship between ideas, create two separate sentences.

Incorrect (run-on): Muslims fast for a period of thirty days this period is called Ramadan.

Incorrect (comma splice): Muslims fast for a period of thirty days, this period is called Ramadan.

Correct *(two separate sentences):* Muslims fast for a period of thirty days. This period is called Ramadan.

2. Connect ideas with a comma followed by a coordinating conjunction. If two ideas are of equal importance and you want to indicate a particular relationship between them—for example, cause and effect or contrast—use a comma followed by a coordinating conjunction. (See 12A.)

Incorrect (run-on): The Emancipation Proclamation freed U.S. slaves in 1863 slaves in Texas were not officially freed until June 19, 1865, called "Juneteenth."

Incorrect (comma splice): The Emancipation Proclamation freed U.S. slaves in 1863, slaves in Texas were not officially freed until June 19, 1865, called "Juneteenth."

Correct (comma followed by a coordinating conjunction): The Emancipation Proclamation freed U.S. slaves in 1863, <u>but</u> slaves in Texas were not officially freed until June 19, 1865, called "Juneteenth."

3. Connect ideas with a semicolon. If you want to indicate a particularly close connection—or a strong contrast—between two ideas, use a semicolon. (See 12B.)

Incorrect (run-on): In ancient times, the swastika was a symbol of good luck after 1935 it became the official emblem of the Nazi party.

Incorrect (comma splice): In ancient times, the swastika was a symbol of good luck, after 1935 it became the official emblem of the Nazi party.

Correct (ideas connected with a semicolon): In ancient times, the swastika was a symbol of good luck; after 1935, it became the official emblem of the Nazi party.

▶ FOCUS ON RUN-ONS AND COMMA SPLICES ◀ WITH CONJUNCTIVE ADVERBS AND TRANSITIONAL EXPRESSIONS

Run-on sentences and comma splices can occur when a conjunctive adverb or transitional expression joins two sentences without the required punctuation.

Incorrect (run-on): Some students have computers, microwaves, and refrigerators in their dorm rooms <u>as a result</u>, electrical circuits are overloaded.

Incorrect (comma splice): Some students have computers, microwaves, and refrigerators in their dorm rooms, <u>as a result</u>, electrical circuits are overloaded.

To correct this kind of run-on or comma splice, simply add the missing semicolon.

Correct: Some students have computers, microwaves, and refrigerators in their dorm rooms; <u>as a result</u>, electrical circuits are overloaded.

---

4. Connect ideas with a subordinating conjunction or relative pronoun. Another way to correct a run-on sentence or comma splice is to use subordination. When one idea is dependent on the other, you can turn that idea into a dependent clause by adding a subordinating conjunction or a relative pronoun.

CHAPTER 14 Avoiding Run-Ons and Comma Splices • 261

> **Incorrect (run-on):** Horace Mann was the first president of Antioch College he encouraged the development of students' social consciences.
>
> **Incorrect (comma splice):** Horace Mann was the first president of Antioch College, he encouraged the development of students' social consciences.
>
> **Correct (clauses joined by subordinating conjunction):** <u>When</u> Horace Mann was the first president of Antioch College, he encouraged the development of students' social consciences.
>
> **Correct (clauses joined by relative pronoun):** Horace Mann, <u>who</u> was the first president of Antioch College, encouraged the development of students' social consciences.

Keep in mind that when you use a relative pronoun to correct a run-on or comma splice, the relative pronoun takes the place of another pronoun in the sentence. See Chapter 13 for lists of subordinating conjunctions and relative pronouns and for advice about punctuating dependent clauses in sentences.

PRACTICE 14-2

Correct each of the following run-on sentences and comma splices either by creating two separate sentences, by connecting ideas with a comma followed by a coordinating conjunction, or by connecting ideas with a semicolon. Be sure punctuation is correct. Remember to put a semicolon before, and a comma after, each conjunctive adverb or transitional expression.

> **Example:** Some people believe chronic sex offenders should be given therapy, however others believe they should be executed.
>
> *Some people believe chronic sex offenders should be given therapy;*
>
> *however, others believe they should be executed.*

Other answers may be correct.

1. Nursing offers job security and high pay, therefore many men and women are choosing nursing as a career.

    Nursing offers job security and high pay; therefore, many men and

    women are choosing nursing as a career.

2. Anne Boleyn was the second wife of Henry VIII her daughter was Elizabeth I.

    Anne Boleyn was the second wife of Henry VIII, and her daughter was

    Elizabeth I.

3. Zaire was previously known as the Congo before that it was the Belgian Congo.

   Zaire was previously known as the Congo; before that, it was the Belgian Congo.

4. Housewife Jean Nidetch started Weight Watchers in 1961 in 1978 she sold the company for $100 million.

   Housewife Jean Nidetch started Weight Watchers in 1961. In 1978 she sold the company for $100 million.

5. Millions of Jews were killed during the Holocaust, in addition Catholics, Gypsies, homosexuals, and other "undesirables" were killed.

   Millions of Jews were killed during the Holocaust; in addition, Catholics, Gypsies, homosexuals, and other "undesirables" were killed.

6. Sojourner Truth was born a slave however she became a leading abolitionist and feminist.

   Sojourner Truth was born a slave; however, she became a leading abolitionist and feminist.

7. First-generation Japanese Americans are called Nisei second-generation Japanese Americans are called Sansei.

   First-generation Japanese Americans are called Nisei; second-generation Japanese Americans are called Sansei.

8. Oliver Wendell Holmes, Jr., was a Supreme Court Justice, his father was a physician and writer.

   Oliver Wendell Holmes, Jr., was a Supreme Court Justice; his father was a physician and writer.

9. Père Noel is another name for Santa Claus, he is also known as Father Christmas and St. Nicholas.

   Père Noel is another name for Santa Claus. He is also known as Father Christmas and St. Nicholas.

10. Latin is one classical language Greek is another.

    Latin is one classical language, and Greek is another.

CHAPTER 14   Avoiding Run-Ons and Comma Splices   • 263

PRACTICE 14-3

Use the list of subordinating conjunctions on page 241 and the list of relative pronouns on page 246 to help you correct the following run-on sentences and comma splices. Be sure to add correct punctuation where necessary.

Examples: Harlem was rural until the nineteenth century ^, when^ improved transportation linked it to lower Manhattan.

The community ^, which^ was soon home to people escaping the crowds of New York City, ~~it~~ became a fashionable suburb.

Other answers may be correct.

1. Harlem ^, which^ was populated mostly by European immigrants at the turn of the century, ~~it~~ saw an influx of Southern African Americans beginning in 1910.

2. ~~This~~ *As this* migration from the South continued for several decades, Harlem became one of the largest African-American communities in the United States.

3. Many African-American artists and writers settled in Harlem during the 1920s, ~~this~~ *which* led to a flowering of African-American art.

4. This "Harlem Renaissance" was an important era in American literary history ^*although*^ it is not even mentioned in some textbooks.

5. ~~Scholars~~ *When scholars* of the era recognize the great works produced then, they point to such writers as Langston Hughes and Countee Cullen and sculptors such as Henry Tanner and Sargent Johnson.

6. Zora Neale Hurston ^, who^ moved to Harlem from her native Florida in 1925, ~~she~~ began work there on her famous book of African-American folklore.

7. ^*Because*^ Harlem was an exciting place in the 1920s, people from all over the city went there to hear jazz and to dance.

264 ▪ UNIT 6 Building Sentences

8. The white playwright Eugene O'Neill went to Harlem to audition actors for his play *The Emperor Jones* ~~it~~ , which made an international star of the great Paul Robeson.

9. ~~Contemporary~~ While contemporary African-American artists know about the Harlem Renaissance, it is still not so familiar to others.

10. ~~The~~ When the Great Depression occurred in the 1930s, it led to the end of the Harlem Renaissance.

PRACTICE 14-4

Correct each run-on sentence and comma splice in the following passage in the way that best indicates the relationship between ideas. Be sure punctuation is appropriate. The first error has been corrected for you.

Other answers may be correct.

Coney Island is a seaside resort located in Brooklyn, New York. In the late nineteenth century it was famous; in fact, it was legendary. Every summer it was crowded, and people sometimes mailed hundreds of thousands of postcards from the resort in one day. Coney Island, which was considered exotic and exciting, ~~it~~ even boasted a hotel shaped like an elephant. Although some ~~Some~~ people saw it as seedy, many thought it was a wonderful, magical place. Coney Island had beaches, hotels, racetracks, and a stadium; however, by the turn of the century it was best known for three amusement parks. They were Luna Park, Steeplechase, and Dreamland. Even though gaslight ~~Gaslight~~ was still the norm in New York, a million electric lights lit Luna Park. While Steeplechase offered many rides, its main attraction was a two-mile ride on mechanical horses. At Dreamland, people could see a submarine; in addition, they could travel through an Eskimo village or visit Lilliputia, with its three hundred midgets. Today, the old Coney Island no longer exists. Fire destroyed Dreamland in 1911, and Luna Park burned down in 1946. In 1964, Steeplechase closed. The once-grand Coney Island is gone. Still, ~~still~~ its beach and its boardwalk endure. Its famous

CHAPTER 14 Avoiding Run-Ons and Comma Splices · 265

roller coaster, the Cyclone, still exists, *and* its giant Ferris wheel, the Wonder Wheel, also remains. Some people still hope the old Coney Island can be reborn.

▶ **FLASHBACK** ◀

Correct any run-ons or comma splices you identified in the previous Flashback exercise, writing two possible corrected versions of each on the lines below.

_____

_____

_____

_____

_____

_____

• • • • • • • • • • • ▶ **REVIEW** ◀ • • • • • • • • • • •

CHAPTER REVIEW: STUDENT WRITING

Read the following student passage, in which sentence errors have been introduced. Then, revise it by eliminating run-on sentences and comma splices, carefully correcting them to indicate the relationships between ideas. Be sure punctuation is correct. The first error has been corrected for you.

Other answers may be acceptable.

```
                    Blood Sports

     Since the time of ancient Rome, citizens have rushed to
                              While
the stadium to see battles. Christians fought lions in an-
```

cient times, today athletes fight each other. Although society ~~Society~~ may have evolved morally to some degree, I believe only our laws keep us from behaving like the ancient Romans. The craving for blood is still evident. For ~~for~~ example, football and hockey fans still yell "Kill him!" and "Rip their faces off!"

I played "barbaric" sports for ten years. My parents, who encouraged my athletic career, ~~they~~ got me started in sports early on. Between the ages of ten and seventeen I was very active in martial arts, and for four years I played high school football. As a young child I competed in karate tournaments, where I received many injuries. I broke my nose three times; I also broke my hand twice and my foot once. As a competitor, I enjoyed the thrill of battle; however, I feared serious injury. Eventually I gave up karate; instead, I concentrated on football.

Extreme force was very important in high school football. I played defense, and often I hurt my opponents. Once I hit a quarterback in his hip with my helmet. The ~~the~~ blow knocked him to the ground. They carried him off the field, and my team's fans went berserk. For weeks people congratulated me; still, I felt uncomfortable. I now believe playing sports requires a great deal of physical aggressiveness and pain. I accept this as part of the game. I just don't want to play anymore.

CHAPTER REVIEW: EDITING PRACTICE

Reread your response to the Paragraph Practice at the beginning of the chapter, and review the two Flashback exercises you did. Then, correct each run-on sentence and comma splice you found, choosing the revision that best conveys your meaning. If you do not find any run-ons or comma splices in your own paragraph, work with a classmate to correct his or her work, or edit written work you did in response to another assignment.

CHAPTER REVIEW: COLLABORATIVE ACTIVITIES

1. Find an interesting passage from a newspaper or magazine article. Working in a group of three or four students, edit it to create run-ons and comma splices. Then, exchange exercises with the other group.
2. Work in a group to correct each run-on and comma splice in an exercise prepared by another group of students. When you have finished, return the exercise to the group that created it.
3. Continuing to work with members of your group, evaluate the other group's work on your exercise, comparing it to the original newspaper or magazine passage. Pay particular attention to punctuation. Where the students' version differs from the original, decide whether their version is incorrect or whether it represents an acceptable (or even superior) alternative to the original.

Review

- A run-on (or fused) sentence is an error that occurs when two sentences are joined without punctuation. (See 14A.)

    Horace Mann was the first president of Antioch College he encouraged the development of students' social consciences.

- A comma splice is an error that occurs when two sentences are joined with just a comma. (See 14A.)

    Horace Mann was the first president of Antioch College, he encouraged the development of students' social consciences.

- A run-on or comma splice can be corrected by using the method listed below that most effectively conveys the writer's meaning. (See 14B.)

    Create two separate sentences: Horace Mann was the first president of Antioch College. He encouraged the development of students' social consciences.

    (continued on the following page)

(continued from the previous page)

Connect ideas with a comma followed by a coordinating conjunction: Horace Mann was the first president of Antioch College, and he encouraged the development of students' social consciences.

Connect ideas with a semicolon: Horace Mann was the first president of Antioch College; he encouraged the development of students' social consciences.

Connect ideas with a subordinating conjunction: When Horace Mann was the first president of Antioch College, he encouraged the development of students' social consciences.

Connect ideas with a relative pronoun: Horace Mann, who was the first president of Antioch College, encouraged the development of students' social consciences.

Unit 6 Review

The collaborative activities, writing practice topics, and student writing sample that follow provide opportunities for you to review what you have learned in Chapters 12 through 14.

COLLABORATIVE ACTIVITIES

1. With three other students, form a company to develop and market one of the new products you wrote about in the Paragraph Practice at the beginning of Chapter 12. Imagine that, as representatives of this company, you were going to deliver a speech to a group of ten-year-olds about how the product was developed and how you expect it to change their lives. You want your audience to understand how the product works, and you want them to enjoy your presentation; most important, you want them to use the product. Your speech should address the children in simple, accessible language. Be careful, however, *not* to use short, choppy sentences. Instead, combine sentences with coordination or subordination. If you like, you can plan visual aids or demonstrations to support your speech.

2. For this exercise, work with a student of the opposite gender. Each of you should make a list of ten short sentences, with each sentence stating an advantage of belonging to your own gender. Review your lists together to make sure each sentence is complete. Then, use coordination and subordination to pair sentences from the two lists to create longer sentences that make the relationship between them (similarity, contrast, causality, and so forth) clear. Be sure to choose coordinating conjunctions, conjunctive adverbs, and subordinating conjunctions with care and to use correct punctuation.

3. Working in a group of three or four students, design your ideal high school, complete with perfect teachers, students, physical plant, facilities, and equipment. Assume that money is no object. What rules and regulations might be required to maintain the state of perfection you describe? Make lists of information to use in a future writing assignment, and then, working as a group, try to develop a one-sentence statement that sums up your feelings about the ideal school: Is it a possibility, or just a dream?

4. Assume that your group has been hired by the admissions office of your school to write a brochure to convince prospective students to visit your campus. Begin your project with each member of the group writing ten short sentences describing the things on campus that prospective students should see. Then, working collaboratively, pool your lists of sentences, and use coordination or subordination to combine as many pairs of sentences as possible into longer sentences.

WRITING PRACTICE

1. Who do you believe has the advantage, males or females? Why? Before you begin to write, review the material you generated for Collaborative Activity 2 in this Unit Review, and be sure to consider the disadvantages as well as the advantages of being male or female.

2. Write about your ideal high school. Using the information developed by your group in response to Collaborative Activity 3 in this Unit Review, write about the students, staff, and facilities you see as ideal. In addition to discussing how to maintain this ideal environment, consider some threats to your school's survival. Remember, funding for your ideal school is unlimited.

3. Using the sentences generated by your group in Collaborative Activity 4 of this Unit Review as a starting point, write the text of a brochure to be sent to all prospective students who request information about your school.

STUDENT WRITING

Revise the passage that follows by combining sentences with either coordination or subordination. Also correct any run-on sentences or comma splices. Finally, be sure all punctuation is accurate. The first sentence has been corrected for you.

Other answers may be acceptable.

The Donner Party

In the 1840s, Americans wanted to go west, *because they* ~~They~~ wanted to escape cholera and malaria outbreaks and an unstable financial climate in the East. They also had "land fever*,*"*;* *m*Many people wanted to own land of their own. *When the* ~~The~~ Donner brothers and their families left Independence, Missouri, in May of 1846*,* *t*They had high hopes. They were heading for California*,* *, which s*~~S~~ome people said ~~California~~ was like Eden.

At first the Donner Party faced heavy rains*, and thunderstorms* ~~Thunderstorms~~ produced flooded rivers and muddy trails. In late June they arrived at Fort Laramie. A man warned them about a shortcut to California, that he said was dangerous. However, the Donner Party ignored the warning. They wanted to take the shortcut, because it would save four hundred miles. The journey was very hard; in fact, the road was almost impassable. After they reached the Great Salt Lake in late August, they traveled across eighty miles of desert.

Because the "shortcut" had actually delayed the travelers, by autumn they were running out of time. Soon snow would block their route to California. When snow blocked the road across the Sierra Nevada mountains in late October, the Donner Party was trapped. They had to spend the winter in makeshift shacks and cabins, while the snow was sometimes five feet deep. When food and water supplies became low, the travelers ate twigs and bark. Eventually, some people died. Then, some survivors ate the dead. Meanwhile, search parties looked for the missing people. By April, all the survivors had been rescued. Forty-six people survived; forty-one died. Although two-thirds of the women and children survived, only one-third of the men did.

The story of the Donner Party's ordeal spread rapidly. People were shocked by the cannibalism; however, the survivors lived normal lives. Some became ranchers, and others bought real estate. One survivor opened a restaurant.

15 Avoiding Illogical Shifts

> **Overview**
>
> In this chapter you will learn
> - To avoid illogical shifts in tense
> - To avoid illogical shifts in person
> - To avoid illogical shifts in number
> - To avoid illogical shifts in discourse
> - To avoid illogical shifts in voice

PARAGRAPH PRACTICE

Write a paragraph about how you think parents can help their teenage children learn to succeed in life. How can parents encourage independence without giving their children too much freedom? What can they say that will motivate their children to set goals and achieve them? Be sure to give some specific examples of the actions and advice you recommend. Use the space below for invention. Then, write your paragraph on the lines that follow.

A **shift** occurs any time a writer changes tense, person, number, type of discourse, or voice. As you write and revise, be sure that any shifts you make are logical—that is, that you make them for good reason.

A AVOIDING ILLOGICAL SHIFTS IN TENSE

Writers make shifts in tense to indicate that actions take place at different times.

> Last year I <u>ran</u> (past tense) three miles a day, but now I <u>am</u> (present tense) tired of running, so I think I <u>will use</u> (future tense) a bicycle instead.

An **illogical shift in tense** occurs when a writer changes tense for no apparent reason.

Illogical shift in tense (past to present)

The dog <u>walked</u> slowly to the fireplace. Then he <u>circles</u> twice and <u>lies</u> down.

Revised (consistent past)

The dog <u>walked</u> slowly to the fireplace. Then he <u>circled</u> twice and <u>lay</u> down.

Revised (consistent present)

The dog <u>walks</u> slowly to the fireplace. Then he <u>circles</u> twice and <u>lies</u> down.

Illogical shift in tense (present to past)

Many trees are cut for use in industry. Paper is one product made from them. Fiberboard was another.

Revised (consistent present)

Many trees are cut for use in industry. Paper is one product made from them. Fiberboard is another.

Revised (consistent past)

Many trees were cut for use in industry. Paper was one product made from them. Fiberboard was another.

Once you have established the tense of a passage, stay with that tense unless there is a reason not to.

▶ FOCUS ON SHIFTS IN TENSE ◀

In general, you can shift from the present to the past tense (or vice versa) for the following reasons.

- To compare something in the present with something in the past

    Today it is sunny and warm, but yesterday it was rainy and cold.

- To provide background

    Most European cities are relatively clean and disease free, but cities were not always such healthy places to live.

- To present an example that occurred in the past

    Although not as well publicized as airplane crashes, train accidents kill a large number of people each year. For example, last year a freight train collided with a passenger train and killed ten people.

PRACTICE 15-1

Edit the following sentences for illogical shifts in tense. If the sentence is correct, write *C* in the blank.

Examples: She was surprised when she ~~receives~~ *received* the news. ____

Last year she was a captain on the force. Now she is chief of police. *C*

1. When Beverly Harvard became the chief of the Atlanta police force in

CHAPTER 15   Avoiding Illogical Shifts • 275

1994, she ~~is~~ *was* the only African-American woman ever to hold that title in a major U.S. city. ____

2. She started on the police force when she was twenty-two, at a time when mostly white men ~~work~~ *worked* as Atlanta police. ____

3. Now more than half the department is African American, and women ~~made~~ *make* up about a quarter of the force. ____

4. Harvard first thought about joining the force because her husband and a male friend said they ~~do~~ *did* not believe women ~~are~~ *were* capable of police work. ____

5. Her husband even ~~agrees~~ *agreed* to pay her $100 if she made it on to the force. ____

6. She accepted the challenge in 1973, and today she looks back on her first years of training with amazement at how little she knew then. *C*

7. In fact, when she entered the police academy, she did not really plan to be a police officer. She just ~~wants~~ *wanted* to prove her husband wrong and to win the $100 bet. ____

8. By the time she ~~graduates~~ *graduated* from the academy, however, she realized that working as a police officer was the career she wanted. ____

9. She started out in the communications department. Then, she ~~spends~~ *spent* a year walking a beat. ____

10. Over the years she ~~moves~~ *moved* up in the ranks and worked as a supervisor in units ranging from criminal investigation to affirmative action. ____

11. One thing that helped her in her progress was her administrative ability. Another ~~is~~ *was* her talent for effective management. ____

12. In addition, she is well educated and ~~held~~ *holds* a master's degree in public administration. ____

13. When it was announced, some veteran officers ~~criticize~~ *criticized* her appointment to police chief, but most younger officers praised the choice. ____

276 • UNIT 7 Revising for Clarity and Effectiveness

14. Now, most members of the force appreciate her accessibility and ~~were~~ *are* happy about her willingness to listen to new ideas and approaches.

    _____

15. Still, Harvard has her work cut out for her. In 1994 Atlanta's violent crime rate was very high for the city's size. __C__

▶ FLASHBACK ◀

Look back at your response to the Paragraph Practice at the beginning of the chapter. Check each sentence to make sure you have not illogically shifted from one tense to another. If you find an incorrect sentence, write it on the lines below, correcting any illogical shifts in tense.

_____

_____

B AVOIDING ILLOGICAL SHIFTS IN PERSON

Person is the form a pronoun takes to indicate who is speaking, spoken about, or spoken to.

	Person	
	Singular	Plural
first person	I	we
second person	you	you
third person	he, she, it, one	they

Writers generally use the same person throughout a passage. Sometimes, of course, a shift in person is necessary for meaning and is perfectly logical.

When *he* (third person) walked into the room, I (first person) stood up.

CHAPTER 15   Avoiding Illogical Shifts   •   277

An **illogical shift in person** occurs when a writer shifts from one person to another for no apparent reason, often from the third person into the second person. To avoid this problem, decide which person you are going to use in a piece of writing, and remain with it throughout—unless a shift is needed to convey your meaning.

Illogical shift from third to second person

The hikers were told that you had to stay on the trail.

Revised (consistent third person)

The hikers were told that they had to stay on the trail.

Illogical shift from third to second person

Anyone can learn to cook if you practice.

Revised

Anyone can learn to cook if he or she practices.

Revised (consistent second person)

You can learn to cook if you practice.

PRACTICE 15-2

The following sentences shift illogically between the second person and the third person. Edit each sentence so that it uses third person pronouns consistently. Be sure to change the verb so it agrees with the new subject.

Example: Before a person gets a job in the fashion industry, *he or she has* ~~you have~~ to have some experience.

1. Young people who want to get into the fashion industry don't always realize how hard ~~you~~ *they* will have to work.

2. They think that working in the world of fashion will be glamorous and that ~~you~~ *they* will quickly make a fortune.

3. In reality, no matter how talented ~~you are,~~ *he or she is* a recent college graduate entering the industry is paid only about $18,000 a year.

4. The manufacturers and retailers who employ new graduates expect ~~you~~ *them* to work for three years or more at this salary before ~~you~~ *they* get promoted.

5. A young designer may get a big raise if ~~you are~~ *he or she is* very talented, but this is unusual.

6. New employees have to pay their dues, and ~~you~~ *they* soon realize that most of ~~your~~ *their* duties are very tedious.

7. One may be excited to land a job as an assistant designer but then find that all ~~you get~~ *one gets* to do is color in designs that have already been drawn.

8. Other beginners in fashion houses discover that ~~you~~ *they* spend most of ~~your~~ *their* time sewing or typing up orders.

9. If one is serious about getting into the fashion industry, ~~you have~~ *one has* to be realistic.

10. For most newcomers to the industry, the ability to do what ~~you're~~ *they're* told to do is more important than ~~your~~ *their* artistic talent or fashion sense.

▶ FLASHBACK ◀

Look back at your response to the Paragraph Practice at the beginning of the chapter. Check each sentence to make sure that there are no illogical shifts in person. If you find an incorrect sentence, write it on the lines below, correcting illogical shifts in person.

_____

_____

C AVOIDING ILLOGICAL SHIFTS IN NUMBER

Number indicates singular (one) or plural (more than one).

Number	
Singular	**Plural**
he/she	they
Fred	Fred and Ethel
man	men
an encyclopedia	encyclopedias
his	their

CHAPTER 15 Avoiding Illogical Shifts • 279

Sometimes a shift in number is necessary to convey a writer's meaning.

When the <u>president</u> (singular) spoke, <u>we</u> (plural) all listened.

An **illogical shift in number** occurs when a writer shifts from singular to plural (or the other way around) for no apparent reason. For example, an illogical shift in number occurs when a writer uses a singular noun or pronoun and then refers to it later in the sentence with a plural pronoun.

Illogical shift in number from singular to plural

Each <u>visitor</u> to the museum must check <u>their</u> cameras at the entrance.

Revised (consistent singular)

Each <u>visitor</u> to the museum must check <u>his or her</u> camera at the entrance.

Revised (consistent plural)

<u>Visitors</u> to the museum must check <u>their</u> cameras at the entrance.

For more on pronoun-antecedent agreement, see 19D.

PRACTICE 15-3

Edit the following sentences for illogical shifts from singular to plural, either by changing the singular element to the plural or by changing the plural element to the singular. Be sure also to change the verb so it agrees with the new subject. If the sentence is correct, write *C* in the blank.

Examples: Each attorney first makes ~~their~~ *his or her* opening speech. _____

Good jurors
~~A good juror~~ takes their time in making their decision. _____

Answers may vary.

1. According to recent studies, a juror may have ~~their~~ *his or her* mind made up before the trial even begins. _____

2. As attorneys offer their opening arguments, a juror may immediately decide whether ~~they think~~ *he or she thinks* the defendant is innocent or guilty. _____

3. This unfounded conclusion often depends on which attorney makes ~~their~~ *his or her* initial description of the case the most dramatic. _____

4. During the trial, that juror will only pay attention to evidence that corresponds to the decision ~~they have~~ *he or she has* already made. _____

280 ▪ **UNIT 7** Revising for Clarity and Effectiveness

5. ~~A juror~~ *Jurors* with poor decision-making skills ~~is~~ *are* also not likely to listen to challenges to their opinions when the full jury comes together to deliberate. ____

6. No matter how wrong they are, such ~~a juror~~ *jurors* argue~~s~~ their positions strongly and urge~~s~~ the strictest sentencing or the highest damage payments. ____

7. Jurors like these feel their responsibility is to argue for their version of the truth rather than to weigh all the evidence and alternative possibilities. *C*

8. Such ~~a juror~~ *jurors* will even make up their own evidence to support their case. ____

9. For example, one juror argued that a man being tried for murder was acting in ~~their~~ *his* own self-defense because the victim was probably carrying a knife, but no knife was mentioned during the trial. ____

10. Studies suggest that ~~a person~~ *people* who jump~~s~~ to conclusions on a jury probably won't take their time when making other important decisions in life. ____

⋯⋯⋯▶ **FLASHBACK** ◀⋯⋯⋯

Look back at your response to the Paragraph Practice at the beginning of the chapter, locating all the sentences in which you use the pronoun *they* or *their*. Check every sentence to make sure each of these pronouns refers to a plural noun or pronoun. If you find an incorrect sentence, write it on the lines below, correcting any illogical shifts in number.

_____

_____

D AVOIDING ILLOGICAL SHIFTS IN DISCOURSE

You use **direct discourse** when you present someone's exact words. Direct discourse is always enclosed within quotation marks and is often accompanied by an **identifying tag**, a phrase that identifies the speaker *(he says, she says, Natalie says)*. You use **indirect discourse** when you summarize someone's words. With indirect discourse you do not use quotation marks, and you often introduce the reported statement with the word *that*. Statements in direct and indirect discourse use different pronouns and different verb tenses.

Direct discourse (first person, present tense)

Carla said, "I'm going to drive to Phoenix."

Indirect discourse (third person, past tense)

Carla said that she was going to drive to Phoenix.

Questions in direct discourse end with a question mark. When recorded as indirect discourse, questions include a word like *who, if, why, whether, what,* or *how* and do not end with a question mark.

Direct discourse

Demi looked at her brother and asked, "What do you think you're doing?"

Indirect discourse

Demi looked at her brother and asked him what he thought he was doing.

An **illogical shift in discourse** occurs when you combine direct and indirect discourse within the same sentence. This shift creates an awkward or ungrammatical sentence that will confuse readers.

Illogical shift

Elena said that "all this studying is not worth the trouble."

Revised (direct discourse)

Elena said, "All this studying is not worth the trouble."

Revised (indirect discourse)

Elena said that all this studying was not worth the trouble.

Illogical shift

Molly asked could she help me plan my trip?

Revised (direct discourse)

Molly asked, "Can I help you plan your trip?"

Revised (indirect discourse)

Molly asked if she could help me plan my trip.

See 24B for more on punctuating direct discourse.

282 • UNIT 7 Revising for Clarity and Effectiveness

PRACTICE 15-4

The following sentences contain illogical shifts in discourse. Edit each sentence so that it consistently uses either direct or indirect discourse. Be sure to punctuate correctly. If the sentence is correct, write *C* in the blank.

Examples: After three dates my husband asked ^*if I* would ~~I~~ marry him. ____

After three dates my husband asked, *"Will you* ~~would I~~ marry ~~him~~ *me?"* ____

Answers may vary.

1. The coach finished his pep talk and then asked ^*if we* were ~~we~~ ready to win. ____

2. One student wondered ~~was~~ *if* this information ^*was* going to be on the test~~?~~. ____

3. The union leaders announced ~~that,~~ "~~the~~ *The* strike is over." ____

4. The attorney asked the witnesses if they had been near the scene of the crime. *C*

5. Oprah Winfrey asked the audience ~~did~~ *if* they ~~sympathize~~ *sympathized* more with the husband or the wife. ____

6. My supervisor said I could read at my receptionist station but asked ^*if I* could ~~I~~ do it after 3:00. ____

7. The report stated, "There is no proven link between cholesterol levels and cancer." *C*

8. Before the 1960s some doctors advised that ~~"~~smoking ~~is~~ *was* a good way of reducing stress.~~"~~ ____

9. The Speaker of the House asked ^, *"Will* ~~would~~ the chamber come to order~~?~~*?"* ____

10. My three-year-old wondered ~~did~~ *if* her baby brother ~~come~~ *came* from outer space. ____

FLASHBACK

Look back at your response to the Paragraph Practice at the beginning of the chapter. Check the sentences in which you have written about what people should say, and make sure you have not mixed direct and indirect discourse. If you find an incorrect sentence, write it on the lines below, correcting any illogical shifts in discourse.

_____

_____

If you do not find any illogical shifts, rewrite one of your sentences on the lines above, changing direct discourse to indirect discourse or changing indirect discourse to direct discourse.

E AVOIDING ILLOGICAL SHIFTS IN VOICE

When the subject of a sentence performs the action, the sentence is in the **active voice.** When the subject of a sentence receives the action, the sentence is in the **passive voice.** Compare these two sentences:

Active voice

Nat Turner launched a slave rebellion in August 1831. (Subject *Nat Turner* performs the action.)

Passive voice

A slave rebellion was launched by Nat Turner in 1831. (Subject *slave rebellion* receives the action.)

The passive form of the verb consists of a form of *be* plus the past participle—*was launched*. (See Chapter 10 for information on forming past participles.) Frequently, but not always, the word *by* follows the passive construction to indicate who or what performed the action *(by Nat Turner)*.

An **illogical shift in voice** occurs when a writer changes from active to passive voice or from passive to active voice for no apparent reason.

Illogical shift in voice (active to passive)

J. D. Salinger wrote *The Catcher in the Rye,* and *Franny and Zooey* was also written by him.

Revised (consistent voice)

J. D. Salinger wrote *The Catcher in the Rye,* and he also wrote *Franny and Zooey.*

Illogical shift in voice (passive to active)

Radium was discovered by Marie Curie, and Watson and Crick described the structure of DNA.

Revised (consistent voice)

Marie Curie discovered radium, and Watson and Crick described the structure of DNA.

Because the active voice places the emphasis on the individual performing the action, it is almost always clearer and stronger than the passive voice. Generally, then, you should use the active voice in most writing. The passive voice is acceptable only when the action is more important than the person performing it or when you do not know who performed an action.

The study was carried out by the Department of Agriculture. (The emphasis is on the study, not on who performed it.)

My suitcase was stolen in the airport. (The writer does not know who stole the suitcase.)

▶ FOCUS ◀ ON CORRECTING ILLOGICAL SHIFTS IN VOICE

To correct an illogical shift in voice, you need to know how to change sentences from passive to active voice and from active to passive voice.

- To change a sentence from the passive to the active voice, determine who or what performs the action, and make it the subject of a new active voice sentence.

    Passive voice: The campus escort service is used by some of my friends. (*Friends* performs the action.)
    Active voice: Some of my friends use the campus escort service.

If the passive voice sentence does not indicate who or what performs the action, you will have to supply a subject for the active verb.

   Passive voice: She was taught to swim. (Who taught her to swim?)
   Active voice: Her father taught her to swim.

- To change a sentence from the active to the passive voice, determine who or what receives the action, and make it the subject of a new passive voice sentence.

   Active voice: César Ritz opened a hotel in Paris in 1898. (*Hotel* receives the action.)
   Passive voice: A hotel was opened by César Ritz in Paris in 1898.

CHAPTER 15   Avoiding Illogical Shifts   •   285

PRACTICE 15-5

The following sentences contain illogical shifts in voice. Revise each sentence by changing the underlined passive voice verb to the active voice.

Example: Several researchers are interested in leadership qualities, and a study of decision making <u>was conducted</u> by them recently.

Several researchers are interested in leadership qualities, <u>and they recently conducted a study of decision making.</u>

1. A local university funded the study, and the research team <u>was led</u> by Dr. Alicia Flynn.

   A local university funded the study, <u>and Dr. Alicia Flynn led the research team.</u>

2. The researchers developed a series of questions about decision making, and then a hundred subjects <u>were interviewed</u> by them.

   The researchers developed a series of questions about decision making, <u>and then they interviewed a hundred subjects.</u>

3. Instinct alone <u>was relied on</u> by two-thirds of the subjects, while only one-third used logical analysis.

   <u>Two-thirds of the subjects relied on instinct alone</u>, while only one-third used logical analysis.

4. After the researchers completed the study, a report <u>was written</u> about their findings.

   After the researchers completed the study, <u>they wrote a report about their findings.</u>

5. The report <u>was read</u> by many experts, and most of them found the results surprising.

   <u>Many experts read the report</u>, and most of them found the results surprising.

PRACTICE 15-6

The following sentences contain illogical shifts in voice. Revise each sentence by changing the underlined active voice verb to the passive voice.

286 ▪ **UNIT 7 Revising for Clarity and Effectiveness**

> **Example:** My hometown was settled in 1865, and people <u>called</u> it Poague's Landing until 1905.
>
> My hometown was settled in 1865, *and it was called Poague's Landing until 1905.*

1. The UFO's landing was reported at noon, and someone <u>spotted</u> little green men soon afterwards.

   The UFO's landing was reported at noon, *and little green men were spotted soon afterwards.*

2. A suspect was detained by local authorities, but they later <u>released</u> the man.

   A suspect was detained by local authorities, *but the man was later released.*

3. *Forrest Gump* was voted 1994's most popular movie, and most critics also <u>praised</u> it.

   Forrest Gump was voted 1994's most popular movie, *and it was also praised by most critics.*

4. Only a week after the town was flooded, a tornado <u>hit</u> it.

   Only a week after the town was flooded, *it was hit by a tornado.*

5. The game was rescheduled when bad weather <u>interrupted</u> it.

   The game was rescheduled when *it was interrupted by bad weather.*

• • • • • • • • ▶ **FLASHBACK** ◀ • • • • • • • •

Look back at your response to the Paragraph Practice at the beginning of the chapter. Check each sentence to make sure there are no illogical shifts in voice. If you find an incorrect sentence, write it on the lines below, correcting any illogical shifts in voice.

CHAPTER 15 Avoiding Illogical Shifts • 287

• • • • • • • • • • • • • REVIEW • • • • • • • • • • • • •

CHAPTER REVIEW: STUDENT WRITING

Read the following student passage in which illogical shifts in tense, person, number, discourse, and voice have been introduced. Identify the shifts you think need to be corrected. Edit the passage to eliminate the unnecessary shifts, making sure subjects and verbs agree. The first sentence has been edited for you.

The Mixing of Cultures

Because the United States is the melting pot of the world, it ~~drew~~ *draws* thousands of immigrants from Europe, Asia, and Africa. Many of them come to the United States because they ~~wanted~~ *want* to become Americans. At the same time, they also want to preserve parts of their original cultures. This conflict confuses many immigrants. Some think that in order to become American ~~you~~ *they* have to give up ~~your~~ *their* ethnic identity. Others think it is possible to become an American without losing ~~your~~ *their* ethnic identity. To me, this is the strength of the United States: Filipino Americans are able to be both Filipino and American. I know of no other country in the world where this ~~was~~ *is* true.

Many Filipino Americans try to maintain their Filipino culture in the United States. For example, they decorate their houses to remind them of traditional houses in the Philippines. Filipinos also try to preserve their native language. Although ~~every Filipino~~ *all Filipinos* speak~~s~~ English, ~~Tagalog is also spoken by them~~ *they also speak Tagalog*—usually at home. On holidays, Filipinos observe the traditions of the Philippines. They sing Filipino folk songs, do traditional dances, and cook

Filipino foods. ~~Everyone tries~~ *They all try* to visit their relatives in the Philippines as often as they can. In this way a Filipino child can often experience ~~their~~ *his or her* ethnic culture firsthand.

My father left the Philippines because of the political persecution he experienced. He was a teacher, and the government did not like some of the ideas he ~~expresses~~ *expressed*. One day, his brother, who worked for the police, warned him that ~~you will~~ *he would* be arrested if ~~you keep~~ *he kept* criticizing the government. The next day my father and mother ~~buy~~ *bought* plane tickets for the United States. Today, he often talks about his life in the Philippines. He describes his village and his boyhood on his father's coffee plantation. He says that he cannot explain how beautiful his home was. As he talks, he ~~got~~ *gets* a faraway look in his eyes. I know that he loves his home and that he ~~missed~~ *misses* it. When I ask him if he would ever want to move back, he says that ~~"~~this is his home now.~~"~~

A Filipino family that wants to hold onto ~~their~~ *its* ethnic background can learn to live in America. Here cultures mix and enrich one another. Each culture has something to offer America--~~their~~ *its* food, language, and traditions. At the same time, America ~~had~~ *has* something to offer each culture--economic opportunity, education, and freedom.

CHAPTER REVIEW: EDITING PRACTICE

Reread your response to the Paragraph Practice at the beginning of the chapter. Revise any illogical shifts in tense, person, number, discourse, or voice. When you have finished, do the same for another paragraph or assignment you are currently working on.

CHAPTER REVIEW: COLLABORATIVE ACTIVITIES

1. On a piece of paper, write five sentences that include shifts from present to past tense, some logical and some illogical. Then, exchange papers with another person in your group, and revise any incorrect sentences.

2. As a group, compose five sentences containing illogical shifts in tense, person, number, discourse, and voice to use as a test. Then, exchange tests with another group in the class. After you have taken their test, compare your answers with theirs.

3. As a group, choose five words from the list below, and use each as the subject of a sentence. Make sure each sentence includes a pronoun that refers to the subject.

    Example:

    Doctors must know their patients.

doctors	anything	a parent	everybody
someone	raccoons	anyone	a woman
workers	no one	children	everyone
something	a book	anybody	people

    Then, make sure that the sentences you have written do not include any illogical shifts in person or number.

Review

- An illogical tense shift occurs when a writer changes tense for no apparent reason. (See 15A.)

    Illogical shift in tense: The dog walked slowly to the fireplace. Then, he circles twice and lies down.
    Revised: The dog walked slowly to the fireplace. Then, he circled twice and lay down.

- An illogical shift in person occurs when a writer shifts from one person to another for no apparent reason. (See 15B.)

    Illogical shift in person: The hikers were told that you had to stay on the trail.
    Revised: The hikers were told that they had to stay on the trail.

    (continued on the following page)

(continued from previous page)

- An illogical shift in number occurs when a writer shifts from singular to plural (or the other way around) for no apparent reason. (See 15C.)

    Illogical shift in number: Each visitor to the museum must check their cameras at the entrance.
    Revised: Each visitor to the museum must check his or her camera at the entrance.

- An illogical shift in discourse occurs when a writer combines direct and indirect discourse within the same sentence. (See 15D.)

    Illogical shift in discourse: Molly asked could she help me plan my trip?
    Revised (direct discourse): Molly asked, "Can I help you plan your trip?"
    Revised (indirect discourse): Molly asked if she could help me plan my trip.

- An illogical shift in voice occurs when a writer changes from active to passive voice or from passive to active voice for no apparent reason. (See 15E.)

    Illogical shift in voice: J. D. Salinger wrote *The Catcher in the Rye,* and *Franny and Zooey* was also written by him.
    Revised: J. D. Salinger wrote *The Catcher in the Rye,* and he also wrote *Franny and Zooey.*

16 Using Parallelism

Overview

In this chapter you will learn
- To recognize parallel structure
- To avoid faulty parallelism
- To use parallelism in certain grammatical constructions

PARAGRAPH PRACTICE

Write a paragraph in which you discuss three things you would change about your college or university. In your topic sentence, identify the three things you are going to discuss in the rest of the paragraph. In the body of your paragraph, explain why you would make each change. Be sure to support your statements with specific examples. Use the blank space below for invention. Then, write your paragraph on the lines that follow.

A RECOGNIZING PARALLEL STRUCTURE

Parallelism is the repetition of similar grammatical patterns to present similar ideas. For example, nouns are linked with nouns, verbs with verbs, adjectives with adjectives, phrases with phrases, and clauses with clauses. Parallelism makes sentences smooth, balanced, and easy to follow.

> ### ▶ FOCUS ON PARALLEL STRUCTURE ◀
>
> When you present two or three similar ideas in a sentence, check to be sure you have used parallel wording.
>
> Casey is a <u>snowboarder</u>, not a <u>skier</u>. (two nouns)
> We saw the ducks <u>fly</u>, <u>swim</u>, and <u>fish</u>. (three verbs)
> The road of life is <u>long</u>, <u>bumpy</u>, and <u>steep</u>. (three adjectives)
> <u>Making the team</u> was one thing; <u>staying on it</u> was another. (two phrases)
> <u>My, what big eyes you have</u>, Grandma! <u>My, what big ears you have</u>! <u>My, what big teeth you have</u>! (three clauses)

CHAPTER 16   Using Parallelism • 293

Faulty parallelism occurs when similar grammatical patterns are not used to present similar ideas. For example, look at how awkward and wordy the sentences that follow are compared to the sentences in the preceding box:

Casey is a snowboarder, but skiing is not something that interests him.
We saw the ducks fly, and some swam, while others were fishing.
The road of life is long, has a lot of bumps, and climbs steeply.
Making the team was one thing, but she was worried about staying on the team.
My, what big eyes you have, Grandma! And you do have big ears. Your teeth are also quite large.

To correct faulty parallelism, reword all your similar points so that they use the same grammatical pattern. For example, use all nouns or all the same verb forms.

▶ FOCUS ON PARALLEL STRUCTURE ◀

Repeating certain key words signals parallel structure and establishes the connections among similar ideas. Don't forget to include *all* the words you need to reinforce parallel structure.

Faulty: He rode on a horse, donkey, and an elephant.
Revised: He rode <u>on a</u> horse, <u>on a</u> donkey, and <u>on an</u> elephant.

PRACTICE 16-1

In the following sentences, decide whether the underlined words are parallel. If so, write *P* in the blank. If not, rewrite them to make them parallel.

Examples: As a shopper, I <u>insist on quality</u>, <u>expect good service</u>, and <u>seek out value</u>. *P*

For me, <u>getting an A on a math test</u> is harder than <s>when I swim</s> *swimming* ten miles. ____

1. People today are <u>working more</u> and <u>playing less</u>. *P*

2. Some smokers say that they smoke cigarettes to help <u>wake themselves up</u>, <u>give themselves a break</u>, and <s>also so that they can</s> <u>keep themselves going</u>. ____

294 ▪ **UNIT 7** Revising for Clarity and Effectiveness

3. They also admit that cigarettes are <u>expensive</u>, <u>smelly</u>, and <s>have dangerous dangers</s>. *dangerous* ____

4. Computer games can be <u>addictive</u> and <u>hypnotic</u>. *P* ____

5. <u>Being happy in life</u> is more important to me than <s>that I make</s> a lot of money. *making* ____

6. The team <u>lost the game</u> even though the quarterback <s>was playing</s> his best. *played* ____

7. Judges must <u>care about justice</u>, <u>uphold the laws</u>, and <s>they should</s> treat defendants fairly. ____

8. <u>According to the newspaper, the economy is getting stronger.</u> <u>According to my wallet, the economy is getting weaker.</u> *P* ____

9. <u>Love is blind</u>, but <s>the feeling of</s> hate is blinder. ____

10. To succeed, <u>set realistic goals</u>, <u>work toward them diligently</u>, and <s>you must also</s> believe in yourself. ____

• • • • • • • ▶ **FLASHBACK** ◀ • • • • • • •

Look back at your response to the Paragraph Practice at the beginning of the chapter. Do you see any examples of faulty parallelism? If so, rewrite one incorrect sentence on the lines below, revising for parallel structure.

_____

_____

B USING PARALLEL STRUCTURE

As you have seen, parallel structure enables you to emphasize the relationship among similar points. Therefore, parallel structure is especially important for paired items, comparisons, and items in a series.

Paired Items

You should use parallel structure when you connect ideas with a coordinating conjunction—*and, but, or, nor, for, so,* and *yet.*

> George believes in <u>doing a good job</u> and <u>minding his own business</u>.
> We must <u>pay for the cleanup now</u> or <u>pay for the cleanup later</u>.

You should also use parallel structure for paired items joined by correlative conjunctions, like *both . . . and, not only . . . but also, either . . . or, neither . . . nor,* and *rather . . . than.*

> Jan is <u>both</u> <u>artistically talented</u> <u>and</u> <u>mechanically inclined</u>.
> The group's new recording <u>not only</u> <u>has a great dance beat</u> but <u>also</u> <u>has thought-provoking lyrics</u>.
> I'd <u>rather</u> <u>eat one worm by itself</u> <u>than</u> <u>eat twenty with ice cream</u>.

Comparisons

Because they present two items as equivalent, comparisons formed with *than* or *as* require parallel structure.

> Success is more a matter <u>of working hard</u> <u>than</u> <u>of getting lucky</u>.
> <u>She cares about her patients</u> as much as <u>she cares about her family</u>.

Items in a Series

Items in a series—words, phrases, or clauses—should be expressed in parallel terms.

> <u>Increased demand</u>, <u>high factory output</u>, <u>and</u> <u>a strong dollar</u> help the economy.
> She is a champion because <u>she stays in excellent physical condition</u>, <u>she puts in long hours of practice</u>, <u>and</u> <u>she has an intense desire to win</u>.

PRACTICE 16-2

Fill in the blanks in the following sentences with parallel elements of your own that make sense in context.

Example: A good teacher ___*knows the subject*___ and

___*respects the students.*___

Answers will vary.

1. Before a test, I am both _____ and _____.

296 • UNIT 7 Revising for Clarity and Effectiveness

2. My ideal mate should be _____, _____, and _____.

3. Next semester I will either _____ or _____.

4. I define success more as _____ than as _____.

5. Rich people _____, but poor people _____.

6. I have noticed that some _____, while other _____.

7. To advance in a job, you must _____, _____, and _____.

8. Three reasons to go to college are _____, _____, and _____.

9. _____ is more important to me than _____.

10. I enjoy _____ more than _____.

PRACTICE 16-3

Rewrite the following sentences to achieve parallel structure.

Example: California's San Gabriel Valley is close to mountains, and beaches and deserts are nearby.

California's San Gabriel Valley is close to mountains, beaches, and deserts.

1. Pasadena and Claremont are major cities in the valley. So is Pomona.

Pasadena, Claremont, and Pomona are major cities in the valley.

_____

CHAPTER 16   Using Parallelism • 297

2. Pasadena offers the famous Rose Bowl stadium, and the Norton Simon Museum and the historic Wrigley house are also there.

   Pasadena offers the famous Rose Bowl stadium, the Norton Simon Museum, and the historic Wrigley house.

3. Watching the big Tournament of Roses Parade is more exciting than it would be to view the Macy's Thanksgiving parade.

   Watching the big Tournament of Roses Parade is more exciting than viewing the Macy's Thanksgiving parade.

4. You can watch from the crowded parade route. The comfort of your living room is also a possibility.

   You can watch from the crowded parade route or from the comfort of your living room.

5. Judges rate the rose-covered floats on their originality, what artistic merit they have, and the overall impact they make.

   Judges rate the rose-covered floats on their originality, artistic merit, and overall impact.

6. Some people enjoy the Rose Bowl game more than they would like the parade.

   Some people enjoy the Rose Bowl game more than the parade.

7. The Rose Bowl game is not only America's oldest collegiate championship but also the bowl game that is the country's most popular.

   The Rose Bowl game is not only America's oldest collegiate championship but also the country's most popular bowl game.

8. Held every fall in Pomona, the Los Angeles County Fair offers carnival rides, popular performers are presented, and there are agricultural shows included.

   Held every fall in Pomona, the Los Angeles County Fair offers carnival rides, popular performers, and agricultural shows.

9. Visitors come to play challenging skill games, and they also can enjoy various ethnic foods.

   Visitors come to play challenging skill games and to enjoy various ethnic foods.

10. The starting gate was introduced at the valley's Santa Anita Race Track, and so was electrical timing, as well as the photo finish.

    The starting gate, electrical timing, and the photo finish were introduced at the valley's Santa Anita Race Track.

▶ FLASHBACK ◀

Look back at your response to the Paragraph Practice at the beginning of the chapter. On the lines below, rewrite three sentences from your response. In one revised sentence, use a correlative conjunction such as *both . . . and;* in another sentence, make a comparison using *than* or *as;* and in a third sentence, present items in a series. (Instead of rewriting sentences from your paragraph, you may write three new sentences on the same topic.) When you have finished, check to make sure you have used parallel structure in each sentence.

1. _____

_____

2. _____

_____

3. _____

_____

CHAPTER 16 Using Parallelism • 299

REVIEW

CHAPTER REVIEW: STUDENT WRITING

Read the following student passage, in which examples of faulty parallelism have been introduced. Identify the sentences you think need to be corrected, and make the changes required to maintain parallelism. In addition, supply all words necessary for clarity, grammar, and sense, adding punctuation as needed. The first sentence has been edited for you.

Questionable Heroes

Heroes are people who are looked up to for their outstanding achievements and ~~are also admired~~ *their admirable* personal qualities. Earlier generations looked up to heroes who played a part in their country's history, who contributed something to society, and ~~they also liked people~~ who showed moral or intellectual superiority. These heroes included colonial Americans, who established this country, *a*bolitionists, who brought an end to slavery, and soldiers, ~~because they~~ *who* served their country in time of war, ~~were also included~~. Most young people today, however, do not understand the real definition of a hero. They find their heroes not in books or in history, but *in* television ~~is the place they look~~. Not only do they admire rock performers, but also *they* admire athletes and movie stars ~~are admired by them~~.

The heroes of today are recognized not for their honesty or leadership, but ~~they are liked~~ for the entertainment they provide. How can big-name celebrities like Arnold Schwarzenegger, Madonna, and Michael Jordan compare to genuine heroes like George Washington, Thomas Jefferson, or

Martin Luther King, Jr.? The answer is that they do not. Washington helped the thirteen colonies gain their independence from Great Britain, *Jefferson drafted* ~~and~~ the Declaration of Independence, ~~was drafted by Jefferson. In addition,~~ *and* Martin Luther King, Jr., risked his life to achieve equal rights. By contrast, the people who are on the covers of magazines today are honored only because of their looks or ~~they can~~ *their ability to* toss a football. Sadly, many of today's heroes are admired not because of anything they have actually done, but ~~people admire them~~ because of the image they project.

Fictional characters have always served as role models for children. Early American heroes like Johnny Appleseed and Molly Pitcher were brave and ~~also acted generously~~ *generous*. Compare these figures to Bart Simpson and Beavis and Butt-head, cartoon characters who have brought the concept of heroism to a new low. Their crude behavior, their lack of interest in school, and ~~the fact that they have~~ *their* questionable values make their attraction a mystery. Sold-out Halloween masks of these crude characters, however, are proof of their great popularity.

Clearly, the stature of heroes has diminished over time. The forgotten heroes of the past who represented honesty, loyalty, and leadership have been replaced by individuals who are sarcastic, ~~and~~ cynical, ~~and they are also~~ juvenile, and mischievous. Heroes like George Washington, Thomas Jefferson, and Martin Luther King, Jr., stand much higher than the slick media creations of today.

CHAPTER REVIEW: EDITING PRACTICE

Reread your response to the Paragraph Practice at the beginning of the chapter. As you read, underline any pairs or series of words, phrases, or clauses you encounter. Then, add parallel constructions where you can to increase emphasis or clarity. When you are finished, do the same for another paragraph or assignment you are currently working on.

CHAPTER REVIEW: COLLABORATIVE ACTIVITIES

1. Working in a group, list three or four qualities that you associate with each word in the following pairs.

   - Brothers and sisters
   - Teachers and students
   - Parents and children
   - City and country
   - Baseball and football
   - Books and television
   - Work and play

2. Write a compound sentence comparing each of the above pairs of words. Use a coordinating conjunction to link the clauses, and make sure each sentence uses clear parallel structure, mentions both words, and draws on the qualities you listed for the words in the preceding activity.

3. Choose the three best sentences your group has written for Collaborative Activity 2. Then one student from each group should write these sentences on the board so the entire class can read them. The class can then decide which sentences make the best use of parallelism.

Review

- Parallelism is the repetition of similar grammatical patterns to present similar ideas. (See 16A.)

    Casey is a snowboarder, not a skier.
    We saw the ducks fly, swim, and fish.

- Use parallel structure when you pair items. (See 16B.)

    George believes in doing a good job and minding his own business.
    Jan is both artistically talented and mechanically inclined.

(continued on the following page)

(continued from the previous page)

- Use parallel structure in comparisons formed with *than* or *as*. (See 16B.)

    Success is more a matter of <u>working hard</u> than of <u>getting lucky</u>.

- Use parallel structure for items in a series. (See 16B.)

    <u>Increased demand</u>, <u>high factory output,</u> and <u>a strong dollar</u> help the economy.

17 Revising for Sentence Variety

Overview

In this chapter you will learn
- To vary sentence types
- To vary sentence openings
- To combine sentences for greater sentence variety
- To vary sentence length

PARAGRAPH PRACTICE

In 1994 California voters approved Proposition 187, a law (since challenged in the courts) that denies free public education and non-emergency health care to illegal immigrants. Would you have voted for or against this measure? Why? Make sure your topic sentence states your position and the rest of the paragraph presents the reasons that support it. Use the blank space below for invention. Then, write your paragraph on the lines that follow.

In earlier chapters, you learned to recognize the basic sentence pattern, to construct different kinds of sentences, and to distinguish correct sentences from faulty ones. Now you are ready to focus on writing sentences that add interest to your writing. One way to accomplish this is by varying the form and length of the sentences you use.

A VARYING SENTENCE TYPES

Most English sentences are **statements.** Others are **questions** or **exclamations.** As you explore your options for increasing sentence variety, you should experiment with all three types of sentences.

> ▶ FOCUS ON SENTENCE TYPES ◀
>
> In addition to statements, questions, and exclamations, writers can also use **commands,** statements that address readers directly. ("Now, consider another argument.") In college writing, this kind of sentence is used frequently in writing instructions (see 3D and 27D), but rarely in other situations.

All of the sentences in the following paragraph are statements.

> In less than twenty years, the image of African Americans in television sitcoms seemed to change dramatically, reflecting the changing status of black men and women in American society. In *Beulah,* the 1950 sitcom that was the first to star an African-American woman, the title character was a maid. Her friends were portrayed as irresponsible and not very smart. *Amos 'n' Andy,* which also appeared in the 1950s, continued these unflattering stereotypes of black characters. In 1968, with the civil rights movement at its height, the NBC comedy hit *Julia* portrayed a black woman in a much more favorable light. A widowed nurse, raising a small boy on her own, Julia was a dedicated professional and a patient and devoted mother. The image of the African American was certainly more positive, but the character was no more balanced or three-dimensional than earlier black characters had been.

In the revised paragraph, a question and an exclamation add variety to the original.

> In less than twenty years, the image of African Americans in television sitcoms seemed to change dramatically, reflecting the changing status of black men and women in American society. <u>But had anything really changed?</u> In *Beulah,* the 1950 sitcom that was the first to star an African-American woman, the title character was a maid. Her friends were portrayed as irresponsible and not very smart. *Amos 'n' Andy,* which also appeared in the 1950s, continued these unflattering stereotypes of black characters. In 1968, with the civil rights movement at its height, the NBC comedy hit *Julia* portrayed a black woman in a much more favorable light. A widowed nurse, raising a small boy on her own, Julia was a dedicated professional and a patient and devoted mother. The image of the African American was certainly more positive, but the character was no more balanced or three-dimensional than earlier black characters had been. <u>Julia was not an object of ridicule; instead, she was a saint</u>!

By adding a provocative question to the revised paragraph, the writer draws readers in and makes them want to read further to find out the answer. The paragraph closes with an exclamation that adds a lively emotional response to the otherwise straightforward discussion.

▶ FOCUS ON SENTENCE TYPES ◀

Exclamations are widely used in informal, personal writing and in dialogue to suggest emotional intensity and emphasis. The more formal the writing is, however, the less often exclamations are used.

306 • UNIT 7 Revising for Clarity and Effectiveness

PRACTICE 17-1

Revise the following passage to vary sentence types. Change two of the statements into questions and one of the statements into an exclamation.

(1) A recent study shows that Americans are getting fatter every year. (2) On the average, adult Americans today are eight pounds heavier than they were ten years ago. (3) ~~Several factors are~~ *What is* responsible for this trend~~.~~ *?* (4) First, Americans are increasingly less active than they have been in the past. (5) In addition, most Americans consume too many high-calorie fast-food meals. (6) Finally, experts believe that the decline in the number of Americans who smoke has contributed to this national weight gain. (7) ~~You may wonder about~~ *What is* the relationship between smoking and weight gain~~.~~ *?* (8) Ex-smokers often replace cigarettes with food, and because nicotine raises the rate at which the body burns calories, smokers burn calories somewhat more slowly after they quit. (9) Therefore, people who quit smoking almost can't help but gain weight. (10) ~~This is~~ *What* a dilemma~~.~~ *!*

••••••••▶ **FLASHBACK** ◀••••••••

Reread your response to the Paragraph Practice at the beginning of the chapter. What questions does your paragraph answer? Write one or two on the lines below.

Question 1: _____

Question 2: _____

If you can, add one of these questions to your paragraph.
    If you think an exclamation would be an appropriate addition to your paragraph, suggest one below.

Exclamation: _____

Where in your paragraph could you add this exclamation?

B VARYING SENTENCE OPENINGS

Varying the way you begin your sentences is another way of adding life to your writing. If you always begin with the subject, your writing is likely to seem dull and repetitive, as does the writing in the paragraph below.

> Scientists have been observing a disturbing phenomenon. The population of frogs, toads, and salamanders has been declining. This decline was first noticed in the mid-1980s. Some reports blamed chemical pollution. Some biologists began to suspect a fungal disease was killing these amphibians. The most plausible explanation seems to be that the amphibians' eggs are threatened by solar radiation. This radiation penetrates the thinned ozone layer, which used to shield them from the sun's rays.

Instead of routinely opening sentences with the subject, you can try beginning with one or more adverbs, as the following paragraph illustrates. (For more on adverbs, see Chapter 20.)

> Scientists have been observing a disturbing phenomenon. <u>Gradually but steadily</u>, the population of frogs, toads, and salamanders has been declining. This decline was first noticed in the mid-1980s. Some reports blamed chemical pollution. Some biologists began to suspect a fungal disease was killing these amphibians. <u>However</u>, the most plausible explanation seems to be that the amphibians' eggs are threatened by solar radiation. This radiation penetrates the thinned ozone layer, which used to shield them from the sun's rays.

You can also begin some sentences with prepositional phrases. A **prepositional phrase** (such as *to the bank, on the town,* or *under my skin*) is made up of a preposition and its object. (For a list of commonly used prepositions, see 21A.) Notice how prepositional phrases add even more variety to the paragraph.

> <u>In recent years</u>, scientists have been observing a disturbing phenomenon. Gradually but steadily, the population of frogs, toads, and salamanders has been declining. This decline was first noticed in the mid-1980s. <u>At first</u>, some reports blamed chemical pollution. <u>After a while</u>, some biologists began to suspect a fungal disease was killing these amphibians. However, the most plausible explanation seems to be that the amphibians' eggs are threatened by solar radiation. This radiation penetrates the thinned ozone layer, which used to shield them from the sun's rays.

FOCUS ON SENTENCE OPENINGS

In addition to adding variety to sentence openings, adverbs and prepositional phrases can also function as transitions, joining your sentences smoothly into a paragraph. (See 2C.)

Remember that a comma usually follows an adverb or prepositional phrase that opens a sentence. (See 22B.)

PRACTICE 17-2

Several sentences in the following passage contain prepositional phrases and adverbs that could be moved to the beginnings of sentences. Revise the passage to vary the sentence openings by moving prepositional phrases to the beginnings of three sentences and by moving adverbs to the beginnings of three other sentences. Be sure to set off these phrases and adverbs with commas. The first sentence has been revised for you.

Other answers are possible.

(1) ~~A~~ *In 1981, a* disaster struck Kansas City ~~in 1981~~, tragically killing over one hundred people. (2) Partygoers were dancing in the crowded lobby of a new hotel, the Hyatt Regency. (3) ~~The~~ *Suddenly, the* dancers ~~suddenly~~ heard a very loud cracking sound. (4) ~~Two~~ *Above them, two* suspended walkways ~~above them~~ were packed with observers stomping heavily in time to the music. (5) The dancers watched in horror as the walkways began to crash into the lobby. (6) ~~The~~ *First, the* top walkway ~~first~~ broke loose from the ceiling and crashed into a second walkway beneath it. (7) ~~Both~~ *With a loud roar, both* concrete walkways then collapsed ~~with a loud roar~~ into the hotel's crowded lobby bar. (8) People who had been having a good time only moments before now screamed hysterically as they watched others die horrible deaths. (9) ~~It~~ *Certainly, it* was ~~certainly~~ a scene the survivors would not soon forget.

PRACTICE 17-3

Listed below are three adverbs and three prepositional phrases. In the passage that follows, add these to the beginnings of sentences in order to

CHAPTER 17 Revising for Sentence Variety • 309

vary sentence openings. Be sure that your additions connect ideas clearly and logically.

Occasionally	Sadly
For example	In fact
With their screams and chants	Of course

Other answers are possible.

(1) Professional football is one of the most popular sports in the country; it is also one of the most dangerous. (2) *Sadly,* Bob Utley and Darryl Stingley are now paraplegics because of injuries they suffered on the field, and the disabled list increases each season.

(3) The league has established new rules to make the game safer, and some of these have cut down on serious injuries. (4) *For example, a* ~~A~~ player cannot tackle a kicker after he has kicked the ball, and a player cannot tackle a quarterback after he has thrown the ball or a runner after he has gone out of bounds. (5) These precautions, however, do not always protect players. (6) *Occasionally, players* ~~Players~~ still tackle other players in violation of the rules because they are angry and frustrated or even as a calculated strategy. (7) *In fact, one* ~~One~~ coach is rumored to have placed bounties on rival players. (8) A team member collects by putting the opposing player out of commission for the entire game.

(9) *Of course, the* ~~The~~ fans also share the blame for the violence of football. (10) *With their screams and chants, they* ~~They~~ encourage players to hit harder or play with more intensity. (11) They believe their team should do anything to win. (12) The unfortunate fact is that as football becomes more dangerous to players, it becomes more popular with fans.

> ●●●●●●●●● ▶ **FLASHBACK** ◀ ●●●●●●●●●
>
> Look back at your response to the Paragraph Practice at the beginning of the chapter. Identify two sentences that you could revise by adding an introductory adverb or prepositional phrase to vary their openings. Write the revised sentences on the lines below.
>
> 1. _____ , _____
>   (adverb or prepositional phrase)   (original sentence)
>
>   _____
>
> 2. _____ , _____
>   (adverb or prepositional phrase)   (original sentence)
>
>   _____

C COMBINING SENTENCES

You learned in Unit 6 to combine sentences with coordination (Chapter 12) and with subordination (Chapter 13). In addition to these methods, you can combine sentences with present participles, with past participles, with compounds, or with appositives.

Coordination

Two sentences

American Sign Language is becoming more sensitive to cultural differences. Some traditional signs still reflect insulting stereotypes.

Combined (coordinating conjunction)

American Sign Language is becoming more sensitive to cultural differences, <u>but</u> some traditional signs still reflect insulting stereotypes.

Two sentences

Many people support tax cuts and reduced government spending. They would rather not give up any of their own benefits.

Combined (conjunctive adverb)

Many people support tax cuts and reduced government spending;

however, they would rather not give up any of their own benefits.

Subordination

Two sentences

Noah Webster is widely known as the first prominent American lexicographer. Many dictionaries include the name *Webster* in their titles.

Combined (subordinating conjunction)

Because Noah Webster is widely known as the first prominent American lexicographer, many dictionaries include the name *Webster* in their titles.

Two sentences

The first Chinese Exclusion Act was passed by Congress in 1882. It banned Chinese laborers from entering the U.S.

Combined (relative pronoun)

The first Chinese Exclusion Act, which was passed in 1882, banned Chinese laborers from entering the U.S.

Present Participles

As explained in Chapter 11, the **present participle** is the *-ing* form of a verb: *using, carrying*. Writers frequently use present participles to combine two short sentences into one longer sentence.

Two sentences

Duke Ellington refused to bow to current fads. He composed over a thousand songs.

Combined (present participle)

Refusing to bow to current fads, Duke Ellington composed over a thousand songs.

Notice that the verb *refused* in the first of the two separate sentences has been changed to the present participle *refusing* in the combined version. Note also that *Duke Ellington* is now the subject of the verb *composed* and that *he*, the original subject of *composed*, has been dropped.

Past Participles

Past participles of verbs are usually formed with *-ed (used, carried)* or *-d*, but there are also many irregular forms *(known, written)*; for a list of these, see 10B. Two sentences can often be combined when one of them contains a past participle.

Two sentences

Nogales, Arizona, is located on the Mexican border. It is a bilingual city.

Combined (past participle)

Located on the Mexican border, Nogales, Arizona, is a bilingual city.

Notice that the form of the verb *be* preceding the participle is dropped when the sentences are combined.

> ### ▶ FOCUS ON PUNCTUATING SENTENCES COMBINED ◀ WITH PARTICIPLES
>
> Use a comma to set off a phrase introduced by a present participle or a past participle.
>
> Remembering his working-class roots, Paul McCartney returned to Liverpool to give a concert.
> Rejected by Hamlet, Ophelia goes mad and drowns herself.

Compound Subjects or Compound Verbs

A **compound subject** consists of two nouns or pronouns, usually joined by *and;* a **compound verb** consists of two verbs, usually joined by *and*. When you combine two sentences with a compound subject or a compound verb, you eliminate repetition between the sentences. At the same time, use of such compounds helps you vary your sentences.

Two sentences

Elijah McCoy was an African-American inventor. Garrett Morgan was also an African-American inventor.

Combined (compound subject)

Elijah McCoy and Garrett Morgan were African-American inventors.

Two sentences

Robert Redford starred in *All the President's Men* in 1976. He directed *Quiz Show* in 1994.

Combined (compound verb)

Robert Redford starred in *All the President's Men* in 1976 and directed *Quiz Show* in 1994.

> **FOCUS ON COMBINING SENTENCES WITH COMPOUNDS**
>
> When you combine sentences with compounds, do not put a comma between the two parts of the compound subject or between the two parts of the compound verb.
>
> **Incorrect:** The fortune-teller read my palm, and told me about my future.
>
> **Correct:** The fortune-teller read my palm and told me about my future.
>
> Also remember that a compound subject takes a plural verb.

Appositives

An **appositive** is a word or word group that identifies or renames a noun or pronoun. Using an appositive is often a good way to combine two sentences about the same subject.

Two sentences

C. J. Walker was the first American woman to become a self-made millionaire. She marketed a line of hair-care products for black women.

Combined (appositive)

C. J. Walker, the first American woman to become a self-made millionaire, marketed a line of hair-care products for black women.

Notice that an appositive can also come at the beginning or the end of a sentence.

The first American woman to become a self-made millionaire, C. J. Walker marketed a line of hair-care products for black women.

Several books have been written about C. J. Walker, the first American woman to become a self-made millionaire.

> **FOCUS ON PUNCTUATING APPOSITIVES**
>
> When combining sentences, set off appositives with commas. See 22C.

314 • UNIT 7 Revising for Clarity and Effectiveness

To see how combining sentences can add interest to your writing, compare the two paragraphs that follow. In the following paragraph, many of the sentences are short, and the effect is choppy.

> Many Native American languages are disappearing. The people who speak them are dying. Young people are not learning the old languages. Before Europeans came to North America, over 700 languages were spoken here. Each culture had its own language. However, nineteenth-century U.S. government officials discouraged the use of these languages. They encouraged Native Americans to speak English. As a result of this policy and of the gradual assimilation of the Native American population, fewer than 200 languages survive today. For example, only a few people speak Tolowa. Tolowa is one Native American language. Other languages in danger of becoming extinct include Kanuk, Yurok, Patwin, Northern Paiute, and Wintu. All are still spoken in California. These languages and many others are classified as endangered. They struggle to survive.

The revised paragraph that follows uses a variety of strategies to combine sentences and add interest.

Subordination
Coordination

Coordination

Compound verb

Appositive

Subordination
Participle

> Many Native American languages are disappearing <u>because</u> the people who speak them are dying <u>and</u> young people are not learning the old languages. Before Europeans came to North America, over 700 languages were spoken here, <u>and</u> each culture had its own language. However, nineteenth-century U.S. government officials <u>discouraged</u> the use of these languages <u>and encouraged</u> Native Americans to speak English. As a result of this policy and of the gradual assimilation of the Native American population, fewer than 200 languages survive today. For example, only a few people speak Tolowa, <u>one Native American language</u>. Other languages in danger of becoming extinct include Kanuk, Yurok, Patwin, Northern Paiute, and Wintu, <u>which</u> are all still spoken in California. <u>Classified as endangered</u>, these languages and many others struggle to survive.

PRACTICE 17-4

Use a present participle to combine each of the following pairs of sentences into a single sentence. Eliminate any unnecessary words, and use a comma to set off each phrase introduced by a present participle.

Example: Chaplin's public accepted him unquestioningly. They saw his early characters as representations of the common man.

<u>Accepting him unquestioningly, Chaplin's public</u>

<u>saw his early characters as representations of</u>

<u>the common man.</u>

1. Charlie Chaplin grew up in the slums of London. He held various jobs and played bits in vaudeville.

   Growing up in the slums of London, Charlie Chaplin held various jobs and played bits in vaudeville.

2. Chaplin came to Hollywood in 1910. He was discovered by the director Mack Sennett.

   Coming to Hollywood in 1910, he was discovered by the director Mack Sennett.

3. Chaplin turned to writing and directing. He made his first famous film, *The Tramp*.

   Turning to writing and directing, Chaplin made his first famous film, The Tramp.

4. He often appeared in his "little tramp" role. He was a sad-looking but humorous clown in baggy pants.

   Often appearing in his "little tramp" role, he was a sad-looking but humorous clown in baggy pants.

5. Chaplin became an independent producer in 1918. He released films through United Artists.

   Becoming an independent producer in 1918, Chaplin released films through United Artists.

6. Chaplin attempted to move from silent to talking pictures. He made *City Lights* and *Modern Times*.

   Attempting to move from silent to talking pictures, Chaplin made City Lights and Modern Times.

7. Chaplin wanted to satirize Nazi Germany. He directed and starred in *The Great Dictator*.

   Wanting to satirize Nazi Germany, Chaplin directed and starred in The Great Dictator.

8. Anticommunist crusaders criticized him for his politics and his personal behavior. They attacked Chaplin in the 1950s.

   Criticizing him for his politics and personal behavior, anticommunist crusaders attacked Chaplin in the 1950s.

9. Chaplin returned to the United States in 1972. He received a special Academy Award.

   Returning to the United States in 1972, Chaplin received a special Academy Award.

10. He lived in England until his death in 1977. He was knighted by Queen Elizabeth II in 1975.

    Living in England until his death in 1977, he was knighted by Queen Elizabeth II in 1975.

PRACTICE 17-5

Use a past participle to combine the following pairs of sentences into a single sentence. Eliminate any unnecessary words, and use a comma to set off each phrase introduced by a past participle.

> **Example:** Langston Hughes was born in Missouri. He was a major African-American writer.
>
> *Born in Missouri, Langston Hughes was a major African-American writer.*

1. Hughes was interested in writing since his high school days. He published his first poem in 1921.

   Interested in writing since his high school days, Hughes published his first poem in 1921.

2. Hughes was surprised to win a magazine's poetry prize. He decided to become a writer.

   Surprised to win a magazine's poetry prize, Hughes decided to become a writer.

3. Hughes was troubled by the treatment of African Americans. He wrote poems about their lives.

   Troubled by the treatment of African Americans, he wrote poems about their lives.

4. Hughes was convinced that African-American music could be translated into poetry. He wrote his first book of poems, *The Weary Blues*.

   Convinced that African-American music could be translated into poetry, he wrote his first book of poems, The Weary Blues.

5. Hughes was celebrated by both white and black critics. He was praised for the freshness of his language and verse.

   Celebrated by both white and black critics, Hughes was praised for the freshness of his language and verse.

6. Hughes was pleased by this recognition. He published a novel and a collection of stories.

   Pleased by this recognition, Hughes published a novel and a collection of stories.

7. Hughes was known primarily as a poet. He nonetheless collaborated on several plays.

   Known primarily as a poet, he nonetheless collaborated on several plays.

8. Hughes was inspired by the people of Harlem. He did some of his most important work after moving there.

   Inspired by the people of Harlem, Hughes did some of his most important work after moving there.

9. Hughes was determined to convey his ideas to a wide audience. He wrote columns for several newspapers.

   Determined to convey his ideas to a wide audience, Hughes wrote columns for several newspapers.

10. Hughes was also interested in black history. He wrote *The First Book of Negroes* (1952) and *Famous American Negroes* (1954).

    Also interested in black history, Hughes wrote The First Book of Negroes (1952) and Famous American Negroes (1954).

PRACTICE 17-6

Combine each of the following sets of sentences into one sentence by creating a compound subject or a compound verb. Remember that a compound subject takes a plural verb.

Example: The NCAA Presidents Commission wants to reform college athletic programs, ~~It~~ *and* has recommended a number of measures for doing so.

318 ▪ UNIT 7 Revising for Clarity and Effectiveness

1. These college presidents *and their supporters* want to improve the academic performance of college athletes. ~~Their supporters also want to improve college athletes' academic performance.~~

2. Their first proposal raises the number of required core courses for entering freshmen, *and* ~~It~~ increases the SAT scores necessary for admittance.

3. A second proposal requires athletes to earn a certain number of credits every year, *and* ~~It~~ mandates a similar advancement in an athlete's grade point average.

4. Many athletic directors see the changes as unfair, *and* ~~They~~ are resisting them.

5. Georgetown basketball coach John Thompson *and many other Big East coaches* oppose~~s~~ the plan. ~~Many other Big East coaches also oppose the plan.~~

6. Thompson believes standardized test scores to be biased, *and* ~~He~~ wants their use in screening student athletes banned.

7. He *and other opponents* also fear~~s~~ that the new rules will force many athletes to choose easy majors. ~~Other opponents fear the same thing.~~

8. According to supporters, however, many athletes under the current system fail to advance academically, *and* ~~They~~ often finish their eligibility fifty or more hours short of graduation.

9. The new rules, they say, give student athletes a fair chance, *and* ~~They~~ also keep them on the graduation track.

10. In their view, lax oversight by athletic directors *and lack of support for academic excellence are* ~~is~~ to blame for the poor performance of student athletes. ~~Lack of support for academic excellence is also to blame.~~

PRACTICE 17-7

Use appositives to combine each of the following sets of sentences into one sentence. Three of your sentences should have the appositive at the be-

CHAPTER 17   Revising for Sentence Variety • 319

ginning, three should have the appositive in the middle, and three should have the appositive at the end. Be sure to use commas appropriately.

Example: Alfred Hitchcock, *an English-American film and television director,* was born in 1899 and died in 1980. ~~He was an English-American film and television director.~~

Answers may vary.

1. His first big success came in 1935 with *The Thirty-Nine Steps,* ~~It was~~ a thriller about an innocent man mistaken for a criminal.

2. His next big English-made hit, *The Lady Vanishes,* brought many offers from Hollywood. ~~It was *The Lady Vanishes*.~~

3. His first Hollywood film was the suspense classic *Rebecca,* ~~It was~~ a 1940 film version of a popular novel by Daphne du Maurier.

4. ~~Spellbound was~~ *One* ~~one~~ of his odder movies of the 1940s, *Spellbound* ~~It~~ is the story of an amnesiac head of a mental institution and includes a surreal dream sequence by Salvador Dali.

5. His most controversial film, ~~was~~ *Psycho,* ~~It~~ stars Anthony Perkins as the mentally unstable proprietor of the Bates Motel, as well as his own "mother."

6. Audiences in 1960 were truly shocked by its infamous depiction of a woman's bloody murder in a shower, ~~This is~~ a scene that represents brilliant use of sound and editing.

7. ~~Hitchcock was a~~ *A* well-known television personality as well as a film director, *Hitchcock* ~~He~~ hosted two successful series in the late 1950s and the early 1960s.

8. His hefty profile and deep voice, ~~were~~ trademarks of the early television shows, ~~They~~ are still recognizable in reruns to viewers today.

9. ~~Hitchcock was one~~ *One* of the great masters of film technique, *Hitchcock* ~~He~~ made movies admired by both popular audiences and academic critics.

320 • UNIT 7 Revising for Clarity and Effectiveness

PRACTICE 17-8

The following passage is made up of short, choppy sentences. Using the various techniques described in this section, combine these sentences so that they flow smoothly and the connections between ideas are clear and sensible. The first sentence has been done for you.

Answers will vary.

(1) Doo-Wop, ~~was~~ a form of rock and roll popular from about 1951 to 1956, (2) ~~It~~ evolved out of street-corner singing. (3) ~~It possessed~~ *Possessing* a simple beauty, (4) Doo-Wop was sung by such groups as the Moonglows, the Flamingos, and the Cadillacs. (5) Frankie Lyman ~~was~~ one of its biggest stars, (6) ~~He~~ sang with the passion of the tenements. (7) Lyman grew up in the Bronx, *and* (8) ~~He~~ made his first record with a group called the Teen Agers. (9) The group's "Why Do Fools Fall in Love?," *which* echoed the yearning of all teenagers, (10) ~~It~~ shot to the top of the charts. (11) Frankie Lyman and the Teen Agers cut one hit after another, *and* (12) ~~They~~ became a legend in Doo-Wop history.

(13) ~~The~~ *When the* British invasion of rock began in the 1960s, (14) ~~It~~ *it* pushed Doo-Wop off the charts. (15) Many Doo-Wop artists returned to the tenements, *and most* (16) ~~Most~~ were soon forgotten. (17) Lyman, *who* had been one of the most successful singers of his time, (18) ~~He~~ died penniless and addicted to heroin. (19) ~~He was buried~~ *Buried* in an unmarked grave in a Bronx cemetery, (20) ~~He~~ *he* seemed forgotten. (21) In 1993 fans of Doo-Wop finally honored Lyman's contribution to early rock and roll, *and* (22) ~~They~~ voted Frankie Lyman and the Teen Agers into the Rock and Roll Hall of Fame.

CHAPTER 17 Revising for Sentence Variety

> ### ●●●●●●●● ▶ FLASHBACK ◀ ●●●●●●●●
>
> Look back at your response to the Paragraph Practice at the beginning of the chapter. Underline two or three pairs of short sentences that you think could be combined. On the lines below, combine each pair of sentences into a single sentence, using one of the methods discussed in 17C. Use a different method for each pair of sentences.
>
> 1. _____
>
> _____
>
> 2. _____
>
> _____
>
> 3. _____
>
> _____

D VARYING SENTENCE LENGTH

A paragraph of short, choppy sentences—or a paragraph of long, rambling ones—is usually monotonous. Mixing long and short sentences, perhaps following a string of several long sentences with a relatively brief one, will enable you to create a more interesting paragraph.

In the following paragraph, the sentences are all quite short, and the result is a dull passage.

> The world's first drive-in movie theater opened on June 6, 1933, in Camden, New Jersey. Automobiles became more popular. Drive-ins did too. By the 1950s there were more than four thousand drive-in movies in the United States. Over the years, the high cost of land hurt drive-ins. So did the rising popularity of television. Now, they have been replaced by the multiplex and the VCR. There are no drive-ins at all in Alaska. There are none in Rhode Island or Delaware either. New Jersey's last drive-in closed in 1991.

The revised paragraph that appears below is more interesting because it mixes long and short sentences.

> The world's first drive-in movie theater opened on June 6, 1933, in Camden, New Jersey. As automobiles became more popular, drive-ins did too, and by the 1950s, there were more than four thousand drive-in movies in the United States. Today, there are fewer than a thousand. Over the years, the high cost of land, combined with the rising popularity of television, hurt drive-ins. Now, they have been replaced by the multiplex and the VCR. There are no drive-ins at all in Alaska, Rhode Island, or Delaware, and New Jersey's last drive-in closed in 1991.

To increase sentence variety, the writer first combined some of the original paragraph's short sentences. Then, a new short sentence ("Today, there are fewer than a thousand") was added for emphasis after a long one.

PRACTICE 17-9

This passage is made up of short, choppy sentences. Revise it so that it mixes long and short sentences. Be sure to use commas and other punctuation appropriately.

Answers will vary.

(1) The AIDS quilt contains thousands of panels. (2) Each panel honors a victim of the disease*, and each* (3) ~~Each~~ tells a story. (4) One panel is for a young man*, who* (5) ~~He~~ was a college student. (6) The panel includes a two-page account of his life*, which is* (7) ~~The pages are~~ protected by cellophane. (8) Another panel is for an eight-year-old boy. (9) It includes his action figures*, and* (10) ~~It~~ proudly displays a baseball cap. (11) A third panel displays a large picture of a young man. (12) It also includes a quotation*, that* (13) ~~The quotation~~ says, "Blood saved his life, and it took it away."

PRACTICE 17-10

The following passage contains a series of short, choppy sentences. Revise it so that it mixes long and short sentences. Be sure to use commas and other punctuation appropriately.

Answers will vary.

(1) Kente cloth is made in western Africa*, and* (2) ~~It~~ is produced primarily

by the Ashanti people. (3) It has been worn for hundreds of years by African royalty/, (4) ~~They~~ *who* consider it a sign of power and status. (5) Many African Americans wear Kente cloth/ (6) ~~They~~ *because they* see it as a link to their heritage. (7) Each motif or pattern on the cloth has a name/, (8) ~~Each~~ *and each* color has a special significance. (9) For example, red and yellow suggest a long and healthy life/, (10) ~~Green~~ *while green* and white suggest a good harvest. (11) African women may wear kente cloth as a dress or head wrap. (12) African-American women, like men, usually wear strips of cloth around their shoulders. (13) Men and women of African descent wear kente cloth as a sign of black pride/, (14) ~~Many~~ *but many* white people do not understand the significance of the cloth.

••••••••▶ FLASHBACK ◀••••••••

Look back at your response to the Paragraph Practice at the beginning of the chapter. Have you varied the lengths of your sentences? Count the number of words in each sentence, and write the results on the lines below.

Sentence 1 ____   Sentence 6 ____

Sentence 2 ____   Sentence 7 ____

Sentence 3 ____   Sentence 8 ____

Sentence 4 ____   Sentence 9 ____

Sentence 5 ____   Sentence 10 ____

Now, revise your Paragraph Practice, combining the sentences you rewrote for the previous Flashback. Then, try writing a new short sentence to follow one of your paragraph's longer sentences. Count the number of words in each sentence of your revised paragraph. Compared to your original version, are your sentences now more varied in length?

324 — UNIT 7 Revising for Clarity and Effectiveness

REVIEW

CHAPTER REVIEW: STUDENT WRITING

The student passage that follows is composed of a series of brief sentences, most of which begin with the subject. It is also missing some transitional words and expressions. Using the revision strategies illustrated in this chapter, revise the passage so its sentences are varied, interesting, and smoothly connected. The first two sentences have been edited for you.

Answers will vary.

Golf Course Management

Many people consider the career of a golf course superintendent a recreational, low-stress occupation/ ~~They think it is a job with~~ *that has* many advantages, such as idle winters and frequent opportunities to play golf. ~~My~~ *Because my* father is a golf course superintendent/, I am often asked the question, "What does your dad do in the winter?" My response is that he works normal hours. ~~His~~ *Obviously, his* summers are more hectic, but his job is demanding all year 'round.

~~A~~ *During the summer, a* golf course superintendent arrives at work about 5:30 a.m. ~~during the summer~~. My dad gets much of his work done in the early morning hours/ ~~The~~ *, when the* golf course is not open to golfers ~~then~~. My dad keeps his crew at work until two or three in the afternoon. During this time, they groom the course/ ~~They also~~ *and* fertilize the greens and fairways.

~~My~~ *my* dad usually returns home during the summer between 4 and 7 p.m. ~~It depends~~ *Depending* on how much he and his crew are able to accomplish/ He sometimes returns to work after dinner for an hour or two in order to irrigate/ ~~He~~ *; thus, he* avoids most

CHAPTER 17 Revising for Sentence Variety • 325

irrigation during the daytime. After all, members would be quite upset if he turned on the irrigation system during their golf game!

Summer hours are often long and tiring for a golf course superintendent because most of the responsibility falls on his shoulders. His crew is able to maintain the course, but they lack the specific training and education of a certified golf course superintendent. For example, my dad has a four-year college degree, as most superintendents do. He knows all about horticulture, soils, and drainage, and he has also studied fertilizing techniques and chemistry. In addition, he knows how to diagnose diseases occurring in grass and trees, and knows how to apply the safest, most effective treatments. Finally, he controls nuisances such as water algae and harmful insects that permeate the grass and trees and, if not stopped, will kill them.

Although the workload decreases considerably as the weather turns colder, a golf course superintendent still has plenty to keep him occupied. For instance, he does paperwork and supervises the year-round employees and attends seminars. Designed to help golf course superintendents, these seminars provide important information about the latest improvements in turf management. Superintendents also find out about current treatments and learn about fertilizers. Many golf course superintendents attend these conferences, which educators and suppliers from around the world also attend.

My father enjoys working as a golf course superintendent~~,~~ *and* ~~He~~ doesn't mind the long hours and stress this job entails. ~~It~~ *However, it* does bother him when people don't take his job seriously or think it is merely a part-time job for a person who likes to play golf.

CHAPTER REVIEW: EDITING PRACTICE

Reread your response to the Paragraph Practice at the beginning of the chapter. Using whichever of the strategies in this chapter seem most appropriate, revise your paragraph so its sentences are varied, interesting, and smoothly connected. When you are finished, do the same to another paragraph or assignment you are currently working on.

CHAPTER REVIEW: COLLABORATIVE ACTIVITIES

Read the following list of sentences.

- Many well-known African-American writers left the United States in the years following World War II.
- Many went to Paris.
- Richard Wright was a novelist.
- He wrote *Native Son* and *Black Boy.*
- He wrote *Uncle Tom's Children.*
- He left the U.S. for Paris in 1947.
- James Baldwin wrote *Another Country, The Fire Next Time,* and *Giovanni's Room.*
- He also wrote essays.
- He came to Paris in 1948.
- Chester Himes was a detective story writer.
- He arrived in Paris in 1953.
- William Gardner Smith was a novelist and journalist.
- He also left the U.S. for Paris.
- These expatriates found Paris more hospitable than America.
- They also found it less racist.

1. Working in a small group, add to the list one sentence that is a question or an exclamation. Then, try beginning one or more of the sentences on the list with an adverb or with a prepositional phrase.

2. Continuing to work in your group, combine sentences on the list to add variety and interest. Use the strategies illustrated in 17C as a guide.

3. When your group's revisions are complete, trade paragraphs with another group, and further edit the other group's paragraph to improve sentence variety and coherence.

> **Review**
>
> - Vary sentence types, using an occasional question or exclamation. (See 17A.)
> - Vary sentence openings. (See 17B.)
>
>   *Open with an adverb:* <u>Now,</u> reports point the blame at ultraviolet radiation.
>   *Open with a prepositional phrase:* <u>At first</u>, some reports blamed chemical pollution.
>
> - Combine sentences. (See 17C.)
>
>   *Use a coordinating conjunction:* American Sign Language is becoming more sensitive to cultural differences, <u>but</u> some traditional signs still reflect insulting stereotypes.
>   *Use a subordinating conjunction:* <u>Because</u> Noah Webster is widely known as the first prominent American lexicographer, many dictionaries include the name *Webster* in their titles.
>   *Use a relative pronoun:* The first Chinese Exclusion Act, <u>which was passed in 1882</u>, banned Chinese laborers from entering the U.S.
>   *Use a participle:* <u>Refusing to bow to current fads</u>, Duke Ellington composed over a thousand songs.
>   *Use a compound:* <u>Elijah McCoy and Garrett Morgan</u> were African-American inventors.
>   *Use an appositive:* C. J. Walker, <u>the first American woman to become a self-made millionaire</u>, marketed a line of hair-care products for black women.
>
> - Vary sentence length. (See 17D.)

18 Revising Words

> **Overview**
>
> In this chapter you will learn
> - To choose exact words
> - To use concise language
> - To avoid trite expressions
> - To use similes and metaphors
> - To avoid sexist language

PARAGRAPH PRACTICE

In the space below, write a paragraph in which you discuss what stereotypes most people have about men and women. Do you think any of these stereotypes are based on fact? Be specific, and include the transitional words and phrases readers will need to follow your discussion. Use the blank space below for invention. Then, write your paragraph on the lines that follow.

CHAPTER 18 Revising Words • 329

Good writing involves more than writing grammatically correct sentences and clear paragraphs. It also involves choosing words that convey your ideas with precision and clarity and that make a positive impact on readers. As this chapter explains, you have to take the time when you write, revise, and edit to use exact words and concise language, avoid trite and sexist expressions, and decide whether or not to include similes and metaphors.

A CHOOSING EXACT WORDS

Good writers take the time to find the right word and do not settle for one that comes close to the mark but somehow misses it. To express their ideas as clearly as they can, experienced writers will choose specific and concrete words and avoid vague and abstract terms whenever they can.

Specific words refer to particular persons, places, things, or ideas. **Vague** words refer to entire classes or groups. Statements that contain specific words are generally more vivid than ones that contain only generalities. Each of the following sentences contains vague words that give little precise information.

   While walking in the woods, I saw an <u>animal</u>.
   The <u>person</u> decided to run for Congress.
   The <u>weapon</u> was used in many murders.
   Dennis bought some new <u>clothes</u>.
   I enjoyed my <u>meal</u> a lot.
   Darrell has always wanted a <u>car</u>.

Notice how the specific words make the following revised sentences clearer and more explicit.

While walking in the woods, I saw a <u>baby skunk</u>.
<u>Rebecca</u> decided to run for Congress.
The <u>Saturday night special</u> was used in many murders.
Dennis bought a new <u>blue vest and baggy jeans</u>.
I enjoyed my <u>pepperoni pizza</u> a lot.
Darrell has always wanted a <u>black '57 Chevy convertible</u>.

Concrete words appeal to your senses by naming things you can see, hear, taste, feel, and smell—for example, *orange, blaring, salty, rough,* and *pungent*. **Abstract** words refer to ideas or qualities you cannot perceive with the senses—*happiness* or *truth,* for example. The more concrete your language is, the more vivid and alive your ideas will be to readers. For example, consider the following sentences:

One night I saw a moth fly into a candle flame. It was interesting.

Certainly, these sentences convey the writer's general idea, but readers have no idea what the scene looked like, sounded like, or smelled like. Why was it "interesting"? Compare the description above with the following one by the nature writer Annie Dillard, which uses concrete language to help readers visualize the scene:

One night a moth flew into a candle, was caught, burnt dry, and held. . . . A golden female moth, a biggish one with a two-inch wingspread, flapped into the fire, dropped abdomen into the wet wax, stuck, flamed, and frazzled a second. Her moving wings ignited . . . and vanished in a fine, foul smoke.

> ▶ **FOCUS** ON CHOOSING EXACT WORDS ◀
>
> One way to strengthen your writing is to avoid **utility words**—general words like *good*, *nice*, or *great* that some writers use instead of taking the time to think of more precise words. For example, when you say the ocean looked *pretty*, do you really mean that it *sparkled, glistened, rippled, foamed, surged,* or *billowed*? If you can't think of the word you need, try consulting a dictionary or a thesaurus, a book that lists synonyms. (Be sure to double-check in your dictionary any words you find in a thesaurus in order to make sure you understand what they mean and how they are used in a sentence.)

PRACTICE 18-1

In the following passage, the writer describes an old store in the town of Nameless, Tennessee. Underline the specific, concrete words in the passage that help you experience the scene the writer describes. The first sentence has been done for you.

(1) The old store, lighted only by three fifty-watt bulbs, smelled of coal oil and baking bread. (2) In the middle of the rectangular room, where the oak floor sagged a little, stood an iron stove. (3) To the right was a wooden table with an unfinished game of checkers and a stool made from an apple-tree stump. (4) On shelves around the walls sat earthen jugs with corncob stoppers, a few canned goods, and some of the two thousand old clocks and clockworks Thurmond Watts owned. (5) Only one was ticking; the others he just looked at.

William Least Heat-Moon, *Blue Highways*

PRACTICE 18-2

Below are ten vague or unspecific words. In the blank beside each, substitute a more specific word. Then, use the more specific word in a sentence of your own. You may, if you wish, use more than one word in the blank and in your sentence, as in the example.

Example: talked   *chattered excitedly*

   All through dinner my six-year-old chattered

   excitedly about his first day of school.

Answers will vary.

1. car

2. walk

3. big

4. animal

5. clothing _____

6. sat down _____

7. talented _____

8. accident _____

9. dwelling _____

10. crowded _____

PRACTICE 18-3

The following paragraph is a vaguely worded letter of application for a job. Decide on a job that you yourself might actually want to apply for. Then, rewrite the paragraph on a separate page, substituting specific language for the vague language of the original and adding details where necessary. Start by making the job itself specific in the first sentence. For example, you might begin with a statement like this: "I would like to apply for the dental technician position you advertised in today's *Post*." Then, go on to include specific information about your background and qualifications, expanding the original paragraph into a three-paragraph letter, and changing anything you wish in the original.

Answers will vary.

    I would like to apply for the position you advertised in today's paper. I graduated from high school and am currently attending college. I have taken several courses that have prepared me to fulfill the duties the position requires. I also have several personal qualities that I think you would find important in a person holding this position. In addition, I have had certain experiences that qualify me for such a job. I would appreciate the opportunity to meet with you to discuss your needs as an employer. Thank you.

> ●●●●●●●●▶ **FLASHBACK** ◀●●●●●●●●
>
> Look back at your response to the Paragraph Practice at the beginning of the chapter. Find a sentence containing vague or abstract words, and write those words on the lines below. Then, provide an alternative that is more specific or concrete than each of the original words. Finally, rewrite the sentence, substituting the words that more precisely express your meaning.
>
> Vague or abstract words   Specific or concrete alternatives
>
> _____   _____
>
> _____   _____
>
> _____   _____
>
> Revised sentence _____
>
> _____

B USING CONCISE LANGUAGE

Concise writing comes right to the point and says what it has to say with the minimum number of words. Too often, however, writers construct wordy sentences full of empty phrases called **deadwood** that add nothing to meaning. A good way to test a sentence for nonessential words is to see if crossing out the words affects its meaning.

The flower was red ~~in color~~.

If it does not, you can safely assume the sentence is better off without the extra words.

Sometimes you have to rewrite, substituting a condensed version of a phrase to make a sentence more concise.

Wordy

Due to the fact that I was tired, I missed my first class.

Concise

I was tired, so I missed my first class.

Wordy

In order to follow the plot, you must make an outline.

Concise

To follow the plot, you must make an outline.

▶ FOCUS ON USING CONCISE LANGUAGE ◀

The following phrases add nothing to a sentence. You can usually delete or condense them with no loss of meaning.

Wordy	Concise
It is clear that	(delete)
It is a fact that	(delete)
The reason is that	Because
It is my opinion that	I think/I believe
Due to the fact that	Because
Despite the fact that	Although
In this day and age	Today/Currently
At that time	Then
In most cases	Usually
In the final analysis	Finally
Subsequent to	After

Like deadwood, **needless repetition** can be eliminated with no loss of meaning. Consider the following sentences:

My instructor told me the book was <u>old-fashioned and outdated</u>.
The <u>terrible tragedy</u> of the fire could have been avoided with a smoke detector.

Although repetition can be used effectively—for example, to emphasize important ideas—the repeated phrases in the two sentences above serve no purpose. (An old-fashioned book *is* outdated; a tragedy is *always* terrible.) Notice how easily these sentences can be edited to eliminate redundancy:

My instructor told me the book was ~~old-fashioned and~~ outdated.
The ~~terrible~~ tragedy of the fire could have been avoided with a smoke detector.

> ### ▶ FOCUS ON USING CONCISE LANGUAGE ◀
>
> Sometimes beginning writers try to impress readers by using elevated language. They mistakenly believe that flowery language, big words, and complex sentences are characteristics of good writing. Such elevated language, however, is nearly always wordy. Remember, good writing is clear and concise.
>
> **Elevated:** When I entered this institution of higher learning, I cogitated about the selections I had before me.
>
> **Revised:** When I came to college, I thought about the courses I could take.
>
> A good rule to remember is never to use ten words when you can say the same thing in five or—as in the examples above—seventeen words when you can say the same thing in thirteen.

PRACTICE 18-4

The following sentences contain deadwood and needless repetition. Cross out any unnecessary words, and make any changes or other revisions that may be needed.

Example: ~~It is a fact that many~~ *Many* grown-up children have trouble getting their parents, ~~their mother and father,~~ to treat them as adults.

Answers may vary.

1. Some parents constantly criticize ~~all the time~~ and offer unwanted advice ~~that their children do not desire to hear~~.

2. Adult children can become frustrated ~~due to the fact that~~ *because* their parents seem to feel they are not capable of making their own decisions ~~by themselves~~.

3. When this happens, the children may begin to whine childishly ~~and in a juvenile manner~~ or even throw a temper tantrum ~~despite the fact that~~ *although* such behavior only reinforces their parents' attitudes.

4. ~~In most cases~~ *Usually* there are better ways to improve one's parents' behavior ~~for the better~~.

5. ~~In order to~~ *To* get parents to stop being critical, an adult child might turn the tables and encourage his or her parents to ~~have a discussion and~~ talk about their own childhoods.

6. The child can then point out any similarities between the parents' behavior ~~then~~ in the past and his or her behavior ~~now~~ in the present.

7. ~~Another thing adult~~ *Adult* children might also ~~do is to~~ explain that while they value their parents' opinion, they are still going to make their own decisions.

8. Finally, an adult child should not sit by idly ~~doing nothing~~ when family stories are being told ~~or related~~.

9. ~~Despite the fact that~~ *Although* parents may have been telling these stories the same way for years ~~and years~~, the child may have a very different perspective on the event.

10. Expressing ~~and talking about~~ this different perspective can help an adult child define his or her position in family myth in a new way ~~that is different from the old way~~.

PRACTICE 18-5

The following passage contains deadwood and needless repetition. Cross out any unnecessary words, and make any revisions that may be needed. The first sentence has been done for you.

(1) Psychologist Marcia Morris began to study flirting when she was ~~a student studying~~ in graduate school. (2) It is her ~~own~~ opinion that in all species the female makes the original choice of mate. (3) First, a female ~~originally~~ chooses the male that interests her. (4) ~~Subsequent to~~ *After* this, she begins to send signals to show that he may approach. (5) Morris wanted to learn what signals women send to let men know they are interested. (6) She and

her assistants visited singles bars to observe and to record their observations ~~of what they saw~~.

(7) To attract a man, they found, women ~~in most of the cases~~ *usually* glance at him first and then smile ~~in a friendly way~~. (8) After they turn away ~~so they are no longer looking at the man~~, they may toss their heads, flip their hair, or laugh. (9) A woman may also sway ~~side to side~~ with the music being played, which typically ~~and most often~~ leads the man to request a dance. (10) ~~In the final analysis~~, *Ultimately* Morris's studies show that a woman's ability to get a man to talk to her depends less on her looks ~~and whether she is beautiful~~ than on her flirting skills. (11) One of Morris's assistants used the techniques their research uncovered and bragged ~~boastfully~~ that it never took her more than ten minutes to reel a guy in.

▶ **FLASHBACK** ◀

Look back at your response to the Paragraph Practice at the beginning of the chapter. Identify a sentence that contains deadwood or needless repetition. Rewrite the sentence on the lines below, editing it so it is more concise.

_____

_____

C AVOIDING TRITE EXPRESSIONS

One way of making your writing fresh and lively is to avoid trite, overused expressions called **clichés.** Such expressions have been used so often they no longer evoke an original response from readers. Nevertheless, writers often plug in these ready-made phrases without giving them much thought. Their effect is to deaden writing with worn-out phrases that do nothing to create interest.

▶ FOCUS ON CLICHÉS ◀

Following is a list of some of the clichés you may find in your own writing.

add insult to injury	lay the cards on the table
better late than never	all things considered
easier said than done	strong as an ox
free as a bird	the last straw
handwriting on the wall	thin as a rail
hard as a rock	tried and true
hit the nail on the head	between a rock and a hard place
last but not least	work like a dog

When you encounter a cliché, you can either substitute a fresh expression of your own, or replace the cliché with a direct statement.

Cliché

When school was over, she felt <u>free as a bird</u>.

Revised (fresh expression):

When school was over, she felt like a bird that had just escaped from its cage.

Cliché

These days you have to be <u>sick as a dog</u> before you are admitted to a hospital.

Revised (direct statement):

These days you have to be very sick before you are admitted to a hospital.

PRACTICE 18-6

Cross out any clichés in the following sentences, and either substitute a fresher expression or restate the idea in direct language.

Example: Lottery winners may think that they will ~~be free as a bird~~ *shed any money worries* for the rest of their lives.

Answers will vary.

1. Many people think that a million-dollar lottery jackpot allows the winner to stop working ~~like a dog~~ *long hours* and start living ~~high on the hog~~ *a carefree life*.

2. ~~All things considered, however~~ *In fact*, the reality for lottery winners is quite different.

CHAPTER 18 Revising Words • 339

3. For one thing, lottery winners who ~~hit the jackpot~~ *win big prizes* do not receive their winnings all at once; instead, payments are usually spread out over twenty years.

4. Of that $50,000 a year, close to $20,000 goes to taxes and anything else the ~~lucky stiff~~ *winner* owes the government, such as student loans.

5. Next come relatives and friends ~~with their hands out~~ *who ask for money*, leaving winners ~~between a rock and a hard place~~ *with difficult choices to make*.

6. They can either ~~cough up~~ *give* gifts and loans or ~~wave bye-bye to~~ *lose the friendship of* many of their loved ones.

7. ~~Adding insult to injury,~~ *Even worse,* many lottery winners have lost their jobs because employers thought that once they were "millionaires," they no longer needed to draw a salary.

8. Many lottery winners wind up ~~way over their heads~~ in *serious* debt within a few years.

9. ~~In their hour of need,~~ *Faced with financial difficulties,* many would like to sell their future earnings to companies that offer lump-sum payments of forty to forty-five cents on the dollar.

10. This is ~~easier said than done,~~ *almost impossible,* however, because most state lotteries won't allow winners to sell their winnings.

▶ **FLASHBACK** ◀

Look back at your response to the Paragraph Practice at the beginning of the chapter. If you have used any clichés, write them below, and then edit them so they are more original and forceful. If you can't think of a more original way of expressing the cliché, state the idea in plain language.

(continued on the following page)

(continued from the previous page)

Cliché	Revised
_____	_____
_____	_____
_____	_____

D USING SIMILES AND METAPHORS

Experienced writers know that similes and metaphors can add a distinctive touch to their writing. A **simile** is a comparison of two unlike things that uses *like* or *as*.

His arm hung at his side <u>like</u> a broken shutter.
He was <u>as</u> happy <u>as</u> a grasshopper in summer.

A **metaphor** is a comparison of two unlike things that does not use *like* or *as*. Instead of saying two things are like each other, a metaphor equates them.

Invaders from another world, dandelions conquered my garden.
He was a beast of burden, carrying cement from sunrise to sunset.

The force of similes and metaphors comes from the surprise of seeing two essentially unlike things being compared. Used in moderation, similes and metaphors can add a lot to your writing. Excessive use of these devices, however, can be distracting.

▶ FOCUS ON USING SIMILES AND METAPHORS ◀

Remember, both similes and metaphors compare two dissimilar things. If the items being compared are too much alike, the result is a plain statement of fact.

Your boat is like my boat.

PRACTICE 18-7

Underline examples of figurative language in the following sentences. Above the similes write *S*, and above the metaphors write *M*.

                                                        M
Example: My workload is <u>a pit it seems I'll never climb out of</u>.

1. Her heart was as fragile as a newly laid egg. [S]
2. My boss's words were a cold shower, bringing me back to reality. [M]
3. It rained so heavily that the atmosphere was like the inside of a jellyfish. [S]
4. Selena's singing career was a skyrocket just waiting to be lit. [M]
5. Looking like a lopsided wedding cake, the old white house seemed about to topple over. [S]

PRACTICE 18-8

Use your imagination to complete each of the following with three appropriate similes.

Example: A boring class is like *toast without jam.*

a straitjacket.

a bedtime story.

Answers will vary.

1. A good friend is like _____

2. A thunderstorm is like _____

3. My current life is like _____

PRACTICE 18-9

Use your imagination to complete each of the following with three appropriate similes.

Example: as hungry as *a baby bird*

the Big Bad Wolf

a crash-dieter after a five-day fast

342 • UNIT 7 Revising for Clarity and Effectiveness

Answers will vary.

1. as soft as _____

2. as restless as _____

3. as old as _____

PRACTICE 18-10

Think of a person you know well. Using that person as your subject, fill in the following to create metaphors. Try to express each metaphor in more than a single word, as in the example.

Example: If _my baby sister_ were an animal, _she_ would be _a curious little kitten._

Answers will vary.

1. If _____ were an animal, ____ would be _____

2. If _____ were a food, ____ would be _____

3. If _____ were a means of transportation, ____ would be ____

4. If _____ were a natural phenomenon, ____ would be _____

5. If _____ were a toy, ____ would be _____

> **FLASHBACK**
>
> Look back at your response to the Paragraph Practice at the beginning of the chapter. Find two sentences in which you present an idea that could be enriched with a simile or a metaphor. Rewrite the first sentence, adding a simile. Rewrite the second sentence, adding a metaphor.
>
> 1. _____
>
>   _____
>
> 2. _____
>
>   _____

E AVOIDING SEXIST LANGUAGE

Sexist language refers to men and women in terms generally perceived to be derogatory or insulting (or, at best, just plain thoughtless). Sexist language is not just words like *hunk, bimbo,* or *babe* that many women and men find objectionable. It can be words or phrases that unnecessarily call attention to gender or that suggest a job or profession is exclusively male or female when it actually is not. It can also be giving information about a woman—for example, her marital status—that you would not offer for a man.

Usually, you can solve the problem of sexist usage by being sensitive and using a little common sense. For every sexist usage, there is a perfectly acceptable nonsexist alternative.

Sexist	Nonsexist
man/mankind	humanity/humankind/human race
businessman	executive/business person
fireman/policeman/mailman	fire fighter/police officer/letter carrier
male nurse/woman engineer	nurse/engineer
congressman	member of congress, representative
stewardess/steward	flight attendant
man and wife	man and woman/husband and wife
manmade	synthetic
chairman	chair/chairperson
anchorwoman/anchorman	anchor

344 • UNIT 7 Revising for Clarity and Effectiveness

> ### ▶ FOCUS ON AVOIDING SEXIST LANGUAGE ◀
>
> Do not use *he* to refer to both genders when your subject could be either male or female.
>
> > Everyone should complete <u>his</u> assignment by next week.
>
> You can correct this problem in three ways:
>
> - Use *he or she* or *his or her*.
>   > Everyone should complete <u>his or her</u> assignment by next week.
>
> - Use plural forms.
>   > Students should complete <u>their</u> assignment by next week.
>
> - Eliminate the pronoun.
>   > Everyone should complete <u>the</u> assignment by next week.

PRACTICE 18-11

Edit the following sentences to eliminate sexist language.

1. Many people today would like to see more police~~men~~ *officers* patrolling the streets.
2. A doctor should be honest with his *or her* patients.
3. The attorneys representing the plaintiff are Geraldo Diaz and ~~Mrs.~~ Barbara Wilkerson.
4. Chris Fox is the ~~female~~ mayor of Port London, Maine.
5. Travel to other planets will be a giant step for ~~man~~ *humanity*.

> ### • • • • • • • ▶ FLASHBACK ◀ • • • • • • •
>
> Look back at your Paragraph Practice exercise. List below any words that could be considered sexist. Then, next to each word, list one or more nonsexist alternatives.
>
> | Sexist | Nonsexist |
> | --- | --- |
> | _____ | _____ |
> | _____ | _____ |

CHAPTER 18   Revising Words   ▪   **345**

REVIEW

CHAPTER REVIEW: STUDENT WRITING

The following student passage has problems with word choice. Read it carefully, and then revise it, making sure your revision contains exact words and concise language. (Add words and phrases that tell what things look, taste, smell, feel, and sound like.) In addition, eliminate elevated or sexist language and trite expressions. If you can, add an occasional simile or metaphor to increase the impact of the essay. Finally, underline language that seems fresh and original. The first sentence has been edited for you.

Answers will vary.

A Day at the Pool

It all begins on a ~~nice~~ *bright* summer day as we ~~transport~~ *carry* our neatly packed pool equipment from the car and head to the pool. We walk across the <u>bumpy, gravel-covered</u> parking lot with our arms piled high with a ~~pretty~~ *bright red* beach bag, a ~~gaily~~ *green and white* ~~striped~~ beach chair, *pink and green* ~~colored~~ beach towels, and ~~an~~ *an orange* ~~interesting~~ drinking cup *with a picture of a lion on it*. We make it through the ~~entrance~~ *blue metal doors* and walk into the ladies' locker room. The walls are lined with *dented metal* lockers, and past the lockers is a metal door held open by a wooden wedge. Walking through the doorway, we proceed to our usual spot in the shaded grass area. This is where we spend our day socializing with other <u>"pool princesses"</u> and checking out the ~~hunks~~ *guys*.

As I sit, I hear the sounds of children crying and laughing and of parents <u>bellowing</u> at them. Suddenly, the noises cease at the sound of a loud, high-pitched whistle. All eyes are on the ~~female~~ lifeguard. She's dressed in a *black one-piece* ~~nice~~ bathing suit covered by a *white* tank top with ~~an unusual design~~ *a pair of sea horses* on the front. She's wearing black Ray-Ban sunglasses, and she holds a silver whistle in her mouth. She sits *regally* on her high wooden platform and raises her hand, pointing her finger at the accused. Then, as quickly as the silence began, it ceases.

~~Due to the fact~~ *Because* I am hungry, I go to the snack bar. I am ~~enticed~~ *drawn in* by the *buttery* scent of freshly popped popcorn, the ~~tantalizing~~ *pungent* aroma of spicy fries, and the equally tempting smell of hamburgers. The choice is difficult. I finally decide on a bright yellow banana popsicle. It tastes ~~good~~ *cold and sweet* and ~~takes care of~~ *quenches* my thirst. I turn and come face-to-face with a small child. His cheeks are ~~red from overexposure to the burning rays of the sun~~ *sunburned*. His nose is a white painted triangle, and his eyes are ~~illuminated~~ *shining* as he ~~converses with~~ *begs* his mother ~~about purchasing~~ *to buy him* more goodies from the snack bar. Slithering around him, I head back to the safety of my towel.

Reaching my chair, I look down to see a strange toddler sitting ~~as quiet as a mouse~~ *quietly on it*. He seems to have claimed my seat as his own. He looks up and smiles as drool slides out of the corner of his mouth. Then, he rises and waddles off, his wet diaper sagging around his knees. I discover that he has left his mark on my chair. At this point, I decide it is time to go home.

We gather our ~~copious~~ *many* belongings and head for the car. Again we pass through the metal door, down the hallway of lockers, and out the exit to the parking lot. We cross the gravel parking lot to our car. After we load our trunk, we get into the car only to find the air is ~~so~~ *as* hot and thick *as pancake syrup*. As

I sit in the hot car, I wonder whether it makes sense to go
through all this ^trouble^ just to spend a couple of hours at the
pool.

CHAPTER REVIEW: EDITING PRACTICE

Reread your response to the Paragraph Practice at the beginning of the chapter. Revise the paragraph, making sure your language is as exact and concise as possible. In addition, be sure you have avoided using trite, elevated, or sexist expressions. When you have finished, do the same for another paragraph or writing assignment you are currently working on.

CHAPTER REVIEW: COLLABORATIVE ACTIVITIES

1. Bring in two or three paragraphs of description from a romance novel, a western novel, or a mystery novel. As a group, choose the paragraphs that seem most in need of revision for clearer, more concise word choice.

2. As a group, revise the paragraphs you brought in for Collaborative Activity 1, making them as clear and concise as possible and eliminating clichés and sexist usage.

3. Exchange your revised paragraphs from Collaborative Activity 2 with another group. Check to make sure you agree with their revisions. Make any additional changes you think the paragraphs need.

Review

- Specific words refer to particular persons, places, things, or ideas. Vague words refer to entire classes or groups. Abstract words refer to ideas or qualities you cannot perceive with the senses—*happiness* or *truth,* for example. Concrete words appeal to your senses by naming things you can see, hear, taste, feel, and smell. (See 18A.)

    Vague: While walking in the woods, I saw an animal.
    Specific: While walking in the woods, I saw a baby skunk.
    Abstract: One night I saw a moth fly into a candle. It was interesting.
    Concrete: One night a moth flew into a candle, was caught, burnt dry, and held. . . .

    (continued on the following page)

(continued from the previous page)

- Concise writing comes right to the point and says what it has to say with the minimum number of words. (See 18B.)

    Wordy: <u>In order to</u> follow the plot, you must make an outline.
    Concise: <u>To</u> follow the plot, you must make an outline.

- One way to make sure your writing is fresh and lively is to avoid overused expressions called *clichés*. (See 18C.)

    Cliché: When school was over, she felt <u>free as a bird</u>.
    Revised: When school was over, she felt like a bird that had just escaped from its cage.

- A simile is a comparison that uses *like* or *as*. A metaphor is a comparison that does not use *like* or *as*. Instead of saying two things are like each other, it equates them. (See 18D.)

    Simile: <u>Like</u> invaders from another world, dandelions conquered my garden.
    Metaphor: Invaders from another world, dandelions conquered my garden.

- Sexist language refers to men and women in terms that are generally perceived to be derogatory or insulting. For every sexist usage, there is usually a perfectly acceptable nonsexist alternative. (See 18E.)

Unit 7 Review

The collaborative activities, writing practice topics, and student writing sample that follow provide opportunities for you to review what you have learned in Chapters 15 through 18.

COLLABORATIVE ACTIVITIES

1. Assume you have been contacted by your local newspaper to write reviews of your three favorite movies. Begin by listing the three movies that you like the best. Then, compare your list to the lists compiled by the other people in your group. Finally, choose the three movies that all the people in the group agree are the best.

2. Write a paragraph about one of the movies your group selected. Begin with a short summary of the movie, and then go on to discuss the specific qualities that make the movie memorable. Your paragraph should have a clear topic sentence that tells what you like about the movie.

3. As a group, edit your paragraphs so they are suitable for the body of an essay. Then, work together to write an introduction and a conclusion. Keep in mind that the introduction should contain a thesis that states the main point of the essay. If you wish, you can duplicate the essay and distribute copies to the rest of the class. Then, as a class, you can examine the essays for illogical shifts, faulty parallelism, and problems with sentence variety and word choice.

WRITING PRACTICE

1. Write about the person whom you most admire. Why do you admire this person? Which of his or her qualities do you think are the most admirable? If you can, give some examples to support your conclusions.

2. Animal activism has attracted support from movie and television personalities as well as many ordinary people. Recently, activists—movie stars included—broke into the home of a well-known fashion designer to denounce his use of leather and furs in his creations. Assume you were a person who witnessed this incident. Write an essay in which you consider whether or not animals should have certain rights. Be specific, and make sure you discuss whether you think the break-in was justified.

3. Assume that a publisher has asked you to rate your textbooks. She says she wants your opinion so that her company can produce better books. Which of your textbooks do you like the best? Which do you like the

350 ▪ UNIT 7 Review

least? What qualities make a textbook good? What qualities make it bad? Write an essay in which you present your conclusions in the form of a letter to the publisher.

STUDENT WRITING

Read the following student essay, in which errors have been introduced. Correct any illogical shifts you find. In addition, identify and correct any instances of faulty parallelism. Finally, revise for sentence variety and word choice. After you have made your corrections, check to make sure that you have supplied all words necessary for clarity, grammar, and sense. The first paragraph has been edited for you.

Answers may vary.

My Cousin Mike

When I was fourteen, I spent the summer in Iowa. ~~Both~~ *Because both* my parents are from Iowa*,* ~~We~~ *we* visit there every year. That summer, however, stands out in my memory.

My mother*,* ~~and~~ father*,* ~~and also my~~ sister*,* and I drove to Iowa in August. We planned to spend three weeks at my great-aunt's house in Ackley. The drive was ~~nice~~ *like one in a new-car commercial*. Along the way we passed green hills, fields of hay, and ~~we also saw~~ small towns. When we got to Iowa, we found that ~~it was hot as blazes~~. *T*~~t~~he temperature typically reached one hundred degrees every day. The hot air ~~rises~~ *rose* in waves over the fields, and ~~across the road~~ dust devils blew in drifts *across the road*. I was not happy.

My second day there, though, something unexpected *transpired* ~~transpires~~. I made a friend. We were introduced at my great-aunt's home.

"Kelly, this is Mike Thompson. He's your third cousin," my mother said.

My first impression ~~is~~ *was* that I ~~don't~~ *didn't* think we ~~are~~ *were* going to get along. He was handsome, had long blond hair, and ~~baggy clothes, were worn by him. Long~~ *wore* baggy clothes, *but long* hair and baggy clothes weren't in style then as they are now. I had never seen anything quite like Mike before. I was afraid to start a conversation, ~~He~~ *so he* started one.

"You're from Philadelphia?" he drawled.

"Yes," I answered timidly.

"That's cool," he said. "I've always lived in Iowa."

And that's how he began his life story. He'd been born in Iowa seventeen years before. He'd spent his life working on his father's farm, ~~He also went~~ *and going* to school. He hated the farm. I asked him ~~"~~how he could hate working on a farm, in the open air and out on the land?~~"~~. He answered that the farm ~~makes me~~ *made him* feel tied down.

As if to emphasize his point, he added, "I like school, but I don't like the farm. My father wants me to stay on the farm, but I won't."

He explained that a lot of young people in Iowa thought ~~you~~ *they* had to get off the farm to make a life for ~~yourself~~ *themselves*. They saw that as the cost of farming went up, income from farming was going down. For this reason, a typical farmer is not able to make ~~his~~ *a* living from farming anymore.

~~Due to the fact that~~ *Because* I stayed three weeks, the two of us had plenty of time to talk about society, politics and ~~we also discussed~~ independence. He told me ~~"~~*that* he admired Thoreau.~~"~~ *At that time,* I didn't know who Thoreau was ~~at that time~~ but I was too embarrassed to ask.

"I'll set an example for society like Thoreau did," Mike said. "Someday I'll get out of here and do something for society. Maybe I'll even show up on your doorstep," he added, laughing. I was young then, and I didn't think much about his comment.

At the end of August, my family and I left for home. Mike and I said goodbye. I knew that even though we had become close friends, we would not exchange letters. Neither of us was a letter writer.

Over the years I heard about Mike. He had gone to community college and then on to Iowa State. I was happy to hear that he was getting an education. Then one day, unexpectedly, I heard a knock at the door of my apartment. I opened it, and there was Mike--still just as handsome as ever and now dressed in a blue blazer and a pair of neatly pressed pants.

"Hi, Cuz," he said. "I told you I might show up someday. Well, guess what? I'm going to start law school next week--here in Philadelphia."

As we hugged, we both started to laugh. Mike had gotten what he wanted, and I had gotten my friend back.

19 Using Nouns and Pronouns

Overview

In this chapter you will learn
- To recognize nouns and form plural nouns
- To recognize personal pronouns
- To understand pronoun case
- To understand pronoun-antecedent agreement
- To make pronouns agree with compound antecedents, indefinite pronoun antecedents, and collective noun antecedents
- To avoid nonspecific or unnecessary pronoun references
- To use reflexive and intensive pronouns correctly

PARAGRAPH PRACTICE

Write a paragraph in which you describe why you like a particular musician or group, a particular television show, or a recent movie. Assume your readers are not familiar with your subject, and explain to them why they would enjoy it. Use the blank space below for invention. Then, write your paragraph on the lines that follow.

A   RECOGNIZING NOUNS AND FORMING PLURAL NOUNS

A **noun** is a word that names a person *(singer, Gloria Estefan)*, an animal *(dolphin, Flipper)*, a place *(downtown, Houston)*, an object *(game, Tetris)*, or an idea *(happiness, Darwinism)*.

> ### ▶ FOCUS ON COMMON AND PROPER NOUNS ◀
>
> Most nouns, called **common nouns**, begin with lowercase letters.
>
>   character   holiday
>
> Some nouns, called **proper nouns**, name particular people, places, objects, and events. A proper noun always begins with a capital letter.
>
>   Homer Simpson   Labor Day
>
> See 24A for more on proper nouns.

A **singular** noun names one thing. A **plural** noun names more than one thing. Most nouns add *-s* to form plurals. Other nouns, whose singular forms end in *s, ss, sh, ch, x,* or *z,* add *-es* to form plurals. Some nouns that end in *s* or *z* double the *s* or *z* before adding *-es*.

Singular	Plural
street	streets
gas	gases
class	classes
bush	bushes
church	churches
fox	foxes
quiz	quizzes

Irregular Noun Plurals

Some nouns are irregular and form plurals in different ways.

- Nouns whose plural forms are the same as their singular forms

one fish	two fish
a deer	some deer
this species	these species
a TV series	two TV series

- Nouns ending in *f* or *fe*, whose plural form is generally *ves*

each half	both halves
my life	our lives
a lone thief	a gang of thieves
one loaf	two loaves
the third shelf	a wall of shelves

    Familiar exceptions: roof (plural *roofs*), proof (plural *proofs*), belief (plural *beliefs*)

- Nouns ending in *y*, whose plural form generally changes *y* to *i* and adds *-es*

another baby	more babies
every worry	many worries

    Note that when the *y* follows a vowel, you just add *s:* monkey (plural *monkeys*), day (plural *days*).

- Hyphenated compound nouns, whose plural form changes the first word in the compound

Lucia's sister-in-law	Lucia's two favorite sisters-in-law
a mother-to-be	twin mothers-to-be
the first runner-up	all the runners-up

- Miscellaneous irregular plurals

that child	all children
a good man	a few good men
the woman	several women
my left foot	both feet
a wisdom tooth	my two front teeth

PRACTICE 19-1

In the blank at the right of each noun listed below, fill in the plural form of the noun. Put checks next to the plural forms of regular nouns. Circle the plural forms of irregular nouns.

Examples: bottle __bottles__ ✓   child __(children)__

1. headache __headaches__ ✓
2. life __(lives)__
3. foot __(feet)__
4. chain __chains__ ✓
5. deer __(deer)__
6. honey __honeys__ ✓
7. bride-to-be __(brides-to-be)__
8. woman __(women)__
9. loaf __(loaves)__
10. kiss __kisses__ ✓
11. beach __beaches__ ✓
12. duty __(duties)__
13. son-in-law __(sons-in-law)__
14. species __(species)__
15. wife __(wives)__
16. city __(cities)__
17. elf __(elves)__
18. tooth __(teeth)__
19. catalog __catalogs__ ✓
20. patty __(patties)__

PRACTICE 19-2

Proofread the underlined nouns in the following paragraph for correct singular or plural form. If a correction needs to be made, cross out the noun, and write the correct form above it. If the noun is correct, write *C* above it.

Example: Many ~~studys~~ *studies* prove this.

(1) I recently talked to a group of my unmarried ~~friend~~ *friends* about what they look for in a person of the opposite sex. (2) Most of the ~~woman~~ *women* said that their ~~standardes~~ *standards* were the same whether they just wanted to date a ~~men~~ *man* for fun or whether they might consider him as a potential ~~mates~~ *mate*. (3) Both just-for-fun ~~date~~ *dates* and potential ~~husband-to-bes~~ *husbands-to-be* were considered real ~~catchs~~ *catches* if they had decent ~~job~~ *jobs* or were working in that direction, if they were considerate and honest, and if they had good ~~sensess~~ *senses* of humor. (4) My male buddies *C*, however, had different ~~ideaes~~ *ideas*. (5) They wanted dates *C* to be good-

looking, to have outgoing ~~personalitys~~ *personalities*, and to have independent ~~lifes~~ *lives* of their own. (6) Potential ~~wifes~~ *wives*, on the other hand, should not be too attractive to other ~~mens~~ *men*, should be homebodies *C*, and should see themselves not as independent but as ~~halfes~~ *halves* of a whole. (7) Sometimes I think the two ~~sexs~~ *sexes* are different ~~specieses~~ *species*.

▶ FLASHBACK ◀

Look back at your response to the Paragraph Practice at the beginning of the chapter. Circle each noun in your paragraph. Which are singular, and which are plural? Copy the nouns in the appropriate columns.

Singular	Plural
_____	_____
_____	_____
_____	_____
_____	_____
_____	_____
_____	_____
_____	_____

Now, circle any irregular plural nouns.

B RECOGNIZING PERSONAL PRONOUNS

A **pronoun** is a word that takes the place of a noun or another pronoun.

Michelle was really excited. Finally, *she* had a job.

The subject of the first sentence above is the noun *Michelle*. In the second sentence, *she* refers to *Michelle*, the person who finally found a job.

Without pronouns, your sentences would be very tedious because you would have to repeat the same nouns over and over again.

Michelle was really excited. Finally, Michelle had a job.

Because they can substitute for nouns, pronouns make your sentences smoother and more natural sounding.

As you will learn later in this chapter, there are many different kinds of pronouns, each with different functions. This section focuses on personal pronouns. A **personal pronoun** takes the place of a person or thing. In the first pair of sentences above, *she* is a personal pronoun that takes the place of the person *Michelle*.

Personal Pronouns	
Singular	**Plural**
I	we
you	you
he, she, it	they

Pronouns, like nouns, can be singular or plural. The personal pronouns *I, he, she,* and *it* are always singular and take the place of singular nouns. The personal pronouns *we* and *they* are always plural and take the place of plural nouns. The personal pronoun *you* can be either singular or plural.

PRACTICE 19-3

In the following sentences, fill in each blank with an appropriate personal pronoun.

Example: __I__ like to be direct with my friends.

1. __I__ pride myself on always being honest.

2. My father always told me that honesty is the best policy, and __he__ was right.

3. Sometimes this hurts my friends' feelings, and __they__ tell me that __I__ am being rude to them.

4. __I__ answer them by saying that __we__ all need to hear the honest truth about ourselves sometimes.

5. My friend Linda understands my point, and __she__ is always eager to let me hear the honest truth about myself whenever __I__ have made a comment about her.

CHAPTER 19 Using Nouns and Pronouns • 359

6. She tells me, "If __you__ are going to dish __it__ out, then __you__ had better learn to take __it__ yourself."

7. It's true that if her comment is really strong, __it__ can upset me for a day or two.

8. But then __I__ remember that it's only Linda's opinion, and __she__ is never right about anything.

▶ FLASHBACK ◀

Look back at your response to the Paragraph Practice at the beginning of the chapter. In the left-hand column below, list each use of the personal pronouns *I, he, she, it, we, you,* and *they*. In the right-hand column, list the noun each pronoun replaces.

Personal Pronoun	Noun
_____	_____
_____	_____
_____	_____
_____	_____
_____	_____
_____	_____
_____	_____

C UNDERSTANDING PRONOUN CASE

A pronoun changes form according to the way it functions in a sentence. When a pronoun functions as a sentence's subject, it is in the **subjective case.**

Finally, <u>she</u> realized that dreams could come true. (The pronoun *she* is the sentence's subject.)

When a pronoun functions as an object (as a direct or indirect object of a verb or as the object of a preposition), it is in the **objective case.**

If Joanna hurries, she can stop <u>him</u>. (The pronoun *him* is the direct object of the verb *stop*.)

Professor Miller sent <u>us</u> information about his research. (The pronoun *us* is the indirect object of the verb *sent*.)

Marc threw the ball to <u>them</u>. (The pronoun *them* is the object of the preposition *to*.)

▶ FOCUS ON OBJECTS ◀

A **direct object** is a noun or pronoun that receives the action of the verb.

      D.O.
I sent a <u>fax</u> yesterday.
     D.O.
I'll call <u>him</u> today.

An **indirect object** is the noun or pronoun to or for whom the action of the verb has been done.

    I.O.   D.O.
I sent <u>Adam</u> a fax.
   I.O. D.O.
I gave <u>her</u> money.

The word or word group introduced by a preposition is known as the **object of the preposition**. (See 21A.)

             O.P.
She ran out of the <u>room</u>.
           O.P.
Kelly worked for <u>them</u>.

When a pronoun shows ownership, it is in the **possessive case.**

Hieu took <u>his</u> lunch to the meeting. (The possessive pronoun *his* shows that the lunch belongs to Hieu.)

Debbie and Kim decided to take <u>their</u> lunches, too. (The possessive pronoun *their* shows that the lunches belong to Debbie and Kim.)

The following chart lists the various forms that pronouns take in subjective, objective, and possessive cases.

Pronoun Case

Subjective	Objective	Possessive
I	me	my (mine)
he	him	his
she	her	her (hers)
it	it	its
we	us	our (ours)
you	you	your (yours)
they	them	their (theirs)

Three special situations can cause problems when you are trying to determine pronoun case. One occurs when a pronoun is *part of a compound,* another occurs when a pronoun is *part of a comparison,* and the third occurs when the pronoun is *followed directly by a noun.*

Pronouns in Compounds

When a pronoun appears alone, you can determine its case by its function in a sentence. Sometimes, however, a pronoun is linked to a noun with *and* or *or* to form a **compound.** In such cases, it is not always easy to determine whether to use a subjective or an objective pronoun. However, the same rules that apply to pronouns alone apply here.

If the compound in which the pronoun appears is the sentence's subject, use the subjective case.

Toby and I (not *me*) like jazz.

If the compound in which the pronoun appears is the object of the verb or of a preposition, use the objective case.

Many people admire Janelle and him (not *he*) for their courage.
The school sent my father and me (not *I*) the financial aid forms.
This fight is between Mike and me (not *I*).

These rules also apply if both parts of the compound are pronouns.

He and I are no longer friends. (subject)
The interviewer asked only her and me to wait. (object)

> ▶ **FOCUS** ON CHOOSING PRONOUNS ◀
> IN COMPOUNDS
>
> One easy way to determine correct pronoun case in a compound is to drop the noun and rewrite the sentence with the pronoun alone.
>
> *(continued on the following page)*

> *(continued from the previous page)*
>
> Toby and [*I* or *me*?] like jazz.
> <u>I</u> like jazz. (not *Me like jazz*)
> Toby and <u>I</u> like jazz.

Pronouns in Comparisons

Sometimes a pronoun appears after the word *than* or *as* in a **comparison**.

John is luckier <u>than</u> I.
The inheritance changed Raymond <u>as</u> much as her.

In such cases, you can determine whether to use the subjective or objective form of the pronoun by completing the comparison.

John is luckier than I [am].

Here the pronoun *I* is the subject of the verb *am*. Therefore, the pronoun is in the subjective case.

The inheritance changed Raymond as much as [it changed] her.

Here the pronoun *her* is the object of the verb *changed*. Therefore, the pronoun is in the objective case.

> ### ▶ FOCUS ON CHOOSING PRONOUNS ◀
> ### IN COMPARISONS
>
> Sometimes your choice of pronoun can change your sentence's meaning. For example, if you say, *I like Cheerios more than he*, you mean that you like Cheerios more than he likes them.
>
> I like Cheerios more than he [does].
>
> If, however, you say, *I like Cheerios more than him*, you mean something quite different. You mean that you like Cheerios more than you like him.
>
> I like Cheerios more than [I like] him.

Pronouns Followed Directly by a Noun

Occasionally, a first-person plural pronoun (*we* or *us*) is followed directly by a noun. When the noun is the subject, use the subjective pronoun (*we*). When the noun is an object, use the objective pronoun (*us*).

CHAPTER 19 Using Nouns and Pronouns · 363

<u>We students</u> deserve a break.
Registration can be torture for <u>us students</u>.

> ▶ **FOCUS** ON PRONOUNS FOLLOWED ◀
> DIRECTLY BY A NOUN
>
> If you aren't sure whether to use the subjective or objective case, try dropping the noun. When you read the sentence without the noun, you should be able to tell at once which pronoun is correct.
>
> <u>We</u> (not *us*) deserve a break.
> Registration can be torture for <u>us</u> (not *we*).

PRACTICE 19-4

In the following sentences, check the underlined pronouns, which are part of compound constructions, for correct subjective or objective case. If a correction needs to be made, cross out the pronoun, and write the correct form above it. If the pronoun is correct, write *C* above it.

Example: The reward was divided between my friend and
         C
    <u>me</u>.

                                                                    me
1. The deejay at the wedding reception asked Dionne and <u>~~I~~</u> to do an encore.
   She   *C*
2. <u>~~Her~~</u> and <u>I</u> enjoy singing together.
                                              him
3. The first time we sang, we really played up to <u>~~he~~</u> and the crowd.
   C   *him*
4. <u>We</u> talked with <u>~~he~~</u> for a few minutes about what we should sing for the encore.
                I
5. Dionne and <u>~~me~~</u> couldn't agree.
  We
6. <u>~~Us~~</u> two are always having trouble deciding on a song.
                                  C   *me*
7. Finally the deejay made the decision for <u>her</u> and <u>~~I~~</u>.
         C   *C*
8. After <u>she</u> and <u>I</u> finished, the guests went wild.
      they
9. Then <u>~~them~~</u> and the servers started chanting, "More, more, more."
                           C
10. It was too much for Dionne and <u>me</u> to believe.

PRACTICE 19-5

Write in each blank the correct form (subjective or objective) of the pronouns in parentheses. If the correct pronoun is subjective, add the unstated verb.

Example: He's a better poker player than __I am__ (I/me).

1. Even Sharon Stone is a better actress than __she is__ (she/her).

2. They are such a mismatched couple. Everybody likes her so much more than __him__ (he/him).

3. No one enjoys shopping more than __she does__ (she/her).

4. My brother and our Aunt Cecile were very close. Her death affected him more than __me__ (I/me).

5. Could any two people have a more perfect relationship than __we do__ (we/us)?

6. I'll admit my roommate drives better than __I do__ (I/me).

7. We at Steer Hut serve juicier steaks than __they do__ (they/them).

8. Even if you are as old as __I am__ (I/me), you're not as smart.

9. That jacket fits you better than __me__ (I/me).

10. The Trumps may be richer than __we are__ (we/us), but I'll bet they don't have as much fun.

▶ **FLASHBACK** ◀

Look over your response to the Paragraph Practice at the beginning of the chapter. Can you find any pronouns used with compounds or comparisons? If so, write one such sentence below, making sure that you use the appropriate pronoun case.

_____

_____

D UNDERSTANDING PRONOUN-ANTECEDENT AGREEMENT

As you learned in 19B, pronouns take the place of nouns or other pronouns. The word a pronoun refers to in a sentence is called the pronoun's **antecedent.** In the following sentence, the noun *leaf* is the antecedent of the pronoun *it*.

The leaf turned yellow, but it did not fall.

A pronoun must always agree in number with its antecedent. If an antecedent is singular, the pronoun must be singular. In the sample sentence above, the antecedent *leaf* is singular, so the pronoun that refers to it is also singular. If the antecedent is plural, the pronoun must also be plural.

The leaves turned yellow, but they did not fall.

Pronouns must also agree with their antecedents in gender. If an antecedent is feminine, the pronoun that refers to it must also be feminine.

Melissa passed her driver's exam with flying colors.

If an antecedent is masculine, the pronoun that refers to it must be masculine.

Matt wondered what courses he should take.

If an antecedent is neuter (that is, neither masculine nor feminine), the pronoun that refers to it must also be neuter.

Lee's car broke down, but she refused to fix it again.

PRACTICE 19-6

In the following sentences circle the pronouns, underline each pronoun's antecedent, and draw an arrow from the pronoun to the antecedent.

Example: College students today often fear they will be the

victims of crime on campus.

1. Few campuses are as safe as they should be, experts say.
2. However, crime on most campuses is probably not really worse than it is

   in any other community.
3. Still, students have a right to know how safe their campuses are.
4. My best friend Joyce never sets foot on campus without her can of Mace.
5. Joyce believes she must be prepared for the worst.

366 • UNIT 8 Nouns, Pronouns, and Other Parts of the Sentence

6. Joyce's <u>boyfriend</u> attended a self-defense program that (he) said was very helpful.

7. My <u>friends</u> won't let fear of crime keep (them) from enjoying the college experience.

8. Our <u>school</u> is doing what (it) can to provide a safe environment.

PRACTICE 19-7

Fill in each blank in the following passage with an appropriate pronoun. The first one has been done for you.

(1) Drive-in movie theaters used to be common in the United States, but now __they__ are fairly rare. (2) In 1958 there were more than four thousand of __them__ across the country. (3) Now, there are fewer than nine hundred. (4) One of the most amazing is the Thunderbird Drive-In in Ft. Lauderdale, Florida. (5) __It__ has twelve different screens. (6) Owner Preston Henn says __it__ is the largest drive-in theater in the world. (7) __He__ opened the theater with only one screen in 1963. (8) __He__ also opened a flea market on the property. (9) __It__ is now one of the largest flea markets in the state, with over two thousand vendors, a circus, and an amusement park. (10) The vendors think __they__ are getting a good deal. (11) As __his__ flea market business grew, Henn began adding screens, and __he__ plans to add two more. (12) One benefit of all the screens to patrons is that __they__ can sneak a peak at the other movies that are playing. (13) While watching Sylvester Stallone flex __his__ pecs, they might also enjoy the sight of Meryl Streep acting __her__ heart out. (14) It's worth a visit if you're ever in Ft. Lauderdale—as long as it's not raining.

CHAPTER 19 Using Nouns and Pronouns • 367

> ▶ **FLASHBACK** ◀
>
> Look back at your response to the Paragraph Practice at the beginning of the chapter. Circle each personal pronoun in your paragraph, and draw an arrow to its antecedent. Do all of your personal pronouns agree with their antecedents? If not, correct your pronouns.

E) SOLVING SPECIAL PROBLEMS WITH PRONOUN-ANTECEDENT AGREEMENT

Special problems in pronoun-antecedent agreement are likely to occur when antecedents are compounds, indefinite pronouns, collective nouns, or nonspecific pronouns or when unnecessary pronouns are added.

Compound Antecedents

A **compound antecedent** consists of two or more words connected by *and* or *or*. Compound antecedents connected by *and* are plural, and they are used with plural pronouns, as in the following sentence:

During the American Civil War, England and France tried to protect their economic interests.

Compound antecedents connected by *or* may take a singular or a plural pronoun. When both elements of a compound antecedent connected by *or* are singular, use a singular pronoun.

Either a dog or a cat must have put its paw in the frosting.

When both elements are plural, use a plural pronoun.

Are dogs or cats more loyal to their owners?

> ▶ **FOCUS** ON SINGULAR AND PLURAL ◀
> ANTECEDENTS CONNECTED BY OR
>
> When one element of a compound antecedent connected by *or* is singular and one is plural, use a pronoun that agrees with the word that is closer to the pronoun.
>
> *(continued on the following page)*

> (continued from the previous page)
>
> Is it possible that European nations or Russia may send <u>its</u> (not *their*) troops?
>
> Is it possible that Russia or European nations may send <u>their</u> (not *its*) troops?

PRACTICE 19-8

In each of the following sentences first underline the compound antecedent and circle the connecting word (*and* or *or*). Then, circle the appropriate pronoun in parentheses.

Example: <u>Groucho</u> (and) <u>Harpo</u> were younger than (his/(their)) brother Chico.

1. <u>Larry</u> (and) <u>Curly</u> were younger than (his/(their)) partner Moe.
2. Either <u>Chip</u> (or) <u>Dale</u> has a stripe down ((his)/their) back.
3. Most critics believe <u>Stan</u> (and) <u>Ollie</u> did (his/(their)) best work in silent comedies.
4. Was it <u>Dorothy</u> (or) <u>Lillian</u> who made ((her)/their) first movie that year?
5. <u>Lucy</u> (and) <u>Ethel</u> never seem to learn (her/(their)) lesson.
6. Either <u>*MASH*</u> (or) <u>*The Fugitive*</u> had the highest ratings for any television show in ((its)/their) final episode.
7. Was it <u>Hannah</u> (or) <u>her sisters</u> who gave (her/(their)) mother a party?
8. Can <u>Warrington</u> (and) <u>Reginald</u> succeed with (his/(their)) new HBO series as they did with (his/(their)) *House Party* movies?
9. Was it <u>Mario Van Peebles</u> (or) <u>his father Melvin</u> who made ((his)/their) directing debut with *New Jack City*?
10. Can there be any doubt that <u>Barbra</u> (or) <u>Bette</u> will always get ((her)/their) way?
11. <u>Film</u> (and) <u>videotape</u> both lose ((its)/(their)) clarity over time.

12. Either Tower or Blockbuster is having (its/their) grand opening today.

13. The popcorn and soft drinks here are expensive for (its/their) size.

14. Do comedies or dramas have a greater impact on (its/their) audiences?

15. Either Tom or Jerry will eat (his/their) words.

Indefinite Pronoun Antecedents

Some pronouns are called **indefinite pronouns** because they do not refer to any particular person or thing.

Indefinite Pronouns

anybody	everyone	nothing
anyone	everything	one
each	neither	somebody
either	nobody	someone
everybody	no one	something

Most indefinite pronouns, such as those listed in the box above, are singular. Therefore, they are used with singular pronouns, as in the following sentence:

Everything was in its place.

Note that some indefinite pronouns—*both, few, many, some, several*—are plural and are used with plural pronouns.

> ▶ **FOCUS** ON *HIS* OR *HER* WITH ◀
> **SINGULAR INDEFINITE PRONOUNS**
>
> Even though indefinite pronouns are usually singular, many people use plural pronouns to refer to them.
>
> Everyone must hand in their completed work before 2 P.M.
>
> Because many people think of *everyone* as plural, sentences like the one above are widely used—and widely accepted—in spoken En-
>
> *(continued on the following page)*

(continued from the previous page)

glish. Nevertheless, *everyone* is singular, and written English requires a singular pronoun. Therefore, you should not use *his* to refer to *everyone*. To do so assumes that *everyone* refers to an individual who is male. (By the same token, using *her* assumes that *everyone* refers to a female.) *His or her*, however, allows for the possibility that the indefinite pronoun may refer to either a male or a female.

Everyone must hand in <u>his or her</u> completed work before 2 P.M.

Although they are precise, however, *he or she, him or her,* and *his or hers* can seem wordy or awkward, especially if they are used several times in a passage. Often, you can avoid using these constructions by replacing the indefinite pronoun with a plural word.

<u>All students</u> must hand in <u>their</u> completed work before 2 P.M.

▶ FOCUS ON INDEFINITE PRONOUNS WITH OF ◀

Sometimes indefinite pronouns are used in phrases with *of*—*each of, either of, neither of,* or *one of,* for example. Even when they are part of such phrases, however, these indefinite pronoun antecedents are singular and take singular pronouns.

Each of the routes has <u>its</u> (not *their*) own special challenges.

For information on subject-verb agreement with indefinite pronouns, see 8D.

PRACTICE 19-9

In the following sentences first circle the indefinite pronoun antecedent. Then, circle the appropriate pronoun in parentheses.

Example: (Each) of the artists will have ((his or her)/their) own exhibit.

1. (Either) of those paintings will be sold with ((its)/their) frame.
2. (Each) of the artist's brushes has ((its)/their) own use.

CHAPTER 19   Using Nouns and Pronouns • **371**

3. (Everything) in the room made (its)/their) contribution to the whole design.

4. (Everyone) must remember to take (his or her)/their) paintbox.

5. (Neither) of my sisters wanted (her)/their) picture displayed.

6. (One) of the men brought both of (his)/their) children to the exhibit.

7. (Each) of the colors must be mixed with (its)/their) contrasting color.

8. When (someone) compliments your work, be sure to tell (him or her)/them) that it's for sale.

9. (Anyone) can improve (his or her)/their) skills as an artist.

10. (Either) of these workrooms has (its)/their) own advantages.

PRACTICE 19-10

Edit the following sentences for errors in pronoun-antecedent agreement. Rather than substituting *him or her* for *their* when the antecedent is singular, you might consider replacing the antecedent with a plural word.

Examples: Everyone will be responsible for ~~their~~ *his or her* own transportation.

~~Each of~~ *All* the children took their books out of their bags and closed their desks.

Answers may vary.

1. Everyone has the right to ~~their~~ *his or her* own opinion.

2. Is everybody planning to eat ~~their~~ *his or her* lunch in the cafeteria?

3. Somebody must have forgotten to take ~~their~~ *his or her* shower this morning.

4. ~~Each of~~ *All* the patients had their own rooms, with their own televisions and their own private baths.

5. Someone in the store has left ~~their~~ *his or her* car's lights on.

6. Simone keeps everything in her kitchen in ~~their~~ *its* own little container.

7. Each of the applicants must have ~~their~~ *his or her* associate's degree.

8. Anybody who's ever juggled a job and children knows how valuable ~~their~~ *his or her* free time can be.

9. Either of the coffeemakers comes with ~~their~~ *its* own filter.

10. ~~Almost everyone waits~~ *Most people wait* until the last minute to file their income taxes.

Collective Noun Antecedents

Collective nouns are words that name a group of people or things but are singular in form. Because collective noun antecedents are usually singular, they are usually used with singular pronouns:

The band played on, but <u>it</u> never played our song.

In the sentence above, the collective noun *band* names a group of individual musicians, but it refers to them as a unit. Because *band* is a singular antecedent, the singular pronoun *it* is used to refer to it.

The following box lists some frequently used collective nouns.

Collective Nouns			
army	club	gang	team
association	committee	government	union
band	company	group	
class	family	jury	

Note that plural forms of collective nouns *(bands, teams)* take plural pronouns:

Twelve marching bands strutted <u>their</u> stuff.

PRACTICE 19-11

Circle the collective noun antecedent in the following sentences. Then circle the correct pronoun in parentheses.

Example: The (jury) returned with ((its)/their) verdict.

1. The (company) provides ((its)/their) employees with very generous benefits.

2. Each study (group) is supposed to hand in ((its)/their) joint project by the end of the week.

CHAPTER 19 Using Nouns and Pronouns • 373

3. Any (government) should be concerned for the welfare of (its/their) citizens.

4. The (Black Students Union) is sponsoring a party to celebrate (its/their) fifteenth anniversary.

5. Every (family) has (its/their) share of troubles.

6. An (army) is only as strong as the loyalty of (its/their) soldiers.

7. Even the best (team) has (its/their) off days.

8. The (band) has just signed a contract to make (its/their) first record.

9. The (gang) is known for (its/their) violent initiation rites.

10. I wouldn't join any (club) that would have me as one of (its/their) members.

PRACTICE 19-12

Check the following passage for correct pronoun-antecedent agreement. First determine the antecedent for each underlined pronoun. (Some will be compound, some will be indefinite pronouns, and some will be collective nouns.) Put a line through any pronoun that does not agree with its antecedent, and write in the correct form above it. If the pronoun is correct, write *C* above it. The first error has been corrected for you.

(1) Diversity has come to the American corporation. (2) Today the average company counts among ~~their~~ *its* employees many more women and members of minority groups than at any other time. (3) The U.S. government has established laws to protect *its* (C) citizens from discrimination in employment. (4) Anyone who can prove discrimination can usually see ~~their~~ *his or her* company punished. (5) This means that a corporation and ~~their~~ *its* board will usually set diversity in the workforce as one of ~~its~~ *their* goals. (6) Having a diverse workforce doesn't mean, however, that an organization has truly met the needs of *its* (C) employees. (7) While a Hispanic employee or a female employee may now find that ~~their~~ *his or her* opportunities are greater, there are still issues to be resolved. (8) Employees and management must first understand ~~its~~ *their* common goals. (9) Then, a company needs to implement the kinds of policies that

will make it possible for each of ~~their~~ *its* employees to work at <u>his or her</u> *C* best.

(10) For example, a vice president or a mail-room clerk may need to take time off to see ~~their~~ *his or her* family through a crisis. (11) Company policy should allow leave time to anyone in the company, regardless of ~~their~~ *his or her* position.

(12) In a truly diverse workforce, workers must be treated fairly.

▶ **FLASHBACK** ◀

Look back at your response to the Paragraph Practice at the beginning of the chapter. Does your paragraph contain any antecedents that are compounds, indefinite pronouns, or collective nouns? If so, list them below.

Compounds	Indefinite Pronouns	Collective Nouns
_____	_____	_____
_____	_____	_____
_____	_____	_____
_____	_____	_____

Have you used the correct pronoun with each of these? If not, correct your pronouns.

Nonspecific Pronoun References

A pronoun should always refer to a specific antecedent. When a pronoun has no antecedent, the sentence will be confusing. The pronouns *it* and *they* can present problems in a sentence because they sometimes do not point to any particular antecedent, as in the sentences that follow:

<u>It</u> says in today's paper that overcrowded prisons are a serious problem.

On the evening news, <u>they</u> said a baseball strike was inevitable.

The following sentences are clearer than the ones above because they eliminate the vague pronouns *it* and *they* and substitute more specific words:

<u>An editorial</u> in today's paper says that overcrowded prisons are a serious problem.

CHAPTER 19 Using Nouns and Pronouns • 375

On the evening news, <u>the sports commentator</u> said that a baseball strike was inevitable.

Unnecessary Pronoun References

When a pronoun serves no purpose in a sentence, it should be eliminated:

The county health officials, <u>they</u> recommended that all children be innoculated against measles and polio.

Here the pronoun *they* is used right after its antecedent *health officials*. It is therefore unnecessary and should be eliminated. (Only an intensive pronoun can directly follow its antecedent. See 19F.)

The following revised sentence, which eliminates the unnecessary pronoun, clearly indicates who made the recommendation:

<u>The county health officials</u> recommended that all children be innoculated against measles and polio.

If the pronoun reference is clear, however—for instance, if it refers to a noun in a previous sentence—you can also revise by using just the pronoun.

<u>They</u> recommended that all children be innoculated against measles and polio.

PRACTICE 19-13

Edit the following sentences for vague or unnecessary pronouns. Cross out any errors, and write in your corrections, if any, above them.

Example: ~~It states in the~~ *The* Constitution *states* that we are all created equal.

1. ~~It predicts in the~~ *The* weather report *predicts* that there will be snow tomorrow.

2. The new president of the college, ~~she~~ is forming a student committee to propose changes in the curriculum.

3. ~~In the~~ *The* encyclopedia ~~it~~ gives Maya Angelou's birth year as 1928.

4. "Honor thy father and thy mother," ~~it tells us in~~ *tells us* one of the Ten Commandments.

5. The Vietnam War, ~~it~~ ended in an American withdrawal in 1975.

6. The Bonneville Salt Flats in Utah, ~~they~~ offer a smooth salt surface that is perfect for auto racing.

7. ~~In the~~ *The* park ~~they have~~ *has* a skating rink and a free zoo.

8. The Cuban Missile Crisis, ~~it~~ followed the Bay of Pigs invasion.

9. ~~They say in my~~ My textbook ^says there should be a comma here.

10. People who have little education, ~~they~~ often have trouble finding jobs.

▶ **FLASHBACK** ◀

Look back at your response to the Paragraph Practice at the beginning of the chapter. Can you spot any confusing or unnecessary pronoun references? If so, revise one incorrect sentence on the lines below.

_____

_____

F UNDERSTANDING REFLEXIVE AND INTENSIVE PRONOUNS

Two special kinds of pronouns, reflexive pronouns and intensive pronouns, also always agree with their antecedents in person and number. Although the functions of the two kinds of pronouns are different, their forms are identical.

Reflexive Pronouns

Reflexive pronouns always end in *-self* (singular) or *-selves* (plural).

Rosanna lost <u>herself</u> in the novel.

You need to watch <u>yourself</u> when you mix those solutions.

Mehul and Paul made <u>themselves</u> cold drinks.

Intensive Pronouns

Intensive pronouns also end in *-self* or *-selves*. However, they always appear directly after their antecedents, and they are used for emphasis.

I <u>myself</u> have had some experience in sales and marketing.

The victim himself collected the reward.

They themselves were uncertain of the significance of their findings.

Reflexive and Intensive Pronouns

Singular Forms

Antecedent	Reflexive or Intensive Pronoun
I	myself
you	yourself
he	himself
she	herself
it	itself

Plural Forms

Antecedent	Reflexive or Intensive Pronoun
we	ourselves
you	yourselves
they	themselves

PRACTICE 19-14

Fill in the correct reflexive or intensive pronoun in each of the following sentences.

Example: Sometimes I find __myself__ daydreaming in class.

1. The leaders gave _themselves_ more credit than they deserved.
2. That woman takes _herself_ too seriously.
3. The President _himself_ visited the AIDS patients.
4. I don't see _myself_ as a particularly funny person.
5. Have you _yourself_ ever actually seen an extraterrestrial?
6. We Americans pride _ourselves_ on our tolerance of diversity, but we can still be discriminatory and narrow-minded.

378 • UNIT 8 Nouns, Pronouns, and Other Parts of the Sentence

7. The bird settled __itself__ on my window ledge.

8. You should all give __yourselves__ a big pat on the back for a job well done.

9. Dorothy and the others hardly recognized __themselves__ after the transformation.

10. I __myself__ am opposed to the legislation, but I don't condemn others who support it.

• • • • • • • • • • • • • **REVIEW** • • • • • • • • • • • • •

CHAPTER REVIEW: STUDENT WRITING

Read the following student passage, in which noun and pronoun errors have been introduced. Check for errors in plural noun forms, pronoun case, and pronoun-antecedent agreement, as well as for any nonspecific or unnecessary pronouns. Make any editing changes you think are necessary. The first sentence has been edited for you.

Answers may vary.

Going Beyond Books

Extracurricular ~~activitys~~ *activities* can be just as important for ~~a~~ college student*s* as their coursework. Two students I myself have met illustrate the truth of this statement. For each of them, ~~their~~ *his or her* extracurricular activity made a real difference.

Julia joined our school's rifle team. As the only female on the team, she had some problems at first. Eventually, though, her teammates saw that she could shoot as well as ~~them~~ *they* and she began to feel comfortable with the group and ~~their~~ *its* routine. In her first year, her team won the state Junior Varsity championship, and judges ranked ~~them~~ *it* third in the region. In her second year, ~~her~~ *she* and the team placed sixth in the championship match held at the United States Military Academy at West Point. Julia ~~she~~ found she enjoyed these triumphs. Like her teammates, she enjoyed rifle shooting because the sport requires precision and concentration in the midst of intense competition. It also gave ~~she~~ *her* and her teammates an occasional escape from their studies. Most important, Julia had the opportunity to visit other campuses when she competed in away matches and to meet other competitors, some of whom were also ~~woman~~ *women*. For Julia, intercollegiate competition offered a lot of benefits.

Chris, a chemistry major, got similar benefits from his participation in the student affiliate of the American Chemical Society (ACS). By the time he was a sophomore, he was president of our school's chapter. Serving in this office taught him how to handle leadership and responsibility. The organization was geared toward educating ~~their~~ *its* members about chemistry through seminars and visits to industry sites. ~~They~~ *It* also encouraged members to attend social functions with other chemistry majors and faculty. Chris was active in organizing all these events. Through the school's ACS chapter, ~~a student~~ *students* could increase their knowledge of chemistry beyond what their textbooks offered.

Many students believe courses are what school is all about, but Julia and Chris would disagree. For students like ~~they~~ *them*, time spent on extracurricular activities can be as valuable as time spent in a classroom or library. Studying and extracurricular activities are two ~~halfs~~ *halves* of a whole educational experience.

CHAPTER REVIEW: EDITING PRACTICE

Reread your response to the Paragraph Practice at the beginning of the chapter. Change every singular noun to a plural noun and every plural noun to a singular noun. Then, edit your pronouns so singular pronouns refer to singular nouns and plural pronouns refer to plural nouns. If you like, you may also do this exercise with a piece of writing you did in response to another assignment.

CHAPTER REVIEW: COLLABORATIVE ACTIVITIES

1. Working in a group, fill in the following chart, writing one noun on each line. If the noun is a proper noun, be sure to capitalize it.

Cars	Trees	Foods	Famous Couples	Cities
___	___	___	___	___
___	___	___	___	___
___	___	___	___	___
___	___	___	___	___
___	___	___	___	___
___	___	___	___	___

Then, write a brief news article that includes as many of the nouns above as you can. Try to make your article clear and coherent. Finally, exchange work with another group. Check the other group's article carefully to be sure the correct pronoun form is used to refer to each noun. Return the article to the original group for editing.

2. Working in a group, write a silly story that uses each of these nouns at least once: *Martians, eggplant, MTV, toupee, kangaroo, Iceland, bat, herd,* and *kayak*. Then, exchange stories with another group. After you have read the other group's story, edit it so that it includes all of the following pronouns: *it, its, itself; they, their, them, themselves*. Return the edited story to its authors. Finally, reread your group's story, and edit once again to make sure pronoun-antecedent agreement is clear and correct.

Review

- A noun is a word that names something. A singular noun names one thing; a plural noun names more than one thing. (See 19A.)
- Most nouns add *-s* to form plurals. Some irregular nouns form plurals in different ways. (See 19A.)
- A pronoun is a word that takes the place of a noun. A personal pronoun takes the place of a person or thing. (See 19B.)

    Michelle was really excited. Finally, she had a job.

- Personal pronouns can be in the subjective, objective, or possessive case. (See 19C.)

    Subjective: Finally, she realized that dreams could come true.
    Objective: Marc threw the ball to them.
    Possessive: Hieu took his lunch to the meeting.

- Pronouns present special problems when they are used in compounds and comparisons. (See 19C.)
- The word a pronoun replaces is called the pronoun's antecedent. (See 19D.)

    The leaf turned yellow, but it did not fall.

- Compound antecedents connected by *and* are plural and are used with plural pronouns. Compound antecedents connected by *or* may take singular or plural pronouns. (See 19E.)
- Most indefinite pronouns are singular. Therefore, they are used with singular pronouns. (See 19E.)

    Everything was in its place.

- Collective noun antecedents are singular and must be used with singular pronouns. (See 19E.)

    The band played on, but it never played our song.

- A pronoun should always refer clearly to a specific antecedent. A pronoun's purpose should always be clear. (See 19E.)
- Reflexive and intensive pronouns must agree with their antecedents in person and number. (See 19F.)

    Reflexive: Rosanna lost herself in the novel.

    Intensive: I myself have had some experience in sales and marketing.

20 Using Adjectives and Adverbs

> **Overview**
>
> In this chapter you will learn
> - To understand the difference between adjectives and adverbs
> - To form comparatives and superlatives of adjectives and adverbs
> - To use the correct forms of irregular comparatives and superlatives
> - To use demonstrative adjectives

PARAGRAPH PRACTICE

Write a cause-and-effect paragraph in which you try to imagine what events or circumstances could lead you to decide to leave your native country. Describe a specific situation that might force you to leave your home forever, and explain your motivation. Where would you go? Why? (If you have already left your native country, explain why.) Use the blank space below for invention. Then, write your paragraph on the lines that follow.

A UNDERSTANDING ADJECTIVES AND ADVERBS

Adjectives and adverbs are words that modify—that is, describe or limit—other words. They help to make sentences more specific and more interesting.

An **adjective** answers the question *what kind? which one?* or *how many?* Adjectives modify nouns or pronouns.

> The Turkish city of Istanbul spans two continents. (*Turkish* modifies the noun *city,* and *two* modifies the noun *continents.*)

> Because of the city's location and history, it is fascinating. (*Fascinating* modifies the pronoun *it.*)

Note that some adjectives, such as *Turkish,* are capitalized because they are formed from proper nouns; also note that numbers, such as *two,* may be used as adjectives.

An **adverb** answers the question *how? why? when? where?* or *to what extent?* Adverbs modify verbs, adjectives, or other adverbs.

> Traffic moved steadily. (*Steadily* modifies the verb *moved.*)

> Still, we were quite impatient. (*Quite* modifies the adjective *impatient.*)

> Very slowly we inched into the center lane. (*Very* modifies the adverb *slowly.*)

384 • UNIT 8 Nouns, Pronouns, and Other Parts of the Sentence

> ▶ **FOCUS** ON DISTINGUISHING ADJECTIVES ◀
> AND ADVERBS
>
> Many adverbs are formed when *-ly* is added to an adjective form.
>
> | Adjective | Adverb |
> |-----------|--------|
> | slow | slowly |
> | nice | nicely |
> | quick | quickly |
>
> Because some adjective and adverb forms look somewhat alike, you can become confused about which to use in a sentence. Remember: Adjectives modify nouns or pronouns, and adverbs modify verbs, adjectives, or other adverbs.
>
> **Adjective:** Let me give you one <u>quick</u> reminder. (*Quick* modifies the noun *reminder*.)
>
> **Adverb:** He <u>quickly</u> changed the subject. (*Quickly* modifies the verb *changed*.)
>
> **Adjective:** Tell me your <u>real</u> name. (*Real* modifies the noun *name*.)
>
> **Adverb:** It was <u>really</u> rude of her to ignore me. (*Really* modifies the adjective *rude*.)
>
> Note: Some adjectives—*lovely*, *friendly*, and *lively*, for example—also end in *-ly*. Do not mistake these words for adverbs.
>
> It was a <u>lovely</u> evening. (Adjective *lovely* modifies the noun *evening*.)

PRACTICE 20-1

In the following sentences, fill in the correct adjective or adverb form from the choices in parentheses.

Example: Women who are __*serious*__ (serious/seriously) walkers or runners need to wear athletic shoes that fit.

1. Doctors have found that many athletic shoes are __*poorly*__ (poor/poorly) designed for women.

2. Women's athletic shoes are __*usually*__ (usual/usually) just scaled-down versions of men's shoes.

CHAPTER 20 Using Adjectives and Adverbs • 385

3. Consequently, they can't provide a __truly__ (true/truly) comfortable fit.

4. Studies have shown that in order to get a shoe that fits __comfortably__ (comfortable/comfortably) in the heel, most women must buy one that is too __tight__ (tight/tightly) for the front of the foot.

5. This can have a __really__ (real/really) negative impact on athletic performance.

6. It can also cause __serious__ (serious/seriously) pain and even physical deformity.

7. Some athletic shoe manufacturers have begun to market athletic shoes that are designed __specifically__ (specific/specifically) for women.

8. Experts say that women must become informed consumers and choose __carefully__ (careful/carefully) when they shop for athletic shoes.

9. One __important__ (important/importantly) piece of advice for women and men is to shop for shoes __immediately__ (immediate/immediately) after exercising or at the end of a work day, when the foot is at its largest.

10. Experts advise that athletic shoes should feel __comfortable__ (comfortable/comfortably) from the moment they are tried on—or else returned to the box.

▶ **FOCUS ON GOOD AND WELL** ◀

Unlike regular adjectives, whose adverb form adds *-ly*, the adjective *good* is irregular. Its adverb form is *well*. Be careful not to confuse *good* and *well*.

Adjective: Fred Astaire was a good dancer. (*Good* modifies the noun *dancer*.)
Adverb: He danced especially well with Ginger Rogers. (*Well* modifies the verb *danced*.)

Note that *well* is always used to describe a person's health.

He really didn't feel well (not *good*) after eating an entire pizza.

PRACTICE 20-2

Fill in the correct form (*good or well*) in the sentences below.

Example: Eating __well__ (good/well) is part of __good__ (good/well) living.

1. Sometimes a particular food can be __good__ (good/well) for you in ways you might not expect.

2. If you're feeling down and just not doing __well__ (good/well) emotionally, you might need a carbohydrate pick-me-up.

3. Some doctors recommend pasta, rice cakes, or pretzels as a __good__ (good/well) source of carbohydrates.

4. If you need to perform __well__ (good/well) mentally—on a test, for example—protein-rich foods may be helpful.

5. Three to four ounces of fish or chicken can be __good__ (good/well) for helping you remain alert.

6. Carbohydrates can be eaten with the protein, but you would do __well__ (good/well) to avoid fats, which can make you drowsy.

7. Most people know that caffeine works __well__ (good/well) to help overcome drowsiness.

8. Caffeine can also be a __good__ (good/well) stimulant for helping one stay alert.

9. High-fat foods encourage the brain to produce endorphins, the same substances that make us feel so __good__ (good/well) when we are with someone we love.

10. However, the most endorphins are produced in people who exercise regularly and eat __well__ (good/well).

CHAPTER 20 Using Adjectives and Adverbs

> ●●●●●●●●●▶ **FLASHBACK** ◀●●●●●●●●●
>
> Look back at the response you wrote for the Paragraph Practice at the beginning of the chapter. Underline each adjective and adverb, and draw an arrow from each to the word it describes or limits. Do all adjectives modify nouns or pronouns? Do all adverbs modify verbs, adjectives, or other adverbs? Have you used *good* and *well* correctly? Revise any incorrect use of modifiers.

B UNDERSTANDING COMPARATIVES AND SUPERLATIVES

Sometimes an adjective or adverb describes something by comparing it to something else. The **comparative** form of an adjective or adverb is used to compare *two* people or things. Adjectives and adverbs form the comparative with *-er* or *more*. The **superlative** form of an adjective or adverb is used to compare *more than two* things. Adjectives and adverbs form the superlative with *-est* or *most*. Compare these two groups of sentences:

Adjectives

This film is <u>dull</u> and <u>predictable</u>.
The film I saw last week was even <u>duller</u> and <u>more predictable</u> than this one. (comparative)
The film I saw last night was the <u>dullest</u> and <u>most predictable</u> one I've ever seen. (superlative)

Adverbs

For beginners, they did needlepoint <u>skillfully</u>.
After they had watched the demonstration, they did needlepoint <u>more skillfully</u> than the other beginners. (comparative)
They did needlepoint <u>most skillfully</u> after they had practiced for many hours. (superlative)

Forming Comparatives and Superlatives

Adjectives

- One-syllable adjectives generally form the comparative with *-er* and the superlative with *-est*.

    great   greater   greatest

(continued on the following page)

(continued from the previous page)

- Adjectives with two or more syllables form the comparative with *more* and the superlative with *most*.

    wonderful   more wonderful   most wonderful

    Exception: Two-syllable adjectives ending in *y* add *-er* or *-est* after changing the *y* to an *i*.

    funny   funnier   funniest

Adverbs

- All adverbs ending in *-ly* form the comparative with *more* and the superlative with *most*.

    efficiently   more efficiently   most efficiently

- Some other adverbs form the comparative with *-er* and the superlative with *-est*.

    soon   sooner   soonest

Never use both *-er* and *more* to form the comparative or both *-est* and *most* to form the superlative.

> Nothing could have been <u>more awful</u> (not *more awfuller*).
> Space Mountain is the <u>most frightening</u> (not *most frighteningest*) ride at Disney World.

PRACTICE 20-3

Fill in the correct comparative form of the word supplied in parentheses.

Example: Children tend to be ___*noisier*___ (noisy) than adults.

1. The weather report says temperatures will be ___*colder*___ (cold) tomorrow.

2. Some elderly people are ___*healthier*___ (healthy) than they look.

3. It has been proven that pigs are *more intelligent* (intelligent).

4. The ___*taller*___ (tall) the building, the more damage the earthquake caused.

5. They want to teach their son to be *more respectful* (respectful) of women than most young men are.

CHAPTER 20 Using Adjectives and Adverbs • 389

6. Zsa Zsa Gabor is __more famous__ (famous) for her husbands and her temper than for her acting.

7. The WaterDrop is __wilder__ (wild) than any other ride in the park.

8. Traffic always moves __more slowly__ (slow) during rush hour than during the evening.

9. When someone asks you to repeat yourself, you usually answer __more loudly__ (loud).

10. You must move __more quickly__ (quick) if you expect to catch the ball.

PRACTICE 20-4

Fill in the correct superlative form of the word supplied in parentheses.

Example: Consumers now pay the __highest__ (high) surcharge ever when they buy tickets for arena events.

1. Ticketmaster is the __largest__ (large) seller of sports and entertainment tickets in the country.

2. The company was the __earliest__ (early) off the mark in selling concert and sporting event tickets both by phone and through retail outlets.

3. It has been __most successful__ (successful) at making deals to keep rival ticket agencies from carrying tickets for large arenas and stadiums.

4. Its markup on tickets is by far the __greatest__ (great) in the business, adding at least 20 percent to the cost of each ticket sold.

5. Because Ticketmaster is the __most powerful__ (powerful) ticket outlet in the country, however, fans have no choice but to pay the price.

6. Critics have argued that Ticketmaster's control of the market is the ___strongest___ (strong) monopoly in the country.

7. In 1994 the rock group Pearl Jam launched the ___most serious___ (serious) offensive to date against the ticket giant.

8. Wanting its fans to be able to buy the ___cheapest___ (cheap) tickets possible, Pearl Jam proposed to lower its own profits as well as Ticketmaster's for its 1994 summer tour. Ticketmaster refused.

9. One of the ___most popular___ (popular) groups in the country, Pearl Jam then could not find enough suitable arenas that were not controlled by Ticketmaster. The group sparked a Congressional investigation.

10. Ticketmaster's president argues that it has succeeded not because of unfairness but because it has been the ___hardest___ (hard) working and ___most aggressive___ (aggressive) company in the business.

▶ **FOCUS** ON IRREGULAR COMPARATIVES ◀
AND SUPERLATIVES

Most adjectives and adverbs form the comparative with *-er* or *more* and the superlative with *-est* or *most*. The adjectives *good* and *bad* and their adverb forms *well* and *badly* are exceptions.

Adjective	Comparative Form	Superlative Form
good	better	best
bad	worse	worst

Adjective	Comparative Form	Superlative Form
well	better	best
badly	worse	worst

Note that the comparative and superlative forms are the same for the adjective *good* and the adverb *well* and for the adjective *bad* and the adverb *badly*.

CHAPTER 20 Using Adjectives and Adverbs

> ▶ **FOCUS** ON TWO SPECIAL SITUATIONS WITH ◀
> **COMPARATIVES AND SUPERLATIVES**
>
> 1. Some adjectives—*excellent, perfect, impossible,* and *unique,* for example—cannot logically be used with the comparative or superlative.
>
>   This sculpture is *unique*. (Unique means "one of a kind," so *more unique* or *the most unique* doesn't make sense.)
>
> 2. Some adverbs that indicate degree—such as *very, somewhat, quite, extremely, rather,* and *moderately*—do not have comparative or superlative forms.

PRACTICE 20-5

Fill in the correct comparative form or superlative form of *good, well, bad,* or *badly.*

Example: She is at her __best__ (good) when she is under pressure.

1. Today in track practice Luisa performed __better__ (well) than she has in weeks.

2. In fact, she ran her __best__ (good) time ever in the fifty meter.

3. When things are bad, we wonder whether they will get __better__ (good) or __worse__ (bad).

4. I've had some bad pizza before, but this one is the __worst__ (bad).

5. The world always looks __better__ (good) when you're in love than when you're not.

6. Athletes generally play __worst__ (badly) when their concentration is poorest.

7. The Sport Shop's prices may be good, but Athletic Attic's are the __best__ (good) in town.

8. There are __better__ (good) ways to solve conflicts than by fighting.

9. People seem to hear __better__ (well) when they agree with what you're saying than when they don't agree with you.

10. Of all the children, Manda took care of her parents __best__ (well).

▶ **FLASHBACK** ◀

Look back at the response you wrote for the Paragraph Practice at the beginning of the chapter. Copy the adjectives and adverbs from your paragraph in the left-hand column. Then, write in the comparative and superlative form for each in the other columns.

Adjective or Adverb	Comparative Form	Superlative Form
_____	_____	_____
_____	_____	_____
_____	_____	_____
_____	_____	_____
_____	_____	_____

C USING DEMONSTRATIVE ADJECTIVES

Some adjectives do not describe other words. These **demonstrative adjectives**—*this, that, these,* and *those*—simply identify particular nouns.

This and *that* identify singular nouns:

<u>This</u> encyclopedia is much more thorough and up-to-date than <u>that</u> one.

These and *those* identify plural nouns:

<u>These</u> words and phrases are French, but <u>those</u> expressions are Creole.

▶ FOCUS ON DEMONSTRATIVE ADJECTIVES ◀

Be sure each demonstrative adjective clearly modifies a particular noun.

I've had lots of bad days, but <u>this day</u> (not *this*) is a complete disaster.

PRACTICE 20-6

Fill in the correct demonstrative adjective in each of the following sentences.

Example: Pay ___*this*___ (this/these) bill now, but hold ___*these*___ (this/these) until next week.

1. The news reported ___*this*___ (this/these) morning that ___*those*___ (that/those) missing children have been found.

2. Will ___*these*___ (this/these) papers be graded by ___*this*___ (this/these) Friday?

3. ___*Those*___ (That/Those) nuts are high in calories, but ___*this*___ (this/these) sesame bar is dietetic.

4. If ___*this*___ (this/these) flooding gets any worse, much of the town will have to evacuate.

5. By ___*that*___ (that/those) time, it may be too late for people to save their property.

● ● ● ● ● ● ● ● ● ▶ FLASHBACK ◀ ● ● ● ● ● ● ● ● ●

Did you use any demonstrative adjectives in the response you wrote for the Paragraph Practice at the beginning of the chapter? If so, underline them, and draw arrows to the nouns they identify.

394 • UNIT 8 Nouns, Pronouns, and Other Parts of the Sentence

● ● ● ● ● ● ● ● ● ● ● ● REVIEW ● ● ● ● ● ● ● ● ● ● ● ●

CHAPTER REVIEW: STUDENT WRITING

Read the following student passage, in which errors in the use of adjectives and adverbs have been introduced. Make any editing changes necessary to correct adjectives incorrectly used for adverbs, adverbs incorrectly used for adjectives, and errors in the use of comparatives and superlatives. You may also add adjectives and adverbs that you feel would make the writer's ideas clearer or more specific. The first sentence has been edited for you.

Answers may vary.

Starting Over

A wedding can be the ~~joyfullest~~ *most joyful* occasion in two people's lives, the beginning of a couple's ~~most~~ happiest years. For some unlucky women, however, a wedding can be the *worst* ~~worse~~ thing that ever happens; it is the beginning not of their happiness but of their battered lives. As I went through the joyful day of my wedding, I wanted so ~~bad~~ *badly* to find happiness for the rest of my life, but what I hoped and wished for did not come true.

I was married in the Savannah belt of the Sudan in the western part of Africa, where I grew up. I was barely twenty-two years old. The first two years of my marriage progressed ~~peaceful~~ *peacefully*, but problems started as soon as our first child was born.

Many American women say, "If my husband gave me just one beating, that would be it. I'd leave." But ~~those~~ *this modern* attitude does not work in cultures where tradition has overshadowed women's rights and divorce is not accepted. All women can do is accept their ~~sadly~~ *sad* fate. Battered women give many rationalizations for staying in their ^abusive marriages, but fear is the ~~commonest~~ ^most common. Fear immobilizes them, ruling their decisions, their actions, and their very lives. This is how it was for me.

Of course, I was ~~real~~ ^really afraid whenever my husband hit me. I would run to my mother's house and cry, and she would always talk me into going back and being more ~~patiently~~ ^patient with my husband. Our tradition discourages divorce, and wife-beating is taken for granted. The situation is really quite ironic: Islam, the religion I practice, sets harsh punishments for abusive husbands, but tradition has so overpowered religion that the laws are only ~~well~~ ^good on the books.

One night, after nine years of torture, I asked myself whether life had treated me ~~fair~~ ^fairly. True, I had a high school diploma and two of the ~~beautifullest~~ ^most beautiful children in the world, but these were not enough. I realized that in order to stand up to the husband who treated me so ~~bad~~ ^badly, I would have to achieve a more better education than he had. That night I decided to get a college education in the United States. My husband ^strongly opposed my decision, but with the support of my father and mother, I was able to begin to change my life.

It has been ~~real~~ ^really difficult for me. I miss my children every day. But I hope that one day I will be able to fight our traditions intellectually and with dignity so that my little daughters will remember even when I am gone that their mother fought back and won. And they <u>will</u> remember.

CHAPTER REVIEW: EDITING PRACTICE

Reread the response you wrote for the Paragraph Practice at the beginning of the chapter. Have you used adjectives and adverbs that effectively communicate the situation you describe? Have you used enough adjectives and adverbs to explain your ideas to readers? Add or substitute modifying words as needed to enrich and clarify your paragraph, deleting any unnecessary adjectives and adverbs.

CHAPTER REVIEW: COLLABORATIVE ACTIVITIES

1. Working in a small group, write a plot summary for an imaginary film. Begin with one of these three sentences.

   - Dirk and Clive were sworn enemies, but that night on Boulder Ridge they vowed to work together just this once, for the good of their country.
   - Genevieve entered the room in a cloud of perfume, and when she spoke her voice was like velvet.
   - The desert sun beat down on her head, but Susanna was determined to protect what was hers, no matter what the cost.

2. Switch summaries with another group. Add as many adjectives and adverbs as you can to the other group's summary. Make sure each modifier is appropriate.

3. Reread your group's plot summary and edit it carefully, paying special attention to the way adjectives and adverbs are used.

Review

- Adjectives modify nouns or pronouns. (See 20A.)

    The Turkish city of Istanbul spans two continents.

- Adverbs modify verbs, adjectives, or other adverbs. (See 20A.)

    Traffic moved steadily.

- To compare two people or things, use the comparative form of an adjective or adverb. To compare more than two people or things, use the superlative form of an adjective or adverb. Adjectives and adverbs form the comparative with *-er* or *more* and the superlative with *-est* and *most*. (See 20B.)

(continued on the following page)

(continued from the previous page)

    big/bigger/biggest
    incredible/more incredible/most incredible

- The adjectives *good* and *bad* and their adverb forms *well* and *badly* are irregular. They use different words to form the comparative and superlative. (See 20B.)
- Demonstrative adjectives—*this, that, these,* and *those*—identify particular nouns. (See 20C.)

    <u>this</u> encyclopedia   <u>that</u> one
    <u>these</u> words   <u>those</u> expressions

21 Using Prepositions

> **Overview**
>
> In this chapter you will learn
> - To identify prepositions and understand their function in a sentence
> - To identify prepositional phrases
> - To use prepositions idiomatically in certain familiar expressions

PARAGRAPH PRACTICE

Write a process paragraph in which you explain a fairly complicated mechanical procedure—for example, installing a new word processing program in a computer or changing the oil in a car. Choose a process with which you are familiar, preferably one you have performed many times. Step by step, using present tense, explain to readers in very specific terms how you generally go about performing this process. Make sure you use transitional words and expressions to help move readers from one step to the next. Use the blank space below for invention. Then, write your paragraph on the lines that follow.

A UNDERSTANDING PREPOSITIONS

Prepositions—words like *at, to, on* and *under*—connect words and word groups in a sentence. Their function is to show the precise relationships between words—for example, to indicate whether a book is *on, under,* or *near* a table.

I thought I left the book <u>on</u> the table or somewhere <u>near</u> the table, but I found it <u>under</u> the table.

Commonly Used Prepositions

about	before	except	off	toward
above	behind	for	on	under
across	below	from	onto	underneath
after	beneath	in	out	until
against	beside	inside	outside	up
along	between	into	over	upon
among	beyond	like	through	with
around	by	near	throughout	within
at	during	of	to	without

Prepositions are combined with nouns or pronouns to form **prepositional phrases.** In a prepositional phrase, the noun or pronoun is the object of the preposition. Additional words describing the noun or pronoun are also part of the prepositional phrase.

Preposition	+	Object	=	Prepositional Phrase
with		long red hair		with long red hair
at		Ted's house		at Ted's house

A prepositional phrase modifies another word or word group in the sentence.

The girl <u>with long red hair</u> was first in line. (*With long red hair* modifies the noun *girl*.)

Ken met his future wife <u>at Ted's house</u>. (*At Ted's house* modifies the verb *met*.)

> ▶ **FOCUS** ON *LIKE* ◀
>
> The preposition *like* can present two special problems.
>
> 1. Sometimes *like* is incorrectly used in place of *as* or *as if*. Because *like* is a preposition, however, it must be followed by a noun or pronoun that serves as its object:
>
>   Tejal wants to be an engineer <u>like</u> <u>her father</u>.
>
>   Use *as* or *as if* to introduce a subject and verb:
>
>   Watch me closely, and do <u>as</u> (not *like*) <u>I do</u>.
>   He stared at me <u>as if</u> (not *like*) <u>we had never met</u>.
>
> 2. Sometimes *like* is incorrectly used to introduce an example:
>
>   **Incorrect:** Playing with fire can be dangerous, like when children experiment with matches.
>   **Correct:** Playing with fire can be dangerous—for example, when children experiment with matches.

PRACTICE 21-1

Fill in the appropriate word (*like, as,* or *as if*) in the following sentences. Remember that *like* is a preposition and is followed by a noun or pronoun object; *as* and *as if* are followed by a subject and verb.

Examples: Whitney doesn't look __like__ (like/as/as if) her

Aunt Aretha.

You must do __as__ (like/as/as if) you are told.

1. Dewey played __like__ (like/as/as if) a real professional.

2. I bowled tonight __as or as if__ (like/as/as if) I had never bowled before.

3. To open the door, you must insert the keys exactly __as__ (like/as/as if) I showed you.

4. Sonia is a careful driver __like__ (like/as/as if) her father.

5. Her brother drives much too fast, __as if__ (like/as/as if) he has a real death wish.

▶ FLASHBACK ◀

Look back at your response to the Paragraph Practice at the beginning of the chapter. Circle every preposition you used, and write five of these prepositions and their objects on the lines below.

Preposition	Object
_____	_____
_____	_____
_____	_____
_____	_____
_____	_____

Have you used *like* correctly? Correct any errors you find.

B USING PREPOSITIONS IN FAMILIAR EXPRESSIONS

Many familiar fixed expressions end with prepositions. Learning to write clearly and *idiomatically*—in keeping with the conventions of written English—means learning which preposition is used in each expression.

The sentences below illustrate idiomatic use of prepositions in various expressions. As you read them, you may notice that sometimes different prepositions are used with the same word. For example, both *on* and *for* can be used with *wait,* to form two different expressions with two different meanings (He *waited on* their table; She *waited for* the bus). Which preposition you choose depends on your meaning. (Pairs of similar expressions that end with different prepositions are bracketed.)

Expression with Preposition	Sample Sentence
acquainted with	It took the family several weeks to become acquainted with their new neighbors.
addicted to	I think Abby is becoming addicted to cheesecake.
agree on (a plan or objective)	It is vital that all members of the school board agree on goals for the coming year.
agree to (a proposal)	Striking workers finally agreed to the terms of management's offer.
angry about or at (a situation)	Taxpayers are understandably angry about (or at) the deterioration of city recreation facilities.
angry with (a person)	When the mayor refused to hire more police officers, his constituents became angry with him.
approve of	Amy's advisor approved of her decision to study in Guatemala.
bored with	Just when Michael was getting bored with his life, he met Sharon.
capable of	Dogs may be able to fetch and roll over, but they certainly aren't capable of complex reasoning.
consist of	The deluxe fruit basket consisted of five pathetic pears, two tiny apples, a few limp bunches of grapes, and one lonely kiwi.
contrast with	Coach Headley's relaxed style contrasts sharply with the previous coach's more formal approach.
convenient for	The proposed location of the new day-care center is convenient for many families.
deal with	Many parents and educators believe it is possible to deal with the special needs of autistic children in a regular classroom.
depend on	Children depend on their parents for emotional as well as financial support.
differ from (something else)	The music of Boyz II Men differs from the music of REM.
differ with (someone else)	I strongly differ with your interpretation of my dream about *The Wizard of Oz*.
emigrate from	My grandfather and his brother emigrated from the part of Russia that is now Ukraine.

grateful for (a favor)	If you can arrange an interview next week, I will be very grateful for your time and trouble.
grateful to (someone)	Jerry Garcia was always grateful to his loyal fans.
immigrate to	Many Cubans want to leave their country and immigrate to the United States.
impatient with	Keshia often gets impatient with her four younger brothers.
interested in	Diana, who was not very interested in the discussion of the Treaty of Versailles, stared out the window.
interfere with	Sometimes it's hard to resist the temptation to interfere with a friend's life.
meet with	I hope I can meet with you soon to discuss my research paper.
object to	The defense attorney objected to the prosecutor's treatment of the witness.
pleased with	Marta was very pleased with Eric's favorable critique of her speech.
protect against	Nobel Prize winner Linus Pauling believed that large doses of Vitamin C could protect people against the common cold.
reason with	When a two-year-old is having a tantrum, it's nearly impossible to reason with her.
reply to	If no one replies to our ad within two weeks, we will advertise again.
responsible for	Parents are not responsible for the debts of their adult children.
similar to	The blood sample found at the crime scene was remarkably similar to one found in the suspect's residence.
specialize in	Dr. Casullo is a dentist who specializes in periodontal surgery.
succeed in	Lisa hoped her MBA would help her succeed in a business career.
take advantage of	Some consumer laws are designed to prevent door-to-door salespeople from taking advantage of gullible buyers.
wait for (something to happen)	Snow White sang while she waited for her prince to come.
wait on (in a restaurant)	We sat at the table for twenty minutes before someone waited on us.
worry about	Why worry about things you can't change?

PRACTICE 21-2

Fill in the correct idiomatic prepositions in the following paragraph. The first sentence has been done for you.

(1) Born in 1828, French writer Jules Verne became interested _in_ (in/with) fantasy at an early age. (2) One story claims that, addicted _to_ (to/with) travel and bored _with_ (about/with) his dull home life, he ran away from home at eleven to become a sailor. (3) When he was caught and returned unhappily to his home, he decided he was capable _of_ (of/to) traveling further in his imagination. (4) That is exactly what he succeeded _in_ (with/in) doing. (5) In fact, he specialized _in_ (in/with) stories of fantastic voyages that dealt _with_ (over/with) travel on remarkable machines piloted by brave crews. (6) Over the course of his long writing career, he was responsible _for_ (for/with) taking his readers to the center of the earth and to the bottom of the sea. (7) In 1865, he wrote *From the Earth to the Moon*, imagining space flight as though he were already acquainted _with_ (to/with) what would happen in the future. (8) The imaginary moon flight he describes in the book is amazingly similar _to_ (with/to) the first NASA flights almost a hundred years later. (9) The spaceship he describes consists _of_ (by/of) command modules almost identical to those of the real NASA ships. (10) It also blasts off from the state of Florida, where NASA's Cape Canaveral space center would eventually be located.

▶ FLASHBACK ◀

Look back at your response to the Paragraph Practice at the beginning of the chapter. Have you used any of the expressions listed on pages 402–403? If so, underline each expression. Have you used the correct prepositions? Make any necessary revisions.

Have you used any other familiar expressions that end with prepositions? Write them on the lines below.

_____

_____

_____

CHAPTER 21 Using Prepositions · 405

REVIEW

CHAPTER REVIEW: STUDENT WRITING

Read the following student passage, in which errors in idiomatic expressions with prepositions have been introduced. Check each underlined phrase. If the preposition is not used idiomatically, cross it out, and write the correct preposition in the space above. If it is correct, write *C* above it. The first sentence has been edited for you.

History and Myth

In 1935, the United States was worrying ~~with~~ *about* a serious economic depression. Rather than write a book that dealt ~~in~~ *with* the grim events around her, Laura Ingalls Wilder chose to write <u>Little House on the Prairie</u>, a book about a time in history similar ~~with~~ *to* the tough days of the 1930s. Written as a novel, the book consists ~~with~~ *of* many historical details of the Ingalls family's life. Like most history, it is part fact and part myth.

In the late nineteenth century, the Homestead Act offered any adult 160 acres, provided that person would live on the land for at least five years. Some, like Wilder's father Charles Ingalls, took advantage ~~for~~ *of* the offer and emigrated from *(C)* the East. The Ingalls family settled on land that was Indian territory, hoping the government would displace the Indians. However, the government interfered ~~in~~ *with* this plan, making farmers like Mr. Ingalls relocate. This is fact.

At the beginning of Chapter 15 of <u>Little House</u>, Wilder casually mentions the presence of mosquitoes. Later in the chapter, she describes the Ingalls family as sick in bed. No one at the time knew why they were sick, but Wilder, looking back on their illness and acquainted ~~to~~ *with* later medical research, notes that the fever was actually malaria, whose spread depended ~~of~~ *on* mosquitoes.

Other details also seem accurate. For example, the children are very grateful ~~for~~ *to* their father when he gives them a penny; this makes sense because very little currency was actually in circulation in the 1870s. Mr. Ingalls seldom purchases goods for money. More often, he and a neighbor agree ~~with~~ *on* a deal by which he trades his services as payment, helping to build a house or dig a well in exchange for something the family needs.

Despite its many facts, though, much of Little House differs ~~with~~ *from* the reality of prairie life. In the book, everything always turns out for the best. Wilder omits many of her family's more negative experiences. The book contrasts ~~to~~ *with* reality in that the family's life is never violent or tragic, and the settlers never seem to be in real danger. By omitting the bleakness and tragedy of her family's life, Laura Ingalls Wilder succeeded ~~on~~ *in* turning history into myth.

CHAPTER REVIEW: EDITING PRACTICE

Reread your response to the Paragraph Practice at the beginning of the chapter. Look closely at each expression that ends with a preposition. (If you did the Flashback exercise on page 404, these expressions will be underlined.) Can you substitute an equivalent word or phrase for any of these expressions? Be careful not to substitute expressions that change your paragraph's meaning. If you like, you may examine your use of familiar expressions ending in prepositions in a piece of writing you did in response to another assignment.

CHAPTER REVIEW: COLLABORATIVE ACTIVITIES

1. Working in a small group, make a list of ten prepositional phrases that include the prepositions *above, around, at, between, from, in, on, over, under,* and *with.* Use very specific nouns as objects of these prepositions, and use as many modifying words as you wish. (Try, for example, to write something like *above their hideously unflattering wedding portrait,* not just *above the picture.*)

2. Exchange lists with another group. Then, still working collaboratively, compose a list of ten sentences—one that includes each of the other group's ten prepositional phrases. Then, give your list of ten sentences to another group.

3. Working with this new list of ten sentences, substitute a different prepositional phrase for each one that appears in a sentence. Make sure each sentence still makes sense.

Review

- Prepositions connect words and word groups in a sentence. They are combined with nouns or pronouns to form prepositional phrases. (See 21A.)

    I thought I left the book <u>on the table</u> or somewhere <u>near the table</u>, but I found it <u>under the table</u>.

- Many familiar expressions are completed by prepositions. (See 21B.)

Unit 8 Review

The collaborative activities, writing practice topics, and student writing sample that follow provide opportunities for you to review what you have learned in Chapters 19, 20, and 21.

COLLABORATIVE ACTIVITIES

1. Imagine that it is the year 2010, and that you and your group are a team of advertising copywriters working under intense pressure to create a press release for a new type of car—the car of the future. Give your vehicle a name, and describe its design, special features, and performance in glowing terms.

2. Exchange press releases with another group. This time, take the point of view of a competing automobile company anxious to discredit the new car. Using the specific information in the press release, write a highly negative review of the new car for an automotive magazine. Your objective is to discourage buyers from test-driving or even going to see your competitor's new car.

3. Imagine that you are game developers who have hit on a terrific idea: You have invented a board game that can make an academic subject (math, history, or biology, for example) interesting as well as educational for elementary school (or middle school) students. You even have a company interested in manufacturing and marketing your game. Now all you have to do is write a specific proposal describing your game and its rules and then provide detailed instructions for playing it. (If you like, you may devise an interactive computer game instead of a board game.)

WRITING PRACTICE

1. As one of the first proud owners of the new car your group praised in its press release in Collaborative Activity 1 above, you are anxious to communicate your reactions to the automakers. Although you are basically satisfied with your new car's looks and performance, it has a few quirks that really annoy you. Write a letter to the director of consumer affairs assessing what you consider to be the automobile's strengths and weaknesses after your first year of ownership.

2. In your first appearance on the Home Shopping Network, you find yourself making a pitch for something you thought you'd never sell—in fact,

it is your most prized possession. In a moving but essentially factual speech, you try to sell this one-of-a-kind item. Write a script for this speech, trying to convince one viewer to buy the item you need to sell. Be very specific about the item's appearance, function, and value.

3. Choose a television program that focuses on a family, and write an essay in which you discuss the myths about American family life that the series creates. Begin by listing examples of relationships, settings, events, and dialog that you consider accurate or true to life. Move from these believable details to the less realistic overall impression the program creates. What misconceptions are perpetuated? For example, is the view of family life too positive? Or is it too negative? Are problems too far-fetched? Are they resolved too easily?

STUDENT WRITING

Read the following student passage, in which errors in the use of nouns, pronouns, adjectives, adverbs, and prepositions have been introduced. Correct all the errors you find. The first sentence has been edited for you.

```
                    Fathers and Sons
                                    with
    Louise Erdrich's Love Medicine deals on two Native

American families, the Kashpaws and the Lamartines. In a

series of interrelated stories, Erdrich focuses on the

characters of Lyman Lamartine (son of Lulu Lamartine and

Nector Kashpaw) and Lipsha Morrissey (son of June Kashpaw
                                            them
and Gerry Nanapush) and the relationships between they and

their families, particularly their fathers.
                                              his
    Each of the men has problems not only with their own
                                his
identity, but with the identity of their father. Lyman was
                with
never acquainted to Nector, and Nector never acknowledged

him. Through most of his life, however, Lyman is surrounded
           women
by the two woman who meant the most to Nector, and Lyman

feels that working with the two women his father loved puts

him in an awkward position. Lipsha must eventually go on a
```

journey to find his father, whose identity he doesn't learn until he is an adult.

When we first meet Lyman in the story "The Red Convertible," he is free spirited and loves having a good time. However, ~~him~~ *he* and other members of his family have a cynical outlook toward the U.S. government and ~~their~~ *its* broken promises. And, when his brother Henry goes off to serve in Vietnam and comes back a ~~real~~ *really* changed man, Lyman feels cut off from him. His ~~worse~~ *worst* fear becomes reality when Henry kills himself. Lyman is left to make the best of his life without the brother he was so attached to. When we meet Lyman again nine years later in "The Tomahawk Factory," he behaves completely ~~different~~ *differently*. After working in his father's factory, he has become ~~ambitiouser~~ *more ambitious*. He sees his future as based on "greed and luck."

Lipsha works in the factory ~~like~~ *as* Lyman does, but he is not at all like Lyman. Lipsha~~,~~ ~~he~~ hasn't done much with his life; he has no focus. Lyman, on the other hand, is very career oriented. Still, Lipsha doesn't wait until his father is dead to get to know things about him. As soon as Lulu tells Lipsha who his father is, Lipsha goes after his hero-father. And, when he finds him, he feels he really belongs.

Both Lyman and Lipsha have problems in their lives with their identities, but both make the best of things. Lyman uses his father's business sense and luck to get ahead in the world, and Lipsha uses all the information about who he is to make peace with himself. At the end of <u>Love Medicine</u>, neither of the men still has ~~their~~ *his* identity problem. They are not their fathers' sons; each is ~~their~~ *his* own person.

22 Using Commas

> **Overview**
>
> In this chapter you will learn
> - To use commas in a series
> - To use commas to set off introductory phrases and transitional words and expressions
> - To use commas with appositives
> - To use commas in dates and addresses

PARAGRAPH PRACTICE

Some colleges have established separate dormitories for students of different races or ethnic groups. Others have separate lounges in student activities centers—or even separate buildings for social and recreational activities. Would you take advantage of such facilities if they were available at your school? Why or why not? State your position in your topic sentence. In the rest of your paragraph, discuss the advantages or disadvantages of giving students the opportunity to associate with only those of their own racial or ethnic group. Use the blank space below for invention. Then, write your paragraph on the lines that follow.

A **comma** separates words or groups of words within sentences. In earlier chapters, you learned to use a comma between two independent clauses linked by a coordinating conjunction (12A). You also learned to use a comma after a dependent clause that comes before an independent clause (13A) and to set off nonrestrictive clauses introduced by relative pronouns (13C). Commas have several other special uses, which are discussed and illustrated in this chapter.

A USING COMMAS IN A SERIES

Use commas to separate elements in a series of three or more words or word groups.

> Leyla, Zack, and Kathleen campaigned for Representative Fattah.
> Either Leyla, Zack, or Kathleen will be elected president of Students for Fattah.
> Leyla made phone calls, licked envelopes, and ran errands for the campaign.
> Leyla is president, Zack is vice-president, and Kathleen is treasurer.

CHAPTER 22 Using Commas • 413

> ▶ **FOCUS** ON USING COMMAS IN A SERIES ◀
>
> Although the comma before the coordinating conjunction in a series of three or more items is usually omitted in newspaper and magazine writing, most college instructors still expect you to use it. In general, don't leave out the comma that comes before the coordinating conjunction. Do not use any commas, however, if all the items in a series are separated by coordinating conjunctions.
>
> Either Leyla <u>or</u> Zack <u>or</u> Kathleen will be elected president of Students for Fattah.

PRACTICE 22-1

Edit the following sentences for the use of commas in a series. If the sentence is correct, write *C* in the blank.

Examples: Costa Rica produces bananas, cocoa, and sugar cane. _C_
The pool rules state that there is no running, or jumping, or diving. ____

1. A triple threat musician, he plays guitar, bass, and drums. ____
2. The organization's goals are feeding the hungry, housing the homeless, and helping the unemployed find work. ____
3. *The Price is Right*, *Let's Make a Deal*, and *Jeopardy* are three of the longest-running game shows on television. _C_
4. In native Hawaiian culture, yellow was the color worn by the royalty, red was worn by priests, and a mixture of the two colors was worn by others of high rank. ____
5. The remarkable diary kept by young Anne Frank while her family was in hiding from the Nazis is insightful, touching, and sometimes humorous. ____
6. A standard bookshelf is sixty inches tall, forty-eight inches wide, and twelve inches deep. ____
7. Most coffins manufactured in the United States are made of elm or oak, and they are lined with either bronze, or copper, or lead. ____
8. Moody, rebellious, and sensitive, Johnny Depp is the 1990s answer to the 1950s actor James Dean. ____
9. California's capital is Sacramento, its largest city is Los Angeles, and its oldest settlement is San Diego. ____
10. Watching television, playing video games, and riding his bicycle are the average ten-year-old boy's favorite pastimes today. _C_

414 • UNIT 9 Special Problems with Punctuation, Mechanics, and Spelling

> ●●●●●●●●●●▶ **FLASHBACK** ◀●●●●●●●●●●
>
> Look back at your response to the Paragraph Practice at the beginning of the chapter. If you have included a series of three or more words or word groups in any of your sentences, did you use commas correctly to separate them? If not, rewrite them below, correcting your punctuation.
>
> _____
>
> _____

B   USING COMMAS TO SET OFF INTRODUCTORY PHRASES AND TRANSITIONAL WORDS AND EXPRESSIONS

Use a comma to set off an introductory phrase from the rest of the sentence.

<u>In the event of a fire</u>, proceed to the nearest exit.
<u>Walking home</u>, Nelida decided to change her major.
<u>To keep fit</u>, students should try to exercise regularly.

Note that if an introductory prepositional phrase consists of fewer than three words, you do not have to use a comma to set it off.

In 1986 the *Challenger* space shuttle exploded on takeoff.

Also use commas to set off transitional words and expressions. Transitional elements may be placed at the beginning, in the middle, or at the end of a sentence.

<u>In fact</u>, Thoreau spent only one night in jail.
He was, <u>of course</u>, bailed out by a friend.
He did spend more than two years at Walden Pond, <u>however</u>.

Note that when a transitional word or expression joins two sentences into a single compound sentence, different punctuation rules apply. (See 12C.)

Frequently Used Transitional Words and Expressions

after all	for instance	instead
also	however	of course
as a matter of fact	in fact	on the other hand
by the way	in other words	therefore
for example	in short	thus

CHAPTER 22 Using Commas • 415

PRACTICE 22-2

Edit the following sentences for the use of commas with introductory phrases. If the sentence is correct, write *C* in the blank.

Examples: From professional athletes to teenagers, people have begun to find alternatives to steroids. ____
Regulated by the Drug Enforcement Administration, steroids are a controlled substance and can only be obtained illegally. _C_

1. During the 1992 Summer Olympics in Barcelona, two American athletes and several athletes from other countries were sent home because they tested positive for banned drugs. ____
2. To the surprise of many fans, these drugs were not steroids. ____
3. For the first time in the games, athletes were accused of taking a drug for animals called clenabutal. _C_
4. In addition to clenabutal, the poison strychnine showed up in one athlete's bloodstream. ____
5. Banned by the rules of the Olympics, these drugs still appeal to athletes because they supposedly enhance performance. ____
6. Because of the laws prohibiting steroids, many athletes are now turning to these and other unregulated substances. ____
7. Often called dietary supplements, these alternative chemicals are claimed to enhance athletic performance in the same way steroids are supposed to. ____
8. According to the *Journal of the American Medical Association*, these dietary supplements do no such thing. ____
9. In fact, they can cause considerable damage to the body. ____
10. Over the course of the last few years, investigators have collected over three thousand samples of such products sold on the black market. ____

PRACTICE 22-3

Edit the following sentences for the use of commas with transitional words and expressions. If the sentence is correct, write *C* in the blank.

Example: Kwanzaa, of course, is a fairly new cultural holiday.

1. As a matter of fact, this yearly African-American celebration is less than thirty years old. ____
2. This holiday to remind us of important African traditions has, however, attracted many celebrants over its short life. ____
3. By the way, the word *Kwanzaa* means "first fruits" in Swahili. ____
4. In other words, Kwanzaa stands for renewal. _C_
5. This can, in fact, be demonstrated in some of the seven principles of Kwanzaa. ____
6. Kwanzaa is, after all, celebrated over seven days to focus on each of these seven principles. ____

7. The focus, first of all, is on unity *(umoja).* ____
8. The second focus, then, is personal self-determination *(kujichagulia).* ____
9. Next, Kwanzaa celebrations emphasize three kinds of community responsibility *(ujima, ujamaa,* and *nia).* ____
10. The other principles of Kwanzaa are creativity *(kuumba)* and, finally, faith *(imani).* ____

▶ FLASHBACK ◀

Look back at your response to the Paragraph Practice at the beginning of the chapter. Underline any introductory phrases and transitional words and expressions you have used. Have you set off each of these with commas when appropriate? Revise any incorrect sentences below, adding commas where needed.

_____

_____

_____

_____

C USING COMMAS WITH APPOSITIVES

Use commas to set off an **appositive**—a word or word group that identifies, describes, or renames a noun or pronoun.

Carlos Santana, leader of the group Santana, played at Woodstock in 1969.

▶ FOCUS ON USING COMMAS WITH APPOSITIVES ◀

An appositive is set off by commas, whether it falls at the beginning, in the middle, or at the end of a sentence.

A dreamer, he spent his life thinking about what he could not have.

He always wanted to build a house, a big white one, overlooking the ocean.

He finally built his dream house, a log cabin.

CHAPTER 22   Using Commas • 417

Single-word appositives are also set off by commas.

> I have visited only one country, Canada, outside the United States.

PRACTICE 22-4

Edit the following sentences for the correct use of commas to set off appositives. If the sentence is correct, write *C* in the blank.

> **Examples:** The Buccaneers haven't joined the Cheese League, the group of NFL teams that holds summer training in Wisconsin. ____
> William Filene, the Boston merchant who founded Filene's department store, invented the "bargain basement." ____

1. Traditional Chinese medicine is based on meridians, channels of energy believed to run in regular patterns through the body. ____
2. Acupuncture, the insertion of thin needles at precise points in the body, stimulates these meridians. ____
3. Herbal medicine, the basis of many Chinese healing techniques, requires twelve years of study. ____
4. Gary Larson, creator of the popular *Far Side* cartoons, ended the series in 1995. ____
5. A musician at heart, Larson has said he wants to spend more time practicing the guitar. _C_
6. *Far Side* calendars and other product tie-ins have earned $500 million, a lot of money for guitar lessons. ____
7. Nigeria, the most populous country in Africa, is also one of the fastest-growing nations in the world. ____
8. On the southwest coast of Nigeria lies Lagos, a major port. ____
9. The Yoruban people, the Nigerian settlers of Lagos, are unusual in Africa because they tend to form large urban communities. ____
10. A predominantly Christian people, the Yoruba have incorporated many native religious rituals into their practice of Christianity. ____

▶ FLASHBACK ◀

Look back at your response to the Paragraph Practice at the beginning of the chapter. Have you used any appositives? If so, underline them and circle the nouns or pronouns they rename or describe. Make sure you have set off appositives appropriately with

(continued on the following page)

> (continued from the previous page)
>
> commas, and use the lines below to revise any sentences that need to be corrected.
>
> _____
>
> _____
>
> _____

D   USING COMMAS IN DATES AND ADDRESSES

Use commas in dates to separate the day of the week from the month and the day of the month from the year.

> The first Cinco de Mayo Yolanda celebrated in the United States was Friday, May 5, 1995.

When a date that includes commas falls in the middle of a sentence, an additional comma comes after the date.

> Friday, May 5, 1995, was the first Cinco de Mayo Yolanda celebrated in the United States.

Do not use commas between a month and the number of the day (May 5) or year (May 1995).

Use commas in addresses to separate the street address from the city and the city from the state or country.

> The office of the famous fictional detective Sherlock Holmes was located at 221b Baker Street, London, England.

When an address that includes commas falls in the middle of a sentence, place an additional comma after the state or country.

> The office at 221b Baker Street, London, England, belonged to the famous fictional detective Sherlock Holmes.

Do not use a comma between the address number and the street name.

PRACTICE 22-5

Edit the following sentences for the correct use of commas in dates and in addresses. Add any missing commas, and cross out any extra commas. If the sentence is correct, write *C* in the blank.

> **Examples:** June 3, 1968, is the day my parents were married.
> Their wedding took place in Santiago, Chile.

1. The People's Republic of the Congo achieved independence on August 15, 1960. ____

CHAPTER 22 Using Commas • 419

2. The Pelican Man's Bird Sanctuary is located at 1705 Ken Thompson Parkway, Sarasota, Florida. ____
3. At 175 Carlton Avenue, Brooklyn, New York, is the house where Richard Wright began writing *Native Son*. ____
4. I found this information in the February 12, 1994, issue of the *New York Times*. ____
5. The Mexican hero Father Miguel Hidalgo y Costilla was shot by a firing squad on June 30, 1811. _C_
6. The Palacio de Gobernio at Plaza de Armas, Guadalajara, Mexico, houses a mural of the famous revolutionary. ____
7. The Pueblo Grande Museum is located at 1469 East Washington Street, Phoenix, Arizona. ____
8. Brigham Young led the first settlers into the valley that is now Salt Lake City, Utah, in July, 1847. ____
9. St. Louis, Missouri, was the birthplace of writer Maya Angelou, but she spent most of her childhood in Stamps, Arkansas. ____
10. Some records list the actress's birthday as May 19, 1928, while others indicate she was born May 20, 1924. ____

REVIEW

CHAPTER REVIEW: STUDENT WRITING

Read the following student passage, in which some commas have been intentionally deleted. Add commas where necessary between items in a series and with introductory phrases, transitional words, and appositives. The first sentence has been edited for you.

```
                    Brave Orchid

     One of the most important characters in The Woman

Warrior, Maxine Hong Kingston's autobiographical work, is

Brave Orchid, Kingston's mother. Brave Orchid, a very complex

character, is an imaginative storyteller who tells vivid

tales of China. A quiet woman, she still impresses her

medical school classmates with her intelligence. She is also

a traditional woman. However, she will stop at nothing to
```

make her family exactly what she wants it to be. Brave Orchid strongly believes in herself; even so, she sees herself as a failure.

In her native China Brave Orchid trains to be a doctor. The other women in her class envy her independence, brilliance, and courage. One day Brave Orchid proves her courageousness by confronting the Fox Spirit, a ghost, and telling him he will not win. First of all, she tells him she can endure any pain he inflicts upon her. Next, she gathers together the women in the dormitory to burn the ghost away. After this event, the other women admire her even more.

Working hard, Brave Orchid becomes a successful doctor in China. After coming to America, however, she cannot work as a doctor because she does not speak English. Instead, she works in a Chinese laundry or picks tomatoes. None of her medical school classmates could have imagined this outcome. During her later years in America, Brave Orchid becomes an overbearing and domineering woman. We see another side of her at this point in the book. She bosses her children around, she tries to ruin her sister's life, and she criticizes everyone and everything around her. Her daughter, a straight-A student, is the object of her worst criticism.

Brave Orchid's intentions are good. Nevertheless, she devotes her energy to the wrong things. She wants the people around her to be as strong as she is. Because she bullies them, however, she eventually loses them. In addition, she is too busy noticing her daughter's faults to see all her accomplishments. Brave Orchid, independent woman and brilliant student, never reaches her goals. She is hard on the people around her because she is, in fact, disappointed in herself.

CHAPTER REVIEW: EDITING PRACTICE

Reread the response you wrote for the Paragraph Practice at the beginning of the chapter. Then, revise your paragraph by making the following additions.

1. Add a sentence that includes a series of three or more words or word groups.
2. Add introductory phrases to two of your sentences.
3. Add an appositive to one of your sentences.
4. Add a transitional word or expression to one of your sentences.

When you have made all the additions, reread your paragraph to check your use of commas with the new material.

CHAPTER REVIEW: COLLABORATIVE ACTIVITIES

1. Bring a homemaking, sports, or fashion magazine to class. Working in a small group, look at the ads that picture people. In what roles are men most often depicted? In what roles are women most often presented? Identify the three or four most common roles for each sex, and give each kind of character a descriptive name—*jock* or *mother*, for example.
2. Working on your own, choose one character from the list your group made in the preceding activity. Write a paragraph in which you describe this character's stereotypical appearance, habits, and so forth. Use references to the appropriate magazine pictures to support your characterization.
3. Rejoining your group, work together to write two paragraphs, one discussing how men are portrayed in the ads and one discussing how women are portrayed.
4. Circle every comma in the paragraph you wrote for Collaborative Activity 2. Work with your small group to explain why each comma is used. If no one in your group can justify a particular comma's use, delete it.

Review

- Use commas to separate elements in a series of three or more words or word groups. (See 22A.)

    <u>Leyla, Zack, and Kathleen</u> campaigned for Representative Fattah.

- Use commas to set off introductory phrases and transitional words and expressions from the rest of the sentence. (See 22B.)

    <u>In the event of a fire</u>, proceed to the nearest exit.
    He was, <u>of course</u>, bailed out by a friend.

- Use commas to set off an appositive from the rest of the sentence. (See 22C.)

    Carlos Santana, <u>leader of the group Santana</u>, played at Woodstock in 1969.

- Use commas to separate parts of dates and addresses. (See 22D.)

    Friday, May 5, 1995
    221b Baker Street, London, England

23 Using Apostrophes

> **Overview**
>
> In this chapter you will learn
> - To use apostrophes to form contractions
> - To use apostrophes to form the possessive case of nouns and indefinite pronouns
> - To revise incorrect use of apostrophes

PARAGRAPH PRACTICE

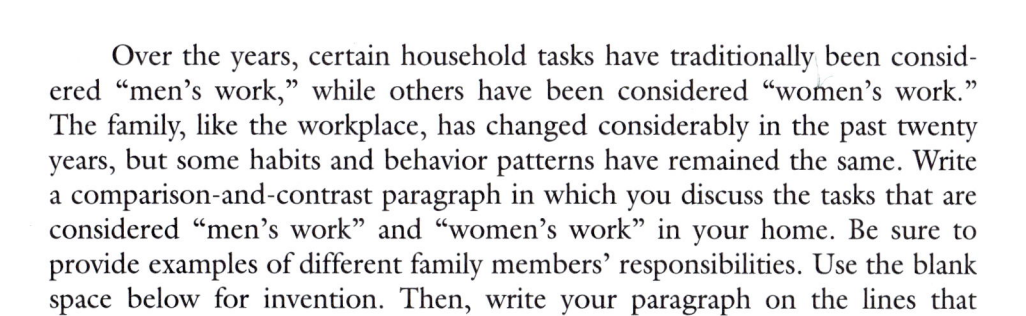

Over the years, certain household tasks have traditionally been considered "men's work," while others have been considered "women's work." The family, like the workplace, has changed considerably in the past twenty years, but some habits and behavior patterns have remained the same. Write a comparison-and-contrast paragraph in which you discuss the tasks that are considered "men's work" and "women's work" in your home. Be sure to provide examples of different family members' responsibilities. Use the blank space below for invention. Then, write your paragraph on the lines that follow.

A   USING APOSTROPHES TO FORM CONTRACTIONS

A **contraction** uses an **apostrophe** to combine two words. The apostrophe takes the place of the omitted letters.

I <u>didn't</u> (*did not*) realize how late it was.
<u>It's</u> (*it is*) not right for cheaters to go unpunished.

Some Common Contractions

I + am = I'm	is + not = isn't
we + are = we're	are + not = aren't
you + are = you're	can + not = can't
it + is = it's	do + not = don't
who + is = who's	will + not = won't
I + have = I've	should + not = shouldn't
I + will = I'll	let + us = let's
there + is = there's	who + is = who's

► FOCUS ON CONTRACTIONS ◄

Keep in mind that contractions are informal. Even though they are acceptable in speech and informal writing, contractions are not used in most college writing. Unless you are writing a journal, a personal essay, or a short story in which you are reproducing dialogue, avoid using contractions.

PRACTICE 23-1

Edit the following sentences for apostrophes in contractions. If the sentence is correct, write *C* in the blank.

Example: If you ~~dont~~ *don't* eat healthy foods, you ~~are'nt~~ *aren't* going to feel your best.

1. ~~Im~~ *I'm* trying hard to watch my diet, but ~~its~~ *it's* not easy. ____
2. Have you ever noticed how ~~wer'e~~ *we're* bombarded by images of high-calorie, high-fat foods? ____
3. Maybe we ~~shouldnt~~ *shouldn't* be so tempted, but it's hard to resist the lure of the fast-food chains. ____
4. They're always presenting commercials showing big, juicy burgers topped with cheese and bacon. *C*
5. Of course, the actual sandwich ~~doesnt~~ *doesn't* look much like the one on television, but that ~~isnt~~ *isn't* the point. ____
6. When ~~your'e~~ *you're* away from home and hungry, ~~its~~ *it's* the picture of that burger that pops into your mind. ____
7. ~~Youll~~ *You'll* be likely to rush to a fast-food place for lunch instead of looking for a meal ~~thats~~ *that's* healthier. ____
8. It ~~should'nt~~ *shouldn't* be so hard to find a fast, healthy meal. ____
9. It ~~isnt~~ *isn't* actually that difficult to offer a salad bar, but most fast-food places ~~dont~~ *don't*. ____

426 • **UNIT 9** Special Problems with Punctuation, Mechanics, and Spelling

10. ~~Theyre~~ *They're* all stuck in the burger rut, and we're the ones who suffer. ____

11. Still, ~~Ive~~ *I've* been avoiding fast-food sandwiches whenever I can. ____

12. If I just ~~ca'nt~~ *can't* avoid fast food, I'll try to find something on the menu ~~thats~~ *that's* a little healthier. ____

13. For example, a grilled chicken sandwich doesn't have nearly the fat or calories that a burger has. *C*

14. ~~Its~~ *It's* still not the perfect meal for a dieter, but it ~~isnt~~ *isn't* too bad. ____

15. When you ~~dont~~ *don't* have many options, ~~youv'e~~ *you've* got to make the best of the situation. ____

• • • • • • • • ▶ **FLASHBACK** ◀ • • • • • • • •

Look back at your response to the Paragraph Practice at the beginning of the chapter, and underline any contractions. Have you used apostrophes correctly to indicate omitted letters? If not, rewrite the contractions correctly on the lines below. If you have not used any contractions, look for any words that could be combined as contractions, and write those contractions below.

_____ _____ _____ _____

_____ _____ _____ _____

B USING APOSTROPHES TO FORM POSSESSIVES

The **possessive** case shows ownership. Personal pronouns have special possessive forms, such as *its* and *his*. (See 19C for information about the possessive forms of personal pronouns.) Nouns and indefinite pronouns do not have special possessive forms. Instead, they use apostrophes to indicate ownership.

Singular Nouns and Indefinite Pronouns

To form the possessive for singular nouns (including names) and indefinite pronouns, add an apostrophe plus an *s*.

Cesar Chavez's goal (the goal of Cesar Chavez) was justice for American farm workers.
The strike's outcome (the outcome of the strike) was uncertain.
Whether it would succeed was anyone's guess (the guess of anyone).

> **FOCUS ON FORMING THE POSSESSIVE OF SINGULAR NOUNS**
>
> Even if a singular noun already ends in *-s*, add an apostrophe plus an *s* to form the possessive.
>
> The class's next assignment was a research paper.
> Dr. Ramos's patients are participating in a double-blind study.

Plural Nouns

To form the possessive of most plural nouns, including names, add just an apostrophe (not an apostrophe plus *s*).

The two drugs' side effects (the side effects of the two drugs) were quite different.
The Johnsons' front door (the front door of the Johnsons) is painted red.

> **FOCUS ON IRREGULAR NOUN PLURALS**
>
> Although most nouns form the plural with *s* and use just an apostrophe to form the possessive, a few nouns have irregular plural forms that do not end in *-s*. See 19A. To form the possessive of these irregular plural nouns, add an apostrophe plus an *s*: *men's* dreams, *children's* toys, the *people's* park.

PRACTICE 23-2

Rewrite the following phrases, changing the noun that follows *of* to the possessive form. Be sure to distinguish between singular and plural nouns.

Examples: the mayor of the city _____the city's mayor_____

the uniforms of the players _the players' uniforms_

428 • UNIT 9 Special Problems with Punctuation, Mechanics, and Spelling

1. the video of the singer   *the singer's video*
2. the scores of the students   *the students' scores*
3. the first novel of the writer   *the writer's first novel*
4. the office of the boss   *the boss's office*
5. the union of the players   *the players' union*
6. the specialty of the restaurant   *the restaurant's specialty*
7. the bedroom of the children   *the children's bedroom*
8. the high cost of the tickets   *the tickets' high cost*
9. the dreams of everyone   *everyone's dreams*
10. the owner of the dogs   *the dogs' owner*

PRACTICE 23-3

Edit the underlined possessive nouns and pronouns in the following sentences for correct use of apostrophes. If a correction needs to be made, cross out the noun or pronoun, and write the correct form above it. If the noun is correct, write *C* above it.

Example: The ~~boss'~~ *boss's* desk is bigger than any of the managers' *C* desks.

1. Her ~~offices'~~ *office's* back wall is covered with various competitors' *C* ads.
2. She believes it is ~~everyones'~~ *everyone's* responsibility to keep up with other ~~businesses's~~ *businesses'* marketing strategies.
3. At the same time, she requires that our ~~firms'~~ *firm's* strategy and all depart- ments' goals be kept as confidential as possible. *C*
4. The company's *C* policy on confidentiality is explained in detail during every single ~~employees'~~ *employee's* initial orientation session.
5. Defend Systems has thirty ~~year's~~ *years'* experience in the home security busi- ness and has installed systems in thousands of people's houses. *C*
6. The company ~~founders'~~ *founder's* name actually is Clarence Defend, much to many of our ~~customer's~~ *customers'* surprise.

CHAPTER 23 Using Apostrophes • 429

7. Now <u>Mr. Defend's</u> daughter runs the ~~familys'~~ business. *(C / family's)*

8. I started at the company three years ago as the ~~bookkeepers'~~ assistant, and now I work as the fifteen ~~installer's~~ administrative coordinator. *(bookkeeper's / installers')*

9. My <u>job's</u> big advantage is that the hours are flexible, which allows me to attend college part-time and still take care of my ~~childrens'~~ needs. *(C / children's)*

10. I don't want to be on <u>Defend Systems's</u> payroll forever, but so far the company has been this working ~~persons'~~ "security." *(C / person's)*

> ▶ **FLASHBACK** ◀

Look back at your response to the Paragraph Practice at the beginning of the chapter. Circle any possessive forms of nouns or indefinite pronouns. Have you used apostrophes correctly to form these possessives? If not, rewrite them correctly in the appropriate columns below.

Singular Nouns or Indefinite Pronouns	Plural Nouns
_____	_____
_____	_____

C REVISING INCORRECT USE OF APOSTROPHES

Be careful not to confuse plural nouns (*boys*) with singular possessive forms (*boy's*). Never use an apostrophe with a plural noun unless it is possessive.

Termites can be dangerous <u>pests</u> (not *pest's*).
The <u>Velezes</u> (not the *Velez's*) live on Maple Drive.

Also be careful not to use apostrophes with personal pronouns that end in *-s*. Personal pronouns indicate the possessive with special forms: theirs (not *their's*), hers (not *her's*), its (not *it's*), ours (not *our's*), and yours (not *your's*).

FOCUS ON PERSONAL PRONOUNS

Be especially careful not to confuse the possessive forms of personal pronouns with sound-alike contractions. Remember, personal pronouns never use apostrophes to form possessives.

Personal Pronoun	Contraction
The dog bit <u>its</u> master.	<u>It's</u> (*it is*) time for breakfast.
The choice is <u>theirs</u>.	<u>There's</u> (*there is*) no place like home.
<u>Whose</u> house is this?	<u>Who's</u> (*who is*) on first?
Is this <u>your</u> house?	<u>You're</u> (*you are*) late again.

PRACTICE 23-4

Check the underlined words in the following sentences for correct use of apostrophes. If a correction needs to be made, cross out the word, and write the correct version above it. If the noun or pronoun is correct, write *C* above it.

Examples: The <u>president's</u> [C] views were presented after several other <u>speaker's</u> [speakers] first presented <u>their's</u> [theirs].

1. <u>Parent's</u> [Parents] should realize that when it comes to disciplining children, the responsibility is <u>their's</u> [theirs].

2. <u>It's</u> [C] also important that parents offer praise for their <u>children's</u> [C] good behavior.

3. In <u>it's</u> [its] first few <u>week's</u> [weeks] of life, a child is already developing a personality.

4. His and <u>her's</u> [hers] towels used to be popular with <u>couple's</u> [couples], but <u>it's</u> [C] not so common to see them today.

5. The <u>Reagan's</u> [Reagans] lived in the White House for eight <u>year's</u> [years], and then they stayed for a while at a <u>friend's</u> [C] home in California.

6. From the radio came the lyrics, "<u>You're</u> [C] the one <u>who's</u> [whose] love I've been waiting for."

7. If you expect to miss any <u>classes'</u> [classes], you will have to make arrangements with someone <u>who's</u> [C] willing to tell you <u>you're</u> [your] assignment.

CHAPTER 23 Using Apostrophes • 431

8. No other school's [C] cheerleading squad ever tried as many tricky stunts as our's [ours] did.
9. Surprise test's [tests] are a regular feature of my economics teacher's [C] class.
10. Jazz's [C] influence on many mainstream musician's [musicians] is one of the book's [C] main subject's [subjects].

• • • • • • • • • • • **REVIEW** • • • • • • • • • • •

CHAPTER REVIEW: STUDENT WRITING

Read the following student passage in which errors in the use of apostrophes have been introduced. Edit it to eliminate errors by crossing out incorrect words and writing corrections above them. (Note that this is an informal response paper, so contractions are acceptable.) The first sentence has been edited for you.

The Women of Messina

In William ~~Shakespeares'~~ [Shakespeare's] play Much Ado about Nothing, the women of Messina, whether they are seen as love objects or shrews, have very few options. A ~~womans~~ [woman's] role is to please a man. She can try to resist, but she probably will wind up giving in. The ~~plays~~ [play's] two women, Hero and Beatrice, are very different. Hero is the obedient one. ~~Heros'~~ [Hero's] cousin, Beatrice, tries to oppose the ~~mans~~ [man's] world in which she lives. However, in a place like Messina even women like Beatrice find it hard to get the respect that should be ~~their's~~ [theirs]. Right from the start, we are drawn to Beatrice. ~~Shes~~ [She's] funny, she has a clever comment for most ~~situation's~~ [situations], and she always speaks her mind about other ~~peoples~~ [people's] behavior.

And, unlike Hero, she tries to stand up to the men in her life, as we see in her and ~~Benedicks~~ *Benedick's* conversations. But even though Beatrice's intelligence is obvious, she often mocks herself. ~~Its~~ *It's* obvious she doesn't have much self-esteem. In fact, Beatrice isn't the strong woman she seems to be.

Ultimately, Beatrice does get her man, and she will end up happy--but at what expense? ~~Benedicks'~~ *Benedick's* last words to her are "Peace! I will stop your mouth" (V. iv. 97). Then, he ~~kisses'~~ *kisses* her. This kiss is a symbolic end to their bickering. It is also the mark of ~~Beatrices'~~ *Beatrice's* defeat. She has lost. Benedick has shut her up. Now, she will be Benedick's wife and do what he wants her to do. Granted, she will have more say in her marriage than Hero will have in ~~her's~~ *hers*, but she is still defeated. Even Beatrice, the most rebellious of ~~Messinas~~ *Messina's* women, finds it impossible to achieve anything of importance in ~~Messinas~~ *Messina's* male-dominated society.

CHAPTER REVIEW: EDITING PRACTICE

Reread your response to the Paragraph Practice at the beginning of the chapter. Because this is an informal exercise, contractions are acceptable; in fact, they may be preferable because they give your writing a conversational sound. Edit the paragraph so that you have used contractions in all possible situations.

Then, add two sentences to your paragraph—one that includes a singular possessive noun and one that includes a plural possessive noun. Make sure these two new sentences fit smoothly into your paragraph and that they, too, use contractions wherever possible.

CHAPTER REVIEW: COLLABORATIVE ACTIVITIES

1. Working in a group of four, and building on your individual responses to the Paragraph Practice at the beginning of the chapter, consider which

specific occupational and professional roles are still associated largely with men and which are associated primarily with women. Make two lists, heading one "women's jobs" and one "men's jobs."

2. Now work in pairs, with one pair of students in each group concentrating on men and the other pair focusing on women. Write a paragraph that attempts to justify why the particular jobs you listed should or should not be restricted to one gender. In your discussion, enumerate the various qualities men or women possess that qualify (or disqualify) them for particular jobs. Use possessive forms whenever possible—for example, *women's drive*, not *women have drive*.

3. Bring to class a book, magazine, or newspaper whose style is informal—for example, a romance novel, *TV Guide*, your school newspaper, or a comic book. Working in a group, circle every contraction you can find on one page of each publication. Then, substitute for each contraction the words it combines. Are your substitutions an improvement? (You may want to read a few paragraphs aloud before you reach a conclusion.)

Review

- Use apostrophes to form contractions. (See 23A.)

    I didn't (*did not*) realize how late it was.
    It's (*it is*) not right for cheaters to go unpunished.

- Use an apostrophe plus an *s* to form the possessive of singular nouns and indefinite pronouns, even when a noun ends in -*s*. (See 23B.)

    Cesar Chavez's goal was justice for American farm workers.
    The class's next assignment was a research paper.

- Use an apostrophe alone to form the possessive of most plural nouns, including names. (See 23B.)

    The two drugs' side effects were quite different.
    The Johnsons' front door is painted red.

- Do not use apostrophes with plural nouns unless they are possessive. Do not use apostrophes with personal pronouns. (See 23C.)

24 Setting Off Proper Nouns, Direct Quotations, and Titles

> **Overview**
>
> In this chapter you will learn
> - To capitalize proper nouns
> - To capitalize and punctuate direct quotations
> - To set off titles of books, stories, and other works

PARAGRAPH PRACTICE

Write a paragraph in which you define an effective television commercial, using exemplification and description to expand your definition. In your paragraph, give examples of particularly memorable, moving, or humorous commercials and mention the names of the shows in which you see them. Be sure to identify the product each commercial advertises, and try to quote particularly effective lines from each commercial. Use the blank space below for invention. Then, write your paragraph on the lines that follow.

A CAPITALIZING PROPER NOUNS

A **proper noun** names a particular person, animal, place, or thing. Proper nouns are always capitalized. The list that follows explains and illustrates specific rules for capitalizing proper nouns and also includes some important exceptions.

1. Always capitalize names of races, ethnic groups, tribes, nationalities, languages, and religions.

    The census data revealed a diverse community of Caucasians, African Americans, and Asian Americans, with a few Latino and Navajo residents. Native languages include English, Korean, and Spanish. Most identified themselves as Catholic, Protestant, or Muslim.

> ▶ **FOCUS** ON BLACK AND WHITE ◀
>
> The words *black* and *white* are generally not capitalized when they designate names of racial groups. The words *Caucasian* and *African American*, however, are always capitalized.

2. Capitalize names of specific people and titles that accompany them. In general, do not capitalize titles used without a name.

   In 1994 President Nelson Mandela was elected to lead South Africa.
   The newly elected fraternity president addressed the crowd.

3. Capitalize names of specific family members and their titles. Do not capitalize words identifying family relationships, including those introduced by possessive pronouns.

   The twins, Aunt Edna and Aunt Evelyn, are Dad's sisters.
   My aunts, my father's sisters, are twins.

4. Capitalize names of specific countries, cities, towns, bodies of water, streets, and so forth. Do not capitalize nonspecific places.

   The Seine runs through Paris, France.
   The river runs through the city.

5. Capitalize names of specific geographical regions. Do not capitalize such words when they specify direction.

   William Faulkner's novels are set in the American South.
   Turn right at the golf course, and go south for about a mile.

6. Capitalize names of specific buildings and monuments. Do not capitalize general references to buildings and monuments.

   He drove past the Liberty Bell and looked for a parking space near City Hall.
   He drove past the bell and looked for a parking space near the building.

7. Capitalize names of specific groups, clubs, teams, and associations. Do not capitalize general references to groups of individuals.

   The Teamsters Union represents workers who were at the stadium for the Republican Party convention, the Led Zeppelin concert, and the Phillies-Astros game.
   The union represents workers who were at the stadium for the political party's convention, the rock group's concert, and the baseball teams' game.

8. Capitalize names of specific historical periods, events, and documents. Do not capitalize nonspecific references to periods, events, or documents.

   The Emancipation Proclamation was signed during the Civil War, not during Reconstruction.
   The document was signed during the war, not during the postwar period.

9. Capitalize names of businesses, government agencies, schools, and other institutions. Do not capitalize nonspecific references to such institutions.

   The Department of Education and Apple Computer have launched a partnership project with Central High School.

CHAPTER 24 Setting Off Proper Nouns, Direct Quotations, and Titles • 437

>   A government agency and a computer company have launched
>   a partnership project with a high school.

10. Capitalize brand names. Do not capitalize general references to kinds of products.

    > While Jeff waited for his turn at the Xerox machine, he drank a can of Coke.
    > While Jeff waited for his turn at the copier, he drank a can of soda.

11. Capitalize titles of specific academic courses. Do not capitalize names of general academic subject areas, except for proper nouns—for example, a language or country.

    > Are Introduction to American Government and Biology 200 closed yet?
    > Are the introductory American government course and the biology course closed yet?

12. Capitalize days of the week, months of the year, and holidays. Do not capitalize the names of seasons.

    > The Jewish holiday of Passover usually falls in April.
    > Passover usually falls in the spring.

PRACTICE 24-1

Edit the following sentences, capitalizing letters or changing capitals to lowercase where necessary.

Example: The third largest ~~City~~ *city* in the ~~united states~~ *United States* is ~~chicago, illinois~~ *Chicago Illinois*.

1. Located in the ~~midwest~~ *M* on ~~lake~~ *L* ~~michigan~~ *M*, ~~chicago~~ *C* is an important port city, a rail and highway hub, and the site of ~~o'hare~~ *OH* ~~international~~ *I* ~~airport~~ *A*, the ~~Nation's~~ *n* busiest.

2. The financial center of the city is ~~lasalle street~~ *L S*, and the lakefront is home to ~~grant park~~ *G P*, where there are many ~~Museums~~ *m* and monuments.

3. To the ~~North~~ *n* of the city, ~~soldier field~~ *S F* is home to the ~~chicago bears~~ *C B*, the city's football team, and ~~wrigley field~~ *W F* is home to the ~~chicago cubs~~ *C C*, an ~~american league~~ *A L* ~~Baseball~~ *b* ~~Team~~ *t*.

4. In the mid-1600s, the site of what is now ~~chicago~~ *C* was visited by ~~father~~ *F* ~~jacques marquette~~ *J M*, a ~~catholic~~ *C* missionary to the ~~ottawa~~ *O* and ~~huron~~ *H* tribes, who were native to the area.

438 ▪ **UNIT 9** Special Problems with Punctuation, Mechanics, and Spelling

5. By the 1700s, the city was a trading post run by john kinzie.
                                                                                 J K

6. The city grew rapidly in the 1800s, and immigrants included germans, irish, italians, poles, greeks, and chinese, along with african americans, who migrated from the south.

7. In 1871 much of the city was destroyed in one of the worst fires in united states history, when, according to legend, mrs. O'Leary's Cow kicked over a burning lantern.

8. Today chicago's skyline is marked by many Skyscrapers, built by businesses like the john hancock company, sears, and amoco.

9. I know chicago well because my Mother grew up there and my aunt jean and uncle amos still live there.

10. I also got information from the chicago chamber of commerce when I wrote a paper for introductory research writing, a course I took at graystone high school.

•••••••▶ **FLASHBACK** ◀•••••••

Look back at your response to the Paragraph Practice at the beginning of the chapter. Underline each proper noun, including brand names of products. Does each begin with a capital letter? Correct any that do not on the lines below.

_____ _____ _____

_____ _____ _____

B   PUNCTUATING DIRECT QUOTATIONS

A **direct quotation** reproduces the exact words of a speaker or of a printed source. Direct quotations are always placed within quotation marks.

    Lauren said, "My brother and Tina have gotten engaged."
    A famous advertiser wrote, "Don't sell the steak; sell the sizzle."

Note that when a quotation is a complete sentence, it begins with a capital letter. When a quotation falls at the end of a sentence, as in the two examples above, the period is placed inside the quotation marks. If the quotation is a question or exclamation, the question mark or exclamation point is placed inside the quotation marks:

The instructor asked, "Has anyone read *Sula*?"
Officer Warren shouted, "Hold it right there!"

> ▶ **FOCUS** ON IDENTIFYING TAGS ◀
>
> Quotations are usually accompanied by an **identifying tag**, a phrase that names the person or work being quoted. When the identifying tag comes *before* the quotation, it is followed by a comma.
>
> Alexandre Dumas wrote, "Nothing succeeds like success."
>
> When the identifying tag comes at the *end* of the sentence, it is followed by a period. In such cases, a comma inside the final quotation mark separates the quotation from the identifying tag.
>
> "Life is like a box of chocolates," stated Forrest Gump.
>
> When the identifying tag comes in the *middle* of a quoted sentence, it is followed by a comma. The first part of the quotation is also followed by a comma, placed inside the quotation marks. Because the part of the quotation that follows the tag is not a new sentence, it does not begin with a capital letter.
>
> "This is my life," Bette insisted, "and I'll live it as I please."
>
> When the identifying tag comes between *two* quoted sentences, it is followed by a period, and the second quoted sentence begins with a capital letter.
>
> "Producer Berry Gordy is an important figure in the history of music," Tony claimed. "He was the creative force behind Motown records."

Remember, even if it is only a single word, directly quoted speech or writing must always be placed within quotation marks.

"Nevermore," said the Raven in Poe's famous poem.

For information on indirect quotations, see 15D.

PRACTICE 24-2

In the following sentences containing direct quotations, first underline the identifying tag. Then, punctuate the quotation correctly, and add capital letters as necessary.

Example: "Why," Darryl asked, "are teachers so out of it?"

1. "We who are about to die salute you," said the gladiators to the emperor.

2. When we turned on the television, the newscaster was saying, "Ladies and gentlemen, President Reagan has been shot."

3. "The bigger they are," said boxer John L. Sullivan, "the harder they fall."

4. "Do you take Michael to be your lawfully wedded husband?" asked the minister.

5. Lisa Marie replied, "I do."

6. "If you believe the *National Enquirer*," my friend always says, "then I've got a bridge I'd like to sell you."

7. When asked for the jury's verdict, the foreman replied, "Not guilty."

8. "I had felt for a long time that if I was ever told to get up so a white person could sit," Rosa Parks recalled, "I would refuse to do so."

9. "Yabba dabba doo!" exclaimed Fred when the brontoburger arrived.

10. "Where's my money?" asked Addie Pray. "You give me my money."

PRACTICE 24-3

Here are some quotations, followed in parentheses by the names of the people who wrote or spoke them. On the blank lines following each quotation, write a sentence that includes the quotation along with an identifying tag in the position that the directions suggest. Be sure to punctuate and capitalize correctly.

Example: Nothing endures but change. (written by the Greek philosopher Heraclitus)

Identifying tag in the middle "Nothing endures," wrote the Greek philosopher Heraclitus, "but change."

CHAPTER 24 Setting Off Proper Nouns, Direct Quotations, and Titles • **441**

1. The heart is a lonely hunter. (written by novelist Carson McCullers)

    Identifying tag at the beginning ___Novelist Carson McCullers wrote, "The heart is a lonely hunter."___

2. I want a kinder, gentler nation. (spoken by former President George Bush)

    Identifying tag at the end ___"I want a kinder, gentler nation," said former President George Bush.___

3. Tribe follows tribe, and nation follows nation. (spoken by Suquamish Chief Seattle in 1854)

    Identifying tag in the middle ___"Tribe follows tribe," said Suquamish Chief Seattle in 1854, "and nation follows nation."___

4. When I'm good, I'm very good. When I'm bad, I'm better. (spoken by Mae West in *I'm No Angel*)

    Identifying tag in the middle ___"When I'm good, I'm very good," said Mae West in I'm No Angel. "When I'm bad, I'm better."___

5. The rich rob the poor, and the poor rob one another. (spoken by Sojourner Truth)

    Identifying tag in the beginning ___Sojourner Truth said, "The rich rob the poor, and the poor rob one another."___

6. Heaven is like an egg, and the earth is like the yolk of the egg. (written by Chinese philosopher Chang Heng)

    Identifying tag in the middle ___"Heaven is like an egg," wrote the Chinese philosopher Chang Heng, "and the earth is like the yolk of the egg."___

7. When I found I had crossed that line, I looked at my hands to see if I was the same person. (spoken by Harriet Tubman, remembering her escape from slavery)

    Identifying tag in the beginning ___Remembering her escape from slavery, Harriet Tubman said, "When I found I had crossed that line, I looked at my hands to see if I was the same person."___

8. If a man hasn't discovered something he will die for, then he isn't fit to live. (spoken by Martin Luther King, Jr.)

   Identifying tag at the end *"If a man hasn't discovered something he will die for, then he isn't fit to live," said Martin Luther King, Jr.*

9. No man chooses evil because it is evil. He only mistakes it for happiness. (written in 1790 by Mary Wollstonecraft)

   Identifying tag in the middle *"No man chooses evil because it is evil," wrote Mary Wollstonecraft in 1790. "He only mistakes it for happiness."*

10. Marriage is an evil, but a necessary evil. (written by the ancient Greek poet Menander)

    Identifying tag in the beginning *The ancient Greek poet Menander wrote, "Marriage is an evil, but a necessary evil."*

● ● ● ● ● ● ● ● ▶ **FLASHBACK** ◀ ● ● ● ● ● ● ● ●

Look back at your response to the Paragraph Practice at the beginning of the chapter. Make sure you have enclosed any direct quotations in quotation marks and inserted other punctuation correctly. Revise any incorrectly punctuated quotations on the lines below.

C SETTING OFF TITLES OF BOOKS, STORIES, AND OTHER WORKS

Some titles are set in *italic* type (or underlined to indicate italics). Others, however, are set within quotation marks. The chart below indicates how to set off different kinds of titles.

CHAPTER 24 Setting Off Proper Nouns, Direct Quotations, and Titles · 443

Italicized Titles	Titles Set within Quotation Marks
Books: *How the Garcia Girls Lost Their Accents*	Book chapters: "The Reading Process"
Newspapers: the *Miami Herald*	Short stories: "The Tell-Tale Heart"
Magazines: *People*	Essays and articles: "Showering with Your Dog"
Long poems: *John Brown's Body*	Short poems: "Richard Cory"
Plays: *Death of a Salesman*	
Films: *The Rocky Horror Picture Show*	Songs: "Lift Every Voice and Sing"
TV or radio series: *Star Trek: The Next Generation*	Individual episodes of TV or radio series: "The Montgomery Bus Boycott," an episode of the PBS series *Eyes on the Prize*

Notice in the previous example that the first letters of all important words in a title are capitalized. Do not capitalize an article (*a, an, the*), preposition (*to, of, around*), or conjunction (*and, but, because*) unless it is the first or last word of the title or subtitle (*On the Road*, "*To an Athlete Dying Young*"; *No Way Out*).

▶ FOCUS ON TITLES OF PAPERS ◀

When you type one of your own papers, be sure to capitalize the first letter of each word in your title—except for articles, prepositions, and conjunctions. Do not underline your title or enclose it in quotation marks.

PRACTICE 24-4

Edit the following sentences, capitalizing letters as necessary in titles.

Example: Eudora Welty's "a worn path" *A Worn Path* is a very moving short story.

444 • **UNIT 9** Special Problems with Punctuation, Mechanics, and Spelling

1. Directed by the wacky Ed Wood, the 1959 movie <u>plan nine from outer space</u> has been called the worst picture of all time. [capitalize: Plan Nine from Outer Space]

2. Gary Larson's cartoon collections include the books <u>in search of the far side</u>, <u>it came from the far side</u>, and <u>valley of the far side</u>. [capitalize: In Search of the Far Side, It Came from the Far Side, Valley of the Far Side]

3. En Vogue's first hit album, <u>born to sing</u>, included the songs "you don't have to worry," "time goes on," and "just can't stay away." [capitalize: Born to Sing; "You Don't Have to Worry," "Time Goes On," "Just Can't Stay Away"]

4. Everyone should read Martin Luther King Jr.'s "i have a dream" and "letter from birmingham jail." [capitalize: "I Have a Dream"; "Letter from Birmingham Jail"]

5. The Fox Network has had hits with shows like <u>married with children</u>, <u>the simpsons</u>, <u>beverly hills 90210</u>, <u>melrose place</u>, <u>martin</u>, and <u>in living color</u>. [capitalize: Married with Children, The Simpsons, Beverly Hills 90210, Melrose Place, Martin, In Living Color]

PRACTICE 24-5

In the following sentences, underline or insert quotation marks around titles. Remember that titles of books and other long works are underlined, and titles of stories, essays, and other shorter works are enclosed in quotation marks.

Example: An article in the <u>New York Times</u> called "It's Not Easy Being Green" is a profile of San Antonio Spurs player Dennis Rodman, who has green hair.

1. Sui Sin Far's story "The Wisdom of the New," from her book <u>Mrs. Spring Fragrance</u>, is about the clash between Chinese and American cultures in the early twentieth century.

2. The rock band Judybats released its single "Sorry Counts" in 1995.

3. Interesting information about fighting skin cancer can be found in the article "Putting Sunscreens to the Test" that appeared in the magazine <u>Consumer Reports</u>.

4. One of the best-known poems of the twentieth century is Robert Frost's "The Road Not Taken."

5. Wayne Wang has directed several well-received films, including <u>The Joy Luck Club</u> and <u>Smoke</u>.

CHAPTER 24 Setting Off Proper Nouns, Direct Quotations, and Titles • 445

6. It is surprising how many people enjoy reruns of the 1960s television series <u>Bewitched</u> and <u>I Dream of Jeannie</u>.

7. The title of Lorraine Hansberry's play <u>A Raisin in the Sun</u> comes from Langston Hughes's poem "Dream Deferred."

8. In his 1994 autobiography <u>Breaking the Surface</u>, Olympic champion Greg Louganis writes about his struggle with AIDS.

FLASHBACK

Look back at your response to the Paragraph Practice at the beginning of the chapter. Circle the titles of the television shows you have mentioned. Are they set off by underlining? Are capital letters used where necessary? Make your corrections on the lines below.

_____   _____

_____   _____

REVIEW

CHAPTER REVIEW: STUDENT WRITING

Read the following student passage in which errors in capitalization and in use of direct quotation and titles have been introduced. Edit the passage to correct any such errors. The first sentence has been edited for you.

<u>The Big Sleep</u>

"<u>The Big Sleep</u>," released in 1946, is a classic movie mystery set in *L*os *A*ngeles, in which Humphrey Bogart plays a *P*rivate *D*etective named Philip Marlowe. In an early scene,

Marlowe learns from his client, General Sternwood, that Sternwood is being blackmailed about his daughter Carmen's gambling habits. Sternwood wants Marlowe to find the blackmailers and get rid of them.

The movie was produced by Warner Brothers, a studio which made many mysteries, and is set up in classic Hollywood style. It includes elements found in many mysteries--murder, suspicion, betrayal--as well as a romantic subplot involving the general's other daughter, Vivian, and Marlowe. By the end of the movie, all the questions about murder and blackmail have been answered. The only questions that remain are about the romance between Marlowe and Vivian.

The movie is full of classic lines. When Vivian learns that Marlowe is a private detective, she says, "I didn't know they existed, except in books--or else they were greasy little men sneaking around hotel corridors." When a character criticizes his manners, Marlowe has a quick comeback. "I don't mind if you don't like my manners," he answers. "I don't like them myself."

The only major criticism of the movie is that, unlike most classic mysteries, it is often very confusing. In fact, one reviewer wrote, "The plot is so fast and complicated you can hardly catch it." Despite any confusion, however, audiences identify strongly with Marlowe, who is clearly a good guy trying to make an honest living. We root for him and want everything to turn out all right for him. So even

CHAPTER 24 Setting Off Proper Nouns, Direct Quotations, and Titles ▪ 447

```
                       T
though the plot of t̶he Big Sleep is hard to follow, the

audience sticks with it, as Marlowe does, until the end.
```

CHAPTER REVIEW: EDITING PRACTICE

Look back at your response to the Paragraph Practice at the beginning of this chapter. If you have quoted specific lines from commercials, try varying the placement of the identifying tags you have used. If your paragraph does not include quotations, try adding one or two. Then, edit carefully for proper use of capital letters, quotation marks, and underlining. When you are finished, do the same for another paragraph or another writing assignment you are currently working on.

CHAPTER REVIEW: COLLABORATIVE ACTIVITIES

1. Imagine that you and the other members of your group are the nominations committee for this year's Emmy, Oscar, or Grammy Awards. Work together to compile a list of categories and several nominees for each category.

    Trade lists with another group. From each category, select the individual artist or work you believe deserves to win the award. Write a sentence about each winner explaining why it is the best in its category.

    After your group finishes all the sentences, exchange papers with another group. Check each other's papers for correct use of capitals, quotation marks, and underlining.

2. Using a separate sheet of paper, work in groups to list as many items in each of the following five categories as you can: planets, islands, musicians or bands, automobile models, sports. Be sure all your items are proper nouns.

    Write six original sentences on the lines below, using one proper noun from each category in each sentence.

    1. _____

    2. _____

    3. _____

    4. _____

5. _____

   _____

3. Working in pairs, write a conversation between two characters, real or fictional, who have very different positions on a particular topic or issue. Place all direct quotations within quotation marks, and include identifying tags that differentiate the two characters' statements. (Note that convention requires you to begin a new paragraph each time a new person speaks.)

   Exchange your conversations with another pair of students, and check their work to see that all directly quoted speech is set within quotation marks and that all other punctuation is used correctly.

> ### Review
>
> - Proper nouns are capitalized. (See 24A.)
>
>   In 1994 President Nelson Mandela was elected to lead South Africa.
>
> - A direct quotation reproduces the exact words of a particular speaker or printed source. It is always placed within quotation marks. (See 24B.)
>
>   Lauren said, "My brother and Tina have gotten engaged."
>
> - An identifying tag can be placed at the beginning, middle, or end of a direct quotation. A direct quotation is separated from the identifying tag by a comma. (See 24B.)
>
>   "Life is like a box of chocolates," stated Forrest Gump.
>
> - In titles, all important words are capitalized, along with the first and the last word. Titles are indicated by italics (underlining) or quotation marks. (See 24C.)

25 Understanding Spelling

Overview

In this chapter you will learn
- To distinguish between spelling and pronunciation
- To decide whether to choose *ei* or *ie*
- To understand the spelling rules for prefixes
- To understand the spelling rules for suffixes
- To distinguish commonly confused words
- To become a better speller

PARAGRAPH PRACTICE

Write a narrative paragraph that summarizes the plot of one of your favorite books or movies or an episode of a favorite television show. Discuss the plot events in the order in which they occur, and make sure you include as many specific details as possible and all the transitional words and expressions readers need to follow your discussion. Do not include your opinions or observations about the book, movie, or television show. Use the blank space below for invention. Then, write your paragraph on the lines that follow.

A UNDERSTANDING SPELLING AND PRONUNCIATION

The best place to find out how to spell a word is a good college dictionary. A dictionary will give you the correct spelling of a word and will break the word into syllables. It will also tell you how a word is pronounced and which syllables are stressed and which are unstressed.

> ### ▶ FOCUS ON VOWELS AND CONSONANTS ◀
>
> Knowing which letters are vowels and which are consonants will help you understand the spelling rules presented in this chapter.
> *Vowels:* a, e, i, o, and u.
> *Consonants:* b, c, d, f, g, h, j, k, l, m, n, p, q, r, s, t, v, w, x, and z.
> *Y* can be considered either a vowel or a consonant depending on how it is pronounced. In *young*, y has a consonant sound; in *truly*, it has a vowel sound.

Because many English words are not spelled exactly as they are pronounced, their spellings must be memorized.

Silent Letters

Some words contain silent letters, which are not pronounced: *island, climb, knight, pneumonia*.

Words Containing Letters Not Pronounced in Informal Speech

Some words contain letters that are not pronounced in everyday speech: *different, library, government, restaurant, surprise*.

Vowels in Unstressed Positions

When *a*, *i*, and *e* appear in unstressed positions at the end of a word, they are often pronounced alike. For this reason, it is impossible to tell from pronunciation alone whether to use *-able* or *-ible*, *-ance* or *-ence*, or *-ant* or *-ent* in word pairs like *capable/susceptible, tolerance/dependence,* and *dependent/defendant*.

Different Forms with Different Spellings

Spelling problems can also occur in the following situations:

- When the verb and noun forms of a word are spelled differently
  advise/advice   describe/description
- When the principal parts of an irregular verb are spelled differently
  bite/bit/bitten   throw/threw/thrown
- When the singular and plural forms of a noun are spelled differently
  wife/wives   woman/women

▶ FOCUS ON SPELLING AND PRONUNCIATION ◀

The following contractions are especially troublesome because they are often incorrectly spelled as they are pronounced, with the word *of* incorrectly used instead of the contraction of *have*.

Correct	Incorrect
could've (could + have)	could of
should've (should + have)	should of
would've (would + have)	would of

PRACTICE 25-1

Following are some pairs of words spelled both correctly and incorrectly (as they are pronounced). Circle the one that is correctly spelled in each pair. If you are not sure, check a dictionary.

Example: coff **(cough)**

1. supprise — **(surprise)**
2. **(night)** — nite
3. goverment — **(government)**
4. lierture — **(literature)**
5. canidate — **(candidate)**
6. **(height)** — hite
7. **(probably)** — probly
8. morgage — **(mortgage)**
9. **(mathematics)** — mathmatics
10. **(nuclear)** — nucular
11. **(recognize)** — reconize
12. **(environment)** — envirement
13. busness — **(business)**
14. **(finally)** — finly
15. **(definitely)** — definitly
16. exellent — **(excellent)**
17. **(before)** — befor
18. Febuary — **(February)**
19. thouht — **(thought)**
20. usely — **(usually)**

PRACTICE 25-2

Following are pairs of words with vowels in unstressed positions spelled both correctly and incorrectly. Circle the one that is correctly spelled in each pair. If you are not sure, check a dictionary.

Example: capabile **(capable)**

1. tolerent — **(tolerant)**
2. **(acceptable)** — acceptible
3. competint — **(competent)**
4. **(guidance)** — guidence
5. impossable — **(impossible)**
6. importent — **(important)**
7. **(maturity)** — maturaty
8. assistents — **(assistants)**

CHAPTER 25 Understanding Spelling

9. (horrible) horrable

10. (consistent) consistint

B DECIDING BETWEEN *IE* AND *EI*

As you have seen, pronunciation is not always a reliable guide for spelling. There are, however, a few dependable rules that can help you become a competent speller.

Most people have memorized the rule that *i* comes before *e*. This rule holds true except when *i* comes after *c* or when the *ei* sound is pronounced *ay* (as in n<u>ei</u>ghbor).

i before *e*	except after *c*	or when *ei* is pronounced *ay*
achieve	ceiling	eight
believe	conceive	freight
friend	deceive	neighbor

> ### ▶ FOCUS ON *IE/EI* COMBINATIONS ◀
>
> There are several exceptions to the rule stated above. For example, *ie* generally comes after *c* if the *c* is pronounced *sh* (*efficient*) or if the *i* is sounded separately (*fancier*). The exceptions follow no pattern, so you must memorize them.
>
> | either | seize |
> |---|---|
> | neither | weird |
> | leisure | conscience |
> | foreign | science |
> | height | species |
> | caffeine | ancient |

PRACTICE 25-3

Proofread the underlined words in the following sentences for correct spelling. If a correction needs to be made, cross out the incorrect word, and write the correct spelling above it. If the word is spelled correctly, write *C* above it.

                       C   receive
Example: It was a <u>relief</u> to <s>recieve</s> the good news.

1. Be sure to ~~wiegh~~ [weigh] the pros and cons before making an important decision, particularly when it comes to friends. [C]
2. When your beliefs [C] are tested, you may be able to ~~acheive~~ [achieve] a better understanding of yourself.
3. In our society [C] many people ~~decieve~~ [deceive] themselves into ~~beleiving~~ [believing] that they are better than everyone else.
4. ~~Cheifly~~ [Chiefly] because they have been lucky, they have reached a certain height [C] in the world.
5. They think that the blood running through their [C] ~~viens~~ [veins] makes them a higher species [C] than the average person.
6. In fact, they are probably ~~niether~~ [neither] smarter nor more talented than others, but they are certainly deficient [C] in humility.
7. ~~Thier~~ [Their] impatient [C] attitude can cause others a lot of ~~greif~~ [grief].
8. I have always ~~percieved~~ [perceived] of myself as thoughtful of others, and my conscience [C] leads me to treat everyone with respect.
9. There are a ~~vareity~~ [variety] of ways to learn a ~~foriegn~~ [foreign] language.
10. *Waterworld* was a really weird [C] movie, even for the ~~feild~~ [field] of science [C] fiction.

••••••▶ **FLASHBACK** ◀••••••

Look back at your response to the Paragraph Practice at the beginning of the chapter, and underline any words that contain *ie* or *ei* combinations. Make sure the words are spelled correctly. If they are not, correct them on the lines below.

_____   _____

_____   _____

C UNDERSTANDING PREFIXES

A **prefix** is a group of letters added at the beginning of a word to change its meaning. For example, the prefix *un-* added to a word means "opposite of" or "contrary to." Thus, *untie* is the opposite of *tie* and *uncaged* is the opposite of *caged*. The addition of a prefix to a word never affects the spelling of the original word. Even if the last letter of a prefix is the same as the first letter of the word to which it is added, the prefix does not change the spelling of the original word.

  dis + service = disservice
  un + able = unable
  co + operate = cooperate
  pre + heat = preheat
  un + natural = unnatural
  over + rate = overrate

PRACTICE 25-4

Write in the blank the new word that results from adding the specified prefix to each of the following words.

Example: dis + respect = *disrespect*

1. un + happy = *unhappy*
2. tele + vision = *television*
3. pre + existing = *preexisting*
4. dis + satisfied = *dissatisfied*
5. un + necessary = *unnecessary*
6. non + negotiable = *nonnegotiable*
7. im + patient = *impatient*
8. out + think = *outthink*
9. over + react = *overreact*
10. dis + solve = *dissolve*

••••••••▶ **FLASHBACK** ◀••••••••

Look back at your response to the Paragraph Practice at the beginning of the chapter. Underline words that have prefixes. Check to make sure they are spelled correctly. If not, correct them on the lines below.

_____   _____

_____   _____

D UNDERSTANDING SUFFIXES

A **suffix** is a group of letters attached to the end of a word that changes its meaning or that changes its part of speech. For example, a suffix can change *happy* to *happily*, *happiness*, or *happier*. Unlike prefixes, suffixes can affect the spelling of the word to which they are added.

Words Ending in Silent -e

If a word ends with a silent (unpronounced) *e*, you have to decide whether to keep or drop the *e* before adding a suffix. In general, you drop the *e* if the suffix begins with a vowel.

Suffix Beginning with a Vowel

Drop the *e*

hope + ing = hoping   dance + er = dancer
continue + ous = continuous   insure + able = insurable

Exceptions

change + able = changeable   courage + ous = courageous
notice + able = noticeable   replace + able = replaceable

In general, you keep the *e* if the suffix begins with a consonant.

Suffix Beginning with a Consonant

Keep the *e*

hope + ful = hopeful   bore + dom = boredom
excite + ment = excitement   same + ness = sameness

Exceptions

argue + ment = argument   true + ly = truly
judge + ment = judgment   nine + th = ninth

PRACTICE 25-5

Write in the blank the new word that results from adding the specified suffix to each of the following words.

Examples: insure + ance = _insurance_
love + ly = _lovely_

CHAPTER 25 Understanding Spelling • 457

1. lone + ly = __lonely__
2. use + ful = __useful__
3. revise + ing = __revising__
4. base + ment = __basement__
5. desire + able = __desirable__
6. true + ly = __truly__
7. microscope + ic = __microscopic__
8. prepare + ation = __preparation__
9. nine + th = __ninth__
10. indicate + ion = __indication__
11. effective + ness = __effectiveness__
12. arrange + ment = __arrangement__
13. fortune + ate = __fortunate__
14. taste + ful = __tasteful__
15. argue + ment = __argument__
16. disable + ed = __disabled__
17. advertise + ment = __advertisement__
18. notice + able = __noticeable__
19. care + less = __careless__
20. judge + ment = __judgment__

Words Ending in -y

When you add a suffix to a word that ends in *-y*, you must decide whether or not to change the *y* to an *i*. Generally, you change the *y* to an *i* if the letter before the *y* is a consonant.

Consonant before Y

Change *y* to *i*

beauty + ful = beautiful
try + ed = tried

busy + ly = busily
friendly + er = friendlier

Exceptions

- Keep the *y* if the suffix starts with an *i*.
    cry + ing = crying   baby + ish = babyish

- Keep the *y* when you add a suffix to some one-syllable words.
    shy + er = shyer   dry + ness = dryness

You generally keep the *y* if the letter before the *y* is a vowel.

Vowel before Y

Keep the *y*

annoy + ance = annoyance
play + ful = playful

enjoy + ment = enjoyment
display + ed = displayed

Exceptions

day + ly = daily
gay + ly = gaily

say + ed = said
pay + ed = paid

PRACTICE 25-6

Write in the blank the new word that results from adding the specified suffix to each of the following words.

Examples: study + ed = _studied_
employ + ment = _employment_

1. happy + ness = _happiness_
2. convey + or = _conveyor_
3. deny + ing = _denying_
4. carry + ed = _carried_
5. ready + ness = _readiness_
6. annoy + ing = _annoying_
7. destroy + er = _destroyer_
8. twenty + eth = _twentieth_
9. forty + ish = _fortyish_
10. day + ly = _daily_
11. cry + ed = _cried_
12. delay + ed = _delayed_
13. busy + ness = _business_
14. lonely + ness = _loneliness_
15. spy + ing = _spying_
16. prepay + ed = _prepaid_
17. lively + hood = _livelihood_
18. ally + ance = _alliance_
19. joy + ful = _joyful_
20. marry + ing = _marrying_

Double the Final Consonant

Some words double their final consonant when you add a suffix that begins with a vowel—for example, *-ed*, *-er*, or *-ing*. You double the final consonant in a word if (1) the last three letters of the word have a consonant-vowel-consonant pattern (cvc) and if (2) the word has one syllable or the last syllable is stressed.

Doubling Consonants

Final Consonant Doubled

cut	+	ing	=	cutting (cvc—one syllable)
bat	+	er	=	batter (cvc—one syllable)
pet	+	ed	=	petted (cvc—one syllable)
commit	+	ed	=	committed (cvc—stress on *last* syllable)
occur	+	ing	=	occurring (cvc—stress on *last* syllable)

Final Consonant Not Doubled

answer	+	ed	=	answered (cvc—stress on *first* syllable)
happen	+	ing	=	happening (cvc—stress on *first* syllable)
act	+	ing	=	acting (no cvc)

PRACTICE 25-7

Write in the blank the new word that results from adding the specified suffix to each of the following words.

Examples: rot + ing = _rotting_
narrow + er = _narrower_

1. hope + ed = _hoped_
2. shop + er = _shopper_
3. rest + ing = _resting_
4. combat + ed = _combatted_
5. reveal + ing = _revealing_
6. open + er = _opener_
7. unzip + ed = _unzipped_
8. trap + ed = _trapped_
9. cram + ing = _cramming_
10. star + ing = _starring_
11. appeal + ing = _appealing_
12. resist + ed = _resisted_
13. refer + ing = _referring_
14. skip + er = _skipper_
15. omit + ed = _omitted_
16. want + ing = _wanting_
17. fat + er = _fatter_
18. fast + er = _faster_
19. repel + ed = _repelled_
20. repeal + ed = _repealed_

▶ **FLASHBACK** ◀

Look back at your response to the Paragraph Practice at the beginning of the chapter. Underline words that have suffixes, and then check to make sure the words are spelled correctly. If they are not, correct them on the lines below.

_____   _____

_____   _____

E LEARNING COMMONLY CONFUSED WORDS

By taking the time to memorize words that are confused because they either look alike or sound alike, you can help yourself become a better speller.

Accept/Except *Accept* means "to receive something." *Except* means "with the exception of" or "to leave out or exclude."

"I <u>accept</u> your challenge," said Alexander Hamilton to Aaron Burr.

Everyone <u>except</u> Darryl visited the museum.

460 • UNIT 9 Special Problems with Punctuation, Mechanics, and Spelling

Affect/Effect *Affect* is a verb meaning "to influence." *Effect* is a noun meaning "result" and sometimes a verb meaning "to bring about."

> Carmen's job could <u>affect</u> her grades.
> Overexposure to sun can have a long-term <u>effect</u> on skin.
> Commissioner Williams tried to <u>effect</u> changes in police procedure.

All ready/Already *All ready* means "completely prepared." *Already* means "previously, before."

> Serge was <u>all ready</u> to take the history test.
> Gina had <u>already</u> been to Italy.

Brake/Break *Brake* means "a device to slow or stop a vehicle." *Break* means "to smash" or "to detach."

> Peter got into an accident because his foot slipped off the <u>brake</u>.
> Babe Ruth bragged that no one would ever <u>break</u> his record of sixty home runs in one season.

Buy/By *Buy* means "to purchase." *By* is a preposition meaning "close to" or "next to" or "by means of."

> The Stamp Act forced colonists to <u>buy</u> stamps for many public documents.
> He drove <u>by</u> but didn't stop.
> He stayed <u>by</u> her side all the way to the hospital.
> Malcolm X wanted "freedom <u>by</u> any means necessary."

PRACTICE 25-8

Proofread the underlined words in the following sentences for correct spelling. If a correction needs to be made, cross out the incorrect word, and write the correct spelling above it. If the word is spelled correctly, write *C* above it.

> **Example:** We must ~~except~~ *accept* the fact that the human heart can <u>break</u>. *C*

1. The ~~affects~~ *effects* of several new AIDS drugs have ~~all ready~~ *already* been reported.

2. *Consumer Reports* gave high ratings to the ~~breaks~~ *brakes* on all new cars tested ~~accept~~ *except* for the Minotaur.

3. Advertisements urge us to ~~by~~ *buy* a new product, even if we <u>already</u> own a *C* comparable item.

4. If you ~~except~~ *accept* the charges for a collect telephone call through the ITC network, you'll probably have to ~~brake~~ *break* your piggy bank to pay their rates.

CHAPTER 25 Understanding Spelling · 461

5. Cigarette smoking <u>affects</u> the lungs <u>by</u> creating deposits of tar that inhibit breathing. *(C, C)*

6. The show was ~~already~~ *all ready* to begin <u>except</u> that the star had not arrived. *(C)*

7. People who live ~~buy~~ *by* the landfill have complained for years about its ~~affects~~ *effects* on the neighborhood.

8. The physical therapy program has ~~all ready~~ *already* ~~excepted~~ *accepted* 20 percent more applicants than it admitted last year.

9. Even a hairline <u>break</u> in a bone can strongly ~~effect~~ *affect* an athlete's performance. *(C)*

10. When they ~~by~~ *buy* their textbooks, most students <u>accept</u> the fact that they'll lose a lot in resale. *(C)*

Conscience/Conscious *Conscience* refers to the part of the mind that urges a person to choose right over wrong. *Conscious* means "aware" or "deliberate."

> After he cheated at cards, his <u>conscience</u> started to bother him.
> As she walked through the woods, she became <u>conscious</u> of the hum of insects.
> Elliott made a <u>conscious</u> decision to stop smoking.

Everyday/Every day *Everyday* is a single word that means "ordinary" or "common." *Every day* is two words that mean "occurring daily."

> *I Love Lucy* was a successful comedy show because it appealed to <u>everyday</u> people.
> <u>Every day</u> Lucy and Ethel would find a new way to get into trouble.

Fine/Find *Fine* means "superior quality" or "a sum of money paid as a penalty." *Find* means "to locate."

> He sang a <u>fine</u> solo at church last Sunday.
> Demi had to pay a <u>fine</u> for speeding.
> Some people still use a willow rod to <u>find</u> water.

Hear/Here *Hear* means "to perceive sound by ear." *Here* means "at or in this place."

> I moved to the front so I could <u>hear</u> the speaker.
> My great-grandfather came <u>here</u> in 1883.

Its/It's *Its* is the possessive form of *it*. *It's* is the contraction of *it is* or *it has*.

> The airline canceled <u>its</u> flights because of the snow.

462 • UNIT 9 Special Problems with Punctuation, Mechanics, and Spelling

It's twelve o'clock, and we're late.
Ever since it's been in the accident, the car has rattled.

PRACTICE 25-9

Proofread the underlined words in the following sentences for correct spelling. If a correction needs to be made, cross out the incorrect word, and write the correct spelling above it. If the word is spelled correctly, write *C* above it.

Example: *C* above It's often difficult for celebrities to adjust to ~~every day~~ *everyday* life.

1. ~~Hear~~ *Here* at Simonson's Fashions, we try to make our customers feel that ~~everyday~~ *every day* is a sale day.

2. The minister was a ~~find~~ *fine* person, and ~~its~~ *it's* a shame that he died so young.

3. That inner voice you hear *C* is your ~~conscious~~ *conscience* telling you how you should behave.

4. In the ~~every day~~ *everyday* world of work and school, it can be hard to ~~fine~~ *find* the time to relax and appreciate life.

5. By the time I became ~~conscience~~ *conscious* of the leaking pipe, ~~it's~~ *its* damage ran to over a hundred dollars.

6. The judge slapped the major corporation with a thousand dollar fine *C* for ~~everyday~~ *every day* that it was not in compliance with the county's safety codes.

7. When immigrants first arrive ~~hear~~ *here* in the United States, they may find *C* that ~~its~~ *it's* difficult at first to adjust to their new home.

8. In ~~every day~~ *everyday* decision making, let your conscience *C* be your guide when it comes to moral issues.

9. Even though they ~~here~~ *hear* over and over about the dangers of drinking and driving, young people always think, "It's *C* not going to happen to us."

10. The college is holding ~~it's~~ *its* fourth annual contest to ~~fine~~ *find* the most popular teacher on campus.

Know/Knew/New/No *Know* means "to have an understanding of" or "to have fixed in the mind." *Knew* is the past tense form of the verb *know*. *New* means "recent or never used." *No* is a word meant to express a negative response.

    I <u>know</u> there will be a lunar eclipse tonight.
    He <u>knew</u> how to install a <u>new</u> light switch.
    Yes, we have <u>no</u> bananas.

Lie/Lay *Lie* means "to rest or recline." The past tense of *lie* is *lay*. *Lay* means "to put or place something down." The past tense of *lay* is *laid*.

    Every Sunday I <u>lie</u> in bed until noon.
    They <u>lay</u> on the grass until it began to rain.
    Tammy told Carl to <u>lay</u> his card on the table.
    Brooke and Cassia finally <u>laid</u> down their hockey sticks.

Loose/Lose *Loose* means "not fastened" or "not attached securely." *Lose* means "to mislay" or "to misplace."

    In the 1940s, many women wore <u>loose</u> fitting pants.
    I don't gamble because I hate to <u>lose</u>.

Mine/Mind *Mine* is a possessive pronoun used to indicate ownership. *Mind* can be a noun meaning "human consciousness" or "intelligence" or a verb meaning "to obey" or "to attend to."

    That red mountain bike is <u>mine</u>.
    A <u>mind</u> is a terrible thing to waste.
    "<u>Mind</u> your manners when you visit your grandmother," Dad said.

Passed/Past *Passed* is the past tense of the verb *pass*. It means "moved by" or "succeeded in." *Past* is a noun meaning "earlier than the present time."

    The car that <u>passed</u> me must have been doing over eighty miles an hour.
    David finally <u>passed</u> his driving test.
    The novel was set in the <u>past</u>.

Peace/Piece *Peace* means "the absence of war" or "calm." *Piece* means "a part of something larger."

    The British Prime Minister thought he had achieved <u>peace</u> with honor.
    My <u>peace</u> of mind was destroyed when the flying saucer landed.
    "Have a <u>piece</u> of cake," said Marie.

PRACTICE 25-10

Proofread the underlined words in the following sentences for correct spelling. If a correction needs to be made, cross out the incorrect word, and write the correct spelling above it. If the word is spelled correctly, write *C* above it.

    Example: I thought I would ~~loose~~ *lose* my <u>mind</u> *C*.

464 • **UNIT 9** Special Problems with Punctuation, Mechanics, and Spelling

1. In the ~~passed~~ [past], many people ~~new~~ [knew] their neighbors well.
2. Today, however, we often ~~loose~~ [lose] touch with our neighbors or do not know [C] them at all.
3. In a search for inner ~~piece~~ [peace] and serenity, we may use relaxation techniques to reach our unconscious minds [C].
4. We may want to ~~loose~~ [lose] ourselves in a place where no [C] other person can reach us.
5. She lay [C] in bed reading for an hour and then ~~lay~~ [laid] the book on the table.
6. Don't mind [C] if you ~~loose~~ [lose] occasionally; ~~know~~ [no] person can be a winner every time.
7. Once they've ~~past~~ [passed] a test, some students put everything they've learned for it out of their minds [C].
8. In the past [C], dress codes in schools were not nearly as ~~lose~~ [loose] as they are today, and most parents ~~lay~~ [laid] down the law about curfews.
9. A musician may ~~no~~ [know] a piece [C] of music by heart and still not ~~mine~~ [mind] listening to it over and over again.
10. You may ~~loose~~ [lose] your way if you wander ~~passed~~ [past] the warning signs.

Plain/Plane *Plain* means "simple, not elaborate." *Plane* is the shortened form of *airplane*.

Sometimes the Amish are referred to as the plain people.
Chuck Yeager was the first person to fly a plane faster than sound.

Principal/Principle *Principal* means "first" or "highest" or "the head of a school." *Principle* means "a law or basic assumption."

She had the principal role in the movie.
I'll never forget the day the principal called me into his office.
It was against his principles to drink liquor.

Quiet/Quit/Quite *Quiet* means "free of noise" or "still." *Quit* means "to leave a job" or "to give up." *Quite* means "actually" or "very."

Jane looked forward to the quiet evenings at the lake.
Sammy quit his job and followed the girls into the parking lot.
"You haven't quite got the hang of it yet," she said.
After practicing all summer, Tamika got quite good at handball.

Raise/Rise *Raise* means "to elevate" or "to increase in size, quantity, or worth." The past tense of *raise* is *raised*. *Rise* means "to stand up" or "to move from a lower position to a higher position." The past tense of *rise* is *rose*.

> Carlos <u>raises</u> his hand when the teacher asks for volunteers.
> They <u>raised</u> the money for the down payment.
> They crowd <u>rises</u> every time their team scores a touchdown.
> Sarah <u>rose</u> before dawn so she could see the eclipse.

Right/Write *Right* means "correct" or "the opposite of left." *Write* means "to form letters with a writing instrument."

> If you turn <u>right</u> at the corner, you will be going in the <u>right</u> direction.
> All students are required to <u>write</u> three short papers.

Sit/Set *Sit* means "to assume a sitting position." The past tense of *sit* is *sat*. *Set* means "to put down or place" or "to adjust something to a desired position." The past tense of *set* is *set*.

> I usually <u>sit</u> in the front row at the movies.
> They <u>sat</u> at the clinic waiting for their names to be called.
> Every semester I <u>set</u> goals for myself.
> Elizabeth <u>set</u> the mail on the kitchen table and went to work.

Suppose/Supposed *Suppose* means "to assume" or "to guess." *Supposed* is both the past tense and the past participle of *suppose*. *Supposed* also means "expected" or "required." (Note that when *supposed* has this meaning, it is followed by *to*.)

> <u>Suppose</u> researchers found a cure for AIDS tomorrow.
> We <u>supposed</u> the movie would be over by ten o'clock.
> You were <u>supposed</u> to finish a draft of the report by today.

PRACTICE 25-11

Proofread the underlined words in the following sentences for correct spelling. If a correction needs to be made, cross out the incorrect word, and write the correct spelling above it. If the word is spelled correctly, write *C* above it.

Example: A <u>principal</u> is <s><u>suppose</u></s> *supposed* to care about his or her students' welfare. *(C above principal)*

1. After a <s>plain</s> *plane* crash is reported in the news, many people vow to <u>quit</u> *C* flying forever.

2. It is not <s>write</s> *right* to expect everyone to agree with your personal <s>principals</s> *principles* of morality in every case.

3. In earlier times, children were always ~~suppose~~ *supposed* to be ~~quite~~ *quiet* and not speak when their elders were talking.

4. My favorite teacher never <u>raised</u> *(C)* his voice in anger, which <u>set</u> *(C)* a good example for students.

5. Surveys have shown that many college students' ~~principle~~ *principal* goal in life is to become <u>quite</u> *(C)* wealthy.

6. <u>Suppose</u> *(C)* for a moment that the defense is ~~write~~ *right* and the district attorney is wrong.

7. It takes ~~quit~~ *quite* a few years of training to learn to fly a ~~plain~~ *plane*.

8. All test-takers are <u>supposed</u> *(C)* to <u>sit</u> *set* their books on the table at the front of the room.

9. Even the strictest high school <u>principals</u> *(C)* cannot always keep the students in hallways ~~quite~~ *quiet* and orderly.

10. Some passengers insist when they fly on a ~~plain~~ *plane* that they have to <u>set</u> *sit* on the <u>right</u> *(C)* side of the aisle, while others insist on sitting to the left.

Their/There/They're *Their* is the possessive form of *they*. *There* means "at or in that place." *There* is also used to introduce a thought (in the phrases *there is* and *there are*). *They're* is a contraction meaning "they are."

> Cesar Chavez wanted farm workers to improve <u>their</u> working conditions.
> I put the book over <u>there</u>.
> <u>There are</u> three reasons I will not eat meat.
> <u>They're</u> the best volunteer firefighters I've ever seen.

Then/Than *Then* means "at that time" or "next in time." *Than* is used to introduce the second element in a comparison.

> He was young and naive <u>then</u>.
> I went to the job interview and <u>then</u> stopped off for a double chocolate shake.
> My dog is smarter <u>than</u> your dog.

Threw/Through *Threw* is the past tense of *throw*. *Through* means "in one side and out the opposite side" or "finished."

> Satchel Paige <u>threw</u> a baseball over ninety-five miles an hour.
> It takes almost thirty minutes to go <u>through</u> the tunnel that connects England and France.

CHAPTER 25 Understanding Spelling • **467**

"I'm <u>through</u>," said Clark as he stormed out of Perry White's office.

To/Too/Two *To* means "in the direction of." *Too* means "also" or "more than enough." *Two* denotes the numeral 2.

During spring break, I am going <u>to</u> Disney World.
My roommates are coming <u>too</u>.
The microwave popcorn is <u>too</u> hot to eat.
"If we get rid of the tin man and the lion, the <u>two</u> of us can go to Oz," said the scarecrow to Dorothy.

Use/Used *Use* means "to put into service" or "to consume." *Used* is both the past tense and past participle of *use*. *Used* also means "accustomed." (Note that when *used* has this meaning, it is followed by *to*.)

I <u>use</u> a soft cloth to clean my glasses.
"Hey! Who <u>used</u> all the hot water?" he yelled from the shower.
Mary had <u>used</u> all the firewood during the storm.
After living in Alaska for a year, they got <u>used</u> to the short winter days.

PRACTICE 25-12

Proofread the underlined words in the following sentences for correct spelling. If a correction needs to be made, cross out the incorrect word, and write the correct spelling above it. If the word is spelled correctly, write *C* above it.

Example: Most chemicals aren't dangerous when ~~their~~ *they're* <u>used</u> *C* properly.

1. ~~Their~~ *There* is more <u>than</u> *C* one way to get ahead in this world.

2. Critics charge that in preventing crime our country's criminal justice system often does ~~two~~ *too* little ~~to~~ *too* late.

3. An appeals judge ~~through~~ *threw* out the evidence that the jury had <u>used</u> *C*.

4. When they think of ~~there~~ *their* past, people often wonder whether they were better off earlier ~~then~~ *than* they are now.

5. Eighty percent of the students who responded ~~too~~ *to* the survey said that ~~their~~ *they're* in favor of a moment of silence but they aren't in favor of school prayer.

6. It ~~use~~ *used* to take more ~~then~~ *than* thirty hours to drive from New York to Miami.

468 ▪ **UNIT 9** Special Problems with Punctuation, Mechanics, and Spelling

7. Before the interstate highway was opened, drivers had to maneuver their [C] cars ~~threw~~ [through] many small towns.

8. Fewer people ~~use~~ [used] to make the trip in the past because it was just ~~to~~ [too] much trouble then [C].

9. When the President threw [C] out the first ball of the baseball season this afternoon, he ~~use~~ [used] his left hand.

10. When ~~too~~ [two] people are in love, ~~their~~ [they're] often unable to see any faults in each other.

11. Retailers say that their [C] sales this holiday season were higher ~~then~~ [than] they were last year.

12. By the time the year is through [C], they expect profits to be higher ~~to~~ [too].

13. Whenever ~~there~~ [they're] involved in an automobile accident, people should try to remain calm and use [C] ~~there~~ [their] common sense.

14. If their [C] injuries are not ~~to~~ [too] great, people should remain right there [C] at the scene of the accident until authorities have arrived.

15. If either car is halfway ~~threw~~ [through] an intersection, then [C] it might be a good idea to try to move it, however.

Weather/Whether *Weather* refers to the state of the atmosphere with respect to temperature, humidity, precipitation, and so on. *Whether* is used in indirect questions.

> The *Farmer's Almanac* says that the weather this winter will be severe.
> Whether or not this prediction will be correct is anyone's guess.

Where/Were/We're *Where* means "at or in what place." *Were* is the past tense of *are*. *We're* is a contraction meaning "we are."

> Where are you going, and where have you been?
> Charlie Chaplin and Mary Pickford were popular stars of silent movies.
> We're doing our back-to-school shopping early this year.

Whose/Who's *Whose* is the possessive form of *who*. *Who's* is a contraction meaning "who is" or "who has."

> My roommate asked "Whose book is this?"

CHAPTER 25 Understanding Spelling • 469

"<u>Who's</u> there?" squealed the second little pig as he leaned against the door.

<u>Who's</u> left a yellow 1957 Chevrolet blocking the driveway?

Your/You're *Your* is the possessive form of *you*. *You're* is a contraction meaning "you are."

"You should have worn <u>your</u> running shoes," said the hare as he passed the tortoise.

"<u>You're</u> too kind," said the tortoise sarcastically.

PRACTICE 25-13

Proofread the underlined words in the following sentences for correct spelling. If a correction needs to be made, cross out the incorrect word, and write the correct spelling above it. If the word is spelled correctly, write *C* above it.

Example: As citizens, ~~were~~ *we're* all concerned with <u>where</u> *C* our country is going.

1. Authorities are attempting to discover ~~who's~~ *whose* fingerprints <u>were</u> *C* left at the scene of the crime.

2. Cancer doesn't care ~~weather~~ *whether* ~~your~~ *you're* rich or poor, young or old, black or white; it can strike anyone.

3. Santa Fe, ~~were~~ *where* I lived for many years, has better <u>weather</u> *C* than New Jersey has.

4. Whenever we listen to politicians debate, ~~were~~ *we're* likely to be wondering ~~whose~~ *who's* telling the truth.

5. You should take <u>your</u> *C* time before deciding ~~weather~~ *whether* to focus <u>your</u> *C* greatest energy on school or on work.

6. The people ~~who's~~ *whose* lives influenced me most <u>were</u> *C* my grandmother and grandfather.

7. You can't just sit around wondering ~~whose~~ *who's* going to make ~~you're~~ *your* dreams come true.

8. When the <u>weather</u> *C* report advises us that it's going to be sunny, ~~were~~ *we're* always careful to carry an umbrella.

470 • **UNIT 9** Special Problems with Punctuation, Mechanics, and Spelling

9. By the time ~~your~~ *you're* in high school, people expect you to have decided ~~were~~ *where* you want to be ten years down the road.

10. Only someone who's *(C)* experienced combat understands the difficulty of deciding ~~weather~~ *whether* to face the enemy or retreat.

11. If ~~your~~ *you're* interested in discovering whose *(C)* movies have made the most money this year, read *Variety*.

12. Last year AIDS activists ~~we're~~ *were* concerned about whether *(C)* or not research funds were going to be cut.

13. If you hope to be a good ballplayer, you're *(C)* first going to have to learn to trust ~~you're~~ *your* reflexes.

14. In deciding ~~whose~~ *who's* the best musician, it doesn't matter whose *(C)* recordings have sold the most.

15. ~~Weather~~ *Whether* or not class will be held outside depends on the weather *(C)*.

•••••••▶ **FLASHBACK** ◀•••••••

Look back at your response to the Paragraph Practice at the beginning of the chapter. Find any words that are on the lists of commonly confused words (pages 459–469), and check to make sure they are spelled correctly. If they are not, correct them on the lines below.

_____   _____

F BECOMING A BETTER SPELLER

At first, learning to spell will take a good deal of time. But by using a systematic approach and following a few steps, you can make this task much easier and become a better speller.

1. *Use the dictionary.* As you write, circle words whose spellings you are unsure of. Then, after you have finished your draft, look up these words in the dictionary to make sure they are spelled correctly.

2. *Use a spell checker.* If you write on a computer, use a spell checker. It will not only correct misspelled words, but it will also identify errors such as transposed or omitted letters.

3. *Proofread carefully.* Keep in mind that a spell checker will only point out words that are spelled incorrectly; it will not help if you have used the wrong word—*to* for *too*, for example. For this reason, you should always proofread your papers for spelling before you hand them in. Be especially careful to look for words your spell checker will not identify as misspelled.

4. *Keep a personal spelling list.* Write down all the words that you misspell. If you keep a writing journal, set aside a few pages in the back for your personal spelling list. As you find new words, add them to your list. Every time you look a word up in the dictionary or your spell checker identifies a misspelled word, write it down. Then, any time you get a chance, review the words on your list.

5. *Look over corrected papers for misspelled words.* Whenever your instructor hands back one of your papers, look for misspelled words—usually circled and marked *sp*. Add these to your spelling list too.

6. *Look for patterns in your spelling errors.* Do you consistently misspell words with *ei* combinations? Do you have trouble forming plurals? Once you figure out which problem you have, you can concentrate on it and take steps to eliminate it.

7. *Learn the basic spelling rules.* Familiarize yourself with the spelling rules in this chapter—especially those that apply to areas in which you are weak. Remember that one rule can help you spell many words correctly. Learning a few rules is certainly more efficient than memorizing long lists of individual words.

8. *Look at the list of commonly confused words in this chapter.* If you have problems with any of these word pairs, add them to your list.

9. *Make flash cards.* Put each word that you have trouble spelling on a 3-by-5-inch card. You can use these cards to test yourself periodically.

10. *Use memory cues.* Use memory cues to help you remember how to spell certain words. For example, thinking of the word *finite* helps you remember that *definite* is spelled with an *i*, not an *a*. Also, thinking of the word *pal* helps you remember that the *principal* of a school (who may or may not be your *pal*) ends with *pal*, not *ple*.

11. Learn to spell some of the most commonly misspelled words. Identify those on the list below that give you trouble, and then add them to your personal spelling list.

Commonly Misspelled Words

a lot	entrance	noticeable	separate
already	environment	occasion	studying
all right	everything	occur	tomato
argument	exercise	occurred	tomatoes
beautiful	experience	occurring	truly
becoming	finally	occurrences	until
believe	forty	occurs	usually
benefit	fulfill	potato	Wednesday
cannot	generally	potatoes	weird
careful	holiday	prescription	window
careless	intelligence	president	withhold
cemetery	interest	professor	woman
certain	interfere	receive	women
definite	loneliness	recognize	writing
definitely	medicine	restaurant	written
dependent	memento	roommate	
develop	minute	secretary	
early	necessary	sentence	

REVIEW

CHAPTER REVIEW: STUDENT WRITING

Read the following student passage, in which spelling errors have been introduced. Identify the words you think are misspelled; then, look them up in the dictionary. Cross out each incorrect word, and write the correct word above the line. The first sentence has been edited for you.

Fudging

The origin of the word fudge is ~~unnown~~ *unknown*. ~~It's~~ *Its* meaning seems to have been adopted from many ~~diffrent~~ *different* sources. At present, it has ~~too~~ *two* meanings. The first is "the smooth chocolate substance that is put on ice cream." The second--

and more ~~intresting~~ *interesting* one--is "to fit together in a clumsy manner."

    ~~Everone~~ *Everyone* can remember fudging on an essay test during his or her academic career. A good ~~freind~~ *friend* of mine, for example, couldn't answer a question on a history test because he didn't know all the causes of World War II. What did he do? He made some causes up and got a B. Some people, like my friend, have had great success and become expert fudgers. Those students who were able to get away with fudging in high school continue to fudge in college and beyond. Many politicians, for example, feel ~~comfortible~~ *comfortable* fudging ~~there campain~~ *their campaign* speeches in order to attract voters. They promise to fight corruption, find homes for the homeless, and put an end to crime. Of course, these are empty promises. How are voters ~~suppose~~ *supposed* to judge a ~~canidate~~ *candidate* if he or she does not tell them the truth?

    Fudging takes place not only in politics but also in many other professions. In ~~sceince~~ *science* people fudge to save time and money. There are many products on the market that are the result of ~~sceintific~~ *scientific* fudging. The researcher manufactured data so that a research project could be finished quickly and cheaply. For example, in the 1980s, a firm fudged data to get the Food and Drug ~~Aministration~~ *Administration* to approve one of ~~it's~~ *its* products: a pill to help people ~~loose wieght~~ *lose weight*. When consumers complained they were getting sick, the FDA ~~puled~~ *pulled* the pill off the market. Of course, ~~weather~~ *whether* or not the researcher was fired makes no difference. The damage was ~~all ready~~ *already* done.

Fudging takes place in society because it works. It saves time and ~~mony~~ *money* and is difficult to detect. If fudging is detected, it is usually only after the harm has been done. In politics fudging is noticed after the politician has been elected. In science it is noticed after a product has been sold to the public. The only sure way to detect fudging before it is too late is to hire people to check the data. Of course, this is both time-consuming and expensive.

For this reason, as long as there are people, there will ~~definatly~~ *definitely* be fudging.

CHAPTER REVIEW: EDITING PRACTICE

On a computer, type your response, as you originally wrote it, to the Paragraph Practice at the beginning of this chapter. If you have time, type in a longer writing assignment you are currently working on. Then, run a spell check. Does the computer pick up all the errors? Which does it identify? Which does it miss?

CHAPTER REVIEW: COLLABORATIVE ACTIVITIES

1. Working in pairs, exchange responses to the Paragraph Practice at the beginning of the chapter. Check each other's paragraphs for spelling errors. Make sure you use a dictionary to check any words that you think are misspelled.

2. Compare the misspelled words you found in Collaborative Activity 1 with those your partner found. How many of the same misspelled words did you find? What patterns of misspelling do you see? What types of spelling errors seem most common?

3. Make a spelling list with your partner, and then pool your findings to create a spelling list for the whole class. When you have finished, determine what types of errors are most common. For example, do most people have trouble with commonly confused words or with adding suffixes?

Review

- You must memorize the spellings of certain words because they are not spelled exactly as they are pronounced. (See 25A.)
- Put *i* before *e*, except after *c*, or in any *ay* sound, as in *neighbor*. (See 25B.)
- The addition of a prefix to a word never affects the spelling of the original word. (See 25C.)

    dis + service = disservice
    un + able = unable

- The addition of a suffix may change the spelling of the original word. (See 25D.)
- In general, drop the *e* if the suffix begins with a vowel. Keep the *e* if the suffix begins with a consonant. (See 25D.)

    hope + ing = hoping
    hope + ful = hopeful

- Generally, when a word ends in *-y*, change the *y* to an *i* if the letter before the *y* is a consonant. Keep the *y* if the letter before the *y* is a vowel. (See 25D.)

    beauty + ful = beautiful
    annoy + ance = annoyance

- Double the final consonant in a word before adding a suffix (1) if the last three letters of the word have a consonant-vowel-consonant pattern (cvc) and (2) if the word has one syllable or the last syllable is stressed. (See 25D.)

    pet + ed = petted (cvc—one syllable)
    commit + ed = committed (cvc—stress on *last* syllable)

- Take the time to memorize the most commonly confused words. (See 25E.)
- Follow the steps to becoming a better speller. (See 25F.)

Unit 9 Review

The collaborative activities, writing practice topics, and student writing sample that follow provide opportunities for you to review what you have learned in Chapters 22 through 25.

COLLABORATIVE ACTIVITIES

1. Work in a group to design a campaign to keep high school students away from cigarettes (or alcohol or drugs). First, come up with a slogan. Then, plan a poster that highlights your slogan. Finally, incorporate the slogan and the poster into a short speech to a high school audience.

2. Assume that your group has been asked to perform a short four-character skit as part of your anti substance-abuse presentation to the high school. Write a script for this skit, but instead of writing each character's lines out as a play does, use quotation marks and identifying tags to set off dialogue. (Remember to begin a new paragraph each time a new person speaks.) Begin by naming your characters and determining the roles they will play.

3. List ten words whose spelling you are not sure of. Compare lists with other members of your group, and work together to choose the twenty most difficult words. Verify the correct spelling and pronunciation of each word in a dictionary. Then, working as a team in competition with another group in your class, conduct a spelling bee. Take turns testing members of the other group by reading each of your twenty words aloud. (Members of the group can work together to come up with the correct spelling.)

WRITING PRACTICE

1. What physical or personal traits do you think people first notice about you? Do these first impressions present an accurate picture of the person you really are? Write an essay in which you answer these questions in very specific terms.

2. How do you expect your life to be different from the lives of your parents? Write an essay in which you identify the various ways in which you expect your life to depart from theirs. You may discuss issues like education, finances, place of residence, social or political values, or professional status. Be sure to use specific examples and explanations.

3. Should local, state, and federal governments continue to enact laws to re-

strict smoking? Which (if any) restrictions are fair, and which are not? For example, should smoking be banned in all public places, including offices, restaurants, and airplanes? Should it be banned only in government-owned buildings, such as libraries and schools? Should smoking be allowed in designated sections of buildings? Should cigarettes be sold to children under eighteen? Write a letter expressing your views. Address your letter to a government official.

4. Imagine you are a travel agent trying to attract tourists to a resort in a particularly unpleasant location—the North Pole, the Sahara Desert, or Mars, for example—for a two-week vacation. Because you know that luring vacationers to this destination will be a challenge, you decide that direct, factual statements will not be enough. Instead, you will need to use other strategies—such as long series of details separated by commas, quoted testimonials from satisfied customers, and even exclamation points—to convey your enthusiasm. Give your "vacation paradise" a name, and write a brochure to be sent to your clients.

STUDENT WRITING

Read the following student essay, in which errors have been introduced. Correct all errors in punctuation, capitalization, and spelling. The first sentence has been edited for you.

Education Internship: First Year

On ~~s~~September 15, when I ~~recieved~~ received a copy of my schedule in the mail, I learned that my hours as an education intern at the ~~a~~Accelerated ~~l~~Learning ~~l~~Laboratory ~~s~~School (the ALL School) would be from nine to ten on Mondays and Wednesdays. On the first day of class, I got to the school extra early. I rang the doorbell, signed in, put on my little visitor sticker, and met the teacher, Eileen Doyle. I was nervous, but I was ready.

The children were still in ~~H~~homeroom. They were ~~suppose~~ supposed to be reading, writing, or doing math. When I looked out at the classroom, though, I saw that most of the sixteen children were out in space somewhere. Mrs. ~~d~~Doyle told me that most of them were in third, fourth, or fifth grade, ~~accept~~ *except* for ~~too~~ *two* girls. One of them was ~~l~~*L*eah, a sixth grader who couldn't read at all.

At nine o'clock, it was time for their investigation groups. Mrs. Doyle's students were all ~~suppose~~ *supposed* to go to different classrooms and interact with other children. The students were ~~studyng~~ *studying* ~~a~~*A*frica, with three teachers team teaching about thirty children. Because this was the end of the month, they were ~~wraping~~ *wrapping* up ~~there~~ *their* study of the ~~c~~*C*ontinent and ~~completeing~~ *completing* work sheets.

My first job was to help Brian, a fifth grader who was a little slow. Brian's problem was that he tended to ~~waist~~ *waste* time and get distracted. I gave him a little firm ~~advise~~ *advice*, however, and eventually got him to work ~~independantly~~ *independently*. Then I moved on to help Andrew, a boy who ~~new~~ *knew* all the answers but had a hard time expressing himself. By the time I had both Brian and Andrew working on ~~they're~~ *their* own, I had to return to our original classroom.

Now Mrs. ~~d~~*D*oyle asked me to work with a girl named Ping. Originally from ~~v~~*V*ietnam, she was twelve years old and didn't speak ~~e~~*E*nglish very well. On a ~~peace~~ *piece* of paper, she had written, "Happy birth<u>en</u> to you." I pointed to <u>birthen</u> and wrote <u>birthday</u>. She wrote <u>birthday</u> and then the whole sentence again, this time with the correct spelling. I asked her when her birthday was, and she counted on her fingers and wrote <u>4/30</u>. I pointed to the <u>4</u> and wrote ~~a~~*A*pril. Then she wrote, "Happy birthday to you, April 30." I wanted to help her more ~~then~~ *than* I had, but by now it was almost ten o'clock.

The ~~principle~~ *principal* was making an announcement over the loudspeaker as I put my coat on. I waved goodbye when I left, and I heard all these little voices saying, "~~g~~*G*oodbye, ~~r~~*R*ebecca."

"Don't worry*,*" I told them, "I'll be back." And I was. I didn't come ~~everyday~~ *every day*, but every Monday and Wednesday for the rest of the year, from nine to ten in the morning, I was ~~their~~ *there*.

Right before the end of the ~~s~~*S*pring semester, I was walking across ~~c~~*C*ampus when I ~~past~~ *passed* a little kid. All of a sudden I heard him yell out, "~~h~~*H*ey, she goes to our school!" He was from the ~~a~~*A*ccelerated ~~l~~*L*earning ~~l~~*L*aboratory ~~s~~*S*chool, and he was pointing at me. His words had an ~~incredable affect~~ *incredible effect* on me. I always ~~use~~ *used* to wonder ~~weather~~ *whether* I'd be a teacher when I grew up. Now I ~~new~~ *knew* I would.

Appendix: Writing Paragraphs and Essays in an Exam Setting

Knowing how to plan, write, and revise paragraphs and essays is a skill you can apply throughout your college years and beyond. One situation in which you will need this skill as a student is during an examination.

Many exam questions call for just a short answer—*yes* or *no*, *true* or *false*. Others ask you to fill in a blank with a few words; still others require you to select the one correct answer from among several choices. In these situations, reading and study skills are clearly more important than writing skills.

In many cases, however, an exam question will specifically tell you to write a paragraph or an essay, and then your writing skills will be important. Knowing in advance exactly what you are expected to do (and how to do it) will give you the confidence you need to perform at your best.

A BEFORE THE EXAM

Exams are usually announced in advance, so you should have plenty of time to prepare. Not making good use of this preparation time deprives you of an important advantage. However, preparation for an exam should begin well before it is announced. In a sense, you begin this preparation on the first day of the semester.

Come to class

It may seem obvious, but regular attendance in class—where you can listen, ask questions, and take notes—lays the best possible groundwork for academic success. If you do have to miss a class, be sure to arrange to copy (and read) another student's notes before the next class so you will be able to follow the discussion.

Do the assigned reading

If you do not keep up with the assigned reading, it will be extremely difficult for you to understand what is being said in class. This means you will not be able to ask intelligent questions or take useful notes.

Take careful notes

Take careful, thorough notes, but be selective. Don't write down everything your instructor says; first listen, then write. Some students find it helpful to reread their notes as soon as possible after taking them; others outline or even recopy their notes. Try different strategies, and do whatever works for you. If you can, though, try to compare notes on a regular basis with another member of the class; working together, you can check for omissions or misinterpretations. Establishing a buddy system also ensures that you review your notes regularly instead of only on the night before the exam.

Study on your own

When an exam is announced, make a study schedule so you will have time to cover everything. Making a schedule—and sticking to it—is especially important if you have more than one exam in a short period of time. Review all your material (class notes, readings, and so on) slowly and carefully, and then review it again. Make a note of anything you do not understand, and keep track of points you think will need extra time. Try to predict the most likely questions, and perhaps practice drafting paragraphs or brief essays that answer these questions.

Study with a group

If you can arrange to study with one or more classmates—and if you are reasonably certain you will actually study during your group sessions—you should certainly do so. Studying with others can often alert you to material you have overlooked or help you to see new interpretations or perspectives.

Make an appointment with your instructor

If your schedule (and your instructor's) permits, you should try to arrange regular conferences throughout the semester. In addition, you should be sure to set up an appointment to meet with your instructor, or with the course's TA, a few days before an exam. Bring to this meeting any specific questions you have about course content and about the format of the upcoming exam. (You should already have reviewed all your material at least once before the meeting.)

Review the material one final time

The night before the exam is not the time to begin your studying; it is the time to review, in a leisurely way, all the material you have studied. When you have finished this review, get a good night's sleep.

B AT THE EXAM

By the time you walk into an exam room, you already will have done all you could do in advance to get ready for the test. Now, your goal is to keep the momentum going and not do anything to undermine all your hard work.

Read through the entire examination

Be sure you understand how much time you have, how much each question is worth (and, therefore, how much time you should spend answering each one), and exactly what each question is asking you to do. For example, are you supposed to write a paragraph? An essay? Should you summarize the assigned readings? Interpret them? Evaluate their ideas? Present your own ideas? If you are not absolutely certain what kind of answer a particular question calls for, ask your instructor or the proctor *before you begin to prepare your response.*

Budget your time

Once you understand how much each section of the exam and each individual question is worth, plan your time, devoting the most time to the questions your instructor sees as most important.

Reread each question

Carefully reread each question on the exam *before you start to answer it.* This time, underline the key words, the ones that give you information about the required *content, emphasis,* and *organization* of your answer. In the following essay question, the key words have been underlined.

> What is mob psychology? Give some specific recent examples of this phenomenon, and explain in each case both the origins and the outcomes of the situations that occurred.

As the underlining reveals, the wording of this question supplies a good deal of useful information. The initial "What is . . . ?" question tells you that you are being asked to define a term. The rest of the question asks you to focus on a few examples and to discuss both causes (origins) and effects (outcomes) of each. Thus, in this question, the key words reveal the expected content and emphasis as well as the patterns of development you are to use.

▶ **FOCUS** ON KEY WORDS ◀

Here are some other helpful key words to look for in exam questions and other assignments.

summarize	define	suggest causes, origins,
trace	take a stand	contributing factors
recount	argue	suggest results, effects,
give examples	support	outcomes
illustrate	compare	analyze
explain	contrast	evaluate
identify	describe	

Remember, even if everything you say is correct, your response is not acceptable if you do not answer the question. For example, a list of nineteenth-century examples of mob psychology (rather than the required *recent examples*) is not an appropriate response to the question; neither is a discussion of *only* causes or *only* effects.

Brainstorm to help you remember your material

Looking frequently at the exam question, use the inside cover of your exam book to **brainstorm**. (See 1B.) Jot down all the relevant points you can think of—what your textbook had to say about the nature of mob psychology, any specific examples mentioned in a collection of assigned newspaper clippings, your instructor's comments (recorded in your class notes) on causes and results of these specific incidents, and so on. The more you can think of now, the more you will have to choose from when you outline your essay.

Write down a central idea

Looking closely at the wording of the exam question as well as at the material on your brainstorming list, write down the central idea of your answer in a single sentence. If your response is in the form of a paragraph, this idea will be your topic sentence; if the answer is a full-length essay, this central idea will be your thesis statement.

Outline your answer

It makes little sense for you to use your very limited (and valuable) time to construct a detailed, multilevel outline; however, a quick outline that lists your main points will be well worth the small amount of time it will take. With such an outline as a guide, you will be able to see a clear direction for your paragraph or essay. Having a realistic plan to follow will help you relax as you write.

Draft your answer

You will spend the greatest percentage of your time actually writing the answer to the question (or questions) on the exam. Follow your outline, keep track of time, consult your brainstorming notes when you need to—but stay focused on the task at hand.

Reread, revise, and edit

When you have finished a draft of your paragraph or essay answer, reread it carefully, making sure you have answered the question very explicitly. Now is the time to add any pertinent supporting details, delete unasked-for information or irrelevant material, and edit to clarify the topic sentences and transitions that will help your instructor follow your reasoning.

C WRITING A PARAGRAPH

Some exam questions call for paragraph-length responses. (For general information about paragraphs, see Chapters 2 and 3.) Typically, these questions are **identifications**, questions that ask you to explain the significance of a person or event and place it in context or to define a key term or concept.

What was the local color movement? (literature)
Who was José Martí? (history)
What is a conditioned response? (psychology)

> ▶ **FOCUS** ON IDENTIFICATIONS ◀
>
> Remember, the more items you are asked to identify on an exam, the less time and space you will be expected to spend on each.

The following is a paragraph written in response to an examination question.

Question: Identify the term *triangular trade*.
Answer:

```
    Triangular trade is the name for a pattern of
trade with three destination points. Triangular
trade routes were often used in colonial times by
ships involved in the slave trade. For example, a
ship could take rum from a New England port to
Africa. There it would trade the rum for slaves,
which it would bring to the West Indies. Then the
slaves would be traded for sugar, molasses, or
spices, which would be brought back to New England,
where it would be distilled into rum. Then the cycle
would begin again, with the African slaves treated
as just another commodity in a commercial
transaction.
```

Topic sentence identifies term to be defined

Definition developed with an extended example

D WRITING AN ESSAY

If an exam calls for an essay-length response, follow the guidelines discussed in Chapter 4. Remember to leave plenty of time to brainstorm and outline before you start to write. In addition, leave time to reread, revise, and edit your draft when you have finished writing.

486 ▪ APPENDIXES

> ▶ **FOCUS** ON INTRODUCTIONS AND CONCLUSIONS ◀
>
> The amount of time you have on an exam is always limited. Therefore, you should devote the bulk of your writing time to the body of your essay rather than to an extended introduction or conclusion. If you have time, it is a good idea to add a title to your essay when you are finished writing.

The following essay was written in response to a question on a midterm exam for a first-year composition course. The exam's purpose was to make sure students had read the course's assigned readings and understood them well enough to develop some original ideas on the subjects those readings addressed. (Note that the question does not ask students to summarize the readings and that it asks them to discuss only three or four essays, not every one they read.)

Question: Several of the essays we have read so far this semester address the concept of personal and social responsibility. Choose three or four reading selections we have studied in class, and give examples from each to explain its author's concept of personal and social responsibility.

Answer:

<pre>
                    Being Responsible

     Although several of the essays we have read
this semester deal, directly or indirectly, with
personal and social responsibility, each author
means something different when he or she considers
what it means to be responsible. Martin Gansberg's
"38 Who Saw Murder Didn't Call the Police," Anna
Quindlen's "The Old Block," and Martin Luther King,
Jr.'s, "I Have a Dream," for example, all suggest
how important it is to be a responsible citizen, but
responsibility means something different for each
writer.
     Gansberg believes that <u>responsibility</u> means
being responsible for others as well as for
ourselves. Maybe Kitty Genovese should have been
considered responsible for her own actions; maybe
she had a responsibility to protect herself by not
exposing herself to the dangers of a dark, deserted
street, but this is not the focus of Gansberg's
article. He believes that the thirty-eight neighbors
who watched her murder and did nothing were the ones
</pre>

Opening sentence echoes wording of question

Essays to be discussed listed

Thesis statement Topic sentence identifies Gansberg's concept of responsibility

who were most guilty of acting irresponsibly. For the people in Gansberg's essay, being responsible would have meant taking action to save Kitty Genovese's life, even if it might have put their own lives at risk (which it apparently would not have). When Gansberg sarcastically criticizes the "respectable" people and exposes their flimsy excuses for not helping, he is criticizing them for their failure to be responsible for another human being.

 Quindlen's essay seems to suggest that responsibility means being responsible not just for oneself or for other individuals but for the community as a whole. When Quindlen tours the old neighborhood and sees its crime, drugs, and burned-out, abandoned buildings, she does not blame politicians for neglecting the cities. She does not even blame her own family for moving away. Instead, she blames the decline of city neighborhoods on all the people who abandoned the cities and moved to the suburbs. Now, she believes, it is the responsibility of those same people to remember where they came from and begin working to save those dying cities. If they do not, she says, the situation will only get worse.

Topic sentence identifies Quindlen's concept of responsibility

 More than Gansberg or Quindlen, Martin Luther King, Jr., sees responsibility as something that is collective rather than individual or personal. King believes all men and women in society share an obligation to act as responsible citizens. He believes it is our responsibility not just to change society gradually, through the choices we make and the behavior we engage in, but sometimes to take specific, immediate action to bring about needed change. Although he is addressing African Americans, his dream goes beyond his hopes for them to his hopes for "all of God's children."

Topic sentence identifies King's concept of responsibility

 Crime, drugs, decaying cities, and racial discrimination are all problems that confront people in our society. As Gansberg, Quindlen, and King show, all of us are responsible, individually and collectively, for working to solve these problems.

Brief conclusion summarizes essay's main points

Appendix: Tips for ESL Writers

Learning English as a second language involves more than just learning grammar. Nonnative speakers of English need to adjust to conventions of usage and ways of thinking that are second nature to native speakers but that may be new to students who grew up speaking another language. This appendix summarizes the areas that typically give nonnative speakers the greatest difficulty.

A INCLUDING SUBJECTS IN SENTENCES

In almost all cases, English requires that every sentence have an explicit subject. In fact, every dependent clause must also have an explicit subject.

Incorrect: My parents don't make much money <u>although work hard</u>.
Correct: My parents don't make much money <u>although they work hard</u>.

English even requires a false or "dummy" subject to fill the subject position in sentences like this one:

<u>It</u> is hot here.

Do *not* write simply: "Hot here" or "Is hot here."
(For more on subjects, see 6A and 7A.)

B AVOIDING SPECIAL PROBLEMS WITH SUBJECTS

In some languages, it is common to begin a sentence with a word or phrase that has no grammatical link to the sentence but that states clearly what the sentence is about. If you speak such a language, you might think of writing a sentence like this one:

Incorrect: Career plans I am studying to be a computer scientist.

A sentence like this cannot occur in English. Even though the phrase *career plans* is in the normal position for a subject, it cannot be a subject because the sentence already includes one, the pronoun *I*, which agrees with the verb *am studying*. In addition, *career plans* is not connected to the rest of the sentence in any other way, such as with a preposition. One way to revise this sentence is to rewrite it so that *career plans* is the subject.

Correct: My career plans are to be a computer scientist.

Another way is to make *career plans* the object of a preposition.

Correct: As for my career plans, I am studying to be a computer scientist.

Standard English also does not permit a two-part subject in which the second part is a pronoun referring to the same person or thing as the first part.

Incorrect: My sister she is a cardiologist.
Correct: My sister is a cardiologist.

When the real subject follows the verb and the normal subject position before the verb is empty, it must be filled by a "dummy" subject, such as *there*.

Incorrect: Are tall mountains in my country.
Correct: There are tall mountains in my country.

C INDICATING WHETHER NOUNS ARE SINGULAR OR PLURAL

Every time you use a noun, ask yourself whether you are talking about one item or more than one, and choose a singular or a plural form accordingly. Consider this sentence:

Correct: The books in both branches of the library are deteriorating.

There are three nouns in this sentence; one is singular *(library)*, and the other two are plural *(books, branches)*. You might think that the modifier *both* is enough to indicate that *branch* is plural and that it is obvious there would have to be more than one book in any branch of a library. It does not matter, however, whether the information is unimportant or obvious or whether it has already been supplied. You must always use a form that indicates explicitly that a noun is plural. (See 19A.)

D UNDERSTANDING COUNT AND NONCOUNT NOUNS

If you compare the nouns *cloud* and *smoke*, you will see that they differ not only in meaning but in the way they are used in sentences.

Correct: The sky is full of clouds.
Correct: The sky is full of smoke.
Incorrect: The sky is full of smokes.

Correct: I can count ten clouds in the distance.
Incorrect: I can count ten smokes in the distance.

Cloud is a **count** noun, and *smoke* is a **noncount** noun. Many English words are count nouns like *cloud*, and many others are noncount nouns like *smoke*. Count nouns usually have a singular form and a plural form: *cloud, clouds*. Noncount nouns usually have only a singular form: *smoke*. The term *noncount* does not mean you cannot use numbers in relation to smoke, but only that English grammar requires you to apply numbers to smoke indirectly: *one wisp of smoke* or *two columns of smoke*, not *one smoke, two smokes*.

Count nouns give the sense of a distinct individual thing or a group of distinct individual things: *a teacher, a panther, a bed, an ocean, a cloud; teachers, panthers, beds, oceans, clouds*. Noncount nouns, on the other hand, give the sense of mass that is not made up of distinct parts: *gold, cream, sand, blood, smoke*. Often, much the same idea can be represented through either the individual focus of a count noun or the more general focus of a noncount noun.

Count	Noncount
people (plural of *person*)	humanity
tables, chairs, beds	furniture
letters	mail
tools	equipment

Abstract nouns are likely to be noncount (see those listed below), but they are not always.

Count	Noncount
suggestions	advice (NOT advices)
facts	information (NOT informations)

(See 18A for more on abstract nouns.)

Some words can be either count or noncount, depending on the meaning intended.

Count: Students in this course are expected to submit two papers.
Noncount: These artificial flowers are made of paper.

Pay attention to how a word is used when you hear or read it. If it has a plural form, then it can be used as a count noun. If it occurs in the singular without a determiner, it is noncount. See the next section for a list of determiners.

> ▶ **FOCUS** **ON COUNT AND NONCOUNT NOUNS** ◀
>
> Here are some general guidelines for using count and noncount nouns.
>
> 1. Use a count noun to refer to a living animal, but use a noncount noun to refer to the food derived from that animal.
>   **Count:** There are several live lobsters in the tank.
>   **Noncount:** This restaurant specializes in lobster.
> 2. If you use a noncount noun for a substance or class of things that
>
> *(continued on the following page)*

(continued from the previous page)

can come in different varieties, you can often make that noun plural if you want to talk about those varieties.

Noncount: Cheese is a rich source of calcium.
Count: Many different cheeses come from Italy.

3. If you want to shift attention from a concept in general to specific instances of it, you can often use an abstract, noncount noun as a count noun.

Noncount: You have a great deal of talent.
Count: My talents don't include singing.

E USING DETERMINERS WITH COUNT AND NONCOUNT NOUNS

Determiners are noun modifiers that differ from most adjectives in the following ways.

1. Determiners do not describe the nouns they modify; instead, they identify or quantify them.
2. When a determiner is accompanied by one or more other adjectives, the determiner always comes first. For example, in the phrase *my expensive new digital watch*, *my* is a determiner; you cannot put *expensive, new, digital*, or any other adjective before *my*.

▶ FOCUS ON DETERMINERS ◀

Determiners include the following words.

1. *a, an, the*
2. *this, these, that, those*
3. *my, our, your, his, her, its, their* (plus the possessive form of a noun: *Sheila's, my friend's*)
4. *whose, which, what*
5. *all, both, each, every, some, any, either, no, neither, many, much, a few, a little, few, little, several, enough*
6. all numerals: *one, two,* and so forth

A singular count noun, whether or not it is modified by other adjectives, must be accompanied by a determiner such as *my watch* or *the new digital watch*, not just *watch* or *new digital watch*. Noncount nouns and plural count nouns, on the other hand, sometimes have determiners but sometimes do not. *This honey is sweet* and *Honey is sweet* are both acceptable, as are *These berries are juicy* and *Berries are juicy*. In each case, however, the meaning is different. You cannot say *Berry is juicy*, however; say instead *This berry is juicy*, *Every berry is juicy*, or *A berry is juicy*.

Some determiners can be used only with certain types of nouns.

1. *This* and *that* can only be used with singular nouns (count or noncount): *this berry, that honey.*

2. *These, those, a few, few, many, both,* and *several* can only be used with plural count nouns: *these berries, those apples, a few ideas, few chairs, many students, both sides, several directions.*

3. *Much* and *a little* can only be used with noncount nouns: *a little honey, little food, much affection.*

4. *Some* and *enough* can only be used with noncount or plural count nouns: *some honey, some berries, enough trouble, enough problems.*

5. *A, an, every,* and *each* can only be used with singular count nouns: *a berry, an elephant, every possibility, each citizen.*

F UNDERSTANDING ARTICLES

The definite article *the* and the indefinite articles *a* and *an* play a significant role in English, allowing the reader to distinguish between different kinds of information.

Definite articles

When the definite article *the* is used with a noun, it indicates that a writer is saying to a reader, "You can identify which particular thing or things I have in mind. The information to make that identification is available to you; either you have it already, or I am about to supply it to you."

A reader can find the necessary information in the following ways.

- By looking at other information in the sentence

    Meet me at <u>the</u> *northeast* corner *of Main Street and Lafayette.*

    In this example, the information needed by the reader is in italic.

- By looking at information in other sentences

    Aisha ordered a slice of pie and a cup of coffee. <u>The</u> pie was delicious. She asked for a second slice.

Here the definite article before the word *pie* in the second sentence indicates that it is the same pie identified in the first sentence. Notice, however, that a noun will not necessarily be preceded by *the* when it is mentioned again. The noun *slice* in the third sentence is preceded by an indefinite article because it is not the same slice referred to in the first sentence. There is no information that identifies it specifically.

- By looking at the surroundings or by referring to general knowledge

    Look at the chart on page 12.
    The earth revolves around the sun.

In the following cases, *the* is always used rather than *a* or *an*.

- Before the word *same: the same day*
- Before the superlative form of an adjective: *the youngest son*
- Usually before a number indicating order or sequence: *the third time*

Indefinite articles

Unlike the definite article, the indefinite articles *a* and *an* occur only with singular count nouns. (See Section D in this appendix.) *A* is used when the next sound is a consonant, and *an* is used when the next sound is a vowel. In choosing *a* or *an*, remember that you have to pay attention to sounds rather than to spelling: *a house, a year, a union,* but *an hour, an uncle.*

When an indefinite article is used with a noun, the writer is saying to the reader, "I don't expect you to have enough information right now to identify a particular thing that I have in mind, except to recognize that what I'm referring to is no more than one."

Consider the following two sentences:

We need a table for our computer.
I have a folding table; maybe you can use that.

In the first sentence, the writer has a hypothetical table in mind, but no actual one. Since it is indefinite to the writer, it clearly is indefinite to the reader, and *a* is used, not *the*. The second sentence refers to an actual table, but because the writer does not expect the reader to be able to identify it specifically, it is also used with *a* rather than *the*.

No article

The absence of an article also has a meaning, but only noncount and plural count nouns can stand without articles: *butter, sweet chocolate, cookies, fresh strawberries,* but *a cookie* or *the fresh strawberry.*

Nouns without articles can be used to make generalizations.

Infants need affection as well as food.

Here, the absence of articles before the nouns *infants, affection,* and *food* indicates that the statement is not about particular infants, affection, or food but about infants, affection, and food in general. Remember not to use *the* in such sentences; in English, a sentence like *The infants need affection as well as food* can only refer to particular, identifiable infants, not infants in general.

Articles and proper nouns

Proper nouns split into two classes: names that take *the* and names that take no article. (See 24A for more on proper nouns.)

1. Names of people usually take no article, unless they are used in the plural to refer to members of a family, in which case they take *the: Napoleon, Mahatma Gandhi,* but *the Kennedys.*
2. Names of places that are plural in form usually take *the: the Andes, the United States.*
3. The names of most places on land (cities, states, provinces, and countries) take no article: *Salt Lake City, Mississippi, Alberta, Japan.* The names of most bodies of water (rivers, seas, and oceans, though not lakes or bays) take *the: the Mississippi, the Mediterranean, the Pacific,* but *Lake Erie* and *San Francisco Bay.*
4. Names of streets take no article; names of highways take *the: Main Street, the Belt Parkway.*

G FORMING NEGATIVES AND QUESTIONS

To form a negative statement, add the word *not* directly after the first helping verb of the complete verb.

Global warming has been getting worse.
Global warming has not been getting worse.

When there is no helping verb, a form of the verb *do* must be inserted before *not.*

Automobile traffic contributes to pollution.
Automobile traffic does not contribute to pollution.

To form a question, move the helping verb that follows the subject in a statement to the position directly before the subject.

The governor is trying to compromise.
Is the governor trying to compromise?

The governor is working on the budget.
What is the governor working on?

As with negatives, when the verb does not include a helping verb, you must supply a form of *do.* To form a question, put *do* directly before the subject.

The governor works hard.
Does the governor work hard?

Remember that when *do* is used as a helping verb, no other helping verb is allowed. Furthermore, the form of *do* used must match the tense and number of the original main verb. Note that the main verb loses its tense and appears in the base form.

Incorrect: Automobile traffic does not contributes to pollution.
Correct: Automobile traffic does not contribute to pollution.

A helping verb never precedes the subject if the subject is a question word or contains a question word.

Who is talking to the governor?
Which bills have been vetoed by the governor?

H INDICATING VERB TENSE

In English you must always indicate when the action referred to by each verb took place (for instance, in the past or in the present). Use the appropriate tense of the verb, even if the time is obvious or if the sentence includes other indications of time (such as *two years ago* or *at present*).

Correct: Yesterday I got a letter from my sister Yunpi.
Incorrect: Yesterday I get a letter from my sister Yunpi.

(For more on verb tense, see Unit 5.)

I RECOGNIZING VERBS THAT ARE NOT USED IN THE PROGRESSIVE TENSES

Some verbs are rarely used in the progressive tenses. (See Chapter 11 for more on the progressive tenses.) The verb *know* is an example. It can be used in the present tense.

Correct: Hiro knows American history backwards and forwards.

To a native speaker, however, the verb sounds strange when used in the present progressive tense.

Incorrect: Hiro is knowing American history backwards and forwards.

Verbs like *know*, called **stative**, usually tell us that someone or something is in a state that is unchanging, at least for a while. In contrast, most English verbs show action, and these action verbs can be used in the progressive tenses without restriction.

▶ FOCUS ON VERBS ◀

Verbs that are stative, at least for some of their meanings, often refer to mental states like *know, understand, think, believe, want, like, love,* and *hate*. Other stative verbs include *be, have, need, own, belong, weight, cost,* and *mean*. Certain verbs of sense perception, like *see* and *hear*, are also stative even though they can refer to momentary events rather than states.

Many verbs have more than one meaning, and some of these verbs are stative with one meaning but not with another. An example is the verb *weigh*.

The butcher is weighing the meat.
The meat weighs three pounds.

In the first sentence above, the verb *weigh* means "to put on a scale"; it is active, not stative, as the use of the progressive shows. In the second sentence, however, the same verb means "to have weight," so it is stative, not active. Therefore, it would be unacceptable to say, "The meat is weighing three pounds."

J PLACING ADJECTIVES IN ORDER

Adjectives and other modifiers that precede a noun usually follow a set order. In some cases, a specific position for a modifier is required; in others, a certain position may be preferred but is not required.

Required order

- Determiners (see Section E of this appendix) always come first in a series of adjectives: *these fragile glasses*. The determiners *all* or *both* always precede any other determiners: *all these glasses*.
- If one of the modifiers is a noun, it must come directly before the noun it modifies: *these wine glasses*.
- All other adjectives are placed between the determiners and the noun modifiers: *these fragile wine glasses*. If there are two or more of these adjectives, the following order is preferred.

Preferred order

- Adjectives that show the writer's attitude generally precede adjectives that merely describe: *these lovely fragile wine glasses*.
- Adjectives that indicate size generally come early: *these lovely large fragile wine glasses*.
- Most other adjectives are placed in the middle.

K LEARNING PREPOSITIONS

Try learning uses of prepositions not in isolation, but as part of a system. For example, to identify the location of a place or an event, you can use either *in*, *on*, or *at*.

The preposition *at* specifies an exact point in space or time.

Please leave the package with the janitor at 150 South Street. I'll pick it up at 7:30 tonight.

Expanses of space or time are treated as containers and therefore require *in*.

Jean-Pierre went to school in Haiti in the 1970s.

On must be used in two cases: with the names of streets (but not an exact address) and with days of the week or month.

We'll move into our new office <u>on</u> 18th Street either <u>on</u> Monday or <u>on</u> the first of the month.

(For more on prepositions, see Chapter 21.)

L UNDERSTANDING PREPOSITIONS IN TWO-WORD VERBS

Consider the following sentence.

Please <u>look at</u> the video monitor.

Here the verb *look* must be followed by the preposition *at*; it is a two-word verb. Here *at* functions as a preposition because it introduces the prepositional phrase *at the video monitor*, and therefore *at* must come at the beginning of the phrase. You cannot change its position.

Incorrect: Please <u>look</u> the video monitor <u>at</u>.

Now consider this sentence:

Please <u>turn off</u> the printer.

Turn off is also a two-word verb, but of a different kind. Here *off*, the second word of the two-word verb, does not introduce a prepositional phrase. Therefore, its position in the sentence can vary.

Correct: Please <u>turn</u> the printer <u>off</u>.

The second word of such a verb can either come before or after the object of that verb; moreover, if the object is a pronoun, the two-word verb must be split and the pronoun must come between the two parts.

Correct: Please <u>turn</u> it <u>off</u>.
Incorrect: Please <u>turn off</u> it.

Other examples of two-word verbs in which the second word does not function as a preposition include *take (it) down, put (it) on, let (it) out*, and *make (it) up*. *The Longman Dictionary of American English* lists at the end of each verb entry the two-word verbs that the verb can form and also indicates whether or not the second word is treated as a preposition.

Appendix: The Reading Process

> **Overview**
>
> In this chapter you will learn
> - To approach a reading assignment with your purpose in mind
> - To highlight a reading assignment
> - To annotate a reading assignment
> - To outline a reading assignment
> - To write a response paragraph
> - To edit your work

Reading is essential to all your college courses. To get the most out of your reading, you need to approach the books and articles you read in a practical way, asking yourself what these works can offer you. You also need to be willing to read and reread. Finally, you need to approach assigned readings critically—just as you approach your own writing. (See 1E.)

Reading critically does not mean finding fault with every point and challenging or arguing with every idea, but it does mean wondering, commenting, questioning, and judging. Most of all, it means *not* being a passive recipient of the ideas you read. To benefit from what you read, you should be an active participant in the reading process. Being an active reader involves approaching a reading assignment with specific questions in mind, highlighting the selection, annotating it, and perhaps outlining it—all *before* you are ready to respond in writing to what you have read.

A   APPROACHING A READING ASSIGNMENT

The first step in the reading process—a step that begins even before you begin to read—is asking yourself some questions about your purpose for reading. These questions can help you understand what you hope to get out of what you are reading and how you will use what you get.

QUESTIONS ABOUT YOUR PURPOSE
- Why am I reading?
- How thoroughly must I understand the reading selection?

- Should I focus on the writer's main idea or on the facts, reasons, and examples that support it?
- Will I be expected to discuss the reading selection in class or with my instructor in a conference?
- Will I have to write about the reading selection? If so, will I be expected to respond informally—for example, in a journal entry—or more formally, in an essay?
- Will I be tested on the material?

Keeping these questions in mind, preview the reading selection. When you **preview,** you look at the title, at *italicized* and **boldfaced** words, at headings, and at illustrations (graphs, charts, photographs, and so on). You also read the first sentence of every paragraph and skim the complete opening and closing paragraphs. As you preview, your goal is not to memorize what you are reading but to get a sense of the writer's main point and key supporting ideas. After you have a general understanding of the passage's subject matter and direction, you can go on to read it more carefully.

PRACTICE C-1

The following article arguing against bilingual education is by Barbara Mujica, a professor of Spanish at Georgetown University in Washington, D.C. (The title, "No Comprendo," is Spanish for "I Don't Understand.") Suppose that your assignment is to prepare first to discuss this article in class and later to write a response paragraph in which you express your own views on the issue of bilingual education.

Preview the article, keeping in mind the Questions about Your Purpose (pages 498–499). When you have finished, restate the author's main point, and list her key supporting ideas.

No Comprendo

1   Last spring, my niece phoned me in tears. She was graduating from high school and had to make a decision. An outstanding soccer player, she was offered athletic scholarships by several colleges. So why was she crying?

2   My niece came to the United States from South America as a child. Although she had received good grades in her schools in Miami, she spoke English with a heavy accent and her comprehension and writing skills were deficient. She was afraid that once she

left the Miami environment, she would feel uncomfortable and, worse still, have difficulty keeping up with class work.

Programs that keep foreign-born children in Spanish-language classrooms for years are only part of the problem. During a visit to my niece's former school, I observed that all business, not just teaching, was conducted in Spanish. In the office, secretaries spoke to the administrators and the children in Spanish. Announcements over the public-address system were made in an English so fractured that it was almost incomprehensible.

I asked my niece's mother why, after years in public schools, her daughter had poor English skills. "It's the whole environment," she replied. "All kinds of services are available in Spanish or Spanglish. Sports and after-school activities are conducted in Spanglish. That's what the kids hear on the radio and in the street."

Until recently, immigrants made learning English a priority. But even when they didn't learn English themselves, their children grew up speaking it. Thousands of first-generation Americans still strive to learn English, but others face reduced educational and career opportunities because they have not mastered this basic skill they need to get ahead.

According to the 1990 census, 40 percent of the Hispanics born in the U.S. do not graduate from high school, and the Department of Education says that a lack of proficiency in English is an important factor in the drop-out rate.

People and agencies that favor providing services only in foreign languages want to help people who do not speak English, but they may be doing them a disservice by condemning them to a linguistic ghetto from which they cannot easily escape.

And my niece? She turned down all of her scholarship opportunities, deciding instead to attend a small college in Miami, where she will never have to put her English to the test.

Barbara Mujica

Author's main point
<u>Because Hispanics are not being encouraged to learn English, their opportunities are limited.</u>

Key supporting ideas

1. <u>Author's niece is afraid to accept a scholarship away from Miami.</u>
2. <u>Students are not required to use English.</u>
3. <u>Many services are provided in Spanish.</u>
4. <u>40% of Hispanics don't graduate from high school.</u>

B HIGHLIGHTING A READING ASSIGNMENT

As you read, you should **highlight** the selection. This strategy will help you to understand the writer's main ideas and to make connections between these ideas when you reread. Because time is precious, highlighting should be selective. Remember, at some point in the future, you will be rereading every highlighted word, phrase, and sentence—so highlight only the most important, most useful information.

Not only should your highlighting be selective, it should also be specifically tailored to your needs. When most people think of highlighting, they assume it just means using a colored highlighting pen to illuminate portions of a passage. But actually, the most useful highlighting uses different symbols for different purposes. When you reread—for example, when you prepare to take an exam or to write a paper—these distinctive symbols will convey specific information to you.

Highlighting Symbols

- <u>Underline</u> key ideas—for example, topic sentences.
- Box or circle words or phrases you want to remember.
- Place a check mark (✔) or asterisk (*) next to an important idea.
- Place a double check mark (✔✔) or a double asterisk (**) next to an especially significant idea.
- Draw lines or arrows to connect related ideas.
- Put a question mark (?) beside a word or idea that you don't understand.
- Number the writer's key supporting points or examples.

The number and kind of highlighting symbols you use when you read a passage are up to you. All that matters is that your symbols are clear and easy to remember.

A student's marks on the following passage, an excerpt from a newspaper column by Anna Quindlen, illustrate the advantages of careful highlighting.

> Consider the recent study at the University of Arizona investigating the attitudes of white and black teenage girls toward body image. The attitudes of the white girls were a nightmare. Ninety percent expressed dissatisfaction with their own bodies, and many said they saw dieting as a kind of all-purpose panacea. "I think the reason I would diet would be to gain self-confidence," said one. "I'd feel like it was a way of getting control," said another. And they were curiously united in their description of the perfect girl. She's 5 feet 7 inches, weighs just over 100 pounds, has long legs and flowing hair. The researchers concluded, "The ideal girl was a living manifestation of the Barbie doll."
>
> While white girls described an impossible ideal, black teenagers talked about appearance in terms of style, attitude, pride, and personality. White respondents talked "thin," black ones "shapely." Seventy percent of the black teenagers said they were satisfied with their weight, and there was little emphasis on dieting. "We're all brought up and taught to be realistic about life," said one, "and we don't look at things the way you want them to be. You look at them the way they are."

from Anna Quindlen, "Barbie at 35"

The student who highlighted this passage was preparing to write an essay about eating disorders. She began by underlining and starring Quindlen's main idea. She then boxed the two key terms the passage compares—*white girls* and *black teenagers*—and underlined two phrases that illustrate how the two girls' attitudes differ (*dissatisfaction with their own bodies* and *satisfied with their weight*). Check marks in the margin emphasize the importance of these two phrases, and arrows connect each phrase to the appropriate group of girls.

The student also circled three related terms that characterize white girls' attitudes—*perfect girl, Barbie doll,* and *impossible ideal*—drawing lines to connect them to one another. Finally, she circled the unfamiliar word *panacea,* which she planned to look up in a dictionary, and put a question mark in the margin beside it. This careful highlighting helped her to understand the passage's ideas and follow the writer's train of thought.

PRACTICE C-2

Look again at the highlighted passage by Anna Quindlen about female teenagers and body image (page 502). How would your own highlighting of this passage be similar to or different from the sample student highlighting?

PRACTICE C-3

Reread "No Comprendo" (pages 499–501). As you reread, highlight the article by underlining and starring main ideas, boxing and circling key words, checkmarking important points, and, if you wish, drawing lines and arrows to connect related ideas. Also, circle each unfamiliar word, and put a question mark in the margin beside it.

C ANNOTATING A READING ASSIGNMENT

To be most effective, highlighting should be accompanied by annotating. Annotating a passage involves making notes—of questions, reactions, reminders, ideas for writing or discussion—in the margins or between the lines. Keeping an informal record of ideas as they occur to you can help prepare you for class discussion and provide a useful source of material for writing.

The following questions are designed to guide your responses as you read and make annotations.

QUESTIONS FOR CRITICAL READING

- What is the writer saying? What do I think the writer is suggesting or implying? What makes me think so?
- What is the writer's purpose?
- What audience is the writer addressing?
- Is the writer responding to another writer's ideas?
- What is the writer's main point?
- How does the writer support his or her points? Does the writer use facts, opinions, or a combination of the two?
- Does the writer include enough supporting details and examples?
- What pattern of development does the writer use to arrange his or her ideas? Is this pattern the best choice?

504 · APPENDIXES

- Does the writer seem well informed? Reasonable? Fair?
- What kind of language does the writer use?
- Do I understand the writer's vocabulary?
- Do I understand the writer's ideas?
- Do I agree with the points the writer is making?
- How are the ideas presented in this reading selection like (or unlike) those presented in other selections I've read?

The following passage illustrates the student's annotations as well as her highlighting.

Consider the recent study at the University of Arizona investigating the attitudes of white and black teenage girls toward body image. The attitudes of the white girls were a nightmare. Ninety percent expressed dissatisfaction with their own bodies, and many said they saw dieting as a kind of all-purpose panacea. "I think the reason I would diet would be to gain self-confidence," said one. "I'd feel like it was a way of getting control," said another. And they were curiously united in their description of the perfect girl. She's 5 feet 7 inches, weighs just over 100 pounds, has long legs and flowing hair. The researchers concluded, "The ideal girl was a living manifestation of the Barbie doll."

While white girls described an impossible ideal, black teenagers talked about appearance in terms of style, attitude, pride, and personality. White respondents talked "thin," black ones "shapely." Seventy percent of the black teenagers said they were satisfied with their weight, and there was little emphasis on dieting. "We're all brought up and taught to be realistic about life," said one, "and we don't look at things the way you want them to be. You look at them the way they are."

Annotations:
- = cure-all
- Need for control, perfection. Why? Media? Parents?
- = plastic, unreal, superficial
- "Thin" vs. "shapely"
- Only 30% dissatisfied —vs. 90% of white girls
- overgeneralization?
- vs. Barbie doll (=unrealistic)

With her annotations this student noted the meaning of the word *panacea*, translated the Barbie doll reference and the contrasting statistics into her own words, and recorded questions she intended to explore further. Her notes reflect her attempts to make sense of the passage's ideas so she would be able to respond intelligently and thoughtfully to them in discussion or in writing.

PRACTICE C-4

Reread "No Comprendo" (pages 499–501). As you reread, keep in mind the Questions for Critical Reading (pages 503–504), and annotate the article by writing down your own thoughts and questions in the margins. Note where you agree or disagree with the writer, and briefly explain why. Quickly summarize any points that you think are particularly important. Also, take time to look up any unfamiliar words you have circled and write brief definitions. Think of these annotations as your preparation for discussing the article in class and eventually writing about your responses to it.

PRACTICE C-5

Trade workbooks with another student, and read over his or her highlighting and annotating of "No Comprendo." How are your written responses similar to and different from the other student's? Do your classmate's responses help you see anything new about the article?

D   OUTLINING A READING ASSIGNMENT

One additional technique you can use to help you better understand a passage you are reading is **outlining.** Formal outlines have fairly rigid conventions, and constructing a formal outline can be time consuming. However, an informal outline—more flexible and simpler to construct—is a valuable reading tool that indicates the progression of a writer's ideas and reveals the relationship of one idea to another.

When you make an **informal outline** of a reading selection, use your highlighted and annotated passage as a guide. Begin by writing the passage's main idea across the top of a sheet of paper. (This will remind you of the passage's focus and help keep your outline on track.) At the left margin, write down the most important idea of the first paragraph or section of the passage. Then, indenting a few spaces, list the examples or details that support this idea. As ideas become more specific, indent further, making sure that ideas that have the same degree of importance are indented the same distance from the left margin. Then, repeat the process with the next paragraph or section of the passage. (You do not need to use complete sentences in your informal outline, and you should not be overly concerned with grammar or style.) After you have finished your informal outline, you should be able to see at a glance what the writer's emphasis is—which ideas are more important than others—and how ideas in different sections of a passage are related.

The student who highlighted and annotated the passage by Anna Quindlen (page 504) made the following informal outline to help her understand the ideas in the passage.

```
Main idea: Black and white teenage girls have very
different attitudes about their body images.
    White girls dissatisfied
        * 90% dissatisfied with appearance
        * Dieting = cure-all
            --self-confidence
            --control
        * Ideal = unrealistic
            --tall and thin
            --Barbie doll
    Black girls satisfied
        * 70% satisfied with weight
        * Dieting not important
        * Ideal = realistic
            --shapely
            --not thin
```

PRACTICE C-6

Individually or in a small group, make an informal outline of "No Comprendo" (pages 499–501). Be sure to refer to your highlighting and annotations as you construct your outline. When you have finished, check to make certain your outline indicates the writer's emphasis and the relationships among ideas.

E WRITING A RESPONSE PARAGRAPH

Once you really understand a passage, you will be in a position to write about it. Sometimes you will be asked to write an essay analyzing a writer's ideas or comparing them with another writer's position. At other times, you will be asked to write a **response paragraph** in which you record your informal reactions to the passage.

Because a response paragraph is informal, no special guidelines or rules govern its format or structure. Your goal is simply to think on paper, letting your mind react to the writer's ideas. As in any paragraph, however, you should include a topic sentence, and your ideas (statements and questions) should be written in complete sentences and linked with appropriate transitions. Still, it is all right to include subjective reactions based on your personal opinions, and an informal style is perfectly acceptable.

The student who highlighted, annotated, and outlined the Quindlen passage wrote this response paragraph.

> Why are white and black girls' body images so different? Why do black girls think it's OK to be "shapely" while white girls are obsessed with being thin? Maybe it's because music videos and movies and

```
fashion magazines show so many more white models,
all half-starved with perfect hair and legs. Or
maybe white girls get different messages from their
parents or the guys they date. Do white and black
girls' attitudes about their bodies stay the same
when they get older? And what about male teenagers'
self-images? Do white and black guys have different
body images too?
```

The process of writing this paragraph was very helpful to the student. The questions she asked raised a number of interesting ideas that she could explore in class discussion or in a longer, more formal and more fully developed piece of writing.

PRACTICE C-7

On a separate sheet of paper, write an informal response paragraph expressing your reactions to and thoughts about "No Comprendo" (pages 499–501) and the issue of bilingual education.

Review

- Ask questions about your purpose before you begin to read. (See Section A.)
- Highlight your reading assignment selectively, using symbols suited to your needs and preferences. (See Section B.)
- Annotate your reading assignment to help you understand the writer's ideas. (See Section C.)
- Outline your reading assignment to increase your understanding of the passage. (See Section D.)
- Write a response paragraph that records your informal reactions to the passage. (See Section E.)

D Appendix: Patterns of Essay Development: Readings for Writers

The twenty-seven selections collected in this appendix—eighteen by professional writers and nine by students—will give you interesting material to read, think critically about, react to, discuss, and write about. In addition, these essays illustrate some of the ways you can organize your ideas in your own papers.

As you read through this appendix, you will notice the selections use the same patterns of development that are used to arrange paragraphs: exemplification, narration, description, process, cause and effect, comparison and contrast, classification and division, definition, and argument. These familiar patterns are not your only options for arranging ideas in essays; in fact, many essays combine several patterns of development. Still, the nine patterns illustrated here suggest some useful strategies for organizing material in your own college writing assignments, and understanding how each pattern works will help you choose the most useful organizational strategy for a particular purpose and audience. (See Chapter 3 for information on using these patterns for developing paragraphs.)

Different assignments call for different patterns of development. For instance, if an exam question asks you to compare two systems of government, you can use comparison and contrast. If your chemistry lab manual asks you to explain the stages of a particular chemical reaction, you can use process. If an English composition assignment asks you to tell a story from your childhood, you can use narration. If a section of a research paper on environmental pollution requires that you provide examples of unsafe waste disposal practices, you can use exemplification.

Each section in this appendix defines one pattern of development, gives examples of how to use it in college writing assignments, and provides several options for organizing an essay and a list of useful transitions. The section introduction ends with a student essay illustrating the pattern and a Writing Checklist outlining the process for writing such an essay.

The pattern of development is then illustrated in two essays by professional writers. Each of these essays is preceded by a brief introduction that comments on its key ideas and pattern of development and suggests what to look for as you read. Each also includes marginal annotations to help you understand the writer's ideas. Every essay is followed by four sets of questions, with asterisks identifying those that can be done in collaboration with other students.

- **Reacting to Reading** questions suggest guidelines for highlighting and annotating the essay
- **Reacting to Words** questions focus on the writer's word choice

508

- **Reacting to Ideas** questions encourage you to respond critically to the writer's ideas and perhaps also consider his or her audience or purpose
- **Reacting to the Pattern** questions ask you to consider how ideas are arranged within an essay and how they are connected to one another

Each section ends with Writing Practice suggestions that give you the opportunity to work with a particular pattern of development either on your own or in collaboration with other students.

A EXEMPLIFICATION

Exemplification is one of the most frequently used patterns of development. Anytime you use one or more examples to answer a question or illustrate a general statement, you are using exemplification.

▶ FOCUS ON TOPICS FOR EXEMPLIFICATION ◀

The wording of your assignment may suggest exemplification. For example, it may ask you to *illustrate* or to *give examples*.

Topic/Assignment	Thesis Statement
Should newly arrived international students be taught only in their native languages or in English as well? Support your answer with an example of a case study.	The success of Sofia Marcus, an eight-year-old from the Dominican Republic, in a bilingual third-grade class shows the value of teaching elementary school students in English as well as in their native languages.
Does *Othello* have to end tragically? Illustrate your position with references to specific characters.	Each of the three major characters in *Othello* contributes to the play's tragic ending.
Discuss the worst job you ever had. Give plenty of examples to support your thesis.	My summer job at a fast-food restaurant was my all-time worst because of the endless stream of rude customers, the many boring and repetitious tasks I had to do, and my manager's insensitive treatment of employees.

Sometimes you can support a thesis statement with a single extended example, as in the first example above. More often, however, you use a series of brief examples—perhaps one illustration per paragraph or perhaps several related examples grouped within each paragraph.

Options for Organizing Exemplification Essays		
Extended Example	**One Example per Paragraph**	**Several Related Examples per Paragraph**
¶1 Introduction	¶1 Introduction	¶1 Introduction
¶2 Single example	¶2 First example	¶2 First group of examples
¶3 Same example	¶3 Second example	¶3 Second group of examples
¶4 Same example	¶4 Third example	¶4 Third group of examples
¶5 Conclusion	¶5 Conclusion	¶5 Conclusion

All the examples you select should relate to your thesis, and your essay's topic sentences should make clear just how each example supports the thesis statement. In addition, transitional words and phrases should introduce each example and show the relationships between one example and another.

▶ **FOCUS** ON TRANSITIONS FOR EXEMPLIFICATION ◀

For example,	For instance,	Specifically,
One example	Another example	The next example
In addition,	Also,	Besides,
Moreover,	Furthermore,	The most important example

The following student essay, "Fighting Fire with Fire Safety Education" by Timothy E. Miles, uses a series of examples to illustrate the need to educate children about fire safety. Some paragraphs group several brief examples together; others develop a single example. Notice how Timothy uses clear topic sentences and helpful transitions to introduce his examples and link them to one another.

```
Fighting Fire with Fire Safety Education

         Timothy E. Miles
```

Since young children suffer more fire-related injuries and fatalities than most others do, fire safety education must be introduced at an early age. This can be done both by parents and by local fire departments. Fire safety for children is an ongoing concern, and adults must take the responsibility for educating and protecting them.

What should small children be taught? First, they should understand what matches are and what the consequences of playing with them can be. They should be taught that matches are not toys and that they can cause great damage. Children should also be taught how to avoid contact burns from stove burners, hot liquids, and electrical appliances.

Another essential part of fire safety education for children is learning how to extinguish fires once they have started. Many children are burned by their own clothing. The chance of injury can be prevented if they are taught how to "Stop, Drop, and Roll." One way of teaching this is for the adult to cut out a "flame" from paper and tape it lightly to the child. When the child actually stops, drops, and rolls on the ground, the "flame" will fall off, thereby "extinguishing" the "fire."

Exit drills in the home can also save lives. These drills need to include information such as how to crawl low to escape smoke, how to feel for hot doors, and how to place towels or clothing under doors to stop smoke from coming into a room. (Children should also understand that smoke and fumes, not the fire itself, cause most deaths.) The need for a meeting place where all family members can be accounted for is perhaps the most important thing to emphasize.

Making sure children know the fire department phone number is another way to reduce fire-related injuries and deaths. It is very important that children know the correct number because not all areas have a 911 system. The numbers of all emergency services should be posted near each phone. Children should know how to dial these numbers and should know the address from which they are calling. To practice reporting a fire, a child can use a toy phone, with an adult assuming the role of the operator.

Finally, children should be aware of what firefighters look like in their equipment. Some children, particularly very young ones, are afraid of firefighters because of their unfamiliar appearance. During a visit to any local firehouse, children can meet firefighters who can answer questions and demonstrate and explain their equipment and gear.

Of course, educating children is not enough in itself to ensure fire safety. Parents and other adults must also educate themselves about what to do (and what not to do) if a fire actually occurs. For example, do not hide or go back into a fire for any reason. Have a meeting place where family members can be accounted for. Do not try to put out a fire; instead, have someone notify the fire department immediately. Also, adults should take the responsibility for getting children involved in fire prevention. Many children learn best by example. Handouts, displays, and videotapes are especially helpful. Demonstration and practice of exit drills in the home and of "Stop, Drop, and Roll" are also useful, particularly during special fire hazard periods such as Halloween and Christmas. Participating in drawing escape plans and making inspections of the home for potential problems also make children feel they are helping. In fact, children can sometimes see things that adults overlook.

By keeping these points in mind, children and their parents can join together to avoid potential disaster. If family members learn about fire safety and if they practice and review what they have learned on a regular basis, lives will be saved.

✓ Writing Checklist: Exemplification

- ❏ Be sure you understand your assignment, audience, and purpose for writing.
- ❏ Use invention strategies to find ideas.
- ❏ Develop a tentative thesis statement.
- ❏ Decide which examples to use to support your thesis statement.
- ❏ Do further invention if necessary to find additional examples.
- ❏ Decide how to arrange your examples.
- ❏ Draft your essay.
- ❏ Revise your thesis statement.
- ❏ Add transitions if necessary to clarify the relationships between the examples.
- ❏ Revise topic sentences and transitions to clarify the relationship between the examples and the thesis.
- ❏ Delete any examples that are not clearly related to your thesis.
- ❏ Revise your introduction and conclusion.
- ❏ Revise sentence structure and word choice.
- ❏ Edit and proofread your essay.

APPENDIX D Patterns of Essay Development

English Is a Crazy Language

Richard Lederer

In this chapter from his book Crazy English, *Richard Lederer uses exemplification to support a surprising thesis: "English is a crazy language." Perhaps because the thesis is so unexpected, Lederer uses a great many examples to support his position. As you read, consider why particular examples are grouped together in paragraphs.*

English is the most widely spoken language in the history of our planet, used in some way by at least one out of every seven human beings around the globe. Half of the world's books are written in English, and the majority of international telephone calls are made in English. English is the language of over sixty percent of the world's radio programs, many of them beamed, ironically, by the Russians, who know that to win friends and influence nations, they're best off using English. More than seventy percent of international mail is written and addressed in English, and eighty percent of all computer text is stored in English. English has acquired the largest vocabulary of all the world's languages, perhaps as many as two million words, and has generated one of the noblest bodies of literature in the annals of the human race.

Nonetheless, it is now time to face the fact that English is a crazy language.

In the crazy English language, the blackbird hen is brown, blackboards can be blue or green, and blackberries are green and then red before they are ripe. Even if blackberries were really black and blueberries really blue, what are strawberries, cranberries, elderberries, huckleberries, raspberries, boysenberries, mulberries, and gooseberries supposed to look like?

To add to the insanity, there is no butter in buttermilk, no egg in eggplant, no grape in grapefruit, neither worms nor wood in wormwood, neither pine nor apple in pineapple, neither peas nor nuts in peanuts, and no ham in a hamburger. (In fact, if somebody invented a sandwich consisting of a ham patty in a bun, we would have a hard time finding a name for it.) To make matters worse, English muffins weren't invented in England, french fries in France, or danish pastries in Denmark. And we discover even more culinary madness in the revelations that sweetmeat is candy, while sweetbread, which isn't sweet, is made from meat.

In this unreliable English tongue, greyhounds aren't always grey (or gray); panda bears and koala bears aren't bears (they're marsupials); a woodchuck is a groundhog, which is not a hog; a horned toad is a lizard; glowworms are fireflies, but fireflies are not flies (they're beetles); ladybugs and lightning bugs are also beetles (and to propagate, a significant proportion of ladybugs must be male); a guinea pig is neither a pig nor from Guinea (it's a South American rodent); and a titmouse is neither mammal nor mammaried.

1 *Introduction*

2 *Thesis statement*
3 *Each body paragraph (3–13) groups related examples*

4

5

Language is like the air we breathe. It's invisible, inescapable, indispensable, and we take it for granted. But when we take the time, step back, and listen to the sounds that escape from the holes in people's faces and explore the paradoxes and vagaries of English, we find that hot dogs can be cold, darkrooms can be lit, homework can be done in school, nightmares can take place in broad daylight, while morning sickness and daydreaming can take place at night, tomboys are girls, midwives can be men, hours—especially happy hours and rush hours—can last longer than sixty minutes, quicksand works *very* slowly, boxing rings are square, silverware can be made of plastic and tablecloths of paper, most telephones are dialed by being punched (or pushed?), and most bathrooms don't have any baths in them. In fact, a dog can go to the bathroom under a tree—no bath, no room; it's still going to the bathroom. And doesn't it seem at least a little bizarre that we go to the bathroom in order to go to the bathroom?

Why is it that a woman can man a station but a man can't woman one, that a man can father a movement but a woman can't mother one, and that a king rules a kingdom but a queen doesn't rule a queendom? How did all those Renaissance men reproduce when there don't seem to have been any Renaissance women?

A writer is someone who writes, and a stinger is something that stings. But fingers don't fing, grocers don't groce, hammers don't ham, and humdingers don't humding. If the plural of *tooth* is *teeth*, shouldn't the plural of *booth* be *beeth*? One goose, two geese—so one moose, two meese? One index, two indices—one Kleenex, two Kleenices? If people ring a bell today and rang a bell yesterday, why don't we say that they flang a ball? If they wrote a letter, perhaps they also bote their tongue. If the teacher taught, why isn't it also true that the preacher praught? Why is it that the sun shone yesterday while I shined my shoes, that I treaded water and then trod on soil, and that I flew out to see a World Series game in which my favorite player flied out?

If we conceive a conception and receive at a reception, why don't we grieve a greption and believe a beleption? If a horsehair mat is made from the hair of horses and a camel's hair brush from the hair of camels, from what is a mohair coat made? If a vegetarian eats vegetables, what does a humanitarian eat? If a firefighter fights fire, what does a freedom fighter fight? If a weightlifter lifts weights, what does a shoplifter lift? If *pro* and *con* are opposites, is congress the opposite of progress?

Sometimes you have to believe that all English speakers should be committed to an asylum for the verbally insane. In what other language do people drive in a parkway and park in a driveway? In what other language do people recite at a play and play at a recital? In what other language do privates eat in the general mess and generals eat in the private mess? In what other language do men get hernias and women get hysterectomies? In what other language do people ship by truck and send cargo by ship? In what other language can your nose run and your feet smell?

How can a slim chance and a fat chance be the same, "what's going on?" and "what's coming off?" be the same, and a bad licking and a good licking be the same, while a wise man and a wise guy are opposites? How can sharp speech and blunt speech be the same and *quite a lot* and *quite a few* the same, while *overlook* and *oversee* are opposites? How can the weather be hot as hell one day and cold as hell the next?

If *button* and *unbutton* and *tie* and *untie* are opposites, why are *loosen* and *unloosen* and *ravel* and *unravel* the same? If *bad* is the opposite of *good*, *hard* the opposite of *soft*, and *up* the opposite of *down*, why are *badly* and *goodly*, *hardly* and *softly*, and *upright* and *downright* not opposing pairs? If harmless actions are the opposite of harmful actions, why are shameless and shameful behavior the same and pricey objects less expensive than priceless ones? If appropriate and inappropriate remarks and passable and impassable mountain trails are opposites, why are flammable and inflammable materials, heritable and inheritable property, and passive and impassive people the same and valuable objects less treasured than invaluable ones? If *uplift* is the same as *lift up*, why are *upset* and *set up* opposite in meaning? Why are *pertinent* and *impertinent*, *canny* and *uncanny*, and *famous* and *infamous* neither opposites nor the same? How can *raise* and *raze* and *reckless* and *wreckless* be opposites when each pair contains the same sound?

Why is it that when the sun or the moon or the stars are out, they are visible, but when the lights are out, they are invisible, and that when I wind up my watch, I start it, but when I wind up this essay, I shall end it?

English is a crazy language.   *Conclusion restates thesis*

Reacting to Reading

1. Preview the essay. Then, read it more carefully, highlighting and annotating as you read.
2. In paragraphs 3 through 13, related examples are grouped together. Annotate several of these paragraphs with descriptive labels that explain why the examples are clustered together. (For instance, the label for paragraph 4 could be *Words for foods*.)

Reacting to Words

*1. Define each of these words: *annals* (1), *culinary* (4), *mammaried* (5), *paradoxes* (6), and *vagaries* (6). Can you suggest a synonym for each word that will work in the essay?
2. Lederer calls English "crazy." What other unexpectedly negative words does he use to characterize the language? What is your reaction to this language?

Reacting to Ideas

1. Do you think English is really as "crazy" as Lederer suggests it is? Can you think of additional examples to support his thesis?

2. Do you think Lederer is trying to make a serious point, or do you think he is just trying to entertain his readers?

Reacting to the Pattern

*1. Chart the exemplification pattern of this essay. Use the chart on page 510 to guide you.
2. Like the body paragraphs, the essay's introductory paragraph also contains a series of examples. What point do all these examples make?

Writing Practice

1. If you speak or have studied a language other than English, write an essay with this thesis: "[Spanish, Korean, or whatever] is [or is not] a crazy language."
*2. Read (or reread) Chapter 25 of this text. Then, write an essay with the thesis "English spelling is completely illogical."
3. Write an exemplification essay in which you use a wide variety of examples to support the thesis "———— is a crazy city."

The Suspected Shopper

Ellen Goodman

Journalist Ellen Goodman wrote "The Suspected Shopper" in 1981 for her syndicated newspaper column. Note that although Goodman develops a single extended example of a "suspected shopper"—herself—throughout her essay, she supports her thesis with a number of specific examples of incidents in which she was suspected. As you read, consider whether the essay is still relevant to readers today—or whether it is perhaps even more relevant.

It is Saturday, Shopping Saturday, as it's called by the merchants who spread their wares like plush welcome mats across the pages of my newspaper. 1

But the real market I discover is a different, less eager place than the one I read about. On this Shopping Saturday I don't find welcomes, I find warnings and wariness. 2

Introductory examples (paragraphs 3–6)

At the first store, a bold sign of the times confronts me: SHOPLIFTERS WILL BE PROSECUTED TO THE FULL EXTENT OF THE LAW. 3

At the second store, instead of a greeter, I find a doorkeeper. It is his job, his duty, to bar my entrance. To pass, I must give up the shopping bag on my arm. I check it in and check it out. 4

At the third store, I venture as far as the dressing room. Here I meet another worker paid to protect the merchandise rather than to sell 5 it. The guard of this dressing room counts the number of items I carry in and will count the number of items I carry out.

In the mirror, a long, white, plastic security tag juts out from the blouse tucked into the skirt. I try futilely to pat it down along my left hip, try futilely to zip the skirt.

Finally, during these strange gyrations, a thought seeps through years of dulled consciousness, layers of denial. Something has happened to the relationship between shops and shoppers. I no longer feel like a woman in search of a shirt. I feel like an enemy at Checkpoint Charlie.[1]

I finally, belatedly, realize that I am treated less like a customer these days and more like a criminal. And I hate it. This change happened gradually, and understandably. Security rose in tandem with theft. The defenses of the shopkeepers went up, step by step, with the offenses of the thieves.

But now as the weapons escalate, it's the average consumer, the innocent bystander, who is hit by friendly fire.

I don't remember the first time an errant security tag buzzed at the doorway, the first time I saw a camera eye in a dress department. I accepted it as part of the price of living in a tight honesty market.

In the supermarket, they began to insist on a mug shot before they would cash my check. I tried not to take it personally. At the drugstore, the cashier began to staple my bags closed. And I tried not to take it personally.

Now, these experiences have accumulated until I feel routinely treated like a suspect. At the jewelry store, the door is unlocked only for those who pass judgment. In the junior department, the suede pants are permanently attached to the hangers. In the gift shop, the cases are only opened with a key.

I am not surprised anymore, but I am finally aware of just how unpleasant it is to be dealt with as guilty until we prove our innocence. Anyplace we are not known, we are not trusted. The old slogan, "Let the Consumer Beware," has been replaced with a new slogan: "Beware of the Consumer."

It is no fun to be Belgium[2] in the war between sales and security. Thievery has changed the atmosphere of the marketplace. Merchant distrust has spread through the ventilation system of a whole business, a whole city, and it infects all of us.

At the cashier counter today, with my shirt in hand, I the Accused stand quietly while the saleswoman takes my credit card. I watch her round up the usual suspicions. In front of my face, without a hint of embarrassment, she checks my charge number against the list of stolen credit vehicles. While I stand there, she calls the clearinghouse of bad debtors.

---
[1] A military security checkpoint.
[2] Country located between France and Germany, enemies in several wars.

Having passed both tests, I am instructed to add my name, address, serial number to the bottom of the charge. She checks one signature against another, the picture against the person. Only then does she release the shirt into my custody. 16

And so this Shopping Saturday I take home six ounces of silk and a load of resentment. 17

Reacting to Reading

1. Preview the essay. Then, read it more carefully, and do whatever highlighting and annotating is necessary to help you understand the writer's ideas.
2. Reread the essay, and review your highlighting and annotations. Then, in the margins of the essay, try to supplement Goodman's examples with one or two examples from your personal experience that support her thesis.

Reacting to Words

*1. Define each of these words: *futilely* (6), *gyrations* (7), *belatedly* (8), *tandem* (8), and *errant* (10). Can you suggest a synonym for each word that will work in the essay?
2. What is Goodman's purpose for choosing words like *mug shot* (11) and *enemy* (7)? How do they help to support her thesis? Can you find additional words or expressions that serve the same purpose?

Reacting to Ideas

*1. Goodman, a middle-class, middle-aged white woman, uses *we* in the sentence "Anyplace we are not known, we are not trusted" (13). Who is this *we*? Do you think Goodman is really part of the group with which she identifies?
2. In paragraph 8 Goodman says the change in attitude she observes is understandable. Do you think she is right?
3. Do you think shoplifting is more or less of a problem today than it was in 1981 when Goodman wrote her essay? What makes you think so?

Reacting to the Pattern

1. List the specific examples of times when Goodman was "treated less like a customer . . . and more like a criminal" (8).
2. How does Goodman arrange the specific examples that support her thesis? Is each discussed in an individual paragraph, or are examples grouped together?
3. Goodman introduces a number of her examples even before she states her thesis. Why do you think she does this?

Writing Practice

1. Have you ever been suspected of shoplifting? Write an exemplification essay in which you use your experience to support a thesis.
*2. Why do you think people shoplift? Write an exemplification essay in which you illustrate a different reason in each body paragraph.
3. What do you think merchants can do to reduce shoplifting without making shoppers feel like criminals? Using exemplification to organize your ideas, write a letter to a store you patronize regularly.
4. Have you ever felt like Belgium, caught between peer pressure and your own sense of right and wrong? Develop an extended example that illustrates what it was like to be caught in the middle and explains how you resolved the problem.

B NARRATION

Narration tells a story, generally presenting a series of events in chronological (time) order, moving from beginning to end.

▶ FOCUS ON TOPICS FOR NARRATION ◀

Sometimes your assignment may suggest narration. For example, it may ask you to *tell, trace, summarize,* or *recount*.

Topic/Assignment	Thesis Statement
Tell about a time when you had to show courage even though you were afraid.	Sometimes a person can exhibit great courage despite being afraid.
Summarize the events that occurred during Franklin Delano Roosevelt's first one hundred days in office.	Although many thought they were extreme, the series of measures enacted by Roosevelt during his first one hundred days in office were necessary to fight the effects of the economic depression.
Trace the development of the Mississippi Freedom Democratic Party.	As the Mississippi Freedom Democratic Party developed, it found a voice that spoke for equality and justice.

520 ▪ APPENDIXES

When you write a narrative essay, you can present one event or several in each paragraph of your essay.

Options for Organizing Narrative Essays	
One Event per Paragraph	**Several Events per Paragraph**
¶1 Introduction	¶1 Introduction
¶2 First event	¶2 First group of events
¶3 Second event	¶3 Second group of events
¶4 Third event	¶4 Third group of events
¶5 Conclusion	¶5 Conclusion

To add interest to your narrative, you may sometimes choose not to use exact chronological order. For example, you can begin with the end of your story and then move back to the beginning to trace the events that led to this outcome. Carefully worded topic sentences and clear transitional words and expressions will help readers to follow your narrative.

▶ **FOCUS** ON TRANSITIONS FOR NARRATION ◀

First. . . second. . . third	Then,	Later,
Now,	Meanwhile,	At the same time,
After that,	Next,	Immediately,
Soon,	As soon as	Earlier,
Before	Two days later,	In 1975,
Finally,		

The following student essay, "Swing Shift" by Mark Cotharn, is a narrative that relates the events of a day in the life of a police officer. Notice that Mark uses present tense to make his dramatic, emotional story more immediate. (Paragraph 3, which moves back in time to summarize events that occurred earlier in the week, uses past tense.) Transitional words and phrases like *after a short briefing* and *within minutes* help link events in chronological order. The mention of specific days and times (as in "Monday it was the guy . . ." or "It's three o'clock in the morning . . .") also helps keep readers on track.

```
             Swing Shift

            Mark Cotharn
```

1   I'm home, safe within familiar walls. Surrounded by my wife and children, I sit at my kitchen table drinking a cold beer, trying to wake up.

2   Today is Thursday, and I've got to pull myself together long enough for one more shift. It's eleven o'clock in the morning, and I've got one hour to prepare mentally for work. This was such a crazy week, I'm not sure if I can.

3   Monday it was the guy on Weeping Willow who was cut up like a side of beef by two parolees. Later on that evening, there was that seventeen-year-old boy who was stabbed to death by his friend. Tuesday brought a father angry at me for giving his kid a citation. The kid didn't tell his old man I threw a bag of dope away, to give him a second chance. Wednesday was the triple gangland execution on Holley. I will never forget the way Teto Gomez looked with most of his head gone and the way his brains decorated the yellow rose bush. But, the worst part of that case was doing CPR on Robert Berassa, who had been shot fourteen times. He was wearing a white T-shirt that was turning crimson. Every time I compressed on his chest, my shirt turned crimson, too. It was too late; Robert was dead.

4   I finish my beer and make my way to the station. Only God can know what the day's events will bring, but I really hope it won't be much.

5   After a short briefing, I begin my shift on patrol. Within minutes, I find myself in pursuit of an armed robbery suspect carrying several handguns and some dynamite. I chase him through the city for almost twelve minutes, at speeds exceeding a hundred miles per hour, before his van quits running and comes to a stop.

6   I stop my unit behind his van. With shotgun in hand, I make my way to approximately twenty feet away from his door. I repeat commands for him to put his hands up, but he won't listen to me. Instead, he opens his door and charges me. I see that he has something in his hand, but I can't tell what it is. I hear two loud booms. The suspect falls to the ground in a pool of blood. Confused, I feel the rotorwash of a helicopter twenty feet over my head and hear the wail of approaching police cars. Still, I don't understand why the

suspect dropped so suddenly until I see smoke rising from the barrel of my shotgun. The suspect is dead, clutching a stick of dynamite.

Unable to let go of my professionalism in public, I detach myself from all emotions or feelings. Many fellow officers come to me and call me Stud, Killer, Ice Man, Exterminator; others come to me and congratulate me on a job well done. 7

Heading back to the station, I turn off the radio and listen to the silence of my thoughts; I know when I get there I will be read my rights and interviewed like a common crook. What did I do wrong? 8

As I expected, I'm met at the door by a shooting team from Internal Affairs. These guys are serious about their job. If the team can find a reason to convict me, they will. The interrogation is lengthy; I'm exhausted. Twelve hours or so have gone by, and the questions are still coming. I recognize the interrogation technique because it's the same one I use. 9

It's three o'clock in the morning. The shooting team is done with me, and I'm headed out the door for home when my chief tells me to go upstairs and talk to the department shrink. Why? I don't need a shrink; I need sleep. 10

The shrink is asking me stupid questions like "How do you feel?" and "Are you going to be OK?" What am I supposed to say? "No"? I tell her I'm just fine, and I'll be back to work in two days. 11

On my way home, alone in my car, I come to. My palms sweat; my chest constricts; my pulse hammers. My mind races back to the intersection of Citrus and Arrow. I can see his face; he's laughing at me. I hear two crisp booms and see him fall. 12

☑ Writing Checklist: Narration

❑ Be sure you understand your assignment, audience, and purpose for writing.
❑ Use invention strategies to find ideas.
❑ Develop a tentative thesis statement that focuses on the incident you will discuss.
❑ Decide which events to include.
❑ Decide how to arrange the events.
❑ Draft your essay.
❑ Revise your thesis statement.
❑ Revise your introduction, making sure it sets the scene, introduces your characters, and states your thesis.
❑ Revise your conclusion.
❑ Add transitions if necessary to clarify the sequence of events.
❑ Revise topic sentences to connect events to the thesis statement.
❑ Delete any events that are not clearly related to your thesis.
❑ Decide whether you need to add dialogue or descriptive detail to make your narrative more interesting.

- ❏ Revise sentence structure and word choice.
- ❏ Edit and proofread your essay.

Falling into Place

Jaime O'Neill

This 1994 essay was written for the New York Times *"About Men" column. In it, Jaime O'Neill, a college English instructor, tells of an experience he had in 1957, when he was thirteen years old and tried in vain to impress a girl. Together, the events support O'Neill's thesis, implied in his essay's last three brief paragraphs, that despite "pain and humiliation," no man (and certainly no adolescent boy) ever really learns that it's pointless to try to impress members of the opposite sex with foolish behavior. As you read, notice how O'Neill uses dialogue to make his story come alive for readers.*

It is 1957 and I am up a tree. Though afraid of heights, I have taken to climbing the trees in the palmetto and mangrove swamp that spreads out from the little clearing where our house sits. *First four paragraphs set the scene*

I cannot now remember what compelled me to climb trees when I was 13 years old, why I both liked and hated the twinge of fear as I scaled my way higher and higher, or what satisfactions might have settled over me when I found a niche between the branches where I could nest, more secure, and survey the swamp from that height. All that returns to me now is the way the breeze blew up there, stirring the leaves, not at all like the breeze on the ground.

The tree I am in towers over a hole, a gash in the sandy Florida soil, six or eight feet deep, packed hard, damp at the bottom. The swamp is slowly being cleared for development; the backhoes and the big Cats have been scraping away the tenacious vegetation, making way for homes. Soon we will have neighbors.

I am thinking about girls. If I thought of other things when I was 13, I can no longer imagine what those things might have been. It is, then, no wonder that I notice two girls who pass under my tree on that warm and humid afternoon, two girls from my class taking a shortcut home through the swamp.

I hear them before I see them; I see them before I know who they are. They are talking and keeping their eyes tight on the ground for fear of snakes, and they don't notice me. As they draw nearer, I know the pleasure of the spy, the Indian scout, the unseen watcher in hidden places. Perhaps I will overhear them saying wonderful things—"this cute boy in class, he just drives me wild"—and it will turn out to be me they are talking about. *Narrative begins in paragraph 5*

No such luck. Still, it is good that they come by. Courage is much better when it has a female audience, and it has taken some courage for me to have climbed so high.

Had I been another kind of boy, I might have let them pass, but the "look at me" impulse is insistent, and one of the girls is exquisite, sporting breasts already like cupcakes under her thin cotton blouse. Perhaps if she sees me up in this tree, a strange and solitary boy, friend of trees, neighbor of sky, mysterious creature of the swamps, she will love me at these heights—love me, and invite me to climb down.

"Hi," I call out. The two of them stop in their tracks, uncertain of where the voice is coming from. I like it that they have to search the trees to find me.

Dialogue adds interest and makes the characters individuals

"What are you," asks the one who is not cute, "some kind of monkey?"

"Tarzan, more like," I say, and I stand upright on my branch and beat my chest with one hand while holding tight to a limb with my other.

"You're going to fall and hurt yourself," the cute girl says. I am further smitten by her concern for me. Smitten, and imperiled. What is it in the male psyche that takes such words as encouragement toward further reckless self-endangerment?

"Nah," I say, and I step carelessly to another branch, "there's nothing to this." I release my steadying grip on the limb and stand barehanded. "See."

What I hope they can't see is that my knees are going a little wobbly with fear.

The not-cute girl shades her eyes, peering up at me. "Well," she says, "why don't you jump if you're so brave?"

I feign interest in her suggestion, survey the depression in the earth below, gauge the distance.

"You think I'm crazy," I say. "It's probably 100 feet down from here." Though this is surely a gross exaggeration, the actual distance is very great.

"Well, what are you, anyway," the girl calls back to me, "some kind of chicken?"

Today, some 35 years later, I am an English teacher, one who routinely tries to convince students of the power of words. There are few words more powerful to an adolescent boy than the word "chicken." For all practical purposes, brain function ceases, superseded by gonadal override.

Still, the chicken side of me, the side I wanted to keep secret, might have protected me from harm if the word had come from the not-cute girl alone. If she wanted to think me chicken, I could live with that.

What I could not live with was when the cute girl echoed the challenge.

"Yeah," she says, "what are you, chicken?"

Climax of story

And so I jump. I cover my eyes with one hand, step purposefully off the branch and plummet like a spear to the hard-packed sand and dirt at the bottom of the Cat-scratched hole. I strike on my heels, fold up like an imploded building. It is as though every molecule of oxygen has been driven out my ears, out my nose, out the very pores of my scalp. In the pit, I cannot move. I gasp raspily, like an old man. The sound scares me; I have never made such a noise before.

Do the girls rush down into the pit, tend to me, beg me to forgive them for their thoughtless challenge? In your dreams, they do. Mine, too.

What they do is laugh and leave. A life lesson.

I will live to know this experience again—the laughing and the leaving—because I am not, as I first suspect, killed.

What I am is unable to move. Faintly, from our house, I can hear the radio playing. I try to call out, but the sound that escapes me is unintelligible and weak, no match for the radio.

Around dusk, I hear my Mom calling me for supper. Then, a while later, I hear movement in the brush and my brother's voice. I groan. He finds me, helps me up.

We hide it all from Mom, of course. My heels are bruised, and for a few days it hurts to stand straight.

Did I learn the life lesson, a lesson gained in pain and humiliation? *Implied thesis*

Hardly.

What man ever really does?

Reacting to Reading

1. Preview the essay. Then, read it more carefully, and do whatever highlighting and annotating is necessary to help you understand the writer's ideas.
2. Underline two or three of O'Neill's statements that you believe are open to question, and write a question in the margin that challenges one of these statements.

Reacting to Words

*1. Define each of these words: *niche* (2), *tenacious* (3), *smitten* (11), *imperiled* (11), *feign* (15), *superseded* (18), *gonadal* (18), *plummet* (22), and *unintelligible* (26). Can you suggest a synonym for each word that will work in the essay?
2. Even though the story he tells occurred in the past, O'Neill uses the present tense to tell what happened. Choose one paragraph, and substitute a past-tense verb for every present-tense verb. Which version do you prefer? Why?

Reacting to Ideas

1. How do you respond to these two statements: "Courage is much better when it has a female audience" (6) and "There are few words more powerful to an adolescent boy than the word 'chicken.'"(18)? Do you think O'Neill's statements are accurate? Do you think they are sexist?
*2. Throughout this essay, O'Neill makes a distinction between the "cute girl" and the "not-cute girl." What is your reaction to this distinction?

3. In paragraph 7 O'Neill says, "Had I been another kind of boy, I might have let them pass. . . ." What do you think he means? What "kind of boy" is he?

Reacting to the Pattern

*1. List the events O'Neill recounts in the order in which he introduces them. Does he follow strict chronological order from beginning to end, or does he move back and forth in time?
2. Paragraph 22 begins with a transitional expression—"And so I jump"—that introduces the story's key event and connects it to previous events. What other transitional words and expressions does O'Neill use to connect events?

Writing Practice

1. Write a narrative essay about a time when you tried unsuccessfully to impress a member of the opposite sex. Your essay can be serious or humorous.
2. Write a narrative essay about a time when you took an unnecessary—and foolish—risk. In your introduction or conclusion, explain what you should have done differently.
3. Write about an incident in which you observed an act of physical courage. Did those who witnessed the act encourage (or discourage) it in any way?

38 Who Saw Murder Didn't Call the Police

Martin Gansberg

This newspaper article recounts in objective language an incident that occurred in New York City over thirty years ago. As Gansberg reconstructs the crime two weeks after it happened, he gives readers a detailed picture of the sequence of events that led up to a young woman's murder—in full view of thirty-eight of her "respectable, law-abiding" neighbors. As you read, consider how you might have acted if you had been a witness to this tragedy.

Introduction summarizes the events (paragraphs 1–3)

1   For more than half an hour 38 respectable, law-abiding citizens in Queens watched a killer stalk and stab a woman in three separate attacks in Kew Gardens.

2   Twice their chatter and the sudden glow of their bedroom lights interrupted him and frightened him off. Each time he returned, sought her out, and stabbed her again. Not one person telephoned the police during the assault; one witness called after the woman was dead.

That was two weeks ago today.

Still shocked is Assistant Chief Inspector Frederick M. Lussen, in charge of the borough's detectives and a veteran of 25 years of homicide investigations. He can give a matter-of-fact recitation on many murders. But the Kew Gardens slaying baffles him—not because it is a murder, but because the "good people" failed to call the police. *Thesis statement*

"As we have reconstructed the crime," he said, "the assailant had three chances to kill this woman during a 35-minute period. He returned twice to complete the job. If we had been called when he first attacked, the woman might not be dead now."

This is what the police say happened beginning at 3:20 A.M. in the staid, middle-class, tree-lined Austin Street area: *Narrative begins*

Twenty-eight-year-old Catherine Genovese, who was called Kitty by almost everyone in the neighborhood, was returning home from her job as manager of a bar in Hollis. She parked her red Fiat in a lot adjacent to the Kew Gardens Long Island Rail Road Station, facing Mowbray Place. Like many residents of the neighborhood, she had parked there day after day since her arrival from Connecticut a year ago, although the railroad frowns on the practice.

She turned off the lights of her car, locked the door, and started to walk the 100 feet to the entrance of her apartment at 82–70 Austin Street, which is in a Tudor building, with stores in the first floor and apartments on the second.

The entrance to the apartment is in the rear of the building because the front is rented to retail stores. At night the quiet neighborhood is shrouded in the slumbering darkness that marks most residential areas.

Miss Genovese noticed a man at the far end of the lot, near a seven-story apartment house at 82–40 Austin Street. She halted. Then, nervously, she headed up Austin Street toward Lefferts Boulevard, where there is a call box to the 102nd Police Precinct in nearby Richmond Hill.

She got as far as a street light in front of a bookstore before the man grabbed her. She screamed. Lights went on in the 10-story apartment house at 82–67 Austin Street, which faces the bookstore. Windows slid open and voices punctuated the early-morning stillness.

Miss Genovese screamed: "Oh, my God, he stabbed me! Please help me! Please help me!"

From one of the upper windows in the apartment house, a man called down: "Let that girl alone!"

The assailant looked up at him, shrugged, and walked down Austin Street toward a white sedan parked a short distance away. Miss Genovese struggled to her feet.

Lights went out. The killer returned to Miss Genovese, now trying to make her way around the side of the building by the parking lot to get to her apartment. The assailant stabbed her again.

"I'm dying!" she shrieked. "I'm dying!"

Windows were opened again, and lights went on in many apartments. The assailant got into his car and drove away. Miss Genovese staggered to her feet. A city bus, O-10, the Lefferts Boulevard line to Kennedy International Airport, passed. It was 3:35 A.M.

The assailant returned. By then, Miss Genovese had crawled to the back of the building, where the freshly painted brown doors to the apartment house held out hope for safety. The killer tried the first door; she wasn't there. At the second door, 82–62 Austin Street, he saw her slumped on the floor at the foot of the stairs. He stabbed her a third time—fatally.

It was 3:50 by the time the police received their first call, from a man who was a neighbor of Miss Genovese. In two minutes they were at the scene. The neighbor, a 70-year-old woman, and another woman were the only persons on the street. Nobody else came forward.

The man explained that he had called the police after much deliberation. He had phoned a friend in Nassau County for advice and then he had crossed the roof of the building to the apartment of the elderly woman to get her to make the call.

"I didn't want to get involved," he sheepishly told police.

Narrative jumps forward in time to describe the aftermath of the incident

Six days later, the police arrested Winston Moseley, a 29-year-old business machine operator, and charged him with homicide. Moseley had no previous record. He is married, has two children and owns a home at 133–19 Sutter Avenue, South Ozone Park, Queens. On Wednesday, a court committed him to Kings County Hospital for psychiatric observation.

When questioned by the police, Moseley also said that he had slain Mrs. Annie May Johnson, 24, of 146–12 133d Avenue, Jamaica, on Feb. 29 and Barbara Kralik, 15, of 174–17 140th Avenue, Springfield Gardens, last July. In the Kralik case, the police are holding Alvin L. Mitchell, who is said to have confessed to that slaying.

The police stressed how simple it would have been to have gotten in touch with them. "A phone call," said one of the detectives, "would have done it." The police may be reached by dialing "O" for operator or SPring 7–3100.

Today witnesses from the neighborhood, which is made up of one-family homes in the $35,000 to $60,000 range with the exception of the two apartment houses near the railroad station, find it difficult to explain why they didn't call the police.

A housewife, knowingly if quite casually, said, "We thought it was a lovers' quarrel." A husband and wife both said, "Frankly, we were afraid." They seemed aware of the fact that events might have been different. A distraught woman, wiping her hands in her apron, said, "I didn't want my husband to get involved."

One couple, now willing to talk about that night, said they heard the first screams. The husband looked thoughtfully at the bookstore where the killer first grabbed Miss Genovese.

"We went to the window to see what was happening," he said, "but the light from our bedroom made it difficult to see the street." The wife, still apprehensive, added: "I put out the light and we were able to see better."

Asked why they hadn't called the police, she shrugged and replied: "I don't know."

A man peeked out from a slight opening in the doorway to his apartment and rattled off an account of the killer's second attack. Why hadn't he called the police at the time? "I was tired," he said without emotion. "I went back to bed."

It was 4:25 A.M. when the ambulance arrived to take the body of Miss Genovese. It drove off. "Then," a solemn police detective said, "the people came out."

Conclusion returns to the day of the fatal incident

Reacting to Reading

1. Preview the essay. Then, read it more carefully, and do whatever highlighting and annotating is necessary to help you understand the writer's ideas.
2. Place a check mark beside each passage of dialogue Gansberg uses. Then, add brief marginal annotations next to three of these quotations, explaining why reproducing the exact words is more effective in each case than just summarizing what was said.

Reacting to Words

*1. Define each of these words: *staid* (6) and *shrouded* (9). Can you suggest a synonym for each word that will work in the essay?
2. What is Gansberg's purpose in using terms like *respectable* (1), *law-abiding* (1), and *good people* (4)? What is your reaction to these words?

Reacting to Ideas

*1. Suppose this essay were written today. How do you think the neighbors would react if the setting and events were the same? What might be different about the situation?
2. What reasons do the witnesses give for not coming to Kitty Genovese's aid? Why do *you* think no one helped her? Do you think the witnesses should be held accountable for their lack of action?

Reacting to the Pattern

1. What other patterns could Gansberg have used to develop his essay? For instance, could he have used comparison and contrast or exemplification? Given the alternatives, do you think narration is the best choice? Why or why not?
*2. Gansberg uses many transitional words and phrases, including references to specific times, to move readers from one event to the next. List as many of these transitions as you can, and note any you believe should be added.

Writing Practice

1. Write a narrative essay about a time when you were a witness who chose not to become involved in events you were observing.

2. Find a brief newspaper article that tells a story about a similar incident in which bystanders witnessed a crime. Expand the article into a longer essay, inventing characters, dialogue, and additional details.
3. Retell Kitty Genovese's story—but this time, have one of the witnesses come to her rescue.

C DESCRIPTION

Description tells what something looks like, sounds like, smells like, tastes like, or feels like.

> ### ▶ FOCUS ON TOPICS FOR DESCRIPTION ◀
>
> Sometimes your assignment suggests description. For example, it may ask you to *describe* or to tell what an object looks like.
>
> | Topic/Assignment | Thesis Statement |
> |---|---|
> | Describe a room that was important to you when you were a child. | Pink-and-white striped wallpaper, tall shelves of cuddly stuffed animals, and the smell of Oreos dominated the bedroom I shared with my sister. |
> | Describe a piece of scientific equipment. | The mass spectrometer is a complex instrument, but every part is ideally suited to its purpose. |
> | Choose one modern painting, and describe its visual elements. | Picasso's *Guernica* is a crowded arrangement of seemingly random images that suggest the senselessness of war. |

When you plan a descriptive essay, your focus should be on selecting details that help your readers see what you see. Your goal is to create a single **dominant impression**, a central theme or idea to which all the details relate. This dominant impression unifies the description so that readers have an overall sense of the person, object, or scene in terms of what it looks like (and, sometimes, what it sounds like, smells like, tastes like, or feels like). Sometimes—but not always—your details will support a thesis, making a point about the subject you are describing.

You can arrange details in many different ways. For example, you can move from least to most important detail (or vice versa). You can also move from top to bottom (or from bottom to top or side to side)—or from far to near (or near to far). Individual paragraphs within your essay may focus on one key characteristic or on several related descriptive details.

Options for Organizing Descriptive Essays		
Order of Importance	Top to Bottom	Far to Near
¶1 Introduction	¶1 Introduction	¶1 Introduction
¶2 Least important details	¶2 Details at top	¶2 Details in distance
¶3 More important details	¶3 Details in middle	¶3 Closer details
¶4 Most important characteristics	¶4 Details on bottom	¶4 Closest details
¶5 Conclusion	¶5 Conclusion	¶5 Conclusion

When you describe a person, object, or scene, you can use **objective description**, reporting only what your senses of sight, sound, smell, taste, and touch tell you ("The columns were two feet tall and made of white porcelain"). You can also use **subjective description**, conveying your attitude or your feelings about what you observe ("The columns were tall and powerful looking, and their porcelain surface seemed as smooth as ice"). Many essays combine the two kinds of description.

Descriptive writing, particularly subjective description, frequently uses **figures of speech**, imaginative comparisons that enrich language by discovering unexpected associations between dissimilar subjects.

- A **simile** uses *like* or *as* to compare two unlike things: Her smile was like sunshine.
- A **metaphor** compares two unlike things without using *like* or *as:* "The fog comes / on little cat feet." (Carl Sandburg)
- **Personification** suggests a comparison between a nonliving thing and a person by giving the nonliving thing human traits: The wind howled angrily.

As you write your descriptions, you should use transitional words and expressions that keep readers on track as you move from one part of your description to another. (Many of these are prepositions or other words and phrases that specify location or distance.)

> **FOCUS ON TRANSITIONS FOR DESCRIPTION**
>
> | | | |
> |---|---|---|
> | The most important | Beyond | Nearby |
> | The least important | Between | In |
> | Next to | Below | Inside |
> | Above | In front of | Outside |
> | On | Behind | Over |
> | On one side . . . on the other side | In back of | Under |

The following student essay, "African Violet" by Alisha Woolery, uses description to create a portrait of a family member. By combining subjective and objective description and using specific visual details—the elderly woman's toothless mouth, her brown eyes, her hands-and-knees position as she works in her garden, her beloved '72 Nova—Alisha creates a dominant impression of her great-grandmother as physically frail yet emotionally spirited.

African Violet

Alisha Woolery

    The black-and-white picture of my great-grandparents is a picture I often bring into my mind when I have decided to look at the "big picture" of life and think all the "deep thoughts." I see their faces, etched into the contrasting grays, so young, so hopeful for their new lives together. My mind then shifts to a more recent picture of my great-grandma with her small, frail body, which in the end gave her more pain than she could handle. I often question the justice of aging, but I also realize, perhaps in not so many words, how much she taught me about life and death--and about everything in between. 1

    My great-grandfather died when I was quite young, and I have only a faint memory of riding his foot like a horse while he recited "Banbury Cross." I have to create an image of him from my relatives' fond memories. Fortunately, however, I knew my great-grandma well, and the conversations we had are among my favorite memories of her. One in particular I recall is her telling me one of the numerous stories of her youth. 2

    "One time I was getting to be about sixteen years 3

old, and there was this boy who asked me on a picnic." Her eyes brightened as she told her story. "He was older than me, and he had a horse and buggy! And WhooWee! That was really something."

The look of astonishment on my face must have been apparent because we laughed until I thought we would keel over. There she was, ninety years old, with absolutely no teeth, telling me how hot this boy who had asked her out was. It was then I realized that the eyes looking out from her aging face were the same brown eyes that had flirted with boys, had fallen in love, and had seen her children and her children's children's children. She had years of experience, and I had very little, but on that warm summer evening, as we sat in her living room, her story bridged the gap between generations.

Besides my grandma's love of telling stories about her life to others, her one true passion was her plants. She loved them all, but her favorites were small plants with dark green leaves and purple blossoms: African violets. I didn't inherit her green thumb, so the miracles she worked with plants were a constant wonder to me. Stems and leaves seemed to flourish under her gentle touch. Plants were her pride and joy, and until she was in her mid-eighties you could still see her, on hands and knees, digging around in the dirt in her front yard.

No, Grandma didn't resign herself to age and let life pass her by; she rode it for all it was worth. This enthusiasm was also apparent in her driving. The woman was a traffic hazard, not because she poked along as so many older folks do, but because she was a speed demon! Poised for action, Grandma strapped herself into her brown '72 Nova and sped out toward destinations unknown with one foot on the gas and the other on the brake. (I am sure she followed the basic traffic laws most of the time, or at least I think so.)

I suppose by all laws of nature, her driving escapades should have done her in, but Grandma died a peaceful death with quiet resolution and acceptance. In fact, she probably had a better outlook on the whole thing than anyone else in the family. She was the closest person to me to die, so it was especially difficult for me to accept that our talks were simply over. I was fifteen at the time and wrote a poem entitled "African Violet" expressing the idea that I didn't feel it was time for her to leave me.

It wasn't until recently that I realized that even by her dying, Grandma was continuing to teach me about life. I saw how bravely she dealt with the increasing pain in her legs as her body deteriorated and how, when she took her last breath, it came as almost a relief to her. I had never thought about death in this way, and she made me question many things about life that I had never truly thought about.

The memories of my great-grandma are very important to me, and sometimes it scares me when a detail escapes my mind because remembering our time together and what I've learned from her is all I have left of her. It is virtually impossible to communicate the impact she has had on me. The only way I feel I can repay her is by telling about her ideas and stories, keeping her memory alive in a legacy of wisdom and laughter.

✓ Writing Checklist: Description

- Be sure you understand your assignment, audience, and purpose for writing.
- Use invention strategies to discover details about your subject.
- Decide what dominant impression your details suggest.
- Develop a tentative thesis statement that expresses the dominant impression of your description.
- Decide which details to include.
- Decide how to arrange the details.
- Draft your essay.
- Revise your thesis statement.
- Revise your introduction, making sure it identifies the subject of your description and includes the dominant impression or thesis statement.
- Add transitions if necessary to signal direction and move readers from one aspect of your subject to another.
- Delete any details that are not relevant to the dominant impression.
- Add details to make your description clearer and more vivid.
- Revise sentence structure and word choice.
- Edit and proofread your essay.

Graduation

Maya Angelou

"Graduation," from Maya Angelou's autobiographical I Know Why the Caged Bird Sings, *presents a vivid picture of a specific time (the 1930s) and place (the rural Arkansas town of Stamps). Against this backdrop, the young African-American students at Lafayette County Training School prepare for their high school graduation. As you read, notice how Angelou moves from a general description of the school and its inhabitants, to a more specific physical description of the school's exterior, and finally to the students eager for graduation.*

The children in Stamps trembled visibly with anticipation. Some adults were excited too, but to be certain the whole young population had come down with graduation epidemic. Large classes were graduating from both the grammar school and the high school. Even those who were years removed from their own day of glorious release were anxious to help with preparations as a kind of dry run. The junior students who were moving into the vacating classes' chairs were tradition-bound to show their talents for leadership and management. They strutted through the school and around the campus exerting pressure on the lower grades. Their authority was so new that occasionally if they pressed a little too hard it had to be overlooked. After all, next term was coming, and it never hurt a sixth grader to have a play sister in the eighth grade, or a tenth-year student to be able to call a twelfth grader Bubba. So all was endured in a spirit of shared understanding. But the graduating classes themselves were the nobility. Like travelers with exotic destinations on their minds, the graduates were remarkably forgetful. They came to school without their books, or tablets or even pencils. Volunteers fell over themselves to secure replacements for the missing equipment. When accepted, the willing workers might or might not be thanked, and it was of no importance to the pregraduation rites. Even teachers were respectful of the now quiet and aging seniors, and tended to speak to them, if not as equals, as beings only slightly lower than themselves. After tests were returned and grades given, the student body, which acted like an extended family, knew who did well, who excelled, and what piteous ones had failed.

1 *Overview of the scene establishes the dominant mood of anticipation and pride*

Unlike the white high school, Lafayette County Training School distinguished itself by having neither lawn, nor hedges, nor tennis court, nor climbing ivy. Its two buildings (main classrooms, the grade school and home economics) were set on a dirt hill with no fence to limit either its boundaries or those of bordering farms. There was a large expanse to the left of the school which was used alternately as a baseball diamond or basketball court. Rusty hoops on swaying poles represented the permanent recreational equipment, although bats and balls could be borrowed from the P.E. teacher if the borrower was qualified and if the diamond wasn't occupied.

2 *Description of the school's exterior*

Over this rocky area relieved by a few shady tall persimmon trees the graduating class walked. The girls often held hands and no longer bothered to speak to the lower students. There was a sadness about them, as if this old world was not their home and they were bound for higher ground. The boys, on the other hand, had become more friendly, more outgoing. A decided change from the closed attitude they projected while studying for finals. Now they seemed not ready to give up the old school, the familiar paths and classrooms. Only a small percentage would be continuing on to college—one of the South's A & M (agricultural and mechanical) schools, which trained Negro youths to be carpenters, farmers, handymen, masons, maids, cooks and baby nurses. Their future rode heavily on their shoulders, and blinded them to the collective joy that had pervaded the lives of the boys and girls in the grammar school graduating class.

3 *Description of the students*

Conclusion reinforces the importance of the occasion

Parents who could afford it had ordered new shoes and ready-made clothes for themselves from Sears and Roebuck or Montgomery Ward. They also engaged the best seamstresses to make the floating graduating dresses and to cut down secondhand pants which would be pressed to a military slickness for the important event. 4

Oh, it was important, all right. Whitefolks would attend the ceremony, and two or three would speak of God and home, and the Southern way of life, and Mrs. Parsons, the principal's wife, would play the graduation march while the lower-grade graduates paraded down the aisles and took their seats below the platform. The high school seniors would wait in empty classrooms to make their dramatic entrance. 5

Reacting to Reading

1. Preview the essay. Then, read it more carefully, and do whatever highlighting and annotating is necessary to help you understand the writer's ideas.
2. Throughout her essay, Angelou implies that the African-American students of Stamps have fewer privileges and opportunities than their white counterparts. Underline phrases that reveal what the black students miss out on. In marginal notes, speculate about what the white students might have access to that Angelou and her classmates do not.

Reacting to Words

*1. Define each of these words: *piteous* (1), *expanse* (2), *collective* (3), and *pervaded* (3). Can you suggest a synonym for each word that will work in the essay?
2. Angelou uses the word *Negro* in her essay; she also uses the word *whitefolks*. What is your reaction to her use of these words? Why do you think she doesn't use *black* or *African American*?

Reacting to Ideas

1. The passage begins with a sense of anticipation, comparing the students to "travelers with exotic destinations on their minds," (1) and ends with the students about "to make their dramatic entrance" (5) into the world. What details suggest that their future may not be quite as bright as they expect?
*2. Do you think the students' race is important or incidental to the point Angelou is making?

Reacting to the Pattern

1. Paragraph 2 focuses on physical description of the school's exterior. What dominant impression does this paragraph convey? In what ways is it an appropriate lead-in to paragraph 3?

*2. This passage communicates a mood that is a mixture of anxiety about and eager anticipation of the future. List the details that help to convey each of these moods.

Writing Practice

1. Describe the mood at your school in the days preceding your own high school graduation. Move from your fellow students to the teachers to your family, and then focus on your own feelings.
2. Describe your high school. Begin with its setting, then move to the exterior of the building, and finally focus on one particular room. (If you prefer, describe your workplace, your home, or some other significant location.)
3. Write the valedictory address you would give if you were graduating from your high school this year. Include detailed descriptions of people and places important to your classmates.

The Grandfather

Gary Soto

Poet and essayist Gary Soto often writes about family members and about his childhood. In this essay he remembers his grandfather with affection, conveying his habits and attitudes by describing the trees in his backyard. As you read, notice how Soto blends objective and subjective description of his grandfather.

Grandfather believed a well-rooted tree was the color of money. His money he kept hidden behind portraits of sons and daughters or taped behind the calendar of an Aztec warrior. He tucked it into the sofa, his shoes and slippers, and into the tight-lipped pockets of his suits. He kept it in his soft brown wallet that was machine tooled with "MEXICO" and a campesino and donkey climbing a hill. He had climbed, too, out of Mexico, settled in Fresno and worked thirty years at Sun Maid Raisin, first as a packer and later, when he was old, as a watchman with a large clock on his belt.

After work, he sat in the backyard under the arbor, watching the water gurgle in the rose bushes that ran along the fence. A lemon tree hovered over the clothesline. Two orange trees stood near the alley. His favorite tree, the avocado, which had started in a jam jar from a seed and three toothpicks lanced in its sides, rarely bore fruit. He said it was the wind's fault, and the mayor's, who allowed office buildings so high that the haze of pollen from the countryside could never find its way into the city. He sulked about this. He said that in Mexico buildings only grew so tall. You could see the moon at night, and the stars were clear points all the way to the horizon. And wind reached all the way

1 *Introduction focuses on grandfather as frugal and hard-working*

2 *Description of backyard*

Focus on avocado tree

from the sea, which was blue and clean, unlike the oily water sloshing against a San Francisco pier.

During its early years, I could leap over that tree, kick my bicycling legs over the top branch and scream my fool head off because I thought for sure I was flying. I ate fruit to keep my strength up, fuzzy peaches and branch-scuffed plums cooled in the refrigerator. From the kitchen chair he brought out in the evening, Grandpa would scold, "Hijo, what's the matta with you? You gonna break it."

By the third year, the tree was as tall as I, its branches casting a meager shadow on the ground. I sat beneath the shade, scratching words in the hard dirt with a stick. I had learned "Nile" in summer school and a dirty word from my brother who wore granny sunglasses. The red ants tumbled into my letters, and I buried them, knowing that they would dig themselves back into fresh air.

Grandfather's frugality reemphasized

A tree was money. If a lemon cost seven cents at Hanoian's Market, then Grandfather saved fistfuls of change and more because in winter the branches of his lemon tree hung heavy yellow fruit. And winter brought oranges, juicy and large as softballs. Apricots he got by the bagfuls from a son, who himself was wise for planting young. Peaches he got from a neighbor, who worked the night shift at Sun Maid Raisin. The chile plants, which also saved him from giving up his hot, sweaty quarters, were propped up with sticks to support an abundance of red fruit.

But his favorite tree was the avocado because it offered hope and the promise of more years. After work, Grandpa sat in the back yard, shirtless, tired of flagging trucks loaded with crates of raisins, and sipped glasses of ice water. His yard was neat: five trees, seven rose bushes, whose fruit were the red and white flowers he floated in bowls, and a statue of St. Francis that stood in a circle of crushed rocks, arms spread out to welcome hungry sparrows.

Focus moves back to avocado tree

After ten years, the first avocado hung on a branch, but the meat was flecked with black, an omen, Grandfather thought, a warning to keep an eye on the living. Five years later, another avocado hung on a branch, larger than the first and edible when crushed with a fork into a heated tortilla. Grandfather sprinkled it with salt and laced it with a river of chile.

"It's good," he said, and let me taste.

I took a big bite, waved a hand over my tongue, and ran for the garden hose gurgling in the rose bushes. I drank long and deep, and later ate the smile from an ice cold watermelon.

Birds nested in the tree, quarreling jays with liquid eyes and cool, pulsating throats. Wasps wove a horn-shaped hive one year, but we smoked them away with swords of rolled up newspapers lit with matches. By then, the tree was tall enough for me to climb to look into the neighbor's yard. But by then I was too old for that kind of thing and went about with my brother, hair slicked back and our shades dark as oil.

Conclusion links Grandfather and avocado

After twenty years, the tree began to bear. Although Grandfather complained about how much he lost because pollen never reached the poor part of town, because at the market he had to haggle over the price of avocados, he loved that tree. It grew, as did his family, and when he died, all his sons standing on each other's shoulders, oldest to youngest, could not reach the highest branches. The wind could move the branches, but the trunk, thicker than any waist, hugged the ground.

tree symbolically

Reacting to Reading

1. Preview the essay. Then, read it more carefully, and do whatever highlighting and annotating is necessary to help you understand the writer's ideas.
2. Circle all the words in the essay that designate colors. Then, write a brief marginal note in which you consider what these words contribute to the essay.

Reacting to Words

*1. Define each of these words: *campesino* (1), *lanced* (2), *hijo* (3), *meager* (4), *laced* (7), and *haggle* (11). Can you suggest a synonym for each word that will work in the essay?
*2. What figure of speech is each of these expressions?

- "the tight-lipped pockets of his suits" (1)
- "large as softballs" (5)
- "a river of chile" (7)

Can you identify any other figures of speech in the essay?

Reacting to Ideas

1. In the first sentence of his essay, Soto says, "Grandfather believed a well-rooted tree was the color of money." Where does Soto refer to this idea again? What do you think he means?
2. Soto calls his essay "The Grandfather." Could you argue that it is not really about the man but about the trees in his backyard—or about one tree in particular? Could you make the point that the essay is really about Soto himself?

Reacting to the Pattern

*1. Soto's grandfather is introduced in paragraph 1. In paragraph 2 we see him sitting in his yard, and then the essay focuses on the avocado tree. Continue tracing the essay's movement from paragraph to paragraph. What is the central focus of each paragraph? Is the essay's progression from one paragraph to the next logical?
2. Does this description use any phrases that convey senses other than sight? Give examples of any phrases that describe sound, smell, taste, or touch.

Writing Practice

1. Write a description of a grandparent or other close relative, focusing on your family member's physical appearance. Move from top to bottom or from least to most striking feature or in some other logical order.
2. Write an essay about a grandparent or other relative in which you characterize your subject by describing his or her favorite possessions.
3. Write an essay about a grandparent or other relative in which you characterize your subject by describing a setting with which you associate him or her—a room, office, or garden, for example.

D PROCESS

Process essays explain the steps in a procedure, telling how something is (or was) done.

> ### ▶ FOCUS ON TOPICS FOR PROCESS ◀
>
> The wording of your assignment may suggest process. For example, it may ask you to *explain a process, give instructions, give directions,* or *give a step-by-step account.*
>
> | Topic/Assignment | Thesis Statement |
> |---|---|
> | Explain the process by which a bill becomes a law. | The process by which a bill becomes a law is long and complex, involving numerous revisions and a great deal of compromise. |
> | Summarize the procedure for conducting a clinical trial of a new drug. | To ensure that drugs are safe and effective, scientists follow strict procedural guidelines for testing and evaluating them. |
> | Write a set of instructions for applying for a student internship in a state agency. | The process of applying for an internship can be quite simple if students follow a few important steps. |

A process essay can be organized as either a process explanation or a set of instructions. **Process explanations**, like the first two examples in the focus box above, generally use present tense verbs ("Once a bill *is* introduced in Congress . . ." or "A scientist first *submits* a funding application . . .") to explain how a procedure is generally carried out. **Instructions**, like the last example in the preceding box, use present tense verbs in the form of commands to tell readers how to perform a particular task ("First, *meet* with your academic advisor..."). Whichever kind of process essay you write, you can either devote a full paragraph to each step of the process or group a series of minor steps in a single paragraph.

Options for Organizing Process Essays	
One Step per Paragraph	**Several Steps per Paragraph**
¶1 Introduction	¶1 Introduction
¶2 First step in process	¶2 First group of steps
¶3 Second step in process	¶3 Second group of steps
¶4 Third step in process	¶4 Third group of steps
¶5 Conclusion	¶5 Conclusion

As you write your process essay, you should discuss each step in the order in which it is performed, clearly identifying the function of each step or group of steps in your topic sentences. If you are writing instructions, you should also be sure to include any warnings or reminders you believe are necessary.

Transitions are extremely important in process essays because they ensure that readers will be able to follow the sequence of steps in the process and, if necessary, perform the process themselves.

▶ **FOCUS** ON TRANSITIONS FOR PROCESS ◀

The first (second, third) step	When	Later,
The next step	Meanwhile,	Soon,
Now,	At the same time,	Then,
As soon as	After that,	Immediately,
Subsequently,	Finally,	The last step

The following student essay, Mai Yoshikawa's "Under Water," explains the process of scuba diving. Because Mai did not think her readers would be likely to have the opportunity to try scuba diving, she did not write her essay in the form of instructions. Instead, she wrote a process explanation, using present tense verbs ("While I *am* floating underwater . . ." or "I *make* sure that the mask *fits* my buddy's face . . ."). Notice how clear transitions ("*Once* I get all this equipment, . . ." "*Then*, I pull the string, . . ." and "*Next*, I place the regulator in my mouth . . .") move readers smoothly through the steps of the process.

```
                         Under Water

                        Mai Yoshikawa
```

1   For most people, their first scuba-diving experience in the ocean does not turn out to be a very good one, and so it was with me. Because I rushed to see the beauty of the seascape, I wasted oxygen and didn't pay much attention to the instructor. Unexpected dangers lie under water, and most first-time divers, like me, are unaware of the risk they are taking when they enter this other world. Now, as a more experienced diver, I have learned that I need to protect myself from trouble by having the right equipment and knowing how to use it well.

2   To ensure a safe dive, you need some basic equipment: an air tank, fins, snorkel, mask, life vest, weight belt, gloves, regulator, pressure and depth gauges, and, occasionally, a wetsuit. The weight belt maintains the diver's neutral buoyancy; therefore, the number of weights a person carries will vary. While I am floating under water, the weight belt and the air pressure work together to enable me to stay at a certain depth without moving up and down. The lighter the diver, the more weights he or she needs. The nylon socks keep my fins from slipping and help me avoid foot injuries. The pressure and depth gauges are connected to the tank where I can easily reach them and check to make sure the numbers on the two instruments correspond. The gauges are set to notify me how deep I can swim with the amount of oxygen left in my tank. Once I get all this equipment and check it, I plan the day's activities and routes with the instructor. The instructor, at that point, becomes my "buddy."

3   The buddy system is extremely important. I check my partner's equipment and make sure every part is in gear, and she checks mine as well. I make sure that the mask fits my buddy's face and that no hair is caught in the rubber lining because any space will allow water to enter. Then, I pull the string on her life vest, examine the jacket as the air inflates, and listen to make sure it holds the air with no leak. Next, I place the

regulator in my mouth, and I try breathing for a while as the oxygen from the tank flows into me each time I inhale. Finally, I open the valve of the tank to its fullest so that my partner will get enough oxygen as she dives.

In order to reduce the risk of accidents, a thorough, careful equipment check must be done. If there are more than two divers, each person pairs up with another person. Usually someone who has had a lot of experience and knows the significance of the inspection, such as an assistant instructor or the owner of the dive shop, is available to help the amateur divers get set up.

As I check to make sure my equipment is working, I get tense and nervous, thinking about possible accidents which, in the worst situation, could kill me. Once this serious phase is finished, however, I am ready for the main event of the day. Usually, the group dive lasts for two or three separate periods, each consisting of approximately twenty to forty minutes. Changing diving spots after every swim gives me the opportunity to enjoy different scenery. On lucky days, I can see rare, enormous fish that I never dreamt of viewing except on the television screen. In most cases, the instructors even give us permission to feed these fish.

Scuba diving is an exciting, breathtaking sport, no matter how many times I experience it. I have learned that I have to be very careful and responsible about the actions I take both before and after I enter the water. But once I start swimming deep into the ocean, I feel so small, yet so free. The fear and panic disappear from my mind with the bubbles of oxygen that flow out from my regulator with my very own, short-winded human breath as it echoes in my ears.

✓ Writing Checklist: Process

- ❏ Be sure you understand your assignment, audience, and purpose for writing.
- ❏ Use invention strategies to find ideas.
- ❏ List each step involved in the process.
- ❏ Decide which steps, if any, need to be explained in detail.
- ❏ Develop a tentative thesis statement that presents an overview of the process.
- ❏ Draft your essay.
- ❏ Revise your thesis statement.
- ❏ Be sure the steps are presented in the proper order.
- ❏ Add cautions or reminders if necessary.
- ❏ Add transitions if necessary to clarify relationships between steps.
- ❏ Revise topic sentences to clarify the function of each step or group of steps.

- ❏ Delete any unnecessary or irrelevant steps.
- ❏ Revise your introduction and conclusion.
- ❏ Revise sentence structure and word choice.
- ❏ Edit and proofread your essay.

Showering with Your Dog

Merrill Markoe

In this humorous essay, Merrill Markoe gives a six-step set of instructions for washing a dog in the shower. Markoe uses a numbered heading to introduce each step, and she begins each section of the essay with the assumption that readers have read the heading. As you read, notice how she talks directly to her readers, using you *to address them.*

Thesis statement

Let's face it. Even the most beloved dog can be very stinky at times. And where pet hygiene is concerned, the enlightened pet guardian (and, of course, by that I mean me) has no choice but to share the indoor facilities with the animal.

Headings identify steps in the process

Step 1: Choosing the Proper Wardrobe

When showering with your dog, it *is* advisable to wear swim wear. I don't know whether the dog would know if you were naked, but *you* would know.

Step 2: Getting the Dog into the Shower

Two alternative steps suggested

Nothing can really proceed until this is accomplished. Often the dog will exhibit a little initial reluctance . . . perhaps because he has watched too many horror movies on TV in which showers are presented in an unfortunate light. Many dogs have never given any thought to the concept of "fiction" and so do not know that most showers are not just another death trap. Rather than confront the animal with a lot of mind-blowing philosophical concepts, I recommend one of two less complicated strategies that work for me. The first is what I call the old "ball in the shower" approach, in which you, the parent or guardian, relocate to the inside of the shower with some favorite sports equipment, making it appear that you have selected the location *not* because of its showering capabilities but simply because it is the best damn place for miles around to hit fungoes. If, after fifteen or twenty minutes of enthusiastic solo sports maneuvers, you have not managed to interest the animal in joining you, I suggest you switch to the immediately effective "chicken skin around the drain" approach. It's a well-documented fact that only a minute amount of chicken skin can accumulate in the lower third of any area of the world before it will be joined by a dog.

Once this has happened, simply close the shower door behind him, or pull the curtain. (For the more squeamish among you who worry about the mess in the shower, you can count on the dog to clean it all up. If he should happen to miss a little, and some chicken skin remains, don't worry. It will simply be taken by any future showerers as a remarkable indication of how seriously you scrub yourself when you wash.)

Step 3: Moistening and Soaping the Animal

This may be trickier than it appears, because the animal tends to move to the parts of the shower where there is no water. And so it becomes your perpetual task to keep moving the water to the parts of the shower where there is a dog. During this phase, apply shampoo and try not to take personally the animal's expression, which indicates a hatred and loathing so extreme that he is trying to figure out how he can reconnect with his long-buried primitive instincts to kill and eat a human being. It may be useful to let the dog know that showering is not a punishment but something *you* actually find pleasurable and relaxing. If this does not help, now is an excellent time to explain to the animal that the legal system is built primarily around the rights of humans, and, if you want to, you can take him back to the pound where you got him and then his life won't be worth a plug nickel.

Step 4: Rinsing

You are now dealing with increasing desperation on the part of the dog, who may be getting ready to make a break for it. This is why nature gave the dog a tail, to help you as you try to restrain him before he runs through the house all matted and soapy and gets big hair-encrusted stains all over your cherished possessions.

Step 5: Toweling the Dog

This process is designed to help you avoid the splattered, soaking mess that results when the dog shakes himself off. No matter how diligently you perform toweling, it is futile. When you're through, the dog will disperse the same astonishing amounts of water and hair as if he had never been toweled at all.

Now you may release the animal, perhaps deluding yourself that he is thrilled at his cleaner condition. You should return immediately to the shower and shovel out the three to five pounds of hair you will find lodged in your drain. This brings me to the final but most important step.

Step 6: Remove Any Bottles of Flea and Tick Shampoo

Take it from someone who has lived through every unfortunate scenario that can result from simply leaving the bottle around. . . . I know I have helped you.

Brief conclusion

Reacting to Reading

1. Preview the essay. Then, read it more carefully, and do whatever highlighting and annotating is necessary to help you understand the writer's ideas.
2. With the exception of the heading that introduces Step 6, Markoe's headings are not complete sentences. In marginal notations, expand each of the other headings into a complete sentence that summarizes the advice Markoe gives in the section.

Reacting to Words

*1. Define each of these words: *exhibit* (3), *reluctance* (3), *fungoes* (3), *minute* (3), *squeamish* (4), *perpetual* (5), *diligently* (7), and *futile* (7). Can you suggest a synonym for each word that will work in the essay?
*2. Markoe refers to the subject of her essay as *the dog* or *the animal*. Does she use any other term? Keeping in mind that this is a humorous essay, what other names would you suggest?

Reacting to Ideas

1. Instead of presenting a fixed set of tasks, Markoe frequently offers her readers alternatives (signaled by words like *if* or *or*). Why do you think she does this? Why do you think her process does not consist of a more rigid set of steps?
2. Markoe's essay is written as a set of instructions. Do you think she actually expects readers to follow these instructions?

Reacting to the Pattern

*1. Markoe's essay has a brief introductory paragraph, but it doesn't have a separate concluding paragraph. If she were to add a concluding paragraph, what advice or information might she include in it?
2. Markoe's headings help to move readers from step to step. What other specific transitions does she use within and between paragraphs to move readers through the process? Do you think she needs any additional transitions? If so, where?

Writing Practice

*1. List the steps in a recipe for preparing one of your favorite dishes. When you have finished, expand your recipe into an essay, adding transitions, cautions and reminders, and an opening and closing paragraph that describe the finished product and tell readers why the dish is worth the trouble.
*2. Write an essay that explains to your fellow students how to study for an exam, write a paper, or take good lecture notes.
3. Write an essay that tells other students how to perform a task associated

with one of your courses—for example, how to dissect an animal, use a graphing calculator, or conduct a survey. Assume your readers have never performed the process before.

Indelible Marks

Joyce Howe

Joyce Howe grew up in Queens, New York, in a neighborhood where everyone knew her father as "the man who ran the Chinese laundry." As his daughter, she had mixed feelings about his occupation and felt ashamed that she and her parents and sisters lived behind the store and helped in the laundry business. In this passage she explains the familiar process by which laundry was sorted, washed, dried, starched, ironed, folded, and wrapped. As you read, try to get a sense of what the process meant to Howe.

In Queens, on the block where we moved, my father was known as the man who ran the Chinese laundry, like Ernie who ran the deli, Benny the upholsterer, and the butcher a few doors down. To all of his customers he was Joe. And they—middle-aged housewives, young bachelors and students, mainly white—were known to him by a first name or by the unique indelible "mark" on their collars and hems. (This "mark," consisting of one or more characters, was written on each item for the duration of a customer's patronage; if he switched laundries, the new establishment usually did not bother changing it.) With all of them, as tickets, laundry bills, and change passed from hand to hand over the wide counter, my father exchanged comments: "Too much of this rain, huh?", "Yeah, the Mets looked lousy last night," or "How's the wife and the kids?"

1 Introduction sets the scene

Saturday was his busiest day. It was not only the day more customers came in and out, but it was also one of the three days on which the long and tedious job of laundry-sorting was done. The entire floor of the store became a dumping ground for soiled clothes. My father divided the laundry into piles: 10 to 15 sheets and pillowcases were bundled up into one sheet and the ticket stubs of the customers whose laundry made up the bundle were then stapled together and put aside for later identification. "Wet items," such as towels, underwear, and socks were separated into two categories—light and dark; shirts were separated into four categories—colored, white, starch, and no starch. Each pile of "wet items" and shirts was then placed in a laundry bag with its respective tag.

2 Process begins

The bags and bundles were picked up Sunday morning by the truck drivers, who had names like Rocky and Louie, from the wholesale laundry or "wet wash" contracted by my father. ("Hand laundry" has been a misnomer since the late 1930s and '40s, when a whole new in-

3

dustry of Chinese-operated wholesale laundries and pressing concerns sprang up and contracted to do the actual washing and pressing for laundrymen.) Every Sunday, we were awakened from our sleep by the sound of the drivers' keys turning in the front door's locks.

Several steps combined in one paragraph

When the "wet wash" drivers returned Monday with the previous day's load, the sheets and pillowcases, or "flat pieces," were wrapped in a heavy brown paper which my mother later would use for tablecloths. The shirts returned in the same bags they went out in. My father pulled out the bag of shirts to be starched and hand-ironed, leaving the rest for the shirt-press truck to pick up that night. On Tuesday night, they returned—clean, pressed, folded—in large square cardboard boxes, each shirt ringed in its own pale blue paper band. 4

For a short time, we had our own automatic dryer to take care of the damp "wet items" when they returned. After it broke down, irreparably, the dryer retired, and was left to hold stacks of comic books and board games. My sisters and I took turns making pilgrimages to the local laundromat, our metal shopping cart bent from the weight of the load. We wheeled those three blocks three times a week. On my turn, I always hoped that no one I knew would see me as I struggled with two hands to keep laundry and cart intact when maneuvering the high curbs. Even then, the irony of going from the laundry to the laundromat was not lost. 5

Process concludes

Of course, there were days when the system was off, when the shirt press might return its load late, or when my father didn't feel well enough to wrap every package. On those days, we were all expected to help. We made sure that the promise my father had made to customers on Saturday that their shirts would be ready by Wednesday was kept. Behind the tan curtain drawn across our plate-glass window every evening at seven and the door's pulled venetian blind, we settled into a tableau. My family formed a late-night assembly line, each member taking his place amid the shelves, boxes, white cones of string, rolls of wrapping paper, and the familiar fragrance of newly laundered cloth. 6

Reacting to Reading

1. Preview the essay. Then, read it more carefully, and do whatever highlighting and annotating is necessary to help you understand the writer's ideas.
2. In the margins of the essay, number the steps in the process that is presented in paragraphs 2 through 6.

Reacting to Words

*1. Define each of these words: *indelible* (1), *duration* (1), *patronage* (1), *tedious* (2), *irreparably* (5), *pilgrimages* (5), and *tableau* (6). Can you suggest a synonym for each word that will work in the essay?
2. Howe's father makes a "unique indelible 'mark'" (1) on the collars of each customer's shirts. Do you think the phrase *indelible mark* could have any other meaning in this passage?

Reacting to Ideas

1. What purpose do you suppose Howe had in mind when she set out to describe this process?
2. Do you think Howe's memories of her childhood as the laundryman's daughter are largely positive or negative? Support your position with specific examples.

Reacting to the Pattern

1. Is this essay a set of instructions or an explanation of how a process is performed? How can you tell?
*2. Using the numbers you wrote in the margins for Reacting to Reading question 2 as a guide, list the individual steps in the process Howe describes. Does the process vary at all, or is it always the same?

Writing Practice

1. Write a process essay explaining the daily routine you followed in a job you held. Include a thesis statement that tells readers how you felt about the job.
*2. Write a process essay in which you tell how to perform a particular task at a job you once held—for example, how to keep a potential customer on the phone, how to clean the deep-fat fryer, or how to set up the housekeeping corner at a day-care center.
3. Write a process essay in which you take readers through the stages of a successful job search. In your conclusion, identify the job you found.

E CAUSE AND EFFECT

Cause-and-effect essays identify causes or predict effects; sometimes they do both.

▶ FOCUS ON TOPICS FOR CAUSE AND EFFECT ◀

The wording of your assignment may suggest cause and effect. For example, it may ask you to *explain why, predict the outcome, list contributing factors, discuss the consequences,* or tell what *caused* something else or how something is *affected* by something else.

(continued on the following page)

(continued from the previous page)

Topic/Assignment	Thesis Statement
What factors contributed to the rise of the women's movement in the 1970s?	The women's movement had its origins in the peace and civil rights movements of the 1960s.
Discuss the possible long-term effects of smoking.	In addition to its physical effects, smoking may also have long-term social and emotional consequences.
How has television affected the lives of those who have grown up with it?	Television has created a generation of people who learn differently from those in previous generations.

A cause-and-effect essay can focus on causes or on effects. When you write about causes, be sure to examine *all* pertinent causes. You should focus on the cause you consider the most important, but you should not forget to consider any minor causes that may be relevant to your topic. Similarly, when you write about effects, consider *all* significant effects of a particular cause, not just the first few that you think of.

If your focus is on finding causes, as it is in the first assignment in the box above, your introductory paragraph should identify the effect (the women's movement). If your focus is on predicting effects, as it is in the second and third assignments, begin by identifying the cause (smoking or television). In the body of your essay, you may devote a full paragraph to each cause (or effect), or you may group several related causes (or effects) in each paragraph.

Options for Organizing Cause-and-Effect Essays	
Identifying Causes	**Predicting Effects**
¶1 Introduction (identifies effect)	¶1 Introduction (identifies cause)
¶2 First cause	¶2 First effect
¶3 Second cause	¶3 Second effect
¶4 Third (and most important) cause	¶4 Third (and most important) effect
¶5 Conclusion	¶5 Conclusion

Transitions are important in cause-and-effect essays because they establish causal connections, telling readers that A caused B and not the other way around. They also make it clear that you are talking about events that have a *causal* relationship (A *caused* B) and not just a *sequential* one (A *preceded* B). Remember, just because one event follows another, the second is not necessarily the result of the first.

> **▶ FOCUS ON TRANSITIONS FOR CAUSE AND EFFECT ◀**
>
> | | | |
> |---|---|---|
> | Because | For | As a result, |
> | Accordingly, | For this reason, | Consequently, |
> | So | Since | Therefore, |
> | The first (second, third) cause | The first (second, third) effect | Another cause |
> | Another effect | The most important cause | The most important effect |

Note: Be careful not to confuse *affect* (usually a verb) and *effect* (usually a noun) in your cause-and-effect essays. (See Section E.)

The following student essay, "How My Parents' Separation Changed My Life," by Andrea DiMarco, examines the effects of a significant event on the author and her family. Andrea begins by identifying the cause—the separation—and then she goes on to explain its specific effects on her family's holiday celebrations, on their day-to-day routine, and on her own outlook on life. Notice that key words and phrases like *changed, different, effect, because*, and *as a result* make her causal connections clear to her readers.

```
         How My Parents' Separation Changed My Life

                      Andrea DiMarco

     Until I was ten, I lived the perfect all-American        1
life with my perfect all-American family. I lived in a
suburb of Albany, New York, with my parents, my sister
and brother, and our dog Daisy. We had a Ping-Pong table
in the basement, a barbecue in the backyard, and two
cars in the garage. My Dad and Mom were high school
teachers, and every summer we took a family vacation.
Then, it all changed.
     One day, just before Halloween, when my sister was      2
twelve and my brother was fourteen (Daisy was seven),
our parents called us into the kitchen for a family
conference. We didn't think anything was wrong at first;
they were always calling these annoying meetings. We
figured it was time for us to plan a vacation, talk
```

about household chores, or be nagged to clean our rooms. As soon as we sat down, though, we knew this was different. We could tell Mom had been crying, and Dad's voice cracked when he told us the news. They were separating--they called it a "trial separation"--and Dad was moving out of our house.

I hardly remember what else we talked about that day. But I do remember how things changed right after that. Every Halloween we'd always had a big jack-o'-lantern on our front porch. Dad used to spend hours at the kitchen table cutting out the eyes, nose, and mouth and hollowing out the insides. That Halloween, because he didn't live with us, things were different. Mom bought a pumpkin, and I guess she was planning to carve it up. But she never did, and we never mentioned it. It sat on the kitchen counter for a couple of weeks, getting soft and wrinkled, and then it just disappeared. I suppose Mom threw it out.

Other holidays were also different because Mom and Dad weren't living together. Our first Thanksgiving without Dad was pathetic. I don't even want to talk about it. Christmas was different, too. We spent Christmas Eve with Dad and our relatives on his side, and Christmas Day with Mom and her family. Of course, we got twice as many presents as usual--I realize now that both our parents were trying to make up for the pain of the separation. The worst part came when I opened my big present from Mom: Barbie's Dream House. This was something I'd always wanted. Even at ten, I knew how hard it must have been for Mom to afford it. The trouble was, I'd gotten the same thing from Dad the night before.

The worst effect of my parents' separation on all three of us was not the big events but the disruption in our everyday lives. Dinner used to be a family time, a chance to talk about our day and make plans. But after Dad left, Mom seemed to stop eating. Sometimes she'd just have coffee while we ate, and sometimes she wouldn't eat at all. She'd microwave some frozen thing for us or heat up soup or cook some hot dogs. We didn't care--after all, now she let us watch TV while we ate--but we did notice.

Other parts of our routine changed, too. Because Dad didn't live with us anymore, we had to spend every Saturday and every Wednesday night at his place, no matter what else we had planned. Usually he'd take us to dinner at McDonald's on Wednesdays, and then we'd go back to his place and do our homework or watch TV. That wasn't too bad. Saturdays were a lot worse. We really wanted to be home, hanging out with our friends in our own rooms in our own house. Instead, we had to do some planned activity with Dad, like go to a movie or a hockey game.

My parents were only separated for eight months, but it seemed like forever. By the end of the school year, they'd somehow worked things out, and Dad was back home again. That June, at a family conference around the kitchen table, we made our summer vacation plans. We decided on Williamsburg, Virginia, the all-American vacation destination. So, things were back to normal, but I wasn't, and I'm still not. Now, eight years later, my mother and father are still OK, but I still worry they'll split up again. And I worry about my own future husband and how I'll ever be sure he's the one I'll stay married to. As a result of what happened in my own family, it's hard for me to believe any relationship is forever.

7

☑ Writing Checklist: Cause and Effect

- ❑ Be sure you understand your assignment, audience, and purpose for writing.
- ❑ Use invention strategies to find ideas.
- ❑ Decide whether to focus on causes or effects.
- ❑ Develop a tentative thesis statement that identifies key causes or effects.
- ❑ Identify all causes or effects relevant to your topic.
- ❑ Decide which cause or effect is most important.
- ❑ Decide how to arrange causes or effects in the body of your essay.
- ❑ Do further invention if necessary to identify additional causes or effects.
- ❑ Draft your essay.
- ❑ Revise your thesis statement.
- ❑ Add transitions if necessary to clarify causal relationships.
- ❑ Revise topic sentences and transitions to clarify the relationship between causes or effects and your thesis.
- ❑ Delete any irrelevant points.
- ❑ Revise your introduction and conclusion.
- ❑ Revise sentence structure and word choice.
- ❑ Edit and proofread your essay.

The Old Block

Anna Quindlen

Former columnist for the New York Times *op-ed page, Anna Quindlen resigned her position at the end of 1994 to devote herself to a career as a novelist. As a columnist, she focused mainly on social and political issues related to women's roles and family life. As you read "The Old Block," a 1992 column, notice how Quindlen moves from an examination of a troubling effect (the poverty of her family's old neighborhood) to the cause of the neighborhood's decline.*

Introduction describes change in the neighborhood (paragraphs 1–4)

The block on which my father grew up half a century ago is a truncated little street that leads nowhere. If it were a foot or two narrower, the map makers might have called it an alley. The houses are identical two-story attached brick buildings with bay windows on the top floor, an overobvious attempt at grandeur.

In this quiet backwater in the southwestern part of the city the children of Irish-Catholic families played in the late afternoons after they had changed from their parochial school uniforms. A police officer walked by twice a day, talking to the people he knew so well.

My father remembers that in one fifteen-minute span when he was eight years old he was hit by four people to whom he was not related: the cop; the neighbor whose window he drew upon with spit; the priest who saw him messing with a statue, and the nun who saw the priest whack him and wanted to second the emotion. So he grew.

Today the kids on the block are black. The house where the seven Quindlen children were raised, the boys packed two to a bed, has long been empty. The small setback porch is still covered with debris from the fire that gutted the building several years ago. There is plywood nailed over the glassless windows and the doorless doorway.

Effect summarized: The neighborhood has deteriorated, while suburbs have prospered

This was a prosperous neighborhood, a way station to something better. Today it is a poor one, a dead end. Charred interiors are common. So are crime, drugs, and a sense of going nowhere.

Since L.A. burst into flames we have cast a net of blame in our search for those who abandoned America's cities.

The answer is simple. We did. Over my lifetime prosperity in America has been measured in moving vans, backyards and the self-congratulatory remark "I can't remember the last time I went to the city." America became a circle of suburbs surrounding an increasingly grim urban core.

In the beginning there was a synergy between the two; we took the train to the city to work and shop, then fled as the sun went down. But by the 1970s we no longer needed to shop there because of the malls. And by the 1980s we no longer had to work there because of the now-you-see-it rise of industrial parks and office complexes. Pseudo-cities grew up, built of chrome, glass, and homogeneity. Half of America now lives in the 'burbs.

First cause: The middle class has abandoned America's cities

We abandoned America's cities.

Ronald Reagan and George Bush did, too, and so did many Democrats, truth be told. And they're going to have to ante up now. But it's not enough anymore to let those boys take all the responsibility. They don't carry it well enough.

I understand how Eugene Lang[1] felt when he gave a speech at his

---

[1] Founder of the I Have a Dream Foundation, which provides counseling and financial support for students in poor urban communities, helping them finish school and enter college.

old grade school and, overwhelmed by the emptiness of words, offered all the students in the class a chance to go to college. I've heard the argument that Mr. Lang's largesse takes government off the hook. But I bet it's not compelling for kids who might have gone down the drain if one man hadn't remembered where he came from, before he moved on to someplace greener, richer, better.

Over the years I've heard about sister-city programs between places here and places abroad, places like Minsk or Vienna. Pen pals. Cultural exchange. Volunteer philanthropy. And all the while, twenty minutes away from the suburbs are cultures and lives and problems about which we are shamefully ignorant. I like the sister-city concept. Short Hills and Newark. South-central L.A. and Simi Valley. Both sides benefit. *Second cause: People in the suburbs are ignorant of urban problems*

The pols will lose interest in the cities again soon enough, because so many city residents are poor and powerless and not white. It would be nice to think of Congress as the home of idealists, but thinking like that makes you feel awfully foolish. America's cities will prosper when America's prosperous citizens demand it. When they remember their roots. *Third cause: City residents are poor and powerless Thesis statement*

I've walked many times down blocks like the one on which my father grew up. I've been a poverty tourist with a notebook, but I never felt ashamed of it until now.

On that little street were the ghosts of the people who brought me into being and the flesh-and-blood kids who will be my children's companions in the twenty-first century. You could tell by their eyes that they couldn't figure out why I was there. They were accustomed to being ignored, even by the people who had once populated their rooms. And as long as that continues, our cities will burst and burn, burst and burn, over and over again. *Conclusion emphasizes cause-effect relationship*

Reacting to Reading

1. Preview the essay. Then, read it more carefully, and do whatever highlighting and annotating is necessary to help you understand the writer's ideas.
2. Circle all the descriptive words and phrases—for example, *glassless windows* (4)—that convey the neighborhood's decline to readers.

Reacting to Words

*1. Define each of these words: *truncated* (1), *grandeur* (1), *backwater* (2), *debris* (4), *charred* (5), *synergy* (8), *homogeneity* (8), *ante* (10), *largesse* (11), and *philanthropy* (12). Can you suggest a synonym for each word that will work in the essay?
2. Quindlen uses *we* throughout her essay—for example, "We abandoned America's cities" (9). Why do you think she does this?
3. In paragraph 14 Quindlen refers to herself as a "poverty tourist." What do you think she means by this phrase? Do you see it as a positive or negative characterization?

Reacting to Ideas

*1. List the differences between the neighborhood Quindlen sees today and "the old block."
2. Do you think Quindlen feels guilty? Do you think she should?

Reacting to the Pattern

1. Which of the three causes Quindlen identifies do you see as most important? Why? What other factors do you think might have played a role in the neighborhood's deterioration?
2. What further effects does Quindlen predict? Do you think her predictions are accurate?

Writing Practice

1. Do you still live in your old neighborhood, or have you or your family moved? Write a cause-and-effect essay explaining why you or your family decided to remain—or to leave.
*2. Why do people leave cities and move to the suburbs? Write a cause-and-effect essay that answers this question.
3. Consider Quindlen's suggestion in paragraph 12. Pair your city or town with a "sister city," and write an essay discussing the possible beneficial effects of a sister-city program.
4. What do you imagine might be the effects of investors' efforts to rebuild Quindlen's old neighborhood? Consider long- and short-term effects, both positive and negative.

Just Say "No," Just Hear "No"

Carol Sanger

Written by a reporter with an interest in legal issues, the following cause-and-effect essay looks at the problem some people have in distinguishing rape from consensual sexual relations. As you read, consider which of the causes Sanger discusses is most important—that is, most responsible for the lack of awareness she identifies.

Introduction (paragraphs 1–4)

1   We are a culture that has learned to think in slogans, and bumper stickers may be a truer gauge of what matters to Americans than newspaper editorials. I am sure about one thing that matters a lot. No surprise here—it is sex.

2   Pick any occupation and there is a bumper sticker bragging about how plumbers or lawyers or cement pourers or accountants "do it": with their briefs on, with their slide rules out, under water, in the air. Lots of people seem to be doing it, or at least thinking about it, and

plastering the news on their fenders. We ride around habituated to these casual, public and slightly sniggering announcements about sex.

There is also another familiar bumper sticker—the "Just Say No" message of drug education fame. We teach children that what they say counts, that if they "just say no," they will be in control, their decisions not to participate will be respected, and they will be safe from the harms of drugs.

Saying "no" may work for kids declining drugs. But it often works less well for women who say "no" to sex, women who do not want to "do it." Saying "yes" or "no" matters tremendously here. It is the difference between sexual intercourse and rape.

Thesis statement

Some people seem confused about the difference between sexual intercourse and rape. The first is a voluntary, often intimate association. The second is a criminal act. The difference between them is not the time of day or the location or what either person was wearing—or what their grades in high school were. The essential difference is consent.

Effect: confusion about what constitutes rape

Consent—agreeing to something—is usually not a hard concept to understand. It may at first appear more complex in the context of rape. One reason is simply its unexpected presence. There is no other crime defined in terms of consent. Only in rape is the victim asked, "Did you agree to it?" Compare "Did you agree to be punched in the face?" "Did you agree to be mugged?"

First cause: unique situation

A second problem has been the language of consent, in most other circumstances no problem at all. Parties to an agreement signal consent by saying "yes." But, so the story goes, everyone knows that women say "no" when they really mean "yes" because "no" is the acceptable social response. With one word—"no"—supposedly standing in for both "yes" and "no," men have understood their job to be to persuade the woman into "yes," and if that fails, to take her "no" for the "yes" that they thought was there anyway, no matter what she said.

Second cause: language of consent

Here the law is a grim conspirator. In most jurisdictions, rape is defined not just as sexual intercourse without the woman's consent but as sexual intercourse without consent *and* as a result of force or the threat of force. So, saying "no" may not be enough. You have to say no, then wait and fear being overpowered, and then resist (complexities that don't fit on a bumper sticker).

Third cause: legal definition of rape in terms of force

By refusing to accept a verbal "no" as the end of the matter, the law requires women to be afraid. Fear is, of course, nothing new to women. We incorporate it into how we negotiate quite ordinary events—where we park, how late we stay, whether we smile at a stranger. Women can inventory the events of any day and list the ways they have been careful, the routinized responses to fear. Rape laws formalize fear. By burdening simple consent with the requirement of resistance, they keep women afraid.

Rape laws undermine consent in another way, too. There are few instances where consenting to something once means you have agreed to it forever. Remember, rape is still defined in many states as sexual intercourse with a woman who is not one's wife, without her consent and

Fourth cause: belief that marriage implies consent

as a result of force or threat of force. So, for married women, having agreed to marry means they have agreed to sex for the duration. In effect, marriage is a waiver of the protection of rape laws. Saying "no" to a husband may not matter at all.

Fifth cause: consent inferred from circumstances

The idea that there is a free zone, like marriage, in which rape can occur without consent leads to yet another problem with the way consent to sexual intercourse is popularly understood—specificity. The law says that rape is sexual intercourse without the woman's consent. That ought to mean that the woman has to consent to the intercourse itself—not just to a ride home, a movie or a walk around the block. Without this explicit consent, every time, intercourse is rape, as much a crime as punching someone in the face without her consent. Yet juries and prosecutors routinely infer consent to sex from the fact that a woman agrees to go on a date, or from the fact that she has chosen to be in a certain place at a certain time. 11

Sixth cause: careless attitudes about sex

There are other, less legal reasons why decisions by women to decline sex are not taken seriously. Go back to the bumper stickers. In many ways we seem to take the view that sex is no big deal, a funny subject for puns on car bumpers. What's the problem? Who wouldn't want it? 12

I think the answer is "lots of people," but I'm only sure about lots of women. 13

Imagine a society—or a legal system—where saying "yes" to intercourse is regarded as skeptically as saying "no" is now. In this imaginary society, spoken words are accompanied by cartoon-like bubbles over one's head that tell what the speaker really wants. We might learn that women consent for many reasons. Sometimes "yes" would mean "Yes, I want to." But other times, I'd bet that "yes" would mean "What's the point in saying 'no'? It's going to happen anyway." Or, "If I say 'no,' he'll get angry, and then what?" 14

Conclusion reinforces thesis

In our world, "yes" always signifies "yes" with regard to sex. That's OK. But if "yes" means "yes," then "no"—just "no"—has got to mean "no." Otherwise, both are confusing. Let's try *that* on a few bumper stickers. 15

Reacting to Reading

1. Preview the essay. Then, read it more carefully, and do whatever highlighting and annotating is necessary to help you understand the writer's ideas.
2. Star the cause you consider most significant. In a brief marginal note, try to explain why it is so important.

Reacting to Words

*1. Define each of the following words: *habituated* (2), *conspirator* (8), *inventory* (9), and *undermine* (10). Can you suggest a synonym for each word that will work in the essay?
2. Is *no* a strong enough word to communicate refusal in the context

Sanger describes? Can you suggest a way a woman can be sure someone hears *no* when she says *no*?

Reacting to Ideas

*1. Do you agree with Sanger that "bumper stickers may be a truer gauge of what matters to Americans than newspaper editorials" (1)? List as many bumper-sticker slogans as you can, and use them to support your position.
2. What does Sanger mean when she says that women routinely "incorporate [fear] into how [they] negotiate quite ordinary events" (9)? Do you agree with her? Do you think men also do this?

Reacting to the Pattern

1. Do Sanger's causes seem to be arranged in any particular order—for example, from least to most important?
2. What transitional words and phrases does Sanger use to connect her causes? Does she need any additional transitions?

Writing Practice

1. In your experience, has what you said always meant what you wanted it to mean? Write a cause-and-effect essay in which you discuss what happened—and why—when something you said was not heard or not interpreted accurately.
2. Sanger blames the attitude that "sex is no big deal, a funny subject for puns on car bumpers" (12), for a lot of the problems people have distinguishing consensual sex from rape. What other consequences do you think this casual attitude toward sex has in our society? Write an essay that analyzes these consequences.
3. Date rape, also called acquaintance rape, seems to be on the rise on college campuses across the country. Write an article for your college newspaper in which you examine various factors that you think account for this rise.

F COMPARISON AND CONTRAST

Comparison-and-contrast essays explain how two things are alike or how they are different; sometimes they discuss both similarities and differences.

When you organize a comparison-and-contrast essay, you can choose either a point-by-point or a subject-by-subject arrangement. A **point-by-point** comparison alternates between the two subjects you are comparing or contrasting, moving back and forth from one subject to the other. A **subject-by-subject** comparison treats its two subjects separately, first fully discussing one subject and then moving on to consider the other subject. In both kinds of comparison-and-contrast essays, the same points of comparison and contrast are applied to the two subjects.

▶ FOCUS ◀ ON TOPICS
FOR COMPARISON AND CONTRAST

The wording of your assignment may suggest comparison and contrast. For example, it may ask you to *compare, contrast, discuss similarities,* or *identify differences*.

Topic/Assignment	Thesis Statement
What basic similarities do you find in the beliefs of Henry David Thoreau and Martin Luther King, Jr.?	Although King was more politically active, both he and Thoreau strongly supported the idea of civil disobedience.
How do the diets of native Japanese and Japanese Americans differ?	As they become more and more assimilated, Japanese Americans consume more fats than their Japanese counterparts do.
Contrast the two sisters in Alice Walker's short story "Everyday Use."	Unlike Maggie, Dee—her more successful, better-educated sister—has rejected her family's heritage.

Options for Organizing Comparison-and-Contrast Essays	
Point-by-Point Comparison	**Subject-by-Subject Comparison**
¶1 Introduction (identifies subjects to be compared or contrasted)	¶1 Introduction (identifies subjects to be compared or contrasted)
¶2 First point of similarity or difference discussed for both subjects	¶2–3 First subject discussed
¶3 Second point of similarity or difference discussed for both subjects	
¶4 Third point of similarity or difference discussed for both subjects	¶4–5 Second subject discussed (points of similarity or difference discussed in same order as for first subject)
¶5 Conclusion	¶6 Conclusion

The transitional words and phrases you select in a comparison-and-contrast essay tell readers whether you are concentrating on similarities or differences. Transitions also help move readers through your essay from one subject to the other and from one point of similarity or difference to the next.

> ### ▶ FOCUS ON TRANSITIONS ◀
> ### FOR COMPARISON AND CONTRAST
>
> | | | |
> |---|---|---|
> | Likewise, | Similarly, | In comparison, |
> | In contrast, | Although | But |
> | Even though | However, | Nevertheless, |
> | On the contrary, | On the one hand, . . . | Whereas |
> | | On the other hand, | |

The following student essay, "Jason Vorhees, Meet Count Dracula" by Cheri Rodriguez, contrasts two well-known horror movie characters. A point-by-point comparison, Cheri's essay alternates between her two subjects, treating the same points in the same order for each. Notice that topic sentences ("Unlike Dracula, Jason Vorhees is a psychotic killer, . . ." "Jason is a much more frightening character than Dracula ever was," and so on) identify the subject under discussion in each paragraph and clearly signal shifts from one subject to the next.

Jason Vorhees, Meet Count Dracula

Cheri Rodriguez

1   Many people like being scared, and horror movies are the best form of entertainment for accomplishing this. In fact, horror movies have gone to extremes to terrify those who watch them. What was considered frightening fifty or sixty years ago seems mild compared to the horror movies of today, whose main characters are so violent and vicious. This difference becomes obvious when we compare early depictions of Count Dracula with the popular contemporary character Jason Vorhees.

2   Count Dracula, a popular character in the 1930s, was an aristocratic man with dark eyes, pale skin, and dark hair. He wore black suits with white shirts and bow ties. A floor-length black cape with a stiff collar set off his attire and made him look like a true count. Tall, slender, and rather handsome, Count Dracula spoke

with a strong foreign accent that made him seem mysterious and distinguished. His movements were graceful and elegant; his pale countenance was meant to strike fear in those who saw him. His dark hair and bluish tinted lips added to his formidable appearance. Still, Dracula was usually polite and charming, even to his victims.

The appearance of Jason Vorhees, the villain in the Friday the Thirteenth movies, is strikingly different from Count Dracula's. Jason's face is horribly deformed, so he hides it behind a hockey mask, which is only removed when he wants to frighten a victim or if it is accidentally torn off his face by someone. He's bald, with a few ugly bumps on his head, and he dresses in a dark, long-sleeved shirt, blue jeans, and boots. Unlike Count Dracula, Jason is tall, stocky, and ugly. He never utters a sound. He moves with a lumbering gait that is neither graceful nor elegant. As a horror movie character, he is gruesome to look at, even with his face covered (as it is most of the time).

As a vampire, Dracula sought out victims so that he could feed on their blood. The lust for blood was a driving force that he could not control, and he attacked people out of a need to survive. Every night, in the form of a bat, he would seek out his victims. Most of the time he had one particular victim in mind, and the audience was kept in suspense, wondering if Dracula would claim his victim or be stopped by the hero of the movie.

Unlike Dracula, Jason Vorhees is a psychotic killer who attacks his victims just for the thrill of it. He's never particular about who his victims are, and if there are five people staying in a cabin in the woods for the weekend, he'll attack all of them. Usually one person out of the group survives, and the audience tries to guess who will be the one to make it out alive.

In their time, the Dracula movies were suspenseful and frightening. Count Dracula's intended victim was usually a beautiful young woman who reminded him of someone he had known centuries before. Dracula's goal throughout each movie was to drink the heroine's blood and make her one of the "undead" like himself so that she could live with him for eternity. His ability to change into a bat and appear in the room of his victim would cause the audience to shiver. The sight of him sinking his fangs into his victim's throat would bring gasps of horror from viewers. Nevertheless, the Dracula movies were more suspenseful than they were violent. Few scenes were bloody (except those in which he bit his victim on the throat). I doubt if the Dracula movies would give today's audiences nightmares or make them afraid of the dark. Viewers know that there is no such thing as a vampire and that they have nothing to fear after leaving the theater.

Jason is a much more frightening character than Dracula ever was. Most of the time he carries a weapon with him, whether it is a knife, a hatchet, or a sledge hammer. If he doesn't have a weapon, he will use anything within his reach. He appears at the most unexpected times and manages to annihilate most of his victims in one evening. Jason's methods of attacking his prey bring screams of horror and revulsion from the audience. Almost every scene includes an act of violence. These movies have no real plot; Jason just goes around killing people. At the beginning of each movie, Jason is revived--no matter how he was destroyed in the preceding movie. The violence is very graphic, and these movies are not for the squeamish or weak-stomached.

Both horror movies and the characters they depict have changed dramatically over the years. The main characters are more gruesome than they used to be, and the movies contain much more graphic violence than before. Although the old movie characters seem corny and old-fashioned to some people, I prefer an evil but elegant villain in a long black cape to an ugly, inarticulate brute in a hockey mask.

☑ Writing Checklist: Comparison and Contrast

❏ Be sure you understand your assignment, audience, and purpose for writing.
❏ Use invention strategies to find ideas.
❏ Decide whether to focus on similarities or differences.
❏ Identify all points of comparison or contrast relevant to your topic.
❏ Develop a tentative thesis statement that identifies key areas of similarity or difference.
❏ Decide whether to organize your essay as a point-by-point or subject-by-subject comparison.
❏ Decide how to arrange points or subjects within your essay.
❏ Do further invention if necessary to identify additional points of comparison or contrast.
❏ Draft your essay.
❏ Revise your thesis statement.
❏ Be sure topic sentences clearly identify each subject or point.
❏ Be sure you have supplied clear transitions that move readers from one subject or point to another.
❏ Be sure you have discussed similar points for each subject.
❏ Delete any irrelevant points.
❏ Revise your introduction and conclusion.
❏ Revise sentence structure and word choice.
❏ Edit and proofread your essay.

That Lean and Hungry Look

Suzanne Britt Jordan

Suzanne Britt Jordan is a freelance writer living in Raleigh, North Carolina, who, in addition to writing regular columns for several newspapers, has published articles in many newspapers and magazines. In "That Lean and Hungry Look," which was first published in Newsweek *in 1978, Jordan uses point-by-point comparison to expose the stereotypes society applies to fat and thin people. This essay later became the basis for her first book,* Skinny People Are Dull and Crunchy Like Carrots *(1982). As you read, think about the stereotypes you yourself apply to each group.*

Introduction

Caesar was right. Thin people need watching.[1] I've been watching them for most of my adult life, and I don't like what I see. When these narrow fellows spring at me, I quiver to my toes. Thin people come in all personalities, most of them menacing. You've got your "together" thin person, your mechanical thin person, your condescending thin person, your tsk-tsk thin person, your efficiency expert thin person. All of them are dangerous.

Thesis statement
First point of contrast: Thin people aren't fun; fat people are nicer

In the first place, thin people aren't fun. They don't know how to goof off, at least in the best, fat sense of the word. They've always got to be a doing. Give them a coffee break, and they'll jog around the block: Supply them with a quiet evening at home, and they'll fix the screen door and lick S&H green stamps. They say things like "there aren't enough hours in the day." Fat people never say that. Fat people think the day is too damn long already.

Thin people make me tired. They've got speedy little metabolisms that cause them to bustle briskly. They're forever rubbing their bony hands together and eying new problems to "tackle." I like to surround myself with sluggish, inert, easygoing fat people, the kind who believe that if you clean it up today, it'll just get dirty again tomorrow.

Some people say the business about the jolly fat person is a myth, that all of us chubbies are neurotic, sick, sad people. I disagree. Fat people may not be chortling all day long, but they're a hell of a lot *nicer* than the wizened and shriveled. Thin people turn surly, mean and hard at a young age because they never learn the value of a hot-fudge sundae for easing tension. Thin people don't like gooey soft things because they themselves are neither gooey nor soft. They are crunchy and dull, like carrots. They go straight to the heart of the matter while fat people let things stay all blurry and hazy and vague, the way things ac-

---

[1]Allusion to Shakespeare's *Julius Caesar*, where Caesar expresses his suspicions of Cassius with these words: "Yond Cassius has a lean and hungry look. He thinks too much; such men are dangerous" (I,ii, 193–94).

tually are. Thin people want to face the truth. Fat people know there is no truth. One of my thin friends is always staring at complex, unsolvable problems and saying, "The key thing is . . ." Fat people never say that. They know there isn't any such thing as the key thing about anything.

Thin people believe in logic. Fat people see all sides. The sides fat people see are rounded blobs, usually gray, always nebulous and truly not worth worrying about. But the thin person persists. "If you consume more calories than you burn," says one of my thin friends, "you will gain weight. It's that simple." Fat people always grin when they hear statements like that. They know better.

5 Second point of contrast: Thin people believe in logic; fat people know life isn't logical or fair

Fat people realize that life is illogical and unfair. They know very well that God is not in his heaven and all is not right with the world. If God was up there, fat people could have two doughnuts and a big orange drink anytime they wanted it.

6

Thin people have a long list of logical things they are always spouting off to me. They hold up one finger at a time as they reel off these things, so I won't lose track. They speak slowly as if to a young child. The list is long and full of holes. It contains tidbits like "get a grip on yourself," "cigarettes kill," "cholesterol clogs," "fit as a fiddle," "ducks in a row," "organize" and "sound fiscal management." Phrases like that.

7

They think these 2,000-point plans lead to happiness. Fat people know happiness is elusive at best and even if they could get the kind thin people talk about, they wouldn't want it. Wisely, fat people see that such programs are too dull, too hard, too off the mark. They are never better than a whole cheesecake.

8

Fat people know all about the mystery of life. They are the ones acquainted with the night, with luck, with fate, with playing it by ear. One thin person I know once suggested that we arrange all the parts of a jigsaw puzzle into groups according to size, shape and color. He figured this would cut the time needed to complete the puzzle by at least 50 per cent. I said I wouldn't do it. One, I like to muddle through. Two, what good would it do to finish early? Three, the jigsaw puzzle isn't the important thing. The important thing is the fun of four people (one thin person included) sitting around a card table, working a jigsaw puzzle. My thin friend had no use for my list. Instead of joining us, he went outside and mulched the boxwoods. The three remaining fat people finished the puzzle and made chocolate, double-fudged brownies to celebrate.

9

The main problem with thin people is they oppress. Their good intentions, bony torsos, tight ships, neat corners, cerebral machinations and pat solutions loom like dark clouds over the loose, comfortable, spread-out, soft world of the fat. Long after fat people have removed their coats and shoes and put their feet up on the coffee table, thin people are still sitting on the edge of the sofa, looking neat as a pin, discussing rutabagas. Fat people are heavily into fits of laughter, slapping their thighs and whooping it up, while thin people are still politely waiting for the punch line.

10 Conclusion begins: main problem with thin people summarized

Conclusion continues: Thin people are downers; fat people are convivial and accepting

Thin people are downers. They like math and morality and reasoned evaluating of the limitations of human beings. They have their skinny little acts together. They expound, prognose, probe and prick. 11

Fat people are convivial. They will like you even if you're irregular and have acne. They will come up with a good reason why you never wrote the great American novel. They will cry in your beer with you. They will put your name in the pot. They will let you off the hook. Fat people will gab, giggle, guffaw, gallumph, gyrate and gossip. They are generous, giving and gallant. They are gluttonous and goodly and great. What you want when you're down is soft and jiggly, not muscled and stable. Fat people know this. Fat people have plenty of room. Fat people will take you in. 12

Reacting to Reading

1. Preview the essay. Then, read it more carefully, and do whatever highlighting and annotating is necessary to help you understand the writer's ideas.
2. Write a brief outline covering the key points expressed in paragraphs 2 through 4 or in paragraphs 5 through 8.

Reacting to Words

*1. Define each of these words: *sluggish* (3), *chortling* (4), *wizened* (4), *surly* (4), *nebulous* (5), *mulched* (9), *cerebral* (10), *machinations* (10), *expound* (11), *prognose* (11), and *convivial* (12). Can you suggest a synonym for each word that will work in the essay?
2. Some of the words Jordan uses—for example, *goof off* (2) and *chubbies* (4)—are quite informal. Identify other informal words, and try to substitute more formal words for some of them. How do your substitutions change the essay?

Reacting to Ideas

1. Jordan clearly intends her essay to be humorous. How can you tell? Which of her statements do you take seriously? Why?
2. What do you think Jordan means in paragraph 9 when she says, "Fat people know all about the mystery of life"? What does she mean in paragraph 10 when she says that thin people are oppressive?
*3. What stereotypes does Jordan seem to assume her readers hold? Do you think she is right?

Reacting to the Pattern

1. What do you think Jordan hopes to show by presenting so many specific differences between thin people and fat people? Do you think she overstates her case?
*2. How would Jordan's essay be different if she had used subject-by-subject comparison? Could she have used a different pattern of development to support her thesis?

Writing Practice

*1. Write a humorous essay in which you develop a point-by-point comparison between tall people and short people or men and women. As you discuss the typical characteristics of each group, cover as many stereotypes of the two groups as possible.

2. In the years since Jordan wrote her essay, overweight people have become more outspoken about the way they are viewed (and treated) by the rest of the population. Taking the point of view of an overweight person who has experienced serious discrimination, write a letter to Jordan in which you compare the way the world treats fat and thin people.

Role Models, Bogus and Real

Brent Staples

Essayist and newspaper columnist Brent Staples frequently writes about current events, particularly issues concerning race. In "Role Models, Bogus and Real," written just days after O. J. Simpson was arrested for murder, Staples examines our attitudes toward our heroes, particularly athletes. As you read, consider who your own role models are and why they qualify.

America deludes itself about why its children behave as they do. In the suburbs we herd them into malls and let them grow up bereft of community, under the impression that what you can buy is who you are. In the cities we raise them in devastated, parentless settings, where drug addiction and random gunfire rule the day.

After all that, when children behave badly we inexplicably lay the blame at the tarnished feet of America's sports gods. We blame Michael Jordan, for gambling. We blame Charles Barkley, for spitting on a fan. This week we're blaming O. J. Simpson, for battering his wife and for being accused of her murder.

The blame of which I speak is indirectly assigned, a consequence of that seemingly innocuous phrase "role model." The term entered the language 30 years ago. Initially a "role model" was someone whose successes other people—and especially children—might emulate. As the television age wore on, there came a subtle shift in meaning. A "role model" became someone who, by virtue of fame and money, was appointed surrogate parent to America's young.

These are peculiar "parents" indeed: They live behind television screens, never meet their "children" and are expected to inspire them by force of fame alone. Any failing on their part is regarded as a betrayal of the nation, and a tragedy for all those doe-eyed kids in television land. These days, the term "role model" is almost exclusively heard

1 *Introduction establishes relationship between adolescent behavior and "role models" (paragraphs 1–3)*

2

3

4 *First subject: bogus role models*

when some modern-day Icarus[1] loses his wings and comes crashing back to earth, proved mortal in the end.

In the days since O. J. Simpson's arrest for murder, there have probably been hundreds of stories lamenting the loss of a vital "role model" for America's young. This despite the fact that Mr. Simpson's glory years as a player ended 20 years ago. In popular culture, 20 years is an eternity. It's a safe bet that until Mr. Simpson's arrest, most kids had barely even heard of him.

Why then the constant "role model" morality play? Partly it's the archaic notion that athletes need to be paragons of virtue and temperance, exempt from mortal flaw. Beyond that, I think, lies a deeper and more unfortunate presumption: that only stars can affect children's lives for the better, that the mere mortals among us are powerless to guide, shape or enlighten. The sadness here is that the reverse is true. The only legitimate "role model" is the person whom children can see, feel and interact with in their daily lives.

Second subject: real role models

Enter Joseph Marshall, Jr., the recipient of a 1994 "genius" award from the MacArthur Foundation and cofounder of San Francisco's Omega Boys Club, a place where young people between the ages of 11 and 25 find friendship, surrogate parents, academic training—and college scholarships. Mr. Marshall says that inner-city kids are confused and violent because they've been "orphaned"—by family, community, government and the media. No athletes, grinning or otherwise, can reach them. His role is to recreate families for these children.

Mr. Marshall is also the host of "Street Soldiers," an extraordinary violence-intervention project. At a time when many radio talk shows have become little more than noise, Mr. Marshall's is the equivalent of a radio "parent," broadcast weekly on San Francisco's KMEL. He reaches an audience of 40,000 to 50,000 young people, many of whom he advises on such pressing matters as how not to shoot people and how to avoid being shot.

The results speak for themselves. "Street Soldiers" has a proven record of averting the reprisal shootings that often follow initial episodes of violence. And since the Omega Boys club opened in 1987, more than 100 young people who might well have gone to jail, or to graveyards, have gone to college instead.

Conclusion states thesis

That's what a role model is: someone who loves and works and encourages and lays on hands. All the rest is noise and empty air.

Reacting to Reading

1. Preview the essay. Then, read it more carefully, and do whatever highlighting and annotating is necessary to help you understand the writer's ideas.

---

[1]Character in Greek mythology who wore wax wings invented by his father but flew too close to the sun and fell to his death when the wax melted.

2. Write brief marginal notes that identify two characteristics of bogus role models and two characteristics of real role models.

Reacting to Words

*1. Define each of these words: *deludes* (1), *bereft* (1), *inexplicably* (2), *tarnished* (2), *innocuous* (3), *emulate* (3), *surrogate* (3), *lamenting* (5), *archaic* (6), *paragons* (6), *temperance* (6), *averting* (9), and *reprisal* (9). Can you suggest a synonym for each word that will work in the essay?
*2. What other words might be substituted for *bogus* in Staples's title? Why do you think Staples selected *bogus*?

Reacting to Ideas

1. In paragraph 3 Staples explains the difference between the original meaning of the term *role model* and its meaning today. What does he say is the difference? Do you think he is right?
*2. Do you agree with Staples's negative characterization of "sports gods" (2) as bogus role models? Can a sports hero be a *real* role model?

Reacting to the Pattern

*1. Staples is contrasting bogus role models, such as "sports gods" (2), with real role models, such as Joseph Marshall, Jr. Exactly how do the two kinds of role models differ?
2. This essay is a subject-by-subject comparison. Why do you think Staples discusses his two subjects in the order in which he does?

Writing Practice

1. Choose your own candidate for each of Staples's two kinds of role models, and write an essay in which you contrast the two people you have selected.
2. In paragraph 5 Staples says, "In popular culture, 20 years is an eternity." Keeping this statement in mind, write an essay in which you contrast your generation's role models with those of your parents' generation. You may interview your parents if you wish.
*3. Write an essay in which you contrast one of your role models with a television or movie hero.
4. All the role models Staples discusses are male. Write an essay called "Female Role Models, Bogus and Real."

G CLASSIFICATION AND DIVISION

Classification-and-division essays break a whole into parts (*division*) and sort various items into categories (*classification*).

> ▶ **FOCUS** ON TOPICS ◀
> ### FOR CLASSIFICATION AND DIVISION
>
> The wording of your assignment may suggest classification and division. For example, it may ask you to *classify* or *divide* or to consider *kinds, types, categories, components, segments,* or *parts* of a whole.
>
> | Topic/Assignment | Thesis Statement |
> |---|---|
> | What kinds of courses are most useful for students planning to run their own businesses? | Courses dealing with accounting, management, interpersonal communication, and computer science are most useful for future business owners. |
> | List the components of the blood, and explain the function of each. | Red blood cells, white blood cells, platelets, and plasma have very distinct functions. |
> | Classify the county's elementary schoolchildren according to their academic needs. | The county's elementary school population includes special-needs students, students with reading and math skills at or near grade level, and academically gifted students. |

Generally, each paragraph of a classification-and-division essay examines a separate category—a different part of the whole. For example, a paragraph could focus on one kind of course in the college curriculum, one component of the blood, or one type of child. Within each paragraph, you discuss the individual items that you have assigned to a particular category—for example, accounting courses, red blood cells, or gifted students. If you consider some categories less important than others, you may decide to discuss those minor categories together in a single paragraph and devote full paragraphs only to the most significant categories.

In a classification-and-division essay, topic sentences clarify the connection between the individual categories and the whole that they form. Transitional words and expressions signal the movement from one category to the next and may also tell readers which category you consider most important.

The following student essay, "Sports Fans Are in a Class by Themselves" by Deborah Ulrich, classifies sports fans into three different categories on the basis of the degree of their involvement in sports. Notice that

Options for Organizing Classification-and-Division Essays

One Category per Paragraph	Minor Categories Grouped Together
¶1 Introduction (identifies whole and its major divisions)	¶1 Introduction (identifies whole and its major divisions)
¶2 First category	¶2 Minor categories
¶3 Second category	¶3 First major category
¶4 Third category	¶4 Second (and most important) major category
¶5 Conclusion	¶5 Conclusion

> ### ▶ FOCUS ON TRANSITIONS ◀
> ### FOR CLASSIFICATION AND DIVISION
>
> The first (second, third) category   The next part
> One kind . . . another kind   The last group
> The most important component   The final type

Deborah discusses one category in each of her body paragraphs, using clear topic sentences to identify and define each kind of fan and relate each category to the group as a whole.

```
    Sports Fans Are in a Class by Themselves

                 Deborah Ulrich

     To say that all sports fans are alike would be as      1
inaccurate as saying that the seasons never change and
are exactly the same all year round. Sports fans are such
a diverse group of people that they cannot be forced into
a single category. Just as each season brings a change in
climate, so it brings various sports activities. No
matter what the season or the sporting event, however,
there are three basic types of sports fans: dedicated,
semidedicated, and totally uninterested fans.
```

Dedicated sports fans prepare weeks ahead of time for the big game. If they plan on attending the sporting event, dedicated sports fans buy their tickets months before the actual game date. They, like the letter carrier, do not let rain, sleet, snow, or blazing sun stand in the way of their passion. They come prepared to withstand all of the elements of Mother Nature, determined to cheer their team to victory. If they plan to view the game at home, they check the television thoroughly in advance to make sure it is in perfect working order. They also clearly circle the time, channel, and date of the event, in red ink, in the <u>TV Guide</u> so they will not forget the game. All the necessities, such as popcorn, chips, and beverages, are already stocked away in the cupboards and labeled "Do Not Touch!" (Remember, whatever you do, do not even whisper while the game is on. In the view of the dedicated sports fan, anything you have to say can wait until the game is over.)

Semidedicated sports fans are different. These fans are not terribly upset if tickets to the game are sold out. After all, it's only a game, and if they happen to be at home they will watch it on television, and if not, they will find out from their buddies who won. Sure, they want their team to win, but semidedicated fans understand that someone has to win and someone has to lose. To them, a sport is not a passion but a leisurely form of entertainment.

At the opposite end of the spectrum from dedicated sports fans are the totally uninterested sports fans. These are people who are usually conned or forced into going along to a sporting event with someone who is really interested in the game. After about an hour of viewing, totally uninterested fans will say, "What sport did you say this is?" and will begin to become more interested in the people around them than in those on the field or court. These fans are very easy to detect because they are the ones who know more about the location of the restroom and snack bar than about the score of the game. You might say that they are the movers and shakers of the game because they are constantly up and out of their seats disturbing everyone else's view of the game. And yes, they are the first to make a mad dash for home when the long ordeal has finally drawn to an end.

For dedicated fans, sporting events are almost always interesting. For semidedicated fans, too, sporting events can be interesting; if they aren't, sometimes just watching the people around them can be just as much fun as watching the game itself. Just ask the totally uninterested fans. They know.

☑ Writing Checklist: Classification and Division

- ❏ Be sure you understand your assignment, audience, and purpose for writing.
- ❏ Use invention strategies to find ideas.
- ❏ Identify the categories you will discuss.
- ❏ Group individual items into categories.
- ❏ Develop a tentative thesis statement that identifies the categories your essay will focus on.
- ❏ Decide how to arrange the categories in the body of your essay.
- ❏ Do further invention if necessary to identify additional categories or to find additional items to group within a particular category.
- ❏ Draft your essay.
- ❏ Revise your thesis statement.
- ❏ Revise topic sentences if necessary so that they clearly connect individual categories to the whole.
- ❏ Revise transitions if necessary so that they clearly introduce each category and distinguish one category from another.
- ❏ Check to make sure you have discussed each category in similar terms.
- ❏ Delete any irrelevant points.
- ❏ Revise your introduction and conclusion.
- ❏ Revise sentence structure and word choice.
- ❏ Edit and proofread your essay.

How Your Body Works

Dave Barry

Best known as a humorist, Dave Barry writes a syndicated column for the Miami Herald. *In a series of irreverent books, he has written on such subjects as fatherhood, home ownership, travel, and American history. "How Your Body Works" is from his book* Stay Fit and Healthy Until You're Dead, *which tackles the subject of physical fitness. This humorous essay divides a whole (the body) into its component parts and groups various characteristics into each category. As you read, consider the essay's use of headings to move readers from one category to the next.*

Your body is like a superbly engineered luxury automobile: if you use it wisely and maintain it properly, it will eventually break down, most likely in a bad neighborhood. To understand why this is, let's take a look inside this fascinating "machine" we call the human body.

Your body is actually made up of billions and billions of tiny cells,

Introduction (paragraphs 1–4)

called "cells," which are so small that you cannot see them. Neither can I. The only people who can see them are white-coated geeks called "biologists." These are the people who wrote your high-school biology textbooks, in which they claimed to have found all these organs inside the Frog, the Worm, and the Perch. Remember? And remember how, in Biology Lab, you were supposed to take an actual dead frog apart and locate the heart, the liver, etc., as depicted in the elaborate color diagrams in the textbook?

Of course, when you cut it open, all you ever found was frog glop, because that is what frogs contain, as has been proven in countless experiments performed by small boys with sticks. So you did what biology students have always done: you pretended you were finding all these organs in there, and you copied the diagram out of the book, knowing full well that in real life a frog would have no use whatsoever for a liver.

Thesis statement

Anyway, biologists tell us that the human body consists of billions of these tiny cells, which combine to form organs such as the heart, the kidney, the eyeball, the funny bone, the clavichord, the pustule, and the hernia, which in turn combine to form the body, which in turn combines with other bodies to form the squadron. Now let's take a closer look at the various fitness-related organs and see if we can't think of things to say about them.

The Skin

First category

Your skin performs several vital functions. For example, it keeps people from seeing the inside of your body, which is repulsive, and it prevents your organs from falling out onto the ground, where careless pedestrians might step on them. Also, without skin, your body would have no place to form large facial zits on the morning before your wedding.

But for fitness-oriented persons like yourself, the important thing about skin is that it acts as your Body's Cooling System. Whenever you exercise or get on an elevator, sweat oozes out of millions of tiny skin holes so it can evaporate and cool the area. Unfortunately, virtually all of these holes are located in your armpits, which is stupid. I mean, you hardly ever hear people complaining about having hot armpits. So what we seem to have here is one of those cases where Mother Nature really screwed up, like when she developed the concept of nasal hair.

The Muscle System

Second category

Your muscles are what enable you to perform all of your basic movements, such as bowling, sniping, pandering, carping, and contacting your attorney. Basically, there are two kinds of muscle tissue: the kind that people in advertisements for fitness centers have, which forms units that look like sleek and powerful pythons writhing just beneath the surface of the skin, and the kind you have, which looks more like deceased baby rabbits.

The beauty of muscle tissue, however, is that it responds to exercise. In a later chapter, we'll talk about how, using modern exercise equipment such as the Nautilus machine in a scientific workout program, you can stretch those pudgy little muscle tissues of yours to the point where you won't even be able to scream for help without the aid of powerful painkilling drugs.

The Skeletal System

How many bones do you think your skeletal system has? Would you say 50? 150? 250? 300? More than 300? 9 *Third category*

If you guessed 50, you're a real jerk. I would say it's around 250, but I don't really see why it's all that important. The only important part of your skeleton, for fitness purposes, is your knees. 10

Knees are God's way of telling mankind that He doesn't want us to do anything really strenuous. When we do, our knees punish us by becoming injured, as you know if you've ever watched professional football on television: 11

ANNOUNCER: The handoff goes to Burger; he's tackled at the six. . . . Uh oh! He's hurt!
COLOR COMMENTATOR: Looks like a knee injury, Bob, from the way that bone there is sticking out of his knee.
ANNOUNCER: Burger's teammates are bending over him. . . . Uh oh! Now *they're* down on the field!
COLOR COMMENTATOR: Looks like they've all injured their knees, too, Bob.
ANNOUNCER: Here comes the team physician, who is. . . . Uh oh! Now *he's* down on the. . . .

So one of the things we're going to stress in our fitness program is knee safety. We're going to get you so aware of this important topic that you won't even discuss racquetball over the telephone without first putting on knee braces the size of industrial turbines. 12

The Digestive System

Your digestive system is your body's Fun House, whereby food goes on a long, dark, scary ride, taking all kinds of unexpected twists and turns, being attacked by vicious secretions along the way, and not knowing until the last minute whether it will be turned into a useful body part or ejected into the Dark Hole by Mister Sphincter. You must be careful about what you eat, unless you want your body making heart valves out of things like bean dip. 13 *Fourth category*

The Central Nervous System

The central nervous system is your body's Messenger, always letting your brain know what's going on elsewhere in your body. "Your nose itches!" it tells your brain. Or, "Your foot is falling asleep!!" Or, "You're hungry!!!" All day long, your brain hears messages like these, thousands of them, hour after hour, until finally it deliberately rests 14 *Fifth category* your hand on a red-hot stove just for the pleasure of hearing your nervous system scream in pain.

Your Respiratory System

Sixth category

Your respiratory system takes in oxygen and gives off carbon monoxide, a deadly gas, by a process called "photosynthesis." This takes place in your lungs, yam-shaped organs in your chest containing millions of tiny little air sacs, called "Bernice." In a normal person, these sacs are healthy and pink, whereas in smokers they have the wretched, soot-stained, anguished look of the people fleeing Atlanta in *Gone with the Wind*. This has led many noted medical researchers to conclude that smoking is unhealthy, but we must weigh this against the fact that most of the people in cigarette advertisements are generally horse-riding, helicopter-flying hunks of major-league manhood, whereas your noted medical researchers tend to be pasty little wimps of the variety that you routinely held upside down over the toilet in junior high school.

The Circulatory System

Seventh and last category

This is, of course, your heart, a fist-sized muscle in your chest with a two-inch-thick layer of greasy fat clinging to it consisting of every Milky Way you ever ate. Your heart's job is to pump your blood, which appears to be nothing more than a red liquid but which, according to biologists (this should come as no surprise), is actually teeming with millions of organisms, some of them with tentacles so they can teem more efficiently.

The only organisms that actually belong in your blood are the red cells and the white cells. The red cells are your body's Room Service, carrying tiny particles of food and oxygen to the other organs, which snork them up without so much as a "thank you." The only reward the red cells get is iron in the form of prunes, which the other cells don't want anyway. If you don't eat enough prunes, your red cells get tired—a condition doctors called "tired blood"—and you have to lie down and watch "All My Children."

The white cells are your body's House Detectives. Most of the time they lounge around the bloodstream, telling jokes and forming the occasional cyst. But they swing into action the instant your body is invaded by one of the many enemy organisms that can get into your bloodstream, these being bacteria, viruses, rotifers, conifers, parameciums, cholesterol, tiny little lockjaw germs that dwell on the ends of all sharp objects, antacids, riboflavin, and the plague. As soon as the white cells spot one of these, they drop whatever they're doing and pursue it on a wild and often hilarious chase through your various organs, which sometimes results in damage to innocent tissue. Eventually they catch the invader and tie its tentacles behind its back with antibodies, which are the body's Handcuffs, and deport it via the bowel.

Conclusion

Of course this is just a brief rundown on your various organs and systems; in the short space I have here, it's very difficult for me to explain all of your body's complexities and subtleties in any detail, or even get any facts right. For more information, I suggest you attend Harvard Medical School, which I believe is in Wisconsin.

Reacting to Reading

1. Preview the essay. Then, read it more carefully, and do whatever highlighting and annotating is necessary to help you understand the writer's ideas.
2. Reread paragraphs 1 through 4. As you read, underline all the *factual* information in these paragraphs. What do you think is the purpose of the paragraphs' *nonfactual* information?

Reacting to Words

*1. Define each of these words: *depicted* (2), *sniping* (7), *pandering* (7), *carping* (7), *turbines* (12), *secretions* (13), *ejected* (13), and *teeming* (16). Can you suggest a synonym for each word that will work in the essay?
*2. Barry uses (not always accurately) a wide variety of scientific and medical terms, such as *cells* (2) and *hernia* (4). He also uses many unscientific terms, such as *frog glop* (3). In two columns, (one for scientific or medical terms and one for nonscientific terms), list the terms Barry uses for scientific processes, body parts, and so on. Why do you suppose he mixed scientific language with colloquial language?

Reacting to Ideas

*1. Barry's essay includes many digressions, such as his comments on smoking in paragraph 15. Identify other discussions you consider to be digressions, and try to explain their presence in the essay.
2. Barry frequently uses **personification** (giving human qualities to nonhuman things) to achieve humor in his essay—for example, calling the red blood cells "your body's Room Service" (17) and the white cells "your body's House Detectives" (18). Identify as many of these figures of speech as you can, and explain why each comparison makes sense.

Reacting to the Pattern

*1. Barry is dividing a whole (the body) into parts (skin, muscle system, and so on), and he signals movement from one component to the next with headings ("The Digestive System," for example). Sometimes, as in paragraph 14, he also includes a topic sentence that explains the function of a particular system. Which categories do *not* have such introductory sentences? Supply any missing topic sentences.
2. For the most part, Barry's treatment of each category is similar. He be-

gins by naming the organ or system, and then he explains its function. What else does he generally include in each section?

*3. Does Barry arrange his categories in any logical order?

Writing Practice

*1. Write a classification-and-division essay in which you discuss the kinds of junk food you find it most difficult to resist. Try to make your essay humorous.

2. What do you read? Classify your reading material, dividing it into four categories: assigned reading, serious personal reading, reading for information, and escape reading. Develop a thesis statement that tells which kind of reading is most important to you, and why. In your essay, support this thesis with specific examples. (If you like, you can write your essay in the form of a speech to be given to elementary school students.)

3. Write a classification-and-division essay in which you consider the three or four kinds of movies that you believe have the most negative impact on teenagers.

Shades of Black

Mary Mebane

Mary Mebane's essay, excerpted from her 1981 autobiography, describes her experiences during the 1950s as a student at North Carolina College at Durham, a historically black college. There, a rigid system of classification according to skin color and social class had an impact on every student. "Shades of Black" identifies the categories into which the population was divided and explains the characteristics of each category. As you read, consider how Mebane's status as a self-described "black black" woman affected her self-esteem.

Introduction (paragraphs 1–3)

During my first week of classes as a freshman, I was stopped one day in the hall by the chairman's wife, who was indistinguishable in color from a white woman. She wanted to see me, she said.

This woman had no official position on the faculty, except that she was an instructor in English; nevertheless, her summons had to be obeyed. In the segregated world there were (and remain) gross abuses of authority because those at the pinnacle, and even their spouses, felt that the people "under" them had no recourse except to submit—and they were right except that sometimes a black who got sick and tired of it would go to the whites and complain. This course of action was severely condemned by the blacks, but an interesting thing happened—such action always got positive results. Power was thought of in negative terms: I can deny someone something, I can strike at someone who can't strike back, I can ride someone down; that proves I am powerful. The concept of power as a force for good, for affirmative response to people or situations, was not in evidence.

When I went to her office, she greeted me with a big smile. "You know," she said, "you made the highest mark on the verbal part of the examination." She was referring to the examination that the entire freshman class took upon entering the college. I looked at her but I didn't feel warmth, for in spite of her smile her eyes and tone of voice were saying, "How could this black-skinned girl score higher on the verbal than some of the students who've had more advantages than she? It must be some sort of fluke. Let me talk to her." I felt it, but I managed to smile my thanks and back off. For here at North Carolina College at Durham, as it had been since the beginning, social class and color were the primary criteria used in determining status on the campus. *[Thesis statement]*

First came the children of doctors, lawyers, and college teachers. Next came the children of public-school teachers, businessmen, and anybody else who had access to more money than the poor black working class. After that came the bulk of the student population, the children of the working class, most of whom were the first in their families to go beyond high school. The attitude toward them was: You're here because we need the numbers, but in all other things defer to your betters. *[Three categories of social class identified]*

The faculty assumed that light-skinned students were more intelligent, and they were always a bit nonplussed when a dark-skinned student did well, especially if she was a girl. They had reason to be appalled when they discovered that I planned to do not only well but better than my light-skinned peers. *[Two categories of skin color identified]*

I don't know whether African men recently transported to the New World considered themselves handsome or more important, whether they considered African women beautiful in comparison with Native American Indian women or immigrant European women. It is a question that I have never heard raised or seen research on. If African men considered African women beautiful, just when their shift in interest away from black black women occurred might prove to be an interesting topic for researchers. But one thing I know for sure: by the twentieth century, really black skin on a woman was considered ugly in this country. This was particularly true among those who were exposed to college. *[Differences in two categories of skin color discussed (paragraphs 6–15)]*

Hazel, who was light brown, used to say to me, "You are *dark*, but not *too* dark." This saved commiserating with the damned. I had the feeling that if nature had painted one more brushstroke on me, I'd have had to kill myself.

Black skin was to be disguised at all costs. Since a black face is rather hard to disguise, many women took refuge in ludicrous makeup. Mrs. Burry, one of my teachers in elementary school, used white face powder. But she neglected to powder her neck and arms, and even the black on her face gleamed through the white, giving her an eerie appearance. But she did the best she could.

I observed all through elementary and high school that for various entertainments the girls were placed on the stage in order of color. And very black ones didn't get into the front row. If they were past caramel-brown, to the back row they would go. And nobody questioned the justice of these decisions—neither the students nor the teachers.

One of the teachers at Wildwood School, who was from the Deep South and was just as black as she could be, had been a strict enforcer of these standards. That was another irony—that someone who had been judged outside the realm of beauty herself because of her skin tones should have adopted them so wholeheartedly and applied them herself without question.

One girl stymied that teacher, though. Ruby, a black cherry of a girl, not only got off the back row but off the front row as well, to stand alone at stage center. She could outsing, outdance, and outdeclaim everyone else, and talent proved triumphant over pigmentation. But the May Queen and her Court (and in high school, Miss Wildwood) were always chosen from among the lighter ones.

When I was a freshman in high school, it became clear that a light-skinned sophomore girl named Rose was going to get the "best girl scholar" prize for the next three years, and there was nothing I could do about it, even though I knew I was the better. Rose was caramel-colored and had shoulder-length hair. She was highly favored by the science and math teacher, who figured the averages. I wasn't. There was only one prize. Therefore, Rose would get it until she graduated. I was one year behind her, and I would not get it until after she graduated.

To be held in such low esteem was painful. It was difficult not to feel that I had been cheated out of the medal, which I felt that, in a fair competition, I perhaps would have won. Being unable to protest or do anything about it was a traumatic experience for me. From then on I instinctively tended to avoid the college-exposed dark-skinned male, knowing that when he looked at me he saw himself and, most of the time, his mother and sister as well, and since he had rejected his blackness, he had rejected theirs and mine.

Oddly enough, the lighter-skinned black male did not seem to feel so much prejudice toward the black black woman. It was no accident, I felt, that Mr. Harrison, the eighth-grade teacher, who was reddish-yellow himself, once protested to the science and math teacher about the fact that he always assigned sweeping duties to Doris and Ruby Lee, two black black girls. Mr. Harrison said to them one day, right in the other teacher's presence, "You must be some bad girls. Every day I come down here ya'll are sweeping." The science and math teacher got the point and didn't ask them to sweep anymore.

Uneducated black males, too, sometimes related very well to the black black woman. They had been less firmly indoctrinated by the white society around them and were more securely rooted in their own culture.

Because of the stigma attached to having dark skin, a black black woman had to do many things to find a place for herself. One possibility was to attach herself to a light-skinned woman, hoping that some of the magic would rub off on her. A second was to make herself sexually available, hoping to attract a mate. Third, she could resign herself to a more chaste life-style—either (for the professional woman) teaching and work in established churches or (for the uneducated woman) domestic work and zealous service in the Holy and Sanctified churches.

16 Three categories of "black black" women identified

Even as a young girl, Lucy had chosen the first route. Lucy was short, skinny, short-haired, and black black, and thus unacceptable. So she made her choice. She selected Patricia, the lightest-skinned girl in the school, as her friend, and followed her around. Patricia and her friends barely tolerated Lucy, but Lucy smiled and doggedly hung on, hoping that someone who noticed Patricia might notice her, too. Though I felt shame for her behavior, even then I understood.

17 First category of "black black" women described

As is often the case of the victim agreeing with and adopting the attitudes of the oppressor, so I have seen it with black black women. I have seen them adopt the oppressor's attitude that they are nothing but "sex machines," and their supposedly superior sexual performance becomes their sole reason for being and for esteeming themselves. Such women learn early that in order to make themselves attractive to men they have somehow to shift the emphasis from physical beauty to some other area—usually sexual performance. Their constant talk is of their desirability and their ability to gratify a man sexually.

18 Second category described

I knew two such women well—both of them black black. To hear their endless talk of sexual conquests was very sad. I have never seen the category that these women fall into described anywhere. It is not that of promiscuity or nymphomania. It is the category of total self-rejection: "Since I am black, I am ugly, I am nobody. I will perform on the level that they have assigned to me." Such women are the pitiful results of what not only white America but also, and more important, black America has done to them.

19

Some, not taking the sexuality route but still accepting black society's view of their worthlessness, swing all the way across to intense religiosity. Some are staunch, fervent workers in the more traditional Southern churches—Baptist and Methodist—and others are leaders and ministers in the lower status, more evangelical Holiness sects.

20 Third category described

Another avenue open to the black black woman is excellence in a career. Since in the South the field most accessible to such women is education, a great many of them prepared to become teachers. But here, too, the black black woman had problems. Grades weren't given to her lightly in school, nor were promotions on the job. Consequently, she had to prepare especially well. She had to pass examinations with flying colors or be left behind; she knew that she would receive no special consideration. She had to be overqualified for a job because otherwise she didn't stand a chance of getting it—and she was competing only with other blacks. She had to have something to back her up: not charm, not personality—but training.

21

Conclusion: how the situation for "black black" women has changed

The black black woman's training would pay off in the 1970s. With the arrival of integration the black black woman would find, paradoxically enough, that her skin color in an integrated situation was not the handicap it had been in an all-black situation. But it wasn't until the middle and late 1960s, when the post-1945 generation of black males arrived on college campuses, that I noticed any change in the situation at all. *He* wore an afro and *she* wore an afro, and sometimes the only way you could tell them apart was when his afro was taller than hers. Black had become beautiful, and the really black girl was often selected as queen of various campus activities. It was then that the dread I felt at dealing with the college-educated black male began to ease. Even now, though, when I have occasion to engage in any type of transaction with a college-educated black man, I gauge his age. If I guess he was born after 1945, I feel confident that the transaction will turn out all right. If he probably was born before 1945, my stomach tightens, I find myself taking shallow breaths, and I try to state my business and escape as soon as possible.

Reacting to Reading

1. Preview the essay. Then, read it more carefully, and do whatever highlighting and annotating is necessary to help you understand the writer's ideas.
2. Mebane's essay addresses a very sensitive issue. What particular parts of her essay, if any, make you uncomfortable or angry? In preparation for class discussion, try to express your feelings in marginal notes.

Reacting to Words

*1. Define each of these words: *pinnacle* (2), *recourse* (2), *nonplussed* (5), *commiserating* (7), *ludicrous* (8), *stymied* (11), *indoctrinated* (15), *stigma* (16), *staunch* (20), and *fervent* (20). Can you suggest a synonym for each word that will work in the essay?
*2. In paragraph 11 Mebane describes a friend as "a black cherry of a girl"; in paragraph 12 she describes another as "caramel-colored." What other words and phrases does she use to describe skin tone? Why do you think she uses such varied and vivid terms?

Reacting to Ideas

*1. In paragraph 4 Mebane identifies the three categories of social class that determined students' status at her school. Do these categories (or others) apply at your school? In your community?
2. How does Mebane account for the "low esteem" (13) in which dark-skinned black women were held? Do you think her explanation makes sense? Does it adequately explain the situation?
3. Mebane describes two kinds of classification systems in her essay, one based on social class and one based on color. Which do you think she considers more important? Do you think the two systems are related?

Reacting to the Pattern

*1. Mebane identifies three categories of social class in paragraph 4, but (because her essay's focus is on *shades* of black) nowhere does she formally list and define all the distinct categories of skin color. List as many categories as you can, beginning with those considered most desirable. Briefly define each category, and give an example of each from Mebane's essay.
*2. List and define the kinds of "black black" women Mebane identifies.

Writing Practice

*1. Write a classification-and-division essay in which you discuss the different kinds of students who attend your school. Make sure you classify them according to only one system—the way they dress, where they congregate, or what their majors are, for example.
2. What occupations have the most and the least status? Write a classification-and-division essay in which you discuss three categories: high-status occupations, neutral-status occupations, and low-status occupations. Be sure to define each category and give plenty of examples.
3. List all the courses you remember taking in high school. From your current perspective as a college student, divide these courses into three categories: those that have already been useful to you, those you expect will be useful to you in the future, and those you now see as a complete waste of time. Write a classification-and-division essay explaining and illustrating each category of course.

H DEFINITION

Definition essays explain the meaning of a term. Most terms, of course, can be defined in one or two sentences. What a definition essay does is present an **extended definition**, using other patterns of development to move well beyond a simple dictionary definition.

▶ FOCUS ON TOPICS FOR DEFINITION ◀

The wording of your assignment may suggest definition. For example, it may ask you to *define* or *explain* or to answer the question *What is x?* or *What does x mean?*

Topic/Assignment	Thesis Statement
Explain the meaning of the term *performance art*.	Unlike more conventional forms of art, *performance art* extends beyond the canvas.

(continued on the following page)

(continued from the previous page)

What did Darwin mean by *natural selection*?	*Natural selection*, popularly known as "survival of the fittest," is a good deal more complicated than most people think.
What is *attention deficit disorder*?	*Attention deficit disorder* (ADD), once narrowly defined as a childhood problem, is now known to affect adults as well as children.

As the above thesis statements suggest, definition essays may be developed in many ways. For example, you can define by telling how something occurred (narration), by describing its appearance (description), by giving a series of examples (exemplification), by telling how it operates (process), by telling how it is similar to or different from something else (comparison and contrast), or by discussing its parts (classification and division). Some definition essays use a single pattern of development; others combine several patterns of development, perhaps using a different one in each paragraph.

Options for Organizing Definition Essays	
Definition Using a Single Pattern of Development	**Definition Combining Several Different Patterns of Development**
¶1 Introduction (identifies term to be defined)	¶1 Introduction (identifies term to be defined)
¶2 Definition by example	¶2 Definition by description
¶3 Additional examples	¶3 Definition by example
¶4 Additional examples	¶4 Definition by comparison and contrast
¶5 Conclusion	¶5 Conclusion

The kinds of transitions used in a definition essay depend on the specific pattern or patterns of development in the essay. (In addition to the transitional words and expressions listed in the box below, you may also use those appropriate for the particular patterns you use to develop your definition essay.)

> **FOCUS ON TRANSITIONS FOR DEFINITION**
>
> One characteristic . . . another characteristic
> Like . . . unlike
> One way . . . another way
> In particular,
>
> For example,
> Also,
> In addition,
> Specifically,

The following student essay, "Street Smart" by Kristin Whitehead, defines the term *street smart*. In the essay's introduction, Kristin defines her term briefly: "To us, being street smart meant having common sense." In the essay's body paragraphs, she expands her definition by providing examples of street-smart behavior and by contrasting her own street-smart behavior with her friends' actions. Notice that the topic sentences of Kristin's three body paragraphs repeat the phrase *being street start means* to remind readers of the essay's focus.

```
                    Street Smart

                  Kristin Whitehead
```

1   I grew up in a big city, so I suppose you could say I was practically born street smart. I learned the hard way how to act and what to do, and so did my friends. To us, being street smart meant having common sense. We wanted to be cool, but we needed to be safe, too. Now I go to college in a big city, and I realize that not everyone here grew up the way I did. Lots of students are from suburbs or rural areas, and they are either terrified of the city or totally ignorant of city life. The few suburban or rural kids who are willing to venture downtown all have one thing in common: They are not street smart.

2   Being street smart means knowing how to protect your possessions. Friends of mine who aren't used to city life insist on wearing all their jewelry when they go downtown. I think this is asking for trouble, and I know better. I always tuck my chain under my shirt and leave my gold earrings home. Another thing that sur-

prises me is how some of my friends wave their money around. They always seem to be standing on the street, trying to count their change or stuff dollars into their wallet. Street-smart people make sure to put their money safely away in their pockets or purses before they leave a store. A street-smart person will also carry a backpack, a purse strapped across the chest, or no purse at all. A person who is not street smart carries a purse loosely over one shoulder or dangles it by its handle. Again, these people are asking for trouble.

Being street smart also means protecting yourself. It means being aware of your surroundings at all times, and <u>looking</u> as if you are. A lot of times I've been downtown with people who kept stopping on the street to talk about where they should go next, or walking up and down the same street over and over again. A street-smart person would never do this. It's important to look as if you know where you're going at all times, even if you don't. Whenever possible, you should decide on a destination in advance, and you should make sure you know how to get there. Even if you are not completely sure where you're headed, your body language should convey your confidence in your ability to reach your destination.

Finally, being street smart means protecting your life. A street-smart person does not walk alone, especially after dark, in an unfamiliar neighborhood. A street-smart person does not ask strangers for directions; when lost, he or she asks a shopkeeper for help. A street-smart person takes main streets instead of side streets. When faced with danger or the threat of danger, a street-smart person knows when to run, when to scream, and when to give up money or possessions to avoid violence.

So how do you get to be street smart? Some people think it's a gift, but I think it's something you can learn. Probably the best way to learn how to be street smart is to hang out with people who know where they are going and do what they do.

☑ Writing Checklist: Definition

❑ Be sure you understand your assignment, audience, and purpose for writing.
❑ Use invention strategies to find ideas.
❑ Decide what pattern or patterns of development to use to develop your definition.
❑ Develop a tentative thesis statement that presents your definition and suggests why you are defining the term.
❑ Decide how to arrange your paragraphs in the body of your essay.
❑ Draft your essay.
❑ Revise your thesis statement.

- Add transitions if necessary to connect different parts of your definition.
- Revise topic sentences if necessary so they clearly introduce the different sections of your definition.
- Delete any points that are irrelevant to your topic.
- Revise your introduction and conclusion.
- Revise sentence structure and word choice.
- Edit and proofread your essay.

Tortillas

José Antonio Burciaga

Bilingual essayist and poet José Antonio Burciaga included this essay in his 1988 collection Weedee Peepo, *an affectionate look at his family and culture. Here he defines the tortilla, remembering its important role in his childhood. As you read, notice how he combines various patterns of development to shape his definition.*

1   My earliest memory of *tortillas* is my *Mamá* telling me not to play with them. I had bitten eyeholes in one and was wearing it as a mask at the dinner table.

Introduction identifies term to be defined

2   As a child, I also used *tortillas* as hand warmers on cold days, and my family claims that I owe my career as an artist to my early experiments with *tortillas*. According to them, my clowning around helped me develop a strong artistic foundation. I'm not so sure, though. Sometimes I wore a *tortilla* on my head, like a *yarmulke*, and yet I never had any great urge to convert from Catholicism to Judaism. But who knows? They may be right.

3   For Mexicans over the centuries, the *tortilla* has served as the spoon and the fork, the plate and the napkin. *Tortillas* originated before the Mayan civilizations, perhaps predating Europe's wheat bread. According to Mayan mythology, the great god Quetzalcoatl, realizing that the red ants knew the secret of using maize as food, transformed himself into a black ant, infiltrated the colony of red ants, and absconded with a grain of corn. (Is it any wonder that to this day, black ants and red ants do not get along?) Quetzalcoatl then put maize on the lips of the first man and woman, Oxomoco and Cipactonal, so that they would become strong. Maize festivals are still celebrated by many Indian cultures of the Americas.

History of the tortilla

4   When I was growing up in El Paso, *tortillas* were part of my daily life. I used to visit a *tortilla* factory in an ancient adobe building near the open *mercado* in Ciudad Juárez. As I approached, I could hear the rhythmic slapping of the *masa* as the skilled vendors outside the factory formed it into balls and patted them into perfectly round corn cakes between the palms of their hands. The wonderful aroma and the speed with which the women counted so many dozens of *tortillas* out of

Process of making tortillas

warm wicker baskets still linger in my mind. Watching them at work convinced me that the most handsome and *deliciosas tortillas* are handmade. Although machines are faster, they can never adequately replace generation-to-generation experience. There's no place in the factory assembly line for the tender slaps that give each *tortilla* character. The best thing that can be said about mass-producing *tortillas* is that it makes it possible for many people to enjoy them.

Ways of eating tortillas

In the *mercado* where my mother shopped, we frequently bought *taquitos de nopalitos*, small tacos filled with diced cactus, onions, tomatoes, and *jalapeños*. Our friend Don Toribio showed us how to make delicious, crunchy *taquitos* with dried, salted pumpkin seeds. When you had no money for the filling, a poor man's *taco* could be made by placing a warm *tortilla* on the left palm, applying a sprinkle of salt, then rolling the *tortilla* up quickly with the fingertips of the right hand. My own kids put peanut butter and jelly on *tortillas*, which I think is truly bicultural. And speaking of fast foods for kids, nothing beats a *quesadilla*, a *tortilla* grilled-cheese sandwich.

Depending on what you intend to use them for, *tortillas* may be made in various ways. Even a run-of-the-mill *tortilla* is more than a flat corn cake. A skillfully cooked homemade *tortilla* has a bottom and a top; the top skin forms a pocket in which you put the filling that folds your *tortilla* into a taco. Paper-thin *tortillas* are used specifically for *flautas*, a type of taco that is filled, rolled, and then fried until crisp. The name *flauta* means *flute*, which probably refers to the Mayan bamboo flute; however, the only sound that comes from an edible *flauta* is a delicious crunch that is music to the palate. In México *flautas* are sometimes made as long as two feet and then cut into manageable segments. The opposite of *flautas* is *gorditas*, meaning *little fat ones*. These are very thick small *tortillas*.

Other uses of tortillas

The versatility of *tortillas* and corn does not end here. Besides being tasty and nourishing, they have spiritual and artistic qualities as well. The Tarahumara Indians of Chihuahua, for example, concocted a corn-based beer called *tesgüino*, which their descendants still make today. And everyone has read about the woman in New Mexico who was cooking her husband a *tortilla* one morning when the image of Jesus Christ miraculously appeared on it. Before they knew what was happening, the man's breakfast had become a local shrine.

Then there is *tortilla* art. Various Chicano artists throughout the Southwest have, when short of materials or just in a whimsical mood, used a dry *tortilla* as a small, round canvas. And a few years back, at the height of the Chicano movement, a priest in Arizona got into trouble with the Church after he was discovered celebrating mass using a *tortilla* as the host. All of which only goes to show that while the *tortilla* may be a lowly corn cake, when the necessity arises, it can reach unexpected distinction.

Thesis statement

Reacting to Reading

1. Preview the essay. Then, read it more carefully, and do whatever highlighting and annotating is necessary to help you understand the writer's ideas.
2. Circle all the Spanish words Burciaga uses in his essay.

Reacting to Words

*1. Define each of these words: *yarmulke* (2), *maize* (3), *infiltrated* (3), *adobe* (4), *edible* (6), *concocted* (7), and *whimsical* (8). Can you suggest a synonym for each word that will work in the essay?
2. Review the Spanish words you circled in Reacting to Reading question 2. Do you think most people who don't know Spanish could determine the meanings of these words from their context?

Reacting to Ideas

*1. List all the uses of the tortilla Burciaga identifies. Then, divide your list into two categories, practical and whimsical uses. Can you suggest any other uses to add to either category?
2. What information does this essay give you about Burciaga and his family? What kind of person do you think he is? What makes you think so?

Reacting to the Pattern

*1. Identify sections of his essay where Burciaga develops his definition with examples, description, and narration. Can you identify any other patterns of development?
2. Burciaga does not include a formal dictionary definition of *tortilla* in his essay. Try writing a one- or two-sentence definition that begins, "Tortillas are . . ."

Writing Practice

1. Is there an ethnic food for which you feel the same affection that Burciaga feels for the tortilla? Write an essay in which you use narration, exemplification, and description to define this food.
*2. Write a definition of one of these food items for an audience that has never seen or heard of the food before: a hot dog, pizza, chili, nachos, grits, or a Big Mac. Begin by defining the food in a single sentence. Then, go on to describe it and show how it is like and unlike other foods with which your readers may be familiar.

History on the Head

Leora Frankel

In response to the popularity of the kaffiyeh (pronounced ka-fee'-a*) as a fashion accessory, this essay appeared in the style section of a major big-city newspaper. Although Frankel acknowledges the kaffiyeh's newfound role in the modern, secular world, she also traces its history and defines it as an important religious and cultural symbol. As you read, note how she quotes a variety of sources to help explain the significance of the kaffiyeh.*

Introduction identifying term to be defined (paragraphs 1–2). First sentence gives brief definition

It is the ultimate cultural survivor in the Middle East: the plain or stitched cotton cloth that Arabs wear on their heads and draped down the back or shoulders. Designed more than 1,000 years ago, it originally protected against the harsh desert climate. Today, it's also an emblem of masculinity, maturity and nationalism. A substitute flag, a mask, a shield. A political or a fashion statement.

It is the kaffiyeh, the headdress, often tasseled, that has been adapted to a multitude of eras, having been embraced all over the Middle East by Muslims, Christians and Druse as well as by tourists and by street vendors in Manhattan.

History of the kaffiyeh

Born in the depths of the deserts, the kaffiyeh (kuh-FEE-yeh) protected wandering Bedouins[1] from lethal sun and sandstorms before Arab workers in all but North Africa started wearing it as a head cover. Over the centuries, it won a class war with the fez, overcame the influx of Western dress and made the leap to the United States and Europe as a fashionable scarf.

The kaffiyeh, whose name may be derived from the Iraqi city of Kufa, is believed to have begun as cream-colored or white. It is now seen in varying colors. Even green and purple stitchings have been spotted.

Kaffiyehs as fashion items for tourists

Tourists in Jerusalem often buy kaffiyehs, usually 40-odd inches square, in wild colors and printed patterns for as little as $3. But an Arab would never wear a print kaffiyeh.

Carol Eisenberg, a New York lawyer visiting her stepson, looked for a white kaffiyeh with red stitching in the Old City. "I thought it would look handsome with my coat," she said. The vendors' hard sell scared her away, but now she wants her stepson to buy her one, despite some fear that people back home might "think I'm like Vanessa Redgrave."[2]

Traditional uses of kaffiyehs

Kaffiyehs can have political, practical and cultural significance. Palestinians beyond middle age wear them out of a sense of dignity. They prefer white in the summer to deflect the heat. When the temperature drops, they wear kaffiyehs made heavier by extensive red or black stitching, the same kind that younger Palestinians wear at nationalist protests year round.

Bedouin boys traditionally receive them from their fathers in their midteens.

"I felt it was the best present in the world—I became like a man," a 77-year-old Bedouin said recently as he poured tea in his tent in the Judean desert, east of Jerusalem. Like others, he considered kaffiyehs to be a sensitive topic and preferred not to be named. "I would fight any person who wants to take my kaffiyeh," he added. "This is my honor."

Some kaffiyehs are made in the West Bank, but the best are from Jordan and cost about $10. "They're softer," said Jamil Tamimi, a vendor, "and the tassels are finer."

---

[1] Nomadic, desert-dwelling people of the Middle East.
[2] Actress who has sparked controversy because of her support for the Palestine Liberation Organization (PLO).

In some Arab societies, the length of the tassels is a sign of status, as is the thickness of the black rings, the iqal, placed on the head over the kaffiyeh. In gold, the iqal is usually reserved for the very wealthy. The iqal (the word is related to the Arabic for wisdom) has come a long way from its origins as a rope for hobbling camels' legs. While women sometimes wear kaffiyehs, particularly in the fields, they never wear iqals because iqals are a symbol of masculinity.

Throwing another man's iqal on the ground is "like rubbing his nose in the dirt," said Ali Khalili, a Palestinian writer and folklore expert. When a Bedouin throws his own iqal on the ground, it is a sign of rage, said Clinton Bailey, an expert on Bedouin culture. "It means," he added, "that he is staking his manhood on a certain point."

Many say the kaffiyeh became a symbol of the Palestinian cause in 1936, during the British mandate over Palestine. It was in an Arab uprising then that the British equated kaffiyeh-wearers with the insurgents. In allegiance, the Palestinian middle and upper classes began wearing kaffiyehs, abandoning the more prestigious Turkish fez. *Relationship between the kaffiyeh and the Palestinian cause*

"There is no other Palestinian kaffiyeh than the black and white one," a 22-year-old activist said, referring to the type favored by the Palestine Liberation Organization chairman, Yasir Arafat. But his style of wearing it—peaked atop his head and draped over a shoulder—mystifies many supporters. Does he use pins? Does the kaffiyeh's outline when his face is in profile represent the map of Palestine, thus a subliminal message?

Palestinians in left-wing organizations like the Popular Front for the Liberation of Palestine wear a white kaffiyeh with red stitching, red being the color of revolution.

When young Palestinians go into the streets to protest and confront Israeli soldiers, or display and use guns, they wrap the kaffiyeh around their neck or hide their face with it. And they never wear an iqal.

The new generation makes shirts and dresses out of kaffiyehs and puts kaffiyeh patterns on book covers and posters. It uses the kaffiyeh instead of the Palestinian flag as a symbol "because the flag is forbidden to us," Mr. Khalili said, adding, "This past year the Israelis also started harassing young people with kaffiyehs."

A high-ranking Israeli security officer said the kaffiyeh is badly misused. "After a criminal activity, it can easily be transformed from a mask into an ordinary accessory," he said. "It is supposed to confuse and embarrass us." But Israeli undercover soldiers who dress as Arabs also rely on kaffiyehs.

A guide to survival behavior in the Middle East would advise you to throw aside your kaffiyeh when Israeli soldiers are looking for suspects or shooting, but to display it as a talisman when confronted with Palestinians throwing stones or burning cars.

Until the Palestinian uprising that began in 1987, Israelis liked to wear them on hikes. Today, the Sinai desert is the only place where they feel comfortable wearing one. *Conclusion: appeal of the kaffiyeh to non-Arabs*

"When I'm in Sinai, I feel that I'm a Bedouin in my soul," said a 29-year-old owner of a Tel Aviv advertising agency who had been seen at the Taba checkpoint wearing a kaffiyeh, given to him by a Bedouin friend. 21

"The kaffiyeh links me to their culture," he said. "It symbolizes a certain purity." 22

Reacting to Reading

1. Preview the essay. Then, read it more carefully, and do whatever highlighting and annotating is necessary to help you understand the writer's ideas.
2. Outline paragraphs 13 through 19.

Reacting to Words

*1. Define each of these words: *lethal* (3), *fez* (3), *influx* (3), *deflect* (7), *hobbling* (11), *mandate* (13), *insurgents* (13), *subliminal* (14), and *talisman* (19). Can you suggest a synonym for each that will work in the essay?
2. Frankel explains the origins of the words *kaffiyeh* and *iqal*. What is the origin of each of these words?

Reacting to Ideas

1. Why do you suppose Frankel quotes so many different kinds of people in her essay?
*2. Do you think Frankel's essay treats the kaffiyeh with respect? Or do you think she trivializes it by devoting so much attention to its popularity as a "fashion statement" (1)?

Reacting to the Pattern

*1. Where in her essay does Frankel develop her definition with examples? With description? Does she use any other patterns of development?
2. Where in her definition does Frankel present historical background? Do you think this background is necessary? Explain.

Writing Practice

1. Do you own an item of clothing as versatile as the kaffiyeh? Write a definition essay in which you begin with a description of the item and then use examples to show its many uses.
2. Is there an item of clothing that has cultural or religious significance for you? Write an essay that defines this piece of apparel, including information about its history as well as its appearance.
3. How do you use the way you dress to project your image to other peo-

ple? Write an essay in which you identify key accessories and articles of clothing in your wardrobe and explain how they work together to create a particular image. In your thesis statement, define the image you wish to project; in your essay's body paragraphs, expand your definition with examples and description.

I ARGUMENT

Argument uses facts, examples, and expert opinion (evidence) to persuade readers to accept a debatable position.

> ### ▶ FOCUS ON TOPICS FOR ARGUMENT ◀
>
> The wording of your assignment may suggest argument. For example, you may be asked to *debate, argue, consider, give your opinion, take a position,* or *take a stand.*
>
> | Topic/Assignment | Thesis Statement |
> |---|---|
> | Explain your position on the debate about national health care. | A system of national health care should be developed, assuming both taxpayers and the government are prepared to pay for it. |
> | Do you believe that General Lee was responsible for the South's defeat at the Battle of Gettysburg? Why or why not? | Because Lee refused to listen to the advice given to him by General Longstreet, he is largely responsible for the South's defeat at the Battle of Gettysburg. |
> | In your opinion, should assisted suicide be legalized? | Although many people think assisted suicide should remain illegal, I believe it should be legal in certain situations. |

An argument essay can be organized *inductively* or *deductively.*

An **inductive argument** moves from the specific to the general: It begins with a group of specific observations and ends with a general conclusion based on these observations. An inductive argument responding to the first of the three topics in the focus box above, for example, could begin with a series of observations about national health care and end with the conclusion that it makes sense if it can be paid for.

A **deductive argument**, however, moves from the general to the specific. A deductive argument begins with a **major premise**—a general statement that the writer believes his or her audience will accept—and then moves to a **minor premise**—a specific instance of the belief stated in the major premise. It ends with a **conclusion** that follows from the two premises. For example, an essay that responds to the third topic above could begin with the major premise that terminally ill patients who are in great pain should be given access to assisted suicide. It could then go on to state and support the minor premise that a particular patient is both terminally ill and in great pain. The essay could conclude by saying that this patient should, therefore, be allowed the option of assisted suicide. In this way, the deductive argument goes through three steps:

Major premise

Terminally ill patients who are in great pain should be allowed to choose the option of assisted suicide.

Minor premise

John Lacca is a terminally ill patient who is in great pain.

Conclusion

Therefore, John Lacca should be allowed to choose assisted suicide.

Options for Organizing Argument Essays		
Induction	**Deduction**	**Combination of Strategies**
¶1 Introduction	¶1 Introduction	¶1 Introduction
¶2 First set of observations	¶2 Major premise	¶2 Induction
¶3 Second set of observations	¶3 Minor premise	¶3 Induction
¶4 Third set of observations	¶4 Evidence supporting minor premise	¶4 Deduction
¶5 Conclusion	¶5 Conclusion	¶5 Conclusion

Before you present your argument, you should decide whether your readers will be hostile, neutral, or in agreement with your thesis. Once you understand your audience, you can determine which arguments you should use.

As you write your argument essay, make sure you begin each paragraph

APPENDIX D Patterns of Essay Development ■ 595

with a topic sentence that clearly relates the discussion to the previous paragraph or to your thesis statement. Throughout your essay try to include specific examples that will make your arguments persuasive. Keep in mind that arguments that rely just on generalizations are not as convincing as those that include vivid details and pointed examples. Finally, strive for a balanced, moderate tone, and avoid name-calling or personal attacks.

Transitions are extremely important in argument essays because they not only signal the movement from one part of the argument to another but also relate specific points to each other and to the thesis statement.

▶ FOCUS ON TRANSITIONS FOR ARGUMENT ◀

But	Indeed,	Truly,	Granted,
Because	In fact,	In conclusion,	To be sure,
Since	Of course,	In summary,	Nevertheless,
Consequently,	On the one hand,	Therefore,	Nonetheless
Moreover,	On the other hand,	Thus,	Despite
Although	Accordingly,	Admittedly,	Certainly

The following student paper, "Why Isn't Pete Rose in the Hall of Fame?" by John Fleeger, is an argument essay. John takes a strong stand in favor of allowing baseball player Pete Rose to be inducted into the National Baseball Hall of Fame, and he supports his thesis with specific facts and examples. The deductive argument that underlies John's essay moves from the major premise (*Qualified players who do not violate major-league rules should be inducted into the Hall of Fame*) to the minor premise (*Pete Rose is a qualified player who did not violate major-league rules*) to the conclusion (*Therefore, Pete Rose should be inducted into the Hall of Fame*).

```
            Why Isn't Pete Rose in the Hall of Fame?

                            John Fleeger

     Nineteen ninety-two marked the first year Pete Rose        1
would have been eligible for the National Baseball Hall
of Fame. Not only was he not elected, his name did not
even appear on the ballot. Why? Has he not established
himself as the all-time best hitter in baseball? Was
he not a member of two championship teams with the
Cincinnati Reds and one with the Philadelphia Phillies?
Did he not help build the foundation for the 1990
championship Reds team? Has he not set or tied several
```

major-league and team records during his career? The answer to all of these questions is "Yes." His dedication to and enthusiasm for the game of baseball earned him the nickname "Charlie Hustle," but not his rightful place in the Hall of Fame. This is unfair and should be changed.

In the late summer of 1989, Pete Rose was banned from professional baseball. The legal agreement reached between major-league officials and Pete Rose does not offer any evidence that Rose bet on any baseball games, and Rose himself does not say that he did. Despite the lack of any confirmation, A. Bartlett Giamatti, Commissioner of Baseball at that time, publicly declared that Rose bet not only on baseball, but also on his own team. Betting on baseball is a violation of major-league rules and is punishable by lifetime banishment from baseball. This was the sentence Pete Rose received.

In 1991 the Hall of Fame Committee along with Fay Vincent, who was then Commissioner of Baseball, decided that as long as a player is banned from baseball, he is ineligible for Hall of Fame selection. This action was taken just a few weeks before Rose's name could have been placed on the ballot, and many believe that Vincent encouraged it specifically to make sure Rose could not be considered for selection. Several of the baseball writers who voted for the Hall of Fame candidates voiced their disapproval of this policy by writing in Rose's name on the ballot. Unfortunately, write-in votes are not counted.

Rose's only hope of making the Hall of Fame depends on his being readmitted to baseball. The commissioner would have to review Rose's application and approve his reinstatement. Chances are not good, however, that the commissioner would reinstate Rose. Therefore, Rose will probably have to wait for a commissioner who is sympathetic to his situation before he applies for reinstatement.

Meanwhile, on the strength of circumstantial evidence and the testimony of convicted felons, baseball has convicted Pete Rose of betting on baseball. He has admitted to betting on horse races and football games but denies ever betting on the sport he loves. He has also admitted that his gambling was a problem and has spent time in counseling. Why is a player who once gambled any worse than the many players who have tested positive for drugs? Those players are suspended from the game for a period of time and are given one or more chances to recover and return to the major league. Why are gamblers not treated the same way as drug abusers?

Many people mistakenly believe that Pete Rose went to prison for betting on baseball and that, for this reason, he should be kept out of the Hall of Fame. The fact is, however, that Rose went to prison for tax-law violations. He failed to pay income tax on his gambling winnings and on the money he made at baseball-card shows. Even so, when has the Hall of Fame ever been reserved for perfect people? Babe Ruth was an adulterer and a serious drinker, but he still holds a place in the Hall. Mickey Mantle and Willie Mays were barred from baseball for being employees of an Atlantic City casino (an obvious gambling connection), but even this decision was eventually overturned.

I have met Pete Rose and, granted, he does not have the greatest personality, but his personal shortcomings are no reason to keep him out of the Hall of Fame. His contributions to the game and his accomplishments as a player more than qualify him to occupy a place beside the greats of the game. Baseball should, in all fairness, let Pete Rose return to the game and allow him to take his rightful place in the Hall of Fame.

☑ Writing Checklist: Argument

- ❏ Be sure you understand your assignment, audience, and purpose for writing.
- ❏ Use invention strategies to find ideas.
- ❏ Be sure your topic is debatable.
- ❏ Develop a tentative thesis statement that accurately presents your position.
- ❏ Determine whether your readers are likely to be hostile, neutral, or in agreement with your thesis.
- ❏ Decide what points you want to make.
- ❏ Determine what evidence you will need to support your points.
- ❏ Decide whether to use an inductive or deductive argument or a combination of the two.
- ❏ Draft your essay.
- ❏ Revise your thesis statement.
- ❏ Add the transitions you need to connect each part of the argument to your thesis.
- ❏ Be sure you have supported your points convincingly.
- ❏ Do further invention if necessary to find additional evidence.
- ❏ Add any facts or examples you need to explain or illustrate your points.
- ❏ Delete any points that are irrelevant to your thesis.
- ❏ Be sure your introduction clearly states your position.
- ❏ Be sure your conclusion follows logically from the points you have made in your essay.
- ❏ Revise sentence structure and word choice.
- ❏ Edit and proofread your essay.

I Have a Dream

Martin Luther King, Jr.

On August 28, 1963, Martin Luther King, Jr., delivered the following speech on the steps in front of the Lincoln Memorial in Washington, D.C. King used the occasion of this speech—the March on Washington in which over two hundred thousand people participated—to reinforce his ideas about racial equality and nonviolent protest. The speech itself is a deductive argument that makes a compelling case for racial justice in the United States. As you read, notice King's effective use of repetition.

Introduction (paragraphs 1–2) provides background

Five score years ago, a great American, in whose symbolic shadow we stand, signed the Emancipation Proclamation. This momentous decree came as a great beacon light of hope to millions of Negro slaves who had been seared in the flames of withering injustice. It came as a joyous daybreak to end the long night of captivity.

But one hundred years later, we must face the tragic fact that the Negro is still not free. One hundred years later, the life of the Negro is still sadly crippled by the manacles of segregation and the chains of discrimination. One hundred years later, the Negro lives on a lonely island of poverty in the midst of a vast ocean of material prosperity. One hundred years later, the Negro is still languishing in the corners of American society and finds himself an exile in his own land. So we have come here today to dramatize an appalling condition.

Major premise: America promises that all citizens are entitled to life, liberty, and the pursuit of happiness

In a sense we have come to our nation's capital to cash a check. When the architects of our republic wrote the magnificent words of the Constitution and the Declaration of Independence, they were signing a promissory note to which every American was to fall heir. This note was a promise that all men—yes, black men as well as white men—would be guaranteed the unalienable rights of life, liberty, and the pursuit of happiness.

Minor premise: Negroes are citizens

It is obvious today that America has defaulted on this promissory note insofar as her citizens of color are concerned. Instead of honoring this sacred obligation, America has given the Negro people a bad check, a check which has come back marked "insufficient funds." But we refuse to believe that there are insufficient funds in the great vaults of opportunity of this nation. So we have come to cash this check—a check that will give us upon demand the riches of freedom and the security of justice. We have also come to this hallowed spot to remind America of the fierce urgency of *now*. This is no time to engage in the luxury of cooling off or to take the tranquilizing drugs of gradualism.

Conclusion: Therefore, Negroes are entitled to life, liberty, and the

Now is the time to make real the promises of Democracy. *Now* is the time to rise from the dark and desolate valley of segregation to the sunlit path of racial justice. *Now* is the time to open the doors of opportunity to all of God's children. *Now* is the time to lift our nation from the quicksands of racial injustice to the solid rock of brotherhood.

It would be fatal for the nation to overlook the urgency of the moment and to underestimate the determination of the Negro. This sweltering summer of the Negro's legitimate discontent will not pass until there is an invigorating autumn of freedom and equality; 1963 is not an end, but a beginning. Those who hope that the Negro needed to blow off steam and will now be content will have a rude awakening if the nation returns to business as usual. There will be neither rest nor tranquility in America until the Negro is granted his citizenship rights. The whirlwinds of revolt will continue to shake the foundations of our nation until the bright day of justice emerges. *pursuit of happiness*

But there is something that I must say to my people who stand on the warm threshold which leads into the palace of justice. In the process of gaining our rightful place we must not be guilty of wrongful deeds. Let us not seek to satisfy our thirst for freedom by drinking from the cup of bitterness and hatred. We must forever conduct our struggle on the high plane of dignity and discipline. We must not allow our creative protest to degenerate into physical violence. Again and again we must rise to the majestic heights of meeting physical force with soul force. The marvelous new militancy which has engulfed the Negro community must not lead us to a distrust of all white people, for many of our white brothers, as evidenced by their presence here today, have come to realize that their destiny is tied up with our destiny and their freedom is inextricably bound to our freedom. We cannot walk alone. *Voice of moderation*

And as we walk, we must make the pledge that we shall march ahead. We cannot turn back. There are those who are asking the devotees of civil rights, "When will you be satisfied?" We can never be satisfied as long as the Negro is the victim of the unspeakable horrors of police brutality. We can never be satisfied as long as our bodies, heavy with the fatigue of travel, cannot gain lodging in the motels of the highways and the hotels of the cities. We cannot be satisfied as long as the Negro's basic mobility is from a smaller ghetto to a larger one. We can never be satisfied as long as a Negro in Mississippi cannot vote and a Negro in New York believes he has nothing for which to vote. No, no, we are not satisfied, and we will not be satisfied until justice rolls down like waters and righteousness like a mighty stream. *Specific instances of injustice*

I am not unmindful that some of you have come here out of great trials and tribulations. Some of you have come fresh from narrow jail cells. Some of you have come from areas where your quest for freedom left you battered by the storms of persecution and staggered by the winds of police brutality. You have been the veterans of creative suffering. Continue to work with the faith that unearned suffering is redemptive.

Go back to Mississippi, go back to Alabama, go back to South Carolina, go back to Georgia, go back to Louisiana, go back to the slums and ghettos of our northern cities, knowing that somehow this situation can and will be changed. Let us not wallow in the valley of despair. *Appeals to emotion*

I say to you today, my friends, that in spite of the difficulties and frustrations of the moment I still have a dream. It is a dream deeply rooted in the American dream.

I have a dream that one day this nation will rise up and live out the true meaning of its creed: "We hold these truths to be self-evident, that all men are created equal."

I have a dream that one day on the red hills of Georgia the sons of former slaves and the sons of former slaveowners will be able to sit down together at the table of brotherhood.

I have a dream that one day even the state of Mississippi, a desert state sweltering with the heat of injustice and oppression, will be transformed into an oasis of freedom and justice.

I have a dream that my four little children will one day live in a nation where they will not be judged by the color of their skin but by the content of their character.

I have a dream today.

I have a dream that one day the state of Alabama, whose governor's lips are presently dripping with the words of interposition and nullification, will be transformed into a situation where little black boys and black girls will be able to join hands with little white boys and white girls and walk together as sisters and brothers.

I have a dream today.

I have a dream that one day every valley shall be exalted, every hill and mountain shall be made low, the rough places will be made plain, and the crooked places will be made straight, and the glory of the Lord shall be revealed, and all flesh shall see it together.

This is our hope. This is the faith with which I return to the South. With this faith we will be able to hew out of the mountain of despair a stone of hope. With this faith we will be able to transform the jangling discords of our nation into a beautiful symphony of brotherhood. With this faith we will be able to work together, to pray together, to struggle together, to go to jail together, to stand up for freedom together, knowing that we will be free one day.

This will be the day when all of God's children will be able to sing with new meaning

> My country, 'tis of thee,
> Sweet land of liberty,
>   Of thee I sing:
> Land where my fathers died,
> Land of the pilgrim's pride,
> From every mountainside,
>   Let freedom ring.

Conclusion (paragraphs 21–23)

So let freedom ring from the prodigious hilltops of New Hampshire. Let freedom ring from the mighty mountains of New York. Let freedom ring from the heightening Alleghenies of Pennsylvania. Let freedom ring from the snowcapped Rockies of Colorado. Let freedom ring from the curvaceous peaks of California.

But not only that. Let freedom ring from Stone Mountain of Georgia. Let freedom ring from Lookout Mountain of Tennessee. Let freedom ring from every hill and molehill of Mississippi. From every mountainside, let freedom ring.

When we let freedom ring, when we let it ring from every village   23
and every hamlet, from every state and every city, we will be able to
speed up that day when all of God's children, black men and white
men, Jews and Gentiles, Protestants and Catholics, will be able to join
hands and sing in the words of the old Negro spiritual, "Free at last!
Free at last! Thank God almighty, we are free at last!"

Reacting to Reading

1. Preview the essay. Then, read it more carefully, and do whatever highlighting and annotating is necessary to help you understand the writer's ideas.
2. Highlight the passage in which King outlines his dream for the United States. In an annotation, explain what he means when he says his dream is "deeply rooted in the American dream" (10).

Reacting to Words

*1. Define each of these words: *score* (1), *beacon* (1), *withering* (1), *languishing* (2), *appalling* (2), *promissory* (3), *unalienable* (3), *hallowed* (4), *gradualism* (4), *invigorating* (5), *inextricably* (6), *redemptive* (8), *wallow* (9), *prodigious* (21), and *curvaceous* (21). Can you suggest a synonym for each word that will work in the essay?
2. King uses a number of words again and again in his speech. Identify some of these words. Why do you think he repeats them? Would the speech have been more or less effective without this repetition?

Reacting to Ideas

1. In paragraph 3 King says that he and the other marchers have come to Washington to cash a check. Does this image accurately represent what he and the other protesters want to achieve? Can you think of another image that might work in the speech?
2. In his speech King is addressing the marchers who came to Washington. Who else do you think he is addressing?
3. Do you think the current racial climate in the United States still warrants King's criticism? Are we any closer today than we were in 1963 to realizing his dream?

Reacting to the Pattern

*1. King uses a deductive argument to present his ideas about racial justice. Do you think an inductive argument would have been more effective?
2. King's argument reaches its conclusion in paragraph 4. What does he do in the rest of his speech?
3. Why do you think King chose to include only a few specific examples to illustrate his points? Does his use of such a small amount of evidence weaken his argument?

602 ▪ APPENDIXES

Writing Practice

1. In paragraph 4 King says, "America has defaulted on this promissory note. . . ." Can you think of some person or organization that has defaulted on its promissory note to you? Write an argument essay in which you make your case. If you wish, you may, like King, use the image of a bad check.
*2. Write an essay in which you argue that if King were alive today, he would (or would not) think his dream of racial justice has been realized.
3. Choose an issue you feel strongly about. Write a letter to the editor of your local paper in which you argue your position.

Animal Tests Saved My Life

Richard Pothier

Richard Pothier is a writer who has received a heart transplant. Understandably, his essay—an inductive argument—takes a position in favor of using animal organs for human transplants. Perhaps because he sees his thesis as controversial, he saves it until the end of his essay. As you read, notice how Pothier arranges information in his essay.

Introductory paragraph provides overview of the issue of using animal organs in humans

In a desperate—and successful—attempt to save the life of a dying man, woman, child or infant sometime in the next few months, surgeons will implant another heart or liver from a baboon or perhaps even a pig into a human body. Then, two things will happen. Doctors will decide whether the recipient will use the animal organ as a "bridge," until a human organ can be located for transplant, or if the patient will keep the animal organ as a permanent transplant. Second, animal-rights activists will picket the hospital where the medical miracle took place.

Last June and just a few weeks ago, men dying of a strain of hepatitis that would most likely have destroyed a human organ received livers from baboons. Both times, the activists sprang into action.

Moderate tone established

I am an animal-rights supporter. I donate money to groups opposing some forms of medical experimentation on animals. I have argued for years, and will today, that animals are sometimes mistreated in such experiments.

Personal example supporting position

But in my chest there beats a heart that used to belong to another person. Now it is mine, and it has already given me nearly four years of a complete and satisfying life after I fell victim to a deadly disease that destroyed my heart.

Had there been no experimentation on dogs, sheep and pigs, you would now be reading another essay by another person. I would have died in 1989. I almost *did* die at Temple University Hospital in

Philadelphia until—just days before my shapeless, bloated heart would offer its last convulsive beat—a donor was found. I awakened from the operation with a strong, 27-year-old heart and a new life at the age of 49. Today, I am 53, healthy and happy. My ultimate life span is unknown. But so is everyone else's.

6   My doctors had to wait until almost the last moment before a suitable donor was found. But now, animal-to-human "xenografts" are nearing routine use as bridges to transplantations and promise a way to destroy the biggest killer in transplantation medicine—the deadly shortage of donor organs.

7   Americans refuse to donate enough organs to help the rest of us to stay alive. The number of heart transplants has peaked at about 2,200 a year. Thousands more of us could be saved from an untimely death. (About a third of recipients are under 44.) But the donor supply has plateaued. The reasons for this mystify transplantation experts. Twenty to 30 percent of those who need a heart transplant will die while they are waiting.   *Specifics of the problem and its extent: shortage of donor organs*

8   Biomedical engineers are working hard on mechanical replacements for hearts, but the human body does not take kindly to such machines. They present problems that may never be solved, and no mechanical solutions at all loom for bad livers, kidneys and lungs.

9   Anti-rejection drugs, however, can successfully allow animal organs to be used in humans. And there is hope that animal hearts, livers and perhaps even lungs could someday permanently replace diseased organs. In the future, genetically altered animals may be bred to provide matched organs for dying humans.

10   But this may never happen if animal-rights activists, with whom I agree on many things, convince society that it is wrong to sacrifice a pig or a baboon or a monkey to save a human. There are already numerous precedents for the use of animals to save lives. Insulin, which keeps diabetics alive, came from animal organs. Many Americans, including my mother, had their lives extended for years through the use of pig heart valves to replace their own faulty valves. I believe it would be a perversion of human sensibility to let infants, young people and men and women die prematurely, out of some bizarre belief that the animal has a greater right to life than the human.   *Precedents for use of animal organs*

11   *New heart*: Both before and after I was diagnosed with cardiomyopathy, a lethal heart-muscle degeneration of unknown cause, I argued—and still do—that some medical experiments on animals were cruel and unnecessary. But before surgeons could implant a donor heart into my chest, they had to practice their skills on animals.   *Arguments for testing procedures on animals*

12   Do those opposing xenografts propose that surgeons practice on people instead? Or that they don't practice at all? Before the surgeons sliced me open with a power saw and cut out my diseased heart, I had to know that I had good odds of awakening.

13   If my son should ever need the same procedure his father needed, and the disgraceful failure of many Americans to donate organs they no longer need continues to kill people, I hope *his* doctors will have available the option of saving his life with an animal's heart—either as a

bridge to a human heart or as his own new heart. I want surgeons to learn their skills practicing on animals—not on my son.

If an activist needed a heart transplant, would he or she reject the use of an animal heart if that were the only organ available? Would he or she reject even a human heart, on the moral ground that thousands of animals had died to perfect this procedure?

Concluding arguments

Right now there are about 30,000 Americans waiting for a lifesaving organ transplant. Every day more names are added to this list of desperate people. Among the newcomers are bound to be some of those who carry the protest signs or write the letters. It is one thing to come up with catchy phrases charging animal abuse; it may be quite another to die because your efforts at propaganda have been successful.

Animal organs can help fill the need. True, the medical problems of animal-to-human transplants have not yet been solved. But for at least 10 years, the problems of human-to-human transplants were not solved, either.

Thesis statement

It may be tough for these well-meaning people to reverse themselves. But it will be tougher for them to carry their signs outside a hospital where a friend, or the child of a friend, is dying.

Reacting to Reading

1. Preview the essay. Then, read it more carefully, and do whatever highlighting and annotating is necessary to help you understand the writer's ideas.
2. Highlight the passages in the essay that reveal Pothier's preconceived ideas about the subject of organ transplants. Use annotations to indicate whether you agree or disagree with his ideas.

Reacting to Words

*1. Define each of these words: *implant* (1), *bloated* (5), *xenografts* (6), *perversion* (10), and *degeneration* (11). Can you suggest a synonym for each word that will work in the essay?
2. In describing his own surgery, Pothier says, "surgeons sliced me open with a power saw and cut out my diseased heart . . . " (12). How does this graphic language affect you? Do you think it is necessary?

Reacting to Ideas

1. In light of his heart transplant, do you think Pothier can be objective? Does the fact that he is a transplant recipient make his argument more or less convincing?
*2. What medical experiments on animals do you believe are justified? What procedures do you think should be limited or done away with entirely?
3. Do you think an animal activist would reject an organ even if it would save his or her life?

Reacting to the Pattern

*1. In addition to Pothier's personal narrative, he includes factual information. Find this information, and decide what purpose it serves in the essay.
2. Pothier begins his essay by describing a situation. How effective is this introduction? Can you think of another introduction that might be more effective?
3. Pothier develops his argument inductively, moving from specific information and examples to a general conclusion. Can you explain the advantages and disadvantages of his organization?

Writing Practice

1. Write an argument essay in which you argue for or against animal experimentation. You may use your own experience with animals to support your position.
*2. Assume you are a person who needs a baboon heart to keep you alive until you can find a suitable human donor. Write a letter to an animal activist explaining why you intend to accept the baboon's heart, or a letter to Pothier explaining why you will not accept it.
3. Do you think animals have rights? Should they have the same rights as humans? What personal observations lead you to your conclusion? Write an essay in which you argue that certain rights of animals should (or should not) be protected by law.

Acknowledgments *(continued from copyright page)*

Ellen Goodman, "The Suspected Shopper" from *Keeping in Touch*. Copyright © 1985 by the Washington Post Company. Reprinted with the permission of Simon & Schuster, Inc.

Joyce Howe, "Indelible Marks" (excerpt) from *The Village Voice* (February 1983). Reprinted by permission.

Martin Luther King, Jr., "I Have a Dream." Copyright © 1963 by Martin Luther King, Jr., renewed 1991 by Coretta Scott King. Reprinted with permission of the heirs to the estate of Martin Luther King., Jr., c/o Joan Daves Agency.

Richard Lederer, "English is a Crazy Language" from *Crazy English,* ed. Elaine Pfefferblit. Copyright © 1990 Pocket Books. Reprinted with the permission of Pocket Books, a division of Simon & Schuster, Inc.

Merrill Markoe, "Showering with Your Dog" and "Men, Women, and Conversation" (excerpt) from *What the Dogs Have Taught Me*. Copyright © 1992 by Merrill Markoe. Reprinted with the permission of Viking Penguin, a division of Penguin Books USA, Inc.

Mary Mebane, "Shades of Black" from *Mary*. Copyright © 1981 by Mary Mebane. Reprinted with the permission of Viking Penguin, a division of Penguin Books USA, Inc.

Barbara Mujica, "No Comprendo," *The New York Times* (January 3, 1995). Copyright © 1995 by The New York Times Company. Reprinted with the permission of *The New York Times.*

Jamie O'Neill, "Falling Into Place," *The New York Times Magazine* (August 15, 1993). Copyright © 1993 by The New York Times Company. Reprinted with the permission of *The New York Times.*

Richard Pothier, "Animal Tests Saved My Life," *Newsweek* (February 1, 1993). Copyright © 1993 by Newsweek, Inc. Reprinted with the permission of *Newsweek.*

Anna Quindlen, "The Old Block" from *Thinking Out Loud*. Copyright © 1993 by Anna Quindlen. Reprinted with the permission of Random House, Inc.

Anna Quindlen, "Barbie at 35" (excerpt), *The New York Times* (September 10, 1994). Copyright © 1994 by The New York Times Company. Reprinted with the permission of *The New York Times.*

Gary Soto, "The Grandfather" from *A Summer Life*. Copyright © 1990 by University Press of New England. Reprinted with the permission of the publishers.

Brent Staples, "Role Models, Bogus and Real," *The New York Times* (June 1994). Copyright © 1994 by The New York Times Company. Reprinted with the permission of *The New York Times.*

Teaching with *Windows on Writing:* A Chapter-by-Chapter Guide

In the sections that follow, we discuss the contents of *Windows on Writing* and offer ideas for working with each chapter in the classroom. For Appendix D (Patterns of Essay Development: Readings for Writers), which is included in *Windows on Writing with Additional Readings,* we also provide discussions of the questions following each of the eighteen professional readings. (Note that answers to the practices in Chapters 1–25 and in Appendix C are provided as annotations with the practices themselves earlier in this annotated instructor's edition.)

▶ WRITING PARAGRAPHS AND ESSAYS (UNITS 1–3)

Units 1–3 provide basic rhetorical instruction. Further instruction in writing essays appears in Appendixes C and D. Many instructors will likely prepare a syllabus that intersperses the chapters in Units 4–9, Revising and Editing Your Writing, among the chapters in Units 1–3 and Appendixes C and D.

Unit 1 The Writing Process

This unit provides an introduction to the writing process, with particular focus on invention strategies and revision. You will probably want to begin by having students work through Chapter 1 either independently or in class. Once they've completed their sample papers, you might give the class an opportunity to discuss the elements of the process they found most useful, most difficult, and most enjoyable. This will give them an opportunity to see that there are many differences among writers and no "one way" of approaching a piece of writing.

Chapter 1 Planning, Drafting, and Revising

Chapter 1 opens with a list of questions about assignment, purpose, and audience. Emphasize to your students that in the course of selecting and arranging details, drafting, and revising, they will need to keep these three issues clearly in mind. Most of the choices they make as writers in school and on the job will depend on their assignment, their purpose, and their audience.

2 – Teaching Notes

The practices in this chapter give students an opportunity to work through the writing process in order to produce a model paragraph. (You might cover Chapter 2 as you discuss revisions to this initial writing assignment; students can then begin to revise specifically for unity, development, and coherence.)

Try to make sure that students complete each of the invention strategies modeled in 1B. While they may find that one or two of these activities work best for them and so not complete all of them for subsequent assignments, they can't know which they can use most successfully without experimenting with them all.

Also make sure that students realize that the process as outlined is not a formula or a rigid series of steps. Some writers do a great deal of invention writing and then map out a clear organization before beginning to draft; they then may consider these drafts finished enough to let others read and comment on before doing any revision. Other writers do less free-form invention writing but spend more time thinking through their ideas; they then make some notes and consider their first—or discovery—drafts more as invention, revising and rewriting them before offering them to readers for comment. Some writers do more invention writing before revising their first drafts, some revise parts of their work as they are drafting, and most edit here and there as they discover errors or ways of rephrasing ideas in the process of rereading what they have written. The elements of the writing process are not so much stages as different kinds of thinking and writing activities that can occur throughout the process of producing a piece of written work.

As they conclude this chapter, let students know that one of their goals over the next few weeks will be to discover for themselves the personal writing process that best suits their habits and inclinations and that will allow them to produce their best work.

Unit 2 Focus on Paragraphs

The first chapter in this unit looks at some basic elements of effective paragraphs; the second provides models of nine common patterns of paragraph development.

Chapter 2 Writing Effective Paragraphs

This chapter focuses on using topic sentences to help unify paragraphs, developing topic sentences with relevant detail, and achieving coherence by connecting ideas clearly.

Most of the practices include sample topic sentences or paragraphs for students to evaluate and discuss productively in class. Others suggest that students evaluate their own work or get comments from others about their work, and then revise accordingly.

Chapter 3 Patterns of Paragraph Development

This is a fairly long chapter, and you will probably only want to assign a section or two of it at a time. If you cover patterns of paragraph development extensively, this may take as much as half of the term.

The patterns of development covered are exemplification, narration, description, process, cause and effect, comparison and contrast, classification and division, definition, and argument. Each is described in the section introduction and then illustrated with two professional and one student example. (The student example appears in a practice, along with questions for analysis; these provide good subjects for class discussion.) Each section ends with a practice that provides students with possible topics for a paragraph, along with a writing guide to help students as they plan, draft, and revise their paragraphs.

If, rather than discrete paragraphs, you have students writing multi-paragraph essays early in the term, you may want to skip this chapter at this point and go on to Chapters 4 and 5, which focus on essays generally. You can then combine study of patterns of paragraph development in Chapter 3 with study of patterns of essay development in Appendix D, as suggested by the second sample syllabus in "Teaching with *Windows on Writing*" in the front of the book. Another possibility is to have students plan, draft, and refine an exemplification paragraph (3A), which they can use as the basis for a multi-paragraph essay, as suggested in Chapter 4. (Exemplification paragraphs can often be readily expanded into essays by the addition of further examples or additional categories of examples; a sample is provided in Chapter 4.) The benefit of this plan is that it helps students transfer paragraph-writing skills directly to essay writing.

Unit 3 Paragraphs into Essays

This unit builds on what students have learned previously about paragraphs—unity, development, and coherence—to help them understand the qualities of effective essays. It also covers introductory and concluding paragraphs. As you have students plan, draft, and revise their first essays of the term, you may want to have them work through both chapters in this unit. If you want them to use a specific pattern of essay development for their first essay, you will also want to cover the treatment of that pattern in Appendix D. (The sample student essay in 4B is a model of cause and effect; the essay in Practice 4-3 is a model of exemplification.)

Chapter 4 Thesis and Support

The first two parts of this chapter provide students with a sense of the shape of an essay and of the way effective essays are composed of unified, well-developed paragraphs. Parts C and D focus on the thesis—moving from topic to thesis, the qualities of an effective thesis, and how a thesis can be supported.

Practices 4-1 through 4-4 and Practice 4-8 build on one another to help students expand a paragraph they have written previously into a multi-paragraph essay. Because students aren't starting their first essays for the class from scratch, many are able to produce more effective first drafts in this way. (Of course, if you wish to have students draft their first essay on a new topic, you may easily skip these practices or use only Practices 4-1 and 4-3 to get students to see the relationship between paragraph structure and essay structure.)

4 – Teaching Notes

You'll probably want to spend at least some class time talking specifically about effective essay topics and thesis statements (see Practices 4-5 through 4-7). Practice 4-7 could serve as a good group activity or an activity in which the entire class could brainstorm and evaluate possible thesis statements. Chapter Review: Student Writing also provides an interesting opportunity for group work.

As students produce their essays, make sure that they continue to work through their personal writing processes. Encourage or provide opportunities for invention, and ask that students revise their first drafts at least once using the techniques discussed in Chapter 1.

Chapter 5 Introductions and Conclusions

This chapter provides an overview of how essays may be introduced and concluded and is best studied as students are drafting or revising the first essays for the term.

Note that for many examples of opening and concluding paragraphs in this chapter, the complete essay appears in Appendix D. Looking at least briefly at these whole essays can provide students with a good sense of how introductions or conclusions work in context. You might spend some time discussing why students think a particular writer chose to begin or end the essay in the way he or she did.

At this point, if you use peer evaluation to provide students with feedback on their drafts, you should be sure to ask peer evaluators to comment on a draft's introduction and conclusion.

▶ REVISING AND EDITING YOUR WRITING (UNITS 4–9)

At this point, the focus of the book shifts from paragraphs and essays to revising and editing at the sentence level (Units 4–9). As mentioned in discussing sample syllabi earlier, there are a variety of ways to use Chapters 6–25. Some instructors will have students work through these chapters fairly sequentially, supplementing their work in Units 1–3 and Appendixes C and D. Others will use the chapters more selectively, depending on the types of essays and paragraphs students are working on (for example, assigning Chapter 20 on adjectives and adverbs in conjunction with description or Chapter 9 on past tense verbs in conjunction with narration). Still others will assign these chapters on an "as needed" basis, for problems that many students in the class are having or even to an individual student when he or she is exhibiting a problem that is not common to the class.

Note that the discussions in these chapters are completely self-contained, so great flexibility is possible in assigning them.

Each chapter in Units 4–9 opens with a Paragraph Practice, in which students are given a prompt to serve as the basis of a draft of a paragraph they will revise and edit based on the information presented in the chapter. These are optional; at your direction, students can easily skip them as they work through the chapter. However, we recommend that you use them at least occasionally, so that students can recognize specific editing issues in context rather than only as part of the practice exercises in the text. See the earlier section "Using Paragraph Practices and Flashbacks" for a fuller discussion.

Unit 4 Writing Simple Sentences

Unit 4 provides basic information about subjects, verbs, and prepositional phrases in simple sentences as a prelude to covering sentence fragments and subject-verb agreement.

Chapter 6 The Basic Sentence Pattern: Subjects and Verbs

Chapter 6 is a very basic review of subjects, prepositional phrases, and verbs and how they function to form complete, simple sentences. All students may not require this review, and you might choose to work through it rather quickly, having students read through it on their own, perhaps only completing a few of the practices. Then, as a class, you might go over the Chapter Review: Student Writing, which provides a good opportunity to review students' understanding of these basic terms and concepts.

You might want to follow study of this chapter with study of Unit 6 on building sentences, which would allow students to see immediately different possibilities of sentence structure based on the basic sentence pattern described in this chapter.

Chapter 7 Avoiding Sentence Fragments

Instructors occasionally note that some of their students don't seem to have trouble with sentence fragments until they assign the chapter on fragments. Yet, because fragments are a problem common to many inexperienced writers, you'll probably need to assign Chapter 7 at least on an "as needed" basis.

In discussing fragments with your students, it's probably best to admit that fragments are commonly accepted in some forms of public writing students read all the time—particularly in advertising. (You might bring in examples yourself or have students bring in examples.) Consequently, they may not have an "ear" for fragments or may feel instinctively that they are using the structure for stylistic effect. You have to let them know that despite their use in some kinds of writing, for academic and professional audiences fragments are almost always considered a mark of an unskilled writer.

Of the three types of fragments covered in this chapter, those with incomplete verbs (7B) and those consisting only of subordinate clauses are the more common. Because individual students often have problems with one sort of fragment more often than with the others, it is important to help them come to recognize the sort they are likely to write rather than just to refer them to fragments generally.

Note that incomplete verb fragments most often occur with the perfect tenses of irregular verbs whose past participle form is different from the simple past form (*He been good/He written a good essay*) and with progressive tenses (*He leaving early*), so you might choose to cover parts of Chapters 10 and 11 in discussing incomplete verb fragments. In addition, you might want to cover parts of Chapter 13 on subordination in discussing subordinate clause fragments.

Chapter 8 Subject-Verb Agreement

The first section in this chapter covers the concept of subject-verb agreement, while the five subsequent sections cover special problems with subject-verb agreement.

This is a longish chapter; if you assign it all, you might do so in two parts. You might also choose to assign only the sections you note that your students have problems with. Agreement problems with *be, have,* and *do* (8B), when words come between the subject and the verb (8C), and when the verb comes before the subject in sentences beginning with *there* (8E) are particularly common.

Note that the second Focus box in this chapter discusses the uses of the present tense, as problems with subject-verb agreement often occur with present tense verbs. You might go over this information with your students before proceeding to the next unit on verbs, which begins by looking at the past tense.

Unit 5 Understanding Verbs

This unit focuses on verb tense and on past and present participles. Some instructors whose classes are made up mainly of native speakers find that, except for a review of irregular past and past participle verb forms (9B–C and 10B) and perhaps some work on choosing between the present perfect and past perfect tenses (10C–D), they need not cover these chapters in depth. Other instructors like to have students work through these chapters fully precisely because they are able to do so fairly easily and confidently.

Chapter 9 The Past Tense

The main focus of this chapter is irregular past tense forms, including detailed treatment of *be* and the commonly confused forms *lie/lay, rise/raise,* and *sit/set*. These three commonly confused pairs can be a bit tricky to teach. One technique is to physicalize these verbs: Ask an uninhibited student to actually *lie* on the desk, *lay* a book down, *rise* from a seat, *raise* his or her hand, *sit* down in a chair, and *set* a notebook on a desk. Then, in each case, have students describe what your demonstrator just did, using the past tense, as you write their sentences on the board, underlining the verb and discussing whether it is in the correct form.

You might use this chapter in conjunction with 3B and 27B on narrative writing and discuss the common use of the past tense in narratives and the different effect of narratives written in the present tense.

Discussion of the past tense forms of *can* (*could*) and *will* (*would*) concludes this chapter.

Chapter 10 Past Participles and the Perfect Tenses

This chapter focuses not only on irregular past participle forms and the present perfect and past perfect tenses, but also on using participles as adjectives. (Note that students need to be concerned about subject-verb agreement with the present perfect tense but not with the past perfect tense.)

One good way of discussing differences in using the past tense, the present perfect tense, and the past perfect tense is to look at the three tenses used in the same piece of writing. Anna Quindlen's essay "The Old Block" in Appendix D is a possibility. She uses both the past tense and the present perfect tense in paragraphs 6, 7, 11, and 14; she uses both the past tense and the past perfect tense in paragraph 15. Read these passages aloud, having students underline the past tense, present perfect tense, and past perfect tense verbs. Then discuss why each tense is appropriate to the writer's meaning in each case.

In discussing participles used as adjectives, you might point out that problems arise most often with regular past participle forms because the *-d* or *-ed* ending may not be sounded clearly in speech (for example, *He is a prejudice person*) and so dropped incorrectly in writing.

Chapter 11   Present Participles and the Progressive Tenses

Because present participles have no irregular forms, they are generally quite easy for students to master. Consequently, this chapter is primarily concerned with uses of the present progressive and the past progressive tenses.

In discussing the present progressive tense, you might want to note the nonstandard use of *be* as a helping verb (*I be going, they be going,* and so forth) to indicate an action about to take place in the future. While in fact a distinct tense in some dialects of English, this usage is unacceptable to most speakers of standard English.

In order to avoid information overload, we have chosen not to cover another progressive tense form that sometimes causes problems, the present perfect progressive tense *(has been going, have been going)*, which indicates an action continuing from the past into the present and perhaps also into the future. You may have students who do not use a form of *have* in expressing this tense *(He been going, they been going)*, in which case you may want to supplement the text discussion a bit.

You might point out that both the present and the past progressive tenses require attention to subject-verb agreement.

Unit 6   Building Sentences

This unit describes two ways of combining sentences (using coordination and using subordination). We also cover run-on sentences and comma splices in this unit because they are a problem of faulty sentence combining and can be corrected by an accepted form of coordination or by subordination.

Some instructors like to introduce methods of sentence combining immediately after covering the simple sentence in Chapter 6. These methods may also be connected to the discussion of revising for sentence variety in Chapter 17.

Chapter 12   Combining Sentences with Coordination

This chapter covers combining sentences with coordinating conjunctions, semicolons alone, and semicolons along with conjunctive adverbs.

8 – Teaching Notes

The discussion of coordinating conjunctions includes examples to help students distinguish the meaning of these conjunctions and the relationship they indicate between the clauses they join. You will probably want to point out the Focus box that explains how to punctuate clauses linked by coordinating conjunctions. Practice 12-2 gives students a chance to combine short sentences with potentially humorous results; you might want to let students read some of their combinations aloud. At this point, you might also want to skip ahead to 14A, which shows students how to identify run-ons and comma splices, and item 2 under 14B, which explains how to correct these using a comma and a coordinating conjunction.

Depending on the level of your students, you may choose not to cover combining sentences with semicolons and with semicolons along with conjunctive adverbs in detail. However, you will probably find that at least some of your students incorrectly link sentences using only a conjunctive adverb or a comma and a conjunctive adverb. (This problem is covered in a Focus box under item 3 in 14B.) If this is the case, you may want to point out the list of conjunctive adverbs and the examples of correctly combined sentences in 12C.

Chapter 13 Combining Sentences with Subordination

This chapter covers combining sentences with subordinating conjunctions and with relative pronouns. It also distinguishes restrictive from nonrestrictive clauses and explains how each is punctuated.

You might point out the list of subordinating conjunctions in 13A, which indicates the relation each conjunction suggests between the sentences it combines. Also make sure that students understand how to punctuate dependent clauses at the beginnings and at the ends of sentences (see the Focus box just prior to the list of subordinating conjunctions). Students are also reminded in 13A that a dependent clause cannot stand by itself as a sentence.

You may want to skip 13B and 13C on combining sentences with relative pronouns, in order to avoid the inevitable confusion associated with the use of restrictive and nonrestrictive clauses. However, if you do have students complete Practices 13-4, 13-5, and/or 13-6 under 13B, make sure that they go back to these exercises to check for correct use of commas with restrictive and nonrestrictive clauses, as suggested in Practice 13-8; to simplify the initial discussion of combining sentences using relative pronouns, the subject of comma use is not discussed until 13C.

Chapter 14 Avoiding Run-Ons and Comma Splices

Here students learn first to recognize run-ons and comma splices and next to correct them by creating two separate sentences or by using any of the accepted methods of combining sentences described in Chapters 12 and 13. If there is any method in Chapters 12 and 13 that you chose not to cover with your students, then you would not want to assign the discussion of that method in 14B.

Unit 7 Revising for Clarity and Effectiveness

The previous unit, while focusing largely on grammatical issues of sentence structure, in fact presents students with a number of stylistic choices for creating and revising sentences. Building on this increasing mastery of writing style, the four chapters in this unit focus more on choices a writer has to make than on errors that need to be corrected.

Chapter 15 Avoiding Illogical Shifts

Five kinds of shifts are covered in this chapter: shifts in tense, person, number, discourse, and voice.

The most common problem students have with shifting tense is shifting from present to past and vice versa, often in personal narratives and in summarizing historical events or fictional plots. You might want to have students review the discussion of the present tense in 8A and of the past tense in Chapter 9.

The most common shift in person is the shift from third person to second person, although the shift from first to second also occurs *(We were told that you had register by today)*. For most academic writing situations, students can simply be advised to avoid using *you* because it is usually inappropriate in any case.

Shifts in number generally involve problems of pronoun-antecedent agreement—using *they* or *their* to refer to a singular antecedent. Students probably hear and even read this usage all the time, so you need to reinforce the fact that most experts still consider it nonstandard. (This topic is also covered in Chapter 19.)

Shifts in discourse are common among student writers, but the concept can be quite difficult for them to grasp. If you feel your students need the work, you might go over Practice 15-4 in detail in class. Each of the eight sentences here in need of revision could be changed either to all direct discourse or all indirect discourse. (Because of limitations of space, the Annotated Instructor's Edition includes only one of these possibilities for each sentence.) Working on the board, have your students revise each sentence both ways. You might want to refer to 24B, which covers punctuating direct quotations.

Finally, we have chosen to cover the passive voice only in this chapter on shifts. It struck us as odd to have a section in the verbs unit in which students practiced changing verbs to the passive voice but then later discourage them from using the passive voice. In Practice 15-6, students have a reason for changing one clause to the passive voice if you wish to have your students do so.

Chapter 16 Using Parallelism

Try to work through some of this fairly brief chapter in class because reading sentences aloud helps a great deal in recognizing parallel structure. Most basic writers grasp the concept of parallelism fairly easily. They don't, however, apply it as readily in their own writing. You might combine study of this chapter with an assignment asking students to revise at least three of their previous papers solely for parallel structure.

You might also combine this chapter with Martin Luther King, Jr.'s, "I Have a Dream" in Appendix D; it provides particularly effective examples of parallel structure.

Chapter 17   Revising for Sentence Variety

This concept has already been introduced in Unit 6, and 17C reviews the techniques for combining sentences covered there and adds three more: using participles, compound subjects/predicates, and appositives. In addition, 17A covers varying sentence types, 17B covers varying sentence openings, and 17D covers varying sentence length. You might cover 17C and 17D together, as varying sentence length will almost always involve combining sentences.

You may want to work through many of the practices in this chapter in class or with students in small groups: most of them do not have single correct answers, the point being that there are different ways of achieving sentence variety. As with Chapter 16, you might combine study of this chapter with an assignment to revise some previous papers solely for sentence variety.

In conjunction with this chapter, you might have students analyze any of the student or professional essays in Appendix A for good examples of varying sentences.

Chapter 18   Revising Words

This chapter focuses on choosing exact words, being concise, avoiding trite language, using figurative language, and avoiding sexist language.

Vagueness is a problem for many student writers. Practice 18-3 is particularly effective for getting writers to see the difference between vague language and exact language.

The concept of conciseness can be difficult to communicate, so you might want to work through Practices 18-4 and 18-5 in class. Similarly, students may not always recognize clichés; ask the class or students in small groups to come up with a list of their own.

Simile and metaphor can be fun to work with, and basic writers can be remarkably creative. You might introduce a few poems at this point. Some readily available possibilities are Langston Hughes's "Harlem (A Dream Deferred)," Robert Burns's "A Red, Red Rose," and Emily Dickinson's "'Hope' Is the Thing with Feathers." You might also look at the uses of simile and metaphor in Martin Luther King, Jr.'s, "I Have a Dream" in Appendix D.

The brief section on sexist language that concludes this chapter may spark some discussion of the extent to which sexist language contributes to sexist assumptions.

Unit 8   Understanding Nouns, Pronouns, and Other Parts of the Sentence

Having covered verbs in Unit 5, here we cover nouns and pronouns, adjectives and adverbs, and prepositions—the other parts of speech that sometimes give students problems. You'll probably use these chapters fairly selectively, focusing perhaps on pronoun case (19C), pronoun-antecedent agreement (19D–E), and the difference between adjectives and adverbs (20A).

Chapter 19   Using Nouns and Pronouns

This chapter defines what nouns are and explains the formation of regular and irregular plurals. It then moves on to a discussion of the use of personal pronouns, pronoun case, pronoun-antecedent agreement, problems with nonspecific and unnecessary pronouns, and the use of reflexive and intensive pronouns. This is a fairly long chapter that covers a number of different issues, so you may want to assign it selectively or in separate stages.

The main problems students have with pronoun case are in compound constructions and in comparisons. The first is easily solved by treating each part of the compound separately: *Bill knows her; Bill knows me; Bill knows her and me*. The second is solved by adding any implied words, particularly if what is implied is a verb: *She is smarter than I [am]*. The main problems of pronoun-antecedent agreement are the use of *they* to refer to singular compound antecedents linked by *or* and to refer to singular indefinite and collective noun antecedents.

The most difficult pronoun problem to discuss with students is nonspecific pronoun reference: *It said on the news. . . .* Advise students to check their work carefully to make sure that *it* and *they* always refer to a specifically named antecedent; if not, they should replace the pronoun with a noun.

Chapter 20   Using Adjectives and Adverbs

The first part of this chapter deals with recognizing the difference between adjectives and adverbs and choosing between them. The second and third parts focus on comparatives/superlatives and demonstratives. Students are likely to have the most trouble with choosing adjectives or adverbs, particularly between *good* and *well*, so you might want to spend some time in class going over Practice 20-2. In your discussion, it might help to review the list of linking verbs in Chapter 6.

Chapter 21   Using Prepositions

Prepositions generally give native English speakers little trouble. The exception is the preposition *like*, which is sometimes used incorrectly in place of *as* or *as if* to introduce a dependent clause; this problem is covered in a Focus box in 21A and in Practice 21-1. The discussion in 21B of idiomatic expressions using prepositions may be most helpful for nonnative speakers. The list here is necessarily incomplete, as there are literally hundreds of such expressions, but it gives an idea of the idiomatic uses of prepositions in English. More advice on these uses is given in Appendix B, L, "Understanding Prepositions in Two-Word Verbs."

12 – Teaching Notes

Unit 9   Special Problems with Punctuation, Mechanics, and Spelling

This unit is not intended as a comprehensive overview of punctuation, mechanics, and spelling, but rather as a guide to some of the problems that basic writing students commonly encounter. Other than the spelling chapter, many instructors will probably choose to assign only parts of these chapters, perhaps only to individual students.

Chapter 22   Using Commas

This chapter discusses four uses of commas: in series, in setting off introductory phrases, with appositives, and in dates and addresses. Other uses of commas have been discussed in previous chapters: in compound sentences (12A), after a dependent clause that comes before an independent clause (13A), and in setting off nonrestrictive clauses (13C). In introducing this chapter, you might want to review these other chapters as well.

Students often neglect to include a comma after the next-to-last item in a series, as is common in journalistic writing. Many experts do consider this use of commas optional unless the lack of a comma could cause confusion. The point you can make to students is that if they get in the habit of always using a comma in this position, they will never run the risk of confusion.

Students often also neglect to use commas with introductory phrases and transitional expressions, so you might want to spend some class time working on this issue.

Chapter 23   Using Apostrophes

The first section in this chapter covers contractions; if you discourage students from using these in academic writing, you'll want to skip this section.

Students can have considerable problems with apostrophes: not using them at all with possessives, misplacing them in forming plural possessives (particularly for irregular nouns) or singular possessives that end in *-s*, using them in the possessive case of personal pronouns and with nonpossessive plural nouns.

Solving problems with apostrophe use in possessives is basically a matter of understanding and remembering the rules. In editing for apostrophes used incorrectly with nonpossessive plural nouns, have students check every noun in which they've used an apostrophe; if they can't substitute the phrase *of the [noun]*, then it is likely the apostrophe is not necessary.

Chapter 24   Setting Off Proper Nouns, Direct Quotations, and Titles

This chapter is something of a catchall, but the topics are connected: Capitalization and the use of quotation marks are the primary focus.

Depending on the kind of writing you have students do, you may want to introduce 24B on direct quotations in conjunction with a narrative assignment or with an assignment in which students are to respond to one of the readings in Appendix D. (For the latter, you might also want to discuss

24C on titles.) Punctuating quotations might also be covered with 15D on shifts between direct and indirect discourse.

Chapter 25 Understanding Spelling

This is a lengthy chapter with a number of different practices focusing on various spelling rules and commonly confused words. It should not be assigned all at once.

Many instructors choose to introduce a few sections in spelling early on and return to new sections throughout the term. If you do this, you might start with 25F, "Becoming a Better Speller," which offers general advice that students can begin to put into practice immediately, along with 25A, which gets students thinking about problems involving spelling and pronunciation.

▶ APPENDIXES A–D

Appendixes A and B are designed for students who need repeated help and reinforcement with two specific writing concerns. Both these appendixes are meant as a reference for students as the need arises, both in and out of the classroom. **Appendixes C and D** provide thorough treatment of reading and of writing in response to reading, as well as guidelines and models (one student and two professional) for writing essays based on the same nine patterns of development discussed for paragraphs in Chapter 3. Instructors who introduce essay-length assignments early in the term will begin using this unit in the first few weeks of class. Instructors who spend more time having students draft and revise individual paragraphs may wait until the final part of the term to introduce this unit; however, it is quite possible that such instructors will want to have students work with individual readings in Appendix D for purposes of class discussion, paragraph assignment topics, or examples of effective style (in conjunction with the chapters in Unit 7).

Appendix A Writing Paragraphs and Essays in an Exam Setting

Here students are given advice for taking written exams. If your students must pass a timed writing assignment test in order to pass the course, you might spend some time talking about test-taking techniques and offer several "practice exams" over the course of the term.

Appendix B Tips for ESL Writers

If you have a number on nonnative speakers in your classes, you might want to familiarize yourself with the coverage in this appendix. It offers advice about some of the more common problems that arise for students with second-language issues.

Appendix C The Reading Process

Here students are presented with a method for reading carefully and critically, including examples of asking questions about purpose, previewing, highlighting, annotating, and outlining. They are also given a model of an

14 – Teaching Notes

informal response paragraph through which they can record their reactions to their reading.

The practices in this appendix carry students through the stages of the reading process using an editorial about bilingual education. You may easily substitute another reading, if you think it might be more suited to your students' interests.

You can assign this appendix to be completed outside of class, but if you have time, you might make it an in-class project, dividing students into groups to share their final response paragraphs.

Appendix D Patterns of Essay Development: Readings for Writers

This appendix provides a concise but thorough course in writing short essays using nine common patterns of essay development. Each of the nine sections opens with a Focus box providing sample assignments that could be developed using the pattern under discussion, along with corresponding thesis statements. Next come a chart outlining different options for organizing an essay using the pattern and a Focus box listing appropriate transitions. These are followed by a student essay and a writing checklist for students to use in completing their own essays. Each section concludes with two professional essays, each followed by four sets of critical reading questions and two or three suggested topics for student papers.

Many instructors will not have students write nine full essays, one for each pattern. We have included nine possibilities, however, to give instructors as much flexibility as possible.

The nine student and eighteen professional selections in this appendix provide useful models for students writing essays organized according to the nine rhetorical patterns. They may also be studied thematically; following are some suggested thematic groupings.

Family Values

  Alisha Woolery, "African Violet"
  Gary Soto, "The Grandfather"
  Joyce Howe, "Indelible Marks"
  Andrea DiMarco, "How My Parents' Separation Changed My Life"
  José Antonio Burciaga, "Tortillas"

What Is a Hero?

  Martin Gansberg, "38 Who Saw Murder Didn't Call the Police"
  Alisha Woolery, "African Violet"
  Gary Soto, "The Grandfather"
  Brent Staples, "Role Models, Bogus and Real"
  John Fleeger, "Why Isn't Pete Rose in the Hall of Fame?"

Social Issues

  Ellen Goodman, "The Suspected Shopper"
  Anna Quindlen, "The Old Block"

Brent Staples, "Role Models, Bogus and Real"
Richard Pothier, "Animal Tests Saved My Life"

Men and Women

Jaime O'Neill, "Falling into Place"
Carol Sanger, "Just Say 'No,' Just Hear 'No'"
Mary Mebane, "Shades of Black"

Prejudice and Inequality

Maya Angelou, "Graduation"
Anna Quindlen, "The Old Block"
Mary Mebane, "Shades of Black"
Martin Luther King, Jr., "I Have a Dream"

Crime and Violence

Ellen Goodman, "The Suspected Shopper"
Mark Cotharn, "Swing Shift"
Martin Gansberg, "38 Who Saw Murder Didn't Call the Police"
Kristin Whitehead, "Street Smart"
Cheri Rodriguez, "Jason Vorhees, Meet Count Dracula"

The Uses of Humor

Richard Lederer, "English Is a Crazy Language"
Merrill Markoe, "Showering with Your Dog"
Suzanne Britt Jordan, "That Lean and Hungry Look"
Dave Barry, "How Your Body Works"

Self-Protection

Timothy E. Miles, "Fighting Fire with Fire Safety Education"
Mai Yoshikawa, "Under Water"
Kristin Whitehead, "Street Smart"

Student essays appear throughout *Windows on Writing* in chapter reviews and unit reviews. They can be studied as examples of rhetorical patterns.

Exemplification

"Geraldine Ferraro" (Chapter 5)
"My First Job" (Chapter 7)
"Cartoon Violence" (Chapter 8)
"Blood Sports" (Chapter 14)
"Going beyond Books" (Chapter 19)
"Women of Messina" (Chapter 23)

Narration

"Escape to Freedom" (Chapter 6)
"Healing" (Chapter 9)

16 – Teaching Notes

"My Life in Haiti" (Chapter 13)
"The Donner Party" (Unit 6)
"Starting Over" (Chapter 20)

Description

"My Father's Life" (Chapter 12)
"A Day at the Pool" (Chapter 18)
"My Cousin, Mike" (Unit 7)
"Brave Orchid" (Chapter 22)

Process

"Preparing for a Job Interview" (Chapter 4)
"Golf Course Management" (Chapter 17)

Cause and Effect

"Reasons for Volunteering" (Unit 3)
"Students from the Caribbean" (Unit 4)
"Making the Team" (Chapter 11)
"Education Internship: First Year" (Unit 9)

Comparison and Contrast

"My Brother's Wedding" (Unit 5)
"Questionable Heroes" (Chapter 16)
"History and Myth" (Chapter 21)
"Fathers and Sons" (Unit 8)

Definition

"The Mixing of Cultures" (Chapter 15)
"Fudging" (Chapter 25)

Argument

"The U.S. War on Drugs" (Chapter 10)

A. EXEMPLIFICATION

Timothy E. Miles, *"Fighting Fire with Fire Safety Education"* (student essay)

Miles's essay is very clearly organized and developed. You might begin by having students underline the thesis statement and each paragraph's topic sentence. Then, ask them to make marginal annotations about the number of examples given to develop each topic sentence. Finally, have them circle all transitional words or phrases. This kind of analysis should provide students with a good sense of how an essay citing multiple examples can be organized.

Richard Lederer, *"English Is a Crazy Language"*

Students will likely enjoy Lederer's irreverent look at the many inconsistencies of English vocabulary. Some of his examples may not be familiar and consequently difficult to explain, but paragraphs 4, 6, 7, 8, 10, 11, and 13 provide examples that nearly everyone should be able to relate to. One general question you might have students discuss: Has Lederer used too many examples? What might be his point in piling up so many?

Reacting to Reading

2. Paragraph 3: *Words about Color;* Paragraph 5: *Words for Animals;* Paragraph 6: *Words That Mean the Opposite of What They Literally Say;* Paragraph 7: *Words Related to Men and Women;* Paragraph 8: *Words That Don't Follow the Pattern One Might Expect;* Paragraph 9: *Inconsistent Prefixes and Suffixes;* Paragraphs 10–12: *Pairs of Words That Have Meanings at Odds with Each Other;* Paragraph 13: *Words That Have Opposite Meanings Depending on How They Are Used.*

Reacting to Words

1. *annals:* records of historical events; *culinary:* relating to cooking or food; *mammaried:* having breasts; *paradoxes:* ideas that seem self-contradictory; *vagaries:* events that are erratic and unpredictable.
2. He also calls English "unreliable" (5) and "bizarre" (6) and refers to its "insanity" (4) and to English speakers being "committed to an asylum for the verbally insane" (10). Note, of course, that he also writes very positively of English in paragraph 1.

Reacting to Ideas

1. Lederer makes a good case for the "craziness" of English. You might suggest that other adjectives ("inconsistent," for example) would put the case more neutrally if students are having trouble accepting his thesis.
2. Most students will probably think that Lederer's predominant purpose is to entertain; but that purpose does not undermine his central point about the eccentricities of the language. He would probably suggest that discovering the humor in the situation is the best thing we can do when faced with this "crazy" language.

Reacting to the Pattern

1. Lederer's essay follows the pattern of several related examples per paragraph. See question 2 under "Reacting to Reading."
2. The examples in paragraph 1 serve to show the power of English, leading nicely into Lederer's ironic thesis.

Ellen Goodman, *"The Suspected Shopper"*

Goodman's essay is more than fifteen years old, a point you might mention at the beginning of your discussion. Most of us have come to take for granted the kind of security measures she describes encountering on her shopping expedition. Do students think that this atmosphere of distrust by retailers might actually contribute to shoplifting in any way?

18 – Teaching Notes

Reacting to Reading

2. Ask students to share their own examples with the class. Do they feel, as Goodman does, that when shopping they have sometimes been considered guilty until they proved their innocence?

Reacting to Words

1. *futilely:* with no hope of success; *gyrations:* twistings and turnings; *belatedly:* beyond the expected time; *(in) tandem:* together; *errant:* straying outside the proper path.

2. Such words support her thesis that in these security-conscious times shoppers are made to feel like "the Accused" (15). Other similar words include "criminal" (8), "suspect" (12), "guilty" (13), "clearinghouse of bad debtors" (15), and "custody" (16).

Reacting to Ideas

1. Young people and minority students may feel that Goodman is not really part of the *we* who "are not trusted." It is pretty obvious, for example, that she exaggerates the clerk's suspicions of her in paragraphs 15–16. Some of your students will probably have encountered worse situations than Goodman describes.

2. This question provides an opportunity for some debate.

3. Along with question 2, students may want to consider the implications of living in a world of increasingly tightened security.

Reacting to the Pattern

1. Examples include the warning sign in paragraph 3, the "doorkeeper" in paragraph 4, the guard in the dressing room and the security tag in paragraphs 5–6, the supermarket and the drugstore incidents in paragraph 11, and the concluding transaction in paragraphs 15–16.

2. See question 1. Most examples are discussed in one or two separate paragraphs.

3. The introductory examples help prepare readers to understand Goodman's thesis. They also set up the scenario that led to her realization that she feels like "an enemy at Checkpoint Charlie."

B. NARRATION

Mark Cotharn, *"Swing Shift"* (student essay)

This essay by an adult working student will probably generate some interesting responses. Cotharn, a police officer, begins by showing himself preparing for a new shift and providing a run-down of the difficult and violent cases he has faced in the days preceding (1–4). The narration proper—the pursuit and shooting of a robbery suspect and the aftermath of this incident at the station—begins in paragraph 5. The conclusion—where

Cotharn finally allows himself to respond to the shooting—is particularly effective. Ask students whether there are any parts of the narration they would like to see expanded. Also have them look at Cotharn's paragraphing. Why does he start each new paragraph as he does?

Jaime O'Neill, *"Falling into Place"*

O'Neill narrates an incident from his early adolescence when he made a fool of himself (almost killing himself in the bargain) by jumping from a high tree in an attempt to impress two passing girls. The essay provides a good opportunity to discuss male and female images and gender roles.

Reacting to Reading

2. If students have trouble finding statements that are open to question, have them look specifically at paragraphs 4–6, 11, and 18–31.

Reacting to Words

1. *niche:* a protected space; *tenacious:* persistent or not easily pulled apart; *smitten:* captivated or charmed; *imperiled:* put into danger; *feign:* pretend; *superseded:* overtaken; *gonadal:* related to gonads, thus hormone-driven; *plummet:* take a steep fall; *unintelligible:* not understandable.
2. Paragraphs 4 and 22 are good choices for changing the present to the past tense. Ask students if they think the present tense makes O'Neill's story seem more immediate.

Reacting to Ideas

1. In discussing whether O'Neill's viewpoint is accurate or sexist, ask students to think specifically about their own—or their children's—experiences in junior high and high school. Does O'Neill's behavior seem typical of adolescent males? Or is he describing a stereotype that has more to do with media images than reality?
2. It's interesting that the "not-cute girl" emerges as the more distinct personality. You might see whether there is a difference in the responses of male and female students to this question.
3. O'Neill was apparently the kind of "strange and solitary boy" (7) who needs attention because he is not very secure or sure of himself. His attempt at showing off for the girls seems more infantile than truly daring.

Reacting to the Pattern

1. O'Neill's story begins with the adolescent writer up a tree in rural Florida in 1957. The first event he relates is the approach of the girls, then his calling them and showing off, then the girls' taunts that culminate with the mocking "chicken," then his jump, followed by their dismissive laughter and his inability to move for several hours. The order is strictly chronological, with paragraph 18 and the final three paragraphs offering the writer's adult commentary.

2. Other transitional words and expressions include "as they draw nearer" (5), "Today, some 35 years later" (18), "Around dusk" (27), and "Then, a while later" (27).

Martin Gansberg, *"38 Who Saw Murder Didn't Call the Police"*

Gansberg's *New York Times* account of the brutal murder of a young woman on the streets of a middle-class neighborhood of New York City while her neighbors overheard her cries but did nothing to help is justly famous. Students should note that Gansberg, unlike O'Neill, writes in the third person rather than the first person. His is not a story about his own experiences; rather he writes as a reporter who interviewed a number of people in order to reconstruct what happened that fateful night.

Reacting to Reading

2. To help students see the different effect of summarizing instead of quoting, you might have them summarize some of the examples of direct quotation they have marked. Which version of each example is more effective?

Reacting to Words

1. *staid:* settled or conservative; *shrouded:* covered as if by a shroud, or burial cloth.
2. These descriptive words stand in contrast to the actual behavior of Kitty Genovese's neighbors. Ask students why they think that "respectable" people would choose not to get involved.

Reacting to Ideas

1. In discussing this question, try to get students to focus on their own actual neighborhoods. If a Kitty Genovese–style assault should occur where they live, what do they think would be the response of the surrounding neighbors? Does the fact that there is more violent crime today than there was thirty years ago mean that people's responses will be different?
2. Excuses given for not helping Genovese ranged from not wanting to get involved, to personal fear, to being too tired and going back to bed. One gets the feeling that these people simply did not know how to respond to what was obviously a brutal attack.

Reacting to the Pattern

1. Given the fact that this was written as a newspaper account, narration makes the most sense. Other possibilities are exemplification (the Genovese story as an extended example of people's apathy) or cause and effect (an attempt to explain *why* no one called the police until too late).
2. Transitions include "Then" (10), "before" (11), "now" (15), "By then" (18), "It was 3:50" (19), "Six days later" (22), and "Today" (25).

C. DESCRIPTION

Alisha Woolery, *"African Violet"* (student essay)

This essay focusing on Woolery's great-grandmother is an excellent model of a description of a family member, a familiar assignment for descriptive essays. You might first have students look for examples of physical description in the essay. (They won't find a great deal.) Then, have them discuss the other techniques Woolery uses to describe her great-grandmother. She relates a specific anecdote (3–4) and describes habitual behavior (5–6). Moreover, she writes at length about her own feelings for her great-grandmother (7–8). Also, focus on Woolery's opening paragraph and her thesis, which focuses on the idea of aging and how her great-grandmother taught her about "life and death—and about everything in between." Students can note how well Woolery develops this thesis and allows it to give the essay real coherence. (This essay and Soto's "The Grandfather" make a nice pairing if you are asking your students to write about a family member.)

Maya Angelou, *"Graduation"*

This excerpt from a longer piece by Angelou describes the atmosphere at her segregated high school in the days just prior to her class's graduation. It includes both physical description and description of the sense of pride and excitement that characterized Angelou and her classmates at this important juncture. You might ask students to start by describing their own experiences prior to high school graduation.

Reacting to Reading

2. Have students look specifically at paragraphs 2 and 3. Are they aware of similar differences among public schools in the United States today?

Reacting to Words

1. *piteous:* to be pitied; *expanse:* a large, open area; *collective:* involving all members of a group or shared; *pervaded:* spread through every part of.
2. Angelou was writing in the 1960s about events in the 1940s; her language was current at the time.

Reacting to Ideas

1. Angelou provides such details explicitly in paragraph 3: In the South in the 1940s, professional opportunities even for blacks who graduated from college were very few.
2. The race of Angelou and her classmates is important to the point being made here. While certain elements of this graduation are universal, the fact of racism and discrimination makes it not simply a happy occasion in Angelou's memory.

Reacting to the Pattern

1. Paragraph 2 paints a fairly bleak picture of the poorly funded school Angelou attended. Paragraph 3 suggests that the students simply accept this as their lot.

22 – Teaching Notes

2. Details communicating the graduates' anxiety include the fact that they "were remarkably forgetful" (1), the boys seeming "not ready to give up the old school" (3), and the idea that the "future rode heavily on their shoulders" (3). Details communicating their eager anticipation include the fact that they "trembled visibly" (1) and their "wait in empty classrooms to make their dramatic entrance" (5).

Gary Soto, *"The Grandfather"*

In this loving portrait, Soto recalls his grandfather, transplanted from the Mexican countryside to the barrios of Fresno, California. Soto sums up his grandfather's gentleness, his frugality, and his persistence by concentrating on his backyard garden and particularly on an avocado tree grown from seed. After the grandfather's death, "all his sons standing on each other's shoulders, oldest to youngest, could not reach the highest branches" (11). You might begin discussion by asking students why they think Soto focuses on the avocado tree. What did it mean to his grandfather, and what does it say about the man?

Reacting to Reading

2. Words referring to color include "soft brown wallet" (1), the "blue" sea (2), the "heavy yellow" lemons (5), and "red and white" roses (6). Soto uses descriptive words such as these to create a sense of the beauty of his grandfather's world.

Reacting to Words

1. *campesino:* rural farmer or dweller in the country (Sp.); *lanced:* pierced, as if with a lance or sword; *hijo:* child, son or daughter (Sp.); *meager:* thin, weak; *laced:* added (something) to increase flavor; *haggle:* bargain over small matters.

2. The first and third are metaphors, the second a simile. Other metaphors include the grandfather "climb[ing]" out of Mexico (1), "A tree was money" (5), and "the smile from an ice cold watermelon." Another simile is "shades dark as oil" (10).

Reacting to Ideas

1. Soto refers to a "tree" as "money" again in paragraph 5. His point is that harvesting the fruit from trees one grows oneself saves one from having to buy the fruit from a vendor.

2. Some students may see the essay as being about Soto and his feelings for his grandfather. The avocado tree—the essay's central symbol—comes to represent the security the grandfather provided for his family.

Reacting to the Pattern

1. Paragraphs 4–11 are arranged essentially chronologically, tracing the stages of the tree's growth from a sapling Soto could jump over (4), to the tree seven and twelve years later producing its first avocados (7–9),

Teaching Notes – 23

to the tree tall enough for Soto to climb (10), to the twenty-year-old tree that finally began to bear fruit, now taller than all the grandfather's sons (11). Paragraphs 5–6 focus on the grandfather and his garden. The progression is logical and easy to follow.

2. Descriptive words other than those focusing on sight include "gurgle" (2), "sloshing" (2), "scream my fool head off" (3), "fuzzy peaches" (3), "ice cold watermelon" (9), and "quarreling jays" (10).

D. PROCESS

Mai Yoshikawa, *"Under Water"* (student essay)

Yoshikawa writes about the process of preparing for a scuba dive, necessary for purposes of safety. (While the essay is written as an explanation of a process, it could easily be adapted as instructions; you might have your students rewrite a paragraph or two to see the difference.) Have students annotate each paragraph, identifying the step being described: first, checking the basic equipment (2); then, checking one's partner's equipment and being checked by one's partner (3–4); and, finally, enjoying the dive (5). Then, ask them to list the substeps for each step. Finally, have them examine Yoshikawa's introduction and conclusion. How does she avoid simply saying something like "I'm going to tell you how to do X" and "Now, you know how to do X."

Merrill Markoe, *"Showering with Your Dog"*

This is a very straightforward instructional process essay, organized into six clearly defined steps. Its humorous tone provides a nice alternative to the blandness of most examples of instructions. You might start by asking students whether they think these are instructions that could actually be followed. How would eliminating the humorous asides affect their response to the essay?

Reacting to Reading

2. Possible expansions of Markoe's headings: *Step 1: Wear a bathing suit. Step 2: Lure the dog into the shower with a ball or a piece of chicken. Step 3: Moisten the dog, and apply shampoo. Step 4: Rinse the dog, trying to keep it in the shower. Step 5: Dry the dog off as well as you can.*

Reacting to Words

1. *exhibit:* show physically; *reluctance:* unwillingness to do something; *fungoes:* fly balls; *minute:* very small; *squeamish:* made sick easily or overly neat; *perpetual:* continual; *diligently:* carefully, with close attention to detail; *futile:* useless, without any effect.

2. Markoe also uses the term *pet* (1). Note that she refers to herself and the reader as the dog's "parent or guardian" (4); logically, she might refer to the dog as "the child" or "baby" or "the ward."

24 – Teaching Notes

Reacting to Ideas

1. Given that she is dealing with a living creature that may react in different ways, Markoe needs to provide alternatives. A single rigid system would not work in every case.

2. While Markoe's purpose may be to entertain more than to instruct, her essay does offer real advice obviously based on extensive personal experience.

Reacting to the Pattern

1. A separate concluding paragraph could do little but summarize what has already been said or offer an unnecessary "So now you know how to shower with your dog." This is probably why Markoe concludes with her final, "most important" step, which provides the essay with a funny, punchy ending.

2. Transitions include "Once this has happened" (4), "During this phase" (5), and "now" (6, 8).

Joyce Howe, *"Indelible Marks"*

Howe's is an informational process essay, explaining the workings of her family's Chinese laundry when she was a child. An interesting discussion might revolve around how students feel about the hard work expected of the children in running the family business.

Reacting to Reading

2. Step 1: Sorting and bundling the laundry (2). Step 2: Pick-up of the laundry for "wet wash" (3). Step 3: Return of the laundry (4). Step 4: Separating hand-ironed shirts from machine-pressed shirts (4). Step 5: Drying the damp items at the laundromat (5). Step 6: Folding and wrapping (6).

Reacting to Words

1. *indelible:* impossible to erase or wash out; *duration:* length (of time); *patronage:* activity as a customer; *tedious:* dull and tiresome; *irreparably:* in a state that cannot be repaired; *pilgrimages:* formal journeys (literally, journeys to a shrine); *tableau:* a formal grouping of figures, as on a stage.

2. Howe is writing about an essential part of her early life and development. Our early experiences often leave "indelible marks" that stay with us the rest of our lives.

Reacting to Ideas

1. Opinion may differ as to Howe's purpose. Certainly, she seems to want to share an important part of her life that few of her readers are likely to have experienced themselves.

2. Except for paragraph 5, which describes her difficulty and embarrassment when wheeling the laundry to a public laundromat, Howe's memories seem mostly positive. She doesn't dwell on any hardships involved, and

even the final paragraph, which details what happens "when the system was off," pictures the family's "late-night assembly line" in an attractive light.

Reacting to the Pattern

1. This is an explanation of a process.
2. See question 2 under "Reacting to Reading." The final paragraph suggests how the process varied. Also, the breakdown of the dryer described in paragraph 5 caused the process to vary.

E. CAUSE AND EFFECT

Andrea DiMarco, *"How My Parents' Separation Changed My Life"* (student essay)

This is a good example of a cause-and-effect essay focusing on personal experience, which many students find easier to accomplish than trying to describe the causes or effects of social or cultural phenomena. Paragraphs 1 and 2 are introductory and describe the situation before the initial cause (DiMarco's parents' separation); then, paragraphs 3–6 focus on specific effects (how the children's lives were different during the separation). Finally, the concluding paragraph suggests the more long-term effects on DiMarco, even after her parents worked things out. You might have students underline the topic sentences for paragraphs 3–6 and note how well DiMarco develops each with specific examples.

Anna Quindlen, *"The Old Block"*

This essay—written for the *New York Times* in the wake of the Los Angeles riots—is somewhat complex both in terms of structure and the point being made. Quindlen revisits the urban neighborhood in which she grew up, once middle-class Irish-Catholic, now largely black and poor (1–4). To her, this neighborhood is representative of many urban areas in the United States. Why do such neighborhoods exist? According to Quindlen, because the middle class has abandoned America's cities; because people in the suburbs are insulated from the problems of the inner city; and because the inner-city poor are powerless and neglected by politicians. Quindlen's purpose is to get her readers to think about our collective responsibility for—and the collective benefits of—alleviating the problems of American inner cities. Do your students believe such a responsibility exists?

Reacting to Reading

2. Other such descriptive words include *covered with debris from the fire that gutted the building* (4), *doorless doorway* (4), and *charred interiors* (5).

Reacting to Words

1. *truncated:* cut short; *grandeur:* state of being important or high ranking; *backwater:* an isolated place (literally, a body of water that is out of the main current of a larger body); *debris:* remains of something broken or

26 – Teaching Notes

destroyed; *charred:* burned, scorched; *synergy:* interaction that benefits both parties; *homogeneity:* sameness, uniformity; *ante:* pay (from the initial stake put up in a poker game); *largesse:* generous giving of money; *philanthropy:* good works to promote human welfare.

2. Your students may not all belong to the *we* to whom Quindlen addresses herself. Have them keep in mind that her original audience was readers of the *New York Times.* She uses *we* to reinforce a sense of collective responsibility.

3. Quindlen was for many years a reporter. As a "poverty tourist," she often visited poor neighborhoods, interviewing their inhabitants—but she could always return to her more comfortable middle-class home when the day was over. Though referring to herself, she seems to use the term "middle class" fairly negatively.

Reacting to Ideas

1. In addition to the physical decline, the "old block" was "a prosperous neighborhood, a way station to something better. Today it is a poor one, a dead end" (5). Do students think such neighborhoods should return to the "self-policing" described in paragraph 3?

2. Quindlen says specifically that she feels "ashamed" (14). She wants her readers to share her shame in order to feel the need to help solve the problem.

Reacting to the Pattern

1. Quindlen never suggests that the residents themselves bear some responsibility for the condition of their lives. What do students think?

2. Quindlen predicts the further effect that as long as the inner cities are ignored, they will "burst and burn, burst and burn, over and over again" (15).

Carol Sanger, *"Just Say 'No,' Just Hear 'No'"*

Sanger takes on the issue of rape, exploring some reasons that "people seem confused about the difference between sexual intercourse and rape" (5). Her point is that women are often not taken seriously as rape victims—and that rape is not taken seriously as a personal violation—because men and the courts don't always take a woman's "no" to mean "no." Asking for your male and female students' views on this subject—whether "no" in a sexual situation always means "no"—may spark some lively discussion.

Reacting to Reading

2. Student answers will vary here. You might begin discussion by suggesting which you find most significant.

Reacting to Words

1. *habituated:* accustomed, used (to); *conspirator:* one who acts with another toward a common, usually unlawful, goal; *inventory:* count up, list; *undermine:* make less firm (literally, excavate the earth from beneath).

2. Related to this question is a point Sanger makes in paragraph 14: Are there times when a woman's "yes" doesn't really mean "yes"?

Reacting to Ideas

1. This is a particularly good small-group activity. Have each group generate a list of bumper-sticker slogans. Then put them all on the board, and discuss them as a class. Bumper stickers may well be "a truer gauge of what matters to Americans than newspaper editorials" because they reflect the views of average people.

2. Sanger's point is that women are always at risk of assault, particularly by men they do not know. Men are far less likely to be assaulted. Do the women in your class agree that "fear" governs aspects of their behavior every day? Do they have to be more cautious than men?

Reacting to the Pattern

1. The causes seem to move from most specific (the language of consent) to most general (societal attitudes toward sex).

2. Transitions include "also" (3), "A second problem" (7), "too" (10), "yet another problem" (11), and "other, less legal reasons" (12).

F. COMPARISON AND CONTRAST

Cheri Rodriguez, *"Jason Vorhees, Meet Count Dracula"* (student essay)

This essay contrasts two horror movie characters: Dracula, as depicted in early Hollywood movies, and the very different contemporary villain from the popular *Friday the Thirteenth* series. Rodriguez presents three points of contrast: the appearance of the two characters (2–3), the motivation for their attacks (4–5), and their level of violence (6–7). Students should have no trouble recognizing this as a point-by-point comparison, but Rodriguez does not directly summarize her three points of contrast. Have students do so for themselves, and perhaps revise Rodriguez's thesis to include the three points. Also, have them consider the level of detail: the essay provides a good model of development through effective use of examples and specific description.

Suzanne Britt Jordan, *"That Lean and Hungry Look"*

This essay is a tongue-in-cheek comparison of "thin people" and "fat people," with Jordan taking the firm stand that fat people are, hands down, the better of the lot. Students sometimes object to Jordan's characterizations as stereotypes, which, of course, they are. Get them to think about her purpose—a defense of fat people, who are in American culture much more often the butt of cruel jokes than thin people are. Do her "reverse" stereotypes make students rethink their attitudes toward fat people at all? Another way to approach this essay is to recognize that some "thin" people are "fat" according to Jordan's definition, while some "fat" people are "thin."

28 – Teaching Notes

Reacting to Reading

2. *Paragraphs 2–4:* (1) Thin people aren't fun; they're always doing things. Fat people don't need always to keep busy. (2) Thin people are always tackling problems. Fat people let things go. (3) Fat people are nicer than thin people. (4) Thin people always want to "go straight to the heart of the matter," to "face the truth"; fat people "know there is no truth." *Paragraphs 5–8:* (1) "Thin people believe in logic"; fat people "realize that life is illogical and unfair." (2) Thin people think logical planning leads to happiness; fat people know that "happiness is elusive at best."

Reacting to Words

1. *sluggish:* slow-moving; *chortling:* laughing, chuckling; *wizened:* shrunken and wrinkled; *surly:* mean, bad-tempered; *nebulous:* vague, without clear distinctions; *mulched:* spread compost around; *cerebral:* pertaining to the brain, intellectual; *machinations:* scheming, plotting; *expound:* set forth in words, make a speech; *prognose:* predict (a verb coined by the writer, based on the noun *prognosis*); *convivial:* happy in the company of others.

2. Other informal words and more formal substitutes include *too damn long (long enough), gooey (soft and sticky), blobs (lumps), spouting off (explaining), full of holes (inaccurate), know all about (understand), figured (thought), whooping it up (having a good time),* and *downers (depressing).*

Reacting to Ideas

1. The exaggerated tone makes it clear that Jordan intends to be humorous, but there is a serious undertone. Jordan seems to want readers to appreciate the ability of "fat people" to enjoy life and not take themselves too seriously.

2. By "know all about the mystery of life," Jordan means that "fat people" recognize that there are no simple answers, that people are never fully in control of their lives, no matter how much they try to manage the world around them. By "oppressive," she means that "thin people" are always trying to be in control.

3. Jordan assumes that her readers see thin people as superior to fat people. She wants to turn this stereotype on its head.

Reacting to the Pattern

1. Jordan probably overstates her case intentionally for comic effect. The many specific instances of differences build her argument almost like a revival sermon.

2. With a subject-by-subject comparison, Jordan could not have contrasted thin and fat people so directly or sharply. No other pattern of development would be as appropriate for this subject.

Brent Staples, *"Role Models, Bogus and Real"*

Sparked by the arrest of O. J. Simpson in 1994, Staples's essay is a subject-by-subject comparison of two types of role models for today's youth: "bogus" role models (like Simpson), created by the media, "who, by virtue of fame and money, [were] appointed surrogate parent to America's young" and real unsung role models, like Joseph Marshall, Jr., who works directly with inner-city youth. You might begin discussion by asking students to name their personal role models. Are these role models media figures or people they know directly?

Reacting to Reading

2. *Examples:* Bogus role models are so "by virtue of fame and money" (3) and "never meet their 'children'" (4). Real role models are people "children can see, feel and interact with" (6); a real role model is "someone who loves and works and encourages and lays on hands" (9).

Reacting to Words

1. *deludes:* misleads, deceives; *bereft:* deprived; *inexplicably:* without explanation; *tarnished:* stained, disgraced; *innocuous:* harmless; *emulate:* imitate; *surrogate:* substitute; *lamenting:* mourning, regretting; *archaic:* outdated, old-fashioned; *paragons:* perfect examples; *temperance:* moderation; *averting:* avoiding; *reprisal:* retaliating, seeking revenge.

2. Possible substitutes include *fake, phony,* and *unreal. Bogus,* however, seems particularly negative, in part because of its sound.

Reacting to Ideas

1. A role model was originally "someone whose successes other people—and especially children—might emulate" (3), according to Staples. Today, role models are wealthy and famous people who "are expected to inspire [children] by force of fame alone" (4).

2. Students will probably come up with examples of star athletes whom they see as role models, but remind them that, according to Staples's definition, a role model must be part of children's daily lives.

Reacting to the Pattern

1. See question 2 under "Reacting to Reading."
2. Staples wants to end with a positive example as a way of making readers realize that we all have the potential to be "real" role models.

G. CLASSIFICATION AND DIVISION

Deborah Ulrich, *"Sports Fans Are in a Class by Themselves"*
(student essay)

This is a very straightforward five-paragraph expository essay: Ulrich sets up her three categories of sports fans explicitly in the thesis at the end of her

30 – Teaching Notes

first paragraph, describes each category separately in the three body paragraphs, and provides a brief summary in the final paragraph. Students might critique this essay as fairly boring. If so, take the opportunity to point out that classification-and-division essays are most interesting when a writer is taking an original slant on a subject (such as Dave Barry does) or is writing about a subject that most readers aren't familiar with (such as Mary Mebane does).

Dave Barry, *"How Your Body Works"*

This opening chapter of a Dave Barry book is a characteristically irreverent look at the divisions that make up the human body: the skin, the muscle system, the skeletal system, the digestive system, the central nervous system, the respiratory system, and the circulatory system. Students are likely to enjoy Barry's humor, and the essay is a good model of the division pattern.

Reacting to Reading

2. The only "factual" information occurs at the beginning of paragraph 2 (unless we count the statement in paragraph 3 that biology students have always pretended to find the organs they are supposed to locate). Barry isn't concerned with "facts."

Reacting to Words

1. *depicted:* pictured; *sniping:* making nasty comments; *pandering:* taking advantage of others, pimping; *carping:* complaining; *turbines:* rotary engines; *secretions:* substances that are secreted (formed and given off); *ejected:* shot out; *teeming:* filled, overflowing.

2. Other examples of scientific terms include *heart, kidney, eyeball, muscle tissue, secretions, oxygen, carbon monoxide, photosynthesis, cyst, bacteria,* and *parameciums.* Nonscientific terms include *funny bone, clavichord, zits, skin holes, Mister Sphincter* (actually, both scientific and nonscientific), *Bernice, snork up, rotifers,* and *conifers.* The juxtapositions provide much of Barry's humor.

Reacting to Ideas

1. Other digressions include the discussion of Biology Lab in paragraphs 2–3 (the end of which is signaled by the "Anyway" that begins paragraph 4) and the football commentary in paragraph 11. They keep the tone informal and humorous.

2. Other personifications include the food taking a "long, dark, scary ride" through the "Fun House" of the digestive system (13), "Mr. Sphincter" (13), and the central nervous system as the body's "Messenger" (14).

Reacting to the Pattern

1. Sections without topic sentences and possible topic sentences for them are the skeletal system ("The skeletal system is made up of a lot of bones

that support the human body"), the respiratory system ("The respiratory system allows you to breathe, except when you hold your breath"), and the circulatory system ("The circulatory system consists of your heart, your blood, and a lot of plumbing").

2. He also includes a series of jokes that play off the functions of the system.

3. There doesn't seem to be a particular order to the presentation. This randomness may be intentional and part of the humor.

Mary Mebane, *"Shades of Black"*

Mebane explores the plight of the "black black" woman in the segregated society of the South in the 1950s, when lighter-skinned blacks had greater status. Even in the all-black schools she attended, lighter-skinned girls were considered more attractive and were more likely to win academic prizes. She shifts in paragraph 16 to set up another system of categories, this time describing the options open to the "black black" woman: attaching herself to a lighter-skinned woman, emphasizing her "sexual performance," or embracing work and "intense religiosity." You might begin discussion by asking students what they would identify as the physical markers of status in their communities today.

Reacting to Reading

2. This activity allows students to vent for themselves what they may find uncomfortable in the reading before participating in a class discussion.

Reacting to Words

1. *pinnacle:* highest point; *recourse:* chance of help or protection; *nonplussed:* perplexed, at a loss for something to say; *commiserating:* sympathizing; *ludicrous:* ridiculous; *stymied:* thwarted, acted as an obstacle; *indoctrinated:* taught a set of principles; *stigma:* mark of shame; *staunch:* faithful; *fervent:* intense.

2. Other terms describing skin tone are *light brown* (7), *caramel-brown* (9), *as black as she could be* (10), *reddish-yellow* (14), and, of course, *black black.* Mebane wants to give readers a sense of the varieties of skin tones and what they represented at the time.

Reacting to Ideas

1. Some variation of these will probably apply for many students.

2. Mebane attributes this low esteem to educated blacks' indoctrination by white society and their attempt to distance themselves from their "blackness."

3. She seems to consider the system based on color as more important, although it seems to be related to social class.

Reacting to the Pattern

1. The main categories of black skin color she refers to are "indistinguishable from white" (such as the chairman's wife), "light-skinned" or

"caramel-colored" (such as Mebane's school rival, Rose), "lighter-skinned" (such as Mr. Harrison, the eighth-grade teacher), and "dark-skinned" or "black black."

2. These are described in the introductory remarks for this reading. (See paragraphs 16–21.)

H. DEFINITION

Kristin Whitehead, *"Street Smart"* (student essay)

This is a good model of defining a cultural concept using specific examples based on personal experience, something students should find useful in choosing topics for their own essays. Have students first analyze Whitehead's introduction: How does she go about generating interest in her topic? Then, consider her three body paragraphs: How many examples does she provide to explain each topic sentence? Do students think Whitehead has given a good sense of what being "street smart" entails?

José Antonio Burciaga, *"Tortillas"*

This lighthearted look at a staple of Mexican cuisine is interesting and immediately accessible as an example of definition. Burciaga develops his definition using narration (paragraphs 1 and 3), cause and effect (paragraph 2), process (paragraph 4), exemplification (paragraphs 5 and 7–8), description (paragraph 6), and comparison (paragraph 6). You might begin discussion by asking students what they remember most clearly from Burciaga's definition; then have them decide why the technique used to make that point was particularly effective.

Reacting to Reading

2. The Spanish words are italicized. You might have to point out that the word *yarmulke* in paragraph 2 is not Spanish.

Reacting to Words

1. *yarmulke:* skullcap worn by Jewish males; *maize:* Indian corn; *infiltrated:* entered secretly behind enemy lines; *adobe:* brick made of earth and straw; *edible:* eatable; *concocted:* prepared, invented; *whimsical:* fanciful, unpredictable.

2. If your class is made up of non-Spanish speakers, you might go through the essay asking about each use of Spanish. Is it clear to students what each Spanish word means? Why, or why not?

Reacting to Ideas

1. Practical uses: filled and eaten as *tacos, quesadillas, flautas,* or *gorditos.* Whimsical uses: a mask, a handwarmer, a hat, an artist's canvas, even the basis for a miraculous vision.

2. In the first paragraph, we see Burciaga as a child being scolded gently for turning a *tortilla* into a mask, and in the second he tells us his family at-

tributes his artistic career to such "clowning around." He also mentions his own children's "truly bicultural" peanut-butter-and-jelly *tortillas*. The impression is of a good-humored man, devoted to his family.

Reacting to the Pattern

1. See the introductory remarks for this reading.
2. A basic definition: *Tortillas* are flat, round cornmeal cakes that may be steamed or fried.

Leora Frankel, *"History on the Head"*

This essay defines the historical, cultural, political, and practical significance of the kaffiyeh, the scarflike cloth worn as a head covering in the Arab world. Devised as a protection against the desert sun (paragraph 3), they have become a symbol of Bedouin manhood (paragraphs 8–9, 11–12) and of the Palestinian cause (paragraphs 13–19), as well as a fashion accessory among non-Palestinians (paragraphs 5–6, 20–22). You might begin discussion by asking students what they found most interesting in this definition essay, and why.

Reacting to Reading

2. (1) The kaffiyeh became a symbol of the Palestinian cause during British rule in the 1930s. (2) It is closely associated with PLO chairman Yassar Arafat. (3) Revolutionary Palestinians wear white kaffiyehs with red stitching because red is the color of revolution; they often use their kaffiyehs to hide their faces during protests. (4) Young people use the kaffiyeh in many ways, in part as a substitute for the Palestinian flag, which is forbidden by Israeli law. (5) Israeli security officers distrust the kaffiyeh because it can so easily become a mask; undercover soldiers use it to disguise themselves as Arabs. (6) It is good advice not to wear a kaffiyeh when Israeli police are looking for suspects but to wear one openly when encountering protesting Palestinians.

Reacting to Words

1. *lethal:* deadly; *fez:* cone-shaped, flat-topped hat, usually with a tassel; *influx:* coming in; *deflect:* repel, ward off; *hobbling:* tying (an animal's legs) together to prevent from wandering; *mandate:* command; *insurgents:* rebels; *subliminal:* acting on the unconscious mind; *talisman:* magical object used as protection from danger.
2. The word *kaffiyeh* probably derived from the Iraqi city of Kufa (4), while an *iqal* was originally a rope for hobbling camels' legs (11).

Reacting to Ideas

1. By quoting so many different kinds of people, Frankel is able to suggest the many different uses for and attitudes toward the kaffiyeh.
2. She seems to treat the kaffiyeh with considerable respect. Note particularly the final paragraphs, which link the kaffiyeh with the "purity" of the Bedouin nomads.

34 – Teaching Notes

Reacting to the Pattern

1. Frankel uses examples in paragraphs 5, 6, 9, 14, 15, 16, 17, 18, and 21–22. She uses description in paragraphs 1, 4, 7, and 10–11. Other patterns include narration (3 and 13) and comparison (19).

2. Historical information is presented in paragraphs 3 and 13. This information is important to explain the origin of the kaffiyeh itself and of its current political significance.

I. ARGUMENT

John Fleeger, *"Why Isn't Pete Rose in the Hall of Fame?"* (student essay)

This is an inductive argument which presents a variety of evidence to support its conclusion that Pete Rose should be readmitted to professional baseball or, at the least, be inducted into the National Baseball Hall of Fame. (Rose was barred from professional baseball after tax problems led to allegations that he had bet on professional baseball games, a violation of major-league rules.) Have students first list the evidence that Fleeger cites: that he was an outstanding player (1); that it was never proved that Rose bet on professional baseball games (2); that rules were imposed by the Hall of Fame Committee that seemed specifically designed to bar Rose (3); that other players who have abused drugs or alcohol or been involved in gambling have not been barred (5–6). Then, have them examine his conclusion, where he states his thesis.

Martin Luther King, Jr., *"I Have a Dream"*

King's speech is one of the landmarks of American oratory, a political document as memorable as the Gettysburg Address, which King begins by echoing in order to suggest how little progress black Americans had made since Lincoln's Emancipation Proclamation a century earlier. Paragraphs 1–9 survey the current situation (America's unfulfilled promise to people of color) and offer an opening call to arms. Paragraphs 10–19 provide the most inspirational and rhetorically stirring language of the speech, describing King's "dream" for a better America. These provide a good opportunity to discuss the importance of pattern and rhythm in effective persuasive prose.

Reacting to Reading

2. The American dream of equal opportunity is the basis for King's dream of brotherhood, freedom, and justice for all, where people "will not be judged by the color of their skin but by the content of their character" (14).

Reacting to Words

1. *score:* equivalent to the number *twenty; beacon:* signal, guide; *withering:* destructive, devastating; *languishing:* lying neglected; *appalling:* horrifying; *promissory:* conveying a promise; *unalienable:* undeniable; *hallowed:* holy, revered; *gradualism:* policy of making progress slowly; *invigorating:* stimulating, energy-giving; *inextricably:* inseparably; *redemptive:* freeing,

Teaching Notes - 35

fulfilling; *wallow:* roll and stretch in a self-indulgent way; *prodigious:* large; *curvaceous:* having curves.

2. Especially notable examples are the repetition of the word *now* in paragraph 4, the phrase "we cannot be satisfied" in paragraph 7, the phrase "I have a dream" in paragraphs 11–18, and the phrase "let freedom ring" in paragraphs 20–23. The repetition establishes a rhythm that can best be demonstrated when the passages are read aloud.

Reacting to Ideas

1. Most readers find the "bad check" image effective. It is concrete and accessible and suggests that the protesters only want what is their due. A possible alternative image might be a contract.
2. He would seem also to be addressing the American public in general, trying to generate support for the civil rights movement.
3. This question is open to debate. Certainly, minorities have greater opportunities today than in 1963, but many would say Americans are no closer to King's dream of brotherhood and racial harmony.

Reacting to the Pattern

1. Most students will probably find King's deductive argument effective.
2. After concluding his central argument in paragraph 6, King uses the rest of the speech to offer a stirring call for change.
3. Given his primary audience—participants in the March on Washington—King didn't really need examples to prove his case that Americans of color were consistently denied their civil rights. Ask students whether readers of today need to be convinced of this fact, or do we accept it as part of U.S. history.

Richard Pothier, *"Animal Tests Saved My Life"*

Pothier, himself the survivor of a heart transplant, argues that animal-rights activists are wrong to attempt to ban medical experimentation using animals or the use of animal hearts as "bridges" to keep heart transplant patients alive until a human donor can be found. While he agrees that "some medical experiments on animals [are] cruel and unnecessary" (11), he asserts that it is not wrong "to sacrifice a pig or a baboon or a monkey to save a human" (10). You might begin discussion by asking students to summarize Pothier's position and compare or contrast it with their own.

Reacting to Reading

2. Such passages include paragraphs 3–5, 10–13, and 14.

Reacting to Words

1. *implant:* insert surgically; *bloated:* swollen, larger than normal; *xenografts:* grafts of tissue from one species to another; *perversion:* corruption; *degeneration:* deterioration, decline in condition.

36 – Teaching Notes

2. Pothier uses such graphic language to suggest the seriousness of the procedure, part of his strategy to convince readers that it is important that such procedures first be performed on animals.

Reacting to Ideas

1. Obviously, Pothier is not "objective," given his own experience as a transplant patient. Some will think that offering himself as an example strengthens the argument, while others may say that it makes his case seem self-centered.

2. Student responses will vary here. To begin the discussion, you might ask how students respond to experiments in which healthy animals are infected with disease.

3. Again, responses will vary. What would Pothier say?

Reacting to the Pattern

1. Factual information is found in paragraphs 1, 2, 7, 8, 9, 10, 15, and 16. These examples and statistics are used to bolster Pothier's argument that heart transplants are essential to saving thousands of lives a year.

2. The introduction effectively sets up the subject of Pothier's argument. Pothier might have begun with the example of himself.

3. The advantage of this organization is that it allows Pothier to present many examples of evidence to support his case. The disadvantage is that if a reader doesn't accept this evidence, then he or she won't accept the argument either.

Index

A, in titles, 443
Abstract words, 330
Accept/except, 459
Action verbs, 127–29
Active voice, 283–86
Addresses, commas with, 418–19
Adjectives, 17, 382–92
   adverbs distinguished from, 384
   comparatives of, 387–92
   definition of, 383
   demonstrative, 392–93
   determiners, 491–92, 496
   ESL writers and, 491–92, 495–96
   good as, 385–86
   order of, 495–96
   past participles as, 202–4
   superlatives of, 387–92
   understanding, 383–87
   without comparatives and superlatives, 391
Adverbs, 17, 382–92
   adjectives distinguished from, 384
   commas with, 308
   without comparatives and superlatives, 391
   comparatives of, 387–92
   conjunctive, 230–33, 260, 310
   definition of, 383
   as sentence openers, 307–10
   superlatives of, 387–92
   understanding, 383–87
   well as, 385–86
Affect/effect, 460
"African Violet" (Woolery), 532–34
"Agony Called Writer's Block, The" (Eddy), 69
Agreement, pronoun-antecedent, 17
Agreement, subject-verb, 16, 147–68
   with indefinite pronouns, 157–58

with irregular verbs, 152–55
with regular verbs, 148–51
with relative pronouns, 160–62
when verb comes before subject, 158–60
when words come between subject and verb, 155–57
All ready/already, 460
Although, as subordinating conjunction, 139
An, in titles, 443
And, compound antecedents and, 367
Angelou, Maya, 534–37
"Animal Tests Saved My Life" (Pothier), 107, 602–5
Annotating, in reading process, 503–505
Antecedents
   collective noun, 372–73
   compound, 367–69
   definition of, 365
   indefinite pronouns, 369–71
   pronoun's agreement with. *See* Pronoun-antecedent agreement
Apostrophes, 17, 423–33
   in contractions, 424–26
   in possessives, 426–29
   revising incorrect use of, 429–31
Appositives, 313–14, 318–19
   commas with, 416–18
Argument
   deductive, 594
   inductive, 593
Argument essays, 593–605
   conclusions of, 601, 604
   introductions of, 598, 602
   options for organization of, 594
   thesis statement for, 593, 604
   topics for, 593
   transitional expressions for, 595
   writing checklist for, 597

Argument paragraphs, 71–75
   audience for, 73
Articles, 492–94
   in titles, 443
As
   comparisons with, 295
   in similes and metaphors, 531
As/as if vs. *like*, 400
Assignment, 1, 97
Audience, 1–3
   for argument paragraphs, 73
   for essays, 508

Background statement, in introduction of essay, 109
Badly/worse/worst, 390
Bad/worse/worst, 390
"Baldness" (Likus), 65
"Barbie at 35" (Quindlen), 502
Barry, Dave, 110, 573–78
Be
   in contractions, 178
   in past progressive tense, 213–15
   past tense of, 177–79
   in present progressive tense, 209–13
   subject-verb agreement with, 152–55
Because, as subordinating conjunction, 139
Best/better/good, 390
Best/better/well, 390
Bishop, Louis Faugeres, 64
Body, of essays, 87, 88, 93–94, 114
   examinations, 486–87
   for exemplification, 495–97, 517
Book of Popular Science, The (Bishop), 64
Books, titles of, 442–45
Born on the Fourth of July (Kovic), 42
Brainstorming, 5–7, 484
Break/brake, 460
Brody, Dan (student), 110

INDEX – 2

Burciaga, José Antonio, 587–89
Burkhart, Susan (student), 48
By/buy, 460

"Camaro Joe" (Burkhart), 47–48
Campbell, Bebe Moore, 47
Can/could, 180–82
Capitalization, 17
   of proper nouns, 435–38
   of titles, 443
Case, 16, 359–64
   objective, 360–64
   possessives, 360–61, 461, 466, 468–69
   subjunctive, 359–64
Cause-and-effect essays, 549–59
   conclusions for, 555, 558
   introductions for, 554, 556–57
   options for organization of, 550
   thesis statement for, 550, 555, 557
   topics for, 549–50
   transitional expressions for, 551
   writing checklist for, 553
Cause-and-effect paragraphs, 53–57
Central ideas. *See* Thesis statement; Topic sentences
Christensen, Sally Thane, 114
Chronological order. *See* Time order
Clarity, editing for, 17
Classification-and-division essays, 569–83
   conclusions of, 576–77, 581–82
   introductions of, 573–74, 578–79
   options for organization of, 571
   thesis statement for, 570, 574, 579
   topics for, 570
   transitional expressions for, 571
   writing checklist for, 573
Classification-and-division paragraphs, 63–67
   definition of, 63, 64
Clauses
   definition of, 240
   dependent (subordinate), 240–52
   independent, 240–46
   relative, 245–52, 260–61
   subordinate (dependent), 260–61
Clichés, 337–40
   list of, 338
Clustering (mapping), 7–8

Coherence, of paragraphs, 28–34
Collective nouns
   as antecedents, 372–73
   definition of, 372
Commands, 304
Commas, 17, 411–22
   with addresses, 418–19
   with adverbs, 308
   with appositives, 313, 416–18
   with conjunctive adverbs, 230
   with coordinating conjunctions, 224, 228, 259–60
   with dates, 418–19
   with introductory phrases, 414–16
   with participles, 312
   with prepositional phrases, 308
   with relative clauses, 250–51
   in a series, 412–14
   with subordinating conjunctions, 241–42
   with transitional expressions and words, 414–16
Comma splices, 257–68
   avoiding, 16
   correcting, 259–65
   definition of, 258
   identifying, 258–59
Common nouns, 354
Comparatives
   of adjectives and adverbs, 387–92
   irregular, 390
"Comparing the British and American Education Systems" (Van Hoboken), 59–61
Comparison-and-contrast essays, 559–69
   conclusions for, 565–66, 568
   introductions for, 564, 567
   options for organization of, 560
   thesis statement for, 560, 564, 568
   topics for, 560
   transitional expressions, 561
   writing checklist for, 563
Comparison-and-contrast paragraphs, 57–63
   point-by-point arrangement in, 58–59
   subject-by-subject arrangement in, 58
Comparisons
   parallel structure for, 295
   point-by-point, 559
   pronouns in, 361–62

   subject-by-subject, 559
   unusual, in introduction of essay, 110
Compass in Your Nose and Other Astonishing Facts about Humans, The (McCuchen), 50
Complete Blader, The (Rappelfeld), 50–51
Complete subjects, 123–24
Complete verbs, 129–30, 137–40
Complex sentences, 240–49
   definition of, 240
   subordinating conjunctions and, 240–45
Compound antecedents, 367–69
Compound sentences, 222–38
   with conjunctive adverbs and transitional expressions, 260
   coordinating conjunctions in, 223–28, 310
   definition of, 223
   semicolons in, 228–33
      conjunctive adverbs, 230–31
      transitional expressions in, 231
Compounds, pronouns in, 361, 362
Compound subjects, 150, 312–13, 317–18
Compound verbs, 312–13, 317–18
Concise language, 333–37
Conclusion, of essays, 88, 94, 111–16
   for argument, 600–601, 604
   avoiding unnecessary phrases in, 112
   for cause-and-effect, 555, 558
   for classification-and-division, 576–77, 581–82
   for comparison-and-contrast, 565–66, 568
   examinations and, 486, 487
   for exemplification, 517
   narrative in, 112–13
   prediction in, 113
   questions in, 113
   quotation in, 114
   recommendation in, 114
   thesis statement in, 112
Concrete words, 330
Conjunctions
   coordinating, 223–28, 259–60, 295, 310
   punctuation with, 241–42

subordinating, 139, 240–45, 260–61, 311
  in titles, 443
Conjunctive adverbs, 230–33, 310
  list of, 230
  run-ons and comma splices with, 260
Conscience/conscious, 461
Consistency, 272–90
  of discourse, 281–82
  of number, 278–80
  of person, 276–78
  of tense, 273–76
  of voice, 283–86
Consonants, 450
  final, doubling of, 458–59
  spelling of, 461, 466, 468–69
  suffixes beginning with, 456
  before *y,* 457
Contractions
  apostrophes in, 424–26
  be in, 178
  list of, 424
  spelling of, 451
Coordinating conjunctions
  compound sentences formed with, 223–28, 310
  list of, 223
  parallel structure and, 295
  punctuation with, 224, 228, 259–60
Coordination, 222–38
  with coordinating conjunctions, 223–28, 310
Corey, Daniel (student), 63
Cotharn, Mark (student), 520–22
Could/can, 180–82
Count nouns, 489–92
Cousins, Norman, 55

Dates, commas with, 418–19
Davia, Megan (student), 108
"Death and Justice: How Capital Punishment Affirms Life" (Koch), 72
-*d*/-*ed* endings, in past tense, 170–73
Deductive argument, 594
Definite articles, 492–93
Definition, in introduction of essay, 108–9
Definition essays, 583–93
  introductions of, 587, 590
  options for organization of, 584
  thesis statement for, 583–84, 588
  topics for, 583–84

transitional expressions for, 585
writing checklist for, 586–87
Definition paragraphs, 67–71
Demonstrative adjectives, 392–93
Dependent (subordinate) clauses, 239–56, 260–61
  definition of, 240
  relative pronouns and, 245–52
  subordinating conjunctions and, 240–45
Descriptive essays, 530–40
  dominant impression created by, 530
  options for organization of, 531
  thesis statement for, 530
  topics for, 530
  transitional expressions for, 532
  writing checklist for, 534
Descriptive paragraphs, 45–49
  objective, 46, 47
  spatial order in, 28, 45, 46
Details
  choosing, 11
  ordering of, 11
    paragraphs, 28–31
  in paragraph development, 26–28
Determiners, 496
  with count and noncount nouns, 491–92
  definition of, 491
Dictionaries, 450, 471
"Did Popeye Watch Too Many Violent Cartoons?" (Woller), 73–74
DiMarco, Andrea (student), 551–53
Direct approach, in introduction of essay, 107
Direct discourse, 281–83
Direct objects, 360
Direct quotation, 438–42
Discourse, consistency of, 281–83
Discovery. *See* Invention strategies
Do, subject-verb agreement with, 153–55
Doyle, Jerry (student), 39
Drafting (drafts)
  at examinations, 484
  first, 13–14
Duong, Anne (student), 44

-*ed*/-*d* endings, in past tense, 170–73
Eddy, Thaddeus (student), 69
Editing
  checklist for, 16–17

at examinations, 484
-*e* ending, silent, suffixes and, 456–57
Effect/affect, 460
Effectiveness
  editing for, 17
  of paragraphs, 19–37
  of thesis statement, 100–102
ei/ie, spelling and, 453–54
"English Is a Crazy Language" (Lederer), 109, 113, 495–516
ESL writers, tips for, 488–97
Espen, Hal, 39
Essays, 86–120, 508–605
  argument, 593–605
  body of, 87, 88, 93–94, 114
  cause-and-effect, 549–59
  classification-and-division, 569–83
  comparison-and-contrast, 559–69
  conclusion of, 88, 94, 111–16
  definition, 583–93
  definition of, 86
  descriptive, 530–40
  at examinations, 503–505
  exemplification, 509–519
  introduction of, 87, 93, 106–11, 114–16
  narrative, 519–30
  process, 540–49
  student. *See* Student essays
  thesis-and-support, 91–97
  thesis statement of. *See* Thesis statement
  titles of, 110–11
Everyday/every day, 461
Examinations, 481–87
  key words in, 483
  preparing for, 481–82
  tips on taking, 482–84
  writing an essay at, 484–85
  writing a paragraph at, 484–85
Examples, in paragraph development, 26–28
Except/accept, 459
Exclamations, 304–6
Exemplification essays, 509–519
  body of, 513–15, 517
  conclusion of, 515, 517
  introduction of, 513, 516–17
  options for organization of, 510
  thesis statement for, 509, 513, 517
  topics for, 509
  transitional expressions for, 510
  writing checklist, 512

Exemplification paragraphs, 38–42
Exemplification sentences, relative pronouns and, 245–49

"Falling into Place" (O'Neill), 523–26
"Fighting Fire with Fire Safety Education" (Miles), 511–13
Figures of speech, 531
Fine/find, 461
Fleeger, John (student), 595–97
Focused freewriting, 3
Frankel, Leora, 109, 589–93
Freewriting, 3–5
 focused, 3
Fused sentences. *See* Run-on (fused) sentences

Gansberg, Martin, 114, 526–30
Good/better/best, 390
Goodman, Ellen, 516–19
Good/well, 385–86
"Graduation" (Angelou), 534–37
Grammar. *See also specific topics*
 editing for, 16–17
"Grandfather, The" (Soto), 113, 537–40
Group study, 182

Haurin, Beth (student), 59
Have
 in past perfect tense, 199–201
 in present perfect tense, 195–99
 subject-verb agreement with, 152–55
Hear/here, 461
Helping verbs, 129–30, 137–39
 can/could and *will/would*, 180–82
 with past participles, 187–89
 in past progressive tense, 213–15
 in present progressive tense, 209–13
Her or *his*, 344
 indefinite pronouns with, 369–70
Highlighting, in reading process, 501–503
"History on the Head" (Frankel), 109, 589–93
Hovis, Ford, 68
Howe, Joyce, 547–49
"How My Parents' Separation Changed My Life" (DiMarco), 551–53
"How Your Body Works" (Barry), 110, 573–78

Ideas
 gathering of. *See* Invention strategies
 main, 19, 86–87. *See also* Thesis statement; Topic sentences
 order of. *See* Order of ideas
 selecting and arranging, 10–12
Identifications, on examinations, 485
Identifying tag, 281
Idioms, prepositions in, 401–4
ie/ei, spelling and, 453–54
If, as subordinating conjunction, 139
"I Have a Dream" (King), 598–602
Illiterate America (Kozol), 54
Illogical shifts, avoiding, 17, 272–90
 in discourse, 281–83
 in number, 278–80
 in person, 276–78
 in tense, 273–76
 in voice, 283–86
Indefinite articles, 493
Indefinite pronouns, 157–58
 as antecedents, 369–71
 definition of, 369
 his or *her* with, 369–70
 list of, 157, 369
 with *of*, 370
 possessives of, 426–27
"Indelible Marks" (Howe), 547–49
Independent clauses, 240–46
 definition of, 240
Indirect discourse, 281–83
Indirect objects, 360
Inductive argument, 593
-ing ending, of present participles, 209
Instructors, discussing exams with, 482
Intensive pronouns, 376–78
Introductions of essays, 87, 93, 106–11, 114–16
 for argument, 598, 602
 avoiding unnecessary statements in, 106
 background statement in, 109
 for cause-and-effect, 554, 556–57
 for classification-and-division, 573–74, 578–79
 common ground established in, 108
 for comparison-and-contrast, 564, 567

 for definition, 587, 590
 definition in, 108–9
 direct approach in, 107
 examinations and, 486
 for exemplification, 513, 516–17
 narrative in, 107
 question in, 108
 quotation in, 110
 thesis statement in, 106
 unusual comparison in, 110
Introductory phrases, commas with, 414–16
Invention strategies (prewriting; discovery), 3–10, 97
 brainstorming, 5–7, 484
 clustering, 7–8
 freewriting, 3–5
 journal writing, 8–10
Irregular verbs
 definition of, 152
 past participles of, 189–95
 past tense of, 173–79, 189–93
 be, 177–79
 -d and *-ed* endings, 173–77
 list of, 174–75
 spelling of, 451
 subject-verb agreement with, 152–55
"Is a Tree Worth a Life?" (Christensen), 114
Italic type, for titles of books, stories and other works, 442–45
Items in a series
 commas with, 412–14
 parallel structure for, 295
Its/it's, 461–62

"Jason Vorhees, Meet Count Dracula" (Rodriguez), 561–63
Jordan, Suzanne Britt, 564–67
Journal writing, 8–10
"Just Say 'No', Just Hear 'No'" (Sanger), 556–59

Kincaid, Willa (student), 40
King, Martin Luther, Jr., 598–602
Kingston, Maxine Hong, 46
Know/knew/new/no, 463
Koch, Edward I., 72
Komanawski, Serge (student), 107, 112
Kovic, Ron, 42
Kozol, Jonathan, 54

Language. *See also* Words, revising of
  concise, 333–37
  sexist, 343–44
"Latina Stereotype, The" (Ortiz Cofer), 43
Lederer, Richard, 109, 113, 513–516
Lie/lay, 463
Like
  as/as if vs., 400
  as preposition, 400
  in similes and metaphors, 531
Likus, Peter (student), 65
Linking verbs, 128–29
Logical sequence. *See* Order of ideas
Loose/lose, 463
-ly ending, for adverbs, 384

McCuchen, Mark, 50
Main idea, 19, 86–87. *See also* Thesis statement; Topic sentences
Main verbs, 129–30, 137
Mapping, 7–8
Markoe, Merrill, 58, 108, 544–47
Marro, Toni-Ann (student), 72
Mebane, Mary, 578–83
Mechanics, editing for, 17
"Men, Women, and Conversation" (Markoe), 58
Metaphors, 340–43, 531
Miles, Timothy E. (student), 511–12
Mine/mind, 463
Morris, Mary, 68
Mujica, Barbara, 499–501

Narrative
  in conclusion of essay, 112–13
  in introduction of essay, 107
Narrative essays, 519–30
  options for organization of, 520
  thesis statement in, 519, 525, 527
  topics for, 519
  transitional expressions for, 520
  writing checklist for, 522
Narrative paragraphs, 42–45
  process paragraphs compared with, 51
  time order in, 28, 42, 43
Negatives, formation of, 494
"No Comprendo" (Mujica), 499–501
Noncount nouns, 489–92
No/new/knew/know, 463

Nonrestrictive clauses, 250–52
Note taking, 482
Nothing to Declare (Morris), 68
Nouns
  capitalization of, 435–38
  collective, 372–73
  common, 354
  count, 489–92
  definition of, 122, 354
  ESL writers and, 489–94
  noncount, 489–92
  number of, 278–80
  as objects, 360
  as objects of prepositions, 125–27, 155
  plural, 16, 354–57, 427–29, 451, 489
  pronouns followed directly by, 362–63
  proper, 354, 435–38, 493–94
  singular, 16, 354, 426–29, 451, 489
  spelling of, 451
  as subjects, 122–25, 148–50
Number
  consistency of, 278–80
  definition of, 278

Objective case, 360–64
Objective description, 531
Objects
  nouns as, 360
  of prepositions, 125–26, 155, 360, 400
  pronouns as, 360–64
Of, indefinite pronouns with, 370
"Old Block, The" (Quindlen), 113, 553–56
O'Neill, Jaime, 523–26
Or, compound antecedents and, 367–68
"Order of Fries, An" (Rodriguez), 51–52
Order of ideas
  sequential, 29–31, 33
  spatial, 28–31, 33, 45, 46
  time, 28, 30, 31, 33, 34, 42, 43, 50
Ortiz Cofer, Judith, 43
Outlining
  at examinations, 484
  in reading process, 505–506

"Pain Is Not the Ultimate Enemy" (Cousins), 55
Paired items, parallel structure for, 295

Papers, titles of, 443
Paragraphs, 19–85
  argument, 71–75
  cause-and-effect, 53–57
  coherence of, 28–34
    defined, 28
    order of details, 28–31
    revising, 32–33
    transitional words and phrases, 31–34
  comparison-and-contrast, 57–63
  definition, 67–71
  definition of, 19
  descriptive, 28, 45–49
  development of, 25–28
    defined, 25
    examples, 26–28
    revising, 26–27
    specific detail, 26–28
  at examinations, 484–85
  exemplification, 38–42
  narrative, 28, 42–45
  process, 28, 49–53
  response, 506–507
  topic sentences of. *See* Topic sentences
  unity of, 19–25
    revising, 21
Parallel structure, 17, 291–302
  definition of, 292
  recognizing, 292–94
  using, 294–98
Participles
  past, 187–95, 311, 316–17. *See also* Past participles
  irregular, 189–95
  regular, 187–89
  present, 137–39, 311, 314–16
Passed/past, 463
Passive voice, 283–86
Past participles, 187–95, 311, 316–17
  as adjectives, 202–4
  of irregular verbs, 189–95
    list, 190–93
  in past perfect tense, 199–201
  in present perfect tense, 195–99
  of regular verbs, 187–89
Past perfect tense, 199–201
Past progressive tense, 213–15
Past tense, 169–85, 214, 274
  could and *would* in, 180–82
  of irregular verbs, 173–79, 189–93
  be, 177–79
  -d and *-ed* endings, 173–77
  of regular verbs, 170–73
Peace/piece, 463

INDEX – 6

Perfect tense, 195–201
  past, 199–201
  present, 195–200
Person
  consistency of, 276–78
  definition of, 276
Personal pronouns, 357–78, 429–30
Personification, 531
Phrases
  definition of, 125
  introductory, 414–16
  prepositional, 125–27, 155–57, 307–10, 400
  transitional, 31–34
Piece/peace, 463
Plain/plane, 464
Planning, of writing, 1–12
  invention strategies and, 3–10
  questions about assignment, audience, and punctuation and, 1–3
  selecting and arranging ideas in, 10–12
Plural nouns, 16, 354–57, 451, 489
  definition of, 354
  irregular, 355, 427
  possessives of, 427–29
Plural pronouns, 358
  pronoun-antecedent agreement and, 367–69, 377
Plural subjects, 124–25, 178
  subject-verb agreement and, 148–50, 152–53
Point-by-point comparisons, 559
Possessive case, 360
Possessives
  apostrophes in, 426–29
  spelling of, 461, 466, 468–69
Pothier, Richard, 107, 602–5
Prediction, in conclusion of essay, 113
Prefixes, 455
Prepositional phrases, 125–27
  commas with, 308
  definition of, 400
  as sentence openers, 307–10
  subject-verb agreement and, 155–57
Prepositions, 17, 398–410
  commonly used, 399
  definition of, 399
  ESL writers and, 496–97
  in familiar expressions, 401–4
  objects of, 125–26, 155, 360, 400
  in titles, 443
  in two-word verbs, 497
  understanding, 399–401
Present participles, 137–39, 311, 314–16
  formation of, 209
Present perfect tense, 195–200
Present progressive tense, 209–13
Present tense, 210, 274
  subject-verb agreement and
    irregular verbs, 152–55
    regular verbs, 148–51
  use of, 149
Preview, in reading process, 481
Prewriting. *See* Invention strategies
Principal/principle, 464
Process essays, 540–49
  options for organization of, 541
  thesis statement for, 540, 544
  topics for, 540
  transitional expressions for, 541
  writing checklist for, 543–44
Process paragraphs, 49–53
  explanation in, 49–50
  instructions in, 50–51
  narrative paragraphs compared with, 51
  time order in, 28, 50
Progressive tense, 208–18
  past, 213–15
  present, 209–13
Pronoun-antecedent agreement, 17, 365–76
  for reflexive and intensive pronoun, 376–78
  special problems with, 367–76
    antecedents, 367–69
    collective noun antecedents, 372–73
    indefinite pronoun antecedents, 369–71
    nonspecific pronoun references, 374–76
    unnecessary, 375–76
  understanding, 365–67
Pronouns, 357–78
  antecedents' agreement with, 17
  case of. *See* Case
  in comparisons, 361–62
  in compounds, 361, 362
  definition of, 122, 357
  followed directly by a noun, 362–63
  indefinite, 157–58, 369–71, 426–27
  intensive, 376–78
  number of, 278–80
  as objects, 360–64
  as objects of prepositions, 125, 155
  personal, 357–78, 429–30
  person of, 276–78
  reflexive, 376–78
  relative, 140, 160–62, 245–52, 260–61
  as subjects, 122–25, 148–49, 152–53, 157–58
Pronunciation, spelling and, 450–53
Proofreading, 471
Proper nouns, 354
  articles and, 493–94
  capitalization of, 435–38
  definition of, 435
Punctuation, 411–33
  apostrophes. *See* Apostrophes
  commas. *See* Commas
  with coordinating conjunctions, 224, 228, 259–60
  editing for, 17
  quotation marks, 281
  semicolons, 228–33, 260
  with subordinating conjunctions, 241–42
Purpose, 1–3
  of essays, 508
  of reading assignment, 498–501

Questions
  in conclusion of essay, 113
  for critical reading, 503–504
  on examinations, 483–87
    essays, 485–87
    paragraphs, 484–85
    rereading, 483–84
  formation of, 494
  in introduction of essay, 108
  about purpose of reading, 498–99
  as sentence type, 304–6
Quiet/quit/quite, 464
Quindlen, Anna, 113, 582, 553–56
Quotation
  in conclusion of essay, 114
  direct, 438–42
  identifying tag and, 439
  in introduction of essay, 110
Quotation marks, 17, 438–45
  in direct discourse, 281
  for direct quotation, 438–42
  for titles, 442–45

Raise/rise, 465
Rappelfeld, Joel, 51

INDEX – 7

Reading process, 498–507
   annotating in, 503–505
   examinations and, 481, 483–84
   highlighting in, 501–503
   outlining in, 505–506
   questions about your purpose and, 498–99
   response paragraphs in, 506–507
Recommendation, in conclusion of essay, 114
Reflexive pronouns, 376–78
Regular verbs
   definition of, 152
   past participles of, 187–89
   past tense of, 170–73
   present tense of, 148–51
   subject-verb agreement with, 148–51
Relative clauses, 245–52, 260–61
   punctuation of, 250–51
   restrictive vs. nonrestrictive, 250–52
Relative pronouns, 245–52, 260–61
   definition of, 245
   list of, 246
   sentence fragments and, 140, 246–47
   sentences combined with, 245–49
   subject-verb agreement and, 160–62
Repetition, needless, 334
Response paragraphs, 506–507
Restrictive clauses, 250–52
Review, before examinations, 482
Revising, 14–18, 303–52
   critical thinking and, 14–16
   editing vs., 16
   at examinations, 484
   of incorrect use of apostrophes, 429–31
   for paragraph coherence, 32–33
   for paragraph development, 26–27
   for paragraph unity, 21
   for sentence variety, 303–27
      combining, 310–21
      length, 321–23
      openings, 307–10
      type, 304–6
   of words, 328–52
      clichés, 337–40
      conciseness, 333–37
      exactness, 329–33
      sexist, 343–44
      similes and metaphors, 340–43

Right/write, 465
Rise/raise, 465
Rodriguez, Cheri (student), 52, 561–63
"Role Models, Bogus and Real" (Staples), 567–69
Run-on (fused) sentences, 257–68
   avoiding of, 16
   with conjunctive adverbs and transitional expressions, 260
   correcting, 259–65
   definition of, 258
   identifying, 258–59

Sanger, Carol, 556–59
Semicolons, 260
   compound sentences formed with, 228–33
   conjunctive adverbs, 230–33
Sentence fragments
   avoiding of, 16, 134–46
      complete verbs, 137–39
      relative pronouns, 140
      subordinating conjunctions, 139
   definition of, 135
   present progressive tense and, 211
   relative pronouns and, 246–47
   subordinating conjunctions and, 242
Sentences
   basic pattern of, 121–33
   complex, 240–49
      relative pronouns, 245–49
      subordinating conjunctions, 240–45
   compound, 222–38
      coordinating conjunctions, 223–28, 310
      semicolons, 228–33
   definition of, 122
   parallel structure of, 17
   run-on (fused), 257–68
   simple, 223
   subject of. *See* Subjects
   topic. *See* Topic sentences
   variety of (revising of), 303–27
      combining, 310–21
      length, 321–23
      openings, 307–10
      type, 304–6
Sequential order, 29–31, 33
   words and phrases that signal, 31
Series, items in. *See* Items in a series
Set/sit, 465

Sexist language, 343–44
"Shades of Black" (Mebane), 578–83
"Showering with Your Dog" (Markoe), 108, 544–47
Silent letters, 451, 456
Similes, 340–43, 531
Simple sentences
   definition of, 223
   joining of. *See* Coordination
Simple subjects, 123–24
Singular nouns, 16, 354, 451, 489
   possessives of, 426–29
Singular pronouns, 358
   pronoun-antecedent agreement and, 367–72, 377
Singular subjects, 124–25, 178
   subject-verb agreement and, 148–50, 152–53
Sit/set, 465
Soto, Gary, 113, 537–40
Spatial order, 28–31, 33, 45
   words and phrases that signal, 31, 46
Specific words, 329–30
Spell checker, 471
Spelling, 17, 449–79
   of commonly confused words, 459–70
   of commonly misspelled words, list of, 472
   of consonants, 461, 466, 468–69
   consonants in, 450, 456–58
   of contractions, 451
   editing for, 17
   ie/ei combinations and, 453
   improvement of, 470–72
   prefixes in, 455
   pronunciation and, 450–53
   suffixes in, 455–59
   understanding, 450–53
   vowels in, 450, 451, 456, 457
Sports Encyclopedia, The (Hovis), 68
"Sports Fans Are in a Class by Themselves" (Ulrich), 570–72
Staples, Brent, 567–69
Statements, 304–6
Stories, titles of, 442–45
"Street Smart" (Whitehead), 585–86
Student essays
   "African Violet" (Woolery), 532–34
   "Fighting Fire with Fire Safety Education" (Miles), 511–512

Student essays *(continued)*
  "How My Parents' Separation Changed My Life" (DiMarco), 551–53
  "Jason Vorhees, Meet Count Dracula" (Rodriguez), 561–63
  "Sports Fans Are in a Class by Themselves" (Ulrich), 570–72
  "Street Smart" (Whitehead), 585–86
  "Swing Shift" (Cotharn), 520–22
  "Under Water" (Yoshikawa), 542–43
  "Why Isn't Pete Rose in the Hall of Fame?" (Fleeger), 595–97
Study habits, 482
Subject-by-subject comparisons, 559
Subjective description, 531
Subjects (of sentence), 122–27
  agreement of. *See* Agreement, subject-verb
  complete, 123–24
  compound, 150, 312–13, 317–18
  ESL writers and, 488–89
  identification of, 122–25
  indefinite pronouns as, 157–58
  plural, 124–25, 148–50, 152–53, 178
  prepositional phrases vs., 125–27
  sentence fragments and, 135–36, 139, 140
  simple, 123–24
  singular, 124–25, 148–50, 152–53, 178
  voice and, 283–86
Subjunctive case, 359–64
Subordinate (dependent) clauses, 239–56, 260–61
  definition of, 240
  relative pronouns and, 245–52
  subordinating conjunctions and, 240–45
Subordinating conjunctions, 139, 240–45, 260–61, 311
  sentence fragments and, 242
Suffixes, 455–59
  after final *e*, 456–57
  after final *y*, 457–58
  definition of, 455
  doubling consonants and, 458–59
Superlatives
  of adjectives and adverbs, 387–92
  irregular, 390

Suppose/supposed, 465
Suspected Shopper, The (Goodman), 516–19
Sweet Summer (Campbell), 47
"Swing Shift" (Cotharn), 520–22
Syllables, 450

Tense
  consistency of, 273–76
  definition of, 149
  ESL writers and, 495
  past. *See* Past tense
  perfect
    past, 199–201
    present, 195–200
  present, 148–51, 210, 274
  progressive, 208–18
    past, 213–15
    present, 209–13
Than, comparisons with, 295
Than/then, 466
That
  with indirect discourse, 281
  as relative pronoun, 140, 160–62, 246
"That Lean and Hungry Look" (Jordan), 564–67
The, in titles, 443
Their/there/they're, 466
Then/than, 466
There is, there are, subject-verb agreement and, 159–60
Thesis-and-support essays, 91–97
Thesis statement, 97–105
  for argument essays, 593, 604
  for cause-and-effect essays, 550, 555, 557
  for classification-and-division essays, 570, 574, 579
  for comparison-and-contrast essays, 560, 564, 568
  in conclusion of essay, 112
  for definition essays, 583–84, 588
  definition of, 87
  for descriptive essays, 530
  effectiveness of, 100–102
  examinations and, 484, 486
  for exemplification essays, 509, 513, 517
  implied, 525
  implied thesis vs., 101
  in introduction of essay, 106
  for narrative essays, 519, 525, 527
  for process essays, 540, 544
  topic vs., 97–99

"38 Who Saw Murder Didn't Call the Police" (Gansberg), 114, 526–30
Threw/through, 466–67
Time order, 28, 30, 33, 34, 42, 43, 50
  words and phrases that signal, 31, 42, 43
Titles
  capitalization of, 443
  of essays, 110–11
  italicizing of, 442–45
  quotation marks for, 442–45
Topic(s). *See also* Invention strategies
  for argument essays, 593
  for cause-and-effect essays, 549–50
  for classification-and-division essays, 570
  for comparison-and-contrast essays, 560
  for definition essays, 583–84
  for descriptive essays, 530
  for exemplification essays, 509
  for narrative essays, 519
  for process essays, 540
  thesis statement vs., 97–99
  topic sentences vs., 20
Topic sentences, 19–28, 502–505
  of argument paragraphs, 72, 73
  of cause-and-effect paragraphs, 54, 55
  of classification-and-division paragraphs, 63, 64
  of comparison-and-contrast paragraphs, 58, 59
  definition of, 19
  of definition paragraphs, 67, 68
  of exemplification paragraphs, 38, 39
  location of, 20–21
  making a point in, 20
  of narrative paragraphs, 42, 43
  in paragraphs and essays, 86–88
  of process paragraphs, 50
  supporting of, 25–28
  in thesis-and-support essays, 93–94
  topic vs., 20
"Tortillas" (Burciaga), 587–89
To/too/two, 467
Transitional expressions
  adverbs and prepositional phrases as, 308
  for argument essays, 595
  for cause-and-effect essays, 551

for classification-and-division essays, 571
for classification-and-division paragraphs, 63
commas with, 414–16
for comparison-and-contrast essays, 561
in compound sentences, 231
for definition essays, 585
for descriptive essays, 532
for descriptive paragraphs, 46
for exemplification essays, 510
list of, 31, 231, 414
for narrative essays, 520
for narrative paragraphs, 42, 43
for paragraph coherence, 31–34
for process essays, 541
in process paragraphs, 50, 51
run-ons and comma splices with, 260
"Trip to a Brand-New Life, The" (Duong), 43–44
Trite expressions, avoiding, 337–40

Ulrich, Deborah (student), 570–72
"Ultimate High, The" (Weckerly), 55–56
"Under Water" (Yoshikawa), 542–43
Unity of paragraph, 19–25
revising, 21
Unless, as subordinating conjunction, 139
Use/used, 467
Utility words, 330

Vague words, 329
Van Hoboken, Lisa (student), 60
Verbs
action, 127–29
agreement of. *See* Agreement, subject-verb
complete, 129–30, 137–40
compound, 312–13, 317–18

definition of, 127
ESL writers and, 495, 497
helping, 129–30, 137–39, 180–82, 187–89, 209–15
identification of, 127–30
irregular, 152–55, 173–77, 451
linking, 128–29
main, 129–30, 137
objects of, 360–64
participles of
past, 311–12
present, 311
regular, 148–52, 170–73
sentence fragments and, 135–40
spelling of, 451
tense of. *See* Past tense; Tense
two-word, prepositions in, 497
Voice, consistency of, 283–86
Vowels, 450
suffixes beginning with, 456
in unstressed positions, 451
before *y*, 457

Wasn't, 178
Weather/whether, 468
Weckerly, Scott (student), 56
Well/better/best, 390
Well/good, 385–86
Weren't, 178
When, as subordinating conjunction, 139
Where/were/we're, 468
Whether/weather, 468
Which, as relative pronoun, 140, 160–62, 246
Whitehead, Kristin (student), 585–86
Who, as relative pronoun, 140, 160–62, 246
Whose/who's, 468–69
"Why Isn't Pete Rose in the Hall of Fame?" (Fleeger), 595–97
Will/would, 180–82
Woller, Tom (student), 74
Woman Warrior, The (Kingston), 46
"Woodstock Wars, The" (Espen), 39

Woolery, Alisha (student), 532–34
Words, 17
commonly confused, 459–70
commonly misspelled, list of, 472
key, in exams and other assignments, 483
revising, 328–52
clichés, 337–40
conciseness, 333–37
exactness, 329–33
sexist, 343–44
similes and metaphors, 340–43
transitional, 31–34
commas with, 414–16
Worst/worse/bad, 390
Worst/worse/badly, 390
Would/will, 180–82
Write/right, 465
Writing process. *See also* Essays; Paragraphs
drafting in, 13–14
editing in, 16–17
for paragraphs
argument, 75
cause-and-effect, 57
classification-and-division, 66–67
comparison-and-contrast, 62–63
definition, 70–71
descriptive, 49
development, 25–28
effectiveness, 19–37
exemplification, 41–42
expansion into essays, 86–97
narrative, 45
process, 53
planning in, 1–12
revising in, 14–18

Y, as vowel vs. consonant, 450
-y ending, suffixes and, 457–58
Yoshikawa, Mai, 542–43
Your/you're, 469
"Youthful Style" (Kincaid), 40, 40*n*